THE TANAGERS

THE TANAGERS
Natural History, Distribution, and Identification

Morton L. Isler and Phyllis R. Isler
Color Plates by Morton L. Isler

SMITHSONIAN INSTITUTION PRESS
WASHINGTON, D.C.

Copyright © 1987 by the
Smithsonian Institution.
All rights are reserved.

This book was edited by Ruth W. Spiegel
and designed by Alan Carter. Production
was coordinated by Kathleen Brown.
Type was set by Graphic Composition, Inc.,
Athens, Georgia.

Cover illustration: Detail from Plate 12,
Piranga (part 1).

♾ The paper used in this publication meets
the minimum requirements of the American
National Standard for Permanence of Paper
for Printed Library Materials Z39.48–1984.

Library of Congress Cataloging-in-Publication Data

Isler, Morton L.

The tanagers : natural history, distribution,
and identification.

Bibliography: p.
Includes index.
1. Tanagers. I. Isler, Phyllis R. II. Title.
QL696.P282I75   1987   598.8'82
85-11747
ISBN 0-87474-552-7
ISBN 0-87474-553-5 (pbk.)

The base map on which geographic ranges
are delineated was prepared by Theophilus
Britt Griswold.

Photography of the original paintings of the
tanager species was by Joe A. Goulait.

To the Memory of

Lillian B. Reynolds and Donald L. Russell

Contents

Foreword, by Theodore A. Parker III 10
Objectives 12
Acknowledgments 13
Sources 15
Plan of the Book 18
Abbreviations 21
Glossary 23
Schematic of a Species Account 28
The Nature of Tanagers 30

The Tanagers: Accounts 41

Color Plates ff. 206
References 374
Index 393

Tables

1. Elevational and Geographic Distribution of Tanagers 32
2. Predominance of Fruit or Insects in Tanager Diets 34
3. The *Chlorospingus* Bush-Tanagers 59
4. Ranges and Selected Characteristics of Common Bush-Tanager Subspecies 61
5. The *Hemispingus* Species 72
6. The *Thlypopsis* Tanagers 84
7. The *Hemithraupis* Tanagers 90
8. The *Chlorothraupis* Tanagers 107
9. The *Lanio* Shrike-Tanagers 114
10. The *Tachyphonus* Tanagers 122
11. The *Habia* Ant-Tanagers 138
12. The *Piranga* Tanagers 147
13. The *Ramphocelus* Tanagers 166
14. The *Spindalis* Tanagers 179
15. The *Thraupis* Tanagers 182
16. Percentage of Palm Tanager Insect-foraging by Substrate in Two Locations 194
17. The *Buthraupis* Species 199
18. The *Anisognathus* Mountain-Tanagers 207
19. The *Iridosornis* Tanagers 214
20. The *Euphonia* Species 223
21. The *Chlorophonia* Species 258
22. The *Chlorochrysa* Tanagers 264
23. The *Tangara* Tanagers 268
24. Percentage of Insect-foraging Records by Branch Size for the Bay-headed Tanager at Two Locations 303

25. The *Dacnis* Species 327
26. The *Cyanerpes* Honeycreepers 340
27. The *Diglossa* Flowerpiercers 350

Color Plates

1. *Orchesticus, Schistochlamys, Neothraupis, Cypsnagra, Conothraupis*
2. *Lamprospiza, Cissopis, Chlorornis, Compsothraupis, Sericossypha*
3. *Nesospingus, Chlorospingus* (part 1)
4. *Chlorospingus* (part 2), *Cnemoscopus, Hemispingus* (part 1)
5. *Hemispingus* (part 2), *Pyrrhocoma, Thlypopsis* (part 1)
6. *Thlypopsis* (part 2), *Hemithraupis, Chrysothlypis, Nemosia*
7. *Phaenicophilus, Calyptophilus, Rhodinocichla, Mitrospingus, Chlorothraupis, Orthogonys*
8. *Eucometis, Lanio*
9. *Creurgops, Heterospingus, Tachyphonus* (part 1)
10. *Tachyphonus* (part 2), *Trichothraupis*
11. *Habia*
12. *Piranga* (part 1)
13. *Piranga* (part 2), *Calochaetes, Ramphocelus* (part 1)
14. *Ramphocelus* (part 2)
15. *Spindalis, Thraupis* (part 1)
16. *Thraupis* (part 2), *Cyanicterus, Buthraupis* (part 1)
17. *Buthraupis* (part 2), *Wetmorethraupis*
18. *Anisognathus, Stephanophorus*
19. *Iridosornis, Dubusia, Delothraupis, Pipraeidea*
20. *Euphonia* (part 1)
21. *Euphonia* (part 2)
22. *Euphonia* (part 3)
23. *Chlorophonia, Chlorochrysa*
24. *Tangara* (part 1)
25. *Tangara* (part 2)
26. *Tangara* (part 3)
27. *Tangara* (part 4)
28. *Tangara* (part 5)
29. *Dacnis*
30. *Chlorophanes, Cyanerpes, Xenodacnis, Oreomanes, Diglossa* (part 1)
31. *Diglossa* (part 2)
32. *Diglossa* (part 3), *Euneornis, Tersina, Nephelornis, Tangara* (addendum)

Genera

Orchesticus 42
Schistochlamys 43
Neothraupis 46
Cypsnagra 46
Conothraupis 50
Lamprospiza 51
Cissopis 51
Chlorornis 54
Compsothraupis 56
Sericossypha 56
Nesospingus 58
Chlorospingus 58
Cnemoscopus 71
Hemispingus 72
Pyrrhocoma 83
Thlypopsis 84
Hemithraupis 90
Chrysothlypis 95
Nemosia 97
Phaenicophilus 100

Calyptophilus 102
Rhodinocichla 103
Mitrospingus 105
Chlorothraupis 107
Orthogonys 110
Eucometis 112
Lanio 114
Creurgops 119
Heterospingus 120
Tachyphonus 122
Trichothraupis 136
Habia 138
Piranga 147
Calochaetes 165
Ramphocelus 166
Spindalis 178
Thraupis 182
Cyanicterus 197
Buthraupis 198
Wetmorethraupis 206

Anisognathus 207
Stephanophorus 212
Iridosornis 214
Dubusia 218
Delothraupis 218
Pipraeidea 220
Euphonia 222
Chlorophonia 258
Chlorochrysa 264
Tangara 267
Dacnis 327
Chlorophanes 337
Cyanerpes 340
Xenodacnis 347
Oreomanes 348
Diglossa 350
Euneornis 369
Tersina 370
Nephelornis 372
Tangara (addendum) 373

Foreword

Tanagers are among the most colorful and vibrant of New World birds. How vividly I recall the spring morning nearly twenty-five years ago when I saw my first Scarlet Tanager amidst the fresh, green foliage of an elm outside my bedroom window. That glowing red bird with velvety black wings seemed curiously out of place in a suburban Pennsylvania neighborhood, and indeed, as I later learned, it was going to remain only a few months in the temperate zone before returning once again to some faraway tropical forest in Ecuador or Peru.

Some of my most exciting moments as a naturalist have taken place on the lower slopes of the Andes in Peru, where as many as forty species of tanagers may be found in a single place. A fruiting tree filled with tanagers—Vermilion, Golden, Saffron-crowned, Flame-faced, and Blue-browed, to name a few—is an unforgettable sight. They dart among the moss-covered, dripping branches like the brilliant fish of a coral reef. Nowhere else on earth can so many colorful birds be seen at once. Not even the lowland forests harbor such a diversity and abundance of these multicolored birds.

Despite their beauty and often conspicuous behavior, only a handful of the more than 240 species of tanagers have been adequately studied in nature. With the exception of four that breed in the United States, most tanagers dwell in the dense and often remote forests of Central and South America. Many pass their lives high above the ground in the tree tops, while others remain in impenetrable undergrowth. The vast majority are difficult to observe. Nevertheless, they remain more conspicuous than most other neotropical forest birds, such as ovenbirds, antbirds and flycatchers, and are therefore suitable subjects for study. A few, like the Blue-gray Tanager or "violinista" of the tropics, are wide-ranging and known to all who live with them, but other tanagers have only recently been discovered and described to science. Isolated high mountain forests in the Peruvian Andes continue to be a source of such discoveries; five previously unknown tanagers have been found there over the past twenty-five years. These include the marvelous Golden-backed Mountain-Tanager, one of the most beautiful members of the family.

This monograph by Phyllis and Morton Isler on the tanagers appears at an appropriate time. As we move from an age of discovery to a time of intensive field study, comprehensive reviews of existing knowledge are of critical importance. This book contains a unique blend of information. In addition to reviewing the literature thoroughly and examining countless museum specimens, the Islers gathered a tremendous amount of unpublished behavioral data from many contemporary ornithologists. They further made numerous trips to South America, including a long and arduous one to the Andes of Peru, to get firsthand experience with many of the birds they were writing about and painting. The result of their labors is a book that gives us a clear picture not only of what is known but—as important perhaps—of what remains to be learned.

Perusal of the species accounts that follow will reveal subjects that require attention, such as reproductive biology and social behavior. Particularly intriguing from the standpoint of community ecology is the coexistence of many similarly sized species in a single locality. I have often seen as many as ten members of the genus

Tangara in the same Andean flock, along with up to a dozen other tanagers and related birds. Much remains to be learned of the factors that promote the formation of such complex flocks. A better understanding of how these tanagers segregate in terms of insect-foraging may in part clarify the situation.

Many tanagers, such as those of the lower Andean cloudforests and coastal forests of Brazil, are presently threatened by the activities of man. Some species, like the Brazilian Tanager, have almost disappeared because of their popularity as cagebirds; others, like the Azure-rumped Tanager of southern Mexico and northern Guatemala, survive in ever-shrinking patches of montane forest. During the next few decades, widespread clearing of tropical forests for agriculture and ranching will endanger more and more tropical animals and plants. As fruit-dispersers, the tanagers represent an integral part of forest ecosystems, particularly in highland areas where they probably outnumber all other frugivorous vertebrates. The survival of some economically valuable Andean trees might depend on the continuing presence of these birds.

We should not forget that many of "our" own breeding birds, such as Scarlet and Summer Tanagers, actually spend most of their lives in the forests of Central and South America. It is therefore imperative that more students of New World birds turn their attention to the problems of the Neotropics, and that they broaden their interests to include, at least in part, the concerns of conservationists. If this does not happen, there may well come a time when spring mornings in Pennsylvania are devoid of one of nature's greatest gifts.

Theodore A. Parker III
Baton Rouge, Louisiana

Objectives

"Colorful" and "conspicuous" are adjectives readily given to tanagers, yet this highly diverse group of 242 species also includes drab and secretive birds. Moreover, some tanagers are almost as stocky and heavy billed as grosbeaks, others as spritely and thin billed as wood-warblers. Honeycreepers and flowerpiercers, now considered tanagers, enhance the diversity further. Tanagers occur from Canada to central Argentina, occupying all types of woodland from elfin forest in the high Andes to mangrove swamps in coastal lowlands. Only a few tanagers have been studied intensively, and many are not well known.

A primary goal of this book is to stimulate field study that will contribute to the understanding and ultimately the conservation of tanagers and the ecosystems of which they are part. To this end, the book systematically draws together existing knowledge of the natural history and distribution of tanagers and identifies knowledge gaps. The book also includes information to assist in field identification. Sexual, age, and subspecific variations in tanager plumages portrayed in this book supplement the growing number of excellent field guides to neotropical birds.

The second principal goal of *The Tanagers* is to provide an up-to-date data base for scientists engaged in ecological, zoogeographic, and taxonomic research. The book makes no taxonomic proposals but employs, without exception, a previously published classification of tanagers, namely the *Check-list of Birds of the World, A Continuation of the Work of James L. Peters* (Storer 1970). Studies currently underway, including biochemical analyses, are likely to propose major modifications of the arrangement of tanager genera and species. We hope that the data contained herein will contribute to formal systematic studies.

Acknowledgments

Our primary base of study has been the National Museum of Natural History of the Smithsonian Institution, without whose collection, library, and staff—especially Storrs L. Olson, Paul Slud, George E. Watson, and Richard L. Zusi—we could not have produced this book. Paul Slud helped us get started and freely shared his knowledge of neotropical birds; Richard Zusi impressed us with the value of making this book; and all four ornithologists encouraged us continuously and willingly helped whenever we asked. In our work at the National Museum of Natural History, we were assisted by many other individuals over the years, especially by J. Philip Angle, Richard C. Banks, Ralph Browning, Anna Datcher, James P. Dean, Bonnie Farmer, Mercedes S. Foster, Freida Hancock, Jack Marquardt, Leslie Overstreet, and John S. Weske.

Our "second home" has been the Museum of Zoology at Louisiana State University where John P. O'Neill, Theodore A. Parker III, James V. Remsen, Jr., Thomas S. Schulenberg, and many of their associates and students stimulated our efforts with their enthusiasm and by generously sharing their encyclopedic knowledge of neotropical birds. Our periodic visits to Baton Rouge always provided us with encouragement and stimulation as we prepared this book.

Our ability to provide descriptions of vocalizations was, in large part, the result of the availability of recordings and the extremely valuable support that we received from Cornell's Library of Natural Sounds. In particular, we are grateful for the help of Gregory F. Budney, James L. Gulledge, Andrea Priori, and David Wickstrom.

In the initial stages of this book, we benefitted from the organizational ideas and suggestions of Steven L. Hilty. Specific suggestions made by Kenneth C. Parkes and Raymond A. Paynter, Jr., helped define the limits of this book as did discussions with Edwin O. Willis regarding the natural history and biogeography of species in the genus *Euphonia*.

The growth of the book was aided substantially in its middle stages by discussions with Theodore A. Parker III and by the generosity of Steven L. Hilty, Gary R. Graves, Paul Slud, Claudia P. Wilds, and Richard L. Zusi, who reviewed intermediate drafts. Lesta Wren and Ruth W. Spiegel helped us develop the style of exposition. William Belton provided translations from Portuguese.

John P. O'Neill regularly reviewed the illustrations as they were being prepared and made many helpful suggestions. We also received encouragement and suggestions regarding the paintings from Lawrence B. McQueen, H. Douglas Pratt, and Guy A. Tudor. John P. O'Neill and Guy A. Tudor supplied information about postures and soft colors, as did Peter C. Alden, Victor L. Emanuel, Rose Ann Rowlett, and others already mentioned. J. P. Myers facilitated our use of the photographic collection of the VIREO program of The Academy of Natural Sciences, Philadelphia; published photographs by Dunning (1970, 1982) and by Norgaard-Olesen (1971) also aided us in making the illustrations.

Our work in the field benefited especially from our having the company at times of Steven L. Hilty and John P. O'Neill and from the opportunity of joining a Louisiana State University field expedition. Many other individuals have advised us, shared our hours in the field, or otherwise helped us. We are sorry that we cannot name them all.

Lastly, we are indebted to the reviewers of our final draft who spent many hours poring over what turned out to be a rather lengthy manuscript. Steven L. Hilty, Theodore A. Parker III, and Robert S. Ridgely were the principal reviewers; each made comments and suggestions throughout the accounts. Gary R. Graves, John P. O'Neill, James V. Remsen, Jr., and Thomas S. Schulenberg reviewed large sections of the book, and William Belton, Claudia P. Wilds, and Richard L. Zusi smaller but important segments. William L. Brown carefully reviewed a large number of the maps. The many comments and suggestions made by our reviewers improved *The Tanagers* substantially, by both adding data and eliminating errors. But the final responsibility for accuracy is ours alone.

The persistence of many field workers produced the data contained in this book. In many tropical areas workers have had to overcome disease, natural disasters, and occasionally vicissitudes of political instability. Today, comforts of civilization are in place in some locations, and bird tours to the Neotropics are popular. But extended stays in remote areas remain difficult, and the information provided in *The Tanagers* reflects the efforts of many individuals who have weathered sometimes inhospitable conditions to bring forth knowledge.

Sources

In preparing this book, we observed tanagers in the field, compiled information from over a thousand references, studied specimens at museums, and perhaps most important, obtained previously unpublished data from a number of individuals and institutions. That *The Tanagers* contains so much information published for the first time is testimony to the willingness of many researchers to share the fruits of their labors. In order to cite data succinctly within the text, major contributions are referenced in special ways. These citations and a description of their sources follow in alphabetical order.

Foster data

Since 1976, Mercedes S. Foster has periodically collected observations in Itapúa, Paraguay, of the feeding behavior of birds, including many tanager species, at fruiting trees of *Allophyllus edulis* (Sapindaceae). The fruit is a 7–10 mm drupe containing an oblong seed, 5–7 mm long and 3–5 mm in diameter, borne on inflorescences. This data set also includes stomach contents and weights obtained from specimens collected in Costa Rica, Peru, and Venezuela, as well as Paraguay.

Hilty data

Steven L. Hilty allowed us to use a data set that was obtained by him and his wife, Beverly, during 16 months of work (1972–1973) in the Western Andes in the Department of Valle, Colombia. The data include over 10,000 individual observations of tanager foraging behavior, habitat, and avian associations. Most were obtained on the Pacific slope at "Alto Yunda" in the upper Anchicayá Valley at about 1050 m (described in Hilty 1980). Accounts of the behaviors of a number of species are drawn primarily from these data.

Isler data

We have seen the majority of tanagers in the field and have had the opportunity to study the behaviors of some species in detail. Where we contributed specific data or substantial amounts of information to an account, we treat ourselves as another source.

LNS recordings

We have described tanager vocalizations primarily from recordings supplied by the Library of Natural Sounds, Laboratory of Ornithology, Cornell University. Here we obtained many fine recordings made by Theodore A. Parker III, Paul Schwartz, William Belton, L. Irby Davis, Arnoud B. van den Berg, and others cited in the text.

LSUMZ data

We obtained a substantial amount of information from the Museum of Zoology, Louisiana State University. Sources included field notebooks of S. E. Allen,

C. S. Cardiff, W. Eley, G. R. Graves, S. M. Lanyon, M. B. Robbins, T. S. Schulenberg, and D. A. Wiedenfeld, as well as unpublished manuscripts. Specimen data from the museum's rapidly expanding collection were especially helpful and include a large number of range extensions.

McDonald data

Mara A. McDonald provided unpublished field observations on tangers of the genus *Phaenicophilus* which she is currently studying in Hispaniola.

Negret data

Alvaro Negret compiled observations made over a number of years near Brasilia, Brazil, on species in the monotypic genera *Neothraupis* and *Cypsnagra*.

O'Neill data

John P. O'Neill supplied field notes from Peru, Ecuador, and Venezuela spanning the years 1965–1985.

Parker data

Theodore A. Parker III provided access to his field notebooks representing over a decade (1973–1984) of intensive field work in the Neotropics during which time he has been recording habitat, avian associations, and foraging behavior. These valuable data were compiled principally in Peru, Bolivia, and Brazil.

Remsen data

Since 1979, James V. Remsen, Jr., has employed a standardized approach to the collection of foraging data during Louisiana State University expeditions to Bolivia; the methodology has been described (Remsen 1985). Individuals who contributed to this growing and important data base are: A. P. Capparella, C. S. Cardiff, L. S. Hale, S. M. Lanyon, T. A. Parker III, M. Sánchez S., T. S. Schulenberg, and D. A. Wiedenfeld. This data set also includes observations made in Peru in 1985 by Remsen.

Stiles data

F. Gary Stiles drew together information that he has collected in Costa Rica over the past decade on two poorly known tanagers of the genera *Lanio* and *Buthraupis*.

Thomas data

Betsy T. Thomas provided records obtained in Venezuela in 1971–1984.

Data received from other individuals

Additional unpublished observations received in writing or recorded on tape are cited with the more usual *in litt.* to distinguish them from the foregoing data sets. In addition to individuals previously identified as providing data sets, contributors include Thomas H. Davis, Gary R. Graves, Russell S. Greenberg, Roger B. Johnson and Lorraine Washington, Eugene S. Morton, Charles A. Munn III, Robert S.

Ridgely, Scott K. Robinson, Mark B. Robbins, Thomas S. Schulenberg, Douglas F. Stotz, Morris D. Williams, Bret Whitney, and Richard L. Zusi. Field recordings of vocalizations not in the LNS collection were supplied by Thomas H. Davis, Gary H. Rosenberg, Rose Ann Rowlett, Thomas S. Schulenberg, and Bret Whitney.

Data obtained from museum collections

In addition to reviewing the collections of the Museum of Zoology at Louisana State University (LSUMZ) and the National Museum of Natural History of the Smithsonian Institution (USNM), we obtained specimen data for selected species in the collections of the Carnegie Museum, Pittsburgh (CM), the American Museum of Natural History, New York (AMNH), and The Academy of Natural Sciences, Philadelphia (ANSP). Additional locational records were obtained from the Field Museum of Natural History, Chicago (FMNH) and the Museum of Comparative Zoology, Harvard University (MCZ).

Plan of the Book

This plan identifies the specific kinds of information sought for *The Tanagers* and the way the data are organized and referenced. We first identify the taxonomy employed, then describe how the book may be used for identification purposes, and finally outline the organization and content of the genus and species accounts.

Taxonomy

We have not made formal studies of the systematics of tanagers but follow without deviation the arrangement of Volume XIII of the *Check-list of Birds of the World, A Continuation of the Work of James L. Peters* (Storer 1970), which is referenced throughout as the *Peters Check-list*. The *Peters Check-list* considers tanagers and the Swallow-Tanager as subfamilies (Thraupinae and Tersininae, respectively) of a large family, the Emberizidae. Furthermore, the *Peters Check-list* includes, as tanagers, twenty-eight species that were formerly considered honeycreepers (Coerebidae).

In providing English names, we typically follow the American Ornithologist Union, 1983, *Check-list of North American Birds*, 6th edition (cited throughout as the *A.O.U. Check-list*) and Meyer de Schauensee, 1970, *The Birds of South America*. A few exceptions have been made in consultation with Robert S. Ridgely to conform to a forthcoming field guide to South American birds.

Species are numbered from 1 to 242 and include five new tanagers described since the publication of the *Peters Check-list* in 1970. Three of these species are inserted into the *Peters Check-list* sequence in the order proposed by the authors of the original species descriptions. These are Parodi's Hemispingus, *Hemispingus parodii* **27**, Rufous-browed Hemispingus, *Hemispingus rufosuperciliaris* **33**, and the Golden-backed Mountain-Tanager, *Buthraupis aureodorsalis* **118**. The book concludes with two newly described species: the Pardusco, *Nephelornis oneilli* **241**, whose affinities are uncertain, and the Green-capped Tanager, *Tangara meyerdeschauenseei* **242**, whose discovery came too late to be included in sequence.

Although our accounts follow the taxonomy of the *Peters Check-list*, we have prepared thirty-seven accounts for taxa that are considered subspecies in the *Peters Check-list* but that are given specific status by other recent authors. In such cases, the species are subdivided into subspecies groups, a term used solely to identify the subdivisions with no taxonomic significance implied. For example, the *Peters Check-list* regards the Spangle-cheeked Tanager, *Tangara dowii* **202**, as a single species that ranges from Costa Rica to eastern Panama, whereas the *A.O.U. Check-list* identifies two geographically isolated species: the Spangle-cheeked, *T. dowii*, of Costa Rica and western Panama and the Green-naped, *T. fucosa*, of eastern Panama. Extra digits added to the species number identify subspecies groups (in the example, **202-1** and **202-2**).

Color Plates

The thirty-two plates illustrate 551 plumages and 23 flight patterns. Multiple plumages are illustrated for species if the plumages seem different enough to cause questions in field identification or if plumage differences reflect sex or age and could be valuable to naturalists undertaking field studies.

We illustrate more than one subspecies of 74 tanagers and as many as six subspecies for some. In deciding which subspecies to illustrate, we usually opted to illustrate extremes. Further variations are described on the facing pages or in the species accounts.

Sexual differences are illustrated for almost half (115) of the tanager species; seasonal differences (alternate plumages), for only three. Postjuvenal plumages of younger birds that have not attained adult (i.e., definitive) plumage are termed subadult and illustrated when they differ significantly from the adult plumages of older birds. The emerging feathers of tanagers molting from subadult to adult plumages (and the few molting into alternate plumages) often create a patchy appearance, but such individuals are not pictured because they can be identified readily by interpolating from other plumages.

In the design of the plates, the following conventions have been adopted: birds touching or perching on the same branch are of the same species, birds of sequential genera face in opposite directions, and the tanagers on each plate are illustrated at the same scale except in pictures of flight patterns which are at one-half the scale of perched birds.

Text Facing the Color Plates

Plumage descriptions are placed opposite each plate so that identification materials may be seen together. Because space is limited, plumage descriptions are amplified in the species accounts when necessary. Common characteristics of species contained in a genus are sometimes provided in the text facing the plates, and this information is not repeated in the species descriptions.

The organization of text facing the plate varies with the species. For example, where subspecific differences are more obvious than age or sexual plumage differences, species descriptions in facing text are organized by subspecies. When subspecies are illustrated, scientific names are used to link the subspecies with geographic range and other information in the species account.

In selecting color names, we sought to follow Smithe (1975 + suppl.), a widely available color guide. When Smithe's color names, such as Smalt Blue, are not in general use, we employ a common color name followed by the name of the particular shade in parentheses, for example, blue violet (Smalt Blue).

Genus Accounts

Genus accounts provide generalizations about habitat, behavior, vocalizations, and nesting. They also include references to hybrids and to studies of competition among closely related species. Large genera (e.g., *Euphonia*, *Tangara*, *Diglossa*) are divided into species groups based on appearance, distribution, behavior (especially foraging behavior), and vocalizations. Species groups have no taxonomic significance but are aimed at making the summaries more manageable, assisting in field identification, suggesting needed field work, and stimulating formal studies of systematics.

Species Accounts

A Schematic of a Species Account is included below, at the end of this section, on pages 28–29. The schematic is the key to the organization of data. It also aids in identifying knowledge gaps in the species accounts, for unless relevant information was found on a subject listed in the schematic, e.g., nest location, we omit the subject from a species account rather than noting that no nests have been found. Only if a major heading, for example, Vocalizations, is devoid of data do we note "No information" in the account. Most of the topics listed in the schematic are self-explanatory; some are defined in the Glossary; but a brief added explanation is needed for a few topics.

The Middle and South American distribution of every species has been replotted and described by major civil subdivisions (e.g., departments) of countries. The ornithological gazetteers published by the Museum of Comparative Zoology, Harvard University, were used extensively in this effort. Ranges north of Mexico were obtained from the recently revised *A.O.U. Check-list*. Range descriptions are taken to the subspecies level if either of two conditions are met: 1) the ranges of the subspecies are clearly disjunct, or 2) the subspecies differ in appearance sufficiently to be illustrated or discussed in the text.

The predominant frequencies of tanager vocalizations were identified by using a Real-time Spectrum Analyzer (*Technics* Model SH-8055). Very High Pitch means that the sound is most intense in a frequency band centered at 16,000 hertz; High Pitch at 8000 hertz; Moderate Pitch at 4000 hertz; Low Pitch at 2000 hertz; and Very Low Pitch at bands centered at 1000 hertz or less. The initial capital letter of these terms signifies that the pitch was determined in this manner; otherwise, the description of pitch is not capitalized.

Sources are referenced in the body of the text only when they are the sole basis for information. In situations where a single source is the basis for a number of sentences or an entire paragraph, the reference is set aside in a separate sentence within parentheses: (Hilty data.) Otherwise sources are provided in the final section of the account. When faced with a large number of references, we limit the primary sources to about ten, giving weight to articles covering a variety of the subjects discussed in the species account. On the other hand, all sources of specialized information on weights, stomach contents, vocalizations, and breeding are listed if they contributed to the account.

Maps

Maps are drawn from the same sources as are the range descriptions. A map accompanies every species account, or subspecies group account if appropriate, except for the North American summer ranges of *Piranga* species. The 263 range maps are at an identical scale and may be compared easily since the maps covering part of a page or column are excerpted from the same full-page base map.

Ranges are pictured on the maps as continuous in areas of similar habitat and elevation (e.g., along the slope of the Andes) unless we know that there has been extensive field work in an area to confirm an apparent range gap, unless subspecific differences suggest a range discontinuity, or unless the apparent range gap is substantial. A question mark has been placed in range gaps or along the boundary of a range where knowledge of habitat suggests that the species range could extend in that direction. A black dot on a map signifies a single record.

Abbreviations

AMNH	American Museum of Natural History, New York
ANSP	The Academy of Natural Sciences, Philadelphia
Aug	August
c	central
ca.	about
cm	centimeter(s)
CM	Carnegie Museum, Pittsburgh
cp.	compare
diam.	diameter
Dec	December
e	eastern
ec	east-central
elev.	elevation
esp.	especially
et al.	and others
etc	a number of unspecified additional persons or things
Feb	February
fide	on the authority of
FMNH	Field Museum of Natural History, Chicago
g	gram(s)
ha.	hectare(s)
I.	Island
Is.	Islands
in.	inch(es)
incl.	including
in litt.	communication in writing or on tape
Jan	January
LNS	Library of Natural Sounds, Laboratory of Ornithology, Cornell University, Ithaca, New York
LSUMZ	Louisiana State University Museum of Zoology, Baton Rouge
m	meter(s)
mm	millimeter(s)
MCZ	Museum of Comparative Zoology, Harvard University, Cambridge, Massachusetts
min.	minute(s)
Mt.	Mount
n	northern (in range descriptions)
N or n	number (except in range descriptions)
nc	north-central
n.d.	not dated
ne	northeastern
nw	northwestern
Nov	November
obs.	observations

Oct	October
p.	page
pers. comm.	personal communication
prep.	preparation
s	southern
sc	south-central
se	southeastern
sec.	second(s)
sensu	in the sense of
Sept	September
sp	species (singular)
spec.	specimen
spp	species (plural)
suppl.	supplement(s)
sw	southwestern
USNM	National Museum of Natural History, Smithsonian Institution, Washington, D.C.
w	western
wc	west-central

Glossary

This glossary includes words or terms that: 1) have a more narrowly defined usage in the book than may be found elsewhere, for example, Breeding date or Weight; 2) may not be found in popular dictionaries, for example, Parapatric; 3) come directly from another language, for example, *varzea*; or 4) may be confusing to readers whose first language is not English.

ADULT PLUMAGE. The plumage that is generally indistinguishable from that of adults of any age; also known as the definitive plumage.

AGONISTIC BEHAVIOR. Behavior that appears to be associated with conflict between birds.

AGGREGATIONS. *See* Feeding aggregations.

ALLOPATRIC. Refers to species that occupy different geographic regions.

ALTERNATE PLUMAGE. A second annual plumage acquired prior to the breeding season; the breeding or nuptial plumage.

AMAZONIA. Refers to lowlands in the drainage of the Amazon River.

ANT-FOLLOWING FLOCK. A group of species that preys on invertebrates and small vertebrates fleeing from advancing swarms of army ants.

ANTING. Refers to birds' putting crushed or live ants among their feathers.

ARAUCARIA FOREST. In southeastern Brazil, wooded areas of Paraná pine, *Araucaria angustifolia*.

ARAUCARIA POMPON. Used to describe large, round, dense, spiny clusters of foliage at the end of long branches of the Brazilian araucaria (see Belton 1985).

BORDER. Used as a synonym for edge (as in forest edge).

BREEDING DATE. Limited to observations of active nests, nest construction, or stub-tailed juveniles; also includes the collection of a female about to lay eggs. Undocumented statements of breeding season and indicators of possible breeding, such as the enlarged gonads of specimens, are not used in this book. Breeding dates are given by month by country; by state in Brazil.

CAATINGA. A habitat in northeastern Brazil of stunted, often thorny, trees with many cacti and other succulents; ground may be bare.

CALL-SONG. Used to describe a vocalization in which a contact call or other call note is delivered repeatedly at a regular cadence.

CANOPY. The uppermost continuous stratum of foliage in the forest; formed by the crowns of the trees.

CERRADO. A habitat of stunted twisted trees growing to heights of about 3–7 m on the Brazilian tableland. Varies from a dense, almost impenetrable tangle of vegetation to a more open scrub where the crowns of trees cover as little as 50% of the terrain.

CORE SPECIES. *See* Nuclear species.

DIAGONAL-LEAN. Insect-foraging in which the bird moves along a branch, regularly stopping to scan the undersides of the branch by leaning over one side of the branch and then the other.

ELFIN FOREST. Humid, often windswept, forest of high elevations; characterized by stunted trees and (usually) abundant epiphytes.

FAMILY GROUP. Parent birds and their offspring.

FEEDING AGGREGATIONS. Stationary heterogeneous groups of birds assembled for the purpose of consuming a single food source. Also known as feeding assemblages.

FLOCK. *See* Mixed-species flock.

FLUTTER-PURSUIT. A foraging method in which the bird darts out after prey that attempts to escape an attack (or possible attack) by flying.

FOREST. Used in a general sense for a large area of mature evergreen trees that form a complete or nearly complete canopy.

FOREST CLEARINGS. Man-made or natural openings surrounded by forest.

FOREST EDGE. The transition habitat (ecotone) between forest and open space or low vegetation.

GALLERY FOREST OR WOODLAND. A narrow strip of trees along water courses in otherwise mostly open country.

GLEAN. Used to describe foraging techniques in which the bird moves along, usually rapidly, examining the surfaces of substrates at close range (generally less than a few centimeters away), selecting and gathering food bit by bit. *Compare with* Peer and pick.

HEAD-DOWN GLEAN. A foraging technique in which the bird turns completely upside down in a more or less vertical position to search for and capture prey on the undersides of branches or leaves.

HIGH-PITCHED. When capitalized, signifies that a vocalization is most intense within a frequency band centered at 8000 hertz.

HOME RANGE. The area over which a species normally travels in search of food without regard to the way boundaries are maintained. *Compare with* Territory.

HOVER-GLEAN; HOVER-PICK. Foraging methods in which the bird hovers at a substrate to attack prey. In the hover-glean, the bird hovers both to examine the substrate for prey and to attack after locating it. In the hover-pick, the bird spots the prey while perched and then plucks it from the substrate in a brief hover. The hover-glean and hover-pick are difficult to separate in the field, so they should be interpreted with caution in the text.

HUMID FOREST. Encompasses moist and wet forest as defined by Holdridge (1967).

INSECT. Used in a general sense to represent all small arthropods.

INSECT-FORAGING. Includes both search and attack.

JUVENAL PLUMAGE. First plumage of contour feathers which, in the case of tanagers, is acquired while the young bird is in the nest; usually worn for a short time. Described in the text only when extraordinarily different from subadult and adult plumages.

LEAF-WALKING. A foraging technique in which the bird walks or hops over the upper surfaces of leaves to obtain prey.

LOCAL. Used to describe a species that is found only in scattered locations within the larger region in which it occurs.

LOWLANDS. Elevations less than about 1000 meters above sea level.

LOW-LYING FOREST. A forest subject to seasonal or year-round inundation from rain or flooding of rivers or other inland bodies of water.

LOW-PITCHED. When capitalized, signifies that a vocalization is most intense within a frequency band centered at 2000 hertz.

MANDIBULATION. The process by which a small plucked fruit is rotated in the bird's mandibles to mash it and often to separate the seed and/or skin that are then dropped.

MATORRAL. Riverine vegetation that is typically lower in height and more open than adjacent forest.

MIXED-SPECIES FLOCK. A group of birds containing two or more species that move together from place to place. *See* Permanent mixed-species flock and Temporary mixed-species flock.

MODERATE-PITCHED. When capitalized, signifies that a vocalization is most intense within a frequency band centered at 4000 hertz.

MONTANE FOREST. Encompasses premontane, or lower montane, as well as the montane forest of Holdridge (1967).

MOSSY FOREST. A high-humidity forest in which the trees are heavily laden with moss and other epiphytic growth. Includes the cloud forest of most other authors.

NESTLING PERIOD. The interval between hatching and the young bird's departure from the nest.

NUCLEAR SPECIES. A species around which mixed-species flocks are formed and maintained.

NORTHERN PERUVIAN LOW. The depression in the Andes occurring in the drainage of the Río Marañón. A major barrier in the distribution of Andean birds. (See Vuilleumier 1984a.)

OMNIVOROUS. Feeding on insects, plant material, and nectar.

PÁRAMO AND PUNA EDGE. Páramo and puna are open formations growing above the upper limit of continuous montane forest in the Andes. Páramo and puna edge is used herein to include transition habitat (ecotone) between high elevation forest and true páramo and puna.

PARAPATRIC. Refers to closely related species whose ranges do not overlap but abut, allowing individuals to come into geographic contact, with no or only limited interbreeding.

PEER AND PICK. An insect-foraging method in which the bird sits on a perch and looks around at surfaces generally more than a few centimeters away and then stretches out acrobatically or flies, glides, or hops to another perch to obtain the prey that is sighted. Movements along perches tend to have a start and stop quality. *Compare with* Glean.

PERIJÁ MOUNTAINS. Located on the northern border between Venezuela (Zulia) and Colombia (La Guajira and Cesar) and given in range descriptions without repeating the names of these departments and countries.

PERMANENT MIXED-SPECIES FLOCK. A mixed-species flock that contains a core of individuals that spend most of the day together, day after day, and defend a common territory.

POMPON. *See* Araucaria pompon.

PROBING AND RUMMAGING. Insect-foraging techniques in which the bird uses its bill, and sometimes feet, to push its way into dead leaf clusters, loose bark, etc. to locate prey without prior visual contact.

PUNA EDGE. *See* Páramo and puna edge.

SALLY TO AIR. After a flying insect is spotted by a perched bird, the bird pursues and attacks its prey in flight. "Hawk" is used by some authors to describe this foraging method, but we reserve "hawk" to mean the searching and pursuing of prey in continuous flight (*sensu* Remsen 1985).

SALLY TO FOLIAGE OR BARK. After prey is spotted by a perched bird, it is picked off a substrate during a continuous flight from one perch to another.

SANTA MARTA MOUNTAINS. In the Departments of Magdalena and Cesar, Colombia. Noted in range descriptions without departmental names.

SAVANNA. Grassland with scattered trees and shrubs.

SAVANNA FOREST OR WOODLAND. Large islands of trees within savanna.

SCARCE. Used to describe a species that one cannot expect to encounter in suitable habitats within its range in a week of field work.

SCRUB. Mature vegetation of low trees and bushes. Sometimes described as dense or open depending upon the proportion of ground covered by woody vegetation.

SECOND-GROWTH WOODLAND OR SCRUB. A regrowth that has not reached maturity. Includes references to capoeira in Brazil.

SEEDS. Seeds listed as found in stomach contents are often ingested as part of berries or other fleshy fruits and, unless so stated, should not be taken to mean the dry fruit (caryopsis) typical of grasses.

SHRUBBY CLEARING. Early regrowth in forest clearings that may be either man-made or natural (i.e., caused by treefalls and landslides).

SONG. A vocalization in which sounds are repeated in a consistent pattern. Includes but is not limited to territorial or advertising songs.

SPECIES GROUP. Used within genera containing many species to identify groupings of species that share some common characteristics of plumage, habitat preference, behavior, and/or vocalizations. Species groups are not defined formally for taxonomic purposes but are aimed at stimulating field work and formal analysis.

SUBADULT PLUMAGE. A plumage worn in the first year or so of a bird's life that is obviously distinct from the adult plumage.

SUBSPECIES GROUP. In situations where recent authors, e.g., the *A.O.U. Check-list*, disagree with the *Peters Check-list* (which we follow) with respect to which taxa constitute species, we have subdivided the species account to allow the reader to examine the available data for components of species, identified as subspecies groups. As used herein, the term has no formal taxonomic significance.

SUPERSPECIES. A group of species derived from a common ancestor that are allopatric and considered too distinct morphologically to be regarded as a single species. We have not formally defined superspecies but report on other authors' considerations.

SYMPATRIC. Refers to species that occur in the same geographic area.

TEMPORARY MIXED-SPECIES FLOCKS. Contain individuals of different species that band and disband frequently without schedule or organization.

TERRA FIRMA. Forest not subject to inundation from rains or flooding. Equivalent to the Portuguese terra firme.

TERRITORY. An area within the home range of a species that is held through overt defense, display, or advertisement.

UNDERGROWTH. Shrubs, small trees, and herbs sometimes growing to a height of 3 to 4 meters above the ground in forest or woodland. Equivalent to ground story.

UNDERSTORY. The vegetation layer between the forest canopy and the undergrowth; formed primarily by shade-tolerant trees of midheights.

VARZEA. Forested areas that are seasonally flooded by river systems; used primarily in the Amazon basin.

VERY-HIGH-PITCHED. When capitalized, signifies that a vocalization is most intense within a frequency band centered at 16,000 hertz.

VERY-LOW-PITCHED. When capitalized, signifies that a vocalization is most intense within frequency bands centered at 1000 hertz or less.

WEIGHT. The mean and range are given in grams. Weights are not included for collected birds whose body fat was described as moderate or heavy; exceptions are so noted. The number of weights used to calculate the mean is given in the section listing sources.

WESTERN VENEZUELAN LOW. The depression in the Andes occurring in Táchira in the drainage of the Río Uribante close to the border with Colombia. A major barrier in the distribution of Andean birds. Also known as the Táchira Depression. (See Vuilleumier 1984a.)

WOODLANDS. Areas of trees that either 1) are evergreen but have an open canopy, i.e., less crown density than forest, or 2) have a more or less closed canopy, but the trees are typically short and/or deciduous.

Schematic of a Species Account

Plate Number (refers to color plate on which species is illustrated)

1. Average length (of museum specimens)
2. Weight: average and extremes (specimens with little or no fat)
3. Number of subspecies (from *Peters Check-list*) and citations for subspecies described since 1970
4. Differences in appearance that are not shown in plates or described in facing text
5. Record of breeding in subadult plumage

Geographic Range

1. Described down to major civil divisions within countries
2. Source, if description differs from that in *Peters Check-list*
3. Ranges of subspecies whose plumages are distinct or whose ranges are disjunct

Elevational Range

1. Above sea level (typical as well as extremes; to nearest 50 m)

Habitat and Behavior

1. Types of habitat and vegetation occupied
2. Seasonal movements between habitats and/or locations
3. Social organization; participation in mixed-species flocks and feeding aggregations
4. Displays, roosting, and anting
5. Distinctive postures, movements, and/or flight
6. Territoriality; adoption of a home range
7. Foraging height and distance to the canopy
8. Percentages of observations of fruit-eating, insect-searching, and feeding at flowers
9. Foraging methods for various types of food
10. Principal fruits taken; sizes; method of eating
11. Types of insects taken; substrates on which insects are sought
12. Stomach contents

Vocalizations

1. Descriptions of various types of vocalizations
2. Predominant frequencies
3. Behavior while vocalizing

Breeding

1. Courtship; nesting territoriality
2. Nest-building behavior
3. Type and location of nest
4. Number and appearance of eggs
5. Length of incubation and nestling periods
6. Feeding and protection of nestlings and fledglings
7. Number of broods
8. Breeding dates (see Glossary)

Sources

1. Primary (maximum: about 10 sources)
2. Weights (incl. number of specimens)
3. Stomach contents
4. Vocalizations (incl. number of recordings)
5. Nests, eggs, and breeding dates

The Nature of Tanagers

Tanagers belong to a very large group of birds known as nine-primaried oscines (or songbirds) because their tenth or outermost wing primary is minute and concealed. Characteristics have never been found that distinguish clearly among the subgroups of New World nine-primaried oscines commonly known as wood-warblers, tanagers, cardinals, and buntings (see Storer 1969; Sibley 1970; Raikow 1978). Despite the unclear boundaries, bill shape and presumed feeding behavior have been used to define families or subfamilies. Wood-warblers generally have slender pointed bills and feed mostly on insects, tanagers have thicker bills (some with a notch on the upper mandible) and eat mostly fruit, and New World finches have the stoutest bills and take mostly seeds. A "nectar feeding" subgroup, the honeycreepers, variously has been defined as a separate group or merged into tanagers and wood-warblers (see Beecher 1951).

Bill form and feeding habits appear less and less to be a good reflection of phylogenetic relationships among the New World nine-primaried songbirds. Recent studies (e.g., Amadon 1950) have shown that bill form can change quite rapidly in evolutionary time. Moreover, feeding behaviors within each of the three groups—wood-warblers, tanagers, and finches—have been found to be highly variable, as exemplified by descriptions herein of tanager feeding behaviors. Initial results of biochemical research (see Sibley and Ahlquist in press) support the idea that only one family is involved and that major shifts of genera among tanagers, emberizine finches, and wood-warblers would better describe their phylogenetic relationships.

Despite the increasing certainty that tanagers are not presently definable as a monophyletic group, we employ the rather traditional taxonomic arrangement of the *Peters Check-list* (Storer 1970). It will take many years to reassess the relationships among the New World nine-primaried songbirds, and in the meantime, it is convenient and appropriate to use a well-known existing taxonomy. Even within the confines of this taxonomy, tanagers exhibit a remarkable variety of morphology and behavior.

Size and Appearance

Taken as a whole, tanagers are fairly small birds; the median length of the 242 species included in this book is 14 cm (about 5.5 inches), and the median weight (known for 204 species) is 19 grams. Size variation is considerable, however, and the low medians reflect the large number of small tanagers of two genera, *Tangara* and *Euphonia*, that together contain seventy-three species. Among the smallest tanagers are the Plumbeous Euphonia and the Short-billed Honeycreeper, which are about 9 cm in length and weigh about 9 grams; the longest, the Magpie Tanager, is about 26 cm; and the heaviest, the White-capped Tanager, weighs about 114 grams. Typically, males and females of the same species are similar in size.

In the tropics, tanagers form a large percentage of the highly visible birds, partly because of their attractive coloration. The majority of tanagers are strikingly marked with brilliant patches of color, some with metallic or opalescent qualities, or with boldly defined areas of black and white. In fewer species, such as the widespread Blue-gray Tanager, a single bright color shades from light to dark. However, the patterns and colors of some tanagers (e.g., *Hemispingus*, *Chlorothrau-*

pis, Habia) are comparatively muted, as are female plumages of a number of other species. Sexual plumage differences apparent in the field occur in 48 percent of the tanagers (115 species). In flight, a number of species (e.g., some *Tachyphonus, Cyanerpes, Diglossa*) show white or yellow underwing-coverts that contrast with body plumage, and a few tanagers (some *Thraupis, Trichothraupis*) exhibit distinctive wing-stripes or -spots.

Tanager bills vary substantially in thickness, length, proportions, and curvature. Bill shapes appear to be related to feeding behavior, especially to the types of insects that are taken. Many heavy-billed genera such as *Lanio, Creurgops, Habia*, and *Chlorothraupis* are primarily insectivorous; the notches on their bills are ideally suited for grasping chitinous insects. Differences in foraging behavior among tanagers may also be reflected in variations in leg musculature (see Raikow 1978) and in the relative weight of leg muscles (see Moermond and Denslow 1985). The strong limbs of many tanagers allow them to reach out acrobatically in all directions when obtaining food (*ibid.*).

In 116 species, the plumage of first-year birds (technically, the first basic plumage) may be distinguished in the field from that of full adults (the definitive plumage). In seventy-seven of these species, both first-year males and females differ from adults, the most extreme case being the Black-faced Tanager, whose adults are black and gray and subadults predominantly yellowish olive-green. In thirty-nine sexually dichromatic species, first-year males resemble females.

Although a few species, including North American *Piranga* tanagers, undergo a partial molt before the breeding season, most tanagers molt only once a year, after the breeding season (see Snow and Snow 1964, Foster 1975). Consequently, year-old tanagers do not undergo their first complete molt until after their first potential breeding season, and a number of species have been found to breed in subadult plumage. Some species take two or more years to attain adult plumage. For example, Schaefer (1953) discovered that the male Swallow-Tanager does not attain fully definitive plumage for four years. Schaefer also found that these males began to breed in their first year.

Distribution and Habitat

Tanagers are encountered in nearly every major type of forested or shrubby habitat in the Western Hemisphere except the north woods of Alaska and Canada and the *Nothofagus* forests of southern Chile and Argentina. Seasonally, tanagers migrate away from the northern and southern reaches of the hemisphere. In tropical regions some species migrate in conjunction with cycles of rainfall and food availability. Such seasonal movements may result in locally reduced populations (e.g., in central Panama, see Greenberg 1981c) or the abandonment of an area by a species (e.g., the Black-and-white Tanager in northwest Peru).

The geographic ranges of two-thirds (163) of the tanager species occur completely within South America (defined to include Panama east of the canal). Conversely, only eighteen species occur year-round solely in North and Middle America west of the Panama Canal. Eight species are endemic to oceanic Caribbean islands.

Approximately equal numbers of species have elevational ranges centered in lowlands and highlands (Table 1). We consider tanagers to be lowland species if they predominantly inhabit regions of less than 1000 meters elevation, or highland species if found predominantly over 1000 meters. Only eighteen species have distinct lowland and highland populations. The geographic ranges of five of these

Table 1 Elevational and Geographic Distribution of Tanagers

Geographic Distribution	Lowlands		Highlands		Both		Total	
	N	%	N	%	N	%	N	%
East of Andes	46	19	7	3	4	2	57	24
Andes	7	3	77	32			84	35
North (and West) of Andes	33	14	13	5			46	19
Caribbean					8*	3	8	3
Both East and North of Andes	14	6					14	6
Both East of Andes and Andes	2	1	1	<1	6	2	9	4
Both North of Andes and Andes	5	2	4	2	1	<1	10	4
East and North of Andes and Andes	7	3			6	2	13	5
Caribbean, East and North of Andes, and Andes					1	<1	1	<1
Total	114	48	102	42	26	9	242	100

*The entire group of Caribbean endemics is placed here because mountains are low in the islands, relative to the mainland, and because most species tend to occur at all elevations.

species (the Black-goggled, Blue-and-yellow, and Fawn-breasted Tanagers; Blue-hooded Euphonia; and Blue-naped Chlorophonia) follow a similar pattern—extending from Andean highlands into temperate lowlands in northern Argentina and southeastern Brazil. About one-fourth of the predominantly lowland species occur regularly above 1000 m in some locations, a few in substantial numbers. Some—the Black-faced, Blue-gray, and Palm Tanagers in particular—seem to have expanded their ranges from lowlands to highlands with clearing of highland forest and increasing human settlement.

The Andes are a major center of tanager radiation. Slightly over one-third (35 percent) of tanager species are confined to Andean slopes, where they form an important part of the region's forest avifauna and where conditions conducive to further speciation remain (see Graves 1985). Only seven of the eighty-four Andean species primarily live at lowland (foothill) elevations, below 1000 m.

The Andes are also a physical barrier separating the geographic ranges of lowland tanagers. Only twenty-one of 114 lowland species occur on both sides of the Andes, and the ranges of ten of the twenty-one are nearly confined to regions east of the Andes and barely extend around the north end. The well known Blue-gray and White-lined Tanagers are among the few species with extensive Central and South American distributions.

We estimate that 149 tanager species (62 percent) inhabit forests or are forest-based; 54 (22 percent) live primarily in semiopen areas in which trees and shrubs are mixed with open spaces; and 39 (16 percent) cannot be reasonably categorized. While tanagers favoring semiopen environments are extending their ranges, some tanagers requiring substantial areas of contiguous forest to survive are increasingly threatened with extinction.

In the Andes, where trees are exposed on steep slopes and stunted at high elevations, tanagers are encountered at all heights in the vegetation, but in towering dense lowland forests, tanagers are almost always found in the canopy or subcanopy and at forest borders and breaks. A few atypical species, such as some ant-tanagers, are encountered at low heights in forest interiors, but only where the light supports rather extensive vegetation. The reasons why most tanager prefer microhabitats that receive substantial amounts of sunlight are not entirely clear, but they almost certainly are related to the availability of fruit and also probably to aspects of insect-foraging behavior.

Social Behavior

After the breeding season, the large majority of tanager species remain in pairs or in small groups of three to five individuals, presumably parents and offspring. Bands of 6–12 individuals, characteristic of some tanager species, are thought to consist of a pair and multiple broods (e.g., White-capped Tanager, Turquoise Tanager) or family groups that have joined together (e.g., some *Chlorospingus* species). Groups of over a dozen or so individuals of the same tanager species are very uncommon. Species in which individuals remain solitary are equally unusual but include the Glossy and Carbonated Flowerpiercers, which defend individual territories outside of the breeding season, and the North American *Piranga* tanagers, which appear to be territorial on their wintering grounds.

Nearly all tanagers participate in mixed-species flocks, but the extent of participation varies greatly by species. The data suggest that, in general, the more insectivorous a species is, the more time it spends with mixed-species flocks. Moreover, as might be expected, lowland tanagers inhabiting forested areas, where mixed-species flocks abound, associate with such flocks more often than do species of semiopen areas, where fewer flocks form. Forested areas, however, also shelter a few interspecifically unsocial tanager species, such as the Dusky-faced Tanager and Swallow-Tanager, that travel in single-species groups.

Studies of color-banded flocks have revealed important distinctions among mixed-species flocks and the role of tanagers in them. Two studies in the highlands of Central America found that mixed-species flocks formed around a single species with other species (often termed attendant species) joining and leaving the flock as the core species traversed its home range. The roles of different species in highland flocks may vary by season or locality. In one study (Buskirk et al. 1972), the core species was the Common Bush-Tanager, but in another location (Powell 1979), the Common Bush-Tanager was found to be an attendant species. In Bolivia, Remsen (1985) noted four different types of highland flocks with overlapping home ranges, but individuals were not color-banded.

In contrast with the single core species found in highland flocks, color-banded lowland mixed-species flocks in Peru (Munn and Terborgh 1979, Munn 1985) and Panama (Gradwohl and Greenberg 1980) have been found to contain a core of permanently associated individuals of 2–6 species that forage together and defend a common territory. Common territorial defense was initially described by Willis (1960b) in Belize where one of the two species involved was the Red-crowned Ant-Tanager. In the Peruvian study area, color-banding showed that the core of each canopy flock consisted of pairs of six species, including three tanagers, and each understory flock had a core of six different species, none of which was a tanager. However, twenty additional tanager species in the Peruvian study area were observed to join at least one of the two types of permanent flocks as transients.

The color-banded flocks studied to date in the Neotropics have been composed primarily of insectivorous species (see Powell 1985). In addition to transitory participation in these flocks, omnivorous tanagers are found in another kind of assemblage, often termed a tanager-honeycreeper flock, but intensive observations of color-marked birds in such aggregations have not yet been undertaken. Munn (1985) has suggested that the omnivorous tanagers of the high canopy and emergents form temporary flocks that assemble and disband frequently, without apparent schedule or organization.

Feeding Behavior

Tanagers typically eat both fruit and insects. In addition, taking nectar or eating flowers has been observed for about one-fourth of the tanagers, and a few species (e.g., *Chlorophanes* and some *Diglossa*) feed extensively on nectar for at least part of the year. Other species (e.g., some *Thraupis*) regularly eat buds and leaves.

Table 2 represents our judgements of the proportion of fruit and insects (putting aside other nourishment) in tanager diets. Although the data are based on piecemeal studies and estimates, the pattern is almost evenly balanced between the two basic food types and suggests that the extent of fruit-eating in tanager diets is often overstated. A bias towards fruit-eating observations probably exists because many tanagers are more easily observed in fruiting shrubs and trees along forest edge than when foraging for insects inside vegetation.

Given the limited nutritional content of many fruits (see below), most tanager species appear to obtain a balanced diet of carbohydrates, protein, and lipids by eating both fruit and insects. The proportions of fruit and insects in tanager diets, however, has been found to vary seasonally in Trinidad (Snow and Snow 1971), and future studies may find that insects are taken more often when birds need protein for molting or egg production (see Moermond and Denslow 1985).

Fruit-Eating

Many tanagers eat small juicy fruits that may be swallowed whole, including seeds. Such fruits are usually high in carbohydrates, low in lipids and protein, and consequently may be inadequate for most species to survive upon exclusively. For example, tanagers often eat fruits of melastomes (Melastomataceae), two species of which have been found to contain 84 percent carbohydrates (by dry weight), whereas the corresponding percentage (median) for 26 plant families was about 54 percent (see Moermond and Denslow 1985).

Table 2 Predominance of Fruit or Insects in Tanager Diets*

	More Insects		More Fruit		About Equally†		Total	
	No.	%	No.	%	No.	%	No.	%
Extensive data‡	24	42	17	30	16	28	57	100
Fair data§	25	27	25	26	43	47	92	100
Total	49	33	41	28	59	40	149	100

*"Predominance" means that more than two-thirds of observations involved either fruit or insects.

†"About equally" indicates that observations were at least one-third insects and one-third fruit. Observations involving food other than fruit or insects, such as nectar, were excluded.

‡"Extensive data" means the judgment was based on at least 50 structured foraging observations (e.g., Snow and Snow 1971; Hilty data), 10 or more stomach contents, and/or judgements of persons who have studied the species extensively in the field; typically more than one approach was used.

§"Fair data" means that less information was available, but enough to make an informed judgement. Ninety-three species were omitted because of insufficient data.

Tanagers typically pick small fruits while perched on branches or leaf stems, often by stretching to reach the fruit. After plucking the fruit, tanagers rotate it in the bill with rapid movement of the mandibles (sometimes termed mandibulation), often mashing the fruit before it is swallowed, a procedure which, so far as known, is employed only by tanagers and other nine-primaried songbirds (Moermond and Denslow 1985). Although large seeds may be extracted and dropped, usually the entire fruit is swallowed. One of the functions of fruit mashing may be to squeeze the juice out of the fruit, for tanagers have the unusual ability to take in juices without tilting back their heads (Moermond 1983). Euphonias and chlorophonias, for example, are often observed squeezing the juice out of berries. Some tanagers (e.g., *Thraupis*) also pick pieces out of large pulpy fruits whose seeds are dropped or left hanging.

Three additional types of fruit deserve special attention because they are mentioned often in the species accounts:

1. Arillate fruits. Arils are fleshy seed coverings that are encapsulated in tough, sometimes woody, pods that open as they mature (see Skutch 1980). Apparently rich in lipids and proteins, arils are an important food source for some tanagers (especially *Chlorophanes*, *Cyanerpes*, *Dacnis*). Thin-billed species of tanagers like *Cyanerpes* often obtain newly ripening arils by inserting their bills into capsules not yet fully opened.

2. Cecropia fruits. Abundant colonizers of forest clearings, the approximately forty-five *Cecropia* species (Urticaceae) typically have fruits that hang down on bundles of small fingerlike catkins (see Skutch 1977, chap. 10) that constitute an especially important food source in the dry season. Typically, after perching head down on the spike itself, tanagers begin eating at the tip and gradually denude the spike of fruit, pulling off pieces of pulp and swallowing them immediately (see Silva 1980; Skutch 1980).

3. Mistletoe. Favorite food of euphonias and chlorophonias, whose intestines appear specialized for their consumption, mistletoe fruits are also taken by other tanager species. The tough rinds of some mistletoe fruits are peeled by mandibulation before the seeds and the gelatinous mass surrounding them are swallowed whole. One mistletoe species has been found to be very high in lipids (Moermond and Denslow 1985).

Insect-Feeding

Just as the insect-foraging behavior of tyrant flycatchers is characterized by stationary search from a perch (Fitzpatrick 1980), tanager insect-foraging typically incorporates movement along branches in trees and shrubs, but within this general stereotype, tanagers have developed many different foraging techniques. In this section, after discussing tanager prey briefly, we compare the foraging techniques of tanagers that take insects mostly from one substrate with the techniques of others whose search is not so focused. We also describe insect-foraging techniques that are applied to particular substrates.

Principal insect food recorded for tanagers include larvae and caterpillars (recorded for 62 tanager species), coleopterans (57 tanager species), hymenopterans (39 tanager species), and orthopterans (34 tanager species). However, these observations are almost certainly biased against small insects less than about 1 cm long, and the paucity of such data for small tanagers (e.g., *Tangara*) is very noticeable in the species accounts. Highland tanagers (e.g., *Hemispingus*) appear to take mostly beetles (coleopterans) and grublike insects, whereas lowland tanagers typically are found to have a wide variety of insects (herein used to include all arthropods) in their diets. To some extent, this is an artifact of the distribution of insect life. For example, orthopterans (e.g., roaches and katydids) occur primarily in lowlands—mostly below 1500 m in Costa Rica (Janzen 1973).

Tanagers that concentrate their search on specific types of substrates tend to be small in size (9–14 cm long), to take small prey or soft prey such as grubs, and to glean by moving over branches and twigs rather methodically, examining the preferred substrates at close range, almost myopically, to locate food items. Substrate specialization is especially apparent among the 47 species of *Tangara*. Of 31 species for which foraging behavior is available, 24 (77 percent) appear to be substrate specialists. Fifteen of these species typically take prey from branches, 5 from leaves, 1 from the undersides of leaves and branches, and 3 mostly take insects in the air. The 15 branch specialists are further divisible into species that favor bare branches and those that favor mossy branches, and each of these categories contains species that prefer different branch sizes. Specialization is most prevalent in the Andes where a large number of *Tangara* species are sympatric.

In contrast to specialists, substrate generalists tend to be large in size (13–20 cm long), to take large prey such as orthopterans, and to locate their prey by peering at substrates beyond their immediate reach; this requires them to move in order to attack their targets. Some species (e.g., *Creurgops*, most *Piranga*) hop along branches deliberately, turn their heads slowly, and stretch out or hop for short distances to snare their prey. Other tanagers (e.g., *Tachyphonus*) move rapidly, looking around quickly, and often attack in darting, acrobatic movements. Some rapidly moving species (e.g., Blue-gray Tanager, see Snow and Snow 1971) flutter-pursue insects that tend to escape predation by movement. A few species (e.g., White-winged Tanager) characteristically alternate rapid and deliberate movements.

Substrates often searched and the methods that tanagers use to obtain insects from them include:

1. Branch undersides. Tanagers (especially small species in the genera *Tangara*, *Cyanerpes*, *Euphonia*) characteristically hop along branches stopping every few centimeters to inspect the undersides by leaning first over one side of the branch and then the other in a patterned maneuver herein termed the diagonal-lean. Some species also hang down so their bodies are entirely below the branch or hover or sally to obtain insects from branch undersides.

2. Leaf undersurfaces. A number of tanagers reach the undersides of leaves by hanging down over the leaf from a perch on a branch, on a leaf petiole, or on the leaf itself. Other species reach up to the underside of a leaf from a perch below it. Some (e.g., Red-crowned Ant-Tanager, Gray-hooded Bush-Tanager) ascend upward-slanting branches or saplings to inspect the undersides of leaves systematically.

3. Leaf uppersurfaces. As a group, tanagers may attack insects on leaf tops proportionately more often than most foliage-gleaning birds (see Greenberg and Gradwohl 1980), and some species appear to have evolved a number of specialized techniques for doing so. For example, the White-shouldered Tanager jumps down to attack insects on leaves below its perch; the Guira Tanager sticks its head up above the canopy to search for insects that it attacks acrobatically; the Black-headed Hemispingus and Drab Hemispingus forage by walking atop stiff leaves found at high elevations; at lower elevations the Palm Tanager walks atop large palm leaves, sometimes also hanging to inspect undersides; and the Masked Crimson Tanager often sallies to pick insects off leaf tops.

4. Moss clusters. Tanagers (e.g., *Chlorospingus*, *Buthraupis*) that live in cloud forests and other habitats with moss-laden trees often stop their movements along branches to inspect large masses of moss. This behavior is also common among small *Tangara* tanagers that typically search the undersides of mossy branches.

5. Epiphytes. A number of the same tanagers that search moss clusters are often seen to pick insects from arboreal epiphytes such as bromeliads. A few species (e.g., Olive-green Tanager) may be epiphyte specialists.

6. Insects in flight. A few atypical tanagers (e.g., shrike-tanagers and the Swallow-Tanager) obtain most of their insect prey in the air, and probably the majority of tanagers sally to air at least occasionally. In some species (e.g., *Chrysothlypis*), such sallies seem to be opportunistic extensions of their usual acrobatic hovering and sallying to leaves. The aerial sallies of others seem to be seasonal, occurring when flying termites emerge (e.g., *Cypsnagra* and many other species) or when bees are plentiful (e.g., many *Piranga* species).

7. Army ant following. The Gray-headed Tanager, the Black-goggled Tanager, and some *Habia* species regularly follow army ant swarms to feed on insects trying to escape the ants. A number of other tanager species, especially *Tachyphonus*, are occasionally seen at swarms.

8. Ground foraging. At least twenty tanager species forage on the ground regularly. For example, two somewhat aberrant species, the Rosy Thrush-Tanager and the Chat Tanager, rummage about in leaves like some thrushes and emberizine finches; the White-lined Tanager often pounces on insects from a perch just off the ground; and some high elevation species (e.g., some *Iridosornis*) are often observed foraging on mossy rocks or banks.

9. Arboreal dead leaves. Over two dozen tanager species (e.g., some *Thlypopsis* and *Habia*) are known to examine dead leaf clusters occasionally, and it is possible that a few of these species may be dead-leaf foraging specialists (*sensu* Remsen and Parker 1984).

10. Damaged leaves. The Blue Dacnis has been found to bypass the typical tanager search movements along branches and to fly directly to damaged leaves to probe for insects (Greenberg and Gradwohl 1980).

Vocalizations

The high-pitched squeaky phrases often heard from *Thraupis* tanagers and the rather weak, simple songs of many *Tangara* have probably contributed to the widespread notion that tanagers are poor songsters. Sound recordings by Parker, Schwartz, Belton, and others credited in the species accounts show, however, that the vocalizations of many tanagers are distinctive and/or pleasant to the ear and that a few tanagers (e.g., *Cypsnagra*, *Rhodinocichla*) employ extraordinary, intricate duetting. Females of some species (e.g., some *Piranga* and *Thraupis*) sing briefer and weaker songs than do males.

Song types tend to be similar within genera and useful for narrowing down identification in the field. For example: *Schistochlamys* species have melodic whistles like those of some cardinal finches (Cardinalinae); *Chlorospingus* species incorporate series of thin chipping and chittering notes; *Chlorothraupis* species rapidly deliver series of whistles, squeals, and wheezy notes; most *Piranga* species repeat thrushlike phrases; and the songs of some *Euphonia* species incorporate imitations of the alarms and other calls of their neighbors.

Much remains to be learned about the behavioral context of tanager song. In a study of the Swallow-Tanager, Schaefer (1953) observed that song seemed to have little attractive influence on females or little relation to hostile or territorial behaviors between neighbors; such vocalizations may be used to maintain pair bonds. Social bonding may also be the function of noisy group vocalizations undertaken by the Dusky-faced Tanager, Hooded Mountain-Tanager, and a number of other species.

Tanagers primarily deliver their songs at dawn, but a number of species (e.g., *Habia*, some *Hemispingus*) have a second distinctive song type that is given during the day. Dawn songs are typically delivered from high, regularly used perches, suggesting they are territorial in nature, whereas day songs are emitted irregularly from lower perches inside vegetation and may be related to pair contact or bonding.

Species of many tanager genera have at least two types of calls: a contact note that tends to be high pitched and relatively thin, and an alarm call that is usually moderate pitched and sharp or harsh. In addition, some species (e.g., *Buthraupis*) have distinct flight calls that are used prior to taking off or while flying. A number of tanagers emit "rattles," "scolds," and aggressive sounding notes in hostile encounters with others of their species.

Breeding Behavior

Tanager breeding seasons generally follow the pattern of most omnivorous or insectivorous birds (see Snow and Snow 1964; Skutch 1976). In temperate latitudes, tanagers typically nest in the spring: March–June in North and Middle America and September–December in southern Brazil and surrounding countries. Closer to the Equator, nesting in each hemisphere continues to be concentrated in these same periods because they mark the transition from dry to wet seasons, a time when fruit and insects are most available to supply the nutrition essential to breeding success. At or near the Equator, lowlands tend to have two dry and two rainy seasons. Here, the breeding seasons of some species, especially those living in semiopen habitats near human settlement (e.g., Palm and Blue-gray Tanagers), are extended, sometimes year-round. Specialized feeders, especially nectarivores, provide exceptions to typical seasonal patterns; for example, in Guatemala, the Slaty Flowerpiercer breeds from November to January when flowers are abundant (Skutch 1954).

For the large majority of tanagers, little is known of such basic aspects of breeding behavior as whether breeding pairs are territorial. The clearest demonstrations of territoriality derive from studies of mixed-species flocks in which individual tanagers were color-banded (see section on Social Behavior above). Certain inhabitants of patchy highland forests (e.g., some *Diglossa*, *Xenodacnis*) also are evidently territorial during the breeding season. In North America, sympatric Summer and Scarlet Tanagers have been found to be interspecifically as well as intraspecifically territorial (see Shy 1984b, 1984c). On the other hand, nests of the Silver-beaked Tanager have been found in close proximity, suggesting an absence of or minimal territoriality—or alternatively, polygamy.

Male tanagers display to females or rival males by exhibiting their brightest or most contrasting feathers. For example, in a rather startling display the Ruby-crowned Tanager (see Plate 10), which normally appears all black, flares out a brilliant red crest, uncovers its white lesser wing-coverts, and opens and closes its wing to show white underwing-coverts. *Ramphocelus* species stretch upward to show off the extensive white base to their lower mandible. In a more complex display, the male and female Swallow-Tanager curtsy with synchronized bows.

Willis (1976b) has noted that the typical precopulatory display of tanagers involves wing-fluttering, tail-lifting, and crouching on a horizontal branch.

Euphonias and chlorophonias build globular nests with side entrances and the Swallow-Tanager nests in cavities, but the majority of species build cup nests. Cup nests vary significantly in construction and placement, and some approach globular nests in appearance. For example, tanagers living in mossy forests often place their nests within clumps of thick moss, constructing a rudimentary cup accessible through a side entrance. At the other extreme, some exposed cup nests (e.g., of *Habia*) are so thin and shallow that the eggs may be seen from below.

A large number of species (especially *Tangara*) place their nests in dense clusters of leaves. Crannies, such as the crotch of a tree or a hollowed-out fence post, are the usual sites for domed nests of euphonias and the cup nests of other species (e.g., the Palm Tanager). At least five species (incl. two *Chlorospingus*) regularly place their nests on the ground in sheltering clumps of grass, ferns, heath, etc. Of the 124 species whose nests remain undiscovered, many live in mossy forest where their nests are likely to be found hidden within dense clusters of mosses or bromeliads.

The female takes leadership in nest-building, but the male sometimes participates by finding and placing nest materials in the nest and helping to shape the nest (see Skutch 1976). Eggs, typically 2–3 for most tanagers and 4–5 for euphonias and chlorophonias, are usually layed on consecutive days. Incubation and brooding is by the female; the only exception found to date has been the Rosy Thrush-Tanager (Schwartz in Gilliard 1958). Males typically remain in attendance near the female and some males feed their mates. Nestlings are usually fed by both sexes.

Insects and nutritious arils (see section on Fruit-Eating above) are most often given to nestlings. At times the insects are so large that the nestlings can barely swallow them; presumably this reduces the number of visits to the nest and helps prevent predators from finding it (see Skutch 1985). Euphonias and chlorophonias appear to digest partially and regurgitate food brought to nestlings. Five tanager species have been found to have helpers, presumably offspring of previous broods, that assist the parents in feeding the nestlings.

Incubation and nestling periods vary substantially. Larger species (e.g., *Habia*) that build nests close to the ground and have been found to suffer extremely high rates of nest predation (see Skutch 1985) typically have short (10–13 days) incubation and nestling periods. Often the young leave the nest before they can fly, creeping out into dense tangles. At the other extreme, euphonias, with their young hidden in domed nests, have incubation and nestling periods of 18–24 days. Medium-sized species (e.g., *Tangara*) whose nests are usually well hidden in dense foliage or moss have incubation and nestling periods in between these extremes.

The Tanagers: Accounts

ORCHESTICUS

The Brown Tanager, the single *Orchesticus* species, has an unusual swollen bill. Its foraging behavior suggests tanagers of the genera *Creurgops* and *Tachyphonus*.

Orchesticus abeillei 1
Brown Tanager
Plate 1

Length 17 cm (6½ in.). Weight 31.5 g. Monotypic.

Geographic Range

Se BRAZIL in Paraná, São Paulo, extreme se Minas Gerais (Mt. Itatiaia, Pinto 1951), Rio de Janeiro (state), and Espírito Santo (casually north to Nova Lombardia Refuge; sight, Sept 1977—Ridgely and Sick).

Orchesticus abeillei

Elevational Range

Ca. 900–1500 m; once at ca. 750 m in Espírito Santo.

Habitat and Behavior

Inhabits montane forest; also occurs in tall trees near human settlements. Encountered in pairs and small groups. A portion of the population apparently migrates out of the northern section of its range in winter (Sick 1985). Often travels with mixed-species flocks, particularly with the Buff-fronted Foliage-gleaner, *Philydor rufus*, which is remarkably similar in coloration (Willis 1976b).

Typically forages in the canopy. Hops deliberately along branches shaded by crown foliage, peers around (especially at leaves in dense foliage), then attacks insects in rapid movements, often by sallying; takes insects from the air (Sick 1985), leaf undersides, and spider webs. Inspects bromeliads, mosses, and lichens. (Parker data.)

Vocalizations

Call note: a High-pitched snappy *tsit*. Song: a thin High-pitched *deh-d-d-d-seeeee*, the ending upward-inflected and somewhat rough and squealing; repeated after pauses of 1–9 sec. Song is delivered at dawn and throughout the day; often sings perched upright on uppermost bare branches. (Parker, LNS.)

Breeding

In Rio de Janeiro: In possible courtship display, a male and female faced each other about 10 cm apart and remained motionless with wings held slightly open and drooping, bodies upright, tails down and fanned open. Their nest was nearby in a bromeliad growing on a tree trunk; one bird appeared to be incubating while its mate remained nearby. (Parker data.) Two eggs (presumably of the same clutch) were pinkish white, blotched pale chestnut and deep reddish brown with a few lavender specks; markings were mostly at the large end (Ogilvie-Grant 1912). Breeding dates: Rio de Janeiro Oct.

Sources

Primary Davis 1945b, 1946; Parker data; Pelzeln 1869; Sick 1985; Willis 1976b. **Weights (n = 1?)** Sick 1985. **Vocalizations** LNS recordings by Parker (3). **Nests, eggs, and breeding dates** Parker data; Ogilvie-Grant 1912.

SCHISTOCHLAMYS

Both *Schistochlamys* species search for insects and fruit in bushes and low trees in semi-open areas. The range of the widespread Black-faced Tanager, *S. melanopis* **3**, almost completely overlaps the more restricted range of the Cinnamon Tanager, *S. ruficapillus* **2**, but where both occur, one or the other species tends to be much more abundant. The two species are sometimes found in close proximity in c Brazil (Sick 1985). Their behavior and vocalizations suggest a saltator (Cardinalinae).

Schistochlamys ruficapillus 2
Cinnamon Tanager
Plate 1

Length 16 cm (6½ in.). Weight 29 g (24.1–38.2 g). Three subspecies.

Geographic Range

E BRAZIL from extreme s Pará (Pinto and Camargo 1957), c Maranhão, sw Piauí, and e Pernambuco southward to e Paraná and São Paulo, and inland to extreme ne Mato Grosso and s Goiás.

Elevational Range

From sea level to ca. 1000 m or higher (see Sick 1985).

Habitat and Behavior

Favors dense scrub in cerrado and caatinga; often near wet places in dry regions; especially common in high mountain meadows above treeline (Sick 1985). Also occurs at forest edge and in second growth, riparian woodland, and parks. Appears to migrate seasonally away from parts of c Brazil (Sick 1985). In winter, said to gather in palm trees planted around habitations in e Brazil (Goeldi 1894). May be expanding its range into deforested areas (Ridgely *in litt.*).

Encountered singly or in pairs. Sits quietly at times in the crowns of trees, possibly acting as a sentinel, but often moves quickly to the interior of thickets when approached. Forages mostly in low trees and bushes, but may go higher at forest edge. Observed eating fruits of mulberry (*Morus* sp), palm species, and herbaceous pokeweed (*Phytolacca* sp). Stomach contents: vegetable matter (1); animal matter (1); both (2). Contents in-

Schistochlamys ruficapillus

cluded seeds, fruit, hymenopterans (incl. ants and bees), and coleopterans.

Vocalizations

Call: a low *kwat* or *tche-it* (Sick 1985). Song: a short, rather monotonous, sweet whistled trill often containing trisyllabic stanzas like *dji, djü, dju-dji-djúi* or *wüídje-wüídje* (as rendered in Portuguese, Sick 1985). Resembles the song of the Black-faced Tanager, *S. melanopis* **3** (Ridgely *in litt.*); is delivered from tops of small trees and shrubs.

Breeding

Eggs (2) are yellowish white, densely spotted dark brown (Ihering 1902). Breeding dates: Brazil (Minas Gerais) Dec.

Sources

Primary Burmeister 1856; Erickson and Mumford 1976; Forbes 1881; Goeldi 1894; Mitchell 1957; Sick 1985; Wied 1830. **Weights (n = 3)** Fry 1970; Sick 1985. **Stomach contents** Moojen, Carvalho, and Lopes 1941; Schubart, Aguirre, and Sick 1965. **Vocalizations** Mitchell 1957; Sick 1985. **Eggs and breeding dates** Erickson and Mumford 1957; Ihering 1902.

SCHISTOCHLAMYS 45

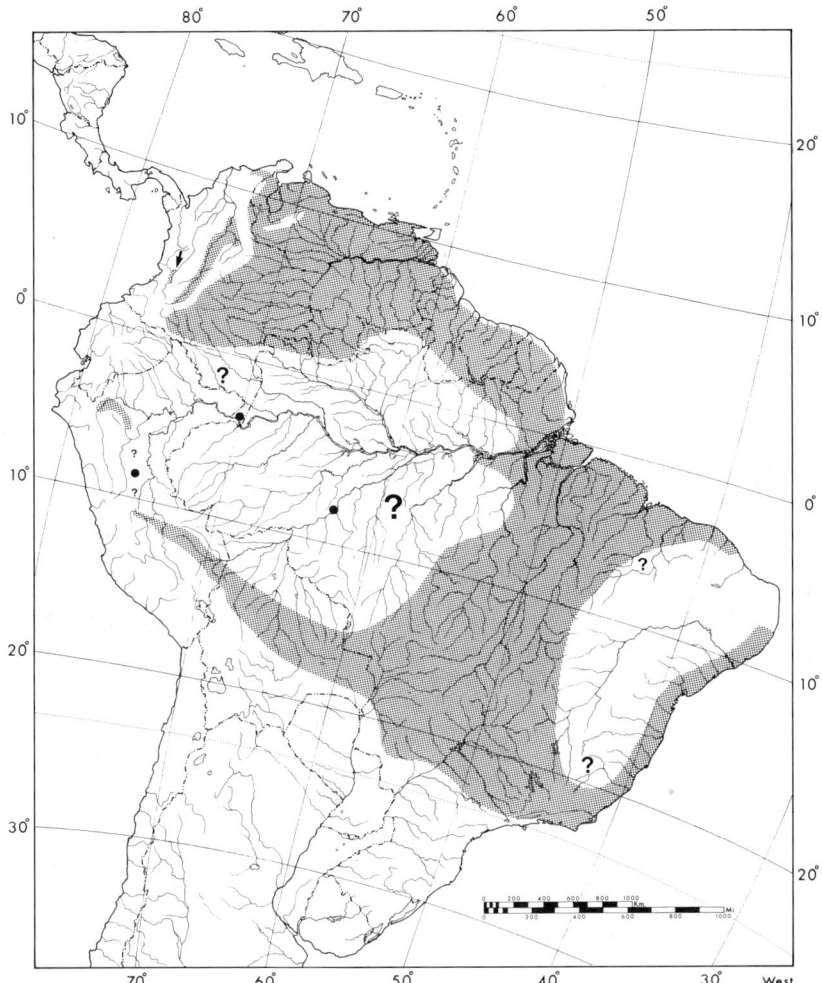

Schistochlamys melanopis

Schistochlamys melanopis **3**
Black-faced Tanager
Plate 1

Length 17 cm (6½ in.). Weight 33 g (29.0–40.0 g). Five subspecies. Breeds in subadult plumage which is sometimes misidentified as the female plumage.

Geographic Range

Encircles a large part of Amazonia. COLOMBIA in the upper Cauca Valley in Valle and the middle and upper Magdalena Valley from Santander to Huila; the Santa Marta and Perijá Mountains eastward through VENEZUELA north of the Andes; east of the Andes in COLOMBIA south to Meta and Vaupés—extending its range further south along the base of the Andes to Putumayo (Hilty and Brown 1986) and one record in extreme s Amazonas (sight, Aug 1974—Remsen)—and eastward through VENEZUELA (except in the llanos) and THE GUIANAS (possibly confined to the savanna belt) to n BRAZIL in ne Pará (Novaes 1980) and Amapá (Novaes 1978); BRAZIL, south of the Amazon River from w Pará (one record from Amazonas) east along the coast to nc Ceará (Pinto and Camargo 1961) and from Maranhão (inland)

and Pernambuco (along the coast) south to São Paulo and ec and s Mato Grosso; west from s Mato Grosso, BRAZIL, through BOLIVIA and thence north (locally) along the e base of the Andes to Cajamarca (Río Marañón Valley), PERU.

Elevational Range

Lowlands and foothills to ca. 1700 m, occasionally slightly higher.

Habitat and Behavior

Inhabits semiopen areas in both dry and humid regions. Prefers bushes and low scrubby trees, especially when grouped together in dense patches on grassy hillsides, in open country such as savanna, or in low gallery forest. Also occurs in open woodland, low second growth, woodland edge, and *Mauritia* palm associations. Invades deforested areas opened for cultivation (Hilty and Brown 1986). Migrates seasonally from parts of c Brazil (Sick 1985). Usually encountered in pairs, sometimes in small family groups. Often disappears into shrubbery when approached.

Typically forages in upper portions and crowns of small trees and shrubs. Flies low across intervening spaces. Not recorded on the ground but observed in tall grass. Stomach contents: vegetable matter (2); animal matter (2); both (2). Contents included fruit, berries, seeds, ants, and other insect remains.

Vocalizations

Song is rhythmic; usually consists of 3 or 4 rich, flutelike, whistled phrases, *tu-whit-WHEER, tu-whit-WHEER, tu-whit*; Low- and Moderate-pitched; sung in about 3 sec. and repeated after a pause of about 10 sec. Call note: a sharp *swit* or *swik* (Snyder 1966). Often calls in flight.

Breeding

Builds an open cup nest of grass in low vegetation at the edge of an open space. In Suriname, a nest was placed 0.4 m above the ground in grass (Haverschmidt 1975). Eggs (2) are grayish or yellowish-white, thickly covered with dark brown spots or blotches. Breeding dates: Venezuela April. Suriname Jan. Brazil (Mato Grosso) Sept.

Sources

Primary Ginés et al. 1951; Haverschmidt 1968; Hilty and Brown 1986; Novaes 1973; Parker data; Schäfer and Phelps 1954; Snyder 1966; Sick 1985. **Weights (n = 22)** Fry 1970; Haverschmidt 1948, 1952, 1968; LSUMZ data. **Stomach contents** Beebe 1909; Haverschmidt 1968;

Schubart, Aguirre, and Sick 1965. **Vocalizations** LNS recordings by Schwartz (2); Snyder 1966. **Nests, eggs, and breeding dates** Allen 1891; Haverschmidt 1975; Peixoto 1932; Santos 1948; Snethlage 1935; Thomas data.

NEOTHRAUPIS and CYPSNAGRA

On the tablelands of central Brazil where both the White-banded Tanager, *Neothraupis fasciata* **4,** and the White-rumped Tanager, *Cypsnagra hirundinacea* **5,** are found, recent field work (Negret data) has shown that the White-banded prefers dense scrub (cerrado) whereas the White-rumped occurs mostly in open grass-covered areas with scattered trees (campo sujo). The foraging behavior of both species reminded one observer (Parker data) of *Tachyphonus* tanagers. The song of the White-rumped Tanager is delivered in a ringing synchronized duet, and the song of the White-banded, which is only slightly less remarkable, is also probably given synchronously by two individuals. Both species employ helpers at the nest.

Neothraupis fasciata **4**
White-banded Tanager
Plate 1

Length 16 cm (6½ in.). Weight 30 g (29.0–32.0 g). Monotypic. Adult plumage appears to be acquired in the second year.

Geographic Range

From s Maranhão and Piauí, BRAZIL, southward through Goiás, w Bahia, and Minas Gerais to São Paulo, BRAZIL, and Amambay, PARAGUAY, and westward through s Mato Grosso, BRAZIL, to e BOLIVIA (Santa Cruz).

Elevational Range

Tablelands to ca. 1100 m (Ridgely *in litt.*); to 550 m in Bolivia.

Habitat and Behavior

On the Brazilian tablelands, primarily lives in dense cerrado where the crowns of trees

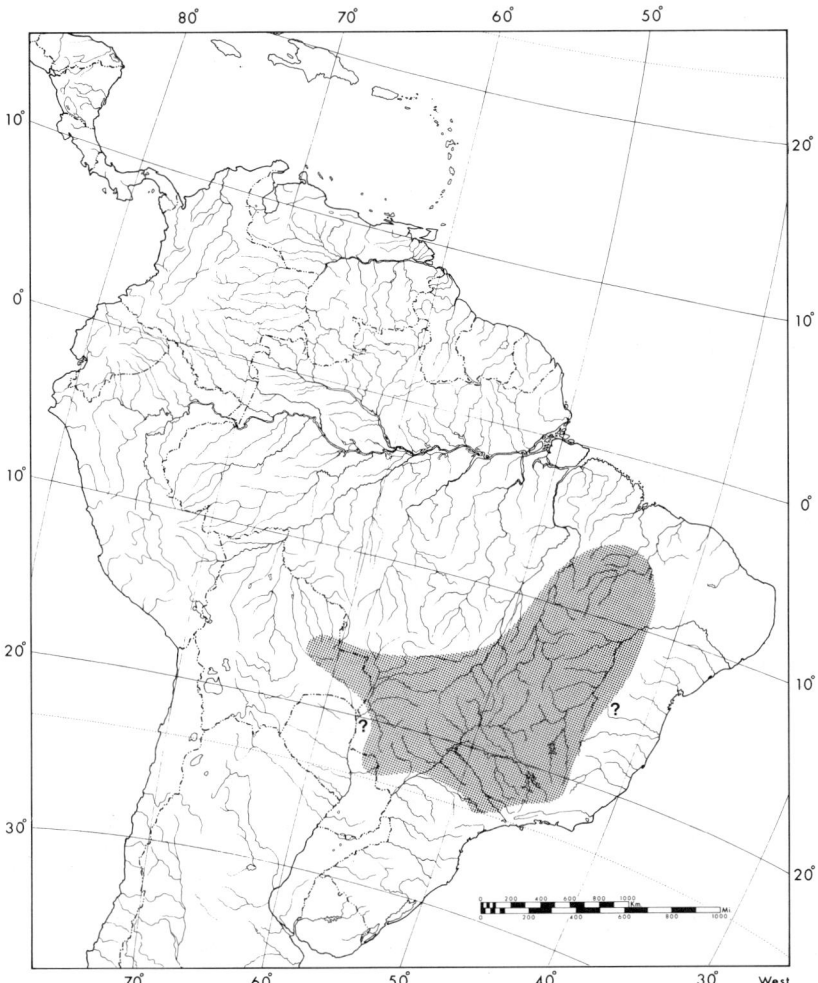

Neothraupis fasciata

cover 50% or more of the terrain; occasionally inhabits groves of semideciduous trees (7–15 m high) where the ground is covered with grass (cerradão); occurs least often in savanna and disturbed areas with scattered shrubs (Negret data). In e Bolivia, encountered in open woodland with heavy grass cover and low bushes (LSUMZ data). In sc Mato Grosso, may migrate seasonally (Allen 1891). Usually lives in groups of 5–12 (most often 7) individuals; groups are smaller during the breeding season (Negret data). Travels with mixed-species flocks in the cerrado; may be a nuclear species.

Forages mostly in grasses and herbaceous vegetation; quickly follows the passage of fire through the cerrado to capture insects on the ground (Negret data). Ground-feeding birds are alerted to possible dangers by a flock mate who perches as a sentinel in the higher vegetation (Negret data). Also moves quickly through woody vegetation; peers and picks insects from leaves, branches, and tree trunks. Foraging behavior is suggestive of a *Tachyphonus* tanager (Parker data). Appears to be primarily insectivorous, but takes fruit from *Annona*, *Miconia*, *Eugenia*, *Palicourea*, *Casearia*, and *Byrsonima* species (Negret data). Stomach contents: insect matter (6); vegetable matter (1). Contents included ants, coleopterans, spiders, seeds, and a small land snail.

Vocalizations

Call: a strident *uit* or *bit* (Sick 1985). Frequent chipping is heard as groups move through vegetation; sentinels give alarm calls. Song: a lively, loud, and liquid melodic whistle, e.g., *whew chid-di-wee-wee-TYOO chid-i-o-WOO chi-d-dee-TYOO*; usually begins with a cueing note followed by 3–6 phrases, each ending emphatically; apparently given by pairs in a synchronized duet; song elements are 5–10 sec. long with pauses of 2–6 sec.; Moderate- and Low-pitched; usually heard only before dawn, ending about 10 min. before good light; delivered from high in bushes and trees (Parker, LNS; Parker data).

Breeding

Usually hides its large deep cup nest, constructed of twigs and straw and lined with fine grass, among leaves and branches of a small tree. Clutch size is generally 3, sometimes 2. Young birds of previous broods help at the nest (Negret data). Breeding dates: Brazil (Goiás) Oct and Nov.

Sources

Primary Negret data; Parker data; Ridgely *in litt.*; Sick 1985. **Weights (n = 3)** LSUMZ data. **Stomach contents** LSUMZ data; Negret data; Pelzeln 1869; Schubart, Aguirre, and Sick 1965. **Vocalizations** LNS recordings by Parker (1); Parker data; Sick 1985. **Nests and breeding dates** Negret data.

Cypsnagra hirundinacea 5
White-rumped Tanager
Plate 1

Length 16 cm (6 in.). Weight 29 g (25.0–34.0 g). Both subspecies are illustrated. Adult plumage is apparently acquired in the second year.

Geographic Range

C. h. pallidigula: north of the Amazon River in the Sipaliwini savanna (Renssen 1974), SURINAME, and Amapá, BRAZIL (Novaes 1978); south of the Amazon River from nw Ceará, BRAZIL, southward to n Bahia and westward through Piauí, c Maranhão, n Goiás, se Pará, and nw Mato Grosso, BRAZIL, to El Beni, BOLIVIA; one record from sc Amazonas, BRAZIL. *C. h. hirundinacea*: s Bahia, BRAZIL, southward to São Paulo (west of the coastal mountains), westward through s Goiás, and s Mato Grosso, BRAZIL, and nc PARAGUAY (Concepción) to ec BOLIVIA (Santa Cruz).

Elevational Range

Lowlands to about 1000 m in Brazil, to 700 m in Bolivia (LSUMZ).

Habitat and Behavior

In the Brazilian tablelands, primarily inhabits grasslands with scattered low trees less than 2 m high (campo sujo); occasionally found in open cerrado where trees and shrubs shade less than 50% of the grasses and herbs; also occurs in agricultural areas and at the fringes of settlements where similar habitat occurs (Negret data). In Bolivia, encountered in open woodland with heavy grass cover (LSUMZ data). Also recorded at woodland edge and in *Mauritia* palm groves within savanna. In c Brazil, usually found in groups of 3–6 individuals; during the breeding season, each group has an extensive territory of about 5 ha. (Negret data). In Bolivia, encountered in pairs and small groups (LSUMZ data).

In c Brazil, captures coleopterans and orthopterans low in the vegetation and also on the ground; seasonally sallies to air for flying ants and termites (Negret data). Also in c Brazil, hopped slowly along interior branches and peered for insects with head up and neck outstretched; caught 4–5 cm orthopterans and a 3 cm caterpillar from inside curled green leaves and from the bottom surface of a leaf; foraging behavior was suggestive of a *Tachyphonus* tanager (Parker data). Highly insectivorous, but eats fruit of *Byrsonima*, *Anonna*, *Eugenia*, and *Erythroxlum* species (Negret data). Stomach contents: animal matter (4). Contents included a large spider. Additional stomach contents included a small beetle and seeds.

Vocalizations

Pairs duet from the tops of low trees, especially in the morning, and may be heard at some distance (at least 200 m). The male and female perch within a half-meter of each other and sit upright with tails shaking as they sing; other individuals of the (family?) group perch nearby, but apparently do not sing. The male begins the song with a churring that becomes a staccato rattle at which time the female joins in with a loud, melodious, wrenlike series that sounds like *wee-o ta-CHEE-o chee-o*, repeated over and over. The contrast between the unmusical and musical vocalizations produces an unusual synchronized duet that is both forceful

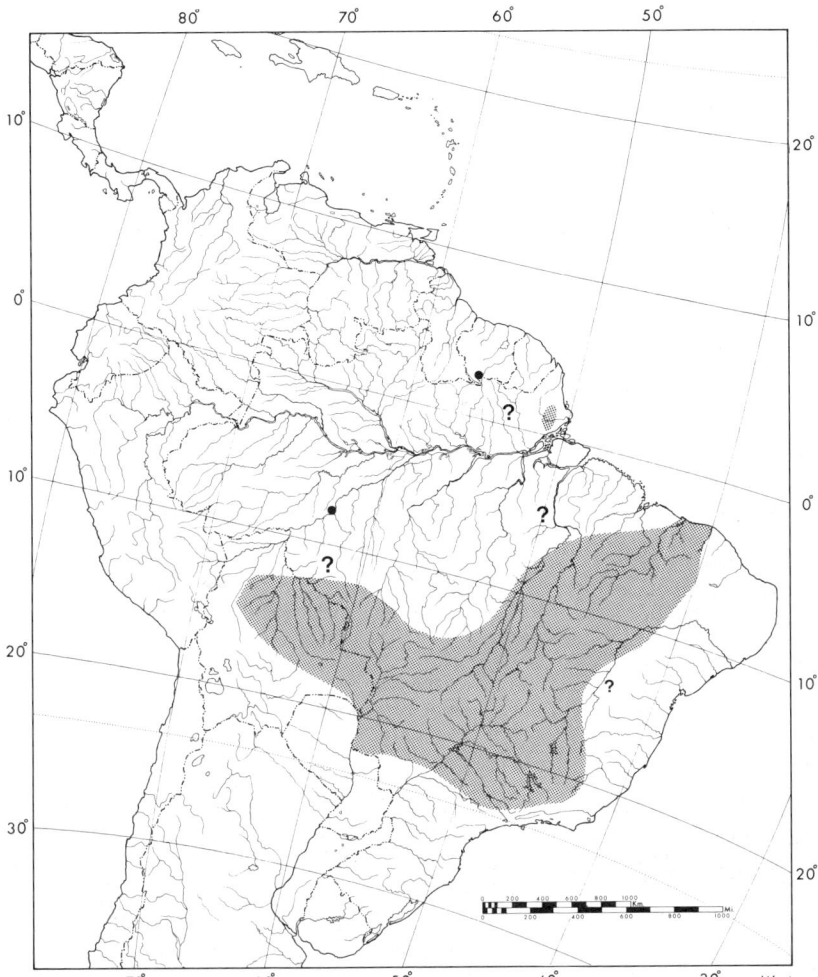

Cypsnagra hirundinacea

and rhythmic. The flat call note, *chak*, suggests a call of the Northern Mockingbird, *Mimus polyglottos* (Parker data).

Breeding

Cup nests are placed in the forks of branches 1–2 m off the ground. Nests are made of tightly woven grasses (sometimes including leaves or twigs) and lined with cottonlike plant material of *Eriotheca*. Eggs (4, sometimes 3) are pale blue, sparsely spotted with black or chocolate dots that tend to form a wreath around the large end. One or 2 birds, probably young of the previous season, typically help at the nest. Breeding dates: Brazil (Goiás) Sept and Nov; (São Paulo) Nov.

Sources

Primary Negret data; Parker data; Pelzeln 1869; Reinhardt 1870; Renssen 1974; Ridgely *in litt.*; Sick 1985. **Weights (n = 7)** LSUMZ data; Sick 1985. **Stomach contents** LSUMZ data; Reinhardt 1870. **Vocalizations** LNS recording by Parker (1); Renssen 1974; Ridgely *in litt.*; Sick 1985. **Nests, eggs, and breeding dates** Ihering 1914; Negret data; Parker data.

CONOTHRAUPIS

Both *Conothraupis* species, the Black-and-white Tanager, *C. speculigera* **6,** and Cone-billed, *C. mesoleuca* **7,** appear to favor open woodland. The behavior of the Black-and-white Tanager has reminded observers of emberizine finches of the genus *Passerina* (Cardiff and Dittman *in litt.*). The plumage pattern of males of both species is strikingly like that of some seedeaters in the genus *Sporophila*. The known ranges of the two *Conothraupis* species are separated by about 1500 km, but the actual gap may prove smaller given the nomadic tendencies of the Black-and-white Tanager.

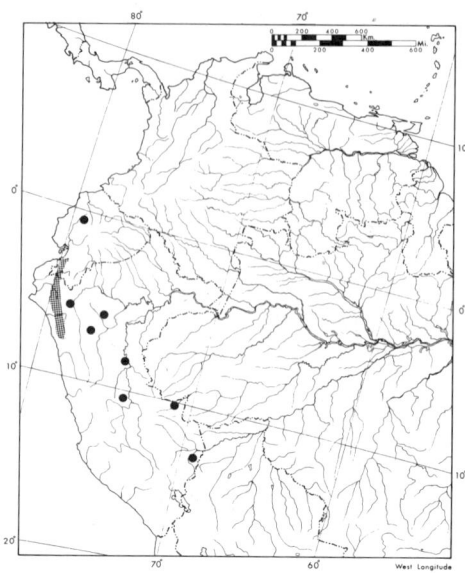

Conothraupis speculigera

Conothraupis speculigera 6
Black-and-white Tanager
Plate 1

Length 16 cm (6 in.). Weight 25 g (23.0–28.0 g). Monotypic.

Geographic Range

West of the Andes in Pichincha (sight, 1980—Ridgely; July 1981—Hilty et al.), Azuay, and Loja, ECUADOR, southward to La Libertad, PERU, and east of the Andes in Amazonas, Cajamarca, San Martín, Ucayali (O'Neill 1966), Pasco (FMNH), and Madre de Dios (sight, July 1981 and Aug 1982—Parker), PERU.

Elevational Range

Ca. 100–1800 m.

Habitat and Behavior

Nomadic in at least part of its range; occurrences in areas of nw Peru are dependent on whether there has been sufficient rainfall for vegetation to develop (O'Neill 1966). For example, at one site regularly visited by LSUMZ personnel in Lambayeque, Peru (elev. 100 m), the Black-and-white Tanager was seen only once prior to 1983, but this species was common after heavy rains in 1983 and 1984 and was encountered in large single-species flocks in September 1984 (Cardiff and Dittman *in litt.*; LSUMZ data; M. Williams *in litt.*). Nesting is documented for the western Andean slope but not the eastern slope, and it is not known whether individuals found in Amazonia travel over the Andes from the western slope or represent an eastern slope or Amazonian nesting population.

Usually encountered singly or in small groups. Also seen in flocks of over 50 individuals. In nw Peru, occurs in bushes and herbaceous vegetation underneath trees in woodlands and tall second growth. Also found in trees and shrubbery at forest edge in humid regions.

In Lambayeque, Peru, single-species flocks foraged primarily in the weedy understory of woodlots of tall mesquite (*Prosopsis* sp), presumably searching for insects, but foraging behavior could not be observed in the dense vegetation. When a flock was approached, the entire group left the understory for higher vantage points in trees, then flew some distance away or dropped back into the weeds if danger passed (Cardiff and Dittman *in litt.*). Also foraged in the trees at heights of 3–12 m above the ground, generally within 1–2 m of the crowns, hopping along thin branches and typically perching upright or reaching out to pick insects off mesquite leaflets (Cardiff and Dittman *in litt.*, 9 obs.). Stomach contents: animal matter (23); animal and vegetable matter (7). Contents included caterpillars (both smooth and hairy), small spiders, a midsized orthopteran, moths, beetles, hemipterans, a small bee or wasp, leaflets, and seeds.

Vocalizations

Song is a series of 3–5 double notes that sound like *chee'ong* or *chee'ouk*, quite loud and icteridlike, with the quality of a Solitary Black Cacique, *Cacicus solitarius* (O'Neill data). On its breeding grounds, a singing male may perch conspicuously on the crown of a bush or sometimes in a tree, sitting fairly erect with head raised and wings slightly drooped.

Breeding

Carriker (1934) flushed a laying female from a thicket of rank grass and weeds growing on a steep slope above an irrigation ditch. He was unable to locate her nest but suspected it was placed on or near the ground since no nests were found in the shrubbery. Breeding dates: nw Peru April.

Sources

Primary Carriker 1933a, 1934; Cardiff and Dittman *in litt.*; O'Neill 1966; O'Neill and Pearson 1974; Ridgely 1980. **Weights (n = 9)** LSUMZ data. **Stomach contents** LSUMZ data. **Vocalizations** Carriker 1934; O'Neill data; Taczanowski 1884b. **Breeding dates** Carriker 1934.

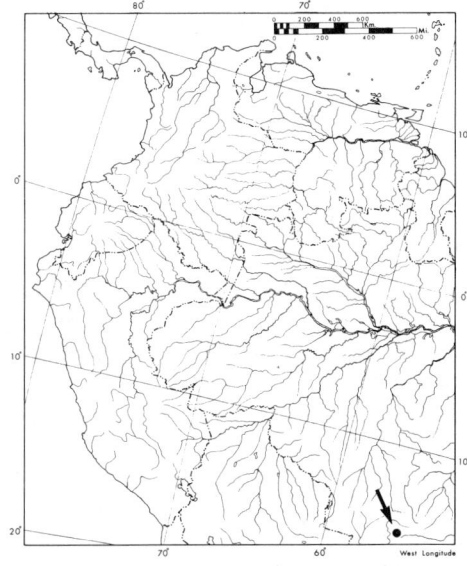

Conothraupis mesoleuca

Conothraupis mesoleuca 7
Cone-billed Tanager
Plate 1

Length 14 cm (5½ in.). Monotypic.

Geographic Range

Known only from the type locality, ne of the city of Mato Grosso, Mato Grosso, BRAZIL.

Elevational Range

Ca. 200 m.

Habitat and Behavior

Taken among bushy vegetation in dry forest.

Vocalizations

No information.

Breeding

No information.

Sources

Primary Berlioz 1939a, 1946.

LAMPROSPIZA and CISSOPIS

The relationships of these two monotypic genera to other tanagers is unclear, but a number of authors have noted that *Lamprospiza* and *Cissopis* resemble one another. Both species are often encountered in small noisy groups.

Lamprospiza melanoleuca 8
Red-billed Pied Tanager
Plate 2

Length 17 cm (6½ in.). Weights 34 g (31.0–42.0 g). Monotypic.

Geographic Range

From Maranhão (photo, Ridgely, *in litt.*) and Amapá, BRAZIL (Novaes 1978), and THE GUIANAS southwestward through Amazonian BRAZIL (Pará, ec Amazonas, and extreme nw Mato Grosso) to BOLIVIA (extreme n Beni) and se PERU (n Puno, Madre de Dios, and Ucayali).

52 LAMPROSPIZA

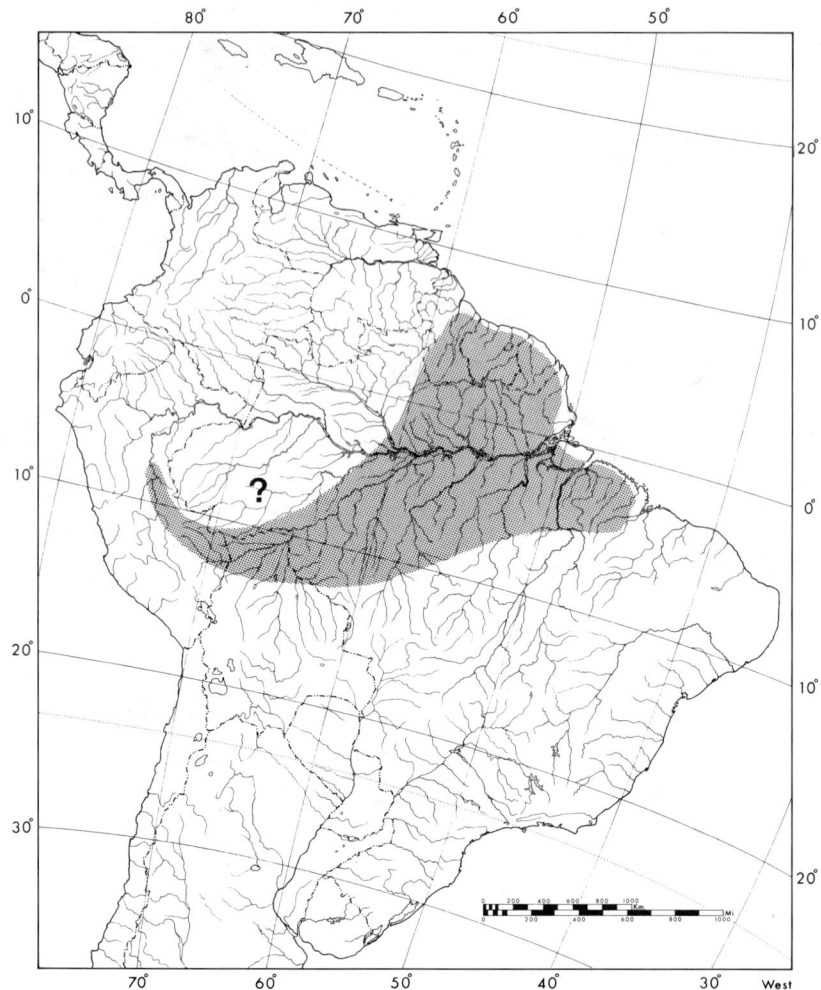

Lamprospiza melanoleuca

Elevational Range

Lowlands.

Habitat and Behavior

Inhabits the interior and edge of terra firma forest; occasionally occurs in savanna woodlands. Typically encountered in small groups of 3–6 individuals. Joins feeding aggregations at fruiting trees and associates with mixed-species flocks, but the duration of such associations is unclear. Often heard or seen flying over treetops, apparently moving between widely separated food sources. Forages in the canopy, usually in the crowns of tall trees but also comes lower in fruiting trees. In Suriname, perched almost horizontally on branches 8–10 cm in diam. and turned from side to side; occasionally sat up vertically. Also seen leaping back and forth among larger open limbs in the crown of a tall tree, opening wings only once or twice to cover a distance of about 3–6 m possibly capturing insects in the air. Observed feeding on *Cecropia* catkins. (Isler data.) Stomach contents: berries, seeds, and coleopterans.

Vocalizations

Groups are noisy. Flock members deliver a buzzy High-pitched *tzee-tzee* or *tzee-tzee-tzee* in rapid succession and, simultaneously, a clearer loud Moderate-pitched *cheer* or *chee-*

cheer (Suriname) or downward-inflected *wheeer* (Brazil and Peru), often followed by a High-pitched *chi-de-de-dit* that may be lengthened or run into a trill. In flight, gives a Moderate-pitched *per-CHEE-chee-chee* suggesting the call of an American Goldfinch, *Carduelis tristis* (T. H. Davis *in litt.*).

Breeding

No information.

Sources

Primary Haverschmidt 1968; Isler data; Munn 1985; Parker data; Pearson 1975b; Willis 1977. **Weights (n = 7)** Haverschmidt 1948, 1968; LSUMZ data. **Stomach contents** Haverschmidt 1968; Pelzeln 1869. **Vocalizations** LNS recordings by Bierregaard (1), T. H. Davis (2), Parker (3); recording by Whitney (1); T. H. Davis *in litt.*

Cissopis leveriana 9
Magpie Tanager
Plate 2

C. l. leveriana: length 26 cm (10½ in.); weight 76 g (73.8–86.0 g). *C. l. major*: length 29 cm (11½ in.); weight 75.8 g (1 male) and 69 g (67.5–71.0, 2 females).

Geographic Range

C. l. leveriana: both slopes of the Andes in VENEZUELA from Táchira and Apure to Mérida and east of the Andes from COLOMBIA southward through ECUADOR and PERU to Santa Cruz (Schmitt et al. in press), BOLIVIA, eastward north of the Amazon River through Amazonas and c Bolívar, VENEZUELA, to GUYANA with scattered records from n Roraima (Pinto 1966), BRAZIL, SURINAME (Zimmerman 1977), and FRENCH GUIANA, and eastward south of the Amazon to c Mato Grosso, se Pará, and s Maranhão, BRAZIL. *C. l. major*: from Goiás and Bahia (one 19th-century record from Pernambuco) south to extreme n Rio Grande do Sul, BRAZIL (Belton 1973), Misiones, ARGENTINA, and PARAGUAY east of the Río Paraguay.

Elevational Range

Lowlands to 1200 m, occasionally higher; to 2000 m in the Andes of Venezuela.

Habitat and Behavior

In Amazonia, lives in semiopen floodplains along rivers (incl. *varzea* forest edge) where thickets and low trees predominate; thought to be expanding its range as forest is opened up in Andean foothills in Peru and Bolivia (Remsen and Parker 1983). North and south of Amazonia, inhabits open woodlands, second growth, reverted clearings, and shrubby places at forest edge; also occurs in plantations (coffee, banana) and areas of human settlements near forest. Encountered in small groups of 3–5 (sometimes up to 10) individuals, in pairs during the breeding season, and occasionally singly. Joins feeding aggregations at fruiting trees but is sporadic in mixed-species flocks. Noisy and conspicuous, bringing to mind a jay or a magpie (Corvidae) in appearance and behavior. Makes long hops; almost seems to leap from branch to branch as it moves through open woodland. Frequently flies about clearings; flight is steady and slow; wings make a whirring noise. Wags its tail vertically; displays white-spotted tail feathers when taking off or startled.

In Amazonia, forages mostly below 12 m off the ground in shrubs and small trees in the flood plain; occasionally goes to the tops of tall trees at forest edge or into forest for a short distance. Elsewhere, forages at all levels, especially the canopy of open woodland, tall second growth, and shade trees in plantations. In c Brazil, seeks fruits of *Hamelia patens* (Rubiaceae) and descends to eat fruits of the herbaceous pokeweed of *Phytolacca* species (Sick 1985). In Argentina, seen at *Cecropia* trees, jumping and fluttering to feed at catkins (Parker data). In Ecuador, ate small hard green buds (Goodfellow 1901). Stomach contents: vegetable matter (9); animal matter (2); both (15). Contents included fruit pulp, seeds, spiders, caterpillars, and hymenopterans.

Vocalizations

Call note: a hard, loud, Moderate-pitched *chek*. *C. l. leveriana*: Also utters a thin squealing *sweeeee* and a squealing *eeCHUK*. The variable yet distinctive explosive song combines Low-pitched raspy rattles with Moderate-pitched squeaky notes, e.g., *t-t-t-t-t-t-t-TEEK TEEK TEEK*, *titl-titl-tleechuk ee-CHUK*, etc; usually delivered for some time at a jerky pace. *C. l. major*: phrases, frequently trisyllabic, are repeated very rapidly (Sick 1985); on one recording the basic phrase sounds like *swikit swee swee* (Parker, LNS).

Breeding

Builds a cup nest made of twigs, plant fibers, and grass (one was decorated with leaves), concealed in dense foliage on a fork of a branch of a shrub or low tree (one nest was about 3.5 m above the ground). Eggs (2)

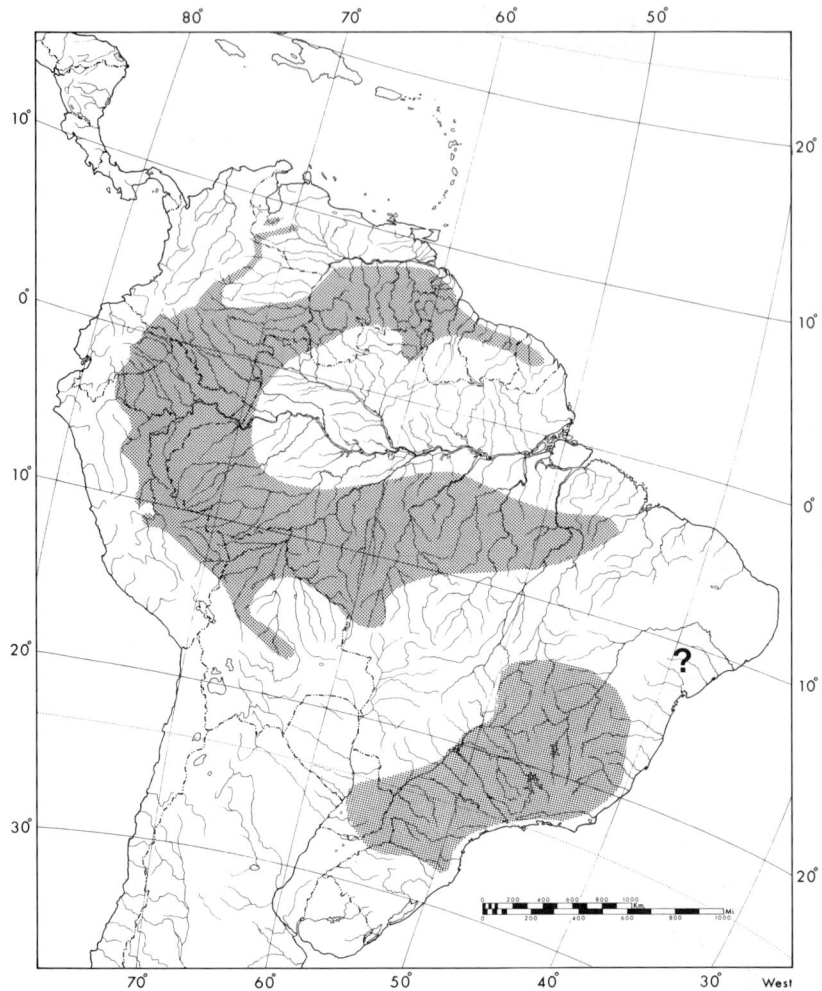

Cissopis leveriana

have an ashy or reddish-brown base covered all over with densely packed brown spots. In captivity, a nest was built 1.4 m up in a tree; incubation took 12–13 days; and the nestling period was 15 days (Norgaard-Olesen 1974). Breeding dates: Brazil (Rio de Janeiro) Oct.

Sources

Primary Burmeister 1856; Descourtilz 1852; Goeldi 1894; Hilty and Brown 1986; LSUMZ data; Mitchell 1957; O'Neill 1974; Parker data; Reinhardt 1870; Sick 1985; Taczanowski 1884b. **Weights (n = 13)** Belton 1985; LSUMZ data; Pearson 1971; Sick 1985; Weske 1972. **Stomach contents** Foster data; LSUMZ data; Moojen, Carvalho, and Lopes 1941; Pelzeln 1869; Schubart, Aguirre, and Sick 1965. **Vocalizations** LNS recordings by Parker (3), Schwartz (1), van den Berg (2); Goeldi 1894; O'Neill 1974; Sick 1985; Snyder 1966. **Nests, eggs, and breeding dates** Ihering 1900; Nehrkorn 1899; Penard and Penard 1910; Snethlage and Schreiner 1929.

CHLORORNIS

In its appearance, the single *Chlorornis* species, the Grass-green Tanager, stands apart from other tanagers, although the Grass-green's habitat, foraging behavior, and vocalizations resemble those of species in the genus *Buthraupis*.

Chlorornis riefferii 10
Grass-green Tanager
Plate 2

Length 20 cm (8 in.). Weight 53 g (42.0–59.0 g). Five subspecies.

Geographic Range

C. r. riefferii, diluta, and *elegans*: the Andes of COLOMBIA (from Boyacá south in the E Andes) southward on the Pacific slope through ECUADOR to Loja and on the e Andean slope through ECUADOR and PERU to n Cuzco (Cordillera Vilcabamba, Weske 1972). *C. r. celata* and *boliviana*: e Andean slope from Puno, PERU, to Cochabamba, BOLIVIA.

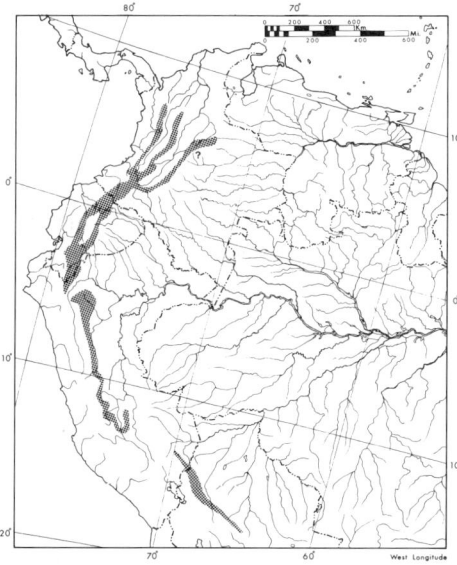

Chlorornis riefferii

Elevational Range

1500–3350 m; mostly 2000–2700 m.

Habitat and Behavior

Prefers wet mossy forest and forest edge; less numerous in tall second-growth woodland. Travels in pairs or small groups of 3–6 (rarely to 10) individuals. Usually encountered in pairs or singly in Bolivia, where seemingly less common than farther north (Schulenberg *in litt.*). Often accompanies mixed-species flocks. Moderately active and conspicuous. Perches for long periods, sometimes sitting back on its legs almost horizontally and, at other times, sitting upright. Flies rather heavily.

Feeds from low in bushes to high in trees but forages most often in the upper half of small trees; foraging heights may vary regionally. Moves a little sluggishly from branch to branch when foraging. Inspects moss and epiphytes and peers at foliage; leans down to pick prey off leaf tops. Examines undersides of mossy branches 3–6 cm in diam. using the diagonal-lean foraging method. Occasionally hangs or flutters clumsily from leaves. Stomach contents: vegetable matter (3); animal matter (2); both (2). Contents included fruit pulp, seeds, a 40 mm worm, and insect remains. Additional stomach contents included berries and caterpillars.

Vocalizations

Contact call is a Moderate to High-pitched, abrupt, squeaking, finchlike, nasal *enk* or *eck*, at times given in twos or threes or strung into a longer stuttering series; sometimes uttered "hysterically." Emits a slow *t-e-e-e-e-k* just prior to or during flight. Dawn song: phrases begin with 1 or 2 short *enk* notes, somewhat like cueing notes of a wren, followed by bursts of 1–5 harsh squeaky double notes that sound like a rusty gate being moved back and forth quickly. Possible day song: repeats a heavy *chink* followed by a higher-pitched *zheet*; about 1 phrase/2 sec. Songs are Moderate- to Low-pitched.

Breeding

In Colombia, a relatively large nest was made of green moss and ornamented with ferns. One egg was gray, freckled lilac gray (Sclater and Salvin 1879).

Sources

Primary Goodfellow 1901; Isler data; Hilty and Brown 1986; LSUMZ data; Niethammer 1956; Remsen 1985; Taczanowski 1884b; Vuilleumier 1970. **Weights (n = 37)** LSUMZ data; Weske 1972. **Stomach contents** LSUMZ data; Taczanowski 1884b. **Vocalizations** LNS recordings by Parker (3) van den Berg (1); recording by R. A. Rowlett (1); Hilty and Brown 1986. **Nests and eggs** Sclater and Salvin 1879.

COMPSOTHRAUPIS and SERICOSSYPHA

The Scarlet-throated, *Compsothraupis loricata* 11, and White-capped, *Sericossypha albocristata* 12, are among the largest tanagers. The two species are similar in plumage, and both have very heavy legs, but their environments and behavior differ greatly. In its behavior, the Scarlet-throated Tanager suggests a *Thraupis* tanager (Sick 1985) or an icterid (Ridgely *in litt.*) whereas the White-capped reminds one of a jay (Corvidae). A recent study supports the placement of *Sericossypha* within the Thraupinae (Morony 1985).

Compsothraupis loricata 11
Scarlet-throated Tanager
Plate 2

Length 21 cm (8½ in.). Weight 72.5 g (1 male). Monotypic. Also known as *Sericossypha loricata*. Red throated males form a distinct minority of individuals encountered. May breed in subadult plumage (Sick 1985).

Geographic Range

Ne BRAZIL from e Maranhão, Piauí, Ceará, Pernambuco, and Alagoas south to wc Goiás, c Minas Gerais and se Bahia.

Elevational Range

Ca. 200–1000 m.

Habitat and Behavior

Inhabits trees in gallery woodland and semi-open areas near water. Usually encountered in small groups of up to 8 individuals even during the breeding season; rarely in pairs. Sluggish; sometimes perches on exposed branches high in trees (Ridgely *in litt.*). Stomach contents: insects.

Vocalizations

Call note is a loud *chirt* (Ridgely *in litt.*), similar to that of the Red-rumped Cacique, *Cacicus haemorrhous* but harsher (Sick 1985). Song: described as a single phrase, rendered in Portuguese as *kjä* or *kjö*, repeated uninterruptedly at dawn at a rate of about 1 phrase/sec. and continued for up to 7 min. at a time; often given again after a brief pause of up to a min.; a session may last up to 45 min.; rarely sings during the day (Sick 1985).

Breeding

During the breeding season, males display white bases of back feathers. Nests are hidden in dense palm crowns, in woodpecker holes in *Mauritia* palm snags, and in abandoned stick nests of the Rufous Cachalote, *Pseudoseisura cristata*. Seen carrying long sticks, presumably to add to a nest, and also observed attacking hawks that came near a nest. (Sick 1985.)

Sources

Primary Pinto 1954; Ridgely *in litt.*; Sick 1985; Wied 1830. **Weight (n = 1)** Sick 1985. **Vocalizations** Ridgely *in litt.*; Sick 1985; Wied 1830. **Nests** Ridgely *in litt.*; Sick 1985.

Sericossypha albocristata 12
White-capped Tanager
Plate 2

Length 24 cm (9½ in.). Weight 114 g (95.0–125.0 g). Monotypic.

Geographic Range

The e slope of the C Andes near the Caldas-Tolima border (sight, Orejuela in Hilty and Brown 1986) and the w slope of the C Andes in Cauca, COLOMBIA; both sides of the upper Magdalena Valley in Huila, COLOMBIA; and the e slope of the Andes from Táchira, VENEZUELA (west of the Western Venezuelan Low), southward locally through COLOMBIA, ECUADOR, and PERU to Junín.

Elevational Range

1600–3200 m.

Habitat and Behavior

Inhabits humid montane forest; also occurs at forest edge and in second-growth woodland. Locally distributed and generally scarce. May wander seasonally (Hilty and Brown 1986). Travels in groups of 4–8 individuals; in Peru, groups typically contain only one male in adult plumage (Schulenberg *in litt.*), suggesting family groups. Larger flocks of up to 20 individuals have been reported.

Flock members usually remain close together. Peers, postures, and cocks tail jay-like; hops and leaps boldly through trees (Silliman in Hilty and Brown 1986). Flock members typically feed in 2 or 3 trees within a small area and then fly as a group to a new foraging site which may be several hundred

Compsothraupis loricata

to a thousand or more meters away. Sails down slopes with wings held open (Parker data). Forages in the tops of trees (mostly tall trees), occasionally lower, to tops of second growth. Stomach contents: vegetable matter (2); animal matter (4); both (1). Contents included fruit pulp, seeds, ants, wasps, bees, coleopterans, dipteran larvae, and a snail shell.

Vocalizations

Very noisy; generally heard long before it is seen. In an erratic and variable fashion, strings together piercing notes (Moderate- to Low-pitched) that include *kip*, *keep*, *peeeaap*, *peeer*, and *peeeur*; delivered at a rate of about 40 notes/min. Turns from side to side or leans forward with each note. Continues calling for some time (over 9 min. in one recording). Often flock members call simultaneously, producing a cacophony of notes.

Breeding

No information.

Sources

Primary Goodfellow 1901; Isler data; Hilty and Brown 1986; LSUMZ data. **Weights (n = 17)** LSUMZ data. **Stomach contents** LSUMZ data. **Vocalizations** LNS recordings by Isler (1), O'Neill (3), Parker (1), van den Berg (1).

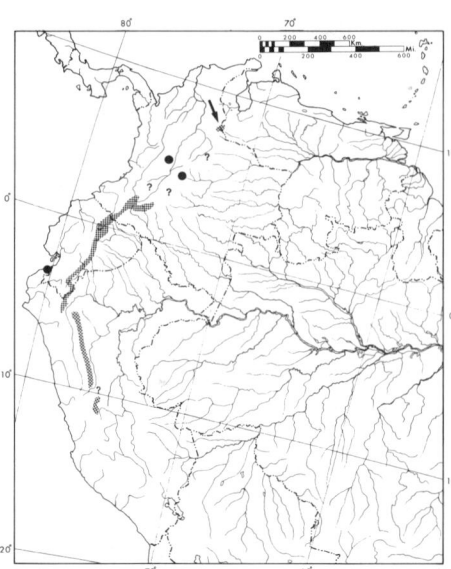

Sericossypha albocristata

Habitat and Behavior

Inhabits humid forests in mountains and descends to palm forests, thickets, and coffee plantations at lower elevations. When not nesting, travels in straggling groups of up to 12 or more individuals. Often stays well hidden within dense foliage. Although it seldom flies for long distances, flight is strong and undulating. Gathers in large flocks to roost; individuals chatter, scold, and fight as they fly to roost sites in palm trees or bamboo clumps. Has been observed anting (see King and Kepler 1970).

Forages in dense vegetation in the forest canopy and also in the understory. Flies and flutters along twigs; examines leaves and the undersides of limbs (Wetmore 1927). Observed eating *Cecropia* and palm fruits. Stomach contents: orthopterans, weevils, spiders, moths, caterpillars, lizards, frogs, fruit, and a few hard grass seeds.

Vocalizations

Calls: a loud sharp *chewp* or a harsh *chuck* that frequently runs into a chatter of varying length, *chi-chi-chit*; also *tsweep tsweep*, a soft short twitter, and a thin *sigh* like a heavy exhale (Raffaele 1983). Song is sweet and warbling with many trills.

Breeding

Nests (3 recorded) are placed 2–9 m off the ground (Raffaele 1983). One cup-shaped nest, loosely woven with feathers and grass, was placed in a small tree (Gundlach 1882). Eggs (2–3) are cream colored heavily speckled brown; one had a few black spots and streaks. Breeding dates: Jan–Aug.

Sources

Primary Biaggi 1970; Raffaele 1983; Wetmore 1927. **Weights (n = 19)** Olson and Angle 1977; Oniki 1975. **Stomach contents** Danforth (?yr). **Vocalizations** Raffaele 1983; Wetmore 1927. **Nests, eggs, and breeding dates** Gundlach 1882; Raffaele 1983.

NESOSPINGUS

The single species, endemic to Puerto Rico, was originally described as a *Chlorospingus*. *Nesospingus* appears to differ substantially from *Chlorospingus* species in morphology, social and feeding behaviors, and vocalizations.

Nesospingus speculiferus **13**
Puerto Rican Tanager
Plate 3

Length 16 cm (6½ in.). Weight 36 g (31.0–39.7 g). Monotypic. Subadult plumage: brownish below; lacks white wing-spot.

Geographic Range

PUERTO RICO; confined to slopes of Sierra de Luquillo, high mountains near Maricao, the Carite-Guavate State Forest, and locally near Cidra (Raffaele 1983).

Elevational Range

From ca. 200 m to mountain tops; mostly at higher elevations.

CHLOROSPINGUS

Chlorospingus bush-tanagers (Table 3) are active little birds whose English name is poorly chosen. Moss-tanager would be a more appropriate name as *Chlorospingus* mostly live in forests laden with mosses and other epiphytes. From forest interiors *Chlorospingus*

Nesospingus speculiferus

species move at times to forest edge or isolated neighboring shrubs or trees to nest and feed.

Noisy and often conspicuous, *Chlorospingus* typically travel in small groups of 4–8 individuals (except while nesting) and their repeated loud call notes seem to help draw and keep mixed-species flocks together. The calls of most species have a buzzy unclear quality, like sputtering or chittering. Songs tend to be composed of strings of notes that run into trills and rattles.

Cup nests of *Chlorospingus* are mostly placed on tree limbs or trunks, hidden inside clumps of mosses, ferns, or epiphytes in a way that provides both camouflage and shelter from inclement weather. Over a

Table 3 The *Chlorospingus* Bush-Tanagers

14	*C. ophthalmicus*	Common Bush-Tanager
15	*C. tacarcunae*	Tacarcuna Bush-Tanager
16	*C. inornatus*	Pirre Bush-Tanager
17	*C. punctulatus*	Dotted Bush-Tanager
18	*C. semifuscus*	Dusky Bush-Tanager
19	*C. zeledoni*	
20	*C. pileatus*	Sooty-capped Bush-Tanager
21	*C. parvirostris*	Yellow-whiskered Bush-Tanager
22	*C. flavigularis*	Yellow throated Bush-Tanager
23	*C. flavovirens*	Yellow-green Bush-Tanager
24	*C. canigularis*	Ashy-throated Bush-Tanager

third of the known nests of the Common Bush-Tanager have been found on the ground, concealed in mosses, ferns, and dense grasses.

Bush-tanagers occur in mountains from central Mexico to northern Argentina in a species distribution that resembles a patchwork quilt. Five species have quite limited ranges. In most localities, only one species occurs; less often two occur together; and we know of no localities where three species are normally found at the same elevation. Consequently, the taxonomy of bush-tanagers is confused and uncertain. The Yellow-whiskered and Yellow-throated seem to replace one another elevationally; they come together at about 1600–1700 m in Ecuador (Ridgely *in litt.*).

Two of the eleven *Chlorospingus* listed in the *Peters Check-list* are not valid species. Zeledon's Bush-Tanager has been found to be a color morph of the Sooty-capped (see Johnson and Brush 1972), and the Dotted a subspecies of the Common Bush-Tanager (see Olson 1981b). On the other hand, the Common Bush-Tanager may be found to consist of more than one species.

Chlorospingus ophthalmicus 14
Common Bush-Tanager
Plate 3

Length 13–14 cm (5–5½ in.). Weight varies from 16 g (13.3–18.0 g) for *bolivianus* to 22 g (16.0–25.5 g) for *hiaticolus*. Twenty-five subspecies, including 3 described recently: *trudis* and *exitelus* (Olson 1983) and *hiaticolus* (O'Neill and Parker 1981). Table 4 identifies subspecific differences in iris color, the presence of a post-ocular spot, and presence of a yellow band across the breast. Additional differences are exemplified by the 6 subspecies illustrated on Plate 3: heads are different shades of brown, gray, and black; throats have varying amounts of spotting and are white, cream, cinnamon, or yellow brown; and bellies are white or pale gray. Dark-eyed individuals occasionally noted in the range of light-eyed subspecies may be young birds.

Geographic Range

See Table 4.

Elevational Range

Generally 1000–2500 m, but reported as high as 3500 m in Mexico and 3000 m in Guatemala, Venezuela, and Bolivia. Descends to lowlands seasonally in some parts of Mexico and Central America.

Habitat and Behavior

Prefers humid mossy epiphyte-laden forest. Frequently moves out to scrub at forest edge or to dense second growth and isolated trees in open areas near forest. Encountered in pairs, family groups, and flocks of 4–10 individuals; seems to form larger single-species groups in Central America than in South America. Participates in mixed-species flocks; was the single core species of flocks forming in a study area in Panama (Buskirk et al. 1972), but at a study site in Costa Rica, was found to be an attendant species (Powell 1979). At these two sites, defended a home range of about 0.5–1.5 ha. (larger in the site where it was a core species). Also joins feeding aggregations at fruiting shrubs and trees. Active and restless; often in motion. Hops quickly and alertly along branches, jerks tail sideways, and flicks wings, constantly flashing white underwings. In Costa Rica, found to roost every night in the same places, in bushes within 3 m of the ground (Buskirk et al. 1972).

Feeds on insects and fruit, occasionally on nectar. Forages from shrubbery to tree tops; in Costa Rica, occasionally hops on the ground to obtain insects and fruit (Skutch 1967a). Appears to forage higher in South America than in Central America (Moynihan 1979). Hops along branches, peering around, examining foliage, stems, moss, epiphytes, and dry leaves. In Costa Rica, typically searches for insects by rummaging through detritus and epiphytes (Powell 1979). Hangs upside down to reach insects or spiders on undersides of substrates; occasionally sallies to a leaf.

Swallows small fruits whole and skillfully removes pulp from tough skins; pecks at large fruits. In Costa Rica, takes a wide variety of fruits, especially from plants in the Ericaceae, Melastomataceae, and Gesneriaceae (see Wheelwright et al. 1984). Presses nectar from flowers by pulling the corolla from its calyx and mashing the basal end (Skutch 1967a). Sometimes probes flower remnants with bill or tongue. In Bolivia, usually picked fruits while perched, rarely snatched them on the wing (Remsen data, 19 obs.). Stomach contents: vegetable matter (1); animal matter (29); both (19). Contents included beetles and other insects, seeds, and fruit juice.

Table 4 Ranges and Selected Characteristics of Common Bush-Tanager Subspecies

Range	Subspecies	Iris Color	Post-Ocular Spot?	Breast Band?
S San Luís Potosí, Hildalgo, state of Mexico, and Guerrero, MEXICO, southeastward through CENTRAL AMERICA to Chiriquí and Bocas del Toro, PANAMA.	albifrons, ophthalmicus, wetmorei, dwighti, postocularis, honduratius, regionalis, novicius	Dark	Yes	Yes
VENEZUELA is the coastal range from Miranda westward, Falcón, Yaracuy, and the Andes from Lara to Táchira; the Perijá Mountains; ne COLOMBIA from the n end of the E Andes south to n Santander.	jacqueti, falconensis, venezuelanus, ponsi, eminens	Light	Yes	Yes
COLUMBIA, in the E Andes from c Santander to Cundinamarca and in Caquetá, C Andes (southward on the w slope to Valle, e slope to Huila), e slope of the W Andes in Antioquia; Macarena Mountains (Meta); both Andean slopes from Pichincha and Napo, ECUADOR, south to El Oro, ECUADOR, and Cajamarca, PERU, and the e slope of PERU from Amazonas to Huánuco west of Río Huallaga (O'Neill and Parker 1981).	flavopectus, trudis, exitelis, nigriceps, macarenae, phaeocephalus, hiaticolus	Light	No	Yes
PERU in e Pasco, Junín, and Ayacucho (O'Neill and Parker 1981); recently collected series from c Pasco (LSUMZ) resemble this race but some specimens show introgression with hiaticolus.	cinereocephalus	Light	No	No
Extreme s PERU in Cuzco (LSUMZ) and Puno.	peruvianus	Light	No	Yes
BOLIVIA in La Paz and nw Cochabamba.	bolivianus	Light	Yes	Yes
BOLIVIA in c and se Cochabamba.	fulvigularis	*	Yes	Yes
Extreme ne Santa Cruz, BOLIVIA to Tucumán, ARGENTINA.	argentinus	Dark	Yes	Yes

*Both light and dark irides have been reported; two subspecies may be involved.

Vocalizations

Calls often; the typical contact note is a squeaky or a hard short *tsit*, given singly or in a spitting series, *t-z-z-z-z-z-z-zit*. In Central America: Expresses alarm or hostility with calls such as *tuck* or *sreee*, given alone or in series, and short High-pitched rattles (some downward-inflected). Separated pairs utter a clear whistle, e.g., *tsoooweee*, *tseeeyooo*. (See Moynihan 1962a.)

Song patterns vary substantially among subspecies. In Central America: The dawn song is a series of unclear *psit* notes; one individual sang 3 notes every 2 sec. (*regionalis*, Whitney recording). Day songs involve highly variable, lengthy series of twittering High-pitched notes that often end in a downward-inflected trill sounding like *reeee-yooo*.

In South America: Subspecies deliver different combinations of High-pitched *psit*s, High- to Moderate-pitched *chit*s and *chid-it*s, and Moderate- to High-pitched trills that usually come at the end of the series. The songs of a few subspecies (e.g., *jacqueti*, *venezuelanus*) seem to be confined to simple rhythmic series of *chit* notes. More compli-

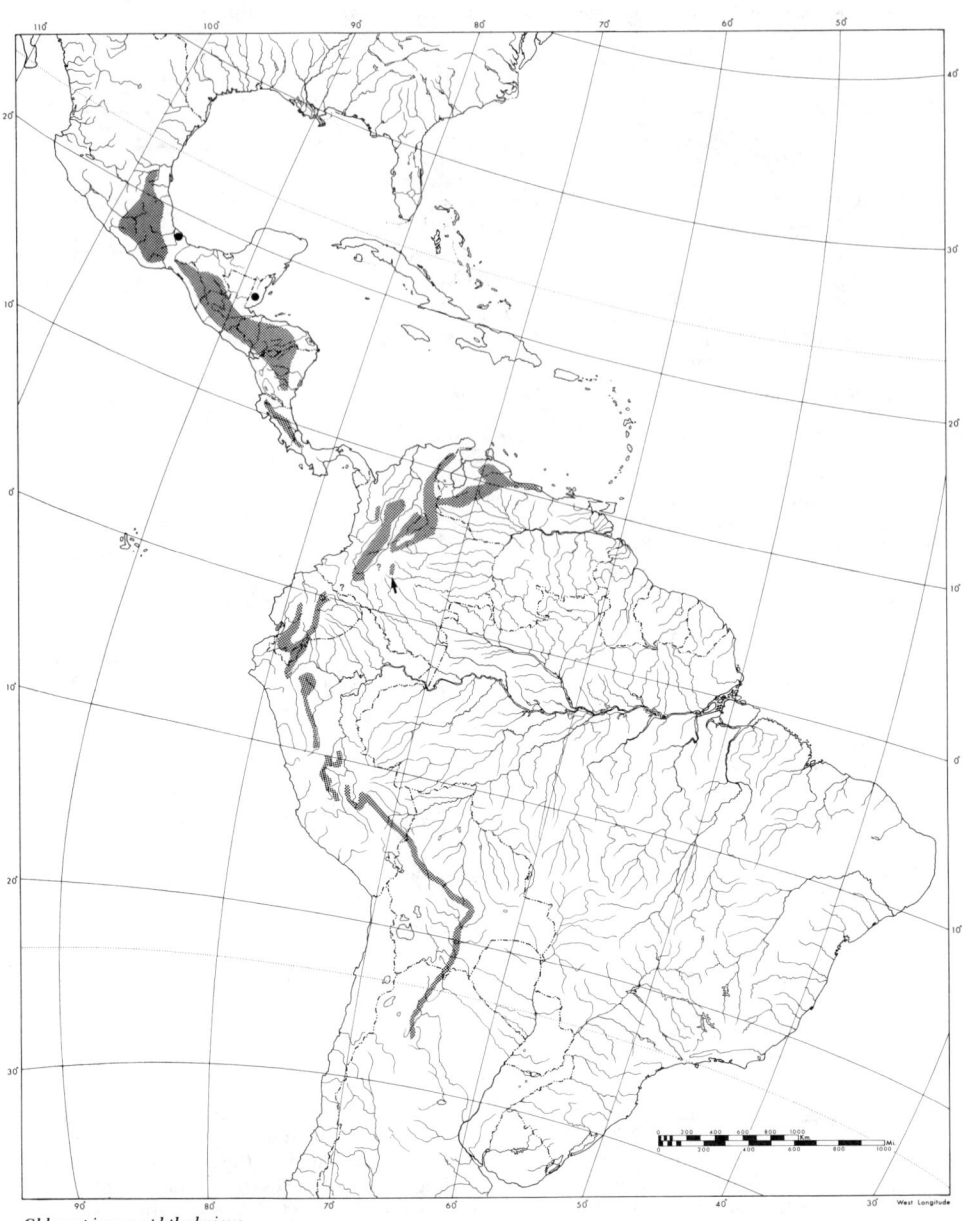

Chlorospingus ophthalmicus

cated versions are exemplified by the song of the Peruvian *hiaticolus* in which a series of *sip* notes becomes a loud, mostly Moderate-pitched, *chip chip chip chidip chidip chidip chidip chidip chew chew chew* that accelerates further (but declines in loudness and sometimes pitch) into a trill. The song of *cinereocephalus* is even more elaborate and deepens into throaty Low-pitched churring trills (Schulenberg recording). In South America, songs are typically restricted to the period around dawn.

Breeding

In Central America, pairs break away from single-species flocks at the outset of the breeding season and defend a nesting territory. Builds a bulky cup nest, made of moss, grass, leaves, and rootlets and lined with fine fibers and fragments of vegetation, in moss or epiphyte-laden trees (9 in Central America) or on the ground (4 in Central America and 2 in Peru). When nesting in trees, hides its nest inside epiphytes or thick mosses growing on tree trunks, heavy limbs, or branches up to 15 m off the ground; nest openings are small. Nest trees often stand free in clearings adjoining forest. Ground nests are placed on steep cut-banks (5 of 6 nests) and situated among mosses, ferns, or dense grasses that tend to roof them over.

Females apparently construct nests alone; males sometimes accompany mates or bring nesting material to nest sites. Eggs (2, less often 3) are dull white, marked with shades of brown or red, sometimes concentrated on the large end. Females incubate alone for 14 days (see Skutch 1967a). Both parents feed nestlings who fledge after about 13 days. At one nest, the pair remained notably silent even with human intrusion (Rowley 1984). In Costa Rica, 2 broods may be reared in a season. Breeding dates: Mexico April–June. Costa Rica March–June. Panama June. Peru (Puno) Nov.

Sources

Primary Buskirk et al. 1972; Dickey and Van Rossem 1938; Hilty and Brown 1986; LSUMZ data; Moynihan 1962a, 1962c; Olson 1983; O'Neill and Parker 1981; Parker data; Remsen data; Skutch 1967a; Slud 1964; Wetmore 1939. **Weights** (*bolivianus* n = 27; *hiaticolus* n = 28; remaining subspecies n = 71): Hartman 1955; Hartman and Brownell 1961; Lowery and Dalquest 1951; LSUMZ data; Oniki 1972; Weske 1972. **Stomach contents** Foster data; LSUMZ data. **Vocalizations** LNS recordings by Isler (2), Morton (2), Parker (17), Schwartz (9); recordings by Schulenberg (4), Whitney (2), R. A. Rowlett (1); O'Neill and Parker 1981; Moynihan 1962a; Skutch 1967a; Slud 1964. **Nests, eggs, and breeding dates** Edwards 1967; LSUMZ data (Schulenberg); Ogilvie-Grant 1912; Rowley 1966, 1984; Sclater and Salvin 1879; Worth 1939.

Chlorospingus tacarcunae 15
Tacarcuna Bush-Tanager
Plate 3

Length 13 cm (5 in.). Weight 17.8 g (1 female). Monotypic.

Geographic Range

Cerro Tacarcuna and its spur Cerro Mali on the border of PANAMA (Darién) and COLOMBIA (Chocó) and Cerro Jefe and Cerro Azul, e Panamá province, PANAMA (Ridgely 1976).

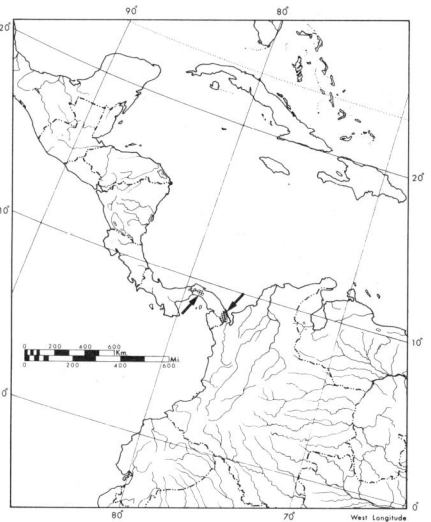

Chlorospingus tacarcunae

Elevational Range

850–1000 m in Panamá province and 1000–1500 m in Darién.

Habitat and Behavior

Inhabits forest and forest edge. Encountered in elfin forest in e Panamá province. Much like other bush-tanagers; usually in small groups and sometimes with mixed-species flocks; perhaps a nuclear species. Forages in the understory of tall forest and at all heights in elfin forest. Stomach contents (1): caterpillars and other insect remains.

Vocalizations

No information.

Breeding

In Panama, a female was seen carrying nesting material in February (Wetmore, Pasquier, and Olson 1984).

Sources

Primary Ridgely 1976, *in litt.*; Wetmore, Pasquier, and Olson 1984. **Weights (n = 1)** Wetmore, Pasquier, and Olson 1984. **Stomach contents** Wetmore, Pasquier, and Olson 1984. **Breeding dates** Wetmore, Pasquier, and Olson 1984.

Chlorospingus inornatus   16
Pirre Bush-Tanager
Plate 3

Length 15 cm (6 in.). Weight 28 g (20.2–36.0 g). Monotypic.

Geographic Range

Extreme e Darién (Cerro Sapo, Cerro Pirre, Cana), PANAMA, and adjacent Chocó, COLOMBIA (Cerro Nique; Robbins, Parker, and Allen 1985).

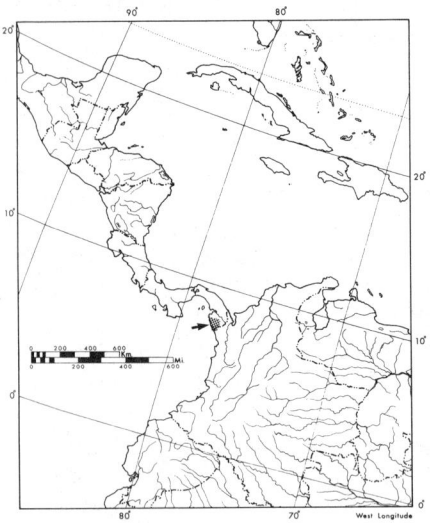

Chlorospingus inornatus

Elevational Range

800–1550 m.

Habitat and Behavior

Inhabits dense foliage, vine tangles, and bamboo in elfin forest; also occurs in the canopy of montane forest. Encountered in groups of 3–6 individuals. Travels with mixed-species flocks or independently. Forages mostly from mid to upper levels of trees and bushes. Searches for insects along thin branches and in dense foliage; gleans leaves and picks at mosses on branches. Also gleans tree-fern fronds (Parker data) and hangs from beneath twigs (Goldman in Wetmore, Pasquier, and Olson 1984). Stomach contents: vegetable matter (3); animal matter (2); both (4). Contents included fruit, larvae, and insect remains.

Vocalizations

Utters 3 kinds of buzzy, somewhat thin, High-pitched notes: *SPEETza, tsip*, and *chuweet?*. These may be given singly or in strings of 2–4 (mostly 4); often gives a string of one type of note and then turns to another (Parker, LNS).

Breeding

No information.

Sources

Primary LSUMZ data; Parker data; Ridgely 1976; Robbins, Parker, and Allen 1985; Wetmore, Pasquier, and Olson 1984. **Weights (n = 14)** LSUMZ data. **Stomach contents** LSUMZ data. **Vocalizations** LNS recordings by Parker (4); Robbins, Parker, and Allen 1985.

Chlorospingus punctulatus   17
Dotted Bush-Tanager
Plate 3

Length 13 cm (5½ in.). Monotypic. Considered a subspecies of the Common Bush-Tanager, *C. ophthalmicus* **14,** by Olson (1981b) and the *A.O.U. Check-list*.

Geographic Range

Both slopes in Veraguas and Coclé, PANAMA.

Elevational Range

850–1400 m.

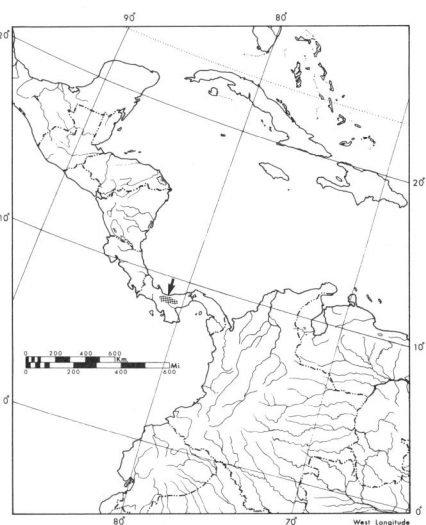

Chlorospingus punctulatus

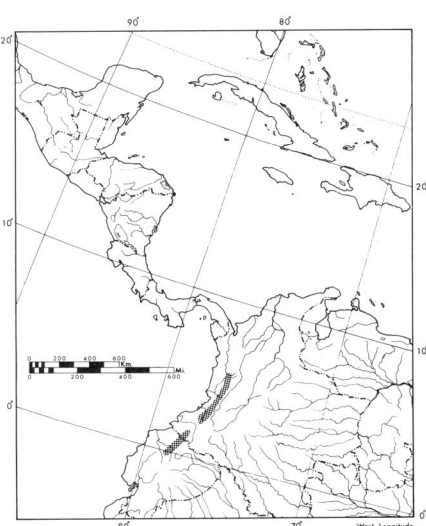

Chlorospingus semifuscus

Habitat and Behavior

Inhabits humid montane forest. Not distinguished behaviorally from the Common Bush-Tanager.

Vocalizations

While foraging, often repeats a squeaky *tsit*, like that of a typical Common Bush-Tanager subspecies (Whitney recording).

Breeding

No information.

Sources

Primary Ridgely 1976; Wetmore, Pasquier, and Olson 1984. **Vocalizations** recording by Whitney (1).

Chlorospingus semifuscus **18**
Dusky Bush-Tanager
Plate 3

Length 14–15 cm (5½–6 in.). Weight 19 g (17.2–23.0 g). Both subspecies are illustrated. Also known as the Dusky-bellied Bush-Tanager.

Geographic Range

C. s. livingstoni: the Pacific slope of the Andes from s Chocó (Cerro Tatamá) to Cauca, COLOMBIA. *C. s. semifuscus*: from Nariño, COLOMBIA, to Pichincha, ECUADOR.

Elevational Range

1200–2500 m; as low as 900 m in Cauca, Colombia.

Habitat and Behavior

Inhabits mossy forest and forest edge. In w Colombia, favors wet foggy forest; more confined to forest than are Common Bush-Tanager, *C. ophthalmicus* **14,** subspecies of Central America and ne Colombia. Comes to forest edge primarily to eat fruit (Hilty *in litt.*). Observed in pairs (Isler data); occurs in mixed-species flocks (Moynihan 1979).

Vocalizations

Song: a series of High-pitched kissing *tsit* notes that become *tsit-it* notes before turning into a slightly lower-pitched buzzy trill; sometimes the trill is omitted (Schulenberg recording). Song has the pattern of some South American subspecies of the Common Bush-Tanager. Calls: a High- to Very-high-pitched abrupt *seet*, often repeated, and a High- to Moderate-pitched buzzy trill like the final element in the song (R. A. Rowlett recording).

Breeding

No information.

Sources

Primary Hilty and Brown 1986. **Weights (n=6)** LSUMZ data. **Vocalizations** recordings by R. A. Rowlett (1), Schulenberg (1); Hilty and Brown 1986.

Chlorospingus zeledoni 19
Zeledon's Bush-Tanager
Plate 3

Length 14 cm (5½ in.). Weight 20.3 g (1 male, moderate fat). Monotypic. Now understood to be a color phase of the Sooty-capped Bush-Tanager, *C. pileatus* **20,** (Johnson and Brush 1972). Completely sympatric with the more common Sooty-capped, Zeledon's Bush-Tanager has not been found anywhere, even locally, in the absence of the Sooty-capped.

Geographic Range

Limited to Volcan Irazú and Volcan Turrialba in c COSTA RICA.

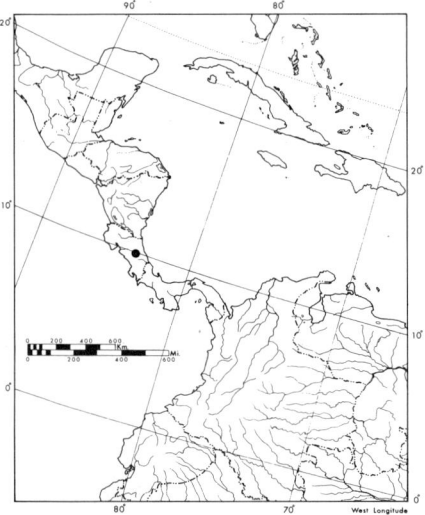

Chlorospingus zeledoni

Elevational Range

From 2500 m to treeline.

Habitat and Behavior

Inhabits montane forest and woodlands. Foraging behavior is like that of the Sooty-capped Bush-Tanager. Travels in pairs, singly, and small groups. Typically seen in company with the Sooty-capped Bush-Tanager.

Vocalizations

Calls: not distinguishable from those of the Sooty-capped Bush-Tanager. Song: a simple warble of 3 parts introduced by a steeply rising *swee* (Johnson and Brush 1972).

Breeding

An obviously mated pair consisting of a Zeledon's and a Sooty-capped was observed, as was a similarly composed pair of begging juveniles (Johnson and Brush 1972).

Sources

Primary Carriker 1910; Johnson and Brush 1972; Slud 1964. **Weights (n=1)** LSUMZ data. **Vocalizations** Johnson and Brush 1972.

Chlorospingus pileatus 20
Sooty-capped Bush-Tanager
Plate 3

Length 14 cm (5½ in.). Weight 21 g (16.0–24.1 g). Two subspecies; said to be invalid by Wetmore, Pasquier, and Olson (1984). Young birds are all yellow below, streaked olive, with a pale yellowish bill.

Geographic Range

COSTA RICA from s Alajuela south along the mountains to Chiriquí (Wetmore, Pasquier, and Olson 1984), PANAMA.

Elevational Range

Treeline down to 1500 m most common above 2600 m in Costa Rica; usually above 1800 m in Panama.

Habitat and Behavior

Inhabits humid montane and elfin forests, forest edge, islands of epiphyte-laden trees, and shrub thickets in pastures. Encountered in small family groups except while nesting. In Costa Rica, families sometimes join together to form large single-species flocks of 8–40 individuals (Johnson and Brush 1972), but said to be territorial year-round in Panama (see Moynihan 1962c). Family groups are sometimes joined by other species.

Habitually flicks open wings and tail. Performs "drooped wing-quivering" and "tail-up" displays in hostile situations (see Moynihan 1962a). Sometimes as tame and confiding as chickadees (*Parus* spp), which it re-

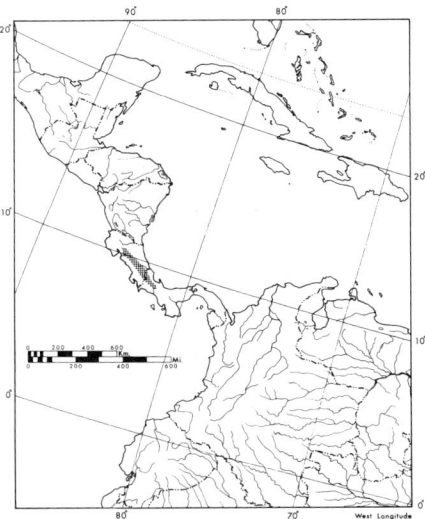

Chlorospingus pileatus

sembles somewhat in behavior and general appearance (Slud 1964). Hunts for insects and fruit in foliage from near the ground to 12 m above the ground, typically at heights of 3–6 m (Johnson and Brush 1972). Often noisily tears arboreal curled dead leaves (Slud 1964).

Vocalizations

Call note is a thin lisping High-pitched *tsit*; sometimes delivers a continuous stream of *tsit*s along with strings of *t-z-z-z-z-zit*, *chat-t-t-t*, *zwee-zwee-zwee*, etc. Displays of hostility are accompanied by a variety of rattles, harsh notes, and flourishes, e.g., *tsee-wee-yoo* or a rapidly repeated jumbled *tsit-wicky* (see Moynihan 1962a). Song: pleasant, somewhat sibilant, rapid *sit-sit SWIee-d-d-d-d-d sit-a-wit*; mostly High-pitched with the third phrase lowest in pitch; 2–3 sec. long; sometimes the final flourish is omitted; intervals between songs are irregular in length but longer than the song element. Typically sings in the early morning and late afternoon and rarely outside the breeding season (Wolf 1976).

Breeding

Defends a territory during the breeding season. Skutch (1967a:173–176) found a nest concealed among ferns and heaths situated at the top of a roadside cut 4 m high. The roomy open cup contained 2 nestlings. Breeding dates: Costa Rica March and July.

Sources

Primary Carriker 1910; Johnson and Brush 1972; Moynihan 1962a, 1962c; Ridgely 1976; Slud 1964; Wolf 1976. **Weights (n = 50)** Hartman 1955; Johnson and Brush 1972; LSUMZ data. **Vocalizations** LNS recordings by Parker (3), van den Berg (2); recording by Whitney (1); Moynihan 1962a. **Nests and breeding dates** Skutch 1967a; Wolf 1976.

Chlorospingus parvirostris **21**
Yellow-whiskered Bush-Tanager
Plate 3

Length 14 cm (5½ in.). Weight 24 g (17.5–28.5 g). Three subspecies; formerly considered subspecies of *C. flavigularis* (see Zimmer 1947b). *C. p. parvirostris* and *huallagae* are illustrated; head colors of *medianus* are intermediate between the other two subspecies. Also known as the Short-billed Bush-Tanager.

Geographic Range

C. p. huallagae: COLOMBIA, at the head of the Magdalena Valley in Huila and the e slope of the E Andes from Cundinamarca south; ECUADOR in Morona-Santiago (MCZ); and PERU from Cajamarca and Amazonas south to La Libertad and San Martín (LSUMZ). *C. p. medianus*: PERU in Junín and Cuzco. *C. p. parvirostris*: Puno, PERU, and La Paz, BOLIVIA.

Elevational Range

1400–2100 m (occasionally slightly higher) in Colombia, 1600–2000 m in Ecuador (Ridgely *in litt.*), and 1500–2600 m in Peru and Bolivia (Graves 1983).

Habitat and Behavior

Inhabits mossy forest and shrubby forest edge; may prefer vegetation bordering or near mountain streams (Weske 1972). Pairs and small groups of up to 6–8 individuals typically travel with mixed-species flocks, at times by themselves (Parker data). Forages in dense canopy foliage within forest; descends to the undergrowth at forest edge; appears to glean foliage (Parker data). Stomach contents: animal matter (5); vegetable matter (1); both (3). Contents included coleopterans and other insects, fruit, and seeds.

CHLOROSPINGUS

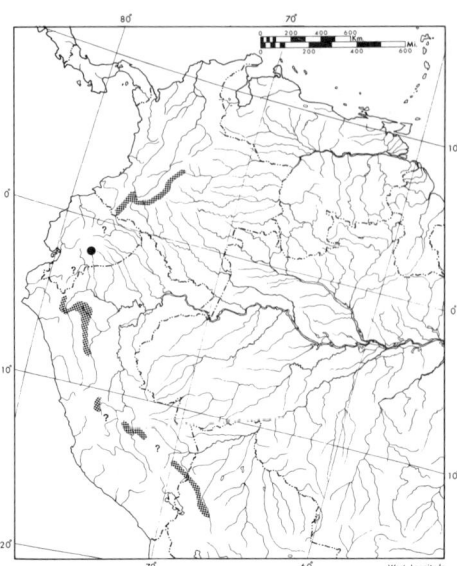

Chlorospingus parvirostris

Vocalizations

Calls: in Colombia, an incessant *tsip* (Hilty and Brown 1986); in Peru, a High-pitched, vibrating, penetrating *seeep* that is sometimes preceded by an abrupt thin *tsip* (Parker, LNS).

Breeding

No information.

Sources

Primary Hilty and Brown 1986; Parker data. **Weights (n = 15)** LSUMZ data. **Stomach contents** LSUMZ data. **Vocalizations** LNS recording by Parker (1); Hilty and Brown 1986.

to the Yellow-whiskered Bush-Tanager, *C. parvirostris* **21,** but ranges do not overlap.

Geographic Range

C. f. hypophaeus: Bocas del Toro and both slopes of Veraguas, PANAMA. *C. f. marginatus*: the Pacific slope from Valle, COLOMBIA, to El Oro, ECUADOR. *C. f. flavigularis*: COLOMBIA at the n end of the W Andes in Córdoba (Hilty and Brown 1986), locally on both slopes of the C Andes in Antioquia, and the head of the Magdalena Valley in Huila; the e slope of the Andes in Boyacá (Hilty and Brown 1986) and from Meta, COLOMBIA, through ECUADOR and PERU to Puno.

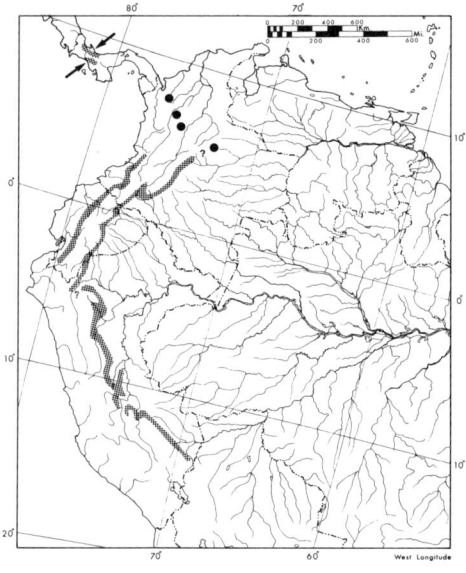

Chlorospingus flavigularis

Chlorospingus flavigularis 22
Yellow-throated Bush-Tanager
Plate 3

C. f. hypophaeus: length 13 cm (5 in.). *C. f. marginatus* and *flavigularis*: length 15 cm (6 in.); weight 28 g (25.0–30.5 g). All 3 subspecies are illustrated. The Panama form (*hypophaeus*) may prove to be a distinct species, in which case its English name would be Dark-breasted Bush-Tanager (*A.O.U. Check-list*). In South America, iris color apparently varies by location. The Pacific coast subspecies, *marginatus*, is similar in throat pattern

Elevational Range

C. f. hypophaeus: 250–900 m. *C. f. marginatus*: 300–1400 m in Colombia (Hilty and Brown 1986). *C. f. flavigularis*: ca. 750–1600 m.

Habitat and Behavior

Inhabits mossy forest and shrubby forest edge; occasionally occurs in second-growth woodland; rarely in open areas adjacent to forest. In Peru, seems to prefer vegetation bordering or near mountain streams (Weske 1972). Groups of 3–8 individuals, pairs, and sometimes single birds almost always travel with mixed-species flocks; possibly a nuclear species in some flocks. Persistently noisy, active, and sometimes unsuspicious.

In Panama (*hypophaeus*), generally forages at middle to upper heights of trees (Ridgely 1976). In Valle, Colombia (*marginatus*), foraged from the ground to the crowns of emergent trees 23 m high; however, median foraging height was about 6 m and only about 25% of all records were above 12 m (Hilty data). In Peru (*flavigularis*), typically foraged 1–10 m off the ground, occasionally ascending to the canopy, especially in fruiting trees (Parker and Parker 1982). Stomach contents (2): animal and vegetable matter, including insects, fruit, and seeds.

In Valle, Colombia (*marginatus*): Of 567 feeding records, 64% were fruit-eating, 29% insect-searching, and 7% at flowers. Ate over 28 species of fruit. Favored melastome fruits (90% of all fruit eaten), especially *Miconia* berries (78% of all melastomes). Also ate buds and flower parts of melastomes. Usually perched upright on twigs or branches to take fruit or flowers (68% of 157 obs.), frequently snatched berries in flight (27%), and occasionally hung down to obtain fruit. Swallowed small fruits whole and squeezed or pecked at larger ones. Searched for insects by hopping along mossy and bare branches of various sizes, including large (0.3 m diam.) slanting tree trunks, stopping to cock head to peer at substrates; also worked among vine tangles and in thickets. Peered and picked prey from branches and leaves about equally (taking insects from both sides of leaves), and reached out to pluck prey off bromeliads, vines, buds, and spider webs. Frequently sallied to leaves, branches, and air (33% of 76 obs.). (Hilty data.)

Vocalizations

Calls incessantly while foraging. In w Ecuador (*marginatus*), utters a chattering spitting Low- to Moderate-pitched *swit* (R. A. Rowlett recording). In w Colombia (*marginatus*), song is described as a weak *chit, twee-twee-twee-twit*, thin and high (Hilty and Brown 1986). In Peru (*flavigularis*), song is a loud, musical *wheet-chew-wheet-wheet-wheet-chew* or a shorter *chip-weet-weet-weet*; flock members utter a variety of *chip* and *seet* notes (Parker and Parker 1982).

Breeding

A cup nest was found embedded in moss 5 m above the ground (Hilty and Brown 1986). Breeding dates: Colombia (*marginatus*) Feb and Sept.

Sources

Primary Hilty data; Hilty and Brown 1986; Parker and Parker 1982; Ridgely 1976. **Weights** (*flavigularis* n = 8) LSUMZ data. **Stomach contents** LSUMZ data. **Vocalizations** recording by R. A. Rowlett (1); Hilty and Brown 1986; Parker and Parker 1982. **Nests and breeding dates** Hilty and Brown 1986.

Chlorospingus flavovirens 23
Yellow-green Bush-Tanager
Plate 4

Length 14 cm (5½ in.). Weight 25 g (1 male). Monotypic.

Geographic Range

Extremely local. Originally known from 2 specimens collected in Pichincha, ECUADOR. Discovered in the upper Anchicayá Valley, Valle, COLOMBIA, by Hilty (1977).

Elevational Range

950–1050 m.

Habitat and Behavior

In Valle, Colombia: Inhabits mossy forest and forest edge; also occurs in adjacent clearings with scattered trees. Usually travels in small groups of 3–5 individuals; often with mixed-species flocks. Typically forages above 7 m off the ground and regularly at canopy heights (22–30 m); rarely descends into thickets or lower vegetation. Median foraging height (95 obs.) was about 12 m. (Hilty data.) Stomach contents (1): vegetable matter including *Ficus* fruit.

Of 91 feeding records in Valle, Colombia, 45% involved taking fruit, 34% were insect-searching, and 21% were at flowers. Ate over 14 species of fruit; took mostly melastomes (75% of all fruit), especially *Miconia* berries; also ate fruits of parasitic and epiphytic plants (13% of all fruit); sometimes traveled directly from one mistletoe clump to another. Took fruit mostly from a perched position; rarely hung from *Cecropia* catkins. Swallowed small fruits whole and mashed larger ones. Primarily searched for insects on all sides of large (>13 cm diam.) mossy branches and on tree trunks; also inspected patches of moss, hanging moss clumps, ferns, and epiphytes. Perched upright, hung upside down, or clung to substrates to pick at prey. Rarely flutter-pursued escaping insects or sallied to moss clumps. Once observed tearing apart a termite nest. (Hilty data.)

CHLOROSPINGUS

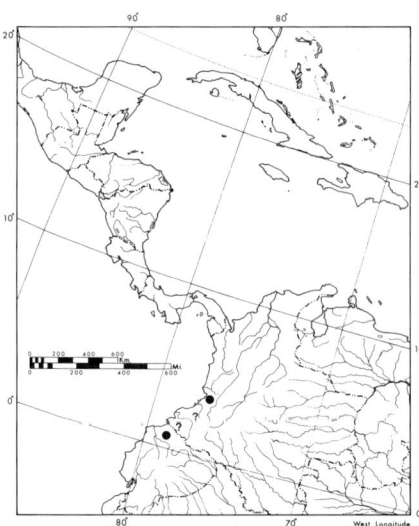

Chlorospingus flavovirens

Vocalizations

Call note: a loud husky *chut* repeated often; coarser and more raspy than notes of other *Chlorospingus* species (Hilty and Brown 1986).

Breeding

Two mossy cup nests were found 5 and 7 m above the ground, one in a mossy tree crotch and the other at the base of palm fronds (Hilty and Brown 1986). Breeding dates: Colombia March–May.

Sources

Primary Hilty data; Hilty 1977; Hilty and Brown 1986. **Weights (n = 1)** LSUMZ data. **Stomach contents** LSUMZ data. **Vocalizations** Hilty and Brown 1986. **Nests and breeding dates** Hilty and Brown 1986.

Chlorospingus canigularis 24
Ashy-throated Bush-Tanager
Plate 4

Length 13–14 cm (5–5½ in.). Weight 18 g (14.5–20.8 g). Five subspecies: *olivaceiceps*, *signatus*, and *conspicillatus* are illustrated; *canigularis* and *paulus* are similar to *conspicillatus*. Some individuals of *paulus* show traces of a white post-ocular streak. Also known as the Ash-throated Bush-Tanager.

Geographic Range

C. c. olivaceiceps: Caribbean slope in c COSTA RICA probably west to Lake Arenal and south along the Talamanca Cordillera (Slud 1964) to Bocas del Toro, PANAMA (sight, July 1982—Ridgely). *C. c. canigularis* and *conspicillatus*: from west of the Western Venezuelan Low in s Táchira, VENEZUELA, and Norte de Santander (USNM), COLOMBIA, southward through the E Andes to Cundinamarca; the C Andes from Caldas to Huila, COLOMBIA; and the Pacific slope from Antioquia (USNM) southward to Cauca and the e slope of the W Andes in Valle and Cauca (Hilty and Brown 1986), COLOMBIA. *C. c. paulus*: the w slope of the Andes from Chimborazo, ECUADOR, to Tumbes, PERU (Wiedenfeld, Schulenberg, and Robbins 1985). *C. c. signatus*: the e slope of the Andes from Napo, ECUADOR, to Cajamarca, PERU, and locally south of the Northern Peruvian Low in San Martín (Parker and Parker 1982), Huánuco (Parker and Parker 1982), n Cuzco (Weske 1972), and ec Cuzco (FMNH), PERU.

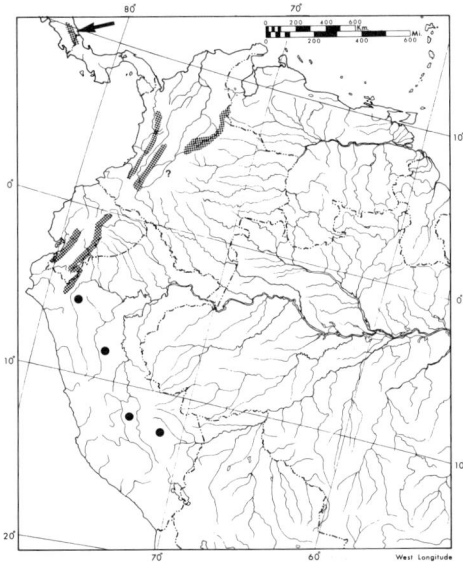

Chlorospingus canigularis

Elevational Range

C. c. olivaceiceps: 300–1500. *C. c. canigularis* and *conspicillatus*: 1200–2600 m. *C. c. paulus*: 300–1500. *C. c. signatus*: 1500–2600 m in e Ecuador, and 1000–1700 m in e Peru.

Habitat and Behavior

Inhabits tall mossy forest canopy and vine-tangled forest edge; also occurs in second growth. In Colombia, often found in vine-crowded forest canopy above steep mountain streams (Hilty *in litt.*). Small active groups of up to 10 individuals are usually joined by other species.

Forages for insects and fruit usually in the canopy within forest but often goes lower, sometimes near the ground at forest edge. Hunts mostly within foliage, searching to the ends of branches, usually slender branches that may be either bare or mossy. Actively gleans leaves and explores vine tangles. Foraging behavior of *olivaceiceps* in Costa Rica (Whitney *in litt.*) appears to be similar to that of South American subspecies.

Vocalizations

Song of *signatus* in Peru: a sharp Moderate-pitched *chut*, a High-pitched *chit*, and a Very-high-pitched *seet* appear to be given simultaneously and accelerated rapidly into a rolling chittering trill, falling then rising in pitch in a distinctive pattern and typically ending abruptly on the highest note; sometimes repeated; songs take 2–7 sec. (Parker, LNS). Call note of *olivaceiceps* in Costa Rica is said to be "a sort of 'tsirt-tsirt'" (Slud 1964).

Breeding

No information.

Sources

Primary Hilty and Brown 1986; Meyer de Schauensee and Phelps 1978; Miller 1963; Parker data; Parker and Parker 1982; Slud 1964. **Weights (n = 12)** LSUMZ data; Miller 1963. **Vocalizations** LNS recordings by Parker (2); Slud 1964.

CNEMOSCOPUS

Ornithologists originally placed the single *Cnemoscopus* species either in the genus *Chlorospingus* or the genus *Hemispingus*. This tanager appears closer to *Hemispingus* in its morphology (Hellmayr 1936), feeding behavior, and vocalizations. Bush-tanager is not an appropriate English name; *Cnemoscopus* forages primarily in trees in humid montane forest.

Cnemoscopus rubrirostris 25
Gray-hooded Bush-Tanager
Plate 4

C. r. rubrirostris: length 17 cm (6½ in.); weight 21 g (18.5 and 23.0 g). *C. r. chrysogaster*: length 15 cm (5½ in.); weight 18 g (13.0–22.5 g).

Geographic Range

C. r. rubrirostris: VENEZUELA in Táchira west of the Western Venezuelan Low; COLOMBIA locally in all 3 Andean ranges (south to Cauca on the Pacific slope); ECUADOR in Napo and Morona-Santiago (LSUMZ); and PERU north of the Northern Peruvian Low near the Piura-Cajamarca border (Parker et al. 1985). *C. r. chrysogaster*: PERU south of the Northern Peruvian Low from s Amazonas to Junín (LSUMZ).

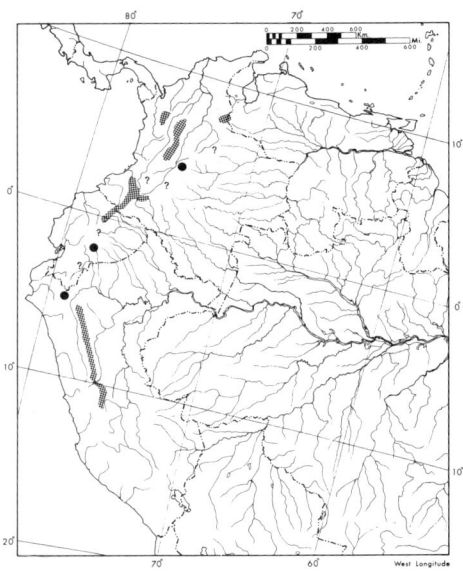

Cnemoscopus rubrirostris

Elevational Range

1900–3350 m. In Colombia, most common 2400–2700 m (Hilty and Brown 1986). In Piura, Peru, 2600–2900 m (Parker et al. 1985).

Habitat and Behavior

Inhabits humid montane forest and forest edge. Travels in pairs and small groups of up to 8 individuals; rarely solitary; typically with mixed-species flocks. Wags or twitches tail downward, often teetering its entire posterior.

Forages from eye level to the subcanopy; less often in the canopy. *C. r. chrysogaster*: Usually flies to the inside of a tree and, in a distinctive manner, creeps along limbs towards outside foliage. Peers around, typically searching for prey on leaf undersides. Occasionally leans over to glean insects on a branch or hangs to probe a dead leaf. After reaching branch tips, regularly sallies to air for insects, making short flights and returning to original perch before flying on.
C. r. rubrirostris: Also creeps along limbs out into foliage. Stomach contents (*chrysogaster*): animal matter (4); vegetable matter (1). Contents included long (2–4 cm) caterpillars and seeds.

Vocalizations

C. r. rubrirostris: Call note: a High-pitched sharp solid *swit*. Song: a 3–4 sec. jumble of Moderate- and High-pitched squeaky sputtering notes, rapidly delivered; sometimes speeded up to a twittering; flows into smacking *chips* for a short interval then begins the song again (Parker, LNS; 90% certain of this species). *C. r. chrysogaster*: Call note: a Moderate-pitched *chip*. Song: a less than 2 sec. jumble of squeaky notes that typically ends in a downward-inflected *sweeee*, e.g., *twitity, twitity, sweeee*; flows into *chips* between groups of phrases (Parker, LNS).

Breeding

Two reports of eggs from Colombia differ: one set, pale greenish white, spotted thickly at the large end with reddish lilac (Sclater and Salvin 1879); the other, bluish white, sparsely marked with black spots (Nehrkorn 1899).

Sources

Primary Hilty and Brown 1986; Isler data; LSUMZ data; Parker data; Ridgely and Gaulin 1980. Weights (*rubrirostris* n = 2; *chrysogaster* n = 32): LSUMZ data; Weske 1972. **Stomach contents** LSUMZ data. **Vocalizations** LNS recordings by Parker (2). **Nests and eggs** Nehrkorn 1899; Sclater and Salvin 1879.

HEMISPINGUS

Hemispingus tanagers (Table 5) are rather plain, medium-sized tanagers that vary in size and bill shape. The majority of these Andean birds have somewhat strong bills, but the bills of four species are thin and pointed. Most species actively forage in dense foliage and remind observers of wood-warblers (Parulinae). Historically, taxonomists have had a difficult time separating some *Hemispingus* from wood-warblers of the genus *Basileuterus*. On the other hand, the Rufous-browed Hemispingus (and perhaps the poorly-known Slaty-backed) is rather lethargic and deliberate in its movements, suggesting an *Atlapetes* brush-finch (Emberizinae).

Table 5 The *Hemispingus* Species

26	*H. atropileus*	Black-capped Hemispingus
	26-1 *atropileus* subspecies group	Black-capped Hemispingus
	26-2 *calophrys* subspecies group	Orange-browed Hemispingus
27	*H. parodii*	Parodi's Hemispingus
28	*H. superciliaris*	Superciliaried Hemispingus
29	*H. reyi*	Gray-capped Hemispingus
30	*H. frontalis*	Oleaginous Hemispingus
31	*H. melanotis*	Black-eared Hemispingus
32	*H. goeringi*	Slaty-backed Hemispingus
33	*H. rufosuperciliaris*	Rufous-browed Hemispingus
34	*H. verticalis*	Black-headed Hemispingus
35	*H. xanthophthalmus*	Drab Hemispingus
36	*H. trifasciatus*	Three-striped Hemispingus

The diversity of *Hemispingus* species is also reflected in their habitat preferences and insect-foraging behaviors. The Black-capped, Orange-browed, Parodi's, and Gray-capped typically forage at or below eye level, searching leaves and stems of bamboo, shrubs, and small trees at high elevations. The Rufous-browed (and probably the Slaty-backed) forages in dense vegetation, near or on the ground. The Superciliaried (except perhaps in Colombia) and the Three-striped forage very similarly, perching on branches to glean outer foliage in tree tops, and replace one another elevationally at about 3100 m in Bolivia where their ranges overlap (see Remsen 1985). The Black-headed and Drab also forage in the canopy but typically walk on the tops of heavy stiff foliage to glean leaf tops. The only two *Hemispingus* of moderate elevations, the Oleaginous and Black-eared, primarily glean leaves in the undergrowth. Only caterpillars and small beetles have been recorded as insect prey of *Hemispingus* (data for 6 spp).

Most *Hemispingus* live in small groups that often appear to function as nuclei of mixed-species flocks. Contact calls are typically brief and sharp, but, while foraging, many *Hemispingus* also utter rapid staccato series of notes intermittently. Often two individuals (possibly more) may vocalize simultaneously. A few *Hemispingus* have dawn songs that are very distinct from their daytime vocalizations.

Hemispingus tanagers live in the Andes; the range of one species extends to the coastal mountains of Venezuela. Most *Hemispingus* are typically found between 2500 m and treeline. The exceptions, the Oleaginous and the Black-eared, have elevational ranges centered at about 1900–2400 m. The geographic distributions of many species are restricted; three species are confined to Venezuela; two species are found solely in Peru, one of which (Parodi's) is known only from the Department of Cuzco. Consequently, most species that appear to occupy the same ecological niche are either allopatric or live at different elevations in areas of range overlap. Ecological distinctions between the Oleaginous and Black-eared are unknown.

Two of the *Hemispingus* species have been described since the publication of the *Peters Check-list* in 1970: the Rufous-browed by Blake and Hocking (1974) and Parodi's by Weske and Terborgh (1974). The Black-headed and Drab Hemispingus form a superspecies; their ranges are separated by the Northern Peruvian Low (see Parker et al. 1985).

Hemispingus atropileus 26
Black-capped Hemispingus

Weske and Terborgh (1974) presented arguments for considering the subspecies of extreme southern Peru and northwestern Bolivia, *calophrys*, as a distinct species. The habitat and foraging behavior of *calophrys* appears similar to that of the subspecies in Peru (*auricularis*).

Hemispingus atropileus (*atropileus* subspecies group 26-1)
Black-capped Hemispingus
Plate 4

H. a. atropileus: length 16 cm (6½ in.). *H. a. auricularis*: length 15 cm (6 in); weight 22 g (18.0–26.0 g). Two subspecies.

Geographic Range

H. a. atropileus: VENEZUELA in sw Táchira west of the Western Venezuelan Low; COLOMBIA in all 3 Andean ranges (locally in the E and W Andes); and ECUADOR on the Pacific slope south to Azuay and the e slope in Napo and Morona-Santiago (LSUMZ). *H. a. auricularis*: PERU on the e slope of the Andes from Piura (LSUMZ) to Cuzco.

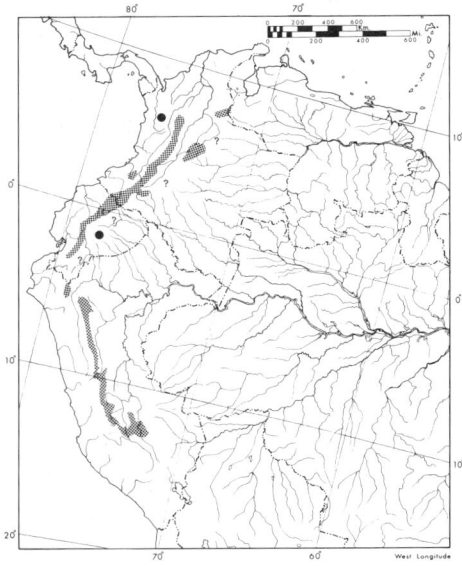

Hemispingus atropileus (*atropileus* subspecies group)

Elevational Range

Ca. 2300–3350 m; rarely down to 1800 m.

Habitat and Behavior

Inhabits humid montane forest, less often broken elfin forest. In Peru, appears to be confined to wetter and denser forests. Prefers *Chusquea* bamboo thickets and dense contiguous tracts of bushes, trees, and second-growth scrub. Typically travels in fast-moving groups of 3–7 (up to 12) individuals, sometimes in pairs. Occasionally encountered in single-species flocks but more often with other species such as the Citrine Warbler, *Basileuterus luteoviridis*. May be nuclear in large mixed-species flocks. Usually forages below eye level in low dense vegetation but occasionally goes higher (to 5 m) in trees. In Peru (*auricularis*): Foraging movements typically begin near the ground. Creeps up bamboo stalks and branches of woody plants, often reaching up to glean the undersides of leaves or to probe bamboo internodes, less often leaning down to pick an insect off the top of a leaf. Sometimes jumps from stalk to stalk of bamboo. Stomach contents: vegetable matter (1); animal matter (11); both (1). Contents included caterpillars and other insects and seeds.

Vocalizations

The light and lively flocking calls (songs?) consist of phrases of rapidly delivered High-pitched notes, such as *d-d-d-d-d-dit* or *z-z-z-z-zeet*. The quality varies from squeaky to chattering; sometimes notes run into a rapid trill that rolls up and down the scale. Phrases are separated by very brief pauses, and the vocalizations may continue for some time. Call note: a sharp High-pitched *tsit*.

The dawn song of *auricularis* is made up of single notes given slowly, evenly, and distinctly: a series of 3–5 rich loud Moderate-pitched *chew* notes is alternated with 6–9 High-pitched *zeeet* notes. Dawn songs are given continuously, perhaps for 15–20 min., from an exposed perch at the top of a tree 5–10 m high. Perches upright, flicks tail continuously from side to side, looks one way and then the other, and periodically jumps around 180 degrees, singing all the time.

Breeding

Builds a cup nest of leaves and stems. Eggs are pale rose with numerous reddish gray spots and streaks, sometimes concentrated on the large end and sometimes evenly distributed (Taczanowski 1884b).

Sources

Primary Hilty and Brown 1986; Isler data; LSUMZ data; Parker data. **Weights (n = 60)** LSUMZ data; Weske 1972. **Stomach contents** LSUMZ data. **Vocalizations** LNS recordings by Isler (4), Parker (5). **Nests and eggs** Taczanowski 1884b.

Hemispingus atropileus (*calophrys* subspecies group   26-2) Orange-browed Hemispingus Plate 4

Length 14 cm (5½ in.). Weight 17 g (14.5–20.5 g). Monotypic if specifically distinct.

Geographic Range

E Andean slope from e Puno (LSUMZ), PERU, to Cochabamba (LSUMZ), BOLIVIA.

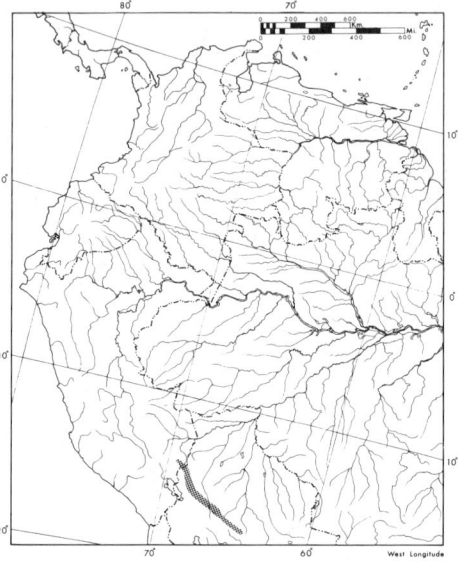

Hemispingus atropileus (*calophrys* subspecies group)

Elevational Range

Ca. 2300–3350 m (treeline).

Habitat and Behavior

Inhabits humid montane forest; less common in elfin forest. Prefers *Chusquea* bamboo thickets inside forest or at forest edge, especially along landslides (Parker *in litt.*). Often encountered in small groups of 4–8 individuals, also in pairs and rarely singly. Found both with and apart from mixed-species flocks.

In Bolivia, foraged primarily in bamboo fairly close to the ground; median foraging height was 3 m not observed higher than 6 m off the ground. Gleaned bottoms and tops of leaves equally (24 of 28 obs.); also gleaned slender branches (1 cm diam.) and moss. Picked prey from substrates mostly without acrobatics (18 of 24 obs.) or reached, hung, or sallied. (Remsen data.) Occasionally probes hanging dead leaf clusters (Remsen and Parker 1984). Stomach contents: animal matter (29); animal and vegetable matter (2). Contents included caterpillars and other insects not identified.

Vocalizations

No information.

Breeding

No information.

Sources

Primary LSUMZ data; Remsen data; Remsen 1985. **Weights (n = 34)** LSUMZ data. **Stomach contents** LSUMZ data.

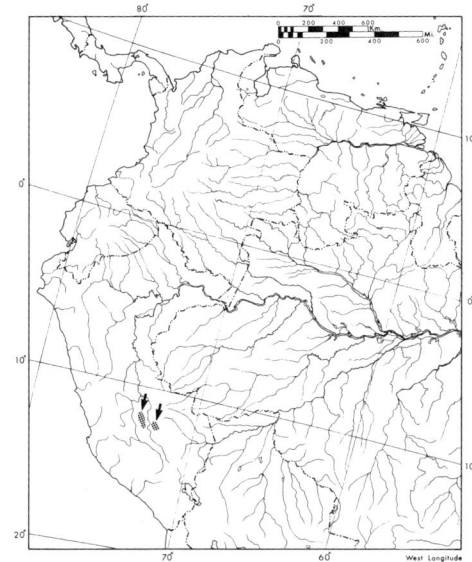

Hemispingus parodii

Hemispingus parodii 27
Parodi's Hemispingus
Plate 4

Length 14 cm (5½ in.). Monotypic.

Geographic Range

Cuzco, PERU. Found to date only in the Vilcanota and Vilcabamba Cordilleras (FMNH; Weske and Terborgh 1975).

Elevational Range

From 2750 (Parker *in litt.*) to ca. 3500 m at or near treeline.

Habitat and Behavior

Inhabits *Chusquea* bamboo thickets in humid elfin forest. Small groups of 3–9 individuals typically travel with mixed-species flocks that include the similar-appearing Citrine Warbler, *Basileuterus luteoviridis*. Forages low in stands of bamboo and in bamboo mixed with other dense foliage; gleans leaves and bamboo internodes. Also hunts at low levels in small trees. Leans down or stretches to pluck prey off substrates. Observed removing a green leaf and mashing it in its bill, possibly to obtain an insect from the leaf underside (Isler data).

Vocalizations

Day song: a string of somewhat labored, rapid, chittering 1–2 sec. phrases, e.g. *p-p-p-psit-sit-sit*, *z-z-z-zit-dit-dit*, and *zh-zh-zh-zhit-zhit-zhit*; Moderate- to High-pitched. Tends to utter a phrase on an even pitch and then abruptly shift to another phrase at a different pitch and quality. Intervals between phrases vary between a fraction of a sec. and 5 or more sec.; intervals sometimes include High-pitched *seet* notes or a harsh, mostly Moderate-pitched *chur-choo-too*. Dawn song: alternates 2 notes, the first High- to Very-high-pitched and the second High- to Moderate-pitched, *pit zzre pit zzre pit zzre* etc; delivered slightly faster than 1 note/sec. and continued for some time (Parker, LNS).

Breeding

No information.

Sources

Primary Isler data; LSUMZ data; Parker data; Weske and Terborgh 1974. **Vocalizations** LNS recordings by Isler (1), Parker (6).

Hemispingus superciliaris 28
Superciliaried Hemispingus
Plate 4

Length 13–14 cm (5–5½ in.). Weight 14 g (11.4–17.2 g). Seven subspecies: *chrysophrys*, *leucogaster*, and *urubambae* are illustrated; *superciliaris*, *maculifrons*, and *nigrifrons* resemble *urubambae*; *insignis* resembles *leuco-*

gaster. No intergrades have been found between the yellow olive and blue gray forms.

Geographic Range

H. s. chrysophrys: VENEZUELA in Táchira, Mérida, and Trujillo. *H. s. superciliaris*: the E Andes of COLOMBIA on the w slope in e Santander (sight, Hilty and Brown 1986), the e slope in n Boyacá, and both slopes in Cundinamarca. *H. s. nigrifrons*: the C Andes of COLOMBIA from Antioquia (Hilty and Brown 1983) southward and both slopes of the Andes from Cauca and Nariño, COLOMBIA, south through ECUADOR to Azuay on the w slope and Morona-Santiago on the e slope. *H. s. maculifrons*: the w slope of the Andes from El Oro, ECUADOR, to c Cajamarca (LSUMZ), PERU, spilling over to the e slope in Piura, PERU, north of the Northern Peruvian Low (Parker et al. 1985). *H. s. insignis* and *leucogaster*: PERU on the e Andean slope south of the Northern Peruvian Low from Amazonas to Junín. *H. s. urubambae*: the e Andean slope from Cuzco, PERU, to Cochabamba, BOLIVIA (Niethammer 1956).

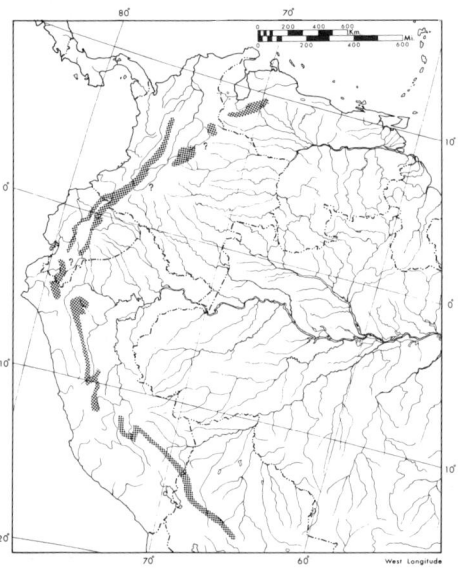

Hemispingus superciliaris

Elevational Range

From 2100 m (rarely lower) to 3350 m in Colombia, more numerous at the higher elevations.

Habitat and Behavior

Frequents forest and forest edge; also occurs in second growth. Found locally (*maculifrons*) in tall *Polylepis* woodland. Pairs, sometimes single birds or small groups of up to 7 individuals, almost always travel with mixed-species flocks; in s Peru and Bolivia, frequently with the Drab Hemispingus, *H. xanthophthalmus* 35. Moves quickly, often seems to flit along. In one forest in c Peru, appeared to roost in dense thickets at the edge of a clearing (Isler data).

In s Peru and Bolivia, forages primarily in the tops of 8–20 m trees but descends to small trees, shrubby growth, and bamboo at forest edge. In Colombia, forages from bamboo and bushy growth to tops of trees on steep slopes, but is seen infrequently in the tops of tall trees (Hilty *in litt.*). In Peru and Bolivia, primarily gleans leaves in dense foliage near branch tips, often foraging where leaf clusters join branches. Mostly forages without acrobatics, but sometimes reaches up or out, leans over, or hangs down to obtain insects. Occasionally gleans branches. In Bolivia: the median foraging height was 11 m and median distance to the top of the canopy was about 2 m Gleaned bottoms, tops, and bases of leaves about equally. (Remsen data, 34 obs.) In Peru, plucked seeds from dry flower heads of a *Vernonia* (Compositae) and shook off attached tassels before eating the seeds (Isler data). Stomach contents (12): insects, including caterpillars and small beetles.

Vocalizations

Call note: a High-pitched sharp brief *tsit* or *tsick*. One individual delivered about 20 notes/min. (Isler, LNS). Song (*maculifrons* and *leucogaster*): a distinctive 3–4 sec. burst of rapidly delivered Moderate- and High-pitched dry harsh notes that become louder while accelerating; bursts may be repeated after short pauses with the cadence of ocean waves rolling in on the shore. Sings primarily just after dawn; sometimes many birds join together to produce a cacophony.

Breeding

No information.

Sources

Primary Hilty and Brown 1986; Isler data; LSUMZ data; Parker data; Remsen data; Remsen 1985. **Weights (n = 41)** LSUMZ data; Weske 1972. **Stomach contents** LSUMZ data. **Vocalizations** LNS recordings by Isler (4), Parker (3).

Hemispingus reyi 29
Gray-capped Hemispingus
Plate 4

Length 14 cm (5½ in.). Monotypic.

Geographic Range

W VENEZUELA in the Andes of Trujillo, Mérida, and Táchira.

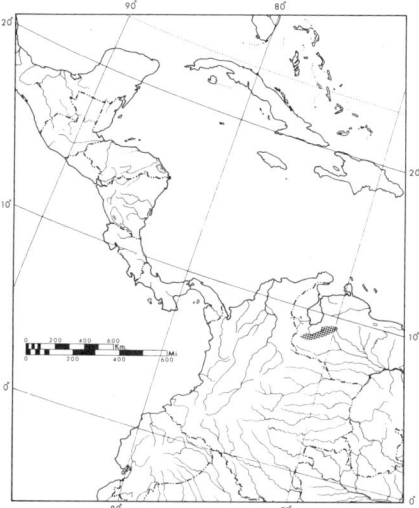

Hemispingus reyi

Elevational Range

1900–3200 m.

Habitat and Behavior

Encountered at shrubby forest edge (Ridgely *in litt.*), *Chusquea* bamboo (Hilty *in litt.*), and habitats similar to those of the Black-capped Hemispingus, *H. atropileus* **26**, (Meyer de Schauensee and Phelps 1978). Most often in groups of about 6 individuals (Ridgely *in litt.*). Often travels with mixed-species flocks; appears to be a nuclear species (Moynihan 1979).

Vocalizations

Repeats a sharp scratchy insistent *tee chew chew*, Moderate- to High-pitched, followed by several single *chew* notes; also utters faster chattering phrases (Schwartz, LNS).

Breeding

No information.

Sources

Primary Meyer de Schauensee and Phelps 1978; Ridgely *in litt.*. **Vocalizations** LNS recording by Schwartz (1).

Hemispingus frontalis 30
Oleaginous Hemispingus
Plate 4

Length 14 cm (5½ in.). Weight 17 g (14.0–20.0 g). Five subspecies: *frontalis*, *hanieli*, and *iteratus* are illustrated; *ignobilis* resembles *iteratus*; *flavidorsalis* resembles *frontalis*.

Geographic Range

H. f. iteratus: ne VENEZUELA in the mountains of Sucre and Monagas. *H. f. hanieli*: n VENEZUELA in the coastal range from Aragua to Miranda. *H. f. ignobilis*: the Andes of VENEZUELA from s Lara west to Táchira. *H. f. flavidorsalis*: the Perijá Mountains. *H. f. frontalis*: the E and C Andes and the W Andes in Antioquia and Cauca, COLOMBIA; the e Andean slope from Nariño through ECUADOR and PERU to c Cuzco.

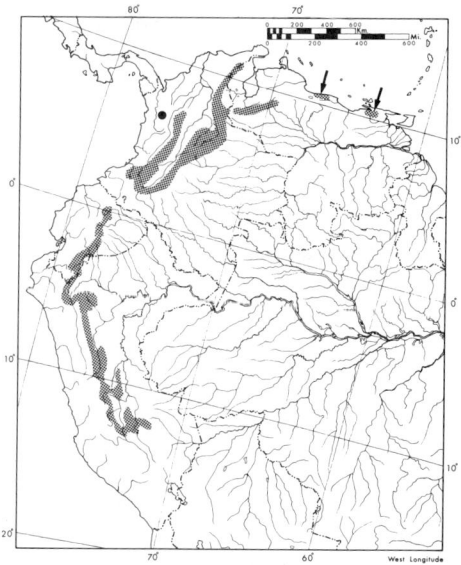

Hemispingus frontalis

Elevational Range

1300–2900 m; generally most numerous 1900–2400 m.

Habitat and Behavior

Inhabits humid montane forest, frequenting patches of thickets, dense shrubbery, and vine tangles; also occurs at forest edge and in clearings. Travels in small groups of 3–4 individuals, rarely in larger groups; in Venezuela and Colombia, encountered often in pairs. In the Andes, frequently accompanies understory mixed-species flocks and may be a nuclear species; rarely with canopy flocks. Twitches or flicks its tail often (Parker data).

Forages primarily in the understory; said to occur in the subcanopy in the Cordillera Vilcabamba in Peru (Weske 1972). In Peru: Deliberately searched foliage, mostly 1–3 m off the ground. Gleaned leaves, including bamboo leaves; hung on leaves at ends of branches; and probed dead leaves. Also foraged in vine tangles. (Parker data.)

Vocalizations

Song: 2 birds duetting produce a series of Moderate- to High-pitched squeaky rattling notes, *chip chip chi-chi-chi-ch-ch-ch-ch* etc, rapidly accelerating and usually running into drawn out, squealing phrases, *wa-CHEW wa-CHEW* etc, typically uttered 3–4 times. Call note: a Moderate- to High-pitched *chip*.

Breeding

Eggs are white and spherical (Nehrkorn 1899).

Sources

Primary Hilty and Brown 1986; LSUMZ data; Meyer de Schauensee and Phelps 1978; Munves 1975; Parker data; Ridgely and Gaulin 1980; Schäfer and Phelps 1954; Terborgh and Weske 1975. **Weights (n = 53)** LSUMZ data; Weske 1972. **Stomach contents** LSUMZ data. **Vocalizations** LNS recordings by Parker (3), van den Berg (1). **Eggs** Nehrkorn 1899.

Hemispingus melanotis **31**
Black-eared Hemispingus
Plate 5

Length 13–14 cm (5–5½ in.). Weight 16 g (13.0–21.8 g). Six subspecies: *melanotis, ochraceus, piurae, berlepschi*, and *castaneicollis* are illustrated; *macrophrys* resembles *piurae*. *H. m. melanotis*: short supercilium is sometimes lacking entirely or, conversely, may extend into a long white supercilium; subadult individuals are slightly olivaceous throughout. *H. m. berlepschi*: adult plumage sometimes has a few white spots above lores as in *melanotis*; subadult with greenish crown, olive-brown back. *H. m. castaneicollis*: subadult plumage parallels that of *piurae* (illus.).

Geographic Range

H. m. melanotis: west of the Western Venezuelan Low in sw Táchira, VENEZUELA, and in the E Andes in Santander (Hilty and Brown 1986), se Boyacá (Ridgely in Hilty and Brown 1986), and Cundinamarca, COLOMBIA; the C Andes from Antioquia south and the e Andean slope from Nariño, COLOMBIA, to Tungurahua, ECUADOR. *H. m. ochraceus*: sw COLOMBIA on the Pacific slope in Nariño and w ECUADOR in Chimborazo. *H. m. piurae*: nw PERU on both slopes of the Andes in Piura and Cajamarca. *H. m. macrophrys*: nw PERU on the Pacific slope of the Andes in La Libertad. *H. m. berlepschi*: e Andean slope from Amazonas to n Cuzco, PERU (Weske 1972). *H. m. castaneicollis*: Puno, PERU, to Santa Cruz (Remsen, Traylor, and Parkes in press), BOLIVIA.

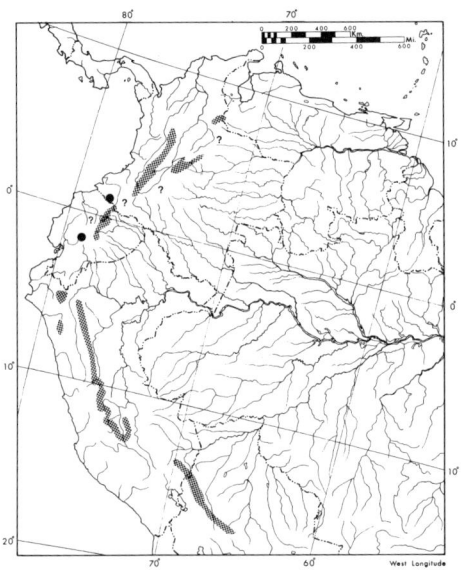

Hemispingus melanotis

Elevational Range

Ca. 1800 m in Venezuela, 1700–2900 m in Colombia, 1500–2600 m in Ecuador, 1200–3050 m in Peru, and 1350–2450 m in Bolivia.

Habitat and Behavior

Inhabits undergrowth and thickets, particularly bamboo thickets in humid forest. Habitat appears to vary geographically. In Colombia (*melanotis*), found in humid to very wet montane forest (Hilty *in litt.*). In nw Peru (*piurae*), in rather dry forest (Parker et al. 1985). In nw Bolivia (*castaneicollis*), mostly in thickets at humid forest edge (Remsen data). Scarce and/or local in many parts of its range. Encountered in small groups of 3–4 individuals, also in pairs or singly. Often travels with understory flocks.

Forages mostly from 1–6 m off the ground, occasionally ascends to crowns of trees. Gleans foliage and hangs from leaves. Stomach contents: animal matter (11); animal and vegetable material (2). Contents included beetles and other insect parts and seeds.

Vocalizations

In Bolivia (*castaneicollis*): Calls: a squeaky or wheezy *jit* or *ja-jit*, Moderate- to High-pitched. When alarmed, repeats calls in short series while flicking wings open. Song is a 2–3 sec. series of call notes; typically speeds up into a rapid twitter, sometimes slowing down to a rhythmic *ji-ja-jit ji-ja-jit ji-ja-jit*; intervals between songs are 3–12 sec.

Breeding

No information.

Sources

Primary Hilty and Brown 1986; LSUMZ data; Parker data; Remsen data; Ridgely and Gaulin 1980. **Weights (n = 52)** LSUMZ data; Weske 1972. **Stomach contents** LSUMZ data. **Vocalizations** LNS recordings by Parker (4); recording by R. A. Rowlett (1).

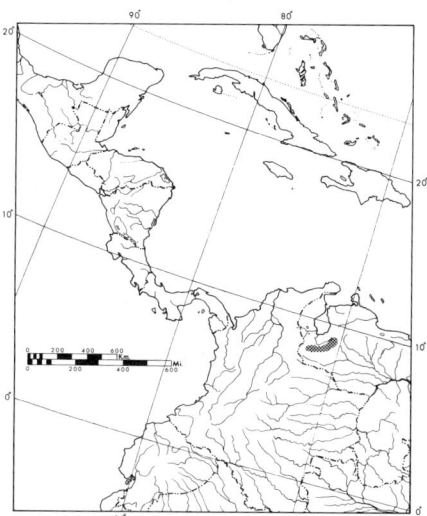

Hemispingus goeringi

Hemispingus goeringi **32**
Slaty-backed Hemispingus
Plate 5

Length 14 cm (5½ in.). Monotypic.

Geographic Range

W VENEZUELA in the Andes of Mérida and Táchira.

Elevational Range

2600–3200 m.

Habitat and Behavior

Inhabits humid montane forest at páramo edge. Forages near the ground, perhaps on the ground. Noted in mixed-species flocks (Moynihan 1979).

Vocalizations

Song: a continuous stream of Moderate-pitched harsh notes, *ch-d-d-d-d-d-d-d* etc, and a more pleasant High-pitched stream of musical, almost tinkling, *chi-ti-tee chi-ti-tee* etc; the 2 types of vocalizations are given simultaneously (probably in a duet); one sequence lasted for over 3 min. (Schwartz, LNS).

Breeding

No information.

Sources

Primary Meyer de Schauensee and Phelps 1978; Moynihan 1979. **Vocalizations** LNS recordings by Schwartz (3).

Hemispingus rufosuperciliaris **33**
Rufous-browed Hemispingus
Plate 5

Length 15 cm (6 in.). Weight 29 g (26.0–33.0 g). Monotypic. Its long legs may be adapted for hopping in thick moss on branches or on the ground.

Geographic Range

Locally on the e Andean slope from Amazonas (south of the Río Marañón) to Huánuco (west of the Río Huallaga), PERU (LSUMZ).

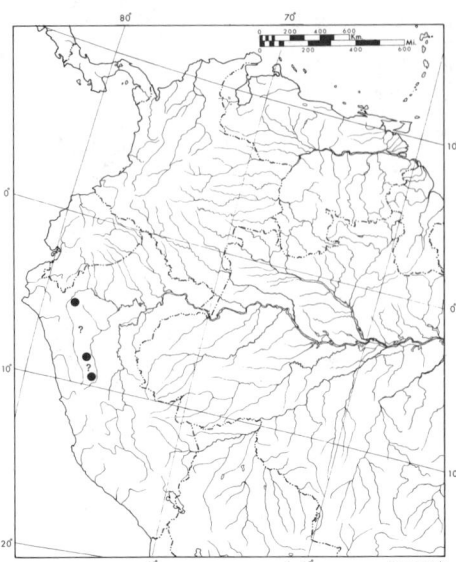

Hemispingus rufosuperciliaris

Elevational Range

2500–3350 m.

Habitat and Behavior

Inhabits humid elfin and montane forest. Lives in forest undergrowth thickly covered with moss, in extensive thickets of bamboo, and in dense shrubby areas adjoining contiguous forest. Pairs and small groups of 3–4 individuals travel alone or accompany mixed-species flocks. Stays well hidden in dense undergrowth habitats. Relatively slow moving for a *Hemispingus* species; behavior is reminiscent of an *Atlapetes* brush-finch (Emberizinae).

Forages typically within 2 m of the ground. Hops deliberately along large limbs with heavy moss jackets. Also encountered hopping between bamboo stalks, on the ground in a *Chusquea* bamboo thicket (Robbins pers. comm.), and in tall grass at the bases of bushes at treeline (Parker *in litt.*). Once observed reaching down or out to pick food out of moss jackets and hanging moss (O'Neill data). Stomach contents: animal matter (4); vegetable matter (2); both (1). Content included beetles, caterpillars, seeds, and rocks.

Vocalizations

Call: a scratchy nasal *chenk*; Moderate- to High-pitched; given in rapid succession by all members of a group (Parker, LNS). Song: short and squeaky nasal notes are mixed with characteristic long and slurred squeals given irregularly; the whole having a "jazzy" rhythm. A segment sounds like *nya-tit-tit-tit-squeal! tit-tit-squeal!, nya-nya tit-squeal!* etc; the powerful song is continued for minutes with only occasional brief pauses; High- and Moderate-pitched.

Breeding

No information.

Sources

Primary Blake and Hocking 1974; Isler data; LSUMZ data; Parker data; Tallman 1974. **Weights (n=21)** Blake and Hocking 1974; LSUMZ data. **Stomach contents** LSUMZ data. **Vocalizations** LNS recordings by Isler (3), Parker (1), van den Berg (1).

Hemispingus verticalis 34
Black-headed Hemispingus
Plate 5

Length 14 cm (5½ in.). Weight 13 g (12.5–14.0 g). Monotypic. Subadult plumage like adult except throat white with grayish spots, short white tufts over eyes, and paler chest.

Geographic Range

VENEZUELA west of the Western Venezuelan Low in sw Táchira; COLOMBIA in the W Andes in Antioquia (Hilty and Brown 1983), the C Andes south to Nariño, and the E Andes in Cundinamarca; ECUADOR along the e Andean slope in Carchi, Napo, and Zamora-Chinchipe (Ridgely 1980); and PERU north of the Northern Peruvian Low in Piura near the Piura-Cajamarca border (Parker et al. 1985).

Elevational Range

Ca. 2600 m to treeline; above 3000 m in Colombia (Hilty and Brown 1986).

Habitat and Behavior

Inhabits bushes and trees in humid montane and elfin forest; sometimes occurs at forest edge or flies to isolated tree groves near treeline. Travels in pairs and groups of 3–5 (once up to 12 or more) individuals; conspicuous members of mixed-species flocks. Seems to be a nuclear species; at one location in Peru, a pair within each mixed-species flock appeared to be territorial (Parker et al. 1985). Restless and fast moving.

Forages primarily in the uppermost leaf

Hemispingus xanthophthalmus   35
Drab Hemispingus
Plate 5

Length 13 cm (5½ in.). Weight 12 g (10.3–15.0 g). Monotypic.

Geographic Range

E Andean slope south of the Northern Peruvian Low from Amazonas, PERU, to La Paz, BOLIVIA (Parker, Remsen, and Heindel 1980).

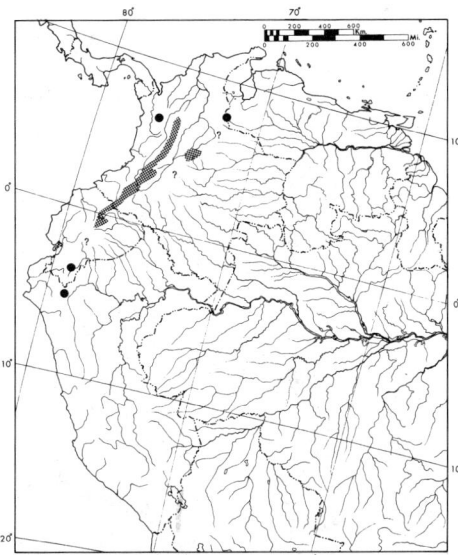

Hemispingus verticalis

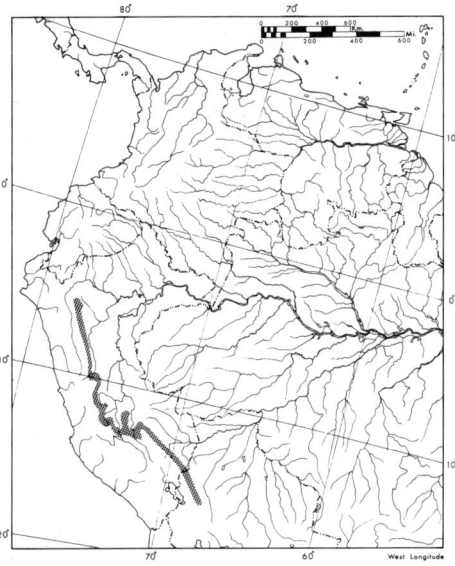

Hemispingus xanthophthalmus

Elevational Range

2400–3500 m in Peru and 2900–3050 m in Bolivia.

Habitat and Behavior

Inhabits humid montane and elfin forest and forest edge. Typically forages in the uppermost foliage of tall bushes and trees, mostly 7–12 m off the ground, as low as eye level, and as high as 18 m. Favors canopy vegetation composed of small stiff closely spaced leaves, but also large (10 x 15 cm) leaves of *Clusia* trees. Groups of 2–5 individuals usually travel with mixed-species flocks. Appears to be an important flock member, probably a nuclear species. clusters of bushes and trees; occasionally observed in bamboo (Parker data). Hops along branches working out towards the tips and walks over leaf clusters. Typically perches horizontally, often atop stiff leaves, and gleans insects from leaf tops. Also walks over foliage to pick fruit (Vuilleumier and Ewert 1978). Stomach contents (2): insects, including caterpillars and beetles. Also feeds on a variety of berries and small fruits including those of melastomes (Parker et al. 1985).

Vocalizations

Song: 5–15 sec. bursts of very squeaky, mostly Moderate-pitched, twittering notes overlaid with a continuous stream of sharp thin High-pitched *seet* or *steet* notes; apparently 2 or more birds sing simultaneously. The lower pitched twittering ends abruptly for intervals of up to 12 sec. during which the High-pitched notes continue alone at a slower pace.

Breeding

No information.

Sources

Primary Hilty and Brown 1986; Isler data; Moynihan 1979; Parker data; Parker et al. 1985. **Weights (n = 5)** LSUMZ data. **Stomach contents** LSUMZ data. **Vocalizations** LNS recordings by Parker (2); Parker et al. 1985.

Walks and hops deliberately across the leaves of dense canopy crowns investigating leaf clusters. Typically bobs head while walking and flutters to new locations. Also searches foliage inside tree canopies; hops along slender branches and twigs working out towards the ends of limbs. Picks prey off leaf tops, twigs, and flower stalks. Occasionally appears to flutter-pursue escaping insects (Isler data). Stomach contents (9): insects.

Vocalizations

Song: a sputtering patternless series of rapidly delivered notes; series and intervals vary from 3 to 8 sec. Notes vary greatly in pitch (from Low to Very High), duration, and quality: most are short or staccato, squeaky, metallic, or spitting, although some are longer with a chirping or squealing quality. Often 2 or 3 birds sing in unison. (Parker, LNS.) Call note is a hard, High- to Very-high-pitched, spitting *tsit* or *tseee* (Isler, LNS).

Breeding

No information.

Sources

Primary Isler data; LSUMZ data; Moynihan 1979; Parker data; Parker and O'Neill 1980; Parker, Remsen, and Heindel 1980; Remsen data; Schulenberg and Remsen 1982. **Weights (n = 30)** LSUMZ data. **Stomach contents** LSUMZ data. **Vocalizations** LNS recordings by Isler (2), Parker (3).

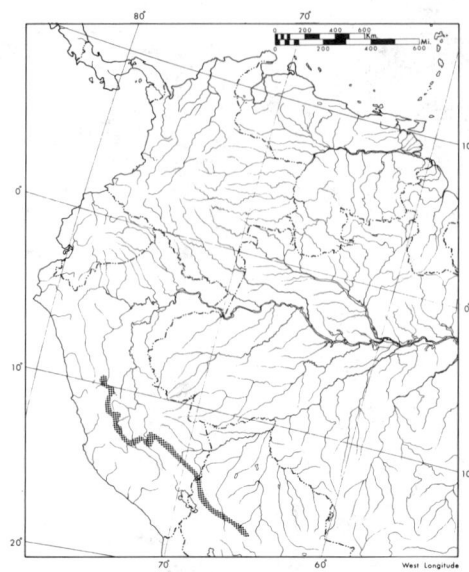

Hemispingus trifasciatus

Hemispingus trifasciatus **36**
Three-striped Hemispingus
Plate 5

Length 13 cm (5 in.). Weight 14 g (12.0–16.0 g). Monotypic. Plumage varies slightly; palest in the northern part of its range, most ochraceous in the south. Juvenal plumage like adult but supercilium tinged buff yellow, crown and cheeks tinged brown. (Remsen 1984.)

Geographic Range

E Andean slope from Huánuco (west of the Río Huallaga, Remsen 1984), PERU, to Cochabamba, BOLIVIA.

Elevational Range

Mostly 3000–3350 m; extremes 2800–4250 m (Remsen 1984).

Habitat and Behavior

Primarily lives in stunted (6–9 m high), small-leaved trees in forest islands and in humid elfin forest at the edge of puna; sometimes occurs in taller trees (to 15 m), rarely in the undergrowth or bamboo thickets. Groups of 2–10 (usually 4–6) individuals travel with mixed-species flocks (seems to be a nuclear species) or occasionally travel by themselves.

Typically forages in dense foliage in the crowns of trees and bushes, usually above eye level. In Bolivia, median foraging height was about 5.5 m and over two-thirds of 58 observations were within 2 m of the tops of vegetation; gleaned insects almost entirely from leaves; took prey about equally off leaf tops and undersides; used simple gleaning motions 87% of the time; rarely reached, hung, or sallied (Remsen data). In Peru, gleaned leaves at or near the ends of limbs; also gleaned twigs and picked at moss and lichens; hung upside down to pick at stems and small leaves (Parker data). Stomach contents (10): insects, including caterpillars.

Vocalizations

Call note: a spitting, mostly High-pitched *swit*, sometimes given rapidly (Parker, LNS). Members of a group often join in a chorus of call notes before crossing an open space to another wooded area (Parker data). Dawn song: repeats *tzit* over and over, at about 40

Pyrrhocoma ruficeps

repetitions/min.; sings from exposed dead limbs protruding above the canopy (Schulenberg *in litt.*).

Breeding

No information.

Sources

Primary LSUMZ data; Parker data; Parker and O'Neill 1980; Remsen data; Remsen 1984, 1985. **Weights (n = 31)** LSUMZ data. **Stomach contents** LSUMZ data. **Vocalizations** LNS recording by Parker (1).

PYRRHOCOMA

The single *Pyrrhocoma* species bears some resemblance to *Thlypopsis* tanagers, but is sexually dichromatic. *Pyrrhocoma* inhabits low dense vegetation; its behavior is not well documented.

Pyrrhocoma ruficeps **37**
Chestnut-headed Tanager
Plate 5

Length 14 cm (5½ in.). Weight 15 g (15 g). Monotypic. Males apparently breed in subadult plumage that resembles female plumage (Belton 1985).

Geographic Range

Se BRAZIL from Rio de Janeiro southward to c Rio Grande do Sul and westward through Misiones, ARGENTINA, to se PARAGUAY in Alto Paraná, Itapúa (Foster spec.), and Paraguarí.

Elevational Range

Varies across range. In Rio Grande do Sul, from near sea level to ca. 1000 m (Belton 1985). In Rio de Janeiro, primarily above 1200 m (Parker data).

Habitat and Behavior

Inhabits dense forest undergrowth, bamboo thickets, tangled shrubbery at forest edge, and dense young second-growth. Encountered in pairs and small groups. Joins mixed-species flocks (Bertoni 1926). Usually forages within 3 m (occasionally to 8 m) above the ground. Stomach contents (1): insects.

Vocalizations

Calls: repeats a thin light High-pitched *tsick*; also utters a scolding High-pitched hissing *pseee* when excited. Song: *pseee-pseee-pseee, tweee-tweee-tweee*; the *pseee* notes are explosive, High-pitched, and hissing; the *tweee* notes (sometimes only 2) are Moderate-pitched, upward-rising, and clearer; length is about 2 sec.; repeated regularly after intervals of about 5 sec.

Breeding

Eggs are white with a few dark spots, mostly at the large end (Ihering 1900).

Sources

Primary Belton 1985; Holt 1928; Olrog 1959; Parker data; Pinto 1951; Sick 1985; Voss 1977; Willis 1979. **Weights (n = 3)** Belton 1985. **Stomach contents** Foster data. **Vocalizations** LNS recordings by Belton (4), Parker (3); Belton 1985; Sick 1985. **Eggs** Ihering 1900.

THLYPOPSIS

Thlypopsis tanagers (Table 6) typically forage within dense shrubby vegetation, often at or just above eye level (the Orange-headed is an exception). Primarily insectivorous; insects are the only recorded food for four species; only the Orange-headed has been found to eat fruit. *Thlypopsis* species forage actively; they appear to take insects primarily off leaves; four species have been found to probe arboreal dead leaves, and four species to probe flowers.

Table 6 The *Thlypopsis* Tanagers

38	*T. fulviceps*	Fulvous-headed Tanager
39	*T. ornata*	Rufous-chested Tanager
40	*T. pectoralis*	Brown-flanked Tanager
41	*T. sordida*	Orange-headed Tanager
42	*T. inornata*	Buff-bellied Tanager
43	*T. ruficeps*	Rust-and-yellow Tanager

Two *Thlypopsis* deliver fairly loud territorial songs in synchronous duets (Parker data), but songs have been recorded infrequently. Some species may deliver songs only during the breeding season although the Orange-headed Tanager sings year-round in se Brazil (Sick 1985). *Thlypopsis* tanagers apparently obtain adult plumage in their second year. Parents and their offspring appear to remain together for a year, as *Thlypopsis* are often encountered in small groups.

One *Thlypopsis*, the Orange-headed Tanager, lives in South American lowlands east of the Andes. The remaining species inhabit montane slopes and valleys and replace each other geographically from coastal Venezuela through most of the Andes to Argentina. Only the ranges of the Rufous-chested and Rust-and-yellow Tanagers overlap significantly, and that overlap may be seasonal as the Rust-and-yellow Tanager is believed to migrate north in the austral winter.

Thlypopsis fulviceps **38**
Fulvous-headed Tanager
Plate 5

Length 12 cm (5 in.). Four subspecies: *fulviceps* and *intensa* are illustrated; *obscuriceps* and *meridensis* resemble *fulviceps*.

Geographic Range

T. f. fulviceps: mountains from Sucre and Monagas west to Carabobo, VENEZUELA, and the e slope of the E Andes in Norte de Santander, COLOMBIA. *T. f. meridensis*: the Andes of Mérida and Táchira, VENEZUELA. *T. f. obscuriceps*: the Perijá moun-

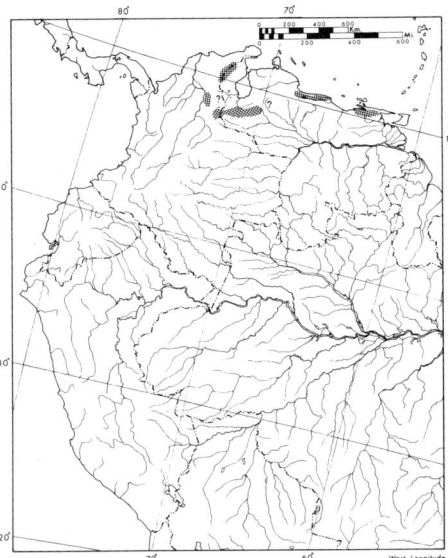

Thlypopsis fulviceps

tains. *T. f. intensa*: the w slope of the E Andes in Norte de Santander, COLOMBIA.

Elevational Range

750–2000 m.

Habitat and Behavior

Inhabits dense thickets, vine tangles, and bamboo at forest edge and in second growth and semiopen areas near forest; also occurs inside humid forest, in open woodland, and in suburban areas. Encountered in pairs, singly, or in groups of up to 10 individuals. Travels restlessly through dense vegetation, alone or with mixed-species flocks. Forages from near the ground to the crowns of trees. In Venezuela, scanned leaves of all sizes; picked insects off both top and bottom leaf surfaces and off petioles; sallied to the underside of a leaf; probed dead leaves in vine tangles and curled dead leaves caught in mistletoe (Parker data). Observed eating a caterpillar (Thomas data).

Vocalizations

Possible song: High- to Moderate-pitched, *chit chit cht-cht-tit-t-t-t-t*; begins slowly then runs together before trailing off into a stutter (10 sec. recording, Schwartz, LNS).

Breeding

No information.

Sources

Primary Hilty and Brown 1986; Meyer de Schauensee and Phelps 1978; Parker data; Schäfer and Phelps 1954. **Vocalizations** LNS recording by Schwartz (1).

Thlypopsis ornata **39**
Rufous-chested Tanager
Plate 5

Length 12 cm (5 in.). Weight 12 g (9.8–14.9 g). Three subspecies.

Geographic Range

The w slope of the C Andes in Cauca, COLOMBIA; the w slope of the Andes from Carchi, ECUADOR, southward through ECUADOR and PERU to Lima; and the e slope of the Andes in PERU from Cajamarca north of the Northern Peruvian Low (Parker et al. 1985) southward (incl. the Marañón Valley) to Junín and in n Cuzco.

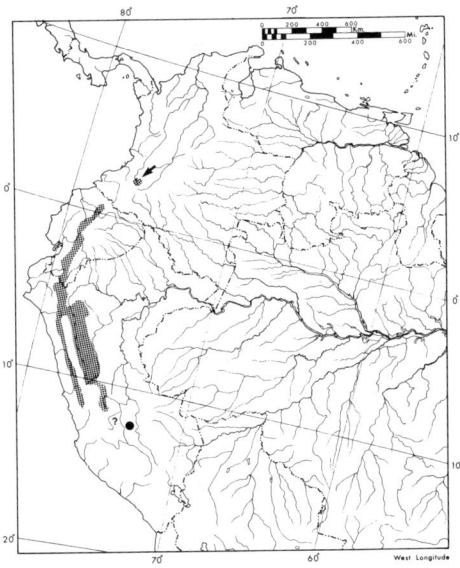

Thlypopsis ornata

Elevational Range

2000–3400 m; mostly 2400–3000 m; as low as 1400 m in Ecuador.

Habitat and Behavior

Inhabits areas of dense shrubbery, bamboo thickets, and second growth at forest edge and away from forest in clearings, in ravines, and on steep slopes; also occurs in *Polylepis* scrub and open woodland. Single birds, pairs, and groups of 3–4 (up to 8) individuals travel by themselves or sometimes with mixed-species flocks. Moves rapidly and actively while foraging in dense foliage from low shrubbery to 6 m up in tree canopies. Gleans leaves, twigs, and arboreal dead leaves; also searches flowers. Occasionally hangs upside down (Parker data). Seen probing incisions of a *Diglossa* species in tubular flowers (Moynihan 1963). Stomach contents (6): animal matter, including beetles. Additional stomach contents included spiders and a caterpillar.

Vocalizations

Call note: *seep* (Parker data).

Breeding

No information.

Sources

Primary Hilty and Brown 1986; Koepcke 1958, 1970; LSUMZ data; Parker data. **Weights (n = 23)** LSUMZ data. **Stomach contents** LSUMZ data; Plenge 1974. **Vocalizations** Parker data.

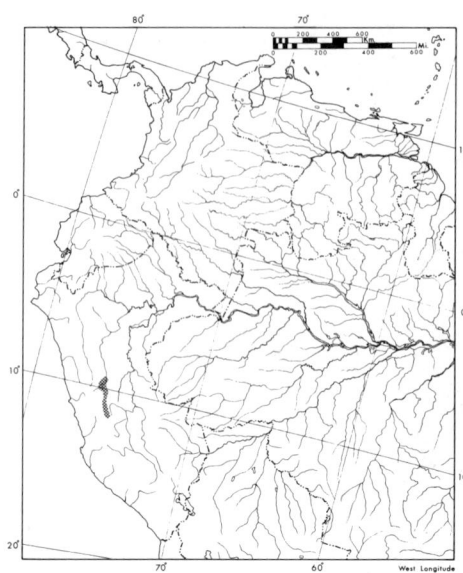

Thlypopsis pectoralis

Thlypopsis pectoralis 40
Brown-flanked Tanager
Plate 5

Length 12 cm (5 in.). Weight 15 g (14.0–17.0 g). Monotypic.

Geographic Range

C PERU in intermontane valleys on the e slope of the Andes in Huánuco, Pasco, and Junín; primarily on the w flank of the e cordillera.

Elevational Range

Ca. 2500–3100 m.

Habitat and Behavior

Inhabits semiopen areas; typically encountered in dense bushes and shrubs bordering cultivation and pastures, alder thickets along streams, and second growth at forest edge. Sometimes observed in tall grass and weeds adjoining thickets (Parker *in litt.*). Pairs usually travel apart from other species, but male and female generally stay within 1–2 m of one another. Occasionally joins mixed-species flocks with the Rufous-chested Tanager, *T. ornata* **39,** where their ranges abut (Parker *in litt.*).

Generally forages for insects just inside the outer foliage of shrubbery. Usually begins foraging within a meter or so of the ground and works upwards, methodically searching for insects, until it reaches a height of about 3 m Forages in the open mostly in the dim light of dawn. During daylight hours, usually remains among interior branches, stems, and vines hopping actively from perch to perch and peering about constantly. Mostly investigates curled dead leaves which are usually taken in the bill and given a twist or shake—if an insect flies out, it is pursued in flight or in a series of short jumps. Also pokes into seed pods and flowers and occasionally seeks insects on bare branches, twigs, leaf stems, and top and bottom surfaces of green leaves. Reaches in all directions or leans over to pick prey off substrates; rarely hangs from leaves. Searches mostly for tiny insects, but also takes caterpillars and small moths.

Vocalizations

While foraging, utters a very soft high pitched *tsit* or a twittery *seet seet seet*.

Breeding

No information.

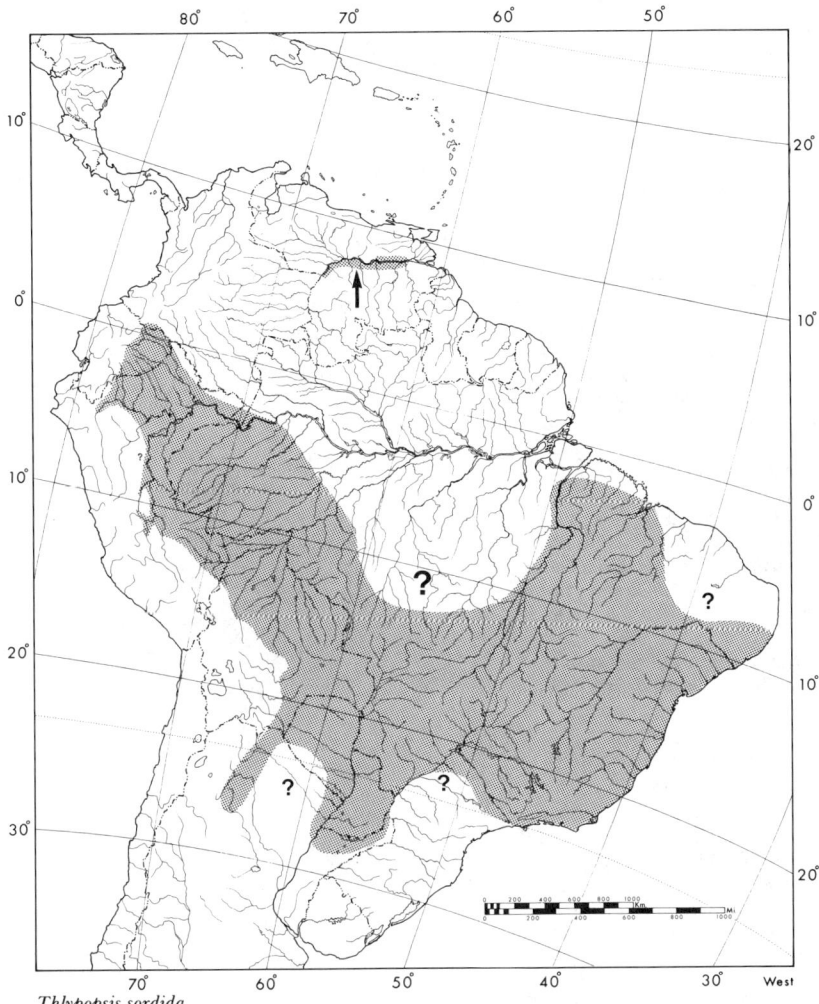

Thlypopsis sordida

Sources

Primary Isler data; O'Neill data; Moynihan 1979; Parker data; Zimmer 1930. **Weights (n = 8)** LSUMZ data. **Vocalizations** Isler data; O'Neill data.

Thlypopsis sordida **41**
Orange-headed Tanager
Plate 5

Length 13 cm (5 in.). Weight 17 g (14.0–19.0 g). Three subspecies.

Geographic Range

T. s. sordida and *chrysopis*: In a band east of the Andes from extreme e Nariño and Amazonas (along the Amazon River), COLOMBIA, southward through ECUADOR, PERU, sw BRAZIL, and BOLIVIA thence along the base of the Andes to Tucumán, ARGENTINA; w and s BRAZIL, w and s PARAGUAY, and n ARGENTINA (e Formosa, e Chaco, n Santa Fe, Corrientes, and Misiones) to w Paraná and e São Paulo, BRAZIL; thence northward through e BRAZIL to extreme e Pará, Goiás, Maranhão, Piauí, Ceará, and Paraíba. *T. s. orinocensis*: VENEZUELA along the Orinoco River in n Bolívar and se Anzoátegui.

Elevational Range

Lowlands to ca. 800 m, occasionally higher; as high as 1300 m in Bolivia (Niethammer 1956).

Habitat and Behavior

In Venezuela and in humid portions of Amazonia, mostly found in shrubbery and low trees in river-created habitats (e.g., successional shrubbery on river islands, see Remsen and Parker 1983); also occurs near water courses in second growth. In the southern portion of its range, occurs in the canopy of open woodland and edge, second growth, gallery forest, swampy woodland, and trees in parks and residential areas. Seasonal movements have been noted in Mato Grosso, Brazil (Allen 1891), and Tucumán, Argentina, where it moves from Andean slopes to lowlands in winter (Dinelli 1918).

Lives in pairs, singly, and in small groups of 3–4 individuals. Forages restlessly from about eye level to tops of small trees. Gleans insects from foliage; seldom hovers or flutters (Hilty and Brown 1986). Stomach contents: vegetable matter (3); animal matter (4); both (1). Contents included orthopterans, coleopterans, dipterans, spiders, fruit pulp, and seeds.

Vocalizations

Calls: rapidly utters a High-pitched *seet* or *sit*, usually doubled or tripled. Also repeats single and double notes, e.g., *seet-a*, at a slower pace, possibly a song. Territorial song (Peru and Bolivia) given by 2 birds, presumably a pair, in a duet: *seet seet t-t-t-t-t-t-t-t-t-d-dit*; the introductory notes High-pitched, the chittering burst that follows is slightly lower in pitch; delivered in flight as well as when perched (Parker, LNS). In Rio de Janeiro, Brazil, sings throughout the year (Sick and Pabst 1968).

Breeding

One nest in Argentina, an open cup about 2 m above the ground, contained 2 bluish white eggs, marked with brown and pale cinnamon (Dinelli 1918). Mitchell (1957) saw an adult feeding 3 well-grown young. Breeding dates: Argentina Dec.

Sources

Primary Dinelli 1918; Hilty and Brown 1986; LSUMZ data; Mitchell 1957; Parker data; Sick 1985. **Weights (n = 29)** Contreras 1979; Fry 1970; LSUMZ data; Weske 1972. **Stomach contents** Foster data; LSUMZ data; Moojen, Carvalho, and Lopes 1941; Schubart, Aguirre, and Sick 1965. **Vocalizations** LNS recordings by Parker (6); Sick 1985. **Nests, eggs, and breeding dates** Dinelli 1918.

Thlypopsis inornata 42
Buff-bellied Tanager
Plate 6

Length 13 cm (5 in.). Weight 15 g (14.0–17.0 g). Monotypic.

Geographic Range

Nc PERU in the drainage of the upper Río Marañón in w Amazonas and Cajamarca.

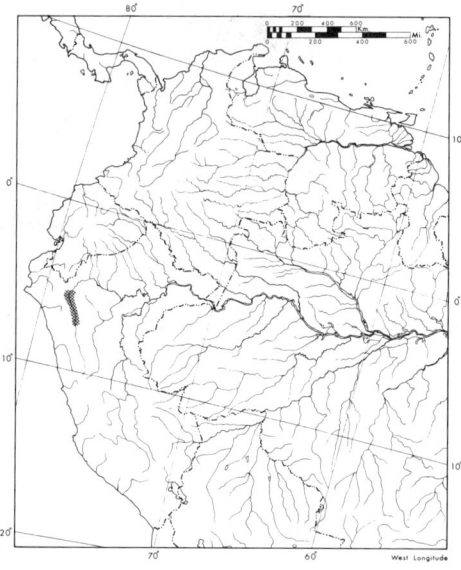

Thlypopsis inornata

Elevational Range

Ca. 450–2000 m.

Habitat and Behavior

Inhabits thickets and dense brushwood in xeric scrub, along rivers, in ravines, and at forest edge. Travels in small groups. Forages mostly at low levels; occasionally ascends to the canopy at forest edge. Gleans small *Acacia* leaves on outer branches, probes composite leaf clusters in shrubbery, and probes flowers (Parker *in litt.*).

Thlypopsis ruficeps

Vocalizations

Calls: *sip* or *seep* while foraging; also *seet-a* repeated several times softly (Parker *in litt.*).

Breeding

No information.

Sources

Primary Dorst 1957a, 1957b; LSUMZ data; Parker *in litt.*; Taczanowski 1884b. **Weights (n = 8)** LSUMZ data. **Vocalizations** Parker *in litt.*

Thlypopsis ruficeps 43
Rust-and-yellow Tanager
Plate 6

Length 12 cm (5 in.). Weight 11 g (9.6–13.1 g). Monotypic.

Geographic Range

The e slope of the Andes from Ayacucho and Cuzco (both slopes above the Río Apurimac, Weske 1972), PERU, southward through BOLIVIA to Tucumán, ARGENTINA. One record from Huánuco (LSUMZ), PERU (in June, possibly a wanderer from the south).

Elevational Range

Ca. 1300–3600 m, rarely lower.

Habitat and Behavior

Inhabits bushes, second growth, bamboo thickets, and low trees in humid forest and at forest edge; also encountered in *Polylepis* woodland. Appears to be partially migratory; leaves parts of Argentina in the austral winter (e.g., Tucumán, Dinelli 1918); possibly migrates northward along the slope of the Andes (Parker *in litt.*). Single birds, pairs, and small groups typically travel with mixed-species flocks. Moves quickly through woodlands often keeping hidden in dense vegetation.

Forages at low and medium heights, but also in the crowns of tall trees. At one site in Bolivia: Foraged primarily in dense foliage in the crowns of bushes and low trees; median foraging height was 3 m; rarely foraged above 9 m. Typically searched for prey on leaves (86% of 40 obs.), primarily taking insects off undersides. Also foraged in flowers and dead leaves and on branches. Picked insects without acrobatic moves (56% of all obs.), or by reaching (Remsen data). In Peru, picked insects off foliage, flower heads, and bamboo leaf bases and internodes (Parker data). Stomach contents (11): insects.

Vocalizations

Pairs duet. Song: a short rapid burst of chittering about 1.5 sec. long; similar to the song of the Orange-headed Tanager, *T. sordida* 41; male and female sit closely (1–2 cm apart) on a branch to sing, then fly together to another branch to sing again (Parker *in litt.*).

Breeding

No information.

Sources

Primary Morrison 1948; Moynihan 1979; Parker data; Parker *in litt.*; Remsen data; Remsen 1985. **Weights (n = 16)** LSUMZ data; Weske 1972. **Stomach contents** LSUMZ data. **Vocalizations** Parker *in litt.*

HEMITHRAUPIS

Hemithraupis tanagers (Table 7) typically forage near the tops of trees in forest canopy, tall second growth, or open woodland. Pairs and small groups move actively through the foliage, frequently in company with mixed-species flocks. *Hemithraupis* appear to forage primarily with the peer and pick method, often stretching their heads above the foliage to search for insects. They pick insects off leaves with a variety of acrobatic techniques, such as reaching out, hanging down, hovering, and sallying. They also eat berries and small fruits. The Guira and Rufous-headed Tanagers constitute a superspecies (Short 1975); they occasionally hybridize in se Brazil, where their ranges abut (see Zimmer 1947a). The Yellow-backed Tanager is sympatric with the other two *Hemithraupis* species.

Table 7 The *Hemithraupis* Tanagers

44	*H. guira*	Guira Tanager
45	*H. ruficapilla*	Rufous-headed Tanager
46	*H. flavicollis*	Yellow-backed Tanager

Hemithraupis guira 44
Guira Tanager
Plate 6

Length 13 cm (5 in.). Weight 12 g (9.5–14.0 g). Eight subspecies: differences in color intensity and size are unimportant in the field; males differ most noticeably in the extent of the yellow borders of the black face and throat.

Geographic Range

H. g. guirina: occurs in 3 disjunct areas in nw South America: *1)* w of the Andes in ECUADOR and adjoining Tumbes, nw PERU (possibly extirpated from Peru); *2)* Cauca Valley, COLOMBIA, from Antioquia to Valle (one sight record on Pacific slope in Valle, Hilty and Brown 1986); *3)* Magdalena Valley, COLOMBIA, from Santander to Huila. *Remaining races*: east of the Andes east and south to n and w Bahia, w Minas Gerais, w São Paulo, and c Rio Grande do Sul, BRAZIL; Misiones, ARGENTINA; e and c PARAGUAY; and along the base of the Andes to Tucumán, ARGENTINA. Not found in e Colombia from Boyacá to Caquetá and n Amazonas, nw Venezuela west of Falcón, sw Venezuela in

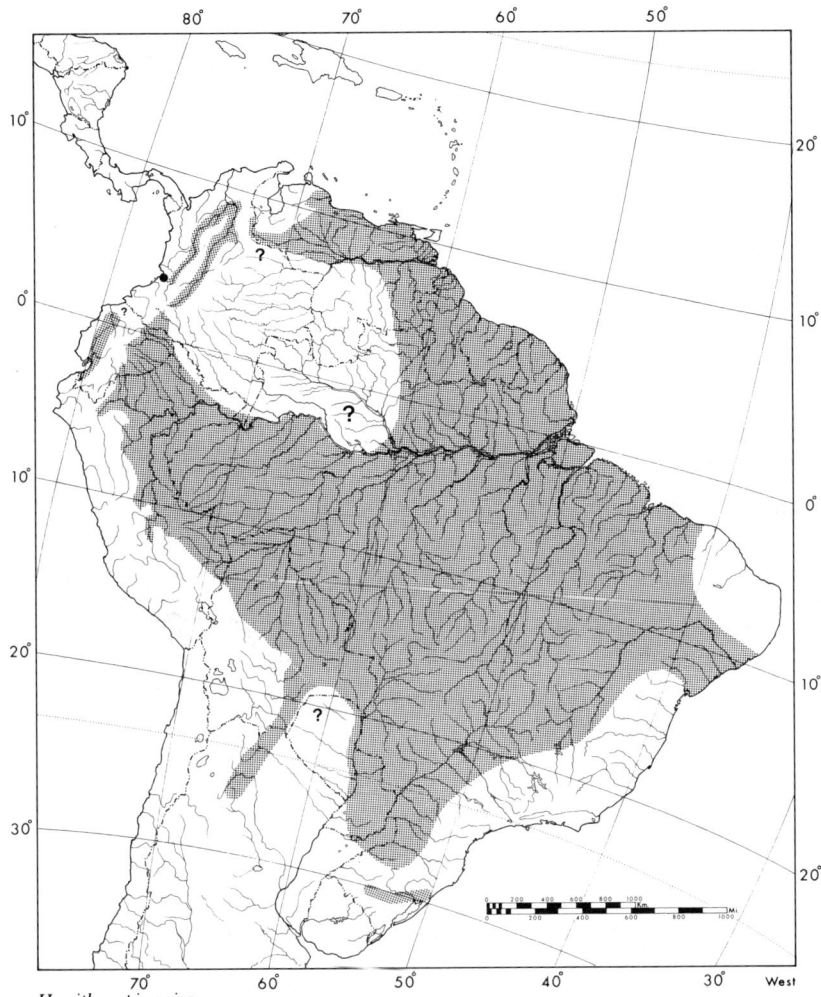
Hemithraupis guira

Amazonas and w Bolívar, and the nw corner of Brazil east of the Río Negro and north of the Amazon River. One suspicious record from Espírito Santo, Brazil (Pinto 1944a).

Elevational Range

Lowlands to 1500 m; to 2000 m in Colombia; mostly below 1000 m.

Habitat and Behavior

In Amazonia, inhabits tall humid terra firma and low-lying forest, also plantations with tall shade trees. Outside of Amazonia, occurs in gallery forest, open woodland, isolated forest preserves and woodlots, second growth, and tall scrub (cerradão); also occurs in orchards. Encountered in pairs or small groups of 3–7 (sometimes up to 25) individuals. Rapidly and actively travels through the canopy, often with mixed-species flocks. In s Peru, occurred at a lower population density than the species comprising the permanent canopy flocks (Munn 1985). In n Venezuela, associates primarily with insectivorous species (Morton 1979).

Flutters actively and acrobatically while foraging for insects in outer foliage of tree crowns, often at the very top of the tree. Pokes head above the foliage to scan leaves. Reaches out to pick prey off bottom (5 obs.) and top (2 obs.) leaf surfaces; hangs from leaves and sallies to foliage; also searches leaf clusters and branches. In Brazil, observed eating *Miconia* berries (Parker data) and examining flower corollas for insects (Santos 1948). Stomach contents: animal matter (8); vegetable matter (1); both (5). Contents included coleopterans, orthopterans (incl. grasshoppers and cockroaches), caterpillars, hemipterans, spiders, fruit, and seeds.

In Paraguay in captivity, took 7–10 mm fruits of *Allophyllus edulis*. Plucked fruit while perched or snatched it in flight. Nibbled, bit, or pecked at fruit taken to a perch, leaving the seed. Sometimes rolled fruit around in its bill to peel off pulp, then dropped the seed. (Foster data.)

Vocalizations

Dawn song: *TIT-de-de-DIT TIT TIT*, *tit-de-de-dit tit*, last note sometimes squealing; cadence very reminiscent of a drummer's roll; Moderate- to High-pitched; about 2.5 sec. long and repeated after 3-sec. pauses. Day song: a rapid series of nasal *chee*s or *chut*s accelerate into a trill of *chit*s, then slows at the end; Moderate- to High-pitched; about 2 sec. long with pauses of 5 sec. Song when agitated: starts with nasal Low- and Moderate-pitched *aauck* or *churr* notes, speeds up into High-pitched trills of *chit*s, and then slows down and speeds up irregularly. The same notes, particularly the *aauck* and *chit* notes, are used as calls.

Breeding

Builds its nest in the tops of trees. In Paraguay, a flimsy cup nest, made of palm fibers and lichens and lined with finer fibers, was placed on the fork of a thin branch. Eggs were white sprinkled with cinnamon brown on the thick end. (Bertoni 1918.) In Suriname, a female was observed feeding fruit to a fledgling (Whitney *in litt.*). Breeding dates: Paraguay, Sept–Oct.

Sources

Primary Belton 1985; Foster data; Haverschmidt 1968; Hilty and Brown 1986; Parker data; Remsen data; Schäfer and Phelps 1954. **Weights (n = 22)** Dick, McGillivray, and Brooks 1984; Fry 1970; Haverschmidt 1952, 1968; LSUMZ data; Short 1971; Sick 1985; Weske 1972. **Stomach contents** Foster data; Haverschmidt 1968; LSUMZ data; Schubart, Aguirre, and Sick 1965; Taczanowski 1884b. **Vocalizations** LNS recordings by Belton (7), Munn (1), Parker (2), Schwartz (1); Hilty and Brown 1986; Short 1971; Sick 1985. **Nests, eggs, and breeding dates** Bertoni 1918; Wetmore 1926.

Hemithraupis ruficapilla 45
Rufous-headed Tanager
Plate 6

Length 13 cm (5 in.). Weight 13 g. Two subspecies.

Geographic Range

E BRAZIL from c Bahia southward to Santa Catarina.

Elevational Range

Lowlands to ca. 1350 m (Parker data).

Habitat and Behavior

Inhabits forest, forest edge, and tall second growth; also occurs in plantations and parks with shade trees. In São Paulo, survives in a remnant woodlot of 250 ha. but not one of 21 ha. (Willis 1979). Encountered in territorial pairs and family groups. Associates with mixed-species flocks; may be a nuclear species (Mitchell 1957). Forages restlessly in the uppermost canopy; rarely in the middle portion of the canopy. Peers about, scanning leaves; picks insects from leaf undersides, also stems (Parker data). Stomach contents: insects. Also eats fruit.

Vocalizations

Call notes: a Moderate- to High-pitched, slightly grating *enk* and a High-pitched *chit*. Song: a rhythmic 2.5 sec. series of rapidly rattled *chit*s, slowing to individual notes; e.g., *chit-t-t-t-t-t-t chew chit-it?* (*chew* note lower in pitch); ends in *chit, chit, chit* in another version. About 2–3 sec. long; delivered at about 12 outbursts per min. Rhythmic and much like the dawn song of the Guira Tanager, *H. guira* **44**. (Parker, LNS.)

Breeding

In Rio de Janeiro in October, a female was seen carrying strips of bamboo(?) into a 5 x 8 cm hole in a hanging clump of *Tillandsia* (Parker *in litt.*).

Sources

Primary Davis 1945a, 1946; Descourtilz 1852; Mitchell 1957; Parker data; Sick 1985; Sick and Pabst 1968; Willis 1979. **Weights (n = ?)** Sick 1985. **Stomach contents** Berla 1944. **Vocalizations** LNS recording by Parker (1). **Nests and breeding dates** Parker *in litt*.

Hemithraupis ruficapilla

Hemithraupis flavicollis 46
Yellow-backed Tanager
Plate 6

Length 13 cm (5 in.). Weight 13 g (11.0–15.0 g). Eleven subspecies; males of *albigularis*, *peruana*, and *ornata* are illustrated. Males of the remaining subspecies resemble *ornata*, differing noticeably in intensity of color and in extent of black barring on the sides. Other than *albigularis* (illus.), females resemble *insignis* (illus.) and, like the males, vary in color intensity, the pale yellow belly approaching white in some races. Young males first resemble females and later resemble adult males but with yellow edgings on wing and tail feathers (see Parkes and Humphrey 1963).

Geographic Range

Several apparently disjunct populations: *H. f. ornata*: Pacific slope from e Darién, PANAMA, to extreme n Chocó, COLOMBIA. *H. f. albigularis*: Antioquia and Santander, COLOMBIA, between the Río Sinú and middle Magdalena Valley. *H. f. peruana*: east of the Andes from w Meta, COLOMBIA, south through ECUADOR to PERU north of the Río Marañón and Amazon River in Amazonas and Loreto. *H. f. sororia* and *cen-*

HEMITHRAUPIS

Hemithraupis flavicollis

tralis: in a band east of the Andes and south of the Río Marañón and Amazon River southward through PERU and n BOLIVIA, thence eastward to extreme se Amazonas and c Mato Grosso, BRAZIL; sight? record in e Mato Grosso (Fry 1970). *H. f. aurigularis, hellmayri*, and *flavicollis*: extreme nw Amazonas, BRAZIL, and extreme e COLOMBIA in Guianía and Vaupés eastward through Amazonas and Bolívar, VENEZUELA, and THE GUIANAS to extreme ne Pará (Novaes 1980) and extreme n Amapá, BRAZIL (Novaes 1978). *H. f. obidensis*: n bank of the Amazon River in w Pará and e Amazonas. *H. f. melanoxantha* and *insignis*: coastal region of e BRAZIL from Pernambuco to s Rio de Janeiro, inland to extreme e Minas Gerais.

Elevational Range

Lowlands to 1000 m.

Habitat and Behavior

In Amazonia, inhabits tall humid terra firma and low-lying (incl. *varzea*) forest and forest edge; also occurs in shaded plantations. Outside Amazonia, mostly in forest and forest edge; also tall second growth, open woodland, shaded plantations, and parks (e Brazil). Encountered in pairs and small groups, sometimes singly. Travels actively through the canopy, usually in company with mixed-species flocks; in se Brazil, may be a nuclear species (Mitchell 1957), but in s Peru, was a transient in permanent canopy flocks (Munn 1985).

Usually forages in the uppermost forest canopy and in emergent trees, less often in lower branches of tree crowns 7–15 m off the ground, occasionally below 7 m Actively searches foliage, primarily in clusters of leaves near the ends of branches. In Colombia, mostly perch gleans; seldom hovers or flutters (Hilty and Brown 1986). In se Brazil and Bolivia, reached to pick insects off both top and bottom leaf surfaces (equally in 6 obs.); frequently hung near branch tips; hovered at leaves; probed flowers; and sallied to air (Parker and Remsen data). In Peru, observed to take fruit at least 30% of the time (Pearson 1975a). Stomach contents: vegetable matter (3); animal matter (6); both (3). Contents included insect parts, a small orthopteran, berries, and fruit. Additional stomach contents included coleopterans, cockroaches, caterpillars, and a leafhopper. Also eats fruits of melastomes, myrtle, and *Urtica* (Descourtilz 1852).

Vocalizations

A small flock produces a variety of call notes: an emphatic Moderate- to High-pitched *tsick*, a High-pitched somewhat squealing *tseet*, an abrupt Moderate- to High-pitched *tut*, and a Moderate-pitched *tyoo*; often given in combinations such as *tut-tsick* or *tyoo-tsick*. Song in Brazil: *si, si, si,* etc., insectlike (Sick 1985).

Breeding

No information.

Sources

Primary Descourtilz 1852; Hilty and Brown 1986; Parker data; Pearson 1969; Remsen data; Sick 1985; Wetmore, Pasquier, and Olson 1984; Willis 1977. **Weights (n = 7)** Greenberg 1981a; LSUMZ data; Pearson 1971. **Stomach contents** Foster data; Haverschmidt 1968; LSUMZ data; Goldman in Wetmore, Pasquier, and Olson 1984. **Vocalizations** LNS recordings by Bierregaard (1), Parker (1); Sick 1985.

CHRYSOTHLYPIS

The common names of the Black-and-yellow Tanager, *C. chrysomelas* **47,** and the Scarlet-and-white Tanager, *C. salmoni* **48,** describe the distinctive males, but the rather plain females are similar to one another. Bills of *Chrysothlypis* are long and slender, and tails proportionately shorter than *Hemithraupis* species. Sharp *Chrysothlypis* bills are often used to pick pieces out of small fruit. While foraging for insects, which are sought primarily on foliage, *Chrysothlypis* tanagers are lively and acrobatic. Their quick darting movements and aerial sallies suggest that they employ peer and pick foraging methods. The two *Chrysothlypis* species are allopatric. The Scarlet-and-white Tanager was formerly placed in the monotypic genus *Erythrothlypis*.

Chrysothlypis chrysomelas 47
Black-and-yellow Tanager
Plate 6

Length 12 cm (5 in.). Weight 13 g (11.0–15.0 g). Three subspecies following Olson (1981b); *titanota* and *ocularis* are illustrated. Male of the nominate race, *chrysomelas*, resembles male of *titanota*; female of nominate race resembles female of *ocularis*. Subadult males resemble females.

Geographic Range

C. c. titanota: the Caribbean slope of COSTA RICA from s Alajuela to Cartago (Slud 1964) and possibly to Bocas del Toro, PANAMA (see Olson 1981b). *C. c. chrysomelas*: from Chiriquí to w Panamá province, PANAMA (Wetmore, Pasquier, and Olson 1984). *C. c. ocularis*: the Pacific slope in e Panamá province and Darién, PANAMA (Wetmore, Pasquier, and Olson 1984). Seen on the PANAMA-COLOMBIA border; probably occurs in adjoining COLOMBIA (Ridgely *in litt.*).

Elevational Range

350–1600 m (Robbins, Parker, and Allen 1985); most numerous around 900 m in Costa Rica; mostly below 1050 m in Panama.

Habitat and Behavior

Inhabits humid forest and forest edge; occasionally strays to semi-isolated trees in adjacent clearings. Usually encountered in single-species groups of 3–8 individuals, also in pairs. Sometimes joins feeding aggregations and associates with mixed-species flocks, for short periods of time (Robbins, Parker, and Allen 1985). Seems to travel through tree tops so quickly that mixed-species flocks are left behind (Parker data).

Spritely and actively forages in the upper canopy. In Costa Rica, made short sallies for

CHRYSOTHLYPIS

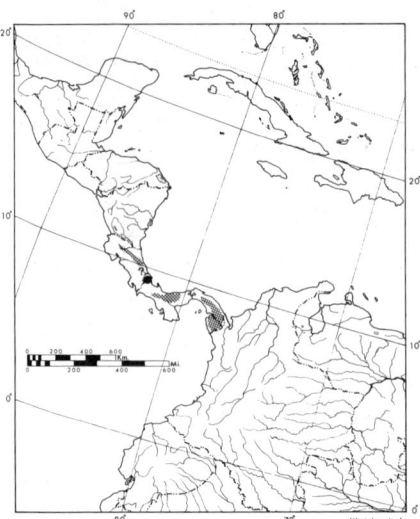

Chrysothlypis chrysomelas

flying insects as well as foraged in foliage (Slud 1964). In Panama: Observed to glean insects from leaves by reaching and hanging; also hovered at surfaces of large leaves and probed dead and dying leaves. Fed at berries of *Miconia*. (Robbins, Parker, and Allen 1985; Parker data.) Stomach contents: vegetable matter (13); vegetable and animal matter (3). Contents included fruit, *Cecropia* seeds, caterpillars, ants, and orthopterans.

Vocalizations

Utters a sharp High-pitched *tzeee*, sometimes doubled. Also a rapid *tzee dit-dit-dit* or *tzee-dizit zit zit* (agitated or hostile calls?) and a weak *tsiss* or *tsiss-it*. Calls often, especially when flying between trees.

Breeding

No information.

Sources

Primary Carriker 1910; Foster and Johnson 1974; LSUMZ data; Parker data; Ridgely 1976; Robbins, Parker, and Allen 1985; Slud 1964; Wetmore, Pasquier, and Olson 1984. **Weights (n = 6)** Greenberg 1981a; LSUMZ data; Strauch 1977. **Stomach contents** LSUMZ data; Olson and Blum 1968; Wetmore, Pasquier, and Olson 1984. **Vocalizations** LNS recordings by Parker (3); recordings by R. A. Rowlett (2), Whitney (1); Robbins, Parker, and Allen 1985; Slud 1964.

Chrysothlypis salmoni 48
Scarlet-and-white Tanager
Plate 6

Length 12 cm (5 in.). Weight 12 g (1 male). Monotypic. Subadult males resemble females for at least a year (Hilty *in litt.*).

Geographic Range

The n end of the W and C Andes in Antioquia, COLOMBIA, southward through COLOMBIA along the Pacific coast to Esmeraldas, nw ECUADOR.

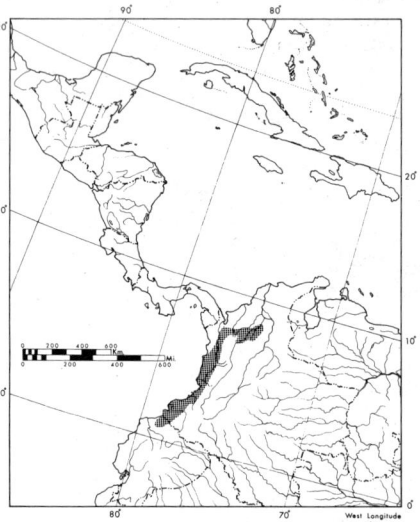

Chrysothlypis salmoni

Elevational Range

Lowlands and foothills to 1100 m mostly in foothills and lower slopes (Hilty *in litt.*).

Habitat and Behavior

Inhabits humid tall second growth, broken forest, forest edge, and dense scrub on ridges and steep canyons; less often inside tall lowland forest; rarely in nearby open areas. Families or groups of 3–6 individuals, also pairs, travel alone or with mixed-species flocks. Active and spritely; often perches upright.

In Valle, Colombia, ate fruit (58% of 180 obs.) and searched for insects (42%), mostly in the crowns of shrubs and trees 4.5–15 m high; rarely foraged below 3 m off the ground or in the crowns of tall trees; median foraging height was 7.6 m. Ate at least 11 species of fruit. Took arillate fruits (51% of all fruit eaten) as capsules were opening and when fruits were ripe; sometimes used openings made by other birds to get at arils. Also ate *Miconia* berries (36%). Perched upright or hung to swallow small berries whole or to peck pieces out of large fruits. Also perched (61% of all insect-foraging) to obtain insects, reaching out with quick darting movements. Took insects mostly off foliage, more rarely off branches less than 3 cm in diam., leaf petioles, flower heads, and fruit surfaces. Captured prey in the air (23% of all insect-foraging), frequently while flying from tree to tree or by flutter-pursuing. Also hovered (8%) and sallied (7%) to leaves and flowers. (Hilty data.)

Vocalizations

Call note while foraging or in flight: a weak sibilant *chip* or *sciip* (Hilty and Brown 1986).

Breeding

In Colombia, stub-tailed fledglings were seen in April and May (Hilty and Brown 1986). First-year birds may help at the nest (Hilty *in litt.*).

Sources

Primary Haffer 1975; Hilty data; Hilty and Brown 1986. **Weights (n = 1)** LSUMZ data. **Vocalizations** Hilty and Brown 1986. **Breeding dates** Hilty and Brown 1986.

NEMOSIA

This genus includes the widespread Hooded Tanager, *N. pileata* **49**, and the extremely rare Cherry-throated Tanager, *N. rourei* **50**. In addition to probing flowers, the highly insectivorous Hooded Tanager often takes insects from twigs, small branches, and leaves.

Nemosia pileata **49**
Hooded Tanager
Plate 6

Length 12 cm (5 in.). Weight 16 g (12.0–20.7 g). Six subspecies.

Geographic Range

N. p. hypoleuca: n COLOMBIA from Córdoba eastward along the coastal region to Magdalena and southward in the Magdalena Valley to extreme s Cesar; n VENEZUELA in Zulia and extreme w Lara (in the region surrounding Lake Maracaibo), Carabobo, the Distrito Federal, and the llanos from Portuguesa (sight, 1976—Isler et al.) and e Apure to Delta Amacuro and n Bolívar. *Remaining subspecies*: along the coast in THE GUIANAS and southward along rivers to c GUYANA; n BRAZIL along the upper Rio Branco, the lower Rio Negro (Roraima and n Amazonas), and the Amazon River from Pará westward to extreme se COLOMBIA (Amazonas) and PERU (e Loreto); and southward east of the Andes to n Ucayali, PERU; BOLIVIA (except extreme w portions); n ARGENTINA in Salta, Jujuy, Formosa (Olrog 1959, Short 1975), and Corrientes (Short 1971) and adjacent BRAZIL in Rio Grande do Sul (Belton 1978); se PARAGUAY; and BRAZIL in São Paulo, Minas Gerais, and Espírito Santo.

Elevational Range

Lowlands to 500 m.

Habitat and Behavior

Encountered in semiopen situations such as thorny or open woodland, forest edge, second growth, shrubby clearings, cerrado, and tall scrub. In some regions including Amazonia, seems to favor low-lying forest (incl. *varzea* forest), gallery forest, coastal mangroves, and other situations near water. Encountered mostly in pairs, sometimes in groups of 3–6 individuals; rarely solitary. Active; travels alone or with mixed-species flocks.

Forages mostly in the upper branches of trees, especially flowering trees, less often in shrubs, but it is unclear whether insects or nectar are taken from flowers. In s Colombia, appeared to favor *Mimosa* and *Cecropia* species (Remsen *in litt.*). Actively searches outer branches for insects by gleaning leaf bases and undersides, picking at bark and slender branches, and hover-picking insects from spider webs. Also eats fruit, including *Miconia* berries. (Parker data.) Stomach contents (4): animal matter. Contents included coleopterans (incl. snout beetles), hymenopterans (incl. ants and bees), hemipterans, homopterans, caterpillars, and spiders.

Vocalizations

Principal call note is a loud sharp insistent *tsip*; sometimes given in rapid succession, es-

Nemosia pileata

pecially in flight (Remsen *in litt.*), or turned into trills or rattles when agitated. Also utters a soft, mostly Moderate-pitched, *sip*; and a variety of sharp Moderate- to High-pitched notes such as *ss-chit*; and a trembling nasal *ts-sn-sn-sn-sn*. Dawn song: an explosive *tsip tsip ti-CHEW ti-CHEW*, or a variant; Moderate-pitched; delivered at a rate of about 7 songs/min.

Breeding

Both sexes build the thin open cup nest, typically binding it with spider webs to a branch high in a tree. Eggs (2) are bluish, spotted brown or lilac gray. Breeding dates: Colombia July. Suriname Aug, Sept, and Dec.

Sources

Primary Dugand 1947; Haverschmidt 1968; Hilty and Brown 1986; Meyer de Schauensee and Phelps 1978; Parker data; Sick 1985; Snethlage 1907, 1913; Todd and Carriker 1922. **Weights (n = 25)** Belton 1985; Haverschmidt 1948, 1952, 1968; LSUMZ data; Sick 1985; Thomas 1982. **Stomach contents** Haverschmidt 1968; Schubart, Aguirre, and Sick 1965. **Vocalizations** LNS recordings by T. H. Davis (1), Parker (2), Schwartz (6); T. H. Davis *in litt.*; Friedmann and Smith 1950; Hilty and Brown 1986; Sick 1985; Snyder 1966. **Nests, eggs, and breeding dates** Haverschmidt 1968; Remsen in Hilty and Brown 1986; Penard and Penard 1910; Sick 1985; Snethlage 1927–1928.

Nemosia rourei

Nemosia rourei 50
Cherry-throated Tanager
Plate 6

Length 14 cm (5½ in.). Monotypic.

Geographic Range

Known only from the type specimen collected in Muriaé, Minas Gerais (n bank of Rio Paraiba), BRAZIL, and a sight record in Jatiboca, Espírito Santo, BRAZIL (Sick 1979).

Elevational Range

900 m in Espírito Santo.

Habitat and Behavior

Seen in a single-species flock of 8 individuals in the forest canopy.

Vocalizations

No information.

Breeding

No information.

Sources

Primary Sick 1979, 1985.

PHAENICOPHILUS

The two Palm-Tanagers are confined to Hispaniola and surrounding small islands. Palm-Tanagers thrive in many types of habitats, foraging for both insects and fruit at all heights in trees and bushes. The two species appear to differ somewhat in their vocalizations.

Phaenicophilus palmarum 51
Black-crowned Palm-Tanager
Plate 7

Length 17 cm (6½ in.). Weight 29 g (24.0–32.0 g). Monotypic. Individuals in subadult plumage are patterned like older birds but dusky gray replaces black on the head with the remainder of head, neck, and breast washed with olive-yellow.

Geographic Range

The DOMINICAN REPUBLIC and HAITI westward to Morne D'Enfer on the w edge of the Massif de La Selle in s Haiti (McDonald data); Soana I.

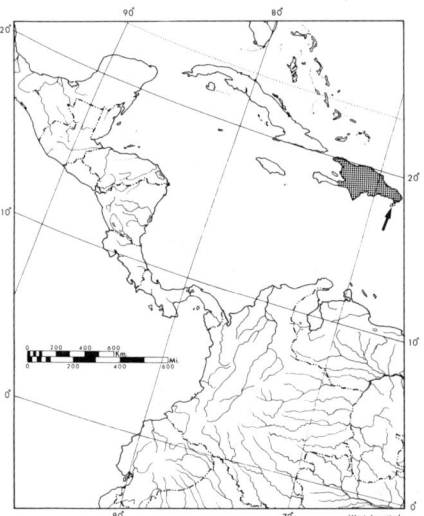

Phaenicophilus palmarum

Elevational Range

From sea level to mountains; mostly in lowlands.

Habitat and Behavior

Inhabits both dry and humid areas in town and country. Encountered in thickets and isolated trees in open situations (incl. urban areas) and in woodland and forest of all types, including cloud forest, pine forest, and mangrove swamps (McDonald data). Very successful in adapting to man's presence. Lives in pairs. After the breeding season, pairs often consist of an adult and an immature bird (McDonald data). Moves about in a slow and leisurely manner, occasionally twitching its tail (Wetmore and Swales 1931). Mostly insectivorous, but young birds seem to take more fruit than adults; about 68% of McDonald's feeding records involved insect-searching, 30% fruit-eating, and 2% at flowers (McDonald data, 739 obs.).

Forages from near the ground to the crowns of tall trees. Tends to forage for some time in one patch of vegetation and then make a long flight to the next patch (McDonald data). Most of McDonald's insect-foraging observations were at foliage, but about 12% were on bark. Clambers over trunks and larger limbs of trees, clinging to rough bark with strong feet (Wetmore and Swales 1931). In the Dominican Republic, observed actively hopping along branches making short flights to change perches, peering about and examining twigs and bark, pecking and pulling at loose bark and at Spanish moss, and flying out and down to catch an insect (Zusi *in litt.*).

Hunts in the mountains for wild berries such as blackberries (Rosaceae) but prefers fruit from the "palo amargo" bush (probably *Celtis trinervia* in the Ulmaceae) and is also fond of pulpy fruit (Dod 1978). Observed eating fruits of Solanaceae and Lauraceae and a *Bocconia* species; occasionally takes nectar (McDonald data). Stomach contents: vegetable matter (3); vegetable and animal matter (2). Contents included fruit seeds, a large tree cricket, a small katydid, a March fly, a leaf-footed bug, and a wasp.

Vocalizations

Calls often when foraging. Call notes: a Low- to Moderate-pitched, buzzy, nasal *pe-u* and a High-pitched penetrating *tseep*, often doubled. Song: repeats a jumble of slightly different, High-pitched, squealing notes that rise in volume, then drop and slow to distinct short *chit* notes (Reynard, LNS). Song varies among locations with a preponderance of buzzy and raspy phrases given in some localities (McDonald data).

Breeding

Deep cup-shaped nests are placed 1–2 m (and probably higher) up in bushes or trees. Often builds near human habitations (a nest was discovered under a tractor); nests are carelessly formed and almost never lined (Dod 1978). Spotted eggs (2–3) vary substantially in size and color (whitish to pale greenish). Staunchly defends its nest (Bond 1943). Incubation period is about 10 days, and the young fledge after about 10 days (McDonald data). Breeding dates: Dominican Republic May–July. Haiti April.

Sources

Primary Bond 1961; Cherrie 1896; Danforth 1929; Dod 1978; McDonald data; Wetmore and Swales 1931; Zusi *in litt.* **Weights (n = 6):** Steadman et al. 1980. **Stomach contents** Danforth 1929. **Vocalizations** LNS recordings by Reynard (6); Bond 1928a; Danforth 1929; McDonald data; Reynard 1981. **Nests, eggs, and breeding dates** Bond 1928a, 1943; Dod 1978; McDonald data.

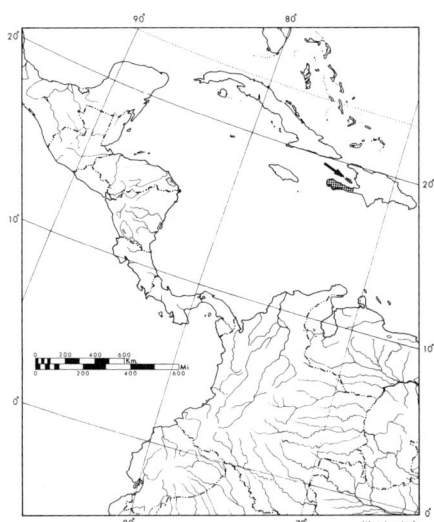

Phaenicophilus poliocephalus

Phaenicophilus poliocephalus 52
Gray-crowned Palm-Tanager
Plate 7

Length 16 cm (6 in.). Two subspecies. Subadult plumage has greenish wash on crown, hindneck, and upper breast (Wetmore and Swales 1931). Subadult individuals of the Black-crowned Palm-Tanager, *P. palmarum* **51,** resemble this species and account for records of the Gray-crowned in the Dominican Republic (Dod *fide* McDonald).

Geographic Range

Southern peninsula of HAITI eastward through the Trouin Valley eastward to ca. 25 km east of Jacmel and to the Cap Rouge (McDonald data); also Île-à-Vache, Grande Cayemite, and Gonâve Islands.

Elevational Range

From sea level to mountain summits.

Habitat and Behavior

Inhabits woodlands, edges, and thickets in dry and humid areas; widespread from mangroves to cloud forests (McDonald data). Lives in pairs; just after the breeding season, pairs often consist of an adult and a subadult (McDonald data); occasionally in small groups of up to 6 individuals. Sometimes sprightly and active, while at other times moves slowly with frequent stops. Forages from the ground to the crowns of tall trees; appears to work through areas of adjoining vegetation without long flights between foraging sites. Primarily gleans foliage; sometimes gleans bark or sallies to air for moths and butterflies; occasionally sallies 15 m or more. Over 90% of McDonald's 489 foraging observations were insect-searching, the remainder fruit-eating. Stomach contents: animal matter (3); animal and vegetable matter (2). Contents contained seeds (5%), a large cockroach, caterpillars, nymphs of hemipterans and homopterans, coleopterans (incl. darkling beetles, weevils, click beetles, and ground beetles) and snails.

Vocalizations

Call note: *peu,* shorter than that of congener (Bond 1928a) and typically doubled (McDonald data). During the nesting season a male sang a canarylike whisper song while approaching the female with outstretched wings (Bond 1944).

Breeding

Builds a deep cup nest 1–9 m up in a bush or tree. Nests are so frail that eggs can often be seen from below. Eggs (2–4) are greenish- or bluish-white marked with buff, brown, or violet gray, tending to form a wreath about the large end. Breeding dates: Gonâve I. May–June. Haiti July.

Sources

Primary Bond 1961; Danforth 1929; Dod 1978; McDonald data; Wetmore and Lincoln 1933;

Wetmore and Swales 1931. **Stomach contents** Danforth 1929. **Vocalizations** Bond 1944, 1961; Dod 1968; McDonald data. **Nests, eggs, and breeding dates** Bond 1928a, 1943; McDonald data.

CALYPTOPHILUS

Calyptophilus frugivorus, the Chat Tanager, is confined to Hispaniola and nearby islands and shares many attributes with *Rhodinocichla rosea*, the Rosy Thrush-Tanager **54**. Both species forage on or near the ground and deliver rich vocalizations (see Bond 1929, 1943, 1982). Two *Calyptophilus* species may be involved. If so, *C. f. tertius* and *abbotti* of Haiti and Gonâve Island would be included in *C. tertius*, the Western Chat Tanager, and *C. f. frugivorus* and *neibae* in *C. frugivorus*, the Eastern Chat Tanager (see Pregill and Olson 1981, Bond 1982, A.O.U. Check-list).

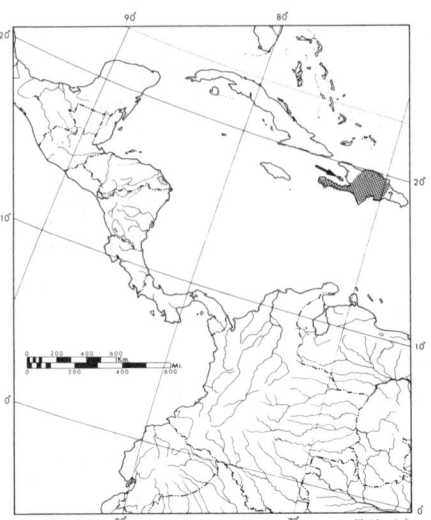

Calyptophilus frugivorus

Calyptophilus frugivorus 53
Chat Tanager
Plate 7

Length 18–21 cm (7–8 in.). Four subspecies; one (*neibae*) was described recently (Bond and Dod 1977). *C. f. frugivorus* is illustrated; *neibae* is smaller, darker, and has a rufescent tail; *abbotti* is smaller and pale gray-brown; and *tertius* is larger, darker in color (the wings and tail deeply rufescent), and lacks the yellow eye-ring (see Bond and Dod 1977).

Geographic Range

C. f. frugivorus: ne DOMINICAN REPUBLIC. *C. f. neibae*: mountains, DOMINICAN REPUBLIC. *C. f. tertius*: sw HAITI. *C. f. abbotti*: Gonâve I.

Elevational Range

C. f. frugivorus: lowlands. *C. f. neibae*: ca. 1550–1950 m. *C. f. tertius*: mountains to at least 2000 m. *C. f. abbotti*: lowlands.

Habitat and Behavior

On the main island, primarily inhabits thick underbrush and dense growth along streams of humid mountain forests, especially in ravines; rare in lowland thickets. On Gonâve I., inhabits semiarid scrub. Lives in pairs, and remains hidden within the densest thickets. Vigorously defends a territory. Primarily forages on or near the ground. Stomach contents: animal matter (1); animal and vegetable matter (1). Contents included 2 seeds, a moth, an ant, 2 hairy spiders, a thrips, and a cockroach ootheca.

Vocalizations

Call note is a dry *tic*. Song of *frugivorus* is a loud, mellow, Low- to Moderate-pitched *swerp swerp* (sometimes slurred or whistled) followed by *chips* given at varying speeds and sometimes running into a short chatter. Song of *neibae* is of similar quality and pattern but notes vary; e.g., *weet-weet-werp chip-cheep-sweet*, also sometimes ending in a short trill. Song of *abbotti* is a weaker, rather buzzy whistled *wee-chee-chee-chee*. Sings mostly at dawn but also during daylight hours when breeding; members of a pair sing responsively; when agitated, sings with much movement of the tail and wings (Dod 1978).

Breeding

One nest, believed to pertain to this species, was built 0.6 m above ground in a fern at the edge of a blackberry patch. The cup-shaped nest contained 1 spotted egg. (Bond 1943.)

Sources

Primary Bond 1928a, 1943, 1961; Bond and Dod 1977; Cherrie 1896; Danforth 1929; Dod 1978; Wetmore and Swales 1931. **Stomach con-**

tents Danforth 1929. **Vocalizations** LNS recording by Dod (1); Bond 1928a, 1961; Danforth 1929; Reynard 1981. **Nests and eggs** Bond 1961.

RHODINOCICHLA

The long-standing question of whether the single ground-dwelling *Rhodinocichla* species belongs in the tanager assemblage has been answered in the affimative by Eisenmann (1962), Clark (1974), and Raikow (1978).

Rhodinocichla rosea 54
Rosy Thrush-Tanager
Plate 7

Length 19–20 cm (7½–8 in.). Weight 18 g (43.0–51.8 g). Five subspecies. Subadult male like female with patches of rose color. Also known as the Rose-breasted Thrush-Tanager.

Geographic Range

R. r. schistacea: the Pacific coast of MEXICO from s Sinoloa to w Michoacán. *R. r. eximia*: the Pacific slope from e San José province, COSTA RICA, to e Panamá province, PANAMA, and locally on the Caribbean slope of PANAMA in Coclé, the region of the canal, and e Cólon (Wetmore, Pasquier, and Olson 1984). *R. r. harterti* and *beebei*: COLOMBIA on the w slope of the E Andes in Cundinamarca and n Tolima; the n end of the E Andes in Norte de Santander (USNM); the Perijá Mountains; and the Santa Marta Mountains (USNM; sight, Hilty and Brown 1986). *R. r. rosea*: VENEZUELA in Falcón (Sierra de San Luis), s Lara, and the coastal region from Yaracuy to Distrito Federal and Miranda.

Elevational Range

Near sea level, rarely to 900 m in Mexico; 250–700 m in Costa Rica; from sea level to 1200 m in Panama; 400–1700 m in Colombia; and 200–1450 m in Venezuela.

Habitat and Behavior

Inhabits thickets and scrub in both dry and humid regions. Lives in dense shrubbery and heavy underbrush in open woodland and woodland edge, second growth, clearings, and plantations; also occurs in undergrowth of thorn forest (Mexico) and in canebrakes along rivers (Costa Rica). Locally distributed within range. Pairs and family groups skulk through thick vegetation. Rarely associates with other species. Exceedingly wary; when approached, moves off, rapidly hopping from limb to limb and making short flights from bush to bush.

Forages on the ground or in lower branches of shrubbery. Flicks aside dead leaves and other ground litter with its bill to hunt for insects. Stomach contents: vegetable matter (3); vegetable and animal matter (3). Contents included seeds (of fruit, grass, and sedge), beetles (4 spp), ants, bugs, a frog bone fragment, and grains of sand.

Vocalizations

Voice is well developed and used freely by pairs to keep in contact. Both males and females sing full, rich, mellow notes. Mates often blend their songs in antiphonal duets. Contact or possibly alarm call: a Low- to Moderate-pitched, clear, whistled *too-wee* or *ter-wee*, second note higher pitched, sometimes followed by a downward-inflected *ta-woo* or a brief, mellow, wrenlike chatter (male and female answering each other). Song: both sexes utter a brief, loud, hard, and sometimes harsh *chew* repeated monotonously, about 1 note/sec. At the nest or in territorial dispute, sing (often antiphonally) a ringing Low- to Moderate-pitched *pa-CHEW* or *whee-choo*, sometimes combined with other notes as in *pa-CHEW, too-too, pa-CHEW*; repeated every 3–4 sec.

Breeding

The cup nest, made of twigs and lined with hairlike fibers, is built low in thickets. In Costa Rica, a shallow bowl-shaped nest, placed on a foundation of coarse sticks, was situated 1 m above the ground among intertangled bushes and vines in a low, dense thicket (Skutch 1962a). Eggs (2–3) are white or pale sky blue with black markings, sometimes in a wreath around the large end. Both sexes build the nest, feed the young, and also take turns incubating the eggs (Schwartz in Gilliard 1958). Breeding dates: Mexico July. Costa Rica Jan–April.

Sources

Primary Carriker 1910; Edwards 1972; Gilliard 1958; Hilty and Brown 1986; Ridgely 1976; Schäfer and Phelps 1954; Skutch 1962a; Wetmore, Pasquier, and Olson 1984. **Weights (n = 14)** Hartman and Brownell 1961; LSUMZ data; Thomas 1982. **Stomach contents** Clark 1913; Hallinan 1924; Goldman in Wetmore, Pas-

Rhodinocichla rosea

quier, and Olson 1984. **Vocalizations** LNS recordings by L. I. Davis (1), Eisenmann and Morton (1), Parker (2), Schwartz (51), van den Berg (1); Edwards 1972; Eisenmann 1952; Ridgely 1976; Skutch 1962a; Slud 1964. **Nests, eggs, and breeding dates** Alden 1969; Gilliard 1958; Skutch 1962a.

MITROSPINGUS

The two *Mitrospingus* species look so much alike that some taxonomists (e.g., Hellmayr 1936) thought they might prove conspecific. Recent field work has shown, however, that the two species differ substantially in many aspects of behavior and voice. The Dusky-faced Tanager, *M. cassinii* **55,** lives apart from other species in small bands that usually stay hidden in low vegetation just inside forest at forest edges and breaks. The Olive-backed Tanager, *M. oleagineus* **56,** is often encountered in mixed-species flocks and usually forages in the open at forest mid-heights.

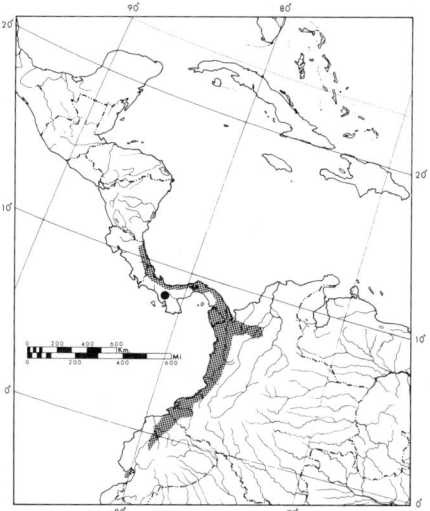

Mitrospingus cassinii

Mitrospingus cassinii 55
Dusky-faced Tanager
Plate 7

Length 18 cm (7 in.). Weight 38 g (33.4–41.0 g). Two subspecies. Subadult birds show semblance of yellow crown patch and underparts are olive-green tinged buff.

Geographic Range

The Caribbean slope from Heredia, COSTA RICA, through COSTA RICA and PANAMA to San Blas; Pacific slope in PANAMA in Veraguas (locally), e Panamá province, and Darién; and from Chocó, COLOMBIA, eastward around the n end of the W Andes to the Río Nechí drainage in ne Antioquia and southward along the Pacific slope to Los Ríos (LSUMZ), ECUADOR.

Elevational Range

Lowlands and foothills to 600 m in Costa Rica (mostly below 300 m), to 1200 m in Panama (LSUMZ), and to 1100 m in Colombia (mostly below 800 m).

Habitat and Behavior

Inhabits tangled shrubbery and dense thickets at forest breaks and edges, especially in the vicinity of forest streams and swampy places; occasionally occurs in low thick second growth adjacent to forest. Usually forages close to the ground, but sometimes goes to higher levels in fruiting trees. Encountered at all seasons in family groups or single-species flocks of up to 15 individuals. While highly sociable intraspecifically, remains apart from other species. Travels rapidly through vegetation, possibly on established rounds. Very active; constantly jerks tail and twitches wings. Almost comical with its mask, pale eye, and excitable disposition (Ridgely 1976). Usually stays hidden inside dense foliage, especially when approached. Sometimes 1 or 2 may perch in a semi-isolated tree 3–9 m above their usual haunts (Slud 1964).

Eats a variety of fruits, especially those of melastomes, Rubiaceae, and Solanaceae; also takes grass seeds (*Lasiacis* sp) and the hard seeds of the arillate fruits of *Alchornea* (Skutch 1972, 1980). In Valle, Colombia, perched on twigs or petioles to pluck berries. Hopped along branches and on large leaves to search for prey, including orthopterans and spiders. Picked insects mostly off foliage, especially off large leaves of *Heliconia* and palm fronds. Sometimes hung upside down from leaves; inspected palm fronds with head down between the leaflets. Probed curled arboreal dead leaves. (Hilty data.) Occasionally observed near ant swarms. Stomach contents (4): vegetable matter, including fruit (incl. *Carludovica palmata*).

Vocalizations

Incessantly chatters Moderate-pitched, harsh, gravelly, sputtering notes such as *chet* or *chet-ut*; when many individuals are calling, the rhythm is like that of strings of small firecrackers going off rapidly in an erratic pattern. Other notes have been described as a wiry high-pitched *wss* or *sszeet?* and a jumble of sharp, pebbly *spssnk*s and *sptzk*s sometimes mixed with a weakly patterned outburst of rapid *swiss* notes (Slud 1964). In Panama, a dawn song was given from the top of a tree along a trail and sounded like *seety, seety, seety, seety, seety* (Wetmore, Pasquier, and Olson 1984).

Breeding

In Costa Rica, a nest, 3 m above a stream, was situated in a young tree growing amid tangled vegetation. The bulky open cup, composed of threadlike flower stems and lined with black fungal filaments, was slung between 2 upright branches that were a few inches apart. One bird appeared to build the nest while flock mates foraged nearby. The 2 nestlings were attended by at least 3, possibly all 7, flock members, the extras apparently unmated helpers or older siblings. Only spiders, grasshoppers, caterpillars, and other arthropods were seen to be fed to the young. (Skutch 1972.) Breeding dates: Costa Rica April. Colombia Sept.

Sources

Primary Carriker 1910; Hilty data; Hilty and Brown 1986; Parker data; Ridgely 1976; Skutch 1972; Slud 1964; Wetmore, Pasquier, and Olson 1984. **Weights (n = 5)** Burton 1975; LSUMZ data. **Stomach contents** LSUMZ data; Olson and Blum 1968. **Vocalizations** LNS recordings by van den Berg (2); Hilty and Brown 1986; Slud 1964; Wetmore, Pasquier, and Olson 1984. **Nests and breeding dates** Hilty and Brown 1986; Skutch 1972.

Mitrospingus oleagineus **56**
Olive-backed Tanager
Plate 7

Length 19 cm (7½ in.). Two subspecies. Subadult lacks gray on forehead, cheeks, and throat.

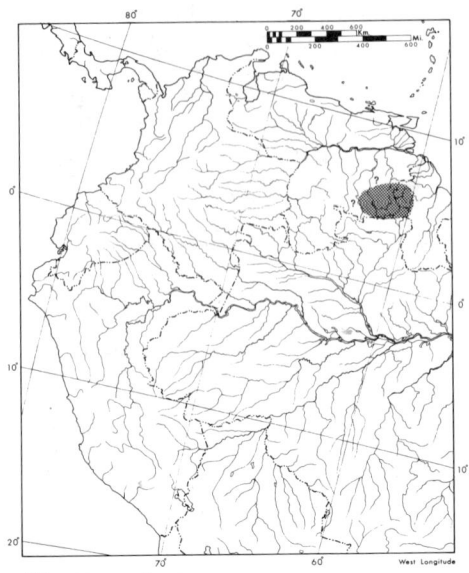

Mitrospingus oleagineus

Geographic Range

Se Bolívar, VENEZUELA, and adjacent GUYANA and BRAZIL.

Elevational Range

900–1800 m.

Habitat and Behavior

Inhabits humid forest and forest edge on slopes of tepuis and mountains. Encountered most often in groups of 6–8 individuals. Sometimes in mixed-species flocks where it appears to be a nuclear species (Parker data). Forages from low in bushes to midlevels of forest in the crowns of 15 m trees. Eats both fruit and insects. In Venezuela, sluggishly sallied upwards from a perch to pluck melastome fruits. Hopped very deliberately along branches searching for insects; picked insects mostly off foliage by reaching up to the undersides of leaves or reaching under the bases of large leaves. Also searched twigs, bark, moss, and dead leaves. (Parker data.)

Vocalizations

Calls: rapidly repeats a harsh *zwer* or *zwee* sometimes accelerated into a raspy churring or rattle. Also emits soft *seep*s and *chip*s. Song: a High-pitched grating squeal, *zweeeee*, sometimes varied to *zweee-eet?* or *zwee-er-eet?*, regularly repeated after intervals of 1–3 sec. (Parker, LNS). Two or 3 individuals of a group may sing at once. Sometimes sings with wings spread open (Parker data).

Breeding

No information.

Sources

Primary Hilty *in litt.*; Parker data. **Vocalizations** LNS recording by Parker (1).

CHLOROTHRAUPIS

The primarily olive *Chlorothraupis* tanagers (Table 8) travel in small troops and chatter noisily as they forage through the understory (an exception to this behavior may prove to be characteristic of the poorly known *C. carmioli frenata* of the eastern slope of the Andes). Foraging behavior of *Chlorothraupis* species closely resembles that of the ant-tanagers, *Habia*, as noted by Willis (1966b). The Olive and the Lemon-spectacled Tanagers constitute a superspecies (A.O.U. Check-list). The Ochre-breasted occurs at higher elevations than the Lemon-spectacled in western Colombia.

Table 8 The *Chlorothraupis* Tanagers

57	*C. carmioli*	Olive Tanager
58	*C. olivacea*	Lemon-spectacled Tanager
59	*C. stolzmanni*	Ochre-breasted Tanager

Chlorothraupis carmioli **57**
Olive Tanager
Plate 7

Length 16 cm (6½in.). Weight 36 g (30.5–44.0 g). Four subspecies. Also known as Carmiol's Tanager.

Geographic Range

C. c. carmioli, magnirostris, and *lutescens*: the Caribbean slope in NICARAGUA, COSTA RICA, and PANAMA (almost certainly in extreme n Chocó, COLOMBIA); the Pacific slope in COSTA RICA near low passes and from Veraguas (locally) to nw Darién, PANAMA (generally north and east of the Río Chepo and Río Chucunaque). *C. c. frenata*: along the e base of the Andes in w Caquetá (sight, June 1981—Hilty) and near the Nariño-Putumayo border, COLOMBIA; San Martín (LSUMZ), PERU; from c Huánuco (LSUMZ) to c Pasco (LSUMZ), PERU; and from c Cuzco, PERU, southward to Cochabamba, BOLIVIA.

Elevational Range

In Central America, 200–1200 m, as high as 1450 m (Wetmore, Pasquier, and Olson 1984); most common between 400–800 m, occasionally on coastal plains adjoining foothills. In South America, ca. 300–1000 m, perhaps higher.

Habitat and Behavior

Behavior may differ between the 3 subspecies in Central America and *frenata* of South America. In Central America, inhabits the undergrowth of humid forest, forest edge, gallery forest, and wooded ravines. In Panama, seems to favor wet areas near rivers (Greenberg 1984). Travels in noisy single-species flocks of up to 15 or more individuals (cp. Wetmore, Pasquier, and Olson 1984); appears to travel along regular routes. Sometimes joined by other species, especially single-species flocks of Tawny-crested Tanagers, *Tachyphonus delatrii* **73**. Primarily forages 2–6 m off the ground, occasionally higher, searching along branches and in vine tangles. Flies more than flits through the understory (Slud 1964). In Panama, observed to take arillate fruits of *Lindackeria* (Greenberg 1981b). Of 59 insect-feeding observations, 63% were on foliage, and of these observations, 65% were off leaf undersides. (Greenberg and Gradwohl 1980.)

In South America (*frenata*), appears to live primarily at midlevels inside forest, to travel in much smaller groups than in Central America, and to be encountered more often with mixed-species flocks (Parker data). Observed eating *Cecropia* catkins and *Miconia* berries (Parker *in litt.*). Stomach contents: animal matter (9); vegetable matter (2); both (2). Contents included fruit, seeds, beetles, and other insects.

Vocalizations

Calls: in Central America, members of a group deliver in succession a variety of single notes, each one often repeated rapidly 2–6 times. Notes include a scolding *chay*, a squeaky *eep*, a churring *wrsst*, an abrupt *chut*, a squeezed out *chee*, and a metallic *wit* (often repeated in flight). Overall, the calls create a noisy chatter. In Peru, repeatedly delivered a grating *kettup* or *keetup* (O'Neill data).

Song: a stream of rapidly delivered, short notes that are repeated in sets of about 3–8

Chlorothraupis carmioli

notes; switches among sets of clear whistles, grating squeals, and sometimes wheezy doubled notes that sound as if the bird is trying to catch its breath; notes are Low- to Moderate-pitched. Songs seem to be delivered more rapidly in Central America than in South America. In Peru, a section of a song was rendered as *chow, chow, chow, chow-chi-chi-chi-chow, chow, chow, whi-chow, whi-chow, wheeup, wheeup, wheeup, wheeup, tic-chow tic-chow tic-chow tic-chow, tic-tic-tic-tic-tic- ch-ch-ch-ch* (O'Neill data). Songs last 10–25 sec. or more.

Breeding

In Nicaragua, a compact nest, made of sticks, leaves, and green moss and lined with fine stems and fibers, was built 1 m up in a bush; eggs (2) were creamy white speckled brown and lavender, especially around the large end (Huber 1932). In Panama, a nest was found about 2 m up in a forest shrub (Wetmore, Pasquier, and Olson 1984). Breeding dates: Nicaragua April. Panama March.

Sources

Primary Hilty and Brown 1986; Howell 1971; LSUMZ data; Parker data; Ridgely 1976; Slud 1964. **Weights (n = 34)** Greenberg 1981a; LSUMZ data. **Stomach contents** LSUMZ data. **Vocalizations** LNS recordings by L. I. Davis (2), Morton (2), Parker (4); recordings by R. A. Rowlett (2); O'Neill data; Slud 1964; Wetmore, Pasquier, and Olson 1984. **Nests, eggs, and breeding dates** Huber 1932; Wetmore, Pasquier, and Olson 1984.

Chlorothraupis olivacea 58
Lemon-spectacled Tanager
Plate 7

Length 17 cm (6½ in.). Weight 39 g (36.0–41.0 g). Monotypic. Also known as the Lemon-browed Tanager or the Yellow-browed Tanager.

Geographic Range

The Pacific slope from se Darién (generally south and west of the valleys of the Río Chepo and Río Chucunaque), PANAMA, southward through COLOMBIA to n Esmeraldas, ECUADOR, and eastward in n COLOMBIA along the n base of the Andes to the Magdalena Valley in Antioquia.

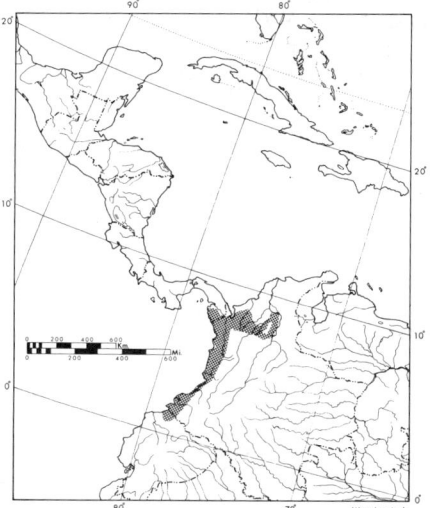

Chlorothraupis olivacea

Elevational Range

Lowlands and foothills to 1500 m; 550–1050 m in Panama; rare in s Colombia above 400 m (Hilty and Brown 1986).

Habitat and Behavior

Inhabits undergrowth of humid forest, second-growth woodland, and edges; especially along streams. Travels in pairs and small groups of up to 6 individuals. Stomach contents: animal matter (2); both animal and vegetable matter (1). Contents included parts of ants, coleopterans (incl. weevils and scarab beetles), caterpillars, and wasps; also seeds (incl. seeds of *Solanum*).

Vocalizations

Delivers a Moderate-pitched, grating, squeaking *cheat cheat cheat cheat*, usually a set of 4–8 notes in 1–2 sec., then a short pause, then another set given at a slightly different pitch, another pause, etc. Also *turee, jee-ut, eep*, and other notes. Chatters incessantly.

Breeding

No information.

Sources

Primary Hilty and Brown 1986; Haffer 1975; Ridgely 1976; Wetmore, Pasquier, and Olson 1984. **Weights (n = 4)** Burton 1975; LSUMZ data. **Stomach contents** LSUMZ data; Goldman in Wetmore, Pasquier, and Olson 1984. **Vocalizations** LNS recording by Parker (1); Hilty and Brown 1986.

Chlorothraupis stolzmanni 59
Ochre-breasted Tanager
Plate 7

Length 17 cm (6½ in.). Weight 40.3 g (1 female). Two subspecies.

Geographic Range

The Pacific slope from Risaralda and s Chocó, COLOMBIA, south to El Oro, ECUADOR.

Elevational Range

Foothills and lower Andean slopes 200–2100 m. In Colombia, most numerous 400–1500 m (Hilty and Brown 1986).

Habitat and Behavior

Inhabits very wet forest and forest edge. Groups of 5–15 individuals travel through low forest levels and are frequently joined by other birds. Stomach contents (1): plant matter.

In Valle, Colombia: Foraged in a somewhat ponderous manner. Searched for food 80% of the time from low to mid levels (1.5–9 m off the ground), rarely on or near the ground, but occasionally to the subcanopy (15 m) or higher. Generally foraged lower for insects than for fruit. Median foraging height was about 5.5 m. Fruit-eating constituted 71% of 232 feeding observations, insect-searching 27%, and at flowers in 2%. Occasionally seen eating frogs and lizards.

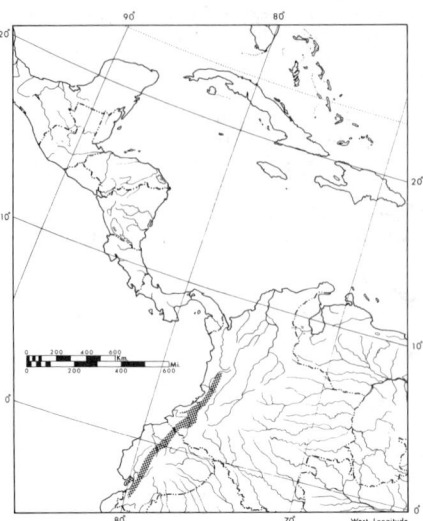
Chlorothraupis stolzmanni

stream for 30 min. or more. (Hilty and Brown 1986.)

Breeding

Builds a rough cup nest 2–5 m above the ground. Eggs (1–2) are white with a dense ring of reddish brown spots, mostly at the large end (Hilty and Brown 1986). Breeding dates: Colombia Jan, Feb, and April.

Sources

Primary Hilty data; Hilty and Brown 1986. **Weights (n = 1)** LSUMZ data. **Stomach contents** LSUMZ data. **Vocalizations** LNS recording by van den Berg (1); Hilty and Brown 1986. **Nests, eggs, and breeding dates** Hilty and Brown 1986.

Took at least 24 species of fruit, primarily melastome fruits (87% of all fruit-eating obs.), especially *Miconia* berries (57% of all melastomes). Perched (occasionally hung) on twigs or sometimes leaves to take fruit and almost as often snatched it in flight. Swallowed small fruits and berries whole and pecked at larger ones. Frequently caught very large insects including katydids, skippers, and moths. Hopped along slender branches less than 2.5 cm in diam. (bare or moss covered, live or dead), stems, and vines. Cocked or turned head from side to side to peer in all directions. Looked at twigs, foliage, hanging moss clumps, and dead leaf clusters. Picked prey off substrates mostly from a perched position. Sometimes hung or leaned over to inspect the undersides of twigs and leaves. Used other acrobatics less often: stretched up and reached under or around leaves and branches, lunged or dove to pursue escaping insects, and very rarely sallied to air. (Hilty data.)

Vocalizations

While foraging, chatters incessantly with rough, very rapid, Moderate- to High-pitched *jeep-jeep-jeep-jeep* phrases; mobs loudly with *jee'ut* and other notes. Song: mostly unmusical, extremely high-pitched *eep* notes; each bird has its own repertoire. Dawn song: from a canopy perch, a fast series, *geegeegee wit'er wit'er tututu, weep, TWEER-TWEER-TWEER, eep'eep k' eep eep eep TWEER-TWEER-TWEER jeep-jeep TWEER*, and so on in an uninterrupted

ORTHOGONYS

The single species resembles tanagers of the preceeding genus, *Chlorothraupis*, and like those species, travels in noisy groups. Unlike *Chlorothraupis* species, the Olive-green Tanager forages primarily in the tops of trees and often searches bromeliads as well as leaves.

Orthogonys chloricterus   **60**
Olive-green Tanager
Plate 7

Length 18 cm (7 in.). Monotypic. Some individuals, possibly in subadult plumage, have clear yellow underparts.

Geographic Range

Se BRAZIL from Espírito Santo to Santa Catarina, doubtfully to Rio Grande do Sul (see Belton 1985).

Elevational Range

Ca. 900–1800 m.

Habitat and Behavior

Inhabits coastal mountain forest and forest edge. Often encountered in groups of about 8 or more individuals, sometimes in smaller groups or pairs. A regular member of mixed-species flocks where it may be a nuclear species. Forages high in tall trees; eats insects and fruit. In Rio de Janeiro: Some members of a large single-species group

Orthogonys chloricterus

often straggled along as much as 75 m behind the leaders. Foraged along branches slowly, hopped 3 or 4 times and then stopped to peer in all directions at foliage and bromeliads, often standing erect on strong legs. Also hopped onto bromeliad leaves to reach inside. In about 60 observations, primarily picked insects from leaves (incl. large leaves 15 x 10 cm) and searched bromeliads; also sallied for flying prey. Observed at *Cecropia* catkins and in vine tangles. (Parker data.)

Vocalizations

Call: a High-pitched, buzzy *tseee*. Song: a chattering bubbly mixture of extended call notes and abrupt Moderate-pitched *pit* notes, often rapidly delivered in series of 3–5 notes with short pauses between series. Groups of Olive-green Tanagers sometimes assemble in noisy congregations (Sick 1985).

Breeding

Observed taking nesting materials to a large bromeliad on a lower limb of a tall tree at forest edge (Parker data). Breeding dates: Rio de Janeiro Nov.

Sources

Primary Davis 1945b, 1946; Goeldi 1894; Holt 1928; Parker data; Santos 1948. **Vocalizations** LNS recordings by Parker (2); Parker data; Sick 1985. **Breeding dates** Parker data.

EUCOMETIS

The single *Eucometis* species occurs from southern Mexico to southeastern Brazil and varies in size and plumage over its range (see Plate 8). Races north of the Andes are considerably more widespread and have a much greater tendency to follow army ant swarms than the races east and south of the Andes.

Eucometis penicillata 61
Gray-headed Tanager
Plate 8

Length 16–17 cm (6–7 in.). Weight 27 g (22.5–35.0 g). Seven subspecies.

Geographic Range

E. p. pallida: the Caribbean slope from Veracruz, n Oaxaca, and the Yucatán Peninsula southward through se MEXICO, BELIZE, and GUATEMALA to Olancho, HONDURAS (plumage grades to next race in se). *E. p. spodocephala*: both slopes of NICARAGUA to Guanacaste (Pacific slope) and Alajuela (Río Frio region, Caribbean slope), COSTA RICA. *E. p. stictothorax*: Pacific slope from Puntarenas, COSTA RICA, southeastward to Veraguas, PANAMA. *E. p. cristata*: from Coclé on the Caribbean slope and from c Panamá province, PANAMA (Wetmore, Pasquier, and Olson 1984), on the Pacific slope eastward through PANAMA, n COLOMBIA, and nw VENEZUELA north of the Andes to Mérida; south in COLOMBIA in the Cauca Valley to Valle (may be extirpated) and the Magdalena Valley to c Huila (Hilty and Brown 1983); and east of the Andes from Arauca, COLOMBIA, to w Barinas, VENEZUELA. *E. p. affinis*: n VENEZUELA from Falcón east to Miranda. *E. p. penicillata*: east of the Andes from Meta and Amazonas, COLOMBIA, southward through ECUADOR to Ucayali, PERU, thence eastward through BRAZIL in a band south of the Amazon River to Maranhão, north of the Amazon from e Amazonas to Amapá, BRAZIL, and north to THE GUIANAS; one record in nw Amazonas, VENEZUELA. *E. p. albicollis*: east of the Andes from extreme nw BOLIVIA (Pando and La Paz) eastward through BOLIVIA and Mato Grosso, BRAZIL, to Goiás and w São Paulo, BRAZIL, and Concepción, PARAGUAY (sight, Aug. 1977—Ridgely; earlier records from "Apa" may refer to this department).

Elevational Range

Lowlands and foothills from sea level to 1700 m mostly below 600 m.

Habitat and Behavior

Habitat and behavior vary geographically. North of the Andes, occurs in both humid and dry regions and inhabits tangled undergrowth and dense shrubbery in forest, open woodland, gallery forest, forest edge, second growth, scrub, and cultivated lands adjacent to forest. The Amazonian race (*penicillata*) is almost always found near rivers, preferring swampy thickets and dense undergrowth of humid low-lying forest (incl. *varzea* forest); in e Amazonia, also occurs in second growth. Southernmost race (*albicollis*) inhabits forest undergrowth and thickets and also has an affinity for river edges (Ridgely *in litt.*).

Encountered in pairs, singly, and in small groups of 3–4 individuals (probably families). Subspecies north of the Andes frequently follow army ant swarms. East of the Andes, rarely reported at ant swarms, but associates with mixed-species flocks away from ants (Oniki and Willis 1972). Usually stays concealed in the undergrowth, especially when approached. Prefers shaded flight paths, often flying up and down watercourses. Darts swiftly through openings, rarely stopping to rest or sing in a small tree or bush. At rest, often twitches its tail and flutters or flicks its wings. Typically forages close to the ground; occasionally goes higher (rarely to 10 m off the ground). Stomach contents (8): insects. Additional stomach contents included cockroaches and their oothecae, berries, and fruit.

North of the Andes: Obtains prey at army ant swarms both by actively darting about and by perching quietly (Slud 1964). Stays at the periphery of ant swarms but goes to the center when dominant antbirds are absent (Willis 1966a). Also eats fruit, including *Miconia* berries, and carries away large arillate seeds plucked from pods hanging on low trees (Skutch 1980). In Costa Rica when army ants were scarce, visited feeding shelves for bananas and seized insects escaping from chickens scratching on the ground at forest edge (Skutch 1977).

Vocalizations

Call notes: a sharp, smacking, unmusical *chup*, *stet*, or *chewp*, Moderate- to High-pitched, sometimes deliberately repeated at

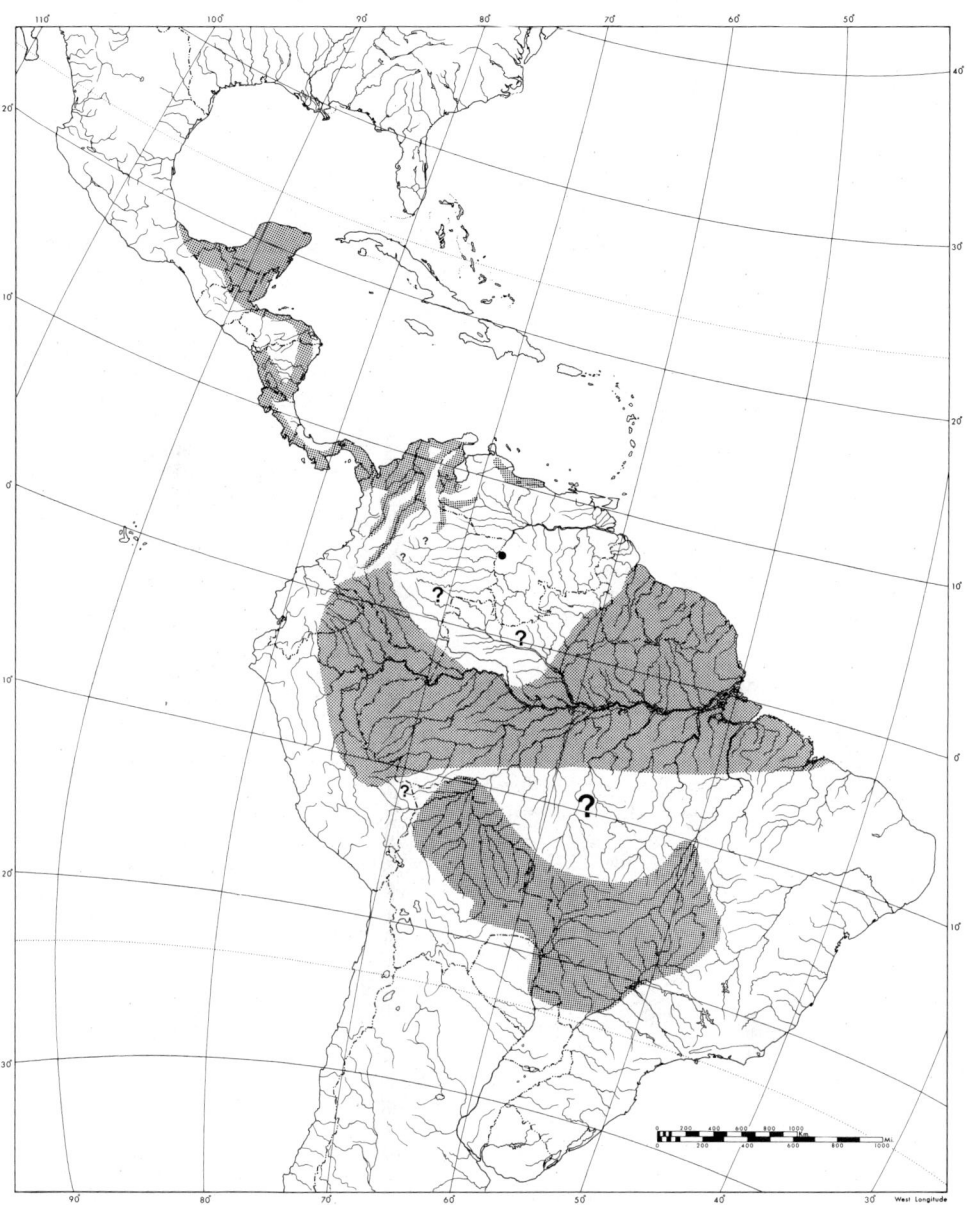

Eucometis penicillata

the rate of about 1 note/sec., and a High-pitched more musical *pseet*. Also delivers a short Low- to Moderate-pitched rattle, possibly an alarm call, and a rhythmic group of 3 High-pitched, squeezed out, squealing phrases, e.g., *tsweee-it tsweee-it tsweee-eat*, delivered in 2–3 sec. (possibly a version of the song). Song varies geographically (Hilty *in litt.*). In Panama, a musical sputter, *eat eat meat chop, 'safurry chew, 'sfurry chew* or the like (Willis and Eisenmann 1979). In Costa Rica, a male sang *whichis whichis whicheery whichis whichu* during nest building (Skutch 1954). In Brazil, a sequence of high whistles with the second part of the stanza descending, *tzee, tzee, tzee, zi, zi, zi, zi zi, zi*, sometimes more varied or prolonged (Sick 1985).

Breeding

Frequently selects a nest site near forest edge in small spiny palms, especially those along water, or in an isolated bush, e.g., coffee, (over 20 nests). Nests have also been found in tall grass and in vines on a bush overhanging a cliff. Sites are typically 0.5–3 m off the ground. Both sexes build the nest, but generally bring nesting material independently. The frail thin-walled shallow cup is usually composed of rootlets and lined with threadlike fibers. Mates call often while building. The male sings even when his bill is full of nesting material or while he is shaping the nest. May not defend a nesting territory (Skutch 1954).

Two (1–3) eggs are laid on consecutive days. Eggs are somewhat variable (may vary by race): ground color is dirty white, gray, pale blue gray, or pale pinkish buff heavily overlaid and mottled with different shades of brown. In Costa Rica: The female incubated alone for 14–16 days, sometimes accompanied by her mate. Both parents fed the young (mostly insects). When alarmed, the parents flitted about, twitched their tails and voiced low complaining notes. At one nest, a female performed a rather poor injury-feigning display. The young left the nest after 11–12 days. (Skutch 1954.) Breeding dates: Belize April. Panama April–Sept. Brazil (Pará) Feb, Sept, Nov, and Dec.

Sources

Primary Dugand 1947; Eisenmann 1952; Hilty and Brown 1986; Novaes 1973; Oniki and Willis 1972; Pinto 1953; Sick 1985; Skutch 1954, 1977; Slud 1964; Wetmore 1943. **Weights (n = 52)** Burton 1975; Haverschmidt 1952, 1968; LSUMZ data; Paynter 1955; Russell 1964; Smithe 1966; Strauch 1977. **Stomach contents** Haverschmidt 1968; LSUMZ data; McDiarmid, Ricklefs, and Foster 1977; Pinto 1953. **Vocalizations** LNS recordings by Parker (2), Schwartz (1), van den Berg (2); recordings by Whitney (2); Sick 1985; Skutch 1954; Slud 1964; Willis and Eisenmann 1979. **Nests, eggs, and breeding dates** Naumberg 1930; Peck 1910; Pinto 1953; Russell 1964; Skutch 1954; Stone 1918; Willis and Eisenmann 1979.

LANIO

The common name of *Lanio* species, shrike-tanager, reflects the characteristic long, toothed bill which ends in a pronounced hook; the bill is very similar to that of a shrike (Laniidae) except that the tooth is farther from the tip (Storer 1969). The four species (Table 9) are allopatric, occurring in dense forests from southern Mexico southward to northern Brazil but are most abundant in Amazonia. They appear to be remarkably similar in their behavior.

Table 9 The *Lanio* Shrike-Tanagers

62	*L. fulvus*	Fulvous Shrike-Tanager
63	*L. versicolor*	White-winged Shrike-Tanager
64	*L. aurantius*	Black-throated Shrike-Tanager
65	*L. leucothorax*	White-throated Shrike-Tanager

Shrike-tanagers typically form part of the nucleus of canopy mixed-species flocks of insectivorous birds (foliage-gleaners, antbirds, etc) that travel through the interior of the forest canopy. Sitting upright, shrike-tanagers peer about rapidly and alertly and call at the approach of predators; consequently, they have important sentinel roles in the flocks. As flocks forage through canopy vegetation, some of their quarry flee, and shrike-tanagers snap up these fleeing insects in sallies and flutter-pursuits, thus reaping the rewards of serving as flock sentinels (see Munn 1984, 1985). The Black-throated and White-throated Shrike-Tanagers constitute a superspecies (*A.O.U. Check-list*) as do the Fulvous and White-winged.

Lanio fulvus

Lanio fulvus 62
Fulvous Shrike-Tanager
Plate 8

Length 15–17 cm (6–7 in). Weight 24 g (19.0–30.0 g); size increases with elevation in the Peruvian Andes (LSUMZ spec.). Two subspecies.

Geographic Range

Along the e base of the Andes from Táchira, VENEZUELA, to Putumayo, COLOMBIA, and more generally east of the Andes from Putumayo and Amazonas, COLOMBIA, southward through e ECUADOR to n PERU (south to n San Martín) and eastward north of the Amazon River to s VENEZUELA (c and s Amazonas and s Bolívar), THE GUIANAS, and Amapá, BRAZIL.

Elevational Range

Lowlands and lower mountain slopes to 1300 m.

Habitat and Behavior

Lives primarily within lowland terra firma forest; occasionally occurs at forest edge. Also inhabits lower montane forest along the base of the Andes and the tepuis of Venezuela. Pairs or single birds are nuclear in mixed-species flocks. Obtains insects mostly in the subcanopy, occasionally in the canopy or in the understory. Quietly perches upright in the vicinity of a moving mixed-species flock and sallies for flying prey that are escaping other birds. Also sallies to foliage and occasionally picks insects off leaves and limbs near its perch. Stomach contents: animal matter (2); vegetable and animal matter (1). Contents included insects and seeds. Additional stomach contents included click beetles, weevils, hemipterans, and homopterans.

Vocalizations

Vocalizes often. Calls: a loud emphatic Moderate-pitched, slightly downward-inflected *tcha*, *tchew*, or *tyoo*; sometimes a strongly downward-inflected *tchee-yee*. Calls are given at irregular intervals, apparently as alarm calls, or sometimes continuously at about 1 note/sec. Also utters a short rattle. Dawn song: 2–3 squeezed out High-pitched notes *tsee-ya tsee-ya tsee-ya* repeated after a variable pause of perhaps 5–17 sec. (Parker, LNS).

Breeding

Said to nest in palm trees (Schomburgk in Chubb 1921).

Sources

Primary Hilty and Brown 1986; Meyer de Schauensee and Phelps 1978; Parker data; Parker, Parker, and Plenge 1982; Willis 1977. **Weights (n = 20)** Dick, McGillivray, and Brooks 1984; LSUMZ data. **Stomach contents** Haverschmidt 1968; LSUMZ data. **Vocalizations** LNS recordings by T. H. Davis (2), Parker (3), van den Berg (1); Hilty and Brown 1986.

Lanio versicolor **63**
White-winged Shrike-Tanager
Plate 8

Length 13–15 cm (5½–6 in.). Weight (*v. versicolor*) 17 g (13.0–20.0 g). Two subspecies.

Geographic Range

Along the e base of the Andes from San Martín, PERU, to Cochabamba, BOLIVIA, and eastward through PERU, extreme n BOLIVIA, and BRAZIL south of the Amazon River to e Pará (Rio Tocantins) and n and w Mato Grosso, BRAZIL.

Elevational Range

Lowlands to ca. 1200 m.

Habitat and Behavior

Primarily lives within terra firma forest; also occurs in low-lying forest. Occasionally wanders to shaded plantations near forest, but was absent from river-edge second-growth in a study area in Peru (Munn 1985). Typically encountered in pairs. The leader of permanent canopy mixed-species flocks (see Munn 1985) in which it also functions as a sentinel. Pairs defend a territory against conspecific pairs in neighboring flocks by countersinging without physical aggression (Munn 1985).

Typically perches upright just below the canopy and sallies to air or flutter-pursues insects dislodged by other species. Also sallies to top and bottom leaf surfaces. Stomach contents: vegetable matter (1); animal matter (3). Contents included insects and fruit pulp.

Vocalizations

Delivers a chattering vocalization while leading long distance (>20 m) flock movements (Munn 1985). Frequently utters somewhat musical Moderate-pitched, downward-inflected *tweeu*, given in alarm at the approach of a predator or in false alarm to provide an advantage over other flock members in capturing fleeing insects (see Munn 1984). Notes of songs resemble this call in quality and pitch. Day song: 1–3 double notes, *too-wee? too-yoo teu-oo*, each note dropping slightly in volume and/or pitch; delivered after irregular pauses of 1–4 sec. Dawn songs: regularly delivered intricate phrases, e.g., *too twee too-wee too-wee-too* (endings vary), about 2 sec. long, pauses of 3 sec. Also at dawn, delivers call notes and phrases from the day song at the rate of about 1 note or phrase/2 sec.

Breeding

In Peru, seen building a nest in November (Munn and Terborgh 1979).

Sources

Primary Munn 1984, 1985; Munn and Terborgh 1979; Parker data; Terborgh and Weske 1969, 1975. **Weights (n = 18)** LSUMZ data; Munn and Terborgh 1979; Weske 1972. **Stomach contents** LSUMZ data. **Vocalizations** LNS recordings by Munn (2), Parker (4), van den Berg (1). **Breeding dates** Munn and Terborgh 1979.

Lanio versicolor

Lanio aurantius 64
Black-throated Shrike-Tanager
Plate 8

Length 20 cm (8 in.). Weight 35 g (29.8–45.0 g). Monotypic.

Geographic Range

The Caribbean slope from c Veracruz, MEXICO, southeastward through MEXICO (except n portion of Yucután Peninsula), BELIZE, and GUATEMALA to Atlántida, HONDURAS.

Elevational Range

Lowlands and foothills from sea level to 1200 m; mostly below 750 m. May wander during winter (Wetmore 1943).

Habitat and Behavior

Not well known but seems to be similar to other *Lanio* species in habitat and behavior. Inhabits interiors of tall humid forest. Travels independently or associates with mixed-species flocks; may be a nuclear species (Edwards and Tashian 1959). Forages usually at midheights but also lower and higher. Quite expert at capturing insects in the air (Willis 1960a).

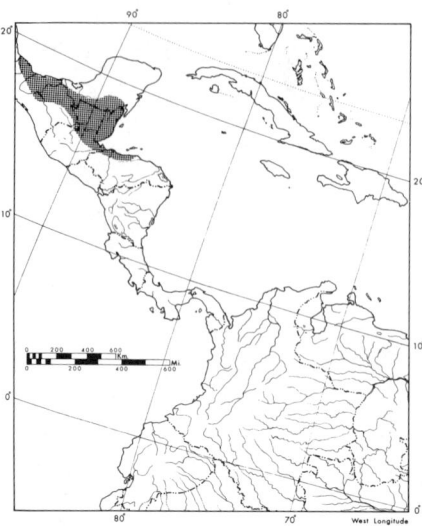

Lanio aurantius

Vocalizations

Alarm notes often arouse other species (Russell 1964). Call or song: *tst, dit, doo, tchew, tchew*; starts at a High pitch and falls with each note, ending with loud, slurred, Moderate-pitched notes (R. A. Rowlett recording).

Breeding

No information.

Sources

Primary Edwards and Tashian 1959; Land 1970; Monroe 1968; Russell 1964; Salvin and Godman 1879–1904; Tashian 1952; Wetmore 1943. **Weights (n = 16)** Paynter 1955; Russell 1964; Smithe 1966. **Vocalizations** recording by R. A. Rowlett (1); Edwards 1972; Russell 1964.

Lanio leucothorax 65
White-throated Shrike-Tanager
Plate 8

Length 19 cm (7½ in.). Four subspecies.

Geographic Range

L. l. leucothorax: the Caribbean slope from Olancho, HONDURAS, southward through NICARAGUA to w Limon, COSTA RICA; spills over to Pacific slope in n Guanacaste, COSTA RICA. *L. l. reversus*: Puntarenas (north of the entrance to the Gulf of Nicoya), COSTA RICA. *L. l. melanopygius*: the Pacific slope from Puntarenas (south of the entrance to the Gulf of Nicoya), COSTA RICA, southeastward to Veraguas, PANAMA; also on the Caribbean slope in Veraguas. *L. l. ictus*: the Caribbean slope in w Bocas del Toro, PANAMA.

Elevational Range

Lowlands and foothills from sea level to ca. 750 m; most numerous at lower elevations in se Costa Rica; mostly in foothills on the Caribbean slope of Panama.

Habitat and Behavior

Inhabits interiors of humid forest. Sometimes found in thinned openings, rarely at forest edge (Slud 1964). Pairs and family groups typically travel with mixed-species flocks; sometimes found singly or in larger groups of 8–10 individuals (2 family groups?). In Costa Rica: Forages from eye level to the canopy, but usually at midheights. Primarily a sally forager, taking insects and sometimes fruit while acting as a sentinel for mixed-species flocks. Sits motionless in the vicinity of a foraging flock, darts out suddenly for prey that has been flushed by another flock member, then flies rapidly to another perch. (Stiles data.) Makes active sweeping sallies among leaves, briefly landing among the foliage, then returning to an open perch (Wetmore, Pasquier, and Olson 1984). Stomach contents: animal matter (2); animal and vegetable matter (2). Contents included orthopterans (incl. cockroaches and katydids), homopterans, beetles, weevils, butterflies, and fruit.

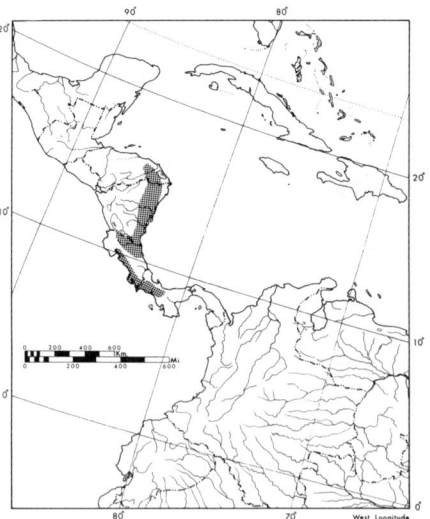

Lanio leucothorax

Vocalizations

Vocalizations appear to contribute to mixed-species flock maintenance. While foraging, often utters a series of 5 or 6 loud, Moderate-pitched, chattered notes, rapidly delivered; pauses between series are short (Whitney recording). Quick to give alarm calls when predators are sighted (Stiles data). Possible song: short, sharp, High-pitched *chip*s and *tick*s, Moderate-pitched chatters, and a variety of other notes (some may be imitative) are interspersed with loud, ringing, slurred, whistled notes that typically are downward-inflected and sound like *tseeer* or *ts tseeer* (Moderate-pitched). Another vocalization sounds like *psee chee chee chee chee*, the *chee* notes dropping in pitch, followed by several additional staggered *chee*s (Slud 1964).

Breeding

In Costa Rica, a nest was found inside forest in a low bush near a stream. Eggs (2) were white with bold chocolate and grayish spots concentrated slightly at the large end. (Smith in Wetmore, Pasquier, and Olson 1984.) Breeding dates: Costa Rica May.

Sources

Primary Carriker 1910; Howell 1957; Monroe 1968; Moynihan 1962c; Slud 1964; Stiles data; Wetmore, Pasquier, and Olson 1984. **Stomach contents** Stiles data; Wetmore, Pasquier, and Olson 1984. **Vocalizations** recordings by Whitney (4); Slud 1964; Stiles data. **Nests, eggs, and breeding dates** Wetmore, Pasquier, and Olson 1984.

CREURGOPS

The heavy bills of the two allopatric *Creurgops* species, the Rufous-crested Tanager, *C. verticalis* **66,** and the Slaty, *C. dentata* **67,** seem to be employed mostly in capturing insects. The *Creurgops* tanagers peer about deliberately and take insects from leaves, thin branches, and moss near the tips of the outermost branches in montane forest canopy.

Creurgops verticalis 66
Rufous-crested Tanager
Plate 9

Length 15 cm (6 in.). Weight 24 g (21.0–27.0 g). Monotypic. Subadult resembles female but gray of upperparts is suffused with buff (USNM spec.).

Geographic Range

Extreme w VENEZUELA in Táchira west of the Western Venezuelan Low; COLOMBIA, locally in the W and C Andes, at the head of the Magdalena Valley in Huila, and along both slopes of the Andes in Nariño; and southward on the e Andean slope through ECUADOR and PERU to n Junín.

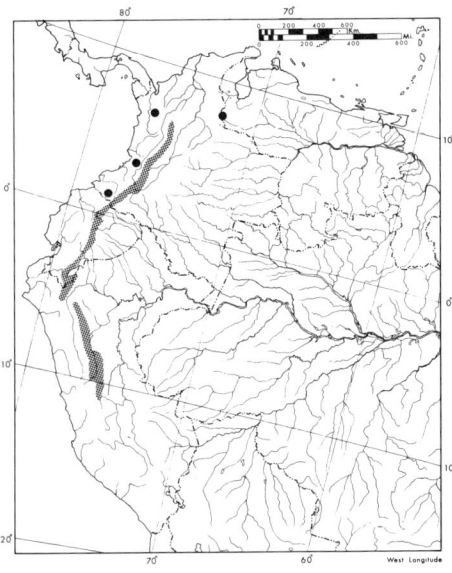

Creurgops verticalis

Elevational Range

From 1150 m (Graves 1983) to 2700 m.

Habitat and Behavior

Inhabits humid mossy forest and forest edge. Forages in the canopy or subcanopy. Pairs, sometimes single birds or groups of 3 individuals, almost always travel with mixed-species flocks. Searches deliberately hopping along slender branches (bare or mossy) into dense outer foliage. Peers at large leaves and twigs, picks at and gleans leaf surfaces, and probes moss. Sallies to air opportunistically

(Ridgely and Gaulin 1980). Stomach contents: animal matter (1); animal and vegetable matter (1). Contents included fruit pulp and insects.

Vocalizations

No information.

Breeding

No information.

Sources

Primary Hilty and Brown 1986; Isler data; LSUMZ data; Parker data; Ridgely and Gaulin 1980. **Weights (n = 6)** LSUMZ data. **Stomach contents** LSUMZ data.

Creurgops dentata **67**
Slaty Tanager
Plate 9

Length 14 cm (5½ in.). Weight 19 g (16.0–19.7 g). Monotypic.

Geographic Range

E Andean slopes from the Cordillera Vilcabamba, Cuzco (Weske 1972), PERU, to Cochabamba (status in Santa Cruz unclear), BOLIVIA.

Elevational Range

1500–2150 m (Weske 1972).

Habitat and Behavior

Inhabits humid montane forest and tall second growth. Usually travels with mixed-species flocks of mainly *Tangara* species. Forages in the canopy and subcanopy 10–30 m above the ground. Works deliberately along slender limbs, carefully searching foliage (Parker and O'Neill 1980). Stomach contents (5): insects, including beetles.

Vocalizations

No information.

Breeding

No information.

Sources

Primary LSUMZ data; Parker data; Parker and O'Neill 1980. **Weights (n = 6)** LSUMZ data; Weske 1972. **Stomach contents** LSUMZ data.

HETEROSPINGUS

The foraging behavior of *Heterospingus* often reminds observers of that of the canopy dwelling *Tachyphonus* species. Authorities disagree as to whether *Heterospingus* consists of one or two species.

Heterospingus xanthopygius **68**
Sulphur-rumped Tanager

The *A.O.U. Check-list* considers *Heterospingus* to consist of two species, but the *Peters Checklist* and Wetmore, Pasquier, and Olson (1984) regard these forms, the Sulphur-rumped and the Scarlet-browed Tanagers, to be conspecific. Haffer (1975) believed that the two forms come in contact in e Darién, Panama, but his data are contradicted by Olson (in Wetmore, Pasquier, and Olson 1984). The behaviors of the two forms appear to be similar.

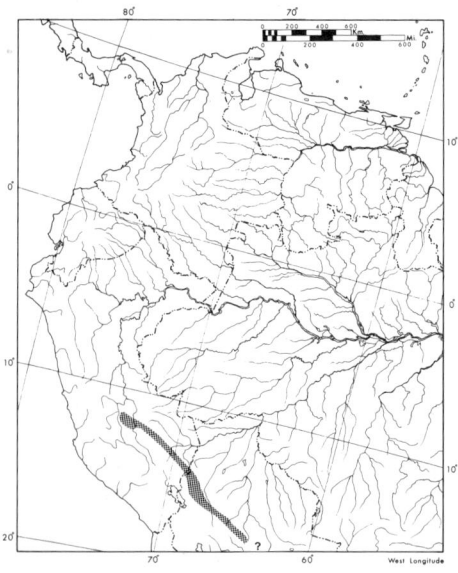

Creurgops dentata

Heterospingus xanthopygius (rubrifrons subspecies group 68-1)
Sulphur-rumped Tanager
Plate 9

Length 15 cm (6 in.). Weight 38 g (36.0 and 40.0 g). Monotypic if specifically distinct.

Geographic Range

The Caribbean slope from Limon, e COSTA RICA, to e San Blas, PANAMA, and the Pacific slope in Veraguas (sight, Wetmore, Pasquier, and Olson 1984) and e Panamá province, PANAMA.

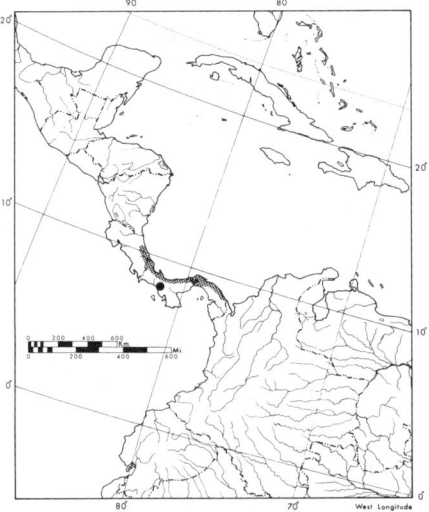

Heterospingus xanthopygius (*rubrifrons* subspecies group)

Elevational Range

Lowlands and foothills to 600 m in Costa Rica and ca. 900 m in Panama.

Habitat and Behavior

Inhabits humid forest and woodland, forest edge, and openings. Typically encountered in small groups (probably families), once in a group of 14 individuals (Ridgely in Wetmore, Pasquier, and Olson 1984); also in pairs. Sometimes accompanies large mixed-species flocks, but often moves so fast that the flock is left behind. Forages mostly in the canopy, lower at forest edge. Of 98 observations (Leck 1971b), 42% were in the tops of trees, 37% at midheights, and 21% at low levels. Observed to eat mistletoe berries and fruits of *Cecropia* and *Hamelia* (Leck 1971b, 1972c). Takes both small and large arthropods (Willis 1980). Of 24 insect-foraging observations in Panama, 50% of prey were taken off foliage, all off leaf tops (Greenberg and Gradwohl 1980). In Costa Rica, examined branches using the diagonal-lean method (Slud 1964).

Vocalizations

Calls often; utters a thin *tsip* or *tseet*, alone or in twitters, and a squeaky rapid chatter. Flight call: repeats a High- to Moderate-pitched *seet* or *silt* (Whitney recording).

Breeding

In Panama, a pair was seen carrying nesting material to an epiphyte-covered branch 20 m off the ground (Ridgely in Wetmore, Pasquier, and Olson 1984). Breeding dates: Panama Dec.

Sources

Primary Carriker 1910; Haffer 1975; Leck 1971b, 1972c; Ridgely 1976; Slud 1964; Wetmore, Pasquier, and Olson 1984; Willis 1972b; Willis and Eisenmann 1979. **Weights (n = 2)** Greenberg 1981a, 1984. **Vocalizations** recording by Whitney (1); Slud 1964; Willis and Eisenmann 1979. **Breeding dates** Wetmore, Pasquier, and Olson 1984.

Heterospingus xanthopygius (xanthopygius subspecies group 68-2)
Scarlet-browed Tanager
Plate 9

Length 17 cm (6½ in.). Two subspecies.

Geographic Range

H. x. xanthopygius: e PANAMA in e Darién eastward through n COLOMBIA along the n base of the Andes to the middle Magdalena Valley in e Antioquia. *H. x. berliozi:* the Pacific slope from w Antioquia and Chocó, COLOMBIA, south to Chimborazo and e Guayas, ECUADOR.

Elevational Range

Lowlands and foothills to 1100 m.

Habitat and Behavior

Inhabits dense humid forest, tall second growth, and forest edge. Typically encountered in pairs, sometimes singly or in groups of 3–4 individuals; accompanies mixed-

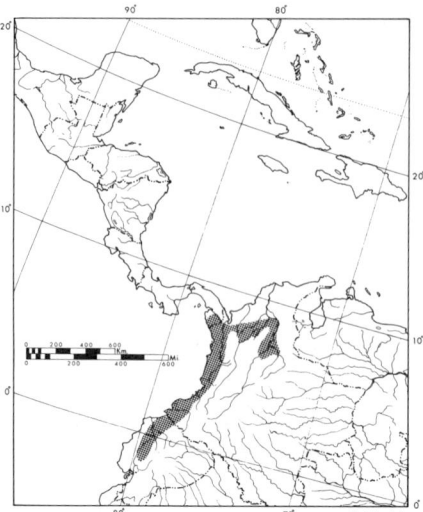

Heterospingus xanthopygius (*xanthopygius* subspecies group)

species flocks. Forages mostly in the canopy, sometimes in the subcanopy, and lower at forest edge. In Valle, Colombia, 9 observations ranged 5.5–33.5 m off the ground (Hilty data).

Moves through the forest very rapidly. Often perches prominently atop tree crowns in the open; sits erect; peers around actively at the tops of leaves, then attacks prey or flies off rapidly to another perch (Hilty *in litt.*). Also sallies awkwardly and flutters in foliage (Hilty and Brown 1986). In Valle, Colombia, observed taking *Cecropia* fruit and *Miconia* berries while perched on branches, twigs, and petioles (Hilty data). In Panama, seen foraging about flowers (Bangs and Barbour 1922). Stomach contents: vegetable matter (1); vegetable and animal matter (1). Contents included beetles, an ant, and seeds of an Oleaceae.

Vocalizations

Often calls loudly while foraging. Call note: a sharp *dzeet* or a forceful *chip*. In Chocó, Colombia, sang a squeaky twittering *cheero-bitty cheero-bitty cherro-pit-sup* (Hilty and Brown 1986).

Breeding

Breeding dates: Panama April. Colombia Dec.

Sources

Primary Haffer 1975; Hilty data; Hilty and Brown 1986; Wetmore, Pasquier, and Olson 1984. **Stomach contents** LSUMZ data; Goldman in Wetmore, Pasquier, and Olson 1984. **Vocalizations** Hilty and Brown 1986; Ridgely in Wetmore, Pasquier, Olson 1984. **Breeding dates** Bangs and Barbour 1922; Hilty and Brown 1986.

TACHYPHONUS

Tachyphonus tanagers (Table 10) are a conspicuous element of the neotropical avifauna, in part because representatives are found in a wide variety of habitats. The eight *Tachyphonus* species are also uncommonly diverse in their social and foraging behavior. Moreover, the Flame-crested and White-shouldered Tanagers are variable in habitat and behavior at the subspecies level.

Table 10 The *Tachyphonus* Tanagers

69	*T. cristatus*		Flame-crested Tanager
	69-1	*cristatus* subspecies group	Flame-crested Tanager
	69-2	*nattereri* subspecies group	Natterer's Tanager
70	*T. rufiventer*		Yellow-crested Tanager
71	*T. surinamus*		Fulvous-crested Tanager
72	*T. luctuosus*		White-shouldered Tanager
73	*T. delatrii*		Tawny-crested Tanager
74	*T. coronatus*		Ruby-crowned Tanager
75	*T. rufus*		White-lined Tanager
76	*T. phoenicius*		Red-shouldered Tanager

Three species—the Flame-crested (except in e Brazil), Yellow-crested, and White-shouldered—are highly insectivorous and primarily live in forest (the Flame-crested and Yellow-crested are parapatric in Amazonia). They are active and fast-moving and flit about slender branches, primarily looking for insects on leaves, most often on leaf tops. These tanagers typically capture prey in short darting or acrobatic movements by reaching out, hanging down, sallying, hovering, and flutter-pursuing. Two species, probably all three, function as core species in permanent mixed-species flocks. In Amazonia, the White-shouldered typically forages at low to midheights, below the foraging heights of the Flame-crested and Yellow-crested Tanagers.

West of the Andes, where the Flame-crested and Yellow-crested do not occur, the White-shouldered usually forages higher off the ground, from midheights to the canopy, than in Amazonia. Here, another *Tachy-*

phonus, the Tawny-crested Tanager, occurs at low heights in the forest. The Tawny-crested is behaviorally quite different from the three aforementioned species; it travels in single-species groups of up to 20 or more individuals that are often independent of other species and that rapidly sweep through forest edge and tall second growth as well as forest.

The *Tachyphonus* tanagers that are found in semiopen country constitute an equally complex array. The Fulvous-crested Tanager is found in both forest and semiopen situations, but seems to occur primarily in forest where poor soil conditions—sandy or periodically inundated soils—create relatively open vegetation. The White-lined and the Ruby-crowned are geographic replacements of each other and are thought to constitute a superspecies (Short 1975). Although their vocalizations are similar, the Ruby-crowned tends to forage at midheights to the canopy of woodlands, whereas the White-lined Tanager typically lives in semiopen situations where it often pounces on ground insects from a low perch, from a stance on the ground, or after hovering briefly. The remaining *Tachyphonus*, the Red-shouldered Tanager, occurs in savanna and similar specialized habitats in and around Amazonia. In some regions, the Red-shouldered and the White-lined are sympatric, but behavioral differences between them are not well understood.

During the breeding season, male *Tachyphonus* often display their wing-coverts, underwing-coverts, and bright crests. Nests of *Tachyphonus* have typically been discovered within a few meters of the ground, sometimes in ground vegetation, but few nests of forest species have been found.

Tachyphonus cristatus 69
Flame-crested Tanager

A single male (and a possibly related female) collected in 1870 in wc Mato Grosso and known as Natterer's Tanager, **69-2,** is considered by some authors (e.g., Meyer de Schauensee 1970) to be specifically distinct, but the *Peters Check-list* considers Natterer's Tanager a subspecies of the highly variable Flame-crested Tanager (also see Zimmer 1945).

Tachyphonus cristatus (*cristatus* subspecies group 69-1) Flame-crested Tanager
Plate 9

Length 15 cm (6 in.). Weight 19 g (16.6–23.0 g). Nine subspecies. In good light, males appear brownish black (esp. south of the Amazon River). Many females are tinged gray on forehead, nape, breast, and/or flanks. Plumages (of both sexes) vary substantially even within the same region.

Geographic Range

T. c. intercedens: VENEZUELA in e Bolívar (east of the Río Caroní), GUYANA, and SURINAME. *T. c. brunneus*: coastal BRAZIL from Paraíba (Pinto and Camargo 1961) southward to São Paulo. *Remaining races*: east of the Andes from Meta and Guainía, COLOMBIA, southward through e ECUADOR to n Cajamarca, n Amazonas, and n Loreto, PERU (mostly north of the Río Marañon and Amazon River); eastward to s VENEZUELA (Amazonas and w Bolívar), FRENCH GUIANA, and c Maranhão, BRAZIL; and thence southward to s Goiás, and c Mato Grosso, BRAZIL, extreme n BOLIVIA (Pando and n El Beni), and se PERU (Madre de Dios).

Elevational Range

Lowlands to ca. 1000 m; to 1400 m in Venezuela (Meyer de Schauensee and Phelps 1978).

Habitat and Behavior

In Amazonia, favors terra firma forest. In e Brazil (*brunneus*), inhabits forest edge, open woodland, gallery and savanna forest, and second growth. Usually seen in pairs, sometimes singly or in small groups of rarely up to 10 individuals. Typically encountered with mixed-species flocks in Amazonia where it is probably a core species; also may be nuclear in mixed flocks in se Brazil (Mitchell 1957). Spritely; actively flutters in outer foliage; perches upright at times.

Forages mostly in the canopy but also comes lower, especially to obtain fruit (e.g., melastomes). In Brazil, considered to be primarily insectivorous (Sick 1985). Works along slender outer branches near dense foliage, gleans or picks insects from leaves of all sizes, and makes short (0.1 m) sallies to leaves; also forages in vine tangles (Parker data). Hangs at tips of branches to obtain in-

TACHYPHONUS

Tachyphonus cristatus (*cristatus* subspecies group)

sects, tender buds, or young shoots (Descourtilz 1852). Stomach contents: vegetable matter (4); animal matter (2); both (2). Contents included fruit, berries, seeds, and insect remains. Additional stomach contents included short-horned grasshoppers. When fruit is scarce in e Brazil, said to eat green seeds from a plant in the sunflower family (Descourtilz 1852).

Vocalizations

In Brazil (*brunneus*), flicks wings as it utters weak, short, flat, Moderate-pitched *chet* calls (Parker, LNS); also delivers a *tzä, tzä, tzä, zititit* (as rendered in Portuguese by Sick 1985). In Colombia, gives thin indistinctive *seeep* notes while foraging (Hilty and Brown 1986).

Breeding

Builds a small open cup nest in bushes or small palms near streams or ponds in the forest understory. Eggs are white to yellowish-pink, spotted red, and sometimes stained black.

Sources

Primary Descourtilz 1852; Haverschmidt 1968; Hilty and Brown 1986; LSUMZ data; Mitchell 1957; Olivares and Hernandez 1962; Parker data; Willis 1977. **Weights (n = 9)** Dick, McGillivray, and Brooks 1984; Haverschmidt 1952, 1968; LSUMZ data; Sick 1985. **Stomach contents** Foster data; Haverschmidt 1968; LSUMZ data; Novaes 1952; Olivares 1962; Olivares and Hernandez 1962. **Vocalizations** LNS recording by Parker (1); Hilty and Brown 1986; Sick 1985. **Nests and eggs** Ihering 1900; Snethlage 1935.

Tachyphonus cristatus
(*nattereri* subspecies group 69-2)
Natterer's Tanager
Plate 9

Length 14 cm (5½ in.). Known from a single (male) specimen collected about 1870. Female ascribed to this form is probably a specimen of *T. c. madeirae* (Zimmer 1945).

Geographic Range

Sw BRAZIL in wc Mato Grosso (near Cáceres).

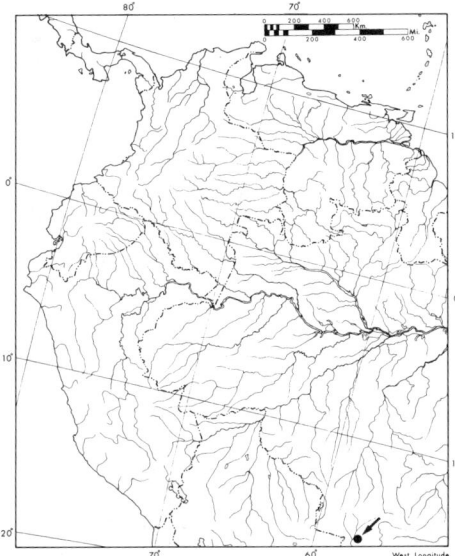

Tachyphonus cristatus (*nattereri* subspecies group)

Elevational Range

Ca. 200 m.

Habitat and Behavior

No information.

Vocalizations

No information.

Breeding

No information.

Sources

Primary Hellmayr 1936; Zimmer 1945.

Tachyphonus rufiventer 70
Yellow-crested Tanager
Plate 9

Length 15 cm (6 in.). Weight 19 g (15.5–19.8 g). Monotypic. Males exhibit a great amount of individual variation in the completeness of the black band across the breast and in the depth of color of crown and underparts. Females vary in the depth of color of throat and undertail-coverts. Subadult plumage is like female but throat yellow like breast, and crown olive like back (Zimmer 1945).

Geographic Range

East of the Andes from s San Martín and c Loreto, PERU, southward to La Paz, BOLIVIA (confined to near the base of the Andes in s Peru and Bolivia), and extreme w BRAZIL south of the Amazon River eastward to the upper Rio Juruá and to the south bank of the Amazon River near the border with COLOMBIA.

Elevational Range

Lowlands to 1400 m in Peru (Weske 1972); to 1650 m in Bolivia.

Habitat and Behavior

Primarily inhabits terra firma forest; also occurs in low-lying forest (incl. *varzea* forest); occasionally encountered in tall second growth and shaded coffee plantations. In se Peru: Occupied tall mature forest; was absent from river-edge second-growth. Pairs (sometimes with offspring) constituted one of six core species that presumably spent all their lives with a single canopy mixed-species flock within a permanent, tightly-drawn territory; occasionally pairs also joined understory flocks. (Munn 1985.)
  Forages primarily at midlevels (10–30 m above the ground) in forest in the upper parts of understory trees but occasionally wanders to the tops of emergent trees or goes low in the understory. In Bolivia, peered at foliage and picked insects off leaf tops (2 obs.); also sallied 0.3 m to a leaf top (Parker and Remsen data). Stomach contents: vegetable matter (1); vegetable and animal matter (1). Contents included fruit pulp and a caterpillar.

Vocalizations

Utters a raspy Moderate-pitched *jjit* and a High-pitched, less raspy *zzeep* in combinations, especially *zzeep? jjit jjit jjeep* (Parker, LNS).

Tachyphonus rufiventer

Breeding

No information.

Sources

Primary Hilty *in litt.*; LSUMZ data; Munn 1985; O'Neill and Pearson 1974; Parker data; Pearson 1969, 1971; Remsen data; Taczanowski 1884b. **Weights (n = 9)** LSUMZ data; Pearson 1971; Weske 1972. **Stomach contents** LSUMZ data. **Vocalizations** LNS recording by Parker (1).

Tachyphonus surinamus **71**
Fulvous-crested Tanager
Plate 9

Length 15–17 cm (6–6½ in.). Weight (*surinamus*) 23 g (20–27 g); (*remaining subspecies*) 19 g (15.0–23.0 g). Four subspecies. Males differ by subspecies in color of sides: *brevipes* has white sides like *napensis* (see Plate 9), *surinamus* has sides tinged buff, and *insignis* (illus.) tinged tawny and buff. Crown patch and rump are cinnamon-rufous in male *napensis*, varying shades of buffy ochraceous in other races. In good light, males are blue black. Female *napensis* is like *brevipes* (illus.) in having underparts tinged buff with only a

Tachyphonus surinamus

light touch of olive on posterior flanks. Female *surinamus* is like *insignis* (illus.) in having a pale grayish throat and belly, brownish across breast, and deep yellow posterior flanks.

Geographic Range

T. s. surinamus: VENEZUELA in se Sucre, e Monagas, Delta Amacuro, Bolívar, and n and c Amazonas; THE GUIANAS; and BRAZIL north of the Amazon River from the Rio Negro eastward. *T. s. brevipes*: east of the Andes in COLOMBIA from w Meta and c Guainía south, sw VENEZUELA in s Amazonas, adjacent nw BRAZIL, and e ECUADOR southward to Amazonas and Loreto (along the Río Marañón and north of the Amazon River), PERU. *T. s. napensis*: south of the Amazon River in nw BRAZIL westward from w Amazonas and Acre (Rio Juruá) to the base of the Andes and extreme s Ucayali, PERU. *T. s. insignis*: south of the Amazon River in BRAZIL from e Amazonas (Rio Madeira) eastward to extreme e Pará.

Elevational Range

Lowlands to 500 m in Colombia and to 1400 m in Venezuela.

Habitat and Behavior

Appears to favor open woody vegetation such as found in areas with sandy soil conditions. Inhabits open terra firma forest and woodland, forest edge, and scrub and second growth near forest; also occurs in open low-lying forest (incl. *varzea* forest). Pairs and family groups travel alone or with mixed-species flocks.

Forages primarily at low and midlevels of forest; at all levels in scrub and second growth. Hops and hovers to glean branches and foliage (Hilty and Brown 1986). Seen briefly over an army ant swarm (Oniki and Willis 1972). Stomach contents: vegetable matter (9) animal matter (8); both (3). Contents included short-horned grasshoppers, fruit, berries, and seeds. Additional stomach contents included bees, weevils, caterpillars, hemipterans, homopterans, and crane flies.

Vocalizations

Calls: Moderate- to Low-pitched, gravelly, abrupt notes, e.g., *chur*, *chur-dit*, or a rattled *chu-di-di-di-dit*; also a High-pitched weak *steep!* sometimes combined with lower-pitched notes as in *steep!-di-dit*.

Breeding

In Brazil, builds a rather deep cup nest placed in bushes or small palms near streams in the undergrowth of terra firma forest; eggs are turquoise blue, spotted black (Snethlage 1935).

Sources

Primary Beebe 1916; Hilty and Brown 1986; Meyer de Schauensee and Phelps 1978; Novaes 1970; Pearson 1972; Snethlage 1907, 1935; Willis 1977. **Weights** (*surinamus* n = ?, remaining subspecies n = 37): Haverschmidt 1968; LSUMZ data. **Stomach contents** Foster data; Haverschmidt 1968; LSUMZ data; Schubart, Aguirre, and Sick 1965. **Vocalizations** LNS recordings by T. H. Davis (1), Parker (1); Hilty and Brown 1986. **Nests and eggs** Snethlage 1935.

Tachyphonus luctuosus **72**
White-shouldered Tanager
Plate 10

Length 13–14 cm (5–5½ in.). Weight 13 g (11.5–15.0 g). Five subspecies.

Geographic Range

T. l. axillaris: the Caribbean slope from Atlántico, HONDURAS, southward through NICARAGUA and COSTA RICA to w Bocas del Toro, PANAMA. *T. l. nitidissimus*: the Pacific slope from San José province, COSTA RICA, to w Chiriquí, PANAMA. *T. l. panamensis*: the Caribbean slope from Coclé, PANAMA, and the Pacific slope from Panamá province, PANAMA, southward through w COLOMBIA and w ECUADOR to El Oro, and eastward through COLOMBIA west and north of the Andes to Zulia, Mérida, and Táchira, VENEZUELA. *T. l. flaviventris*: TRINIDAD and extreme ne VENEZUELA in n and e Sucre. *T. l. luctuosus*: along the e base of the Andes from Barinas, VENEZUELA, to Meta, COLOMBIA; thence more broadly east of the Andes southward through e ECUADOR and e PERU to Santa Cruz, BOLIVIA; and eastward north of the Amazon River through c Amazonas, BRAZIL, s and e VENEZUELA (Amazonas, Bolívar, n Monagas, s Sucre, and Delta Amacuro), GUYANA, SURINAME, and FRENCH GUIANA (Tostain 1980) to Amapá, BRAZIL; south of the Amazon to e Pará, wc Goiás (Ridgely *in litt.*), and Mato Grosso (Rio Paraguai), BRAZIL.

Elevational Range

Lowlands mostly below 1000 m; as high as 2200 m in Colombia (Hilty and Brown 1986).

Habitat and Behavior

Encountered in pairs and family groups of 3–6 individuals, rarely in larger groups. In c Panama, average group size was 2.57 (Greenberg and Gradwohl 1985, 47 obs.). In Peru, some pairs and family groups were core species in permanent canopy mixed-species flocks, but other individuals were seen with permanent understory mixed-species flocks suggesting a high population density in which different pairs are members of the two different types of flocks (see Munn 1985). Flutters about actively in foliage, then rapidly disappears. Males flash white underwing coverts and puff up shoulder patches in display.

Habitat and foraging height appear to vary regionally. In Central America and South America west and north of the Andes, occurs in tall second growth, forest, and forest edge. Forages at all levels, but especially at midheights. On Barro Colorado Island, Panama: About 45% of 75 foraging observations were between 9.5 and 15 m above the ground and about 35% were higher. Sought insects mostly on leaf tops (75% of 75 obs.), also on leaf bottoms, twigs, and in the air. The majority (60% of 70 obs.) of insect-attacks involved lunges, leaps, and sallies; 40% were without acrobatics. Typically foraged in outer foliage; often hopped along a branch toward the tip and then jumped down to a leaf top to attack prey. (Greenberg 1984.) Of 52 observations of large prey, 62% were orthopterans, 15% larvae, and

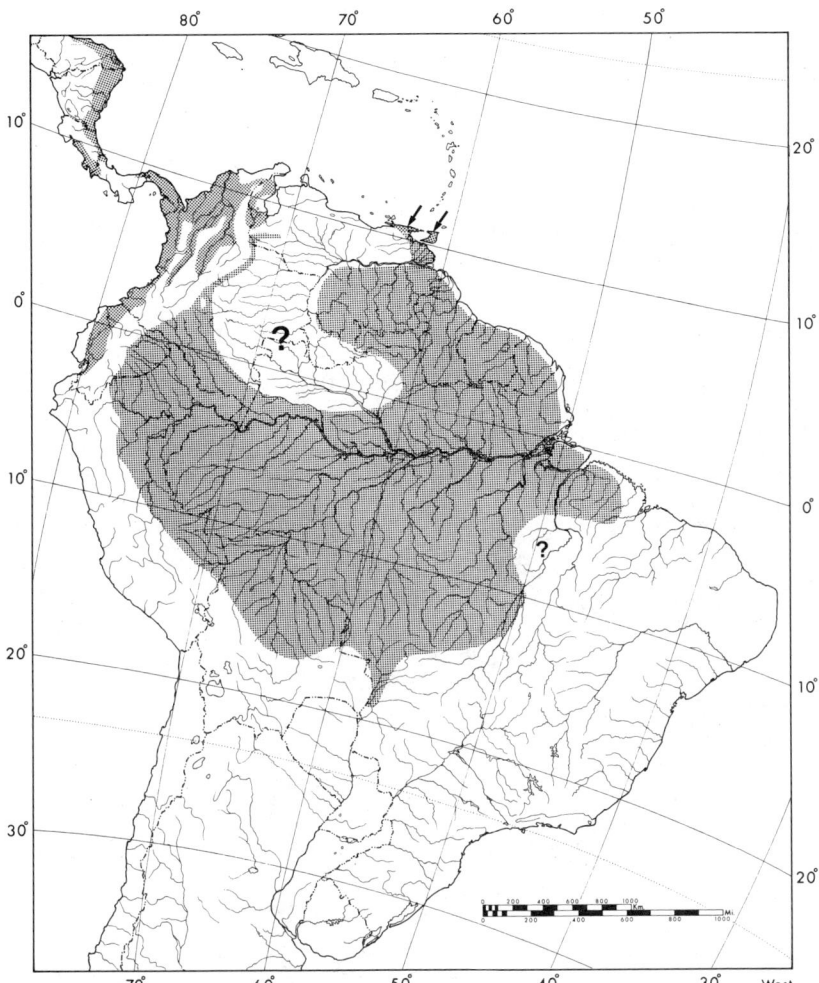

Tachyphonus luctuosus

23% other (Greenberg 1981a). Of 223 feeding observations, only 12% involved plant material, primarily fruit (Greenberg 1981b). In Central America, frequently seen to eat arils of *Casearia*. Also observed eating fruits of many species including *Miconia, Zanthoxylum, Xylopia,* and *Lindackeria* (Greenberg *in litt.*) and peeling edible portions off mistletoe berries and dropping the seeds (Leck 1972c). Stomach contents (1): insect remains.

In Trinidad: Found in forest, at forest edge, and in second growth. Of 49 observations, 71% were insect-searching and 29% were eating fruit. Of the insect-searching, 94% were on leaves, 3% on twigs, and 3% on aerial sallies. Ate a green stick-insect. Foraged mostly at heights of 3–15 m; higher for insects (8–15 m) than for fruit. Seen eating only 4 species of fruit, including *Miconia* berries and a bromeliad. (Snow and Snow 1971.)

In South America east of the Andes, encountered in forest but favors dense foliage and vine tangles in treefalls and other forest openings; also occurs at forest edge, in tall second growth, and in shaded plantations. Appears to forage mostly at heights of 5–10 m above the ground, but sometimes goes higher (up to 30 m, Remsen data). Flits swiftly among rather thick vegetation. Forages acrobatically primarily by searching uppersides of medium-sized green leaves and flutter-pursuing escaping prey (Remsen data, 9 obs.). Also picks insects off leaves while perched and sallies to foliage. Occasionally searches arboreal dead leaves (Remsen and Parker 1984). Stomach contents: vegetable matter (1); animal matter (2). Contents included spiders, termite workers, long-horned grasshoppers, coleopterans, and fruit. Also observed eating a lepidopteran, an orthopteran, and a mantis (Remsen data).

Vocalizations

Calls frequently. In Costa Rica, delivers characterless *tsir* or *tchrit* notes in series of about 5 or a descending set of 3; also a reedy *tsit*, a rising slow *wirst*, and other notes (see Slud 1964). In e Panama, calls include an abrupt Moderate-pitched nasal soft finch-like *chaa*, *chay*, or *chee*; sometimes *chay-dit* or *chay-di-dit*, lower pitched at the end (Parker, LNS); also *tsip, tsip* (Eisenmann 1952). In Trinidad, utters a slight unmusical *tchirrup* or a squeaky *tswee*, often repeated (ffrench 1973). In Guyana, an accelerating 6-syllable *ch-ch-ch-chchch* (Snyder 1966).

Breeding

In Trinidad, fairly deep open cup nests (2), made of dried grass and lined with fine fibers, were placed 1–1.5 m above the ground in the undergrowth. Three eggs from one nest were rich buff, blotched reddish brown; eggs of the second set were pale cream, marked with blackish brown and faintly with pale gray. (Belcher and Smooker 1937.) Breeding dates: Trinidad April, June, and Sept.

Sources

Primary Greenberg 1984, *in litt.*; Hilty and Brown 1986; Howell 1957; Monroe 1968; O'Neill 1974; Parker data; Ridgely 1976; Slud 1964; Snow and Snow 1971. **Weights (n=27)** Burton 1975; ffrench 1973; Greenberg 1984; Greenberg and Gradwohl 1980; LSUMZ data; Strauch 1977; Willis 1980. **Stomach contents** Beebe 1909; Brosset 1964; Foster data; Schubart, Aguirre, and Sick 1965. **Vocalizations** LNS recordings by Parker (2); Eisenmann 1952; Slud 1964; Snyder 1966. **Nests, eggs, and breeding dates** Belcher and Smooker 1937; ffrench 1973.

Tachyphonus delatrii **73**
Tawny-crested Tanager
Plate 10

Length 14 cm (5½ in.). Weight 17 g (14.5–21.1 g). Monotypic. Subadult plumage like female but darker overall; molting subadult male may develop orange tawny crown before black body feathers (Ridgely 1976).

Geographic Range

The Caribbean slope from Gracias a Dios, HONDURAS (sight, Marcus 1983), southward through NICARAGUA and COSTA RICA to San Blas, PANAMA; the Pacific slope in Veraguas (sight, Ridgely 1976), PANAMA, and from Darién, PANAMA, southward through COLOMBIA and ECUADOR to Chimborazo; Gorgona I., COLOMBIA; and along the n base of the Andes in COLOMBIA eastward to the middle Magdalena Valley in e Antioquia.

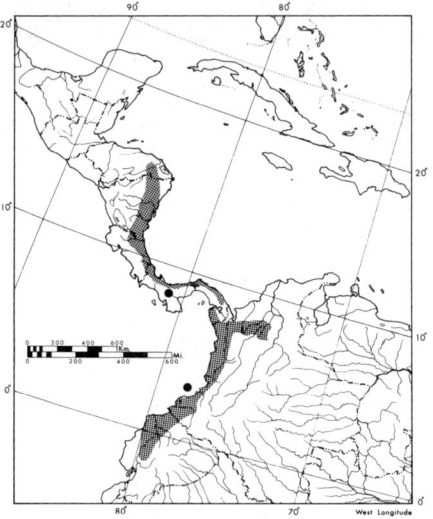

Tachyphonus delatrii

Elevational Range

Lowlands mostly below 800 m but recorded as high as 1500 m in Colombia and Ecuador.

Habitat and Behavior

Inhabits humid shrubby forest edge, tall second growth, and forest interiors. Gregarious; encountered in lively single-species groups of up to 20 or more individuals; in Colombia, usually in groups of 8–12 individuals on the coastal plain and in groups of 3–4 at higher elevations (Hilty data). Groups usually travel independently but sometimes are joined by other species, especially other tanagers, or are united temporarily with large mixed-species flocks. Sweeps rapidly through the forest understory and along forest edge on what appear to be established foraging rounds.

Forages mostly at heights of 2–8 m above the ground in low trees, tall shrubs (not generally inside thickets), and midheights of taller trees. Sometimes forages higher, especially when in large single-species flocks. Probably hunts for insects and fruit about equally; eats a variety of fruit including *Miconia* and other melastomes (Hilty data). Active and acrobatic when foraging. In Colombia, peered around fluttering and hopping among foliage, pecked at prey, hung from and hovered at leaves, and sallied to air; rarely examined branch surfaces (Hilty data). In Honduras, seen dismembering a grasshopper with its bill and then eating individual pieces (Marcus 1983).

Vocalizations

Chatters continuously while foraging; makes kissing and sibilant sounds, mixed with heavier sharper ones. Calls include a squeaky strong *chit* or *tswik* given singly, doubled, tripled, or in simple repetition (Slud 1964).

Breeding

No information.

Sources

Primary Carriker 1910; Hilty data; Hilty and Brown 1986; Isler data; Karr 1971; Marcus 1983; Ridgely 1976; Slud 1960, 1964; Wetmore, Pasquier, and Olson 1984. **Weights (n = 4)** LSUMZ data. **Vocalizations** Slud 1964.

Tachyphonus coronatus **74**
Ruby-crowned Tanager
Plate 10

Length 16 cm (6 in.). Weight 27 g (26.0–29.0 g). Monotypic.

Geographic Range

Extreme s Mato Grosso (Pinto 1944a), s Minas Gerais, and Espírito Santo southward to c Rio Grande do Sul, BRAZIL; Misiones and extreme ne Corrientes (Short 1971), ARGENTINA, and Neembucú, PARAGUAY. One record west of the Río Paraguay in extreme se Presidente Hayes, PARAGUAY.

Elevational Range

Mostly in lowlands; also lower mountain slopes to 1200 m in some regions.

Habitat and Behavior

Inhabits open woodland and thickets and dense second growth at forest edge. Also occurs in orchards, plantations, parks, gardens, and cleared areas where there is thick vegetation. Survives in small woodlots after forest is cleared (Willis 1979). Seen singly, in pairs, and in (family?) groups of 3–4 individuals, and sometimes in larger feeding aggregations (Belton 1985). Rarely in mixed-species flocks (Davis 1946). Moves about restlessly, making short flights between foraging sites. May also be partially migratory as numbers fluctuate seasonally in the former state of Guanabara, Brazil (Sick 1985). Habitually flicks wings showing white lesser coverts and underwing-coverts, and displays red crest when excited.

Usually forages from midheights to the canopy in woodlands but descends lower at forest edge. Eats fruit and insects. Reported to feed on a variety of fruit and flowers: melastomes (incl. *Leandra* sp), *Cecropia*, palms, persimmons, bananas, oranges, and *Eucalyptus* blossoms; also eats leaves. Also eats small fruits of the bromeliads *Neoregelia* and *Nidulariam*, pulling at the fruits, which are hidden in the base of the rosette, until it finds a ripe one that comes off; squeezes and swallows juice and seeds, leaving the fiber (Sick 1985). Comes to feeding trays for papaya (Parker data). Occasionally follows army ant swarms. Fond of sweet secretions of plant lice (Sick 1985). Stomach contents: animal matter (8); vegetable matter (1); both (13). Contents included orthopterans, coleopterans (incl. weevils and leaf beetles), hymenopterans (incl. ants), fruits, and seeds (incl. *Ficus* seeds).

In Paraguay when eating 7–10 mm fruits of *Allophyllus edulis*: Hopped around inside tree crowns; reached out to pluck a fruit, sometimes flying with it to another perch. Rolled the fruit around in its bill to mash it and to clean the pulp off the seed. Usually dropped the seed but sometimes swallowed fruit whole and regurgitated the seed. (Foster data.)

Vocalizations

Sings in a leisurely fashion delivering rich, melodious, loud phrases one after the other. Usually sings from midheights, sometimes from the tops of trees. Song varies with individuals but typically contains a *ch* sound regularly interspersed with 1 or 2 other sounds (Belton 1985). Notes are Low- to Moderate-pitched. Examples are: *whit-it CHEW; chew-chew*; an upward-inflected whistled *whildit* followed by *dit* or *deo* or *whilt cheo; chit chur whee-o; whit dittle chit*; etc. Call notes: both

Tachyphonus coronatus

male and female often deliver an emphatic, heavy, Moderate-pitched note, e.g., *chet* or *tsick* (Belton, LNS). Calls continuously, even with fruit in its bill (Foster data).

Breeding

Conceals its cup nest, composed of grass and lined with rootlets, less than 2 m off the ground in thickets, coffee bushes, or other dense vegetation such as new shoots of a tree stump; often builds in streamside vegetation. Three (sometimes 2) eggs are pink (sometimes white), blotched and smeared with shades of red and brown, especially at the large end; sometimes scrawled with black. In captivity, the incubation period was 13 days; both parents fed the young which left the nest after 9 days (Norgaard-Olesen 1974). Breeding dates: Brazil (Rio de Janeiro) Oct, Dec, and Jan; (São Paulo) Nov.

Sources

Primary Belton 1985, *in litt.*; Davis 1946; Descourtilz 1852; Erickson and Mumford 1976; Euler 1867; Foster data; Holt 1928; Mitchell 1957; Santos 1948; Sick 1985. **Weights (n = 6)** Belton 1985; Short 1971; Sick 1985. **Stomach contents** Moojen, Carvalho, and Lopes 1941; Schubart, Aguirre, and Sick 1965. **Vocalizations** LNS recordings by Belton (10), Parker (2); Parker *in litt.*; Sick 1985. **Nests, eggs, and breeding dates** Euler 1867, 1900; Holt 1928; Ihering 1900; Nehrkorn 1899; Norgaard-Olesen 1974; Ogilvie-Grant 1912; Snethlage and Schreiner 1929.

Tachyphonus rufus 75
White-lined Tanager
Plate 10

Length 17 cm (7 in.). Weight 33 g (25.7–40.0 g); in Trinidad, 36 g (31.0–42.5 g). Monotypic. Some otherwise adult males have cinnamon-rufous feathers in the center of the crown; these feathers may be the residual of the subadult male plumage which resembles the female plumage (Thomas *in litt.*).

Geographic Range

COSTA RICA on the Caribbean slope (except for the Río Frío region) and a sight record on the Pacific slope in s Alajuela (Slud 1964); PANAMA on the entire Caribbean slope and locally on the Pacific slope in w Chiriquí and from w Panamá province eastward (Wetmore, Pasquier, and Olson 1984); COLOMBIA in the Andean region, the n and w slope of the Santa Marta Mountains, and the ne region; VENEZUELA north of the Orinoco River (except nw region), and in n Amazonas, n Bolívar, Delta Amacuro, and Margarita I.; TRINIDAD AND TOBAGO; THE GUIANAS (distribution in the interior is unclear); BRAZIL north of the Amazon River in extreme ne Pará (Novaes 1980) and Amapá (Novaes 1978), and south of the Amazon in Pará (along the Amazon River east of the Rio Tapajos), Maranhão, Piauí, Ceará, and Paraíba southward to Mato Grosso and n and w São Paulo (absent from coastal regions south of c Bahia); e BOLIVIA in Santa Cruz (Remsen and Traylor 1983); PARAGUAY (west of the Río Paraguay and east of the Río Paraguay in Concepción and Central); ne ARGENTINA (e Formosa, e Choco, n Santa Fe, w Misiones, Entre Ríos, and n Buenos Aires). In ECUADOR, reported from Zamora-Chinchipe (MCZ), Morona-Santiago (sight, June 1984—Ridgely), and the w slope in Imbabura and Bolívar (Orces 1944). In PERU, in the Urubamba Valley in Cuzco and in the Marañon-Huallaga drainage in Cajamarca, Amazonas, and San Martín.

Elevational Range

In most regions, occurs from lowlands to ca. 1500 m, but mainly 600–1500 m in Colombia; as high as 2700 m in Colombia (Hilty and Brown 1986) and 2400 m in Venezuela (Isler data).

Habitat and Behavior

Typically lives in thickets, shrubs, and dense second-growth trees in semiopen areas. Frequents forest borders, second growth, and scrubby patches in agricultural and disturbed areas. Also occurs in gallery forest, open woodland, savanna, and gardens in suburban areas. Lives mostly in pairs; also in small family groups for a short time after nesting; rarely solitary, rarely in larger groups of up to 10 or more individuals. Sometimes several gather together in high bare branches before roosting (ffrench 1973). Rarely joins mixed-species flocks. Restless and active; flits wings to expose white shoulder patch. Often flies low across an opening as one member of a pair darts after the other.

Usually forages less than 3 m off the ground and often on the ground; occasionally ascends higher, especially to feed on fruit. In Trinidad, of 238 observations, 60% involved fruit-eating, 30% insect-searching, and 10% were at flowers (Snow and Snow 1971). Stomach contents: animal matter (11); vegetable matter (7); both (4). Contents included ants, coleopterans, hemipterans, dipterans, spiders, feather fragments, fruit, berries, and seeds.

In Trinidad, took 28 species of fruits, especially those of epiphytic plants (35% of all fruit eaten), *Miconia* (20%), and *Cecropia* (14%). Often hovered to take bromeliad fruits and then flew to a nearby perch to mash them; swallowed the pulp and small seeds and dropped the spiny skins; mashed and dropped inedible parts of 3 other kinds of fruit; swallowed others whole. Picked flowers and crunched the bases to squeeze out nectar. (Snow and Snow 1971.) Hangs on leaves or catkins to obtain *Cecropia* fruit. Seen eating wild guavas (Thomas data) and exploits commercially grown fruits such as pineapples, papayas, bananas, and oranges. Readily comes to feeding tables for fruit and sugar.

Of 74 insect-foraging records in Trinidad, 51% were on the ground, 32% in foliage, 14% in aerial sallies, and 3% on branches and twigs. Foraged on the ground by pouncing down on insects from a low (e.g., 0.3 m) perch; also stood upright on the ground or hovered briefly about 15 cm above the ground to snap up prey. Hopped rapidly along small branches, peered all around, and sometimes darted up or forward to pick insects from a leaf or twig. The Snows never saw it closely examine leaves, twigs, or branches. Occasionally fed at army ant swarms, jumping down to the ground to

Tachyphonus rufus

take fleeing insects. (Snow and Snow 1971.) In Colombia, Hilty observed similar insect-foraging techniques; he also saw White-lined Tanagers make short sallies after flying termites from the top of an 18 m tree (Hilty data). In Venezuela, observed eating caterpillars, a moth, and a katydid (Thomas data).

Vocalizations

Call notes: a short Low-pitched *che* or *check* and a weak *seep* or *sip*. In flight: *wist-wist* (Sick 1985). Song: delivers somewhat musical Low- to Moderate-pitched phrases, e.g., *chip-chiwer*, *chip-chur*, *chip-wheeeo*, *cheerU*, *CHEEP-chooi*, or *chip-chip-wheer*. Given at the rate of 100/min (ffrench 1973). Dawn song: repeats a series of 2–4 song phrases after pauses of 5–6 sec. (Schwartz, LNS).

Breeding

Bulky loosely constructed cup nests, made of leaves and grass and lined with thin fibers, are typically situated within 2 m of the ground but occasionally placed up to 12 m off the ground. Usually builds in bushes or trees; once in high grass (Sclater and Salvin 1879). Eggs (2–3, occasionally 1) are white to purplish, marked with very dark brown or black and pale lavender. The female incubates alone for 14–15 days. Both parents feed the young. Courtship feeding by the male was observed before egg laying (Haverschmidt 1968).

In captivity, courtship flight was slow, like a butterfly, with the white feathers fully displayed. The incubation period was 12–13 days and the young left the nest after 12–14 days. One male took over the feeding of fledglings which became independent after 3 weeks. (Norgaard-Olesen 1974.) Breeding dates: Panama May. Venezuela Feb, April–June, and Oct. Trinidad Feb–Aug and Nov (mostly April–June). Peru Jan–March. Brazil (Pará) Oct, Nov, and Jan; (Mato Grosso) Oct; (state uncertain) Dec.

Sources

Primary ffrench 1973; Friedmann and Smith 1950; Ginés et al. 1951; Hilty data; Hilty and Brown 1986; Haverschmidt 1968; Miller 1963; Novaes 1973; Schäfer and Phelps 1954; Slud 1964; Snow and Snow 1971; Todd and Carriker 1922; Wetmore 1926. **Weights** (in Trinidad, n = 84; remaining n = 88): ffrench 1973; Fry 1970; Hartman 1955; Hartman and Brownell 1961; Haverschmidt 1948, 1968; LSUMZ data; Miller 1963; Strauch 1977; Thomas data; Thomas 1982. **Stomach contents** Forbes 1881; Hallinan 1924; Layard 1873; Novaes and Pimentel 1973; Olivares 1963; Schubart, Aguirre, and Sick 1965; Sick 1958. **Vocalizations** LNS recordings by Schwartz (16), D. W. Snow (2); ffrench 1973; Sick 1985; Slud 1964; Snyder 1966. **Nests, eggs, and breeding dates** Allen 1891; Belcher and Smooker 1937; Cherrie 1916; Euler 1900; ffrench 1973; Gilliard 1959; Haverschmidt 1968; Herklots 1961; Norgaard-Olesen 1974; Ogilvie-Grant 1912; Peixoto 1932; Pinto 1953; Sclater and Salvin 1879; Snethlage 1935; Snethlage and Schreiner 1929; Snow and Snow 1964; Stone 1918; Taczanowski 1884b; Thomas data.

Tachyphonus phoenicius **76**
Red-shouldered Tanager
Plate 10

Length 15 cm (6 in.). Weight 21 g (17.0–25.0 g). Monotypic. In subadult plumage (possibly limited to juvenal plumage), both males and females are streaked on the breast and belly.

Geographic Range

East of the Andes in 3 apparently disjunct regions. COLOMBIA (s Meta eastward to Vaupés, Vichada, and Guainía) eastward through s VENEZUELA (Amazonas and Bolívar), and THE GUIANAS to extreme ne Pará (Novaes 1980) and e Amapá (Novaes 1978), BRAZIL. BRAZIL on the n bank of the Amazon River near the Amazonas-Pará border and south of the Amazon from e Amazonas (along the Rio Madeira) eastward and southward to extreme se Pará and nw Mato Grosso. PERU from w Loreto (south of the Río Marañón) to San Martín and n Ucayali (LSUMZ).

Elevational Range

Lowlands and tablelands to ca. 400 m; to ca. 1350 m in San Martín, Peru (O'Neill *in litt.*); to 2000 m on the tepuis in s Venezuela.

Habitat and Behavior

Inhabits semiopen areas of savanna and scrub; has a patchy distribution from Suriname to Colombia following regions of poor soil conditions including sandy savannas and scrubby areas surrounding exposed granite plates and bases of quartzite domed mountains. Frequents bushes and patches of low trees at forest edge and in savannas, open woodland, second growth, and scrub. Generally travels in pairs; also singly and in small groups. Occurs apart from and in mixed-species flocks. Forages low in vegetation, rarely more than 6 m above the ground. However, regular in upper foliage of palms and woodland patches in n Peru (Parker *in litt.*). Flutters and gleans in foliage (Hilty and Brown 1986). Stomach contents: animal matter (7); vegetable matter (2). Contents included ants, coleopterans (incl. weevils), hemipterans, and seeds. Additional stomach contents included spiders.

Vocalizations

Call notes: a weak Low- to Moderate-pitched *chup* or *cheup*, a high-pitched *tsit*, and soft *chip*s while foraging.

Breeding

In Suriname, open cup nests of grass are placed on the ground concealed in clumps of grass or near bushes. Eggs (1–2) are grayish, spotted and blotched chocolate brown completely covering the large end. Breeding dates: Suriname Feb and March.

Sources

Primary Haverschmidt 1968; Hilty and Brown 1986; Isler data; Meyer de Schauensee and Phelps 1978; Olivares 1959. **Weights (n = 43)** Haverschmidt 1952, 1956, 1968; LSUMZ data. **Stomach contents** Haverschmidt 1968; Olivares 1959; Schubart, Aguirre, and Sick 1965. **Vocalizations** LNS recording by T. H. Davis (1); T. H. Davis pers. comm.; Hilty and Brown 1986. **Nests, eggs, and breeding dates** Haverschmidt 1956, 1968, 1975.

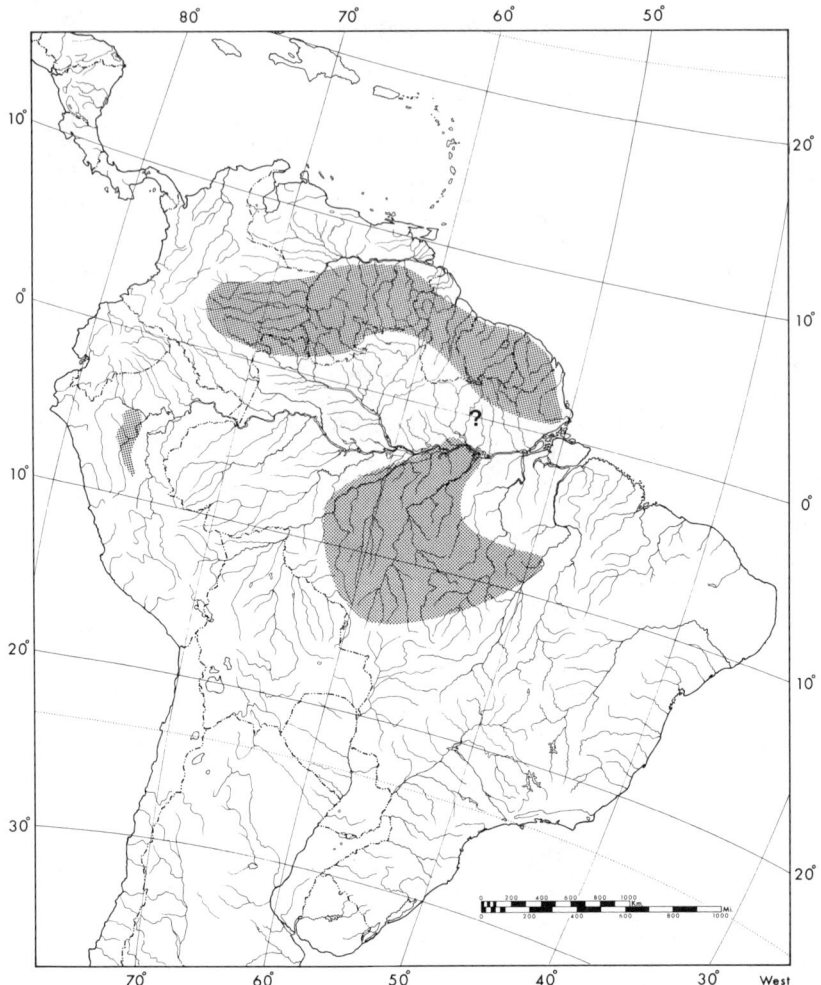

Tachyphonus phoenicius

TRICHOTHRAUPIS

The Black-goggled Tanager, the single species in the genus, usually forages below mid-heights in forest and is often observed following army ants. Its pattern of vocalizations parallels that of *Habia* ant-tanagers, and its foraging behavior also suggests that of *Eucometis* or some species of *Tachyphonus*.

Trichothraupis melanops **77**
Black-goggled Tanager
Plate 10

Length 16 cm (6 in.). Weight 23 g (16.2–26.0 g). Monotypic.

Geographic Range

The e slope of the Andes from s Amazonas and San Martín (Huallaga drainage), PERU, southward through PERU and BOLIVIA to extreme n Salta, ARGENTINA (Olrog 1979); se BRAZIL from s Bahia, s Goiás, and s Mato Grosso southward to n Rio Grande do Sul and adjacent ARGENTINA

Trichothraupis melanops

in Misiones and Corrientes (Short 1971); and PARAGUAY east of the Río Paraguay and the west bank in e Presidente Hayes (Laubmann 1940).

Elevational Range

Ca. 1000–1700 m on Andean slopes; descends to 200 m in c Bolivia (LSUMZ). In Brazil, Argentina, and Paraguay, primarily lowlands but as high as 1200 m.

Habitat and Behavior

Inhabits interiors of forests and woodlands that contain substantial foliage in the understory and midstory. Also occurs in semiopen situations such as shrubbery and low trees at forest edge and along watercourses, second growth, and brush in reverted clearings. Survives in remnant woodlots as small as 21 ha in se Brazil (Willis 1979). Scarce and/or local in the Andes, but not in the eastern portion of its range. Lives in pairs and small groups (presumably families), occasionally up to a dozen individuals. Often travels with mixed-species flocks, especially understory flocks in Andean forests (Parker data) and ant following flocks in se Brazil. Constantly moves from branch to branch; perches horizontally (Parker data).

Forages mostly in the forest understory, frequently dropping to the ground when foraging at army ant swarms; sometimes eats ants. Sallies to foliage and to air; forages in vine tangles (Parker data). Ascends to crowns of trees to eat fruit. Stomach contents: animal matter (22); vegetable matter (6); both (3). Contents included beetles, fruit, seeds, and pieces of a snail shell. Also eats butterflies and wasp larvae (Descourtilz 1852).

In Paraguay when eating 7–10 mm fruits of *Allophyllus edulis*: Foraged mostly in densely foliaged areas of the crown but also in all other sections of the tree. Reached out, leaned over, or made quick sallies to pick fruit; rarely hovered. Peeled fruit by rolling it around in the very tip of its bill. Usually dropped the seed, but sometimes swallowed fruit whole. (Foster data.)

Vocalizations

Calls: a burry spitting Moderate-pitched *tswick* or *twzt* and a sharp High-pitched *tst*; calls often, even with fruit in its bill; flicks wings when calling, exposing white linings. Two types of songs have been recorded in Brazil. The first is a repetition of a 3–4 sec. series of mostly slurred penetrating whistles that shift among Low, Moderate, and High-pitched notes, e.g., *wheee whur whur whit? pheee peee*; in one recording, the series included sweet and warbled notes; often intersperses call notes between series. The second song type is an indefinitely long series of squeals, long slurred whistles, buzzy notes, and short *psps* in which the same note is often repeated 2–5 times.

Breeding

Eggs are pinkish white, marked with brown, lavender, and black, especially at the large end. A cup nest was found 1 m above the ground in a clump of bamboo in the forest; 3 young were observed (Euler 1867). Breeding dates: Brazil (São Paulo) Oct; (Rio de Janeiro) Nov.

Sources

Primary Belton 1985; Chubb 1910; Descourtilz 1852; Erickson and Mumford 1976; Foster data; Goeldi 1894; Holt 1928; Mitchell 1957; Parker data; Pereyra 1951; Sick 1985; Willis 1979. **Weights (n=21)** Belton 1985; LSUMZ data; Short 1971; Sick 1985. **Stomach contents** Belton 1985; Foster data; LSUMZ data. **Vocalizations** LNS recordings by Belton (3), Parker (5); Belton 1985; Foster data; Sick 1985. **Nests, eggs, and breeding dates** Euler 1867; Ihering 1900; Ogilvie-Grant 1912.

HABIA

No other tanager genus has been investigated as thoroughly as has *Habia* (Table 11). Edwin O. Willis began studing *Habia* in 1957 and published a series of research reports that culminated with a comparative review of the taxonomy and behavior of all five species (Willis 1972a). Four of the five are allopatric; the Red-crowned and Red-throated are sympatric in Central America. All except the Crested live in lowlands and/or foothills.

Table 11 The *Habia* Ant-Tanagers

78	*H. rubica*	Red-crowned Ant-Tanager
79	*H. fuscicauda*	Red-throated Ant-Tanager
80	*H. atrimaxillaris*	Black-cheeked Ant-Tanager
81	*H. gutturalis*	Sooty Ant-Tanager
82	*H. cristata*	Crested Ant-Tanager

Ant-tanagers share many ecological and behavioral characteristics; for example, all five species forage in leafy vegetation at low levels. Differences discovered by Willis suggest, however, that the Red-crowned and Crested Ant-Tanagers should be discussed as one group and the Red-throated, Black-cheeked, and Sooty Ant-Tanagers as another (the Red-throated and Sooty are considered a superspecies by the *A.O.U. Check-list*).

Red-throated, Black-cheeked, and Sooty Ant-Tanagers primarily inhabit second growth and areas of patchy woodland; they forage at about 2–3 m above the ground. These three species typically perch on bare branches to peer at nearby substrates or to watch flying insects to see where they land. If prey is seen, ant-tanagers relocate rapidly to a perch where they can reach their quarry, or they make short sallies or hover briefly to capture their prey. If prey is not located quickly, they fly to another perch at about the same height from the ground to search again. Consequently, they move through the undergrowth rapidly. Red-throated, Black-cheeked, and Sooty Ant-Tanagers follow ant swarms frequently and dart after insects attempting to escape from the ants.

In most areas within their range, Red-crowned Ant-Tanagers live in forests with substantial amounts of low and midlevel vegetation. Crested Ant-Tanagers live along ravines and overgrown landslides on mountain slopes. Both species forage at a median height of about 4–5 m off the ground, higher than their congeners. Moreover, they tend to forage for insects by hopping upward through saplings, inspecting leaves and twigs within reach of each perch, picking off prey, and then dropping down to lower levels in the next tree where they start up again. Red-crowned and Crested Ant-Tanagers follow ants only sporadically.

All five species regularly take prey larger than their bills, such as beetles and orthopterans, that they often dismember before eating. Fruit seems to form a smaller part of their diet than insects. *Habia* obtain fruit while perched or in short hovers but rarely remain long in a fruiting tree or shrub.

Ant-tanagers live in pairs or small family groups. Offspring remain with their parents until the next nesting season. They are territorial throughout the year and often join or are joined by other species within their territory.

Some observers have marvelled at the contrast between the harsh notes and the whistled songs of *Habia* species. Songs are given primarily during the breeding season, but contact calls are given often, and grating scolds warn of the presence of intruders.

The female builds the loosely constructed cup nest and incubates the 2–3 eggs alone, although the male remains nearby. Mostly the female feeds nestlings, but both parents feed fledglings (observations of 2 species). Ant-tanagers seem to suffer heavy nest predation, and possibly because of predation, young creep out of the nest into dense vegetation before they can fly.

Habia rubica 78
Red-crowned Ant-Tanager
Plate 11

Length 17–19 cm (6½–7½ in.). Weight (male) 34 g (27.7–42.9 g); (female) 31 g (22.5–37.0 g). Seventeen subspecies. Subadult males resemble females but are darker; may breed in subadult plumage (Wetmore 1943).

Geographic Range

H. r. holobrunnea, rosea, affinis, nelsoni, rubicoides, vinacea, and *alfaroana*: Pacific slope from Nayarit, MEXICO, southeastward through MIDDLE AMERICA to Darién, PANAMA; the Gulf slope from s Tamaulipas, MEXICO, southeastward on the Gulf-Caribbean slope (incl. the Yucatán Peninsula, BELIZE, and GUATEMALA) to HONDURAS (except the extreme east). *H. r. rubra*: TRINIDAD. *H. r. coccinea*: from the e Andean slope in Boyacá, COLOMBIA, northeastward along the base of the Andes to the s Andean slope in Lara, VENEZUELA, and the w slope of the E Andes in Norte de Santander (USNM), COLOMBIA. *H. r. crissalis*: the coastal range in Sucre and Anzoátegui, VENEZUELA. *H. r. mesopotamia*: e Bolívar (along the Río Yuruán), VENEZUELA. *H. r. perijana*: the Perijá Mountains; COLOMBIA along the n end of the W Andes (upper Sinú Valley). *H. r. rhodinolaema, peruviana,* and *hesterna*: east of the Andes from s Meta (Macarena Mountains) and Vaupés (Hilty and Brown 1986), COLOMBIA, southward through e ECUADOR and e PERU to Cochabamba, BOLIVIA, and eastward in BRAZIL north of the Amazon River to the Rio Uaupés and upper Rio Negro, and south of the Amazon to nw Mato Grosso and w and n Pará (Rio Tapajos and lower Rio Xingu). *H. r. bahiae* and *rubica*: e BRAZIL (Pernambuco south to c Rio Grande do Sul), Misiones, ARGENTINA, and se PARAGUAY (San Pedro and Canendiya southward).

Elevational Range

Lowlands and foothills to as high as 1500 m in El Salvador and 2250 m in Panama (Wetmore, Pasquier, and Olson 1984); mostly below 1000 m (below 500 m in Colombia).

Habitat and Behavior

Inhabits leafy undergrowth inside terra firma forest and woodland; frequently found along streams or other situations where there is thick vegetation, but avoids forest edge. Less common in undergrowth of river-edge and low-lying forest and in tall (over 6 m high) scrub and second growth near forest. In se Brazil, survives in remnant woodlots as small as 21 ha. (Willis 1979).

Lives in pairs and small family groups that are often joined by other species of insectivorous birds. In Belize, defends a common territory with the Tawny-crowned Greenlet, *Hylophilus ochraceiceps*, and the two species appear to form the core of mixed-species flocks (see Willis 1960b); forages within a territory of 4–5 ha.; sometimes families forage together along territorial boundaries, but never during the breeding season (Willis 1960a). Moves quickly through the forest. When alarmed, flits wings and flips from side to side (Willis 1972a) or depresses wings and cocks up tail (ffrench 1973). Quickly disappears among dense foliage when approached but often betrays its presence with chatters.

Usually forages at less than 10 m from the ground, occasionally up to 20 m or higher in the subcanopy. At a Peruvian site, the mean

140 HABIA

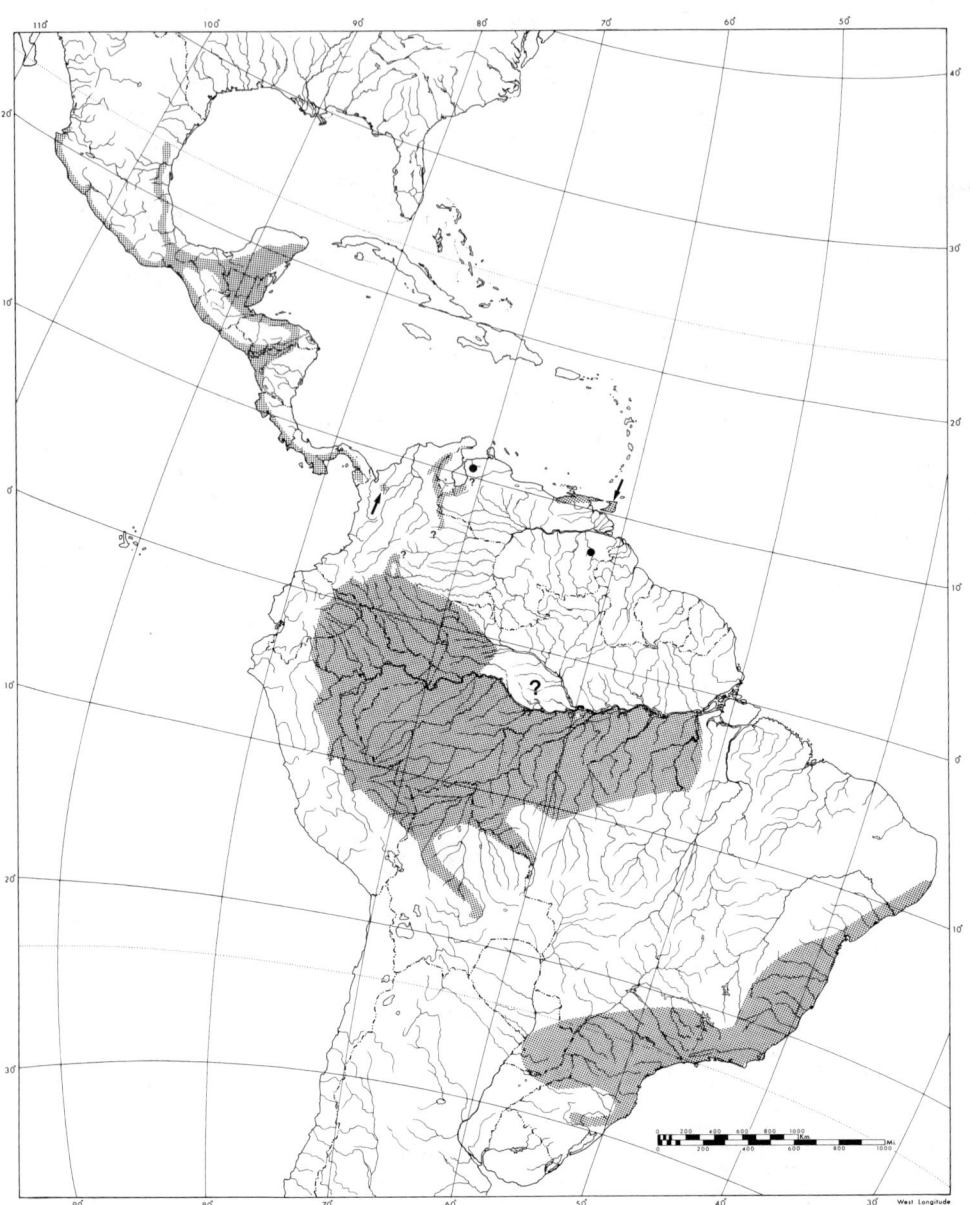

Habia rubica

foraging height was 3.63 m (Munn and Terborgh 1979); in Belize, the median was about 5 m (Willis 1960a). Primarily insectivorous. Stomach contents: animal matter (18); vegetable matter (2); both (4). Contents included beetles, weevils, ants, caterpillars, millipedes, mantises, snails, berries, and fruit.

When insect-foraging, typically hops, leaps, and flutters upward through the vegetation, then drops in flight to begin another set of upward moves. Peers in all directions for food. Usually waits for an insect in flight to alight rather than capturing it in the air. Prey are picked off twigs and foliage or sometimes captured in chasing maneuvers. To obtain prey from underneath leaves or twigs, usually leans over while perched on a horizontal branch, sometimes hovers, and rarely clings to undersides of twigs or limbs. Occasionally hovers or clings to a vine or epiphyte to pick an insect from a large limb or tree trunk. In Trinidad, forages mostly on branches and twigs (ffrench 1973).

Regularly searches arboreal dead leaves, and when prey is found, takes the whole leaf to a perch, works the leaf over in its bill, and extracts and crushes the insect. In Belize, also searches for insects in aerial debris collected in foliage. If an insect drops to escape, sometimes the bird flutter-pursues but more often it scrutinizes the ground above where the insect hit, at times tossing leaves to uncover its quarry. Tears apart large insects with its bill.

Propensity to follow ant swarms varies from region to region. Seems to follow ants least often in Amazonia, more often, yet irregularly, in Central America, and perhaps most often in Trinidad.

Eats berries, including those of *Miconia* and *Solanum*. Flutters up or clings briefly to a branch to pluck large berries. Takes some fruits to a perch where it rotates the fruit with tongue and/or bill while biting off the pulp until the seed drops. Pecks at some fruit until it falls to the ground where it eats the pulp; also eats large fruits that have already fallen to the ground (Willis 1960a).

Vocalizations

Diversified vocalizations range from harsh call notes to musical whistled song phrases. Song patterns vary somewhat between regions. In Central America, 3 principal song types have been identified. They are 1) a breeding season dawn song, 2) a day song, and 3) a soft day song used in various contexts. The first is only given by males during the breeding season (usually at dawn) and delivered in 1.5–3 sec. with pauses of 4–6 sec. Phrases are typically loud and flutelike but differ among individuals. Examples: *peter* (Moderate to Low pitch) repeated; *peer p'yerk pewk peer* (each note slightly lower pitched than the last) and *pee-er cho-cho pe-er* (the *cho-cho* lower in pitch and somewhat staccato). In Costa Rica and c Panama, the song is likely to consist of 3 syllable phrases sounding like the words *peter-bird* or *intervene*. Phrases are typically repeated 6 or more times in Costa Rica, 3–5 times in Panama. The dawn song is given from midlevels near forest openings (Belize) or from low perches in the undergrowth (southeastern Central America).

The day song is typically burry and monotonous, e.g., a Low-pitched whistled *cheer cheer cheer* etc, sometimes rising or falling in pitch and often preceded by rough chattering call notes. The day song may have the function of keeping pairs in touch or maintaining pair bonds. Day songs do not seem to be given south of Mexico and Belize, but may be represented in Amazonia by *peir peir peir peir*, given as the male flies and the female follows (Willis 1972a).

The soft day song has been noted only in Belize and Costa Rica where Skutch (1954) called it "a softly warbled refrain of singular beauty." Commonly includes phrases such as *turee-e-e-e* and *kiss'l* (Willis 1960c). Day song is given while bringing food to young, in territorial disputes, and after bathing.

In South America, the dawn song is also highly variable. In Peru, an example is *peer pyoo peer peeee!*; Low- and Moderate-pitched; the third or fourth note usually highest in pitch and loudest; delivered in 2 sec. with irregular pauses of mostly 5–10 sec. In se Brazil, songs delivered at dawn are mostly monotonous, slightly burry, whistles, *pee pee* etc, repeated up to 9 times; occasionally, rapidly repeats *pe-ter pe-ter* (Belton, LNS).

Call notes are quite different from songs in quality. In most regions, a grating *chat* or *chook* at a Moderate pitch sometimes strung together in a chatter: rapid (ca. 4–6 notes/sec.) staccato series of 5–15 (up to about 50 notes) or shorter chatters that combine different notes. In Amazonia, calls usually are only a single or double *chij* (Willis 1972a). Another call is a higher pitched *tchitit* or *tchititit*.

Breeding

In Belize, pairs defend a breeding territory. The female is most active in selecting the nesting site. Chattering frequently, she sits in one possible site after another. After she flies, the male sits in the same spot and pecks at the air in the same fashion as she did, seemingly moving strands of nesting material (Willis 1961).

Cup nests are typically built inside the forest, often near streams, and placed in crotches of saplings, branch forks in saplings or bushes, or in dense vine vegetation. The shallow cup is constructed mostly of rootlets, other plant fibers, and/or twigs; the nest is so thin that the eggs are sometimes visible from underneath. The female builds the nest, often accompanied by her mate who rarely carries nesting material or shapes the nest. In Belize, the nests discovered were usually over half of the way up in saplings 1.4–7 m high; most nests were 1–4 m above the ground, and the highest was 5.7 m (Willis 1961).

Two or 3 eggs, rarely 1 or 4, are white or bluish with light cinnamon or yellow-brown spots, especially at the large end where the markings form a wreath. The female incubates for 13–14 days. Young are fed by both parents but mostly by the female (Willis 1961). Food consists of larvae and mature insects, many so large that the nestlings have difficulty swallowing them, even after much mashing by the parent. An adult was seen feigning injury to lead intruders away from the nest (Sick 1985). The young leave the nest at about day 10; they cannot fly but are enticed by their parents onto twigs or vines that lead into dense thickets. One pair successfully raised a second brood (Willis 1961). Breeding dates: Mexico May and June. Belize April–July. Guatemala March. Costa Rica Feb and (mostly) April–June. Panama Aug. Trinidad Feb–Aug and Oct. Brazil (Pará) Feb and April; (Rio de Janeiro) Sept, Nov, and Dec.

Sources

Primary ffrench 1973; Foster data; Parker data; Skutch 1954; Wetmore, Pasquier, and Olson 1984; Willis 1960a, 1960b, 1960c, 1961, 1972a. **Weights** (male n = 79; female n = 47): Belton 1985; ffrench 1973; Hartman 1955; LSUMZ data; Munn and Terborgh 1979; Paynter 1955; Russell 1964; Sick 1985; Smithe 1966; Tashian 1952; Weske 1972; Willis 1980. **Stomach contents** Beebe 1909; Dickey and van Rossem 1938; Foster data; LSUMZ data; Schubart, Aguirre, and Sick 1965; Tashian 1952. **Vocalizations** LNS recordings by Belton (3), L. I. Davis (11), Lancaster (1), Morton (1), Parker (11), D. W. Snow (1), Thurber (3), van den Berg (1); Belton 1985; Davis 1972; Edwards 1972; ffrench 1973; Hilty and Brown 1986; Ridgely 1976; Skutch 1954; Slud 1964; Willis 1960c, 1961, 1972a. **Nests, eggs, and breeding dates** Allen 1905; Alvarez del Toro 1952; Andrle 1967; Belcher and Smooker 1937; Euler 1867, 1900; ffrench 1973; Herklots 1961; Nehrkorn 1899; Ogilvie-Grant 1912; Rowley 1966; Skutch 1954; Snethlage and Schreiner 1929; Wetmore, Pasquier, and Olson 1984; Willis 1961, 1972a.

Habia fuscicauda 79
Red-throated Ant-Tanager
Plate 11

Length 18–20 cm (7–7½ in.). Weight (male) 41 g (32.9–46.5 g); (female) 36 g (29.0–44.0 g). Six subspecies. Males of races that are not illustrated are slightly darker than male of *insularis* (illus.). Female of *salvini* is closest to *fuscicauda* (illus.); female of *erythrolaema* is closest to *willisi* (illus.); remaining races are intermediate. Subadult male plumage, which is similar to the female plumage, is retained for a year (Willis 1972a).

Geographic Range

H. f. salvini: the Gulf coast from s Tamaulipas and e San Luis Potosí, MEXICO, southward (except n and e Yucatán Peninsula and n Guatemala) along the Caribbean coast through BELIZE to HONDURAS, and the Pacific coast from Oaxaca, MEXICO, southward through GUATEMALA and EL SALVADOR to HONDURAS. *H. f. insularis*: se MEXICO (n and e Yucatán Peninsula and Meco and Mujeres Is.) and the n half of GUATEMALA.
H. f. discolor: NICARAGUA (except in extreme south; may be absent from the Pacific slope, A.O.U. Check-list). *H. f. fuscicauda*: the Caribbean slope from extreme s NICARAGUA through COSTA RICA to w PANAMA (Bocas del Toro), and the Pacific slope in COSTA RICA from Guanacaste to San José province (Slud 1964).
H. f. willisi: PANAMA on the Caribbean slope from Veraguas eastward to w San Blas and on the Pacific coast locally in Veraguas, w Panamá province, and the Canal Zone (Wetmore, Pasquier, and Olson 1984).
H. f. erythrolaema: from sw Atlántico southward to Bolívar, COLOMBIA; formerly (?) westward through Sucre and Córdoba to the Río Sinú (Hilty and Brown 1986).

Elevational Range

Lowlands and foothills from sea level to 1200 m (mostly at lower elevations) in Mexico and Central America; to 200 m in Colombia.

Habitat and Behavior

Inhabits thickets and dense vegetation in the understory of woodland, second growth, forest edge, and open swampy forest; also wanders to thick scrub in open areas near forest. Scarce in extensive areas of tall humid forest (Willis 1972a). In Colombia, *erythrolaema* may be endangered (Hilty 1985).

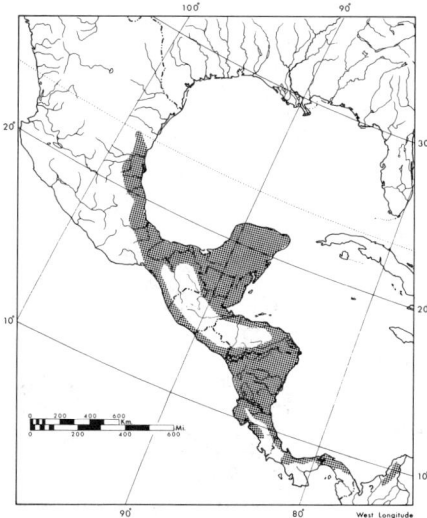

Habia fuscicauda

Encountered in pairs or family groups of 3–5 (rarely 6–8) individuals. Pair bonds seem very strong (see Wetmore, Pasquier, and Olson 1984). Contact calls of forerunners draw family members along in irregular formation, usually 3–10 m apart. Sometimes associates with mixed-species flocks of other insectivorous birds, but primarily joins other species at ant swarms.

In Belize, territories of 4–5 ha. are defended during the breeding season (Willis 1960a). During the nonbreeding season, multiple Red-throated Ant-Tanager families sometimes forage at the same army ant swarms, but the families quarrel or maintain their distance (Willis 1972a). Displays at boundaries by pointing bill upward stiffly and turning the body back and forth in a wigwag or sparring motion. Also spreads tail when excited. Performs broken-wing distraction displays (Wetmore, Pasquier, and Olson 1984). Sits upright while resting or preening, more horizontally while foraging. Observed anting (Alvarez del Toro in Whitaker 1957).

Forages at low heights. In Belize, about 75% of about 4000 foraging observations were below 5 m median height was slightly less than 2 m above the ground; foraged on the ground mostly at ant swarms (Willis 1960a). Stomach contents: animal matter (2); vegetable matter (1); both (2). Contents included coleopterans and other insects, fruit, grass seeds, berries, and a small snake. Also eats ants, caterpillars (up to 3 times the length of the bird's bill), and long-horned grasshoppers (Willis 1972a).

Regularly follows army ant swarms (Willis 1960a, 1972a). Usually occupies a more or less horizontal perch less than 1 m above the ants at the center of swarm activity. Peers around rapidly, turns from side to side, and frequently makes an about-face. Hops along low branches very rapidly, darting after escaping insects. Hops to the ground briefly to snap up prey. Occasionally flutters up to grab prey from the underside of a leaf, hovering briefly, or sallies for flying insects. Batters insects energetically and swallows them whole or piecemeal.

Away from army ants, forages rapidly through the undergrowth, maintaining about the same distance to the ground (Willis 1960a, 1972a). Hops along mostly horizontal branches, 1–2 cm in diam., and tends to peer for insects horizontally. Perches alongside intended prey or leans over to pick prey from underneath leaves or twigs. Sometimes hovers briefly or partly clings to a vine or epiphyte to pluck insects off undersurfaces and tree trunks. Darts quickly after falling insects. Investigates hanging dried rolled-up leaves; if prey is found, takes the whole leaf to a steady perch or the ground to extract the insect. Also probes debris collected among palm fronds and bromeliads.

Picks berries and rotates large ones with the tongue while biting off pulp, letting the seeds drop; swallows *Miconia* and other small berries whole. Occasionally goes to the ground to feed on fallen fruits.

Vocalizations

Highly vocal. Calls are of 3 principal types. The first, the scold, consists of throaty, raspy, Low- or Moderate-pitched notes given at the rate of 2–3 notes/sec., usually in groups of 2–20 notes; high-pitched scolds sound like heavy paper being torn. The second type of call has the rhythm and quality of long-distance radio static (Willis 1972a) and sounds like *scack ack-ack*, etc. This call is often heard as birds flee from an intruder. The third is the contact call, a soft *wik* in Belize and a faint *chak* in Panama.

Songs, mostly given during the breeding season, consist of a twilight song and a day song. The twilight song is a measured, mellow, whistled chant. In Mexico and Belize, delivered in phrases of 3 Low-pitched notes sounding like *chuck per chick*, or in L. I. Davis' words, *be-care-ful*, with different syllables emphasized in different versions; usually repeats 3–6 phrases in a song and delivers 5–6 songs/min. Sings mostly in the late afternoon and for a brief period at dawn; given from low vegetation. In Panama, this song is 4-noted, somewhat squeaky, Low- to Moderate-pitched, and whistled, e.g., *whoo wher, ta-bek*.

In Belize, the day song may be given at any time, most often in the morning. It consists of a rapid Low-pitched series of double-noted mellow whistles usually on a slightly rising scale and volume, *churkle teerkle teekle teekle teekle teep*; length and speed vary considerably, averaging 12 notes at 5 notes/sec. In Panama, the day song appears to be a soft whistled *wheh-cherk-wuh, wher-cherk-weh, wherk chee*.

Breeding

In Belize, 33 nests were found inside forests, most often in saplings between the trunk and small branches or the petioles of large leaves. Saplings used were 1.4–7 m high; nests were placed one-quarter to nine-tenths of the way up (highest was 3.7 m). (Willis 1961.) In other localities, nests were placed 1–5 m up in shrubs and spiny small palms; once in a cluster of orchids on a vine 0.2 m off the ground.

In Belize, the female alone builds the loose cup nest of leaves, vines, and other bulky material. Males accompany mates and sometimes inspect the nest. Occasionally other female-plumaged birds (presumably subadults) follow and help a female build her nest. Two to 4, usually 3, white eggs are incubated by females for 12–14 days. Both parents, and sometimes the female-plumaged helpers, feed the young. Food is carried hidden in the bill.

The large majority of eggs and nestlings are lost to predators. On about the 9th day after hatching, and before they can fly, nestlings are led from the nest by the parents and hidden in the undergrowth. Parents display to distract intruders when young are near or on the ground. After fledging, young are led through the forest in a characteristic fashion—as the male scolds, the female utters a series of rapid *week* notes and low scolds until the young birds follow. As soon as one takes wing, one or both parents crisscross its path in a shielding flight. Rarely raise a second brood. (Willis 1961.) Young birds associate with their parents for their first year (Willis 1972a). Breeding dates: Mexico April, May, and Aug. Belize May–July. El Salvador June. Panama May.

Sources

Primary Willis 1960a, 1960c, 1961, 1972a. **Weights** (male n = 86; female n = 62): Hartman 1955; Hartman and Brownell 1961; Klaas 1968; LSUMZ data; Paynter 1955; Russell 1964; Smithe 1966; Strauch 1977. **Stomach contents** Hallinan 1924; Stone 1918. **Vocalizations** LNS recordings by L. I. Davis (13), Morton (4), Lancaster (1), Parker (1), and Thurber (4); Davis 1972; Edwards 1972; Slud 1964; Willis 1960c, 1972a. **Nests, eggs, and breeding dates:** Alvarez del Toro 1952; Dickey and van Rossem 1938; LSUMZ data; Peck 1910; Stone 1918; Sutton, Lea, and Edwards 1950; Wetmore, Pasquier, and Olson 1984; Willis 1961, 1972a.

Habia atrimaxillaris 80
Black-cheeked Ant-Tanager
Plate 11

Length 19 cm (7½ in.). Weight 48.9 g (1 male). Monotypic.

Geographic Range

S COSTA RICA around the Golfo Dulce region in s Puntarenas.

Elevational Range

Lowlands.

Habitat and Behavior

Inhabits undergrowth of tall second growth, broken forest, and streamside woodlands; occasionally occurs inside patches of fairly tall forest. Lives in pairs or groups of 3–4 individuals, presumably families. Sometimes accompanies mixed flocks of small insectivorous species. Active but sedentary; occupies a territory of 4–6 ha. (Willis 1972a).

Eats mostly animal matter including spiders, roaches, and long-horned grasshoppers but regularly squeezes juice from small fruits. Forages in the understory 1–6 m above the ground. Peers about, mostly from perches on horizontal bare twigs 1–2 cm in diam. Picks insects from leaves and branches, often after darting or fluttering to snatch prey. Shakes leaf clusters; inspects rotten limbs and vine tangles.

Wanders widely over army ant swarms. Very active at swarms when in areas of second growth and forest openings but does not follow swarms in tall forest. Commonly carries prey to the ground beyond the ants for dismembering and mashing.

Vocalizations

Calls: include scolds that sound like paper tearing, a harsh *zurzurzurzurzur*, *chak* grunts, and contact calls sounding like *chek* or *chuk*. Also emits static (like that of a long-distance radio), an apparent alarm call. Male often gives a rattle when approaching the female (Willis 1972a). Dawn song: mellow whistled phrases, 6–11 (most often 7) phrases/song,

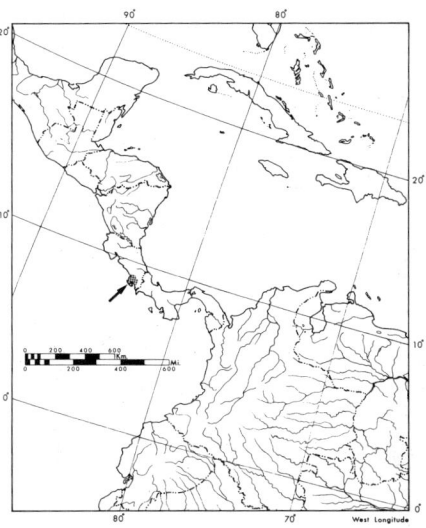

Habia atrimaxillaris

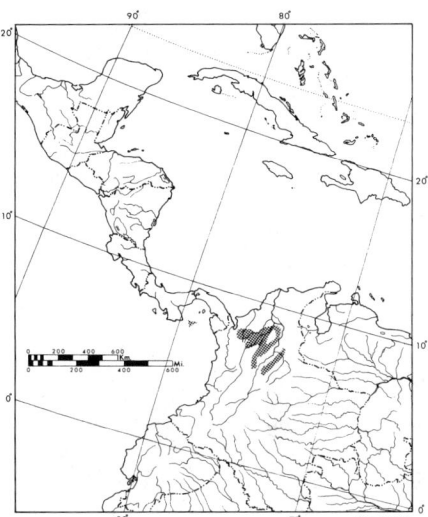

Habia gutturalis

7–8 songs/min.; usually sounds like *chonk TWEEah, chonk TWEEah*, etc, often ends with a single *chonk*; typically Low-pitched, sometimes Moderate-pitched; occasionally alternates pitch. Stays hidden in the underbrush while singing.

Breeding

Willis (1972a) observed repeated courtship feeding by the male of one pair and precopulatory display and calls by the female.

Sources

Primary Slud 1964; Willis 1972a. **Weights (n = 1)** LSUMZ data. **Vocalizations** LNS recordings by L. I. Davis (8); Slud 1964; Willis 1972a.

Habia gutturalis 81
Sooty Ant-Tanager
Plate 11

Length 20 cm (7½ in.). Monotypic.

Geographic Range

Nw COLOMBIA along the n base of the Andes from Córdoba eastward to Santander and thence southward along both sides of the Magdalena Valley to n Tolima and n Cundinamarca.

Elevational Range

Ca. 100–1000 m.

Habitat and Behavior

Inhabits undergrowth of tall second growth and patchy woodland, frequently along streams. May have benefitted from forest destruction (see Willis 1972a). Lives in pairs or family groups of 3–4 individuals. Often associates with mixed-species flocks of insectivorous birds. Travels slowly in company with mixed flocks; wary and fast-moving when alone. Defends a home territory; neighbors do not appear to trespass even at army ant swarms. Hostile encounters involve chattering, sudden wing flits, and tail flicks. In response to song imitations, males usually fly back and forth with crests raggedly spread, bodies compressed and upright, and tails closed and down. (Willis 1972a.)

Highly insectivorous; usually forages 1–5 m above the ground, higher (4–10 m) in patches of tall forest (Willis 1972a). Searches for insects from bare horizontal perches with good views of foliage; makes horizontal flights to other perches or sudden sallies to foliage to capture prey. Follows army ant swarms; repeatedly sallies to foliage above the ants but also captures insects on the ground. Tends to wander over or around swarms. While Willis did not observe fruit eating, Salmon recorded fruit as food (Sclater and Salvin 1879).

Vocalizations

Utters a fast chatter, *chak-cha-cha-cha-cha-cha*, 5–15 notes at 5 notes/sec., often ending with one or more *chagat* notes, like static on a radio. Delivers *chak* notes while foraging. Contact notes: *wik*, rattles, and other notes. Dawn song: the most musical of ant-tanagers; typically a series of 2–3 rich thrushlike whistles repeated at 2 notes/sec. with 6–11 notes/song. Examples of notes include *cheh*, *wher*, *whereyeh*, *whoa*, *pong*, and *where'erer*. Songs are sung near the nest or when the female is out of sight. The female often gives a chatter and static in answer. At dawn and dusk, songs are given loudly and regularly, 6–9 songs/min. as the male moves from place to place low in dense second growth or along forest edge. (Willis 1972a.)

Breeding

Willis (1972a) found a nest 0.5 m above a creek in a patch of tall forest. The rather leafy cup was set in the crown of a fishtail palm and contained 2 young who were fed by both parents. Salmon (in Sclater and Salvin 1879) describes deep cups, loosely made of roots and fibers and lined with ferns, placed in low bushes alongside mountain streams. Eggs are white or pale gray, marked with reddish brown and lilac, especially at the large end. Breeding dates: Colombia April and May.

Sources

Primary Sclater and Salvin 1879; Willis 1972a. **Vocalizations** Willis 1972a. **Nests, eggs, and breeding dates** Ogilvie-Grant 1912; Sclater and Salvin 1879; Willis 1972a.

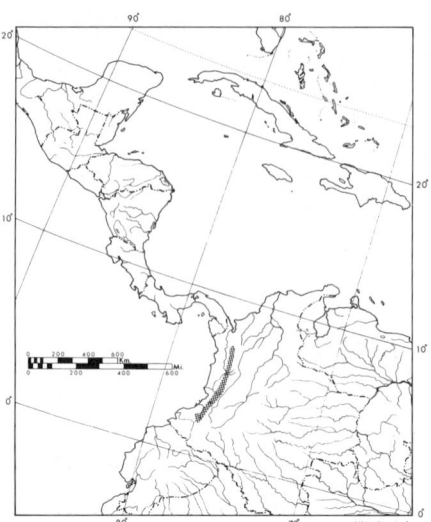

Habia cristata

Habia cristata **82**
Crested Ant-Tanager
Plate 11

Length 19 cm (7½ in.). Monotypic.

Geographic Range

COLOMBIA on the w slope of the W Andes from Antioquia southward to s Cauca (Cerro Munchique); locally on the e slope of the W Andes (Willis 1972a).

Elevational Range

700–1800 m.

Habitat and Behavior

Inhabits thick vegetation in areas where landslides maintain low forest tangles along mountain rivers rushing through deep cut gorges. Usually remains within dense growth but occasionally crosses openings to woodlots and isolated trees in pastures. May be endangered (Hilty 1985). Pairs and small groups of 2–5 individuals, probably families, move rapidly through the undergrowth on irregular routes; individuals usually stay 1–10 m apart. Frequently associates with mixed-species flocks and may be a flock leader. Briefly joins feeding aggregations at fruiting trees.

Appears to forage over a territory of about 5–8 ha. In a boundary dispute between 2 families, most group members intermingled, foraging and calling, while 2 males postured about 1 m apart at the center of activity. The combatants spread and raised crests, fluffed out feathers, and spread tails. At the same time, they alternated facing each other and turning in opposite directions. After about an hour, the families parted.

Eats mostly insects including caterpillars; also fruit. Normally forages 1–10 m above the ground, occasionally higher on steep slopes or in fruiting trees; rarely descends to the ground. Searches for food primarily from perches with good visibility, usually atop horizontal bare branches less than 3 cm in diam. on the outer parts of low trees and bushes. Mostly scans foliage for 5–10 sec. from a perch but sometimes peers around for as long as a min. Often works upward from perch to perch, and then drops to near the base of the next tree or bush. Occasionally ascends or descends a sloping sapling, vine, or tree fern while pivoting back and forth. (Willis 1966b.)

Captures prey by reaching out to twigs or

leaves above or below its perch. Also flutters or hovers briefly to pick insects or fruit, and sallies to snap prey off substrates or to catch falling prey. Uses its bill to extract insects from plucked off dead rolled-up leaves and hunches over to mash or dismember large prey or fruit. Regularly eats *Miconia*, palm, and a variety of other fruits, but usually takes only a few fruits at any one time. (Willis 1966b.)

Ten individuals were observed at an army ant swarm at 1700 m. They foraged mainly 1–2 m off the ground along the edge of and in front of the swarm. (Gochfeld and Tudor 1978.)

Vocalizations

Scolds intruders violently. With body pointed downward, head extended horizontally, and yellow gape flashing conspicuously, the bird utters a very loud sharp *chiv-eek* or *guy-eek* that starts like paper tearing and then glides upward to a piercing squeak; normally given 2–4 times at about 2 notes/sec. Darts among perches or pivots from side to side on the same perch, the long crest raised slightly and tail somewhat spread. (Willis 1966b.)

Other calls: a sharp loud *chip!* to keep in contact; *ch'ree ch'ree* or a sharp series of loud *chee* notes when joining others or fleeing; and a soft series of *chie* notes used by the female soliciting copulation. Dawn song: rather unmusical and monotonous *che'ik* sounds, 1–12 notes at a rate of 1.7 notes/sec. (1 individual); 2–4 sec. between songs. Males often sing from perches overhanging rivers. Sings rather upright with crest folded. Another song, given after a boundary dispute, sounded like *check, eek, chek, eek, check* (or *chraik teef*), 3–7 notes/song at 2 notes/sec. (Willis 1966b.)

Breeding

No information.

Sources

Primary Willis 1966b. **Vocalizations** Willis 1966b.

PIRANGA

Most *Piranga* tanagers (Table 12) live in the upper portions of trees, and although they regularly come lower, preferred trees are usually the tallest in the area. Exceptions are the Rose-throated, Red-headed, and some races of the Hepatic Tanager, all of which are often encountered in low scrubby vegetation.

Table 12 The *Piranga* Tanagers

83	*P. bidentata*	Flame-colored Tanager
84	*P. flava*	Hepatic Tanager
	84-1 *hepatica* subspecies group	Northern Hepatic-T.
	84-2 *lutea* subspecies group	Highland Hepatic-T.
	84-3 *flava* subspecies group	Lowland Hepatic-T.
85	*P. rubra*	Summer Tanager
86	*P. roseogularis*	Rose-throated Tanager
87	*P. olivacea*	Scarlet Tanager
88	*P. ludoviciana*	Western Tanager
89	*P. leucoptera*	White-winged Tanager
90	*P. erythrocephala*	Red-headed Tanager
91	*P. rubriceps*	Red-hooded Tanager

Piranga species take both insects and fruit, but most appear to be mainly insectivorous, locating insects by peering about and then capturing them by reaching out or lunging forward, less often through short sallies to vegetation. Most *Piranga* tanagers also obtain a substantial number of insects in aerial sallies; the Summer Tanager and some races of the Hepatic Tanager skillfully catch bees and wasps in the air.

Piranga tanagers are not very gregarious and are most often encountered in pairs. The species that nest in North America tend to be solitary on their wintering grounds although they form small groups when returning north in the spring, as do the Hepatic Tanagers in Argentina when they migrate in the austral winter.

Typical *Piranga* songs are composed of series of Low- to Moderate-pitched mellow phrases that when put together have a caroling quality—suggesting the songs of many *Turdus* thrushes. The Red-hooded and White-winged Tanagers are exceptions; their songs incorporate high thin notes.

In the boreal summer, the Summer and Scarlet Tanagers are sympatric over a wide area of eastern North America. In these areas of sympatry, the Summer Tanager tends to establish territories in more open habitats than it does in regions where its congener is absent, and the Scarlet Tanager tends to establish territories in denser habitats than it does where there is no range overlap. Moreover, in sympatry, both species respond aggressively to the other's song, and they countersing. As a result, sympatric Scarlet and Summer Tanagers typically occupy neighboring, nonoverlapping territories. (See Shy 1984b, 1984c.)

The geographic ranges of the Western

and Hepatic Tanagers, the other two *Piranga* species in the USA, overlap little with one another or with the ranges of the Scarlet and Summer Tanagers. Where the Western, Hepatic, and Summer Tanagers are sympatric in the southwestern USA, they tend to segregate by elevation and by habitat. The Scarlet and Western Tanagers may hybridize (see Mengel 1963).

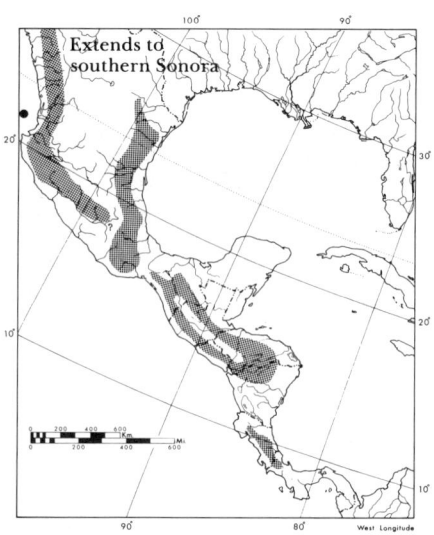

Piranga bidentata

Piranga bidentata 83
Flame-colored Tanager
Plate 12

Length 18–19 cm (7–7½ in.). Weight 34 g (29.8–39.0 g). Four subspecies. Breeds in subadult plumage (Skutch 1967a). Also known as the Stripe-backed Tanager.

Geographic Range

P. b. bidentata: the Pacific slope from s Sonora and s Chihuahua southward to Guerrero and eastward to the states of México and Morelos, MEXICO. *P. b. flammea*: Tres Marías Is., Nayarit, MEXICO. *P. b. sanguinolenta*: the Atlantic slope from c Nuevo León and s Tamaulipas southward to Puebla and Veracruz, MEXICO, and both slopes (probably) in Oaxaca, MEXICO, and from Chiapas, MEXICO, through GUATEMALA, HONDURAS, and EL SALVADOR, to nc NICARAGUA (*A.O.U. Checklist*). *P. b. citrea*: both slopes from s Alajuela, COSTA RICA, to c Chiriquí (Ridgely *in litt.*), w PANAMA.

Elevational Range

Highlands from ca. 800 m to treeline; rarely lower, to near sea level in Guatemala (Land 1970). Mostly above 1800 m in Costa Rica and 1200 m in Panama.

Habitat and Behavior

Primarily inhabits forest and forest edge, but also occurs in open woodland, including pine-oak woods, scattered trees in neighboring fields and pastures, and gardens and other suburban areas where there are large trees. Wanders widely when not breeding. Usually solitary or in pairs, sometimes in small groups. Joins feeding aggregations. Occasionally associates with mixed-species flocks (Moynihan 1962c).

Typically forages in the highest branches of tall trees but sometimes descends to lower levels, even to fruiting bushes; rarely on or near the ground. Takes a variety of fruits including those of melastomes and *Ficus*, and appears to eat insects (no insect-foraging data recorded). In Costa Rica, eagerly ate the berries of *Satyria Warszewiczii* taking a whole berry and skillfully manipulating it in the bill to remove the contents from the tough skin; swallowed both pulp and seeds (Skutch 1967a).

Vocalizations

Calls: a loud harsh Moderate- to Low-pitched *prreck*, a very rapid *chit-t-t-i-tuk*, and a musical *chirrup*. Song: a rich but somewhat throaty or tremulous caroling of 1–6, usually 3–4, bisyllabic notes, *churWEE chirROO churREEZ*; Moderate- and Low-pitched; delivered at about 1 note/sec., sometimes faster; pauses 4–6 sec. between groups of notes. In Costa Rica, males sing in the tops of shade trees isolated in pastures, sometimes on the topmost spire (Skutch 1967a). While a male sang in one tree, a female called *prr-rt prr-rt* from a neighboring tree (Skutch 1967a).

Breeding

Four nests: One was placed within dense foliage at the top of a midsized tree, and another was about 7.5 m up on an exposed shoot at the top of a *Viburnum*; both tree and shrub were standing in pastures (Skutch 1967a). The third nest was located 1 m above the ground in a tangle of bushes and vines, and the fourth was 2.5 m up in a coffee tree (Blake 1956). The loosely constructed open cup is made of rootlets and twigs and lined with grass. Eggs (2–3) are pale or greenish blue, lightly speckled reddish brown or shades of lavender, chiefly at the large end. A male was seen to feed the young at one nest (Skutch 1967a). Breeding dates: Costa Rica April and May. Panama May.

Sources

Primary Blake 1956; Edwards 1972; Leck 1972b; Leck and Hilty 1968; Ridgely 1976; Skutch 1967a; Slud 1964; Wetmore, Pasquier, and Olson 1984. **Weights (n = 14)** LSUMZ data; Martin, Robins, and Heed 1954. **Vocalizations** LNS recordings by L. I. Davis (3), Morton (1), Parker (2), Thurber (1); Chapman 1898; Edwards 1972; Peterson and Chalif 1973; Ridgely 1976; Skutch 1967a; Slud 1964; Sutton and Pettingill 1942. **Nests, eggs, and breeding dates** Blake 1956; Ogilvie-Grant 1912; Skutch 1967a.

Piranga flava 84
Hepatic Tanager

Although it extends from the southeastern USA to northern Argentina, the range of *Piranga flava* is discontinuous, and ecological differences among subspecies have created uncertainty as to whether more than one species is involved. Zimmer (1929a) concluded that there was only one species, and the *Peters Check-List*, which we follow, agrees. However, to provide a clearer understanding of the natural histories of the various forms of *Piranga flava*, we have separated the data into three subspecies groups following another possible arrangement noted in the *A.O.U. Check-list*.

The northernmost races, ranging from the USA to Nicaragua and comprising the *hepatic* subspecies group, have a predilection for pine forest or pine-oak associations. As a separate species, the English name would be Northern Hepatic-Tanager. The central subspecies, ranging from eastern Central America to western and northern South America (mostly in mountains and foothills) and comprising the *lutea* subspecies group, prefer open broad-leafed woodlands and forest borders. If specifically distinct, the English name would be Highland Hepatic-Tanager. The southernmost subspecies, ranging east of the Andes and comprising the *flava* subspecies group, inhabit islands of savanna and other semiopen situations in Amazonia and are more widely distributed in open woodlands and semiopen situations south of Amazonia to Argentina. As a separate species, the English name would be Lowland Hepatic-Tanager. In addition to habitat differences, vocalizations differ somewhat among the groups.

Piranga flava
(*hepatica* subspecies group   84-1)
Northern Hepatic-Tanager
Plate 12

Length 18 cm (7 in.). Weight 37 g (32.0–47.4 g). Five subspecies. First year males retain and breed in subadult plumage resembling female plumage (Dickey and van Rossem 1938). Streaked brown in juvenal plumage.

Geographic Range

P. f. hepatica, *dextra*, and *albifacies*: from extreme s California, Arizona, New Mexico, and w Texas (casually to c California, s Nevada, s Wyoming, and Louisiana, LSUMZ; and accidental in Illinois, *A.O.U. Check-list*), USA, and Nuevo León and Tamaulipas, MEXICO, southeastward through the highlands (nearby lowlands in winter) of MEXICO, GUATEMALA, EL SALVADOR, and HONDURAS to nc NICARAGUA.
P. f. figlina: BELIZE and e GUATEMALA.
P. f. savannarum: extreme e HONDURAS and ne NICARAGUA.

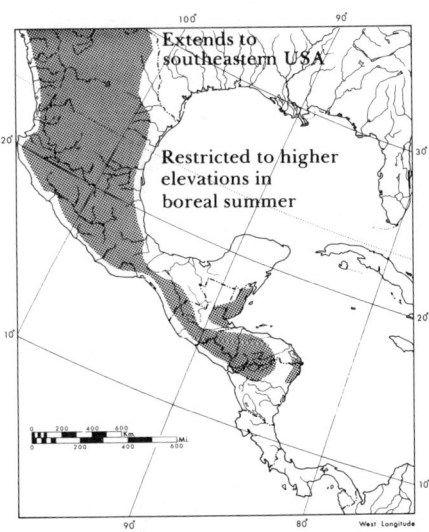

Piranga flava (*hepatica* subspecies group)

Elevational Range

P. f. hepatica, dextra, and *albifacies*: ca. 1000–2500 m, locally higher; mostly 1600–2300 m in the USA; ca. 1100 m in El Salvador; and 600–1800 m in Honduras. Withdraws from n portion of its range and descends to lowlands in boreal winter. *P. f. figlina* and *savannarum*: near sea level.

Habitat and Behavior

Prefers groves of tall trees, typically pine-oak associations in highlands. (See Shy 1984c for tree density and other measures of habitat characteristics in the sw USA.) Lowland subspecies live in pine savannas and occasionally wander for short periods into adjacent broad-leafed woodland edge or coffee plantations. Also lives in pure pine or pure oak woodlands in highlands and, in winter months, occurs in parks and gardens where there are numerous trees. Lives in pairs, sometimes in groups of 4–6 (rarely to 10) individuals during the nonbreeding season. Members of a pair follow each other in swift flight. Strongly territorial in the breeding season; pairs frequently bicker and chase each other when boundaries are crossed (Marshall 1957).

Forages mostly in foliage, from low in small oak trees to the upper branches of tall pines; also visits fruiting shrubs and trees; rarely descends to the ground. Appears to be primarily insectivorous. In the USA, hops slowly and rather awkwardly among branches, constantly stopping to peer at foliage; reaches out deliberately among leaves to pick off prey. Flies low from one tree to the next. Usually takes flying insects by deviating slightly from a direct course to a new perch; occasionally makes long graceful aerial sallies in spaces between trees. One bird sallied to outer foliage on its way to the next tree; another fed by leaping from branches into foliage. (Marshall 1957.)

Eats a variety of vegetable material including domestic peppers, wild grapes and cherries, and *Miconia* berries. Attracted to flowers of agaves, madrones, and oaks. Observed taking nectar at flowering trees (Cruden and Hermann-Parker 1977). Stomach contents (6): insects, including large ants.

Vocalizations

Song: a musical caroling of 5–7 rising and falling bisyllabic phrases, clear and mellow, *twee-hee chu-WAITE cha-ha* etc; Low- to Moderate-pitched, delivered in 3–4 sec. (see Shy 1984b); 9–10 sec. between songs (1 bird). Sometimes the bisyllabic phrases are delivered in pairs in the manner of the Summer Tanager, *P. rubra* 85. In the USA, at dawn during the breeding season, males sang for about half an hour from a favorite perch in a pine, then they moved about singing from various trees for a while, and finally fell quiet until the next day (Marshall 1957). Call note: a soft abrupt Moderate- to Low-pitched *tchuk* or *chuck*. One bird delivered one song phrase at a time frequently uttering *tchuk* before and after the phrase (Stein and Angstadt, LNS).

Breeding

Loosely constructed cups, made of plant fibers and twigs and sometimes lined with pine needles, are typically built in oak or pine trees at the ends of branches 2–15 m above the ground. One observation each of a male carrying nesting material and of a female building a nest accompanied by her mate (Howell 1972). The female appears to incubate alone. Eggs (3–5, usually 4) are pale blue or greenish blue, marked brown, often concentrated in a wreath at the large end. In defense of young, scolds intruders with harsh tones (Henslow in Bent 1965). Breeding dates: USA May–July. Mexico May and June. Belize Aug. Nicaragua April.

Sources

Primary Dickey and van Rossem 1938; Edwards 1972; Howell 1965, 1972; Marshall 1957; Martin, Robins, and Heed 1954; Rand and Traylor 1954; Rowley 1966; Russell 1964; Shy 1984b. **Weights (n = 72)** LSUMZ data; Martin, Robins, and Heed 1954; Poole 1938; Russell 1964; Schaldach 1969. **Stomach contents** Howell 1972; Marshall 1957. **Vocalizations** LNS recordings by L. I. Davis (1), Fish (1), Stein and Angstadt (1); Bent 1965; Edwards 1972. **Nests, eggs, and breeding dates** Bent 1965; Howell 1972; Martin, Robins, and Heed 1954; Nehrkorn 1899; Robins and Heed 1951; Rowley 1962, 1966, 1984; Willis in Russell 1964; USNM.

Piranga flava
(*lutea* subspecies group   84-2)
Highland Hepatic-Tanager
Plate 12

Length 17 cm (7 in.). Weight 34 g (28.0–40.4 g). Six subspecies. Subadult male resembles female but is irregularly tinged red.

Geographic Range

P. f. testacea: both slopes from n Guanacaste, COSTA RICA, to Darién (Cana) and San Blas, PANAMA. *P. f. toddi* and *faceta*: the

Piranga flava (*lutea* subspecies group)

n end of the E Andes in Cesar and Norte de Santander, COLOMBIA; the Santa Marta Mountains, COLOMBIA; the Perijá Mountains; n VENEZUELA in Táchira and from e Zulia, Falcón, and Lara eastward to Sucre; and TRINIDAD. *P. f. haemalea*: the tepuis in s VENEZUELA (Amazonas and Bolívar) and adjacent n BRAZIL (Serro Imerí) eastward through c GUYANA and c SURINAME (Davis 1980; probably this race).
P. f. desidiosa and *lutea*: locally on both slopes above the Cauca Valley from Antioquia to Cauca, COLOMBIA; the Pacific slope from Valle, COLOMBIA, southward through w ECUADOR and w PERU to Lima; and the e Andean slope from the Northern Peruvian Low southward through PERU and nw BOLIVIA to Cochabamba.

Elevational Range

Mostly foothills and mountains, descending to sea level along the Pacific coast in Ecuador and Peru; 600–1200 m in Costa Rica and Panama; 800–1800 m in Venezuela; 200–1800 m in the Santa Marta Mountains; 1500–2200 m in w Colombia; as high as 3150 m in Peru but typically much lower.

Habitat and Behavior

Prefers tall trees in open woodland, second growth, adjacent clearings and coffee plantations, at forest edge, along streams and rivers, and in orchards, parks, and suburban areas. Also occurs in humid forest in Costa Rica (Slud 1964) and montane scrub in Peru (Parker, Parker, and Plenge 1982). In e Panamá province, Panama, survived the substantial deforestation of an area (Ridgely in Wetmore, Pasquier, and Olson 1984). Single birds or pairs usually travel alone but at times associate with mixed-species flocks. Apparently covers a large territory daily; flight is slightly undulating (Slud 1964). In Trinidad, the male points his bill skyward in display, showing the bright throat, and moves his head from side to side (ffrench 1973).

Forages mostly high in trees (in Colombia, 15 m or higher, Miller 1963) but occasionally descends to quite close to the ground; comes to the ground at times to dismember prey (Hilty data). Peers deliberately at foliage and twigs (Hilty and Brown 1986) and searches the undersides of branches (Slud 1964). In Valle, Colombia, also sallied to air and to branches and flutter-pursued; observed smashing a large beetle against a limb, and one bird ate a 10 cm caterpillar (Hilty data). In Trinidad, prey included butterflies (ffrench 1973). In Peru, put a curled dead leaf in the fork of a branch to pry it open (Parker data).

Also eats buds, berries, and other fruit. Seen probing flowers (Parker data). Said to be a pest in corn fields (Ginés et al. 1952). Stomach contents: animal matter (5); vegetable matter (1); both (2). Contents included beetles, caterpillars, a bee, an orthopteran, and seeds.

Vocalizations

Calls: In the Andes, an abrupt *chup*, loud yet soft in quality, delivered rapidly when alarmed; also *jree uree?* In Panama and Costa Rica, calls include *chup chitup* or longer variants, e.g., a rapid *chup-ti-ti-tup*; Low- to Moderate-pitched. Also a high-pitched *chip-i-ty, chip-i-ty, chicky-tick-tick* (Wetmore, Pasquier, and Olson 1984). Song: consists of abrupt single and double notes that may be soft or slightly throaty, *chup wher wheet-ti choo wheet cher!* etc; Moderate- and Low-pitched; delivered in long sequences at the rate of 1–2 notes/sec. and at a rather even pace, somewhat like the song of a *Turdus* thrush; pauses 2–6 sec. between sequences.

Breeding

In Trinidad, a nest made of dry grass was situated 6 m above the ground amidst the sprouting vegetation of a trimmed forest tree at a clearing edge (ffrench 1973). In Colombia, nests were frail flat structures of fine rootlets: 2 were placed among roots under an overhanging bank by a roadside on a mountain slope, and a third was 0.6 m up in a small shrub on top of the bank along a road (Todd and Carriker 1922). Eggs (2) are blue or greenish, spotted with gray, violet, or brown. Both parents feed the young (ffrench 1973). Breeding dates: Trinidad Feb, July, and Oct.

Sources

Primary ffrench 1973; Hilty data; Hilty and Brown 1986; Morton 1979; Parker data; Ridgely 1976; Slud 1964; Todd and Carriker 1922; Wetmore, Pasquier, and Olson 1984. **Weights (n = 37)** ffrench 1973; LSUMZ data; Miller 1963; Strauch 1977. **Stomach contents** LSUMZ data; Stolzmann in Taczanowski 1884b; Goldman in Wetmore, Pasquier, and Olson 1984. **Vocalizations** LNS recordings by Parker (2), Schwartz (12), van den Berg (1); recording by R. A. Rowlett (1); ffrench 1973; Parker data; Ridgely 1976; Slud 1964; Wetmore, Pasquier, and Olson 1984. **Nests, eggs, and breeding dates** ffrench 1973; Nehrkorn 1899; Todd and Carriker 1922.

Piranga flava
(*flava* subspecies group   84-3)
Lowland Hepatic-Tanager
Plate 12

Length 18 cm (7 in.). Weight 35 g (30.3–40.6 g). Four subspecies. First year male subadult plumage resembles female plumage (Wetmore 1926). Streaked brown in juvenal plumage.

Geographic Range

P. f. macconnelli: from e Roraima, BRAZIL, and s GUYANA southeastward through s SURINAME (Davis 1980; probably this race) and FRENCH GUIANA (probably). *P. f. saira, rosacea,* and *flava*: c Pará and Amapá (Novaes 1978), BRAZIL; c Maranhão and Alagoas (Pinto 1954), BRAZIL, southward through e BRAZIL to n Rio Grande do Sul and westward to e and s Mato Grosso, BRAZIL; BOLIVIA (Cochabamba and Santa Cruz southward); PARAGUAY; and sw Rio Grande do Sul, BRAZIL, southward through w URUGUAY, and ARGENTINA to Mendoza (Vigil 1973), Córdoba, and n Buenos Aires.

Elevational Range

Sea level to ca. 2050 m.

Habitat and Behavior

Inhabits open forest or woodland and open areas with scattered trees and bushes such as savanna, riparian woodland, and cerrado;

Piranga flava (*flava* subspecies group)

also eucalyptus groves in se Brazil (Sick 1985); mostly occurs in deciduous woodlands in the south and savanna in the n portion of its range. Is expanding its distribution in Brazil with deforestation (Sick 1985). Migrates north from the extreme s part of its range in the austral winter; only found in the former state of Guanabara, Brazil, in the winter (Sick 1985). Seasonally moves from wooded mountain ravines to valleys in Córdoba, Argentina (White and Sclater 1883). Usually encountered in pairs; in Argentina, forms groups in migration. Tends to stay hidden within foliage; rests in the highest branches (Vigil 1973). When excited, wags tail slowly and regularly; flight is undulating (Wetmore 1926).

Forages mostly in the upper branches of the tallest trees, sometimes lower, but rarely descends to the ground. Favors bees and wasps; captures insects in flight with great skill (Vigil 1973). Eats a variety of berries (Lillo 1889) and fruit, especially figs (Descourtilz 1852). Stomach contents: animal matter (1); animal and vegetable matter (3). Contents included termites, coleopterans, hymenopterans, hemipterans, feathers, and fruit pulp. Also eats caterpillars and spiders (Bertoni 1898).

Vocalizations

Calls: variously rendered as a soft *chef* (Ridgely *in litt.*), *chu chu* (Wetmore 1926), and a loud *tchip* or *tcherit* (rendered in Portuguese, Sick 1985). Song: a frequently repeated *tschip-tschurr* (rendered in Spanish, Vigil 1973); melodious but little varied (Sick 1985).

Breeding

Builds a loosely woven, flat, cup-shaped nest made of dry leaves, roots, grass stems, etc, usually placed on the highest branches of trees but also as low as 2 m above ground in bushes. Eggs (3–4) are greenish-blue or white, marked reddish brown or cinnamon. Breeding dates: Brazil (Rio Grande do Sul) Nov. Paraguay Oct.

Sources

Primary Descourtilz 1852; Pereyra 1938; Sick 1985; Vigil 1973; Wetmore 1926. **Weights (n = 8)** Belton 1985; Fry 1970; LSUMZ data; Sick 1958. **Stomach contents** Moojen, Carvalho, and Lopes 1941; Schubart, Aguirre, and Sick 1965. **Vocalizations** Ridgely *in litt.*; Sick 1985; Vigil 1973; Wetmore 1926. **Nests, eggs, and breeding dates** Belton 1985; Bertoni 1898, 1918; Santos 1948; Vigil 1973.

Piranga rubra **85**
Summer Tanager
In Boreal Summer
Plate 12

Length 17–18 cm (6½–7 in.). Weight 26 g (23.9–38.1 g). Two subspecies. First year males resemble females, but often acquire patches of red during the first winter (Bent 1965). Lightly streaked in juvenal plumage.

Geographic Range

In Boreal Summer: from se California, s Nevada, sw Utah, c Arizona, c New Mexico, c and ne Texas, c Oklahoma, e Kansas, se Nebraska, c Iowa (formerly), c (formerly n) Illinois, s Wisconsin (formerly), c Indiana, c Ohio, sw Pennsylvania, West Virginia, Virginia, e Maryland, s Delaware, and s New Jersey, USA (often wanders further north, to s CANADA; accidental in the British Isles), southward to ne Baja California, se Sonora, n Durango, se Coahuila, and c Nuevo León, MEXICO, and s Texas, the Gulf coast, and s Florida, USA. (*A.O.U. Check-list.*)

Elevational Range

In Boreal Summer: lowlands to ca. 1500 m; sometimes higher, to 1900 m (Ligon 1961) in sw USA.

Habitat and Behavior

In the eastern portion of its range, primarily inhabits open woodlands of mixed oak and other hardwood trees and oak-pine woodlands. In the west, typically lives in riparian woodlands of cottonwoods, willows, or mesquites; occasionally in oak woodland. (See Shy 1984c for measures of tree density and other habitat characteristics.) Also occurs in orchards, parks, and roadside trees. Pairs (solitary before and after the breeding season) typically stay concealed in the upper foliage of the tallest trees. In display, the adult male spreads his wings and tail and raises his bill skyward (Sutton in Bent 1965). Observed anting (Thomas 1941).

Forages primarily in the tops of trees. Appears to be primarily insectivorous. Typically sallies to air for flying insects; favors bees which it takes to a perch to knock off the protruding abdomen (stinger) before eating. Frequently attacks wasps until they desert their nest, then devours their larvae. Also hovers at leaves and searches along branches, moving slowly and deliberately, peering around, and picking at leaves, bark, flowers, and fruit.

In a willow-dominated habitat in Arizona, foraged at all heights from just above the ground to the tops of 21 m trees; rarely dropped to the ground; foraged mostly in the outer portions of trees, usually from branches less than 7.5 cm in diam. Prey taken (mostly flying insects) were less than 30 mm long (Rosenberg, Ohmart, and Anderson 1982). Stomach contents: animal matter (17); vegetable matter (1); both (1). Contents included mostly wasps. Also reported to consume cicadas, grasshoppers, beetles, ants, spiders, caterpillars, dragonflies, weevils, and other arthropods and small fruits such as blackberries and whortleberries.

Vocalizations

Call: a distinctive, mellow, rattling *pit-ti-tuck* or *pit-t-tuck-i-tuck*; Moderate-pitched. Song: utters melodious, clear, bisyllabic notes that are typically given in pairs to form what sometimes sound like a 4-syllable phrase; often delivers about 5 phrases in 3–4 sec., but song is highly variable and may last as long as 44 sec. (see Shy in press); often repeated after pauses of 6–12 sec.; Low- to Moderate-pitched. Songs in the eastern USA are lower in pitch than songs of western populations (see Shy 1983). Compared to the Scarlet Tanager, *P. olivacea* **87,** phrases and songs of the Summer Tanager are more sustained and phrases have purer (sweeter) tones. Songs are mostly delivered from mid-heights (Shy 1983).

Breeding

Courtship appears to begin with frequent, sudden, and spirited pursuits of the female by the male (Fitch and Fitch 1955). The shallow cup nest, made of dry herbaceous vegetation (especially plant stems and grass) and lined with fine grass, is placed on a horizontal branch 2.5–10.5 m above the ground in trees. The female builds the nest alone, accompanied by her mate. Eggs (3–4, rarely 5) are pale blue or greenish blue, heavily spotted reddish brown and faintly marked lilac gray, sometimes forming a cap or wreath at the large end. Incubation by the female takes 11–12 days. Both parents feed the young. Breeding dates: USA May–Aug.

Sources

Primary Bent 1965; Fitch and Fitch 1955; Isler data; Rosenberg, Ohmart, and Anderson 1982; Shy 1983, 1984b, 1984c. **Weights (n = 155)** Child and Marshall 1970; Connell, Odum, and Kale 1960; LSUMZ data; Norris and Johnson 1958. **Stomach contents** Bent 1965; LSUMZ data. **Vocalizations** LNS recordings by L. I. Davis (2), McChesney (2), Stein and Angstadt (1), Stein and Gunn (1); Bent 1965; Peterson 1947; Shy in press. **Nests, eggs, and breeding dates** Bent 1965; Fitch and Fitch 1955; Harrison 1975; Ligon 1961; Nehrkorn 1899; Ogilvie-Grant 1912; Pough 1946; Rosenberg, Ohmart, and Anderson 1982; USNM.

Piranga rubra **85**
Summer Tanager
In Boreal Winter
Plate 12

Length 17–18 cm (6½–7 in.). Weight 28 g (21.6–32.0 g). Two subspecies.

Geographic Range

In Boreal Winter: from s Baja California, s Sinaloa, Mexico State, and Veracruz, MEXICO (rare or casual further north), southward through CENTRAL AMERICA; COLOMBIA; VENEZUELA; TRINIDAD; ECUADOR; and PERU east of the Andes (rare migrant in w PERU, Parker, Parker, and Plenge 1982) southward to Cochabamba (sight, Remsen in press) and El Beni, BOLIVIA (one record in Antofagasta, n CHILE, Prescott 1974); Amazonas, nw BRAZIL (to the Rio Negro and Rio Madeira); GUYANA; and SURINAME (Davis 1979). In migration: n MEXICO, BAHAMA ISLANDS, CUBA, JAMAICA, the CAYMAN ISLANDS, and islands in the w Caribbean Sea (Swan, Providencia, and San Andres); casual or accidental on islands further east——see *A.O.U. Check-list*.

Elevational Range

In Boreal Winter: sea level to around 3100 m; once at treeline in Colombia (Hilty and Brown 1986); generally below 1200 m in Middle America; in n South America, most numerous on lower slopes of mountains.

Habitat and Behavior

Inhabits open woodland and tall second growth, gallery forest, forest edge, shaded plantations, and trees in parks and gardens and along city streets. Also occurs in scrub and low open forest; uncommon inside very dense forest. Often solitary, occasionally in pairs (Morton *in litt.*), and sometimes joins mixed-species flocks, especially at forest borders; also joins feeding aggregations at fruiting trees. Often perches inactively within foliage inside tree canopies, then moves in sudden bursts.

Appears to eat insects more often than fruit. Hunts from mid to upper levels within trees but also comes lower, especially to feed in fruiting shrubs and bushes. Has a liking for bees and wasps; plunders wasp nests and beehives for larvae and pupae. Frequently sallies to air with rapid swooping flights or short sallies. Peers and picks, mostly at leaves. Hovers at foliage, then drops to a nearby perch to swallow its prey. Sometimes mashes insects before eating. Observed attending army ant swarms (Slud 1964), once at 0.5 m above the ground (Willis 1966a).

Also eats a variety of fruit including those of *Miconia*, *Ficus*, and *Cecropia*, mistletoe berries, and arillate fruits. Picks some fruits, including *Cecropia* catkins, in flight. Swallows fruit whole, nibbles around seeds, or squeezes out juice. Pecks holes in oranges still hanging on trees and eats the pulp (Carriker 1910). Stomach contents (7): animal matter, including hymenopterans and dipterans.

Vocalizations

Call: often utters the same distinctive, mellow, rattling, Moderate-pitched *pit-ti-tuck* that is given in summer. In Venezuela, this call is delivered regularly at the rate of 30 calls/min. as an evening song (Schwartz, LNS); also sings this call song in Ucayali, Peru, for about a week in December (O'Neill *in litt.*).

156 PIRANGA

Piranga rubra (in Boreal Winter)

In Costa Rica, sings to establish winter territories on first arrival but rarely thereafter (Skutch 1976).

Breeding

See account for Summer Tanager in Boreal Summer.

Sources

Primary Alvarez del Toro 1950; Dickey and van Rossem 1938; Hilty data; Hilty and Brown 1986; Monroe 1968; Olivares 1969; Parker data; Ridgely 1976; Ridgely and Gaulin 1980; Slud 1964. **Weights (n = 56)** Hartman and Brownell 1961; Leck 1975; Miller 1947, 1963; Rogers and Odum 1966; Smithe 1966; Tashian 1953. **Stomach contents** Brosset 1964; Ginés et al. 1951; Hallinan 1924; LSUMZ data. **Vocalizations** LNS recordings by L. I. Davis (1), Schwartz (1); ffrench 1973; Hilty and Brown 1986; Moynihan 1962c; Slud 1964; Snyder 1966.

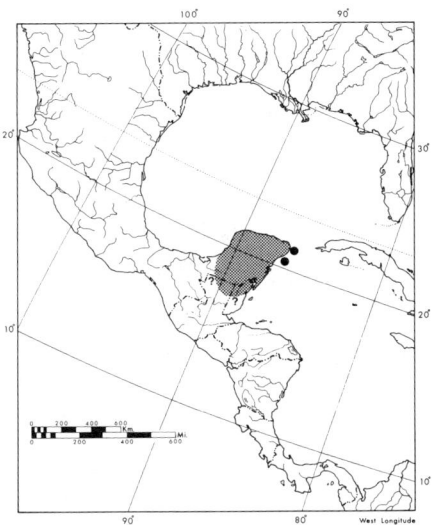

Piranga roseogularis

Piranga roseogularis 86
Rose-throated Tanager
Plate 12

Length 16 cm (6 in.). Weight 24 g (20.7–29.9 g). Three subspecies. First year males resemble females (Chapman 1896).

Geographic Range

Yucatán Peninsula (Campeche, Yucatán, and Quintana Roo) and offshore islands (Cozumel, Meco, and Mujeres), MEXICO, southward to n GUATEMALA (Petén) and BELIZE (Barlow et al. 1972).

Elevational Range

Near sea level.

Habitat and Behavior

Appears to prefer forest edge and scrubby forest with thick undergrowth; also occurs in open country with scattered trees and low scrubby growth. Apparently scarce inside tall forest. Mostly solitary; encountered in pairs during the breeding season and occasionally in small aggregations at a rich food source. Forages from middle to upper levels of midsized trees. Willis (in Russell 1964) saw them foraging in the undergrowth and in saplings. Visits fruiting trees.

Vocalizations

Call: *myaaa*; somewhat plaintive and mewing; Low-pitched, often upward-inflected. Song: 2 clear rich Moderate-pitched notes are followed by several mellow warbled Moderate to Low-pitched phrases and/or single notes, e.g., *wheet cheep wee-ho tu-wee-ho* or *wheet chip whir choo-cho wheer*; typically delivered in 2–4 sec. with pauses of 5–7 sec.

Breeding

No information.

Sources

Primary Barlow et al. 1972; Chapman 1896; Edwards 1972; Land 1970; Paynter 1955; Russell 1964; Smithe 1966; Traylor 1941. **Weights (n = 21)** Barlow et al. 1972; Klaas 1968; LSUMZ data; Paynter 1955; Smithe 1966. **Vocalizations** LNS recordings by L. I. Davis (2), Waide (3).

Piranga olivacea 87
Scarlet Tanager
In Boreal Summer
Plate 12

Length 17 cm (6½ in.). Weight 25 g (23.5–33.0 g). Monotypic. First year male subadult plumage (illus.) is maintained until late winter; bodies of first year males in alternate plumage may be orange red, orange, or yellow (Bent 1965). Streaked brownish in juvenal plumage.

Geographic Range

In Boreal Summer: from e North Dakota, USA, se Manitoba and w Ontario, CANADA, ne Minnesota and n Michigan, USA, s Ontario, sw Quebec, and New Brunswick, CANADA, and c Maine, USA, southward to c Nebraska, w Kansas, nc and se Oklahoma, c Arkansas, wc Tennessee, n Alabama, n Georgia, nw South Carolina, w North Carolina, c Virginia, and Maryland, USA (*A.O.U. Check-list.*) Casual in w North America and ne North America north of breeding range; accidental in Alaska and the British Isles (see *A.O.U. Check-list*).

Elevational Range

In Boreal Summer: lowlands and mountains.

Habitat and Behavior

Inhabits deciduous forest and woodland; also occurs in pine-oak woodland, parks, orchards, and large shade trees in suburban areas. (See Shy 1984c for measures of tree density and other habitat characteristics.) Lives in pairs during the breeding season, mostly solitary at other times. Typically stays concealed within tree foliage, sometimes perching motionless for long periods. Observed anting (Groskin 1943, 1950).

Forages primarily at midheights, generally 6–18 m off the ground, but occasionally descends to the ground or ascends to the topmost tree branches. In New Hampshire, USA, the mean foraging height was 12.8 m where the top of the canopy was 22 m (Sabo and Holmes 1983). Searches for insects on leaves, twigs, and branches, examining the substrates in a leisurely and deliberate manner; often picks at dense leaf clusters in the outer tips of limbs. Also typically sallies for flying insects, particularly hymenopterans (bees, wasps, etc).

Appears to be mostly insectivorous. Prescott (1965) has summarized the literature regarding the food of the Scarlet Tanager, including stomach contents. In addition to hymenopterans captured by aerial sallies, the principal insects taken in summer are lepidopterans (especially caterpillars and moths) and coleopterans (both adult beetles and their larvae). Other animal foods recorded include spiders, dragonflies, orthopterans, and dipterans. In early spring, before foliage has developed or in cold or wet weather, sometimes forages on the ground and in grass for grasshoppers, ground beetles, earthworms, and other terrestrial prey. Eats cultivated fruit such as cherries as well as a variety of wild fruits and berries; also eats tender buds.

Vocalizations

Call: *chip-churr*, first part Moderate-pitched, second part Low-pitched; call varies regionally. When agitated, flicks wings while calling. Other calls include a distress call which is a high-pitched screech descending in pitch; a soft call, e.g., *sweeeee*, given in courtship between pairs; and a nasal, whistlelike call given when one member of a pair arrives at the nest with food (Prescott 1965). Song: suggests a *Turdus* thrush, e.g., the American Robin, but with a hoarse burry quality; 4–5 phrases of double and single (sometimes triple) notes; Low- to Moderate-pitched; songs are typically 2–3 sec. long, and given 4–6 (1–15) times/min.; variable (see Shy 1984a). The male sings from the tops of the highest trees when establishing a breeding territory, afterwards at midheights. The female also sings, usually while gathering nesting material or food; the female's song is softer and shorter than the male's; sometimes male and female alternate song (Prescott 1965).

Breeding

In Michigan, USA: Upon arrival at the breeding grounds, the male establishes a territory by singing almost continuously from conspicuous perches high in the crowns of mature trees. Females are attracted to the singing male, and once paired, the male keeps his mate inside his territory, driving her back if she happens to wander outside the boundaries. Territorial boundaries are not rigid, and males frequently dispute, especially when the female is present. In display, the male holds his wings slightly out from the body, with the wing-tips below the somewhat elevated tail, and utters call notes. If this does not drive the intruder away, both occupant and intruder may adopt the threat-display or may fly at each other until one bird gives way. (Prescott 1965.)

Once paired, the male abandons the high perches and accompanies the female as she forages in lower branches; at times, he sings softly. In courtship, the male descends to low perches on branches projecting 1–2 m up from the forest floor and displays to the female above him by drooping his wings and stretching his neck to expose and elongate the scarlet back patch. The female peers down at her mate from perches 6–9 m above him, pausing when he displays and flying when he does. (Prescott 1965.)

The female chooses the nest site and

builds the nest alone, occasionally accompanied by her mate who resumes his singing loudly and conspicuously from low to medium heights within their territory. The shallow cup nest, made of plant stems, rootlets (ocassionally twigs), and grass and lined with fine fibers, is placed on a horizontal branch 1.2–23 m (mostly 6–18 m) above the ground; nests are sometimes so loosely woven that eggs can be seen from below. Eggs (2–5, mostly 3–4) are dull white to greenish blue, marked with brown, especially at the large end. The female incubates for 12–14 days and is often fed by her mate. Both parents feed insects and fruit to the young. Nestlings depart the nest after 9–15 days. Fledglings are usually independent after 2 weeks. Only one brood is raised. Breeding dates May–July.

Sources

Primary Bent 1965; Harrison 1975; Pough 1946; Prescott 1965; Shy 1983, 1984b, 1984c. **Weights (n = 41)** Baldwin and Kendeigh 1938; Connell, Odum, and Kale 1960; LSUMZ data; Stewart and Skinner 1967. **Stomach contents** LSUMZ data; Prescott 1965; USNM. **Vocalizations** LNS recordings (26); Bent 1965; Mathews 1904; Peterson 1947; Prescott 1965; Shy 1984a. **Nests, eggs, and breeding dates** Bent 1965; Hales 1896; Harrison 1975; Ogilvie-Grant 1912; Patterson and Allen 1968; Pough 1946; Prescott 1964, 1965; USNM.

Piranga olivacea 87
Scarlet Tanager
In Boreal Winter
Plate 12

Length 16 cm (6½ in.). Weight (in migration) 35 g (32.0–38.0 g). Monotypic.

Geographic Range

In Boreal Winter: primarily east of the Andes from COLOMBIA through ECUADOR and PERU to La Paz, BOLIVIA. Extent of range into Amazonian lowlands is unclear; extends at least to Iquitos, Loreto, PERU (Parker *in litt.*). Scattered winter records from the PANAMA lowlands, COLOMBIA north and west of the Andes, and single records from along the Pacific slope in La Libertad (Koepcke 1961) and Lima (Plenge et al. 1985), PERU. Migrates primarily through Caribbean lowlands of MIDDLE AMERICA (from Yucután, MEXICO, south) and COLOMBIA; rare on Caribbean islands.

Elevational Range

In Boreal Winter: mostly 100–1300 m; to 2000 m in Colombia (sight record at 3000 m Hilty and Brown 1986).

Habitat and Behavior

Infrequently observed and poorly known in South America. Primarily appears to inhabit forest canopy (both terra firma and lowlying); also encountered at forest edge and in tall second growth. In migration, occurs in more open habitats such as woodlands, parks, and gardens as well as forest. Usually solitary, but in spring migration, sometimes several gather together in loosely associated groups. Joins mixed-species flocks in the canopy and aggregations at fruiting trees (Parker *in litt.*). Usually forages in outer top branches of tall trees, but may occur at any height. In migration in w Colombia, perched on *Cecropia* branches, peered around, and hung from petioles to pick off insects; also ate *Cecropia* fruit (Hilty data).

Vocalizations

Occasionally utters the throaty *chip-burr* heard further north.

Breeding

See account for Scarlet Tanager In Boreal Summer.

Sources

Primary Hilty data; Hilty and Brown 1986; Parker *in litt.*; Pearson 1972; Ridgely 1976. **Weights (n = 6)** Cruz 1974; Graber and Graber 1962. **Vocalizations** Hilty and Brown 1986; Ridgely 1976.

Piranga ludoviciana 88
Western Tanager
In Boreal Summer
Plate 12

Length 17 cm (6½ in.). Weight 30 g (24.6–36.0 g). Monotypic. First year males resemble females until the early spring when body (but not wing and tail) feathers are molted into a duller version of adult male (Bent 1965). Streaked brownish in juvenal plumage.

Geographic Range

In Boreal Summer: from se Alaska, USA, n British Columbia, s Mackenzie, n Alberta, and s Saskatchewan, CANADA, southward

Piranga olivacea (in Boreal Winter)

to n Baja California, MEXICO, s Nevada, sw Utah, c and se Arizona, s New Mexico, and w Texas, USA, and eastward to e Montana, w South Dakota, nw Nebraska, c Colorado, and c New Mexico, USA. Casual or accidental further north and east in North America. (*A.O.U. Check-list*.)

Elevational Range

In Boreal Summer: mostly 1000–3050 m; as low as 450 m or less in Washington, USA, and mostly above 2300 m in the sw USA.

Habitat and Behavior

Inhabits open coniferous forest; also encountered in mixed coniferous-deciduous forest and mature aspen and alder groves. (See Shy 1984c for measures of tree density and other habitat characteristics.) Lives in pairs during the breeding season. Flight is in an unwavering line with fairly rapid wing beats (Bent 1965). Forages in the canopy of coniferous and mature alder forest. Appears to be mostly insectivorous. Sallies to air for insects including flying ants and termites; often remains perfectly motionless except for moving its head from side to side while scanning the air for prey; once flew straight up 12 m, then dropped vertically to its original perch (Bent 1965). Also searches foliage in a deliberate manner, or jumps upon a spray of leaves, then crawls in a leasurely fashion while reaching to pick objects off foliage; also picks food from flowers (Marshall 1957) In Utah, USA, picked insects off substrates (mostly foliage) and sallied to air almost equally; rarely lunged or hovered (Airola and Barrett 1985, 40 obs). In Oregon, USA, fed on refuse in the streets of a logging camp (McAllister and Marshall 1945).

Stomach contents (47 collected April–Aug, Beal in Bent 1965): 82% insects and 18% fruit. Insects were hymenopterans (56%, increasing to 75% in Aug), mostly wasps and some ants; beetles (12%), mostly click-beetles and wood-borers; hemipterans (8%) including stink-bugs and a few cicadas; grasshoppers (4%); and caterpillars (2%). Fruit appeared to be of some large kind like peaches or apricots; also elderberry seeds, seeds and stems of mulberries, and a raspberry or blackberry seed. Other stomach contents: hemipterans (1); fruit and plant matter (2). Also observed eating juniper and cotoneaster berries (Johnson 1964) and wild cherries (Swarth 1904).

Vocalizations

Call: *pit-ick* or *pit-er-ick*; also utters a rather plaintive, soft, purring *tu-weep* (Pough 1946). Song: 4–5 phrases of rising and falling inflections; Low- to Moderate-pitched; like that of the American Robin, *Turdus migratorius*, but less sustained. Resembles the song of the Scarlet Tanager, *P. olivacea* **87,** but phrases tend to be more complex and delivered at a slower rate (see Shy 1984b).

Breeding

The cup nest, made of twigs, rootlets, grasses, and pine needles and lined with hair or fine rootlets, is placed 1.8–20 m above the ground on outer horizontal limbs of a (typically) fir or pine tree. Trees are often in open areas (14 nests, Tatschl 1967). One nest was placed on the ground under a rock ledge (Wiggins and Wiggins 1939). Eggs (3–5) are pale blue or greenish blue, marked with brown or gray green, especially at the large end. Incubation by the female takes 13 days; both parents feed the young insects and larvae (Bent 1965). Breeding dates: May–July.

Sources

Primary Bent 1965; Marshall 1957; Salt 1957; Shy 1984b; Stiles 1980. **Weights (n = 7)** LSUMZ data. **Stomach contents** Beal in Bent 1965; LSUMZ data; Marshall 1957. **Vocalizations** LNS recordings (21); Bent 1965; Peterson 1969; Pough 1946. **Nests, eggs, and breeding dates** Bent 1965; Hayward 1935; Nehrkorn 1899; Pough 1946; Sibley 1955; Tatschl 1967; Wiggins and Wiggins 1939; USNM.

Piranga ludoviciana 88
Western Tanager
In Boreal Winter
Plate 12

Length 17 cm (6½ in.). Weight 30 g (28.0–34.5 g; most with heavy fat). Monotypic.

Geographic Range

In Boreal Winter: s Baja California, Jalisco, and s Tamaulipas, MEXICO (rarely further north), southward (except in Caribbean lowlands) through GUATEMALA, EL SALVADOR, HONDURAS, and NICARAGUA to c COSTA RICA; casual (but may be increasing) in w Chiriquí, w PANAMA. Mostly on the Pacific slope. Accidental in the Bahama Islands and Cuba (*A.O.U. Check-list*).

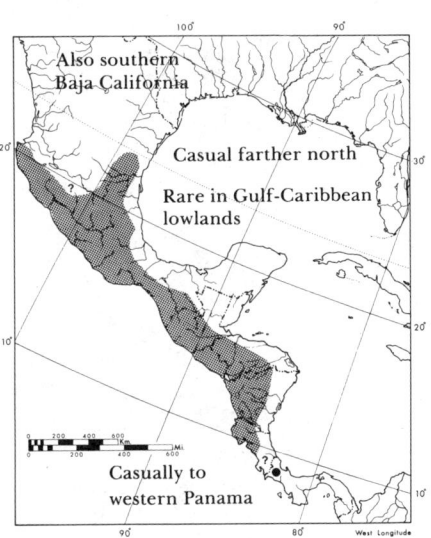

Piranga ludoviciana (in Boreal Winter)

Elevational Range

In Boreal Winter: sea level to 3050 m mostly 600–1400 m. In El Salvador, appears to arrive in the highlands and spread out to lowlands during winter, then return to above 600 m shortly before spring migration (Dickey and van Rossem 1938).

Habitat and Behavior

Prefers pine and pine-oak woodlands, low scrubby forest, forest edge, nearby coffee plantations, and open areas with many scattered trees. During migration, often in more open habitats including arid scrub, orchards, parks, and gardens. Usually solitary, but forms groups of up to 30 or more individuals during migration. In Nicaragua, once noted in large numbers at a feeding aggregation with Clay-colored Robins, *Turdus grayi* (Howell 1964). Forages in the middle or upper branches of trees (Edwards 1972). In El Salvador, said to eat fruit (Rand and Traylor 1954).

Vocalizations

Apparently very quiet. The call, *wit* or *weet*, recalls a Bobolink, *Dolichonyx oryzivorus*, of North America (Sutton and Pettingill 1942).

Breeding

See account for Western Tanager In Boreal Summer.

Sources

Primary Dickey and van Rossem 1938; Edwards 1972; Howell 1964; Land 1970; Monroe 1968; Slud 1964. **Weights (n = 6)** Tashian 1953. **Vocalizations** Sutton and Pettingill 1942.

Piranga leucoptera 89
White-winged Tanager
Plate 12

Length 13 cm (5½ in.). Weight 16 g (13.3–20.0 g). Four subspecies: width of white wing-bars differs noticeably among subspecies (narrowest in *leucoptera*).

Geographic Range

P. l. leucoptera: from extreme s Tamaulipas, MEXICO, southward along the Gulf-Caribbean slope (except the Yucatán Peninsula) through MEXICO, BELIZE, GUATEMALA, and HONDURAS to c NICARAGUA; the Pacific slope from nw GUATEMALA and EL SALVADOR to n NICARAGUA. *P. l. latifasciata*: from n COSTA RICA (c Alajuela) to Veraguas, w PANAMA. *P. l. venezuelae* and *ardens*: VENEZUELA in the coastal ranges from Sucre and Monagas west to Carabobo, in the Andes, and in scattered locations in s and nc Bolívar; the Perijá Mountains (one record in Cesar, COLOMBIA, USNM); very local in COLOMBIA in Norte de Santander, Cundinamarca (one record), both slopes of the C Andes from Antioquia to Valle and Tolima, and on the Pacific slope in Risaralda and Valle; also on the Pacific slope from Nariño, COLOMBIA, south through ECUADOR to El Oro; and on the e slope of the Andes from Tungurahua, ECUADOR, southward through e PERU to extreme w Santa Cruz (Remsen, Traylor, and Parkes in press), BOLIVIA.

Elevational Range

P. l. leucoptera: mostly 500–1500 m, but regularly down to sea level. *P. l. latifasciata*: mostly 900–2600 m, centered at ca. 1500–1800 m. *P. l. venezuelae* and *ardens*: in Venezuela, 650–2500 m north of the Orinoco, 1000–1800 m south of it; in Colombia (except Nariño), 1500–2200 m; from Nariño, Colombia, south to Bolivia, mostly 900–1500 m, extremes 800–2050 m (Graves 1983).

Habitat and Behavior

Inhabits forest and forest edge; also occurs in second growth and scattered trees in areas near forest. In the north (*leucoptera*), often occurs in pine-oak associations and shaded coffee plantations. In the Andes, mostly found in epiphyte-laden cloud forest. Encountered in pairs, occasionally solitary or in small groups. Frequently travels with mixed-species flocks, perhaps less often at high elevations in Panama (cp. Moynihan 1962c). Seems to forage actively for a short time, then pauses to rest.

Typically forages for insects and fruit high in trees, usually in or near the canopy. Sometimes comes lower at forest edge, but rarely near the ground. Peers and flutters among outer twigs and foliage. Perches on twigs or branches to take insects from leaves. In Bolivia, picked insects from upper surfaces of leaves at the very tops of 7.5–30 m trees (Remsen data, 14 obs.). In Costa Rica, searched foliage and the bark of leafy branches and examined earthy, overturned stumps at woodland edge (Slud 1964). Stomach contents: animal matter (2); vegetable matter (1); both (1). Contents included large caterpillars, other insects, and seeds. Also took moths (Collins and Watson 1983), and is possibly attracted to mistletoe berries (Dickey and van Rossem 1938).

Vocalizations

Most commonly utters a sweet High-pitched *wheet!* and a sharp, slightly lower-pitched *pit*; each is given alone or combined as in *pit-wheet!* or *pit-wheet-wheet*. Also delivers a buzzy *wheet wheet*, a trill of 6–10 notes, and (possibly a type of song) *wheet! di-di-dit* (last 3 notes rapid and at a lower pitch). The latter vocalization has many variants, e.g., *wheet,*

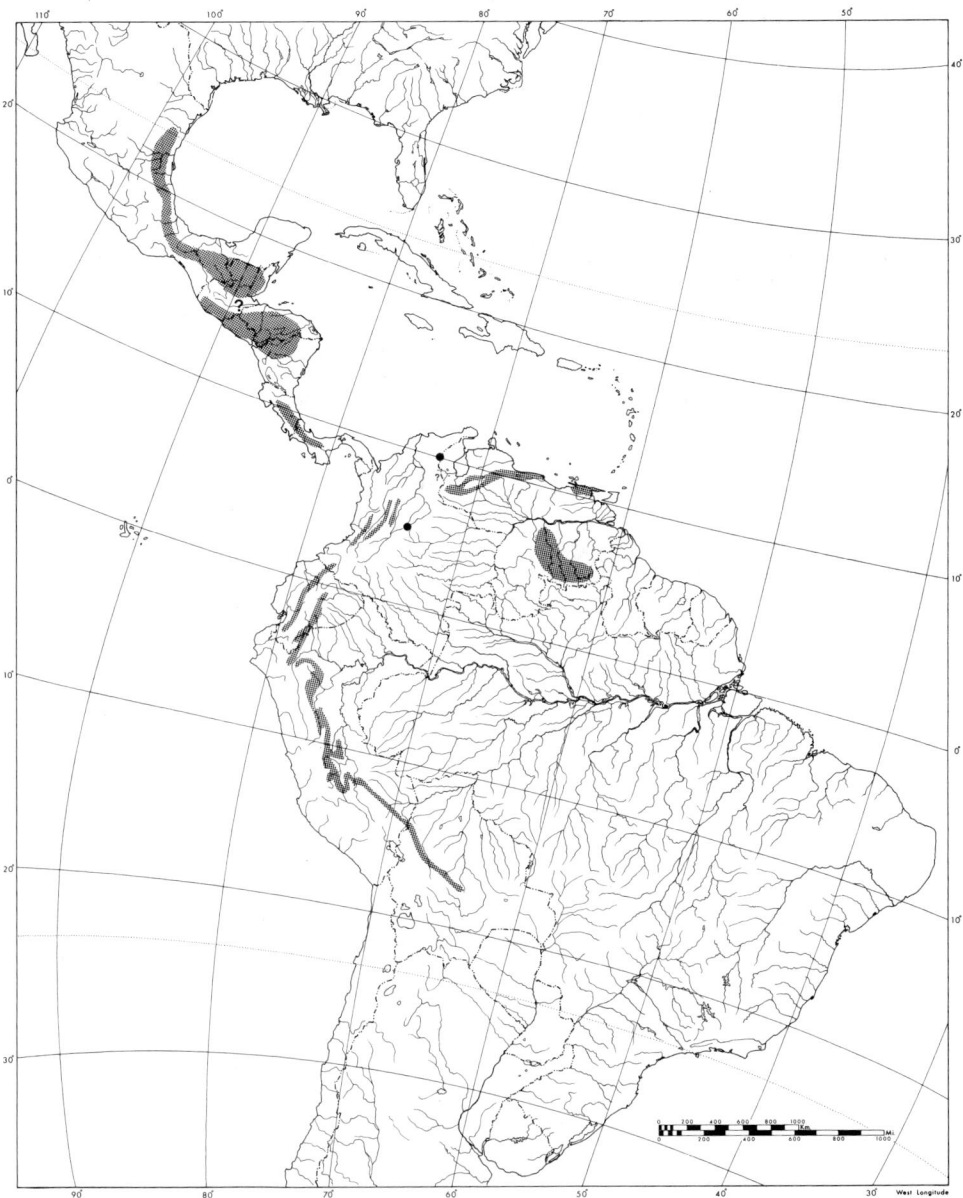

Piranga leucoptera

de-de-dee, *tsupeet*, and may be given so fast that it almost becomes a twitter. In Mexico, also utters a stream of squeaks and twitters, with an occasional emphatic squeal; mostly Moderate- to High-pitched; hesitates occasionally for 1–2 sec., then continues on (Whitney recording). It is unclear whether the large variation in song patterns reflects differences among localities, differences among individuals, or different behavioral situations.

Breeding

No information.

Sources

Primary Hilty and Brown 1986; Dickey and van Rossem 1938; Parker data; Ridgely 1976; Russell 1964; Schäfer and Phelps 1954; Slud 1964; Smithe 1966; Wetmore 1939. **Weights (n = 58)** Hartman and Brownell 1961; Hubbard 1967; LSUMZ data; Russell 1964; Smithe 1966; Tashian 1953. **Stomach contents** Ginés et al. 1951; LSUMZ data. **Vocalizations** LNS recordings by Parker (3), Schwartz (6); recording by Whitney (1); Edwards 1972; Hilty and Brown 1986; Ridgely 1976; Slud 1964.

Piranga erythrocephala 90
Red-headed Tanager
Plate 13

Length 15 cm (5½ in.). Weight 19.9 g (1 male); 24.5 g (1 female). Two subspecies.

Geographic Range

MEXICO on the Pacific slope from se Sonora and Chihuahua southeastward to e Oaxaca (Isthmus of Tehuantepic).

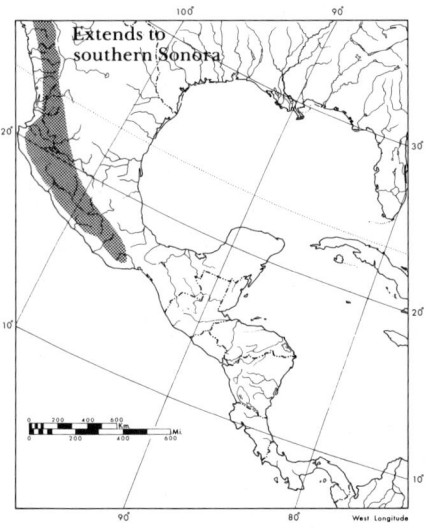

Piranga erythrocephala

Elevational Range

900–2600 m.

Habitat and Behavior

Inhabits montane forest and pine-oak associations, second growth, and forest edge; also occurs in open gallery forest and scrub mixed with woodland. Encountered singly, in pairs, and in small groups; once in a group of 4 individuals in subadult plumage (Zimmerman and Harry 1951); joins mixed-species flocks. Usually stays concealed within foliage, occasionally coming into view when foraging on the outer tips of branches. Forages at midheights of midsized trees; usually below 6 m (Whitney *in litt.*). Eats both insects and small fruits, including blackberries and berries of nightshade (*Solanum* sp).

Vocalizations

Call: a High-pitched *chit* or *chit-t-t-t* (Whitney recording). Song: an indefinitely long series of somewhat throaty, abrupt, single and double notes, e.g., *chur chew che-wier CHEE-chur wee chur cheer CHEE-chur* etc; delivery slightly faster than 1 note/sec. The notes are separated clearly, and the song bounces between upward-inflected Moderate-pitched notes and downward-inflected Low-pitched notes in a somewhat jerky rhythm (L. I. Davis, LNS).

Breeding

No information.

Sources

Primary Alden 1969; Edwards 1972; Hutto 1980; Rowley 1966; Schaldach 1963, 1969; Salvin and Godman 1879–1904; Whitney *in litt.* Weights (n = 2): LSUMZ data. **Vocalizations** LNS recording by L. I. Davis (1); recording by Whitney (1).

Piranga rubriceps 91
Red-hooded Tanager
Plate 13

Length 17 cm (7 in.). Weight 35 g (28.0–40.0 g). Monotypic.

Geographic Range

Locally distributed in the Andes of COLOMBIA from Antioquia and Boyacá southward; the e slope of the Andes from Putumayo, COLOMBIA, through ECUADOR (records on the w slope of ECUADOR may represent individuals that have wandered from the e slope, Ridgely *in litt.*) and n PERU south to Huánuco (FMNH).

Elevational Range

1700–3000 m; 2000–2600 m in Peru (Graves 1983).

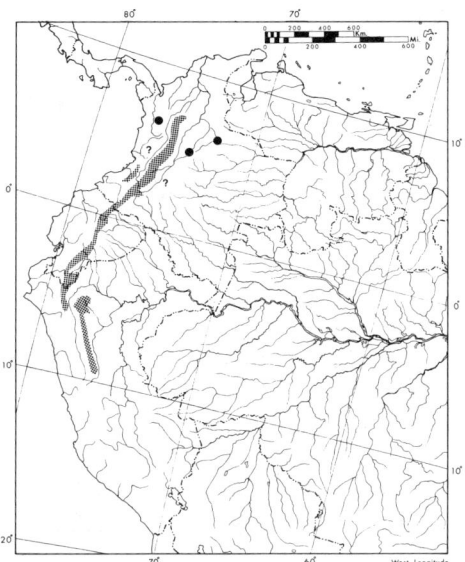

Piranga rubriceps

Habitat and Behavior

Inhabits forest and forest edge. Generally scarce and local. Encountered singly, in pairs, or in groups of 3–6 individuals. Joins feeding aggregations. Mostly independent (Hilty and Brown 1986) but sometimes associates with mixed-species flocks (Moynihan 1979). Forages in upper, sometimes middle, levels for insects and fruit. Peers and hops sluggishly along limbs or in leaves (Hilty and Brown 1986). Perches frequently atop foliage (Parker data). Stomach contents: animal matter (2); animal and vegetable matter (3). Contents included beetles, caterpillars, fruit pulp, and seeds.

Vocalizations

Advertising song(?): a rapid thin High-pitched trill, *ti-ti-ti-ti-ti-ti*, is alternated with sweet, evenly paced, Moderate-pitched notes, *da-dee-dee* or *da-dee-da-dee-dee*; pauses of 2–4 sec. between phrases. Sometimes the foregoing phrases are combined with other Moderate- and High-pitched notes, e.g., *weet-check* and a hoarse *whirt* or *wirst* in a choppy series. Also repeats a rapid *ti-t-t-t-DEE*. (Parker, LNS.)

Breeding

No information.

Sources

Primary Hilty and Brown 1986; LSUMZ data; Moynihan 1979; Parker data. **Weights (n = 7)** LSUMZ data. **Stomach contents** LSUMZ data. **Vocalizations** LNS recordings by Parker (4).

CALOCHAETES

This monotypic genus has been placed near the genera *Piranga* and *Ramphocelus* by most authors, presumably on the basis of similarity of plumage colors. Unlike most species of those genera, the sexes are alike in *Calochaetes*. In its cloud-forest habitat, moss-searching behavior, and thin vocalizations, *Calochaetes* suggests a Mountain-Tanager or a *Tangara* species of mossy habitats, such as the Flame-faced Tanager, *T. parzudakii* **182**.

Calochaetes coccineus 92
Vermilion Tanager
Plate 13

Length 15 cm (6 in.). Weight 46 g (42.0–49.0 g). Monotypic.

Geographic Range

The e slope of the Andes from w Caquetá, COLOMBIA, southward through ECUADOR and PERU to Ayacucho (LSUMZ) and the Cordillera Vilcabamba, Cuzco (Weske 1972).

Elevational Range

Ca. 1100–2000 m; occasionally lower, to 600 m.

Habitat and Behavior

Inhabits tall mossy forest and forest edge. Primarily encountered in small groups of 3–5 individuals, sometimes up to 8 (O'Neill *in litt.*); also in pairs or alone. Associates with mixed-species flocks of other tanagers. Feeds on fruit, especially *Cecropia* catkins and large fruits of tall melastome trees, but rarely observed eating small berries of *Miconia* (Parker data). In Peru, foraged for insects by hopping along mossy branches (both heavily and lightly covered) from inside the tree crown out to open foliage at ends of branches; scanned the branches and

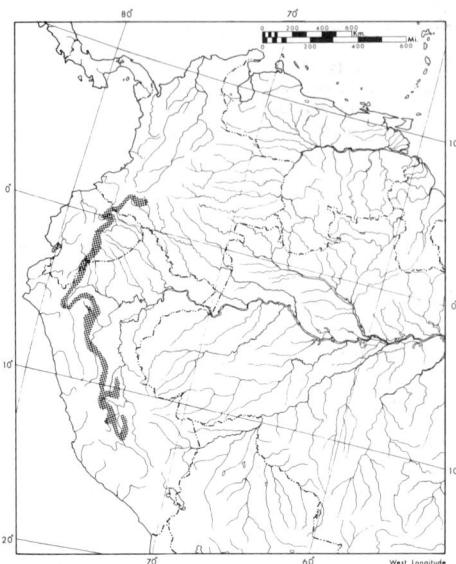

Calochaetes coccineus

Table 13 The *Ramphocelus* Tanagers

⌈	93 *R. sanguinolentus*	Crimson-collared Tanager
⌊	94 *R. nigrogularis*	Masked Crimson Tanager
⌈	95 *R. dimidiatus*	Crimson-backed Tanager
⁞	96 *R. melanogaster*	Huallaga Tanager
⁞	97 *R. carbo*	Silver-beaked Tanager
⌊	98 *R. bresilius*	Brazilian Tanager
⌈	99 *R. passerinii*	Scarlet-rumped Tanager
⌊	100 *R. flammigerus*	Flame-rumped Tanager
	100–1 *icteronotus* subspecies group	Lemon-rumped Tanager
	100–2 *flammigerus* subspecies group	Flame-rumped Tanager

Note: Brackets to the left of the table refer to suggested superspecies (solid lines) and the species groups (dotted lines) discussed in the genus account.

also peered from side to side, investigating bark, moss, and leaves; rarely sallied to air (Parker data). Stomach contents (1): *Cecropia* seeds.

Vocalizations

Utters sharp High- to Very-high-pitched *chip*s and *zit*s that are accelerated into a flat trill, *chip chip zit-t-t-t* (1 brief Parker recording, LNS).

Breeding

No information.

Sources

Primary Hilty and Brown 1986; LSUMZ data; Parker data; Parker and Parker 1982. **Weights (n = 3)** LSUMZ data. **Stomach contents** LSUMZ data. **Vocalizations** LNS recording by Parker (1).

RAMPHOCELUS

Ramphocelus tanagers (Table 13) typically are found in semiopen situations at forest edge and in second growth. They peer around and then reach or dart out to capture prey, primarily from leaves. *Ramphocelus* also sally to air for flying insects. The enlarged lower mandibles of males (except the Crimson-collared) shine almost white and are pointed upward in display during the breeding season. The bill may also function to keep sticky juices away from feathers (cp. Storer 1969), but fruits taken in studies of two species were not especially juicy.

Songs of *Ramphocelus* species are rich and whistled, usually consisting of one and two-syllable notes repeated at a regular pace in long sequences. Calls typically include both a sharp Moderate-pitched alarm note and a drawn out High-pitched contact note. A variety of other calls are used less commonly in displays (see Moynihan 1962b, 1966).

Nests are typically constructed low in bushes and are sometimes quite exposed. Eggs are almost always blue, marked with gray, brown, or lavender. Nestling periods are only about 12 days, when (in at least one species) the young are led away from the nest into thickets despite the fact that they can hardly fly.

Ramphocelus tanagers appear to fall into three species groups. After studying the distribution and morphology of *Ramphocelus* species, Novaes (1959) concluded that the Crimson-backed, Huallaga, Silver-beaked, and Brazilian Tanagers constitute a superspecies. The Silver-beaked and Brazilian Tanagers are parapatric and have interbred in Minas Gerais, Brazil (Sick 1985). However, the habitat preferences and vocalizations of the Brazilian Tanager appear more similar to those of the Masked Crimson Tanager than the Silver-beaked (Parker *in litt.*).

The Scarlet-rumped and Flame-rumped Tanagers are considered to form another superspecies (Novaes 1959; *A.O.U. Checklist*). The colorful rumps of the black males of both species are puffed up in display. The remaining two species, the Crimson-collared and Masked Crimson Tanagers, have similar black and red plumages (see Plate 13) although until recently, the Crimson-collared was placed in its own genus, *Phlogothraupis*.

Ecological differences among the three species groups of *Ramphocelus* are poorly understood. The Masked Crimson Tanager shows a strong preference for riparian habitats; the Brazilian and Crimson-collared perhaps only slightly less so. The Masked Crimson generally forages higher off the ground than its congeners; the Crimson-collared also tends to stay higher in trees and shrubs. The Crimson-collared is usually encountered in pairs; the remaining *Ramphocelus* typically are found in small groups.

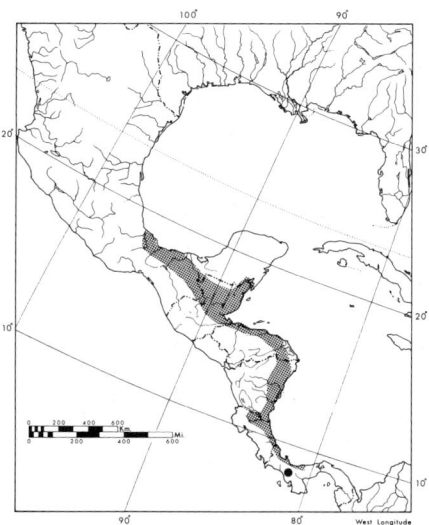

Ramphocelus sanguinolentus

Ramphocelus sanguinolentus 93
Crimson-collared Tanager
Plate 13

Length 17 cm (7 in.). Weight 41 g (34.7–48.1 g). Two subspecies.

Geographic Range

The Gulf-Caribbean slope from s Veracruz, n Oaxaca, Tabasco, and e Chiapas, MEXICO, n GUATEMALA, and s Quintano Roo, MEXICO, southeastward through BELIZE, GUATEMALA, HONDURAS, NICARAGUA, and COSTA RICA (barely spilling over passes onto the Pacific slope in the northwest, Slud 1964) to Bocas del Toro, PANAMA, and locally further east to w Panamá province; also on the Pacific slope in Veraguas, PANAMA (Ridgely 1976).

Elevational Range

Lowlands to 1200 m.

Habitat and Behavior

Favors dense areas of shrubs, second growth, and low trees at forest edge and in clearings, often near watercourses. Also occurs in areas adjacent to forest such as abandoned plantations and tree-studded pastures. Appears to wander after the breeding season. Numbers increase as forest is cleared for cultivation (Berrett 1962). Wide ranging, wary, and not as vocal as the sympatric Scarlet-rumped Tanager, *R. passerinii* **99**. Typically lives in pairs, rarely solitary or in groups (except for a period after the breeding season). Occasionally joins feeding aggregations at fruiting trees. Generally forages 2–10 m up in the tops of tall shrubs and the lower portions of trees. Observed in a fruiting melastome (Land 1963) and feeding in a small fig tree (Peters 1929).

Vocalizations

Calls: an abrupt, Moderate-pitched, somewhat grating *chuck* (alarm note?) and a whistled High- to Very-high-pitched *teer-eest* (contact note?). A patterned call consists of *wirss* notes, first given singly and rising in pitch, then doubled and uttered at the same pitch. The song is a leisurely series of sibilant short phrases with high-pitched *sissing* notes randomly interspersed; delivered from an elevated perch (see Slud 1964).

Breeding

Builds a rather compact cup nest of leaves and small vines (sometimes covered with green moss) 1–2.5 m above the ground in bushes (one was in a cluster of vines on a banana plant). Eggs (3) are pale blue, spotted brownish black and faintly marked lavender, especially at the large end. Breeding dates: Belize May. Nicaragua March–May. Costa Rica May.

Sources

Primary Howell 1957; Lowery and Dalquest 1951; Richmond 1893; Ridgely 1976; Russell 1964; Slud 1960, 1964; Wetmore 1943. **Weights (n = 27)** LSUMZ data; Russell 1964. **Vocalizations** LNS recording by van den Berg (1); recordings by R. A. Rowlett (1), Whitney (1); Slud 1964. **Nests, eggs, and breeding dates** Huber 1932; Nehrkorn 1899; Richmond 1893; Russell 1964; USNM.

Ramphocelus nigrogularis 94
Masked Crimson Tanager
Plate 13

Length 17 cm (6½ in.). Weight 31 g (27.0–36.0 g). Monotypic. Subadult male resembles female. Also known as the Masked Crimson Silverbeak.

Geographic Range

East of the Andes from s Meta, w Caquetá, extreme s Nariño, Putumayo, and Amazonas, COLOMBIA, southward through e ECUADOR and PERU to Madre de Dios, and eastward through Acre and Amazonas (mostly south of the Amazon River), BRAZIL, to c Pará.

Elevational Range

Primarily lowlands to 600 m; rarely higher, once to 1100 m in Peru (LSUMZ).

Habitat and Behavior

Typically encountered along oxbow lake margins and riverbanks at forest edge (incl. *varzea* forest edge) and in second growth; does not occur, however, in early successional vegetation along rivers (Madre de Dios, Peru, Robinson *in litt.*). Also found in shrubby clearings and cultivated areas near water. Usually in groups of 3–8 individuals, occasionally in pairs, and rarely in larger groups of up to 14 individuals, although sometimes large flocks gather to roost in bushes and canebrakes. Groups usually consist of 2–4 adults and a variable number of first year birds (Robinson *in litt.*). Associates with mixed-species flocks, often with the Silver-beaked Tanager, *R. carbo* 97.

Forages at about 2–25 m above the ground, occasionally higher. Picks fruit while perched. In Madre de Dios, Peru, observed eating fruits of melastomes, *Cecropia*, *Coussapoa*, *Ficus*, *Trichostigma*, and *Pera*; hopped and flew short distances through the foliage, gleaning insects from nearby leaves; observed taking spiders (11 obs.), caterpillars (10 obs.), katydids (3 obs.), and unidentified prey less than 1 cm (26 obs.); Robinson *in litt.*. At another site in Madre de Dios, Peru, peered at mostly large (>30 cm long) leaves and picked insects off both upper and undersides; sometimes reached out or clung to the leaf itself (Remsen data, 15 obs.). In Brazil, ate guavas, custard-apples (probably *Annona* sp), and fruits of the family Passifloraceae (Descourtilz 1852). Stomach contents (3): vegetable matter, including fruit pulp, berry pits, and seeds.

Vocalizations

Calls: a sharp metallic Moderate- to High-pitched *tchi* or *tsit*, apparently given in hostility or alarm, and *whi-it* or *wheeeeet*, probably a contact call. A rapid rattle of 4–8 short hard Moderate-pitched *tsur* notes was used repeatedly in an attempt to drive away a Shiny Cowbird, *Molothrus bonariensis*.

Two song types: one seems to be given only at dawn, the other during the day. Apparent dawn song: either *wheet chu* (second note lower pitched) or *chuck wheet?* repeated monotonously at about 1 phrase/sec.; relieved occasionally with single notes and/or brief pauses; Moderate- to Low-pitched. Apparent day song: phrases like *wheeet, chu-chu wheeet wheeet, chu-chu wier wheeet*, and *chu-chu wheeet, chu-chu whirt*; rich and slow, Moderate- to Low-pitched; with occasional pauses.

Breeding

Eggs are said to be like those of the Brazilian Tanager, *R. bresilius* 98: pale blue, sparingly spotted black with small underlying markings of gray and blackish gray (Ogilvie-Grant 1912).

Sources

Primary Descourtilz 1852; Goodfellow 1901; Hilty and Brown 1986; Moynihan 1962c; Novaes 1958; Parker data; Pearson 1972; Remsen *in litt.*; Robinson *in litt.* **Weights (n = 10)** LSUMZ data. **Stomach contents** LSUMZ data. **Vocalizations** LNS recordings by Parker (6), van den Berg (2); Moynihan 1962c; Remsen *in litt.* **Eggs** Ogilvie-Grant 1912.

Ramphocelus dimidiatus 95
Crimson-backed Tanager
Plate 14

Length 16 cm (6½ in.). Weight 28 g (23.8–34.0 g). Five subspecies: differences are minimal (see Wetmore, Pasquier, and Olson 1984). The subadult male resembles the female; probably breeds in subadult plumage (Todd and Carriker 1922). Also known as the Crimson-backed Silverbeak.

Geographic Range

From w PANAMA (Chiriquí on the Pacific slope and Veraguas on the Caribbean slope) eastward through PANAMA (including Coiba and Pearl Is.) and n COLOMBIA to the w slope of the E Andes; southward on the Pacific slope to n Chocó, in the Atrato Valley to c Chocó, in the Cauca Valley to Cauca, and in the Magdalena Valley to

Ramphocelus nigrogularis

Huila; also in nw VENEZUELA (Zulia except east of Lake Maracaibo, n Mérida, and n Táchira) and adjacent COLOMBIA east of the Andes in Norte de Santander.

Elevational Range

Lowlands and foothills; to 1600 m (rarely) in Panama; to 1300 m in Venezuela; and to 1700 m (rarely to 2200 m, Munves 1975) in Colombia.

Habitat and Behavior

Inhabits thickets, shrubbery, and low trees at forest edge and in clearings, plantations, gardens, areas of human habitation, scrub, and second growth. Rarely inside dense forest with local exceptions (Coiba I., Panama, Wetmore, Pasquier, and Olson 1984). Readily colonizes forested areas cleared for cultivation (Olivares 1970).

Lives mostly in pairs and family groups, rarely in larger groups or singly. Travels independently or associates with other species. In Panama, seen with orioles and flycatchers (see Moynihan 1962c). Flies often and rapidly across cleared areas. In Panama, several dozen gathered at a roost (Wetmore, Pasquier, and Olson 1984).

In Panama: Tends to be somewhat hostile towards other birds and defends a territory against members of its own species. Agonistic behavior includes erect posture, crouch posture, ruffling, tail-fanning, and gaping.

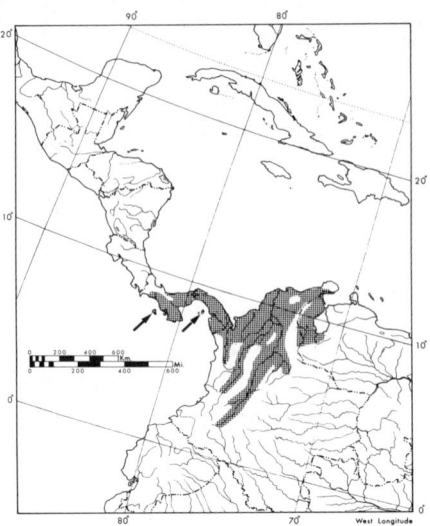

Ramphocelus dimidiatus

Typically flicks tail and (sometimes) wings when preparing to fly. (See Moynihan 1962b.)

Generally forages at low levels. Observed feeding on ripe mangoes on the ground (Wetmore, Pasquier, and Olson 1984). Comes to feeding tables for bananas (Skutch 1954). Stomach contents: vegetable matter (3) animal and vegetable matter (3). Contents included soft seeds (incl. grass seeds), larvae, lepidopterans, a hemipteran, and a spider.

Vocalizations

Calls: most common is a distinctive nasal Moderate-pitched *wah, whanh,* or *anh,* uttered by both sexes, typically in hostile situations. Also a highly variable, hoarse *whaah, wheeaah,* or *zhawhee* uttered in series of 2–4 (up to 10) notes; given as a threat before or during actual fighting or sometimes when greeting a mate. Contact call: a High Pitched *wheeeeet* or *sseeeeeeet*; somewhat loud and sibilant; sometimes doubled.

Dawn song is confined largely to the breeding season and delivered by males from favorite exposed perches 3–12 m above the ground. Typically a clear and melodious Moderate-pitched double note followed by a single note (or vice versa). Precise quality varies; rendered as *sweet, you do*; *chee'awee*; or *keeyoo kew*. When agitated, becomes a somewhat shrill and squeaky *tew-wheet sweeee*. Repeats phrases regularly for varying lengths of time; stops calling when a female approaches.

Day song: call notes are delivered in a regular rhythm from the same perches used at dawn. Notes may be evenly spaced or organized into doublets. Combinations of notes are sometimes given, e.g., *wheeet wah-heee, chikee'o,* or *tsee-hee tsuh-weeeee*.

Breeding

Selects a nesting site 1–3 m above the ground in bushes, hedges, or low trees. The cup nest is constructed of dead leaves and plant fibers (sometimes roots, twigs, or bark) and lined with finer materials. Eggs (2), laid on consecutive days, are pale blue or greenish blue, sparingly marked with deep chocolate, black, or lilac, most heavily at the large end.

In Panama: The female built the nest and incubated alone, often accompanied by the male who sang from a neighboring tree. Incubation took 12 days. Both parents fed the young; at one nest, the female fed only insects to the nestlings for at least the first 6 days while the male brought berries. On day 10 or 11, the young, which could scarcely fly, were led into thick vegetation where they remained hidden for at least 19 days. One pair raised 3 broods in a season. Offspring from the first brood remained with their parents but were not observed helping at the nest. (Skutch 1954.) In captivity, the incubation period was 14 days; one pair raised a second brood; the offspring from the first brood helped feed the young of the second (Norgaard-Olesen 1974). Breeding dates: Panama Feb–June. Colombia March and May.

Sources

Primary Hallinan 1924; Ridgely 1976; Moynihan 1962b, 1962c; Skutch 1954; Todd and Carriker 1922; Wetmore, Pasquier, and Olson 1984. **Weights (n=34)** Burton 1975; Hartman 1955; Hartman and Brownell 1961; LSUMZ data; Miller 1947; Strauch 1977. **Stomach contents** Hallinan 1924; Goldman in Wetmore, Pasquier, and Olson 1984. **Vocalizations** LNS recordings by Schwartz (4), van den Berg (2); recording by Whitney (1); Moynihan 1962b; Skutch 1954; Willis and Eisenmann 1979. **Nests, eggs, and breeding dates** Allen 1905; Hallinan 1924; Ogilvie-Grant 1912; Sclater and Salvin 1879; Stone 1918; Skutch 1954; Todd and Carriker 1922; Willis and Eisenmann 1979; Wyatt 1871.

Ramphocelus melanogaster 96
Huallaga Tanager
Plate 14

Length 17 cm (6½ in.). Weight 25 g (1 male). Two subspecies. Also known as the Black-bellied Tanager and the Huallaga Silverbeak.

Geographic Range

East of the Andes in PERU in San Martín and Huánuco (Río Huallaga drainage); currently extending range to extreme nw Ucayali (Río Ucayali drainage) east of Tingo María (O'Neill *in litt.*).

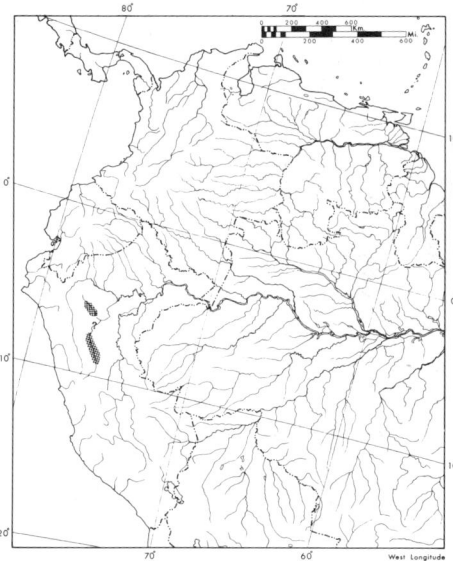

Ramphocelus melanogaster

Elevational Range

800–2100 m.

Habitat and Behavior

Inhabits forest edge, scrub, second growth, river-edge woodland, cultivated areas, gardens, and trees near habitations. Often in small flocks of 6–8 individuals.

Vocalizations

Call note: an abrupt, Moderate-pitched, and slightly burry *chwip* or *chwick* (van den Berg, LNS) similar to notes given in alarm or hostility by other *Ramphocelus* species. Day song is very similar to that of the Silver-beaked Tanager, *R. carbo* **97** (Parker *in litt.*).

Breeding

No information.

Sources

Primary LSUMZ data; Parker data; Tallman 1974; Zimmer 1930. **Weights (n = 1)** LSUMZ data. **Vocalizations** LNS recordings by van den Berg (3).

Ramphocelus carbo 97
Silver-beaked Tanager
Plate 14

Length 16–17 cm (6½ in.). Weight varies from 24 g (21.5–27.0 g) for *atrosericeus*, to 28 g (23.5–37.5 g) for the remaining subspecies. Eight subspecies. Also known as the Common Silverbeak.

Geographic Range

East of the Andes from COLOMBIA southward through ECUADOR and PERU to Santa Cruz, BOLIVIA, and eastward through VENEZUELA (except the llanos) to THE GUIANAS, and through BRAZIL to Amapá, Pará, Maranhão, Piauí, w Bahia, Minas Gerais, w São Paulo, and w Paraná, BRAZIL, and Alto Paraná (no recent records), PARAGUAY; TRINIDAD.

Elevational Range

From sea level to 1900 m; mostly below 1200 m.

Habitat and Behavior

Prefers second growth and bushy habitats in semiopen situations at forest edge, along rivers, lakes, and roadways, and in savannas, cultivated areas, and abandoned plantations. Also occurs in open woodland, but rarely penetrates dense forest. Lives mostly in groups of 4–8 individuals. Occasionally up to 30 or more join a feeding aggregation at a fruiting tree. Individual pairs do not appear to defend a territory. Typically travels in groups of its own; sometimes associates with mixed-species flocks. Flies from tree to tree with long rhythmic flight; group members follow the leaders closely. Flicks wings and tail when about to fly. In display, points bill skyward showing the bright lower mandible. Also assumes erect and crouch postures and silently gapes in hostile situations (see Moynihan 1962b).

Ramphocelus carbo

Usually forages from the ground to about 12 m up, occasionally higher to the canopy of 25 m fruiting trees. In Trinidad, about half of 541 foraging observations were at 3 m or less off the ground; typically foraged higher when feeding at flowers (Snow and Snow 1971). May also forage higher when accompanying mixed-species flocks (see Pearson 1971). In Trinidad, of 588 observations, 50% involved insect-foraging, 45% fruit-eating, and 5% were at flowers (Snow and Snow 1971). In Peru, of 15 observations, 8 were eating fruit and 6 involved insect-searching (Remsen data).

Typically searches for insects by peering at foliage. In Trinidad, insect-searching was 77% on foliage, 13% on grass and weeds, 7% in aerial sallies, and the remainder on seed heads, twigs, and branches. Hopped over foliage fairly rapidly, sometimes darting forward. Its usual prey seemed to be insects that rely on movement to escape. (Snow and Snow 1971.) Observed at army ant swarms in Brazil (Oniki and Willis 1972).

In Trinidad, the Snows recorded this tanager eating 40 species of fruit. Favored melastomes (64% of all fruit-eating records), especially *Miconia* (11 spp) and *Clidemia* berries. Also ate fruits of epiphytes (8%), *Cecropia* (6%), and *Ficus* (2%). Swallowed most fruits whole, but occasionally pecked pieces out of large fruits or crushed them to reduce their size. In Brazil, clung upside down to pendant *Cecropia* catkins and nibbled at the tiny fruits beginning with those at the tip of the catkin and working methodically upwards towards the base (see Silva 1980). In Trinidad, mandibulated bromeliad fruit to eat pulp and seeds and dropped the spiny skin. Took nectar from 3 species of trees and 2 species of vines; broke into the base of flowers of the vine *Dioclea guianensis*, presumably to get at the nectar. (Snow and Snow 1971.) In Brazil, pierced large flowers of the *Norantea* vine to obtain nectar (Sick 1985).

Stomach contents: vegetable matter (14); animal matter (7); both (10). Contents included *Cecropia* fruit, seeds, caterpillars, coleopterans (incl. snout and leaf beetles), spiders, orthopterans, ants, and hemipterans. Additional stomach contents included berries of the families Solanaceae and Loranthaceae, cactus fruit (*Cereus* sp), and flying termites.

Vocalizations

Calls: A Moderate-pitched harsh or sharp *chak* or *chick*, probably given in alarm or hostility, is often delivered rapidly by multiple individuals of a group. Also a High-pitched *zweeet* or *tseeet* which is probably a contact note. Calls frequently. Dawn song: a variety of somewhat harsh and squeaky phrases sounding like *WHEET-zur eeet? zur-eat? WHEET-zur eow WHEET-it zeer WHEET-it zur-ir*; primarily Moderate-pitched; at times the song is broken by a pause or a harsh *CHAK*; notes and phrases are delivered at the rate of 1/sec. or faster. Day song: *CHICK chit-ti-wee* (the last phrase sibilant and sometimes repeated), sometimes shortened to *CHICK*, repeated monotonously; Moderate-pitched; delivered at the rate of 20–25 phrases/min. (Parker, LNS). Skutch (1968) heard a whisper song that was a flutelike flow of slight varied musical notes.

Breeding

Typically selects a nesting site 1–2.5 m above the ground in a low dense bush (records are from a few cm to 7.6 m). The female alone builds the deep compact cup nest which is usually composed of dead leaves and fibers and is sometimes finished on the outside with green leaves. Two (rarely 1 or 3) eggs, laid on consecutive days, are blue or greenish blue, sparingly marked with blackish brown and gray and/or lilac, especially at the large end. The female incubates for 12 days. Both parents feed the young. Beebe (1909) observed a pair carrying grubs to their nestlings. The nestling period is 12 days. Two females, apparently without attending mates, were observed nesting 1 m apart (Skutch 1968; see also Ingels 1977). In Suriname, nests are often reused (Haverschmidt 1968). Breeding dates: Colombia Jan–March. Venezuela April and May. Brazil (Pará) Sept–Feb; (Mato Grosso) Nov. Suriname Dec–Aug and Oct. French Guiana July and Aug. Trinidad Dec–Sept.

Sources

Primary Carvalho 1957; ffrench 1973; Ginés et al. 1951; Haverschmidt 1968; LSUMZ data; Moynihan 1962b; Novaes 1969, 1973; Parker data; Remsen data; Skutch 1968; Snow and Snow 1971; Willis 1977. **Weights** (*atrosericeus* n = 21, remaining races n = 261): Dick, McGillivray, and Brooks 1984; ffrench 1973; Fry 1970; Haverschmidt 1948, 1952, 1968; LSUMZ data; Pearson 1971; Thomas data; Thomas 1982; Weske 1972. **Stomach contents** Beebe 1909; Foster data; Friedmann and Smith 1950; Haverschmidt 1968; LSUMZ data; Novaes 1973; Novaes and Pimentel 1973; Schubart, Aguirre, and Sick 1965. **Vocalizations** LNS recordings by Bierregaard (2), T. H. Davis (2), Isler (2), Parker (5), Schwartz (11), D. W. Snow (2), van den Berg (2); ffrench 1973; Moynihan 1962b; Sick 1985; Snyder 1966. **Nests, eggs, and breeding dates** Allen 1891; Belcher and Smooker 1937; Carvalho 1957; Haverschmidt 1968; Furniss in Hilty and Brown 1986; Ingels 1977, 1978; LSUMZ data (Schulenberg); Niethammer 1956; Novaes 1980; Pinto 1953; Skutch 1968; Snethlage 1935; Taczanowski 1884b.

Ramphocelus bresilius 98
Brazilian Tanager
Plate 14

Length 18 cm (7 in.). Weight 31 g (1 male). Two subspecies.

Geographic Range

Coastal BRAZIL from Paraíba south to Santa Catarina; also reported along the Río Uruguay in Misiones, ARGENTINA (Hoy 1976). Also known as the Brazilian Silverbeak.

Elevational Range

Mostly near sea level; less commonly to ca. 800 m, perhaps higher.

Habitat and Behavior

Primarily encountered near water. Occurs in bushes and trees in marshes near the ocean and low scrubby growth along rivers, streams, ponds, and edges of swampy woodland. Also found in open woodlands, parks, and large gardens. Pairs and small groups fly among low vegetation, but they usually

174 RAMPHOCELUS

Ramphocelus bresilius

stay hidden in dense bushes during the heat of the day.

Tends to aggregate in the austral winter (Mitchell 1957). Prefers pulpy fruits, especially pitangus berries, *Eugenia* species (Descourtilz 1852). Stomach contents: vegetable matter (2); animal matter (2); both (1). Contents included seeds, fruit pulp, insects, and a small quantity of white sand.

Vocalizations

In the wild (as described in Portuguese by Sick 1985): Calls include a hard *jep*, *jip*, *ist*, and *sst-sst*. Song is a melodious tri-syllabic trill, leasurely repeated, *djüle-djüle-djüle*. Small groups make a harsh chattering. In captivity (Moynihan 1962b): uttered a single *wheeeee* (probably a contact note) and *chuck* or *chup* notes (probably alarm or hostile notes). Dawn song (?): long series of *wheeeee* or *wheee-eeee* notes. Whisper song (?): phrases of *chup chuh-wheeee* were combined with call notes in a melodious jumble that lasted about 10 min.

Breeding

Builds an open cup woven of grasses and vines or other fibers. Nests are placed in bushes and low trees or hidden among clumps of marsh grass. Eggs (2–3) are greenish blue, sparingly marked with black and gray. In captivity, the female incubated alone for 13 days and young were fed by both parents (Norgaard-Olesen 1974).

Breeding dates: Brazil (state uncertain) Oct and Dec; (São Paulo) Nov; (Rio de Janeiro) Nov.

Sources

Primary Descourtilz 1852; Euler 1867; Forbes 1881; Goeldi 1894; Mitchell 1957; Parker data; Santos 1948; Sick 1985. **Weights (n = 1)** Sick 1985. **Stomach contents** Berla 1944; Moojen, Carvalho, and Lopes 1941; Schubart, Aguirre, and Sick 1965. **Vocalizations** Moynihan 1962b; Sick 1985. **Nests, eggs, and breeding dates** Euler 1900; Goeldi 1894; Guimarães 1924; Ihering 1900; Ogilvie-Grant 1912; Peixoto 1932; Snethlage and Schreiner 1929.

Ramphocelus passerinii **99**
Scarlet-rumped Tanager
Plate 14

Length 16 cm (6½ in.). Weight 32 g (25.5–37.0 g). Two subspecies; females of both subspecies are illustrated. The intensity of the orange rump and breast band of females of *costaricensis* subspecies varies, possibly with age (see Skutch 1954). Aberrant plumages (e.g., males with orange rumps) occur with some frequency, and young males appear to breed in a subadult plumage resembling that of adult females (see Wetmore, Pasquier, and Olson 1984).

Geographic Range

R. p. passerinii: the Gulf-Caribbean slope from se MEXICO (extreme sw Veracruz, Tabasco, and n Chiapas; not on Yucatán Peninsula) and BELIZE southeastward through CENTRAL AMERICA to Bocas del Toro, PANAMA, and on the Pacific slope in COSTA RICA in c Guanacaste and n Puntarenas (see Slud 1964). *R. p. costaricensis*: the Pacific slope from Puntarenas (except in the north), COSTA RICA, southeastward to w Veraguas (Wetmore, Pasquier, and Olson 1984), PANAMA.

Elevational Range

From sea level to ca. 1000 m; locally higher, to 1700 m in Costa Rica (Skutch 1954) and 1550 m in Panama (Wetmore, Pasquier, and Olson 1984).

Habitat and Behavior

Inhabits semiopen areas with low dense vegetation, including second-growth scrub, thickets, low trees, and tall weeds and grasses. Encountered at forest edge, in clearings, pastures, plantations, and abandoned fields, and along riverbanks and roadsides. Also occurs in gardens near human habitations. Never ventures far into forest undergrowth, but occurs occasionally in the forest canopy (Slud 1964).

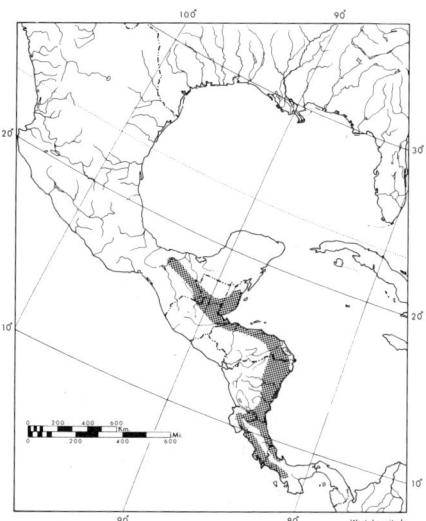

Ramphocelus passerinii

Lives in pairs, families, and in groups of 6–12 individuals. Often stays hidden in dense cover, but actively darts about the vegetation, chattering noisily. Occasionally travels with rapidly moving mixed-species flocks (see Moriarty 1977). Easily excited to mobbing; sometimes mobs harmless objects such as a bedraggled moth or a pair of shoes (see Skutch 1954). May not defend a territory; rarely fights with its own kind or with other species (Skutch 1962b:108). Expresses hostility by posturing with an open bill, and males often perch in the open with wings drooped and scarlet rump feathers expanded. Gathers in groups of up to a dozen or more individuals to roost in low dense vegetation (Skutch 1954).

Typically forages low, usually below 7 m off the ground, sometimes on the ground. In Costa Rica, reported to forage at average heights of 21 m when with mixed-species flocks (n = 5), and 7 m when in single species groups (n = 29; see Moriarty 1977).

Eats a wide variety of fruits and insects. Favors melastomes and several species of arillate fruits; occasionally eats *Cecropia* fruit. Comes to feeding tables for ripe bananas and plantains. In Costa Rica, pecked pieces of aril from seeds still attached to the woody capsule, sometimes carrying the whole seed away; also observed eating leaves. Searched for caterpillars, spiders, and other insects in foliage, and hunted for grasshoppers on the ground. Also sallied for flying termites. Observed once at an army ant swarm in second growth. (Skutch 1954, 1972, 1980.)

Vocalizations

Calls: most commonly utters a harsh, mostly Moderate- and Low-pitched, *ik*, *wac*, or *wah* (possibly expressing hostility); alarm note is a sharp *whip*. Contact note (also delivered when taking flight) is a sharp dry *pzzt*, *pzzt-weet*, or *hist*. Excited phrases given when pairs encounter each other are Moderate- and High-pitched squeaky notes, delivered sharply and rapidly, such as *zweet*, *zzt-not*, *chee*, and a distinctive *churry, churry, churry*.

Dawn song: Repeats the same phrase; one example is *wah-wait chu*, Moderate-pitched (first part upward-inflected, second nasal or harsh), occasionally interrupted with *witchy-wit* (squeaky, higher pitched, and somewhat buzzy). Sometimes a basic phrase is modified, e.g., *vireo viree vireo viree viree*. Quality varies among individuals and ranges from rich and full to slight and weak. During the breeding season, males deliver the dawn song for about 10–15 min. or more, first from their roosting place, then from a favorite perch close to their roost. Perches are apparently unrelated to nest sites (see Skutch 1954). Expands its scarlet rump feathers while singing. Dawn songs are occasionally given during cloudy days. The male is also reported to have a flight song (Slud 1964). The Pacific race (*costaricensis*) sings more and is more musical than the Caribbean race.

Breeding

In Costa Rica (105 nests): Females usually chose the nest site, most often in a thicket or small tree in a field; also among sugar cane, coarse grasses, or ferns. About two-thirds of the nests were situated 1–4 m off the ground (range was 0.36–6.1 m); higher nests were usually concealed in foliage, whereas lower ones were exposed. The open cup, woven of dead leaves, fibers, and grasses, was often decorated with green ferns. The female built the nest alone, accompanied by her mate; she often stole material from neighboring nests. (Skutch 1954.)

Eggs (2, rarely 3), laid on consecutive days, vary from pale blue to pale gray, rarely greenish blue, sparsely marked with black, brown, or pale lilac, usually forming a wreath at the large end. In Costa Rica: Females incubated alone for 12–13 days, attended more or less by their mates. Both parents typically fed nestlings insects, some of considerable size but well mangled. The nestling period was 11–13 (usually 12) days. Upon leaving the nest, young were led into low dense thickets where they remained hidden for about 3 weeks. Very rarely raised a second brood. (Skutch 1954) Breeding dates: Nicaragua March–May and July. Costa Rica Feb–Sept (mostly March). Panama May and June.

Sources

Primary Ridgely 1976; Skutch 1954; Slud 1964; Wetmore, Pasquier, and Olson 1984. **Weights (n = 37)** Hartman 1955; LSUMZ data; Russell 1964. **Vocalizations** LNS recordings by L. I. Davis (7), Parker (2); Eisenmann 1957; Russell 1964; Skutch 1954; Slud 1964. **Nests, eggs, and breeding dates** Carriker 1910; Huber 1932; Ogilvie-Grant 1912; Richmond 1893; Skutch 1954; Wetmore, Pasquier, and Olson 1984.

Ramphocelus flammigerus 100
Flame-rumped Tanager

The two subspecies are sometimes considered distinct species, the Flame-rumped Tanager, *R. flammigerus*, and Lemon-rumped, *R. icteronotus*. The latter form is also known as the Yellow-rumped Tanager. The two forms apparently had been separated by forest and have interbred after forest destruction allowed their ranges to expand and come into contact (Hilty *in litt.*). Intermediates have become fairly common at an elevation of about 800 m, but the extent to which intermediates will continue to occur remains to be seen.

Ramphocelus flammigerus (*icteronotus* subspecies group 100-1)
Lemon-rumped Tanager
Plate 14

Length 18 cm (7 in.). Weight 33 g (29.6–35.6 g). Monotypic if distinct. Subadult males resemble females but underparts, especially undertail-coverts, are often marked with brownish black; breeds in subadult plumage. Also known as the Lemon-rumped Silverbeak.

Geographic Range

The Caribbean slope from Bocas del Toro, PANAMA, eastward to n Antioquia, COLOMBIA, and thence along the n base of the Andes to the Magdalena Valley and

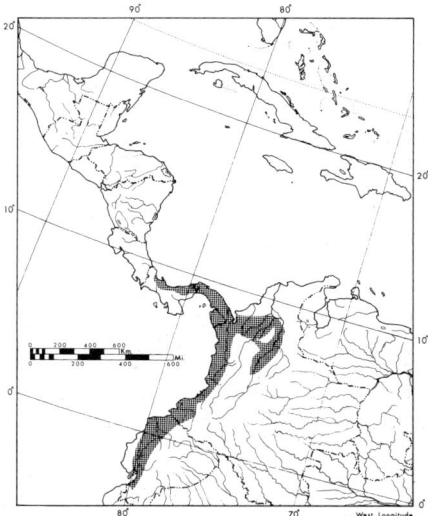

Ramphocelus flammigerus (*icteronotus* subspecies group)

southward in the middle Magdalena Valley to Tolima; and on the Pacific slope in Coclé (El Valle) and from Panamá province eastward and southward through Darién, PANAMA (locally), COLOMBIA, and ECUADOR to Loja near the Peruvian border.

Elevational Range

Lowlands to ca. 800 m; in Colombia, sometimes occurs to 1400 m, rarely to 2100 m (Hilty and Brown 1986).

Habitat and Behavior

Inhabits thickets and second growth at forest edge, in overgrown clearings, and in plantations. In Panama, appears to prefer shrubby places near water. Lives mostly in pairs and family groups, sometimes in groups of up to 12 individuals when not breeding. Individuals, usually young birds, are occasionally seen alone (Hilty data). Small, tightly-knit groups typically travel independently of other species, but readily join feeding aggregations at fruiting trees.

Flicks wings and tail often, especially when preparing to fly. Hostile displays include erect and crouch postures, tail-fanning, and gaping; adult males also have a variety of feather ruffling displays including head, back, and belly fluffing (see Moynihan 1966). Males often sit in the open with wings drooped and rump exposed.

In Valle, Colombia: Foraged mostly below 9 m (median height was about 7.5 m off the ground) but often went higher, even to the tops of 25 m trees. Ate over 22 species of fruit (72% of 170 feeding records) including those of melastomes (30% of all fruit eaten), especially *Miconia* berries, *Cecropia* (27%), and *Ficus* (19%). Typically perched on a twig or branch to pick berries and swallowed them whole. Perched on large fruits (e.g., bananas and fruit capsules) to peck out pieces and hung from *Cecropia* catkins. Rarely took a berry in flight or ate flowers (2% of all feeding records). Sallied to air in about half of 48 insect-feeding attempts. Also peered and picked insects off foliage, grass, ferns, and other substrates. Sometimes acrobatic; occasionally hung from leaves or twigs to obtain prey. (Hilty data.) Stomach contents: vegetable matter (6); animal and vegetable (2). Contents included orthopterans, beetles, fruit, and seeds.

Vocalizations

Most common call notes: a Moderate- to Low-pitched nasal *anh* or *cha* (used in alarm or hostility and may serve as a contact note) and a High-pitched, hard-sounding *tzzheet* (probably a contact note). Other calls include a hoarse *zraa*, various bisyllabic notes (e.g., *tseeee-yah*) and rapid rattles of low pitched, wooden-sounding notes used in hostile encounters (Moynihan 1966).

Dawn song: repeats the same phrase in a regular cadence; most commonly gives a bisyllabic call note, such as *tseee-yah*, but sometimes utters a melodious, rather soft *kioo*; usually repeats the same note, but sometimes varies it slightly; occasionally the series of melodious notes is interrupted by a harsh note. Dawn songs are given only during the breeding season. (Moynihan 1966.)

Breeding

In Panama, males defend breeding territories (Moynihan 1966). Builds its nest in bushes and low trees, 2–5 m off the ground. The compact open cup of leaves and plant fibers is sometimes decorated with leaves and lichens. Eggs (2) are blue or greenish blue marked with black, brown, or lavender, sometimes in a wreath about the large end. In captivity: a female built a deep cup 1 m up in a tree; occasionally the male carried nesting material. Incubation by the female took 11–14 days; both parents fed the young; and nestlings fledged after 12–14 days. (Norgaard-Olesen 1974.) Breeding dates: Panama Feb–May. Colombia Jan–April and Dec.

Sources

Primary Hilty data, Hilty and Brown 1986; Moynihan 1966; Ridgely 1976; Wetmore, Pasquier, and Olson 1984. **Weights (n = 13)** Burton 1975; Hartman 1955; LSUMZ data; Strauch 1977. **Stomach contents** Brosset 1964; LSUMZ data; Wetmore, Pasquier, and Olson 1984. **Vocalizations** LNS recordings by Parker (4), van den Berg (1); Moynihan 1966. **Nests, eggs, and breeding dates** Goodfellow 1901; Hilty and Brown 1986; Norgaard-Olesen 1974; Ogilvie-Grant 1912; Sclater and Salvin 1879; Scamell 1970; Stone 1918; USNM; Wetmore, Pasquier, and Olson 1984.

Ramphocelus flammigerus (*flammigerus* subspecies group 100-2)
Flame-rumped Tanager
Plate 14

Length 18 cm (7 in.). Monotypic if specifically distinct. Also known as the Flame-rumped Silverbeak.

Geographic Range

W COLOMBIA on the Pacific slope from Risaralda (headwaters of the Río San Juan) to nw Nariño, both slopes of the Cauca Valley from c Antioquia southward, and in the upper Río Patía drainage in Cauca.

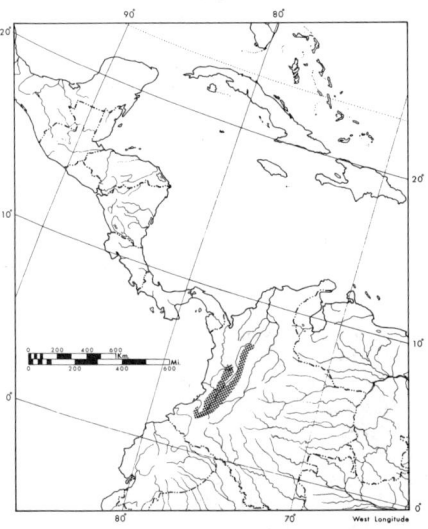

Ramphocelus flammigerus (*flammigerus* subspecies group)

Elevational Range

800–2000 m.

Habitat and Behavior

Inhabits shrubby areas and second growth in overgrown pastures and at forest edge. Behavior is reported to be similar to that of the *icteronotus* subspecies group (Hilty and Brown 1986).

Vocalizations

Voice is reported to be similar to that of the *icteronotus* subspecies group (Hilty and Brown 1986).

Breeding

In Valle, Colombia, a cup nest was found in low weeds (Hilty and Brown 1986). Eggs are pale blue marked with dark brown or black spots (and sometimes a few short lines) that may coalesce in a wreath about the large end. Breeding dates: Feb.

Sources

Primary Hilty and Brown 1986. **Eggs and breeding dates** Hilty and Brown 1986; Ogilvie-Grant 1912.

SPINDALIS

This genus is restricted to Caribbean islands. *Spindalis* may be related to the widespread *Thraupis* tanagers, especially the Blue-and-yellow Tanager, *T. bonariensis* **109**, which *Spindalis* resembles in plumage and feather structure (*Peters Check-list*).

Spindalis zena **101**
Stripe-headed Tanager

As with many taxa that occur across a constellation of islands, the Stripe-headed Tanager exhibits pronounced geographic variation in plumage and size. Although the *Peters Check-list* considers the variety of forms to fall within a single species, plumage variation is especially apparent among female Stripe-headed Tanagers and has led some ornithologists (e.g., Bond 1956) to conclude that three species may be involved. Given this possibility, information regarding *Spindalis* has been organized into subspecies groups (Table 14).

Table 14 The *Spindalis* Tanagers

101	*S. zena*	Stripe-headed Tanager
101-1	*zena* subspecies group	Western Stripe-headed Tanager
101-2	*dominicensis* subspecies group	Eastern Stripe-headed Tanager
101-3	*nigricephala* subspecies group	Jamaican Stripe-headed Tanager

Spindalis zena
(*zena* subspecies group 101-1)
Western Stripe-headed Tanager
Plate 15

Length 14 cm (5½ in.). Weight *zena* and *townsendi* 21 g (17.0–24.5 g); *benedicti* 30 g (26.9–35.2 g). Five subspecies.

Geographic Range

S. z. townsendi: n BAHAMAS. *S. z. zena*: c BAHAMAS east to Mayaguana; irregularly to s Florida, USA. *S. z. pretrei*: CUBA and the Isle of Pines. *S. z. salvini*: Grand Cayman, THE CAYMAN ISLANDS. *S. z. benedicti*: Cozumel I., Quintana Roo, MEXICO.

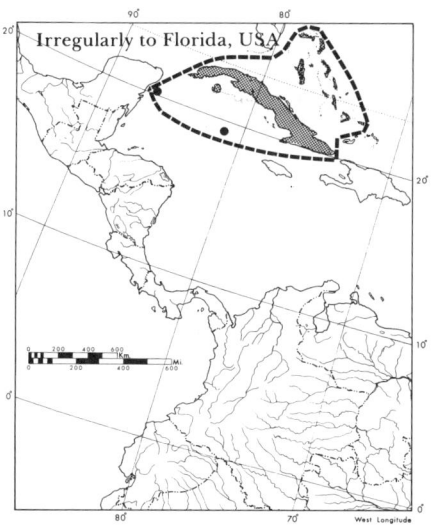

Spindalis zena (*zena* subspecies group)

Elevational Range

At all island elevations.

Habitat and Behavior

Inhabits open woodland, forest edge, scrub, second growth, and tangles of shrubbery in semiopen country. On Cozumel I., most abundant where vegetation has been cut considerably (Paynter 1955). In the Bahamas, found mostly in pines during the breeding season (Brudenell-Bruce 1975). Encountered in pairs and in small groups outside the breeding season. Larger groups reported by Gundlach (1855) in Cuba seemed to have vanished, probably as a result of trapping.

Except when foraging, typically perches high in a tree and is difficult to observe (Brudenell-Bruce 1975). Flight-display: flies up from the top of a tree, circles around with slowly beating wings and in full song, and then dives down to the same or another perch (Brudenell-Bruce 1975). During this display, opens wing and tail feathers to make noise against the air (Waide, LNS). Forages from low in shrubbery to upper branches of trees. Feeds mostly on berries; also eats tender tips of leaves and small plants. Observed attempting to consume a snail (Brudenell-Bruce 1975).

Vocalizations

Calls: *seeip*; members of a group continually utter a soft *tsit-tsit-tsit*. Song: combines thin, squeaky, sibilant, High-pitched *see-tee* doublets (sometimes sounding like an inhale-exhale) with High-pitched *seet* and Moderate-pitched reedy *deet* notes and sometimes with twittering; songs are 3–5 sec. long; pauses are less than 10 sec., at times almost undetectable. Usually sings from a high perch, often the very top of a tree; the song is weak but becomes more vigorous as the breeding season progresses. Another song type is described as a soft warble of discrete notes, 5–6 notes/sec., lasting 1–2 sec. (Reynard 1982). Flight song: a High-pitched sibilant *seet sit-t-t-t-t*. Also sings a lyrical subsong that is so soft it is almost inaudible.

Breeding

In the Bahamas, builds a flimsy nest made of palm fibers and placed in bushes or small trees. In Cuba, nests are said to be built on the outermost branches of tall trees (Gundlach 1855). On Grand Cayman I., one nest was located 3 m above the ground. In defense of young at this nest, the female dropped toward the ground while the male flew to a conspicuous perch at the top of a bush; both spread out wings and tails horizontally, and fluffed out feathers, moving about constantly (English 1916). Breeding dates: Cuba April. Grand Cayman I. May.

Sources

Primary Barbour 1943; Bond 1956; Brudenell-Bruce 1975; Edwards 1972; English 1916; Gundlach 1855. **Weights** (*zena* and *townsendi* n = 16; *benedicti* n = 12): Klaas 1968; LSUMZ data; Paynter 1955; Steadman et al. 1980. **Vocalizations** LNS recordings by Kellogg and Dean (2), Waide (2); Brudenell-Bruce 1975; English 1916; Griscom 1926; Reynard 1982. **Nests and breeding dates** English 1916; Gundlach 1855.

Spindalis zena (*dominicensis* subspecies group **101-2**) Eastern Stripe-headed Tanager
Plate 15

Length 17 cm (6½ in.). Weight 31 g (29.1–33.2 g). Two subspecies.

Geographic Range

S. z. dominicensis: HISPANIOLA and Gonâve Island. *S. z. portoricensis*: PUERTO RICO.

Elevational Range

Sea level to mountain tops; mostly at higher elevations on larger islands; scarce in lowlands of Hispaniola.

Habitat and Behavior

Occupies many kinds of habitats, but seems to prefer humid areas with thickets and low vegetation in or near montane forest and woodland (incl. pine forests). Away from forest, found mainly in areas with groves of trees, especially plantations. Found least often in overgrown clearings and arid scrub. Attracted to fruiting shrubs and trees; moves about regionally as food supplies shift with the changing seasons; numbers are locally affected by drought (see Faaborg 1982).

Encountered in pairs and small groups of 3–4 individuals. Congregates at times in large numbers where fruit is ripening. Flies from perch to perch with a heavy rattle of wings (Wetmore and Swales 1931) and travels with strong undulating flight, sometimes alighting for a minute or two before passing on (Wetmore 1927). Rests quietly high in trees or in bushes.

Forages from low in bushes to the tops of fruiting trees. Observed to eat fruit of *Cecropia*, *Miconia*, *Ficus*, *Brunellia*, *Solanum*, and *Passiflora*, blackberries (*Rubus* sp), and rose apples (*Jambosa jambos*); tears large openings in ripe oranges to extract pulp and juice. Also eats seeds and tender green leaves. Typically takes insects from foliage (McDonald data, 86 obs.); also attacks insects that live in or on fruit (Dod 1978). Their food was thought by Bowdish (1903) to consist of about 70% fruit and 30% insects, but 93% of McDonald's observations (McDonald data, 546 obs.) were at fruit. In Puerto Rico, observed picking aphids from the underside of a leaf (Danforth 1926). In Hispaniola, perched in one spot until all berries were consumed and then suddenly darted to another clump of berries (Verrill and Verrill 1909). In Puerto Rico, in less than half an hour Wetmore (1927) watched a pair consume 2 prickly-skinned fruits (*Annona muticata*) that were about 25 cm long and 13 cm in diam. Stomach contents: fruit.

Vocalizations

Calls: a weak but sharp *tseep* and a drawn-out mournful High-pitched *seeeee*, sometimes followed by rapid dry ticking notes, e.g., *ti-ti-ti*. Fighting males utter harsh scolding notes rendered as *krukky-krurr-r-r-r*. Songs are described as a prolonged weak sibilant *tsee see see see*, a fine squeaky unmusical wiry *tswee tswee tsweey*, and *ZEE-tit-ZEE-tittit-ZEE*, the *ZEE* sounding like an inhale; insectlike. The female sings a whisper song that is a jumble of notes from the song of the male, centered at Moderate Pitch (Reynard 1981, 1982). Sings from exposed perches such as branches of *Cecropia* trees or from inside dense thickets, but usually silent.

Breeding

The surprisingly small cup nest, loosely constructed entirely of dry grass, is placed 1–4.5 m up in trees and bushes. Eggs (3) are whitish with brown spots mostly on the large end. May raise a second brood (Dod 1978). Breeding dates: Hispaniola May and June. Puerto Rico March and June.

Sources

Primary Bond 1956; Bowdish 1903; Danforth 1926, n.d.; Dod 1978; Leck 1972a; Verrill and Verrill 1909; Wetmore 1927; Wetmore and Swales 1931. **Weights (n = 5)** Olson and Angle 1977; Terborgh and Faaborg 1973. **Stomach contents** Christy 1897; Danforth n.d. **Vocalizations** LNS recording by Reynard (1); Bond 1961; Danforth n.d.; Leck 1972a; Raffaele 1983; Reynard 1981, 1982; Verrill and Verrill 1909; Wetmore 1927; Wetmore and Swales 1931; Zusi *in litt*. **Nests, eggs, and breeding dates** Biaggi 1970; Bond 1943; Bowdish 1903; Danforth n.d.; Dod 1978; Raffaele 1983.

Spindalis zena (*dominicensis* subspecies group)

Spindalis zena
(*nigricephala* subspecies group
101-3)
Jamaican Stripe-headed Tanager
Plate 15

Length 18 cm (7 in.). Weight 43 g (42.1–47.2 g). Monotypic if specifically distinct.

Geographic Range

JAMAICA.

Elevational Range

At all elevations but scarce near sea level.

Habitat and Behavior

Primarily inhabits fruiting trees and shrubs in forest and at forest edge. Encountered in family groups and in feeding aggregations of up to 8–10 individuals that interact with much chattering and scolding (Taylor 1955). Rests in tree tops. Flight is rapid and undulating. Feeds on fruit and berries including oranges, pimentos, and Royal Palm fruits. Hangs in all positions from twigs while picking berries (Gosse 1847). Observed taking *Ficus* and *Cecropia* fruit from a perched position and by hovering below or in front of fruit (Cruz 1974), taking fruit of *Dunalia* (Cruz 1981), and eating orange blossoms (Jeffrey-Smith 1956). Stomach contents (2): fruit seeds.

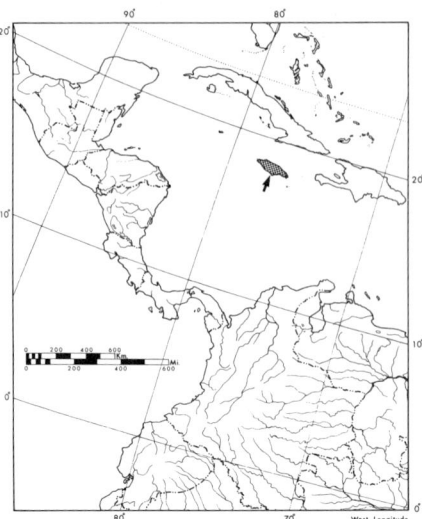

Spindalis zena (*nigricephala* subspecies group)

Vocalizations

Usually silent; utters a low sibilant note during flight (Gosse 1847). Male delivers churrs or rattles when disturbed or in hostile situations (Reynard 1982). A female sang a harsh *chirruky* note when gathering nesting material (Jeffrey-Smith 1956). A female was recorded singing a whisper song that lasted almost 3 min.; song consisted of about 4 sec. phrases, each nearly identical, sounding like *chu wheet, chee see whee see, chu wheet*; in a second recording, paused 3–5 sec. between sets of phrases (Reynard 1982).

Breeding

Builds a small rough cup nest composed of grass and rootlets. Eggs (2–3) are greenish white or pale gray, marked with brown or gray, especially about the large end. Breeding date: June.

Sources

Primary Cruz 1974; Danforth 1928; Gosse 1847; Jeffrey-Smith 1956; Taylor 1955. **Weights (n = 16)** Cruz 1974; Steadman et al. 1980. **Stomach contents** Danforth 1928. **Vocalizations** Reynard 1982. **Nests, eggs, and breeding dates** Gosse 1847; Jeffrey-Smith 1956; March 1863; Ogilvie-Grant 1912; Taylor 1955.

THRAUPIS

The flashing forms and squeaky voices of *Thraupis* species (Table 15) are commonplace sights and sounds of the Neotropics. Occurring from Mexico to Argentina, *Thraupis* spans more of the New World than any other tanager genus except *Piranga*, and *Thraupis* species are generally more common and widespread than *Piranga* species except in North America.

Table 15 The *Thraupis* Tanagers

102	*T. episcopus*		Blue-gray Tanager
103	*T. sayaca*		Sayaca Tanager
	103-1	*sayaca* subspecies group	Sayaca Tanager
	103-2	*glaucocolpa* subspecies group	Glaucous Tanager
104	*T. cyanoptera*		Azure-shouldered Tanager
105	*T. ornata*		Golden-chevroned Tanager
106	*T. abbas*		Yellow-winged Tanager
107	*T. palmarum*		Palm Tanager
108	*T. cyanocephala*		Blue-capped Tanager
109	*T. bonariensis*		Blue-and-yellow Tanager

Prominent in town and country, some *Thraupis* tanagers even inhabit the centers of large cities. Most species adapt well to man-made environmental changes, although their fondness for plantation fruits often makes them unwelcome. Writing a century ago, for example, D'Orbigny described the Blue-and-yellow Tanager as a "terror" to farmers. Despite occasional persecution, most *Thraupis* species remain abundant.

These tanagers typically inhabit semiopen and intermediate types of vegetation such as trees in cultivated areas, forest edge and clearings, savannas, and open woodland. Most species shun forest, although the very local Azure-shouldered Tanager appears to favor forest environments. *Thraupis* tend to forage from midheights to the tops of trees. Typically omnivorous, they appear to subsist mostly on fruit. Favorite fruits include those of melastomes, *Cecropia*, *Ficus*, palms, and pulpy fruits such as oranges and papaya.

Outside of Trinidad, there are few records of insect-feeding behaviors of *Thraupis* tanagers. About half of the species have been observed sallying for flying insects, especially flying termites. In addition to fruit and insects, *Thraupis* obtain nectar by eating flowers; some species consume buds and young leaves.

Most *Thraupis* species live in pairs that are

joined by their recent offspring during the nonbreeding season. Pairs often quarrel among themselves and with other species they meet in fruiting trees. *Thraupis* conspicuously fly from tree to tree, and when hidden in high foliage, their squeaky call notes and songs typically betray their presence. Vocalizations often incorporate distinctive squeezed out notes that may sound unpleasant, although the Blue-and-yellow and Yellow-winged deviate from this pattern. The typical song is a series of 5–10 single or double notes, then a pause, then another series, etc. *Thraupis* typically emit a variety of call notes, including an upward-inflected *seeee*.

After selecting a site that is usually well hidden in dense foliage, both sexes work together to build a cup nest. Blue-gray and Palm Tanagers also nest in man-made structures. Some species occasionally steal materials from or pirate nests. Females incubate alone. Individuals of many, perhaps all, *Thraupis* species breed in subadult plumages.

The Blue-gray and Sayaca Tanagers constitute a superspecies and are possibly conspecific (Short 1975).

Thraupis episcopus 102
Blue-gray Tanager
Plate 15

Length 16 cm (6½ in.). Weight 35 g (27.0–45.0 g). Thirteen subspecies. Some races are bluer, some grayer, and some tinged with green or violet. The most noticeable difference among subspecies are the wing-coverts which may be lavender, blue, or white. Where the range of the Blue-gray Tanager abuts that of the Sayaca, *T. sayaca* **103-1,** in s Peru, Bolivia, and e Brazil, the Blue-gray has white wing-coverts and the Sayaca has blue gray wing-coverts, that is if one considers *T. sayaca boliviana* to be a race of the Blue-gray (see account for **103-1** below). In subadult plumage, wing-coverts of both the Blue-gray and the Sayaca are gray, and in this plumage the two species probably cannot be separated in the field.

Geographic Range

S MEXICO from e San Luis Potosí on the Caribbean slope (rare or absent on the Yucatán Peninsula) and Oaxaca on the Pacific slope southward through CENTRAL AMERICA (including Pearl Is., Coiba I., and other islands off PANAMA) and N SOUTH AMERICA west of the Andes to Lambayeque, PERU, and throughout N SOUTH AMERICA east of the Andes to the s and e edges of Amazonia (extreme nw BOLIVIA in Pando; extreme n Rondônia, s Amazonas, se Pará, e Maranhão, and extreme w Piauí along the Rio Parnaíba, BRAZIL); TRINIDAD AND TOBAGO. Introduced into Lima, PERU.

Elevational Range

From sea level to ca. 2600 m in the Andes, lower in Central America (e.g., to 1500 m in Guatemala). Most numerous in lowlands.

Habitat and Behavior

Prefers semiopen areas including second growth, forest edge (incl. margins of rivers and oxbow lakes), and trees in cultivated lands, savannas, and human settlements; rarely strays far into forest. Quickly colonizes new forest clearings and often lives near buildings. Scarce or absent from very dry regions in Central America.

Lives in pairs. Appears to form single-species flocks in some regions and, in Panama, pairs come together to roost in large numbers (Wetmore, Pasquier, and Olson 1984). Typically joins but does not follow mixed-species flocks that pass through the Blue-gray's home range (e.g., see Buskirk et al. 1972). Frequently at gatherings in fruiting trees. Sometimes aggressive towards each other and other species. Active and restless; often twitches from side to side when perched as though about to take off. When one takes flight, its mate usually follows, but they do not fly side by side or perch together while at rest (Slud 1964). Often seen in strong rapid flight crossing open spaces between trees.

Forages primarily in upper levels of trees; occasionally descends lower or drops to the ground for fallen fruit, especially when food is scarce. In Trinidad, 82% of 211 foraging observations were above 8 m off the ground, whereas only 6% were below 3 m (Snow and Snow 1971). In Costa Rica, especially fond of *Ficus* fruits and bananas; frequently eats *Miconia* berries and less often, arillate fruit (Skutch 1954, 1980). Feeds on large fleshy commercially grown fruits such as papaya. Occasionally eats leaves and flowers or takes nectar. In Trinidad, feeding records were 53% fruit-eating, 37% insect-foraging, and 10% at flowers (Snow and Snow 1971). Stomach contents (11): vegetable matter. Additional stomach contents included mistletoe berries, termites, spiders, and caterpillars.

In Trinidad, fed on 21 species of fruit. Favored *Didymopanax morototoni* of the family

184 THRAUPIS

Thraupis episcopus

Araliaceae (23% of all fruit-eating obs.), *Cecropia* (18%), and *Miconia* (12%). Took small fruits and berries from a perched position, swallowing some fruits whole and mashing others. Clung to large fruits to remove pulp and hung from *Cecropia* catkins. Broke off long catkins of *Piper* and placed them across branches to eat pieces (Snow and Snow 1971). In Brazil, clung upside down to pendant *Cecropia* catkins and nibbled at the tiny fruits beginning with those at the tip of the catkin and working methodically upwards towards the base (see Silva 1980).

Often searches for insects by moving quickly through foliage and reaching up to leaf undersides, stretching out to tops of leaves, or darting forward to snatch prey. Also examines the undersides of branches and twigs using the diagonal-lean foraging method, flutter-pursues escaping insects, and sallies to air. In Trinidad, obtained insects 56% of the time on foliage, 17% on branches and twigs, 11% on flowers and seed heads, and 16% in aerial sallies. Typically sought prey that tried to escape by moving rather than prey that remained hidden (Snow and Snow 1971).

Vocalizations

Call notes: squeaky or squealed notes, often drawn out with a variety of inflections; most common call notes seem to be *seeee* and *cheeup*. Song: a series of very squeaky, squealed, or drawn out notes, typically alternating 1 or 2 High-pitched notes with 1 or 2 Moderate-pitched notes, e.g., *seee seee chaa chaa sweez cha sweez cha-cha*. Pattern may be repeated or may be changed with every series. Speed of delivery varies, perhaps regionally, about 2–5 notes/sec.; the series often speeds up toward the end; some songs end in a trill; pauses between songs are about 3–5 sec. long. Sometimes 2 birds sing simultaneously, producing a jumble of notes. Females deliver briefer and weaker songs than males (Skutch 1954).

Breeding

Establishes nesting territories after agile, darting aerial contests (Ginés et al. 1951). Nests are usually placed 3–20 m above the ground, but have been found from on the ground to 30 m up. The nest is normally well concealed in the fork of a leafy bough in a small tree, tall shrub, or among palm fronds. Nests have also been found under shed roofs, in the domed chamber of a thornbird (*Phacellodomus* sp) nest, and among shoots growing out of a stump (Skutch 1954, 1972). Sometimes pirates nests or steals materials from unfinished or even occupied nests.

Both sexes usually work together to build a deep, neatly constructed, open cup with thick, soft, but substantial walls; nesting materials include rootlets, green moss, grass, ferns, leaves and fine vegetable fibers for the lining. Eggs (1–3, usually 2) are laid on consecutive days. Egg colors range from almost white to grayish-blue or grayish-green, thickly mottled with brown and/or lilac gray; sometimes streaked black. Markings on eggs within a clutch may differ considerably.

Females incubate eggs for 12–14 days (14–15 days in captivity), but both parents feed the nestlings. Young rarely leave the nest before 17 or 18 days at which time they can fly fairly well. Often 2 broods are reared in a season. In captivity, parents hunted for insects more eagerly during rearing of young than at other times, and they tolerated offspring from the first brood all through the rearing of the second brood (Ciarpaglini 1971). Breeding dates: Belize April–June. El Salvador July. Costa Rica Feb–July (mostly March–May). Panama Jan, April, May, and July. Colombia April, May, Oct, and Dec. Venezuela July–Sept. Suriname all months. Guyana Jan–June. French Guiana Aug–Sept. Trinidad all months except Sept (mostly May). Brazil (Pará) May.

Sources

Primary Belcher and Smooker 1937; Ginés et al. 1951; Haverschmidt 1954; Hilty data; Parker data; Skutch 1954, 1969, 1972; Slud 1964; Snow and Snow 1971; Williams 1922. **Weights (n = 181)** Collins 1972; Dick, McGillivray, and Brooks 1984; ffrench 1973; Hartman 1955; Haverschmidt 1948, 1952, 1954, 1968; Leck 1975; LSUMZ data; Miller 1963; Oniki 1972; Paynter 1955; Ricklefs 1976; Russell 1964; Strauch 1977; Thomas 1982; Weske 1972. **Stomach contents** Foster data; Ginés et al. 1951; Haverschmidt 1968; LSUMZ data; Williams 1922. **Vocalizations** LNS recordings by L. I. Davis (1), T. H. Davis (1), Little and Kimball (1), Parker (6), Schwartz (8), D. W. Snow (1); Eisenmann 1952. **Nests, eggs, and breeding dates** Allen 1905; Beebe 1916; Belcher and Smooker 1937; Ciarpaglini 1971; Cherrie 1916; Dickey and van Rossem 1938; ffrench 1973; Hallinan 1924; Haverschmidt 1954, 1968; Hilty and Brown 1986; Ingels 1978; Ogilvie-Grant 1912; Pinto 1953; Ramo and Busto 1984; Russell 1964; Sick 1985; Skutch 1954, 1972; Snow and Snow 1964; Thomas data; Todd and Carriker 1922; Wetmore, Pasquier, and Olson 1984; Williams 1922; Willis and Eisenmann 1979; Young 1929.

Thraupis sayaca 103
Sayaca Tanager

Parkes (*Peters Check-list*:322) suggested that the geographically isolated *glaucocolpa* is a full species, a proposal accepted by Meyer de Schauensee and Phelps (1978).

Thraupis sayaca
(*sayaca* subspecies group 103-1)
Sayaca Tanager
Plate 15

Length 16–17 cm (6½ in.). Weight 32 g (27.9–34.4 g). Three subspecies: *boliviana* may be a race of the Blue-gray Tanager, *T. episcopus* **102,** as suggested by Meyer de Schauensee (1957); in adult plumage the lesser and median coverts of *boliviana* are white tinged blue gray and head is distinctly paler than the back in ANSP specimens; these are characteristics of the Blue-gray Tanager.

See the Blue-gray and Azure-shouldered, *T. cyanoptera* **104,** accounts for plumage comparisons in areas of range overlap. Subadult plumage: brownish, and probably not separable in the field from subadult plumage of the Blue-gray Tanager (illus.). Breeds in subadult plumage.

Geographic Range

T. s. sayaca and *obscura*: e South America from Rio Grande do Norte and e Maranhão, southward through BRAZIL, URUGUAY, and PARAGUAY to Buenos Aires, Córdoba, and probably La Rioja, ARGENTINA, and westward to the extreme se corner of Pará and c Mato Grosso, BRAZIL, e La Paz and e El Beni, BOLIVIA, and the base of the Andes. Sight identifications (Donahue *in litt.*, Isler, et al.) from Tambopata, se Madre de Dios, PERU, should be confirmed with specimens. *T. s. boliviana*: nw Bolivia in ec La Paz and wc El Beni.

Elevational Range

Mostly below 1000 m but found up to 3200 m in the Andes of Bolivia.

Habitat and Behavior

Inhabits open woodland, second growth, scrub of many types, and hedgerows, trees, and shrubs in cultivated lands. Successful near areas of human settlement including parks, residential areas, and the centers of large cities. Readily colonizes small isolated woodlots that can no longer support other frugivores (Willis 1979). Occasionally occurs inside forest when favorite fruits are ripe. In the austral winter, partially withdraws from the southern portions of its range as far north as parts of Rio Grande do Sul, Brazil (Belton 1985).

Travels quickly through tree tops in pairs or, when not nesting, in small groups of 3–4 individuals (occasionally up to 12). Joins feeding aggregations and sometimes associates with mixed-species flocks (Davis 1946). Flies with undulating flight, at times for long distances between woodland groves. When perched, continuously turns body from side to side (Belton 1985). Tends to keep well hidden in tree top foliage, but can be located easily by vocalizations.

Usually forages in tree tops; occasionally descends lower to fruiting shrubs. Especially fond of papaya, oranges, palm fruits, and wild figs. Takes commercially grown fruits and can be a pest to farmers. In se Brazil, recorded eating 36 species of fruit (see Voss and Sander 1980, 1981), and eats leaves and buds of trees and shrubs and eucalyptus flowers (Sick 1985). Stomach contents: vegetable matter (12); animal matter (1); both (7). Contents included fruit pulp and seeds (incl. seeds of *Cecropia*, *Ficus*, and *Schinus*) and hymenopterans (incl. ants).

In Paraguay when eating 7–10 mm fruits of *Allophyllus edulis*: Perched on a branch and leaned over or stretched way out to pluck fruit and then frequently took it to an adjacent tree for eating. Mostly swallowed fruit whole, but sometimes mashed it in its bill or held it against a branch to remove pulp, then dropped the seed. Took fruit rapidly, usually remaining for less than 1 min. in a tree. (Foster data.)

Sallies to air for insects, especially flying termites. In Brazil, crept about flower heads, probing into the base of closed blade-shaped flowers, possibly feeding on insects and/or nectar; also feasted on small wild bees (Mitchell 1957). In Argentina, fed on meat hung to dry outside a restaurant (Short 1975).

Vocalizations

Calls include a Moderate-pitched *chup* and a High-pitched *tzit*. Song: a highly variable series of mostly short, choppy, Moderate- to Very-high-pitched squeaky notes that is characterized by one or more long, loud, slurred, Moderate-pitched notes, usually given in the middle or towards the end of a series. Phrases of 6–9 notes are delivered in

Thraupis sayaca (*sayaca* subspecies group)

2–3 sec. Typically repeats the same sequence of notes, but the song varies considerably regionally and/or individually.

Breeding

Typically hides its nest in thick foliage on forks of outer branches. Nests have been found 1.5–9 m above the ground, frequently in isolated trees near habitations. The carefully woven compact nest is made of grass, flower stems, rootlets, and/or moss, and is sometimes decorated with lichens. Males accompany females during nest building and probably during incubation. Eggs (3, more rarely 2) are variable in color: yellowish white, gray, or greenish, heavily or lightly marked with shades of brown. Females incubate for 12–14 days. Both parents feed the young (Mitchell 1957) which leave the nest after about 20 days. Families appear to remain together for a long time. In Paraguay, pairs seemed to use the same nesting site year after year, and only one brood was raised in a season (Chubb 1910). Breeding dates: Brazil (Minas Gerais) Nov and Dec; (Mato Grosso) Oct and Nov; (Rio de Janeiro) Jan, April, and Sept–Dec; (Rio Grande do Sul) Feb, Sept, Nov, and Dec. Bolivia Nov. Paraguay Oct–Dec.

Sources

Primary Belton 1985; Descourtilz 1852; Foster data; Mitchell 1957; Niethammer 1956; Ruschi 1979; Short 1975; Wetmore 1926; Wied 1830.

Weights (n = 27) Belton 1985; Contreras 1979; LSUMZ data. **Stomach contents** LSUMZ data; Schubart, Aguirre, and Sick 1965. **Vocalizations** LNS recordings by Belton (4), Parker (1), Ward (1); Belton 1985. **Nests, eggs, and breeding dates** Allen 1891; Belton 1982, 1985; Chubb 1910; Eisentraut 1935; Erickson and Mumford 1957; Euler 1867; Mitchell 1957; Norgaard-Olesen 1973; Ogilvie-Grant 1912; Pereyra 1938; Snethlage and Schreiner 1929; Smyth 1928.

Thraupis sayaca
(*glaucocolpa* subspecies group **103-2**)
Glaucous Tanager
Plate 15

Length 16 cm (6½ in.). Weight 33 g (31.3–37.3 g). Monotypic if specifically distinct.

Geographic Range

The Caribbean slope from ne Bolívar, COLOMBIA, eastward to Sucre, VENEZUELA, and south of the coastal range of VENEZUELA to Guárico, Anzoátegui, and Monagas; also Margarita I.

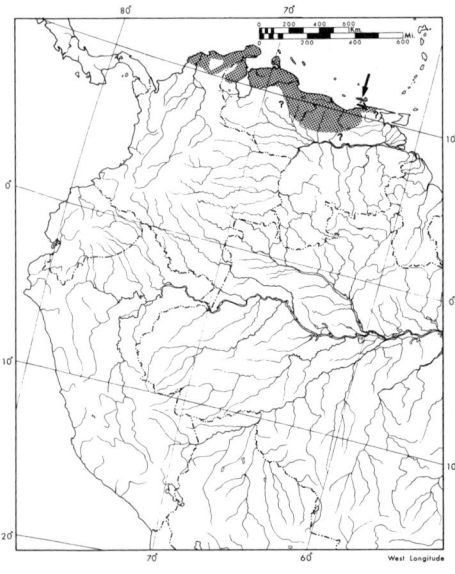

Thraupis sayaca (*glaucocolpa* subspecies group)

Elevational Range

From sea level to 800 m, usually below 500 m.

Habitat and Behavior

Inhabits woodlands and open areas with groves of trees, even though the groves may be far apart. Also frequents tall second growth, and trees in cultivated lands, parks, and gardens. In ne Venezuela, more common where trees are 12–15 m high and scarcer in deciduous seasonal woodland where trees are 5–9 m high (Friedmann and Smith 1950). Encountered in pairs, more rarely alone, and sometimes in small groups of 3–5 individuals. Forages for fruit, primarily in the tree tops.

Vocalizations

Call is a High-pitched smooth sibilant upward-inflected *seeeep*. Song is said to be weak and rambling.

Breeding

In Venezuela, a pair carried nesting material into an unfinished nest of a Plain-fronted Thornbird, *Phacellodomus rufifrons*, located in a low exposed tree growing by a stream (Skutch 1969). Another pair tore up the nest of a Bananaquit, *Coereba flaveola*, probably to steal nesting materials (Friedmann and Smith 1950). Breeding dates: Venezuela April, May, and July.

Sources

Primary Friedmann and Smith 1950; Meyer de Schauensee and Phelps 1978; Schäfer and Phelps 1954; Thomas 1979. **Weights (n = 12)** Thomas 1982. **Vocalizations** LNS recording by Parker (1); Friedmann and Smith 1950. **Breeding dates** Skutch 1969; Thomas data.

Thraupis cyanoptera **104**
Azure-shouldered Tanager
Plate 15

Length 18 cm (7 in.). Weight 44 g (41.0–46.0 g). Monotypic. Subadult is separable from the similar Sayaca Tanager, *T. sayaca* **103,** by early signs of the blue violet (Smalt Blue) wing-coverts, by its comparatively heavier bill and larger size, and by the buffier tone to the Azure-shouldered's underparts.

Geographic Range

The coastal states of se BRAZIL from Espírito Santo to n Rio Grande do Sul. Reports from other localities almost certainly confused this species with the Sayaca Tanager (Naumberg 1924).

Thraupis cyanoptera

Elevational Range

Lowlands to at least 950 m.

Habitat and Behavior

Inhabits forest, open woodland, second growth, and edges. Joins mixed-species flocks in Espírito Santo (Parker *in litt.*), although at a study area in Rio de Janeiro State, was never seen to associate with mixed-species flocks (Davis 1946). Recorded in Rio Grande do Sul only during the austral winter when encountered in close-knit single-species flocks of 15–20 individuals (Belton 1985). Interspecifically aggressive towards the Sayaca Tanager, *T. sayaca* **103** (Sick 1985). Forages in tall trees. Eats fruit, including those of melastomes and palms (*Livistona* sp). In Espírito Santo, searched moss on large limbs and branches (Parker data, 2 obs.).

Vocalizations

Call notes: *sweee* (like other *Thraupis* spp) and other squeaky notes. Song sounds like *look here, right here, drink-drink jrrr*; repeated 2–3 times; the *here* notes are long drawn-out uneven whistles, whereas the *drink-drink* is abrupt; Moderate-pitched; usually about 8–10 sec. long with variable pauses (Parker, LNS). Resembles the song of the Golden-chevroned Tanager, *T. ornata* **105,** but notes and song are much more drawn out.

Breeding

Eggs (2) are pale blue, sparingly marked all over with small purplish black spots (Ogilvie-Grant 1912). Breeding dates: Brazil (Espírito Santo) Oct.

Sources

Primary Belton 1985; Davis 1945b, 1946; Hamilton 1871; Holt 1928; Parker data, *in litt.*; Sick 1985. **Weights (n = 5)** Belton 1985; Sick 1985. **Vocalizations** LNS recording by Parker (1). **Eggs and breeding dates** Ogilvie-Grant 1912; Parker data.

Thraupis ornata 105
Golden-chevroned Tanager
Plate 15

Length 18 cm (7 in.). Monotypic. The subadult plumage is patterned like the adult but is generally duller with only a tinge of blue violet on head, chest, and flanks; subadult is darker than the Sayaca Tanager, *T. sayaca* 103 (Sick 1985).

Geographic Range

The coastal region of se BRAZIL from Bahia south to Santa Caterina and inland to e Minas Gerais.

Elevational Range

From sea level to 1750 m (Parker data).

Habitat and Behavior

Inhabits forest, forest edge, shrubby clearings, plantations, orchards, and areas of human habitation. Is partially migratory; numbers decrease in the mountains in winter; and found in the former state of Guanabara only in winter (Sick 1985). Usually encountered in pairs during the breeding season (Parker data). Outside the breeding season, found in small groups and occasionally in larger flocks of up to 25 or more individuals. Flock members frequently bicker and chase each other. Occasionally, possibly regularly, associates with mixed-species flocks. Quarrels with other species and continually battles for dominance in fruiting trees. Active and restless; often flies rapidly between trees, then disappears quickly inside foliage (Isler data). Observed anting (Sick 1985).

Usually forages in tree tops. Occasionally comes lower to fruiting shrubs and sometimes goes to the ground to eat fallen fruit, e.g. palm fruits. Eats fruits of *Livistona* (Palmae) whole (Sick 1985). Also attracted to wild figs (Holt 1928) and bananas (Descourtilz 1852). Searches for insects in lichens and moss on large limbs and hops along slender branches, scanning and picking at leaves and twigs (Parker data).

Vocalizations

Call: a High-pitched upward-inflected *seeeee*. Song: a 3–4 sec. series of about 7–9 squeaky notes that tend to be squeezed out into pleasant slurred or sliding whistles; Moderate- to High-pitched. Often the same series is repeated after intervals of 3–5 sec.; the pattern differs among individuals. Only the males sing (Descourtilz 1852).

Breeding

Sometimes selects a nesting site close to human habitations, building the nest l.5–9 m above ground in foliage of outer branches of trees and bushes (Goeldi 1894). Nests are placed among large epiphytic bromeliads (Sick 1985) and in Rio de Janeiro, pairs were observed carrying grasslike nesting material into bromeliads that were located over 15 m above the ground in isolated trees near forest (Parker data, 2 obs.). Also in Rio de Janeiro, Mitchell (1957) found a nest placed between the trunk of a Paraná Pine and a bromeliad. In Espírito Santo, Ridgely (*in litt.*) discovered a pair nesting in an oven nest built by a Rufous Hornero, *Furnarius rufus*. Eggs (3) are white or reddish white, marked with brownish black, purplish gray, or deep purplish brown. Females probably incubate alone (Davis 1945a). Breeding dates: Espírito Santo Nov; Rio de Janeiro Oct; São Paulo Oct.

Sources

Primary Davis 1946; Descourtilz 1852; Goeldi 1894; Hamilton 1871; Holt 1928; Mitchell 1957; Parker data; Sick 1985. **Vocalizations** LNS recordings by Parker (5), Ward (1). **Nests, eggs, and breeding dates** Goeldi 1894; Mitchell 1957; Nehrkorn 1899; Ogilvie-Grant 1912; Parker data; Ridgely *in litt.*; Sick 1985.

Thraupis abbas 106
Yellow-winged Tanager
Plate 15

Length 17 cm (6½ in.). Weight 45 g (38.0–55.0 g). Monotypic. Birds in subadult plumage often lack bluish tinge on head but show wing pattern. Breeds in subadult plumage (Dickey and van Rossem 1938).

Thraupis ornata

Geographic Range

The Gulf slope from s Tamaulipas and San Luis Potosí, MEXICO, southward along the Caribbean slope to c NICARAGUA (Zelaya), and on the Pacific slope from Oaxaca, MEXICO, southward to s HONDURAS (possibly NICARAGUA).

Elevational Range

From sea level to between 1400 and 1800 m.

Habitat and Behavior

Inhabits open woodland, gallery forest, forest edge and clearings, tall second growth, orchards, plantations, and areas of human habitation. Readily colonizes areas opened up by man; avoids forest interiors. Lives in pairs, sometimes in groups of 3–10 individuals. Very quarrelsome and aggressive. Joins feeding aggregations in fruiting trees but sometimes its belligerence drives away other species. Perches on high deadwood between feeding sessions, chattering and scolding. In Guatemala, roosted in tall timber bamboo (Skutch 1976).

Travels often, sometimes flying considerable distances. Forages for fruit and insects usually high in trees but also lower. Moves rather deliberately among branches. Especially fond of *Ficus* fruit; eats orange pulp through holes drilled by woodpeckers.

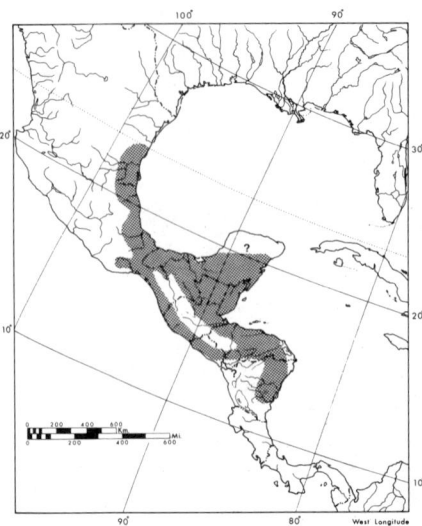

Thraupis abbas

Vocalizations

Call note: a High-pitched *weees*, sometimes upward-inflected, and other squeaky notes. Song: a 2–4 sec., mostly flat trill, *che-che-che-che-che*; predominately High-pitched; often preceded by a call note.

Breeding

Builds its nest 3–18 m above the ground on horizontal branches of thickly foliaged trees or deep in palm fronds. In Belize, observed carrying nesting material to a large tree cavity (Willis in Smithe 1966). Both sexes work together to construct the nest of small twigs, grass, leaves, and fine fibers for the lining. Eggs (2–3) are pale bluish gray, thickly spotted with reddish brown. Nestlings are possibly fed by regurgitation (see Edwards and Tashian 1959). Breeding dates: Mexico April, June, and July. Belize Feb. Guatemala May. El Salvador April.

Sources

Primary Berrett 1962; Dickey and van Rossem 1938; Edwards 1972; Land 1970; Skutch 1954:195; Smithe 1966; Wetmore 1941, 1943. **Weights (n = 42)** Klaas 1961; LSUMZ data; Paynter 1955; Russell 1964; Smithe 1966; Tashian 1953. **Vocalizations** LNS recording by van den Berg (1); recordings by Whitney (2); Edwards 1972; Smithe 1966. **Nests, eggs, and breeding dates** Dickey and van Rossem 1938; Edwards and Tashian 1959; Ogilvie-Grant 1912; Russell 1964; Sclater and Salvin 1859; Smithe 1966; Sutton and Burleigh 1940; USNM.

Thraupis palmarum 107
Palm Tanager
Plate 15

Length 17 cm (6½ in.). Weight 39 g (27.0–48.0 g). Four subspecies.

Geographic Range

T. p. atripennis, violilavata, and *melanoptera*: extreme se NICARAGUA, COSTA RICA (rare or absent from nw Pacific coastal areas), PANAMA, COLOMBIA, ECUADOR (except xeric areas along the coast), VENEZUELA, Margarita I., TRINIDAD, and THE GUIANAS; PERU and BOLIVIA east of the Andes south to Santa Cruz, BOLIVIA; and BRAZIL north of the Amazon River and south of the Amazon west of the Rio Tocantins (e Pará) southward to s Mato Grosso. *T. p. palmarum*: BRAZIL east of the Rio Tocantins (e Pará) southward to s Mato Grosso, w Paraná, and ne Rio Grande do Sul; one record from Alto Paraná, PARAGUAY.

Elevational Range

From sea level to ca. 2200 m; most numerous below 1200 m; in Colombia, occasionally to 2600 m.

Habitat and Behavior

Inhabits trees, especially palm trees, mostly in semiopen habitats such as forest edge, second growth, clearings, savanna, and areas of human habitation. Also occurs in the forest canopy, especially on lower Andean slopes (Parker *in litt.*). Travels in pairs, less often alone or in small groups. Sometimes roosts in large flocks of 10 or more (once as many as 75) individuals. Easily excited and often aggressive towards its own and other species. Commonly joins feeding aggregations and occasionally associates with mixed-species flocks, often with the Blue-gray Tanager, *T. episcopus* **102**. Moves actively from one site to another with swift strong flight. Usually perches horizontally, rarely upright. Appears to maintain a home range throughout the year (Moynihan 1962c).

Typically seeks food high in trees. In Colombia and Trinidad, foraged at heights above 7.5 m about 80% of the time. About half of the observations at each site involved insect-searching (Hilty data, 79 obs.; Snow and Snow 1971, 319 obs.). Stomach contents: vegetable matter (12); animal and vegetable matter (1). Contents included fruit pulp, seeds, and chitin fragments. Additional stomach contents included mistletoe

Thraupis palmarum

berries and termites. Observed eating caterpillars.

Perches on branches or twigs to take berries or other small fruits. Swallows most fruits whole, including fruits as large as 13 cm in diam. Feeds on nectar in large flowering trees. In Trinidad, ate 24 species of fruit, especially those from *Didymopanax morototoni* of the family Araliaceae (29% of all fruit-eating obs.), *Miconia* (21%), and *Cecropia* (11%), and fed at flowers 9% of the time (Snow and Snow 1971). In Colombia, almost half of the fruit-eating records were of *Cecropia* fruit; often hung from leaves to take *Cecropia* catkins (Hilty data). In Brazil, clung upside down to pendant *Cecropia* catkins and nibbled at the tiny fruits beginning with those at the tip and working methodically upwards towards the base (see Silva 1980). Also in Brazil, said to be fond of papaya (Mitchell 1957).

Searches for insects mostly on leaves (Table 16), especially on the undersides of large leaves such as palm fronds and *Cecropia* and banana leaves, often while hanging upside down. Alights on the upper surface of a large leaf, hops to the tip, and hangs head down to search the underside as the leaf bends with added weight. Also sallies for termites and other flying insects. Occasionally forages on dead branches, flutter-pursues escaping insects, and searches for prey under eaves and on screens of buildings.

Table 16 Percentage of Palm Tanager Insect-foraging by Substrate in Two Locations

Substrate	Trinidad (255 obs.)	Colombia (45 obs.)
Foliage	89%	44%
(Large leaves)	(66%)	(75%)
Branches and twigs	1%	9%
Moss and epiphytes	—	7%
Air (sallies)	10%	40%

Sources: Snow and Snow (1971); Hilty data.

Vocalizations

Calls: a lisping Moderate- to High-pitched *seeeee?*, a downward-inflected *see-you*, an upward-inflected *wheerst?* (Low- to Moderate-pitched), a piercing metallic *weert* or *whit*, and a rapid *pip-pip*. Song: a 3–6 sec. series of twittering notes, many of which are squeaky and sibilant, e.g., *sit, seet*; or *sit-it*, rapidly delivered, Moderate- to High-pitched. A typical version might be rendered as *SU-suri SU-suri, sit-IT sit-IT sit-IT, seet seet wheerst?, sreee sreee*. Repeats the series after intervals of up to 20 or more sec. Often sings from the top spike of a palm (Sick 1985).

Breeding

Typically hides its nest in dense foliage or in recesses of structures. Favors inner depths of isolated palm trees at the base of palm fronds; less frequently, chooses other tall isolated trees with dense crowns and bare lower trunks. Also nests in protected places high in structures such as on exposed beams under porches, or nooks and crannies under eaves.

Male and female together build the cup nest which is often made of long broad-bladed dry leaves and lined with fibers. Eggs (1–3, usually 2) are colored cream or white, marked with brown, lavender gray, or black. Females incubate for 14 days and fledging takes 17–21 days. Both parents feed the nestlings; young are possibly fed by regurgitation (Mitchell 1957). Multiple broods are often raised. In Trinidad, pairs have been known to breed 4 times in a season with intervals of 1½–6 weeks between broods (Snow and Snow 1964). Breeding dates: Panama Jan, March, and June. Colombia July–Sept and Dec. Guyana Jan. Suriname Dec–Sept. French Guiana July. Trinidad all months. Brazil (Pará) Oct; (Rio de Janeiro) Dec; (Rio Grande do Sul) Nov and Dec.

Sources

Primary ffrench 1973; Haverschmidt 1968; Hilty data; Hilty and Brown 1986; Mitchell 1957; Moynihan 1962c; Ridgely 1976; Schäfer and Phelps 1954; Slud 1964; Snow and Snow 1971. **Weights (n = 82)** ffrench 1973; Hartman 1955; Haverschmidt 1948, 1968; Leck 1975; LSUMZ data; Miller 1947, 1963; Pearson 1971; Ricklefs 1968, 1976; Snow and Snow 1971; Strauch 1977; Willis 1980. **Stomach contents** Foster data; Haverschmidt 1968; Layard 1873; LSUMZ data; Novaes and Pimentel 1973; Schubart, Aguirre, and Sick 1965; Young 1929. **Vocalizations** LNS recordings by T. H. Davis (1), Isler (1), Morton (1), Parker (5), D. W. Snow (1), van den Berg (2), Ward (3); Eisenmann 1952; Slud 1964. **Nests, eggs, and breeding dates** Belcher and Smooker 1937; Belton 1985; Chubb 1921; ffrench 1973; Haverschmidt 1968; Herklots 1961; Ingels 1978; Lamm 1948; Mitchell 1957; Moynihan 1962c; Norgaard-Olesen 1973; Pinto 1953; Sclater and Salvin 1879; Snow and Snow 1964; Wetmore, Pasquier, and Olson 1984; Williams 1922; Willis and Eisenmann 1979; USNM.

Thraupis cyanocephala 108
Blue-capped Tanager
Plate 16

Length 16 cm (6½ in.). Weight 36 g (27.0–47.0 g). Eight subspecies; underparts extensively blue in *olivicyanea* (illus.); underparts gray in the 7 other races; *auricrissa* and *annectens* are more heavily tinged blue below than *subcinerea* and *cyanocephala* (illus.); *margaritae* is tinged blue down to a sharp line on the center of the breast; and *buesingi* has a whitish malar stripe like *subcinerea* (illus.).

Geographic Range

T. c. subcinerea and *buesingi*: ne VENEZUELA in the coastal mountains of Sucre and Monagas; TRINIDAD. *T. c. olivicyanea*: n VENEZUELA in the littoral chain of the coastal range from Aragua to Miranda. *T. c. auricrissa* and *hypophaea*: w VENEZUELA in the Andes from s Lara to Táchira, the Perijá Mountains, and COLOMBIA on both slopes of the E Andes south to Meta. *T. c. margaritae*: n COLOMBIA in the Santa Marta region. *T. c. annectens*: the W and C Andes of COLOMBIA south to Nariño and Putumayo. *T. c. cyanocephala*: w slope of the Andes from Pichincha, ECUADOR, to c Cajamarca, PERU (LSUMZ); e slope of the Andes from Piura and Cajamarca, PERU, to Cochabamba, BOLIVIA.

Elevational Range

Generally 1500–3000 m, centered at ca. 2000–2300 m. In Bolivia, wanders to 3300 m (Remsen 1985). As low as 800 m in Venezuela and 550 m in Trinidad.

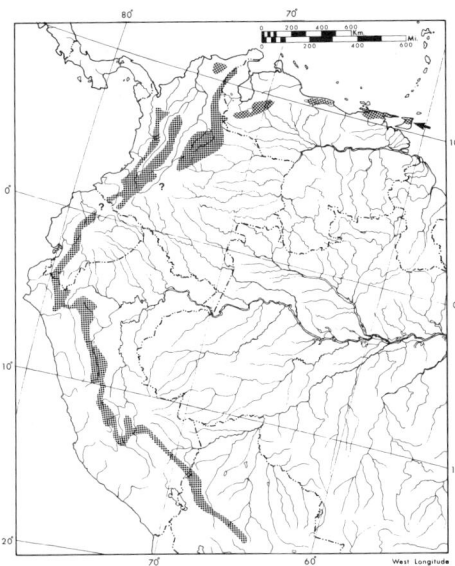

Thraupis cyanocephala

Habitat and Behavior

Inhabits shrubby clearings, second growth, forest edge, and open woodland; also occurs in forest (especially in Peru) and adjacent coffee plantations. Typically lives in pairs; also encountered singly and sometimes in groups of 3–8 (occasionally 15) individuals. Frequently occurs at feeding aggregations and occasionally in mixed-species flocks, especially outside the breeding season. Restless, noisy, and often conspicuous.

Typically forages in the upper levels of shrubs and trees. Reported to eat melastome and coffee berries (ffrench 1973) and to snatch berries in flight (Jelski and Stolzmann in Taczanowski 1884b). In Peru, sallied to air for insects; once abruptly changed flight course to capture an insect; and worked up a sapling, gleaning undersides of leaves (Isler data). Stomach contents: vegetable matter (19); vegetable and animal matter (2). Contents included berries, fruit pulp, seeds, and insects.

Vocalizations

Call note is a High-pitched sharp *tsit*. Songs appear to vary regionally: in Peru, 2–5 phrases of sharp squeaky notes, e.g., *swick-IT*, *swick-it-CHEW-y*, or *swickity-chew*; Moderate- to High-pitched; uttered in a 2–5 sec. series; pauses between songs are variable. This song may be confused with that of the Lacrimose Mountain-Tanager, *Anisognathus lacrymosus* **121,** but phrases of the Blue-capped are usually more flowing and less heavily accented. Also in Peru, another vocalization typically consists of 3 *tsee* notes followed by 10–12 *cha*s at a slightly lower pitch that sounds like the rhythmic shaking of a gourd rattle; the High-pitched series lasts about 3 sec. In Venezuela, a squeaky squealing song consists of 2–3 short piercing High-pitched whistles, followed by a jumble of Moderate- to High-pitched notes.

Breeding

In Trinidad, a deep cup nest was found 8 m above the ground in the crotch of a tree at forest edge. Eggs (2) in Trinidad are pale greenish blue with sepia or blackish markings (Belcher and Smooker 1937); in Colombia, cream colored, boldly marked with purplish brown or gray, more numerous at the large end (Ogilvie-Grant 1912); and in Bolivia, reddish gray with red brown markings (Nehrkorn 1899). Breeding dates: Trinidad June.

Sources

Primary ffrench 1973; Hilty and Brown 1986; Isler data; Schäfer and Phelps 1954; Taczanowski 1884b. **Weights (n = 53)** ffrench 1973; LSUMZ data; Weske 1972. **Stomach contents** LSUMZ data. **Vocalizations** LNS recordings by Isler (1), Parker (4), Schwartz (3). **Nests, eggs, and breeding dates** Belcher and Smooker 1937; Ogilvie-Grant 1912; Nehrkorn 1899.

Thraupis bonariensis 109
Blue-and-yellow Tanager
Plate 16

Length 17 cm (6½ in.). Weight 36 g (28.2–46.5 g). Four subspecies. In Bolivia, black-backed males sometimes have back feathers edged olive or have an olive band between back and rump (Eisentraut 1935). In se Brazil, females show yellow orange on breast in breeding season (Belton 1985).

Geographic Range

T. b. darwinii: the Andes from Pichincha and Napo, ECUADOR, south through PERU to extreme n CHILE (Tarapacá) on the w Andean slope, and to La Paz, BOLIVIA, on the e slope. *T. b. composita, schulzei*, and *bonariensis*: Cochabamba and Santa Cruz, BOLIVIA, southeast through PARAGUAY and Misiones, ARGENTINA, to Paraná (Sick 1985) and Rio Grande do Sul, BRAZIL, and southward through URUGUAY and n ARGENTINA to Buenos Aires, ex-

Thraupis bonariensis

treme ne Río Negro, La Pampa, and Mendoza.

Elevational Range

T. b. darwinii: mostly 2000–3000 m (records to 3600 m) descending to about 1000 m in dry intermontane valleys and to sea level along the Pacific coast of Peru in the Department of Lima. *Remaining races*: from sea level to 2550 m.

Habitat and Behavior

Inhabits trees and shrubbery in open woodland, gallery forest, and semiopen areas such as scrubby hillsides, savanna, parks and gardens, orchards, and various other types of cultivated lands; rarely inside forest. Typically found in trees near water in very dry portions of its range, such as c Argentina and coastal Peru. Departs the extreme southernmost part of its range in the austral winter and is scarce in other parts of Argentina at this season when large numbers migrate north (Albarce and Lucerno 1977). Its status appears to have been enhanced by human settlement even though many are killed by fruit growers.

Lives in pairs, sometimes singly or in small groups of 3–4 individuals. Joins feeding aggregations but is intraspecifically and interspecifically aggressive. Observed with montane mixed-species flocks in n Peru (Moynihan 1979). Flies with swift undulating flight from one group of trees to another.

Forages from low vegetation, including weeds, to the tops of trees. Eats fruit, including cultivated fruit such as apples, pears, plums, and cherries; also eats leaves, buds, pods, and flowers. Pecks pieces out of large fruits and can be very destructive to orchards and gardens. In intermontane valleys of Bolivia, feeds primarily on cactus fruits (Remsen *in litt.*). In Argentina, especially fond of oranges; perches on stems, pecks holes in the skin, and extracts pulp and juice, sometimes until only an empty skin remains (Casares 1944). In Brazil, observed eating eucalyptus flowers (Sick 1985). Stomach contents: vegetable matter (18); animal(?) and vegetable matter (1). Contents included fruit, seeds, moyé berries (probably *Schinus* sp), and pieces of a mollusk shell. In Rio Grande do Sul, Brazil, recorded eating 16 species of fruit (see Voss and Sander 1980, 1981).

Vocalizations

Song: 4–6 sharp bisyllabic notes, *SWEET-sur, SWEET-sur SWEET-sur, SWEET-sur*; Moderate- to High-pitched; given in 3–4 sec. and repeated after pauses of 10–20 sec.; may end or start with a short trill (esp. in flight) or a single note. Sings from constantly-changing perches in the tree tops between intraspecific chases (Sick 1985). Also delivers a series of single Moderate- to High-pitched notes given at an uneven rate but averaging about 1 note/sec., e.g., *sweet, tsick, chuck*, and a jumbled series of these types of notes.

Breeding

Usually selects a nesting site in the crown of a small tree or bush, sometimes as low as 2 m off the ground. Often places the cup nest in the fork of a horizontal branch. Eggs (2–4, mostly 3) vary in color even in the same clutch: dirty white, pale blue, or pale green, thickly marked with dark gray, especially at the large end. A second brood may be raised. In captivity, both parents fed the young (Norgaard-Olesen 1973). Breeding dates: Peru April. Bolivia Nov and Dec. Chile March and April. Argentina Dec and Jan. Brazil (Rio Grande do Sul) Nov and Dec. Uruguay Jan.

Sources

Primary Belton 1985; Descourtilz 1852; Eisentraut 1935; Friedmann 1927; Koepcke 1954, 1958; Pereyra 1938; Short 1975; Taczanowski 1884b; Vigil 1973; Wetmore 1926; Zimmer 1930. **Weights (n=41)** Belton 1985; LSUMZ data; Weske 1972. **Stomach contents** Aplin 1894; Friedmann 1927; LSUMZ data. **Vocalizations** LNS recordings by Belton (3), Isler (2), Parker (4); Sick 1985. **Nests, eggs, and breeding dates** Belton 1985; Dinelli 1924; Eisentraut 1935; Johnson 1967; Koepcke 1958; Mason 1985; Pereyra 1938; Wetmore 1926.

CYANICTERUS

Cyanicterus, a monotypic genus, has a large, unusually shaped, curved bill and bears an uncertain relationship to other tanagers. Storer (1970:326) placed it near the genus *Buthraupis* in the *Peters Check-list* because of similarity of color, pattern, and plumage texture. Meyer de Schauensee (1966) put *Cyanicterus* close to *Chlorothraupis*, and it may be related to *Tachyphonus* (Ridgely *in litt.*).

Cyanicterus cyanicterus 110
Blue-backed Tanager
Plate 16

Length 17 cm (6½ in.). Weight 34 g (1 male). Monotypic. Back and rump of males become greenish blue as plumage wears. Subadult plumage like adult but colors slightly less intense, bill brownish black. (See Parkes 1969a; Ingels 1981).

Geographic Range

THE GUIANAS and adjoining VENEZUELA (e Bolívar); also near Manaus, BRAZIL.

Elevational Range

Ca. 100–600 m in Venezuela (Parker *in litt.*).

Habitat and Behavior

Inhabits humid forest and forest edge; more rarely savanna forest. Seen in pairs and in a group of 4 individuals (once) accompanying mixed-species flocks. Forages in the canopy and subcanopy, moving deliberately, apparently searching for insects (Ridgely *in litt.*). Stomach contents: coleopterans, hemipterans, and homopterans.

Vocalizations

Call or possible song: 2–4 notes (usually 2) sounding like *pseet seet*; thin and penetrating, the second note lower-pitched than the first; occasionally preceded by a *pit* note which is also delivered in a series when excited. Sug-

198 CYANICTERUS, BUTHRAUPIS

Cyanicterus cyanicterus

gests a vocalization of the White-winged Tanager, *Piranga leucoptera* **89.** Male and female may alternate delivery; sits upright while singing, occasionally twitching wings. (Parker, LNS, *in litt.*)

Breeding

No information.

Sources

Primary Davis 1980; Haverschmidt 1968; Ingels 1981; Parkes 1969a; Parker *in litt.*; Ridgely *in litt.* **Weights (n=1)** Haverschmidt 1968. **Stomach contents** Haverschmidt 1968. **Vocalizations** LNS recording by Parker.

BUTHRAUPIS

The *Peters Check-list* brings together two distinct species groups into the genus *Buthraupis* (Table 17), but ornithologists disagree whether one or two genera should be maintained. The five smaller species (**111–115,** Plate 16), formerly constituting the genus *Bangsia,* are confined to foothills and middle montane elevations from Costa Rica to the Pacific slope of Ecuador. The larger Mountain-Tanagers (**116–119,** Plate 17) live at high Andean elevations. Despite their bulk, *Buthraupis* tanagers of both species

Table 17 The *Buthraupis* Species

⌐	111	*B. arcaei*	Blue-and-gold Tanager
│	112	*B. melanochlamys*	Black-and-gold Tanager
│	113	*B. rothschildi*	Golden-chested Tanager
│	114	*B. edwardsi*	Moss-backed Tanager
└	115	*B. aureocincta*	Gold-ringed Tanager
⌐	116	*B. montana*	Hooded Mountain-Tanager
├	117	*B. eximia*	Black-chested Mountain-Tanager
├	118.	*B. aureodorsalis*	Golden-backed Mountain-Tanager
└	119	*B. wetmorei*	Masked Mountain-Tanager

Note: brackets to the left of the table refer to suggested superspecies (solid lines) and species groups (solid plus dotted lines) discussed in the genus account.

groups may easily go unnoticed when these birds are foraging quietly; the colors of their plumages blend surprisingly well with the vegetation.

The small *Buthraupis* tanagers

Something of the ecology and behavior is known only for three species in this group: the Blue-and-gold, Golden-chested, and Moss-backed Tanagers. All three species are found in the canopy or subcanopy of humid forests where they are usually encountered in pairs and to varying degrees with mixed-species flocks. These tanagers appear to feed mostly on fruit. They usually reach out to pick fruit, but also snatch berries in flight. When insect-foraging, the small *Buthraupis* tanagers hop adroitly along branches, stopping often to peer around slowly or to probe moss and epiphytes. Two species have been observed eating flower bases to obtain nectar. Although the Golden-chested and Moss-backed Tanagers live in the same region of Colombia, they occur at different elevations and are not encountered together (Hilty *in litt.*).

The large *Buthraupis* mountain-tanagers

The Black-chested, Golden-backed, and Masked Mountain-Tanagers primarily live in elfin forest near treeline. The Hooded lives mostly in montane forest and is more widely distributed than other members of the group. The Black-chested and Golden-backed form a superspecies, their ranges separated by the Northern Peruvian Low (Parker et al. 1985).

Buthraupis Mountain-Tanagers are usually encountered in small groups, but the Hooded occasionally occurs in large single-species flocks. The Black-chested and Masked, often in company with mixed-species flocks, forage within dense vegetation and dart quickly across intervening open spaces. Hooded and Golden-backed Mountain-Tanagers are often seen flying long distances between foraging sites.

After arriving at a foraging site, Hooded and Golden-backed Mountain-Tanagers are lethargic in their insect-searching and tend to remain for some time in a small area. Most often, they peer down and pick into clumps of moss or capture their prey from under mossy limbs by hanging down, sometimes quite acrobatically. Fruit also seems to be picked in a head-down maneuver.

Buthraupis arcaei   111
Blue-and-gold Tanager
Plate 16

Length 15 cm (6 in.). Two subspecies.

Geographic Range

B. a. caeruleigularis: the Caribbean slope of COSTA RICA from extreme se Guanacaste to Cartago (Slud 1964). *B. a. arcaei*: PANAMA (locally) in Bocas del Toro (sight, July 1982—Ridgely), Chiriquí, Veraguas (on both slopes), and e Panamá province in the Cerro Jefe area (Wetmore, Pasquier, and Olson 1984).

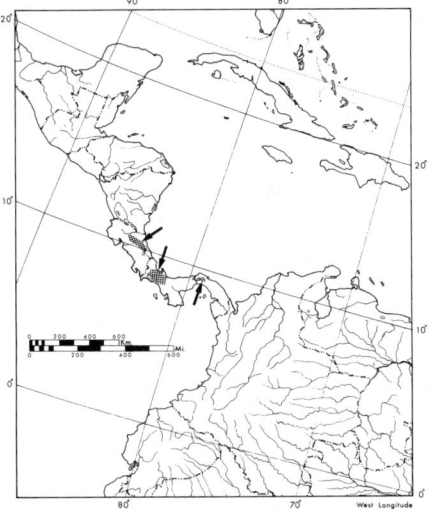

Buthraupis arcaei

Elevational Range

300–1200 m.

Habitat and Behavior

Inhabits humid and wet forest, forest edge, and adjacent tree-studded clearings. Usually lives in pairs; also singly or in small groups. Sometimes travels alone but more often accompanies flocks of other tanagers, especially *Tangara* and *Chlorospingus* species. Flight is abrupt, rapid, and buzzy on fast-fluttering wings; like that of a barbet (Capitonidae); Stiles data.

In Costa Rica: Typically forages in the canopy, lower in isolated trees or at forest edge. Frequently feeds on fruit; perches on twigs and plucks fruit, sometimes reaching far below its perch; occasionally snatches fruit in flight. Mashes up fruit (e.g., Ericaceae spp and melastomes), swallows the pulp, and drops the husk and most (or all) of the seeds. Hops along branches seeking insects; alternates heavy fast hops and sluggish stops. Often perches for several seconds peering and probing deliberately into tufts of moss; rummages in bromeliads. Although heavy-bodied, has very strong tarsi and returns easily to an upright position after leaning over in search of food. Animal food noted: cockroaches, an ant queen, and spiders. Also perches to yank off flowers, notably of epiphytic Ericaceae; mashes the flower in its beak squeezing out the nectar, then discards the flower. (Stiles data.)

Vocalizations

In Costa Rica: utters a thin High-pitched *tseeee-eeeet*, sometimes shortened to *tseeee*; often alternated with a few thin High-pitched *sip* or *tit* notes. One individual perched in a vertical position on a dead branch 12 m above the ground and sang with head tipped back and tail pointed straight down (Whitney *in litt.*). In Panama: sings a 2–3 sec. High-pitched series of sharp notes, *ti-sick-ti-sick-ti-sick* or *chit chit ti-sick-ti-sick-ti-sick*. Sang while perched on a dead twig near the top of a 9 m tree. (Whitney recording.)

Breeding

Nests have been found in Bocas del Toro, Panama (1981, Ridgely *in litt.*), and in Heredia, Costa Rica (1982, Whitney *in litt.*). The Costa Rica nest was being built about 12 m off the ground inside a clump of moss that clung to the side of a dead, branchless tree trunk. The presumed female, making numerous trips, carried what appeared to be matted rootlets into the moss cavity, while the presumed male sang nearby. The Panama nest was in a moss clump that was situated on a heavily festooned horizontal branch, about 10 m above the ground; the entry hole was about 4 cm in diam. An adult brought food, apparently mashed pulpy red fruit, on two occasions about 18 min. apart. Breeding dates: Costa Rica April. Panama July.

Sources

Primary Ridgely *in litt.*; Slud 1964; Stiles data; Whitney *in litt.* **Vocalizations** LNS recordings by van den Berg (3); recordings by R. A. Rowlett (1), Whitney (2); Ridgely in Wetmore, Pasquier, and Olson 1984. **Nests and breeding dates** Ridgely *in litt.*; Whitney *in litt.*

Buthraupis melanochlamys 112
Black-and-gold Tanager
Plate 16

Length 15 cm (6 in.). Monotypic.

Geographic Range

COLOMBIA at the nw end of the C Andes in Antioquia and on the w slope of the W Andes on the slopes of Cerro Tatamá near the common boundary of Chocó, Risaralda, and Valle.

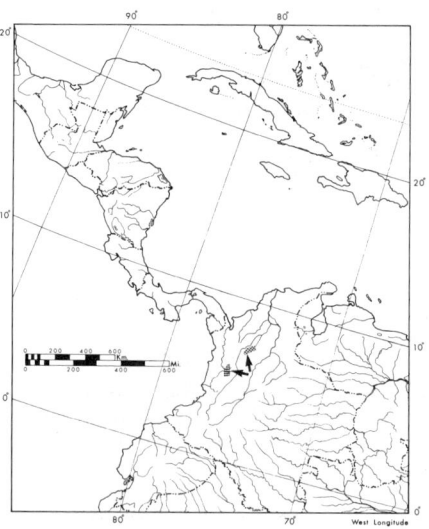

Buthraupis melanochlamys

Elevational Range

1300–2450 m.

Habitat and Behavior

Inhabits humid forest with heavy undergrowth. May be endangered; population at nw end of the C Andes may be extirpated as area is now largely deforested (Hilty 1985).

Vocalizations

No information.

Breeding

No information.

Sources

Primary Hilty and Brown 1986.

Buthraupis rothschildi 113
Golden-chested Tanager
Plate 16

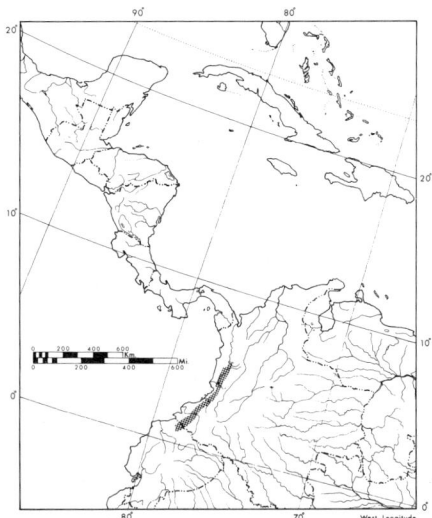

Buthraupis rothschildi

Length 15 cm (6 in.). Monotypic.

Geographic Range

The Pacific slope from c Chocó, COLOMBIA, southward to Esmeraldas, ECUADOR.

Elevational Range

From ca. 150 m (Hartert 1898) to 1100 m; mostly 300–500 m in Valle, Colombia (Hilty and Brown 1986).

Habitat and Behavior

Inhabits humid forest and forest edge. Pairs or single birds are typically encountered in mixed-species flocks of frugivores; usually stays within foliage. When perched on open branches, turns completely around with tail cocked and head low (Hilty and Brown 1986). Travels very directly between trees with a buzzy and somewhat heavy flight (Hilty *in litt.*).

In Valle, Colombia: Primarily foraged inside outer foliage in the crowns of midsized (10.5–17 m) trees; occasionally descended lower. Ate over 10 species of fruit including those of melastomes, epiphytes, mistletoe, *Cecropia*, and *Ficus*. Usually perched to take fruits; also snatched berries in flight and hovered in front of fruit. Swallowed some berries whole and mashed others before eating. Removed fruits or seeds from partially opened capsules. Peered and probed for insects while hopping sluggishly along branches. Searched for prey on bare and mossy branches and leaf stems; also sallied to air. Peeled petals off flowers to eat nectar-laden centers. (Hilty data, 28 obs.)

Vocalizations

Song: a buzzy, insectlike *tiz-ez-ez-ez-ez-ez* repeated up to 10 times a min. Call: a shrill, high-pitched *kjeee*. (Hilty and Brown 1986.) Sings infrequently, but was observed once, singing for several minutes from an exposed perch above the canopy (Hilty 1977).

Breeding

In Colombia, observed carrying nesting material in June (Hilty 1977).

Sources

Primary Hilty data; Hilty 1977; Hilty and Brown 1986; Parker data. **Vocalizations** Hilty and Brown 1986. **Breeding dates** Hilty 1977.

Buthraupis edwardsi 114
Moss-backed Tanager
Plate 16

Length 15 cm (6 in.). Monotypic.

Geographic Range

The Pacific slope from Valle, COLOMBIA, to Pichincha, ECUADOR.

Elevational Range

400–2100 m; in Colombia, mostly above 900 m in Nariño and 1200 m in Valle (Hilty and Brown 1986).

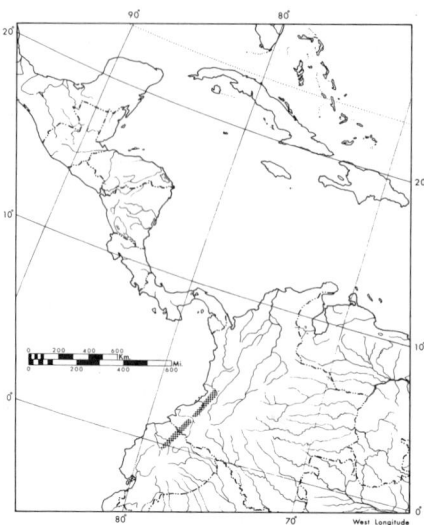

Buthraupis edwardsi

Habitat and Behavior

Inhabits wet and mossy forest, less often forest edge, and rarely trees in clearings. Encountered mostly in pairs, sometimes singly. Travels independently or accompanies mixed-species flocks. Flies directly from one tree to another with a heavy, buzzy flight. Lethargic, almost unsuspicious (Hilty and Brown 1986). In Nariño, Colombia, frequently seen perching quietly on a high stub overlooking the forest (Hilty *in litt.*).

In Valle, Colombia: Usually foraged from mid to upper levels, occasionally descended lower to fruiting shrubs. Mostly ate fruit including fruits of melastomes, epiphytes, and parasitic plants. Picked berries from a perched position and pulled soft parts from palm nut clusters and fruit capsules. Searched for insects on mossy branches and trunks and in heavy mats of moss. Slowly hopped along branches peering deliberately into moss and foliage; picked insects off foliage and flutter-pursued escaping prey; sometimes sallied to air. (Hilty data, 37 obs.) Also in Valle, seen pecking pieces from fruit spikes (Araceae) by clinging to the sides of the fruit (Isler data).

A pair was observed for 12 min. at an ant swarm at an elevation of 1250 m where it alternated between eating berries at a nearby melastome shrub and foraging for insects 1–2 m above the swarm. Sallied and lunged at prey disturbed by the ants; occasionally fluttered lower (to 0.4 m to capture insects. (Hilty 1974.)

Vocalizations

Presumed song of one individual: a trilled *tr'e'e'E'E'e'e'r tr'e'e'E'E'e'e'r*, uttered for nearly one min. without interruption (Hilty and Brown 1986). Contact note: short spitting *psheee*, mostly High-pitched.

Breeding

In Colombia, a stub-tailed juvenile was observed in January (Hilty and Brown 1986).

Sources

Primary Hilty data; Hilty 1974; Hilty and Brown 1986. **Vocalizations** LNS recording by van den Berg (1); recording by Whitney (1); Hilty and Brown 1986. **Breeding dates** Hilty and Brown 1986.

Buthraupis aureocincta 115
Gold-ringed Tanager
Plate 16

Length 16 cm (6½ in.). Monotypic.

Geographic Range

Cerro Tatamá (near the common boundary of Chocó, Risaralda, and Valle) and n Valle, COLOMBIA.

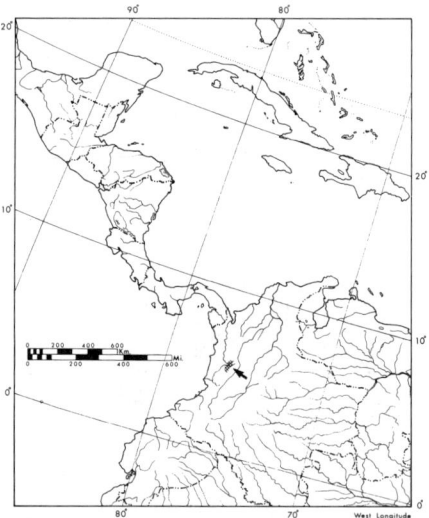

Buthraupis aureocincta

Elevational Range

2100–2200 m.

Habitat and Behavior

Wet mossy forest. May be endangered (Hilty 1985).

Vocalizations

No information.

Breeding

No information.

Sources

Primary Hilty and Brown 1986.

Buthraupis montana 116
Hooded Mountain-Tanager
Plate 17

B. m. montana: length 21 cm (8½ in.); weight 79 g (69.0–91.0 g). *Remaining subspecies*: length 23 cm (9 in.); weight 96 g (72.0–116.0 g). Five subspecies: all resemble *cucullata* (illus.) except *montana* (illus.). Intermediates between the forms illustrated have the nape touched with silver and are found in Puno, Peru (LSUMZ). Individuals in subadult plumage are very pale yellow below with some yellowish throat feathers.

Geographic Range

B. m. montana: the e slope of the Andes in La Paz and Cochabamba, BOLIVIA. *Remaining subspecies*: Táchira, VENEZUELA, west of the Western Venezuelan Low; the Perijá mountains; COLOMBIA throughout all 3 Andean ranges (Hilty and Brown 1986), the Andes in ECUADOR, and the e Andean slope throughout PERU (LSUMZ).

Elevational Range

Ca. 2000–3500 m.

Habitat and Behavior

Inhabits montane forest and forest edge; also occurs in second-growth woodland, partially cleared areas, and scrubby hillsides near forest. Lives in groups of 3–10, occasionally up to 25, individuals. Single-species flocks seem to attract other birds. Travels independently or with mixed-species flocks; often with the Mountain Cacique, *Cacicus leucorhamphus*. Restless and wide-ranging; roams up and down steep forested slopes and sometimes flies for considerable distances above the forest or across open spaces between woodlots. Flocks are often strung

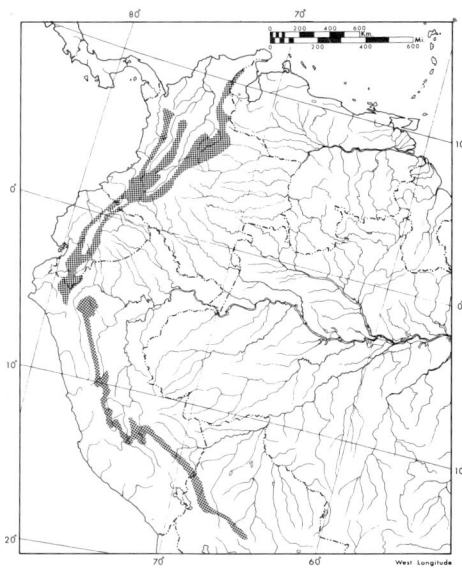

Buthraupis montana

out with stragglers hurrying to keep up (Hilty and Brown 1986). When leaving a tree, typically dives down and then rises into the sky.

Forages most often on moss-covered limbs in the subcanopy of tall trees, but feeds at all levels in trees and shrubs. In Bolivia, median foraging height was about 6 m above the ground and distance to the canopy was about 2 m (Remsen data, 35 obs.). Sits quietly eating fruit which it picks without acrobatics or by leaning head-down. Forages for insects sluggishly, often remaining in a large tree for 10–30 min. Slowly hops along limbs, peers around, and frequently looks down into moss and epiphytes. Often reaches for insects with head-down and diagonal-lean foraging methods. Also inspects dense foliage near the ends of branches and picks prey from the undersides of leaves. Occasionally probes flowers, seed pods, and dead-leaf clusters. Stomach contents: vegetable matter (34); vegetable and animal matter (1). Contents included fruit pulp, berries, seeds (incl. seeds of Gramineae), leaves, and beetles.

Vocalizations

In the early morning, individuals join in a chorus that can be heard over long distances. Disturbances, such as a truck passing by on a nearby highway, may trigger similar outbursts later in the day. Calls consist of sharp squealing (sometimes nasal or raspy)

Moderate-pitched *weeck* and *toot* notes repeated rapidly (up to 3 notes/sec) and interrupted often by series of up to 15 double-noted phrases *toot-weeck* or *weeck-toot* (the *weeck* note upward-inflected). Also utters many weak *ti* notes, singly or in rapid series while foraging (Hilty *in litt.*) and a series of High-pitched *seet* or *ti* notes during a flight display in which the Hooded Mountain-Tanager rises up into the sky on deep wing beats. In an apparent dawn song, a single bird monotonously repeated *weeck!* or *toot-weeck* at a rate of about 1 phrase/sec.

Breeding

No information.

Sources

Primary Hilty and Brown 1986; Isler data; LSUMZ data; Parker data; Remsen data; Remsen 1985; Remsen and Parker 1984. **Weights** (*montana* n = 17; remaining races n = 35): LSUMZ data; Weske 1972. **Stomach contents** LSUMZ data. **Vocalizations** LNS recordings by Isler (2), Parker (6), van den Berg (1); Hilty *in litt.*; Hilty and Brown 1986.

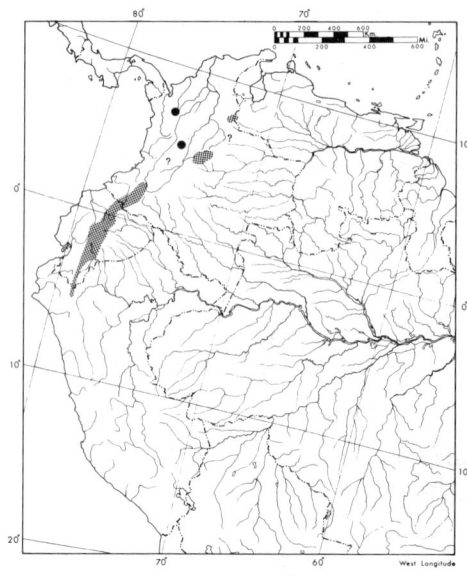

Buthraupis eximia

Buthraupis eximia **117**
Black-chested Mountain-Tanager
Plate 17

Length 18–20 cm (7–8 in.). Weight (*cyanocalyptra*) 63 g (50.0–70.0 g). Four subspecies.

Geographic Range

B. e. eximia: the Andes west of the Western Venezuelan Low in Táchira, VENEZUELA, and adjoining Norte de Santander, COLOMBIA, and the E Andes in Cundinamarca, COLOMBIA. *B. e. zimmeri*, *chloronota*, and *cyanocalyptra*: locally in the C and W Andes in Antioquia and Risaralda, COLOMBIA, and from Huila and Cauca, COLOMBIA, southward through ECUADOR to e Piura and n Cajamarca, PERU, north of the Northern Peruvian Low.

Elevational Range

2000–3800 m, mostly 2800–3400 m in Colombia (Hilty and Brown 1986).

Habitat and Behavior

Inhabits elfin forest at or near treeline; occasionally descends to low, mossy, montane forest. Encountered in small groups of 3–6 individuals, sometimes in pairs or singly. Travels alone or with mixed-species flocks where it may be a nuclear species (Moynihan 1979). Moves rather heavily and quietly (Hilty and Brown 1986). Tends to stay within dense foliage of trees and shrubs.

Searches leaves, mossy branches, and epiphytic growth. Noted in melastomes and other fruiting trees. In Peru, chewed the rinds off large fruits of *Schefflera* but swallowed all the pieces (Parker data). Stomach contents (7): vegetable matter, including seeds and fruit.

Vocalizations

Song: a long, fairly elaborate, series that sometimes continues for up to 30 sec. The repeating element of one song was *tititi-turri-tititi-tee-ter-turry* etc. Call notes: occasionally utters soft *seep*s and *chip*s while feeding (Parker data).

Breeding

No information.

Sources

Primary Hilty and Brown 1986; LSUMZ data; Olivares 1969, 1970; Parker data; Parker et al. 1985. **Weights (n = 14)** LSUMZ data. **Stomach contents** LSUMZ data. **Vocalizations** Parker data; Parker et al. 1985.

Buthraupis aureodorsalis **118**
Golden-backed Mountain-Tanager
Plate 17

Length 23 cm (9 in.). Weight 85 g (75.0–94.0 g). Monotypic. Described by Blake and Hocking (1974).

Geographic Range

The e Andean slope from La Libertad to Huánuco. PERU.

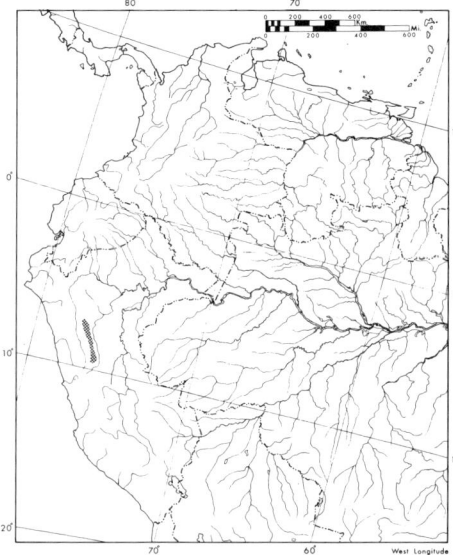

Buthraupis aureodorsalis

Elevational Range

Ca. 3150–3500 m.

Habitat and Behavior

Inhabits elfin forest, especially large islands of forest surrounded by grassland. Occasionally occurs in scattered low trees and scrub in open areas near forest. Small groups of 3–5 (sometimes up to 7) individuals or pairs travel by themselves or sometimes link up with mixed-species flocks, probably for only short periods. Flies just above tree tops between widely separated foraging sites; flight is slightly undulating. After settling into vegetation, becomes difficult to observe; sometimes rests quietly for long periods, looking around. Prior to flight one bird will begin calling; after taking off, it is quickly followed by others, one bird at a time.

Forages from the ground to tree tops but most often at midheights of small trees and bushes. Feeds deliberately on berries and fruit (e.g., those of *Miconia* and *Cecropia*) and insects. In Huánuco, Peru, a flock of 5 individuals, studied for over 45 min., was feeding in moss-laden trees less than 3 m high that were scattered across grassland at the edge of a bog. Each individual foraged for some time without much movement in one tree before flitting on to the next. Hung or leaned down to pick food out of mosses and lichens on branches; less often gleaned leaves. Flew from shrubs to nearby stubble to glean twigs and leaned over to pick food (presumably insects) off grass. (Isler data.) Stomach contents: vegetable matter (5); vegetable and animal matter (2). Contents included fruit pulp, seeds, and an 8 mm beetle.

Vocalizations

Calls from a foraging flock: sharp, metallic, abrupt, squeaky *chit*, *wheet*, and *heet* notes (sometimes in twos or threes or mixed together), chitters, and thin *sweet* or *sweee* notes; notes are High-pitched and surprisingly weak for so large a bird. Calling bouts may follow substantial periods (5–15 min.) of silence at a foraging site. Raises crest at a 45 degree angle when calling. Playback of a recording of these foraging notes brought a flock back down a hillside (perhaps 75–100 m). (Isler data.) Flight call is a sharp High-pitched *steet-steet*. Song: staccato notes, "wheedles," squeals, and churrs are delivered rhythmically and rapidly, and perhaps a little frantically; each note is repeated 4–6 times and then another group is begun in the manner of a mockingbird or thrasher (Mimidae); each group of notes is delivered in 2–5 sec. with hardly a pause between groups; notes are Low- to Moderate-pitched; recorded at dawn and in the early morning. Sometimes pieces of the song are combined with a series of call notes.

Breeding

No information.

Sources

Primary Isler data; LSUMZ data; Parker data. **Weights (n = 10)** LSUMZ data; USNM. **Stomach contents** LSUMZ data. **Vocalizations** LNS recordings by Isler (2), Parker (1); recording by G. H. Rosenberg (1).

Buthraupis wetmorei 119
Masked Mountain-Tanager
Plate 17

Length 20 cm (8 in.). Weight 62.5 g (62.0 and 63.0 g). Monotypic.

Geographic Range

Known from 4 localities: sw COLOMBIA at the s end of the C Andes in Cauca and Huila (both slopes in or near Puracé National Park); sc ECUADOR in Morona-Santiago (e slope of the Andes near Mt. Sangay) and Azuay; and Piura, PERU, near the Piura-Cajamarca boundary (Parker et al. 1985).

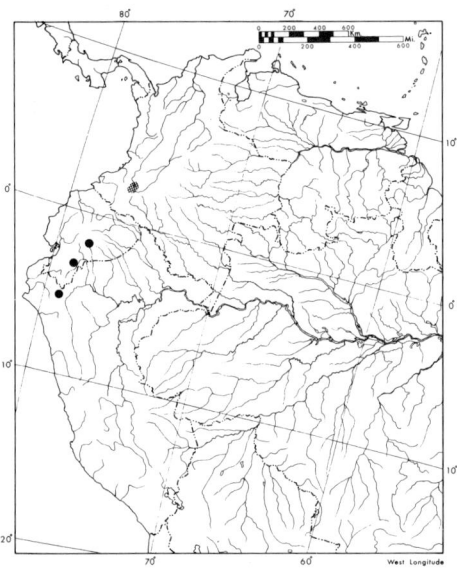

Buthraupis wetmorei

Elevational Range

2900–3650 m.

Habitat and Behavior

Inhabits dense treeline shrubbery and mossy elfin forest near treeline. In Morona-Santiago, Ecuador, prefers islands of mossy scrub surrounded by tall grass and rarely goes to contiguous forest at lower elevations (O'Neill *in litt.*). Encountered singly and in small groups of 3–4 individuals; associates with mixed-species flocks. Flies quickly across openings. Forages in low trees and shrubs for fruit and insects, hopping sluggishly and furtively within dense foliage. In Colombia, observed sallying clumsily for a flying insect (Hilty and Brown 1986). Stomach contents (1): full of seeds.

Vocalizations

No information.

Breeding

No information.

Sources

Primary Hilty and Brown 1986; Isler data; Moore 1934; Parker data; Parker et al. 1985. **Weights (n = 2)** LSUMZ data. **Stomach contents** LSUMZ data.

WETMORETHRAUPIS

The plumage of the single *Wetmorethraupis* species seems similar in appearance to the small *Buthraupis* tanagers, **111–115,** and observers (Parker, O'Neill pers. comm.) noticed a behavioral similarity as well.

Wetmorethraupis sterrhopteron 120
Orange-throated Tanager
Plate 17

Length 17 cm (7 in.). Weight 55 g (54.0–56.0 g). Monotypic. The throat is much duller (more yellowish) in the subadult plumage.

Geographic Range

Nc Amazonas, PERU, from near the Ecuador border to just south of the Río Marañón in hills west of Urakusa (LSUMZ).

Elevational Range

Chiefly 600–800 m.

Habitat and Behavior

Inhabits mature forest. Pairs and small groups of up to 5 individuals sometimes join mixed-species flocks. Forages in the canopy; seems to forage over a large area (O'Neill *in litt.*). Scans leaves and searches mosses and small bromeliads on branches (Parker data). In Amazonas, hovered and then, presumably, picked hanging fruits off the tips of

Color Plates

Plate 1 Orchesticus, Schistochlamys, Neothraupis, Cypsnagra, Conothraupis

ORCHESTICUS 1 *O. abeillei* BROWN TANAGER. Coastal mountains, se Brazil. Bill swollen; upperparts buffy olive-brown, darkest on nape; forehead cinnamon-rufous; underparts cinnamon; wings and tail cinnamon-rufous; underwing-coverts orange buff; irides red. *p. 42*

SCHISTOCHLAMYS–CONOTHRAUPIS
Four genera of thick-billed species. Adult plumages: black, gray, and white; some species with buff or cinnamon; all have white or whitish underwing-coverts. Subadult plumages: typically olive or brown, may be retained through first breeding season. Tail rounded in *Schistochlamys*.

2 *Schistochlamys ruficapillus* CINNAMON TANAGER. E and c Brazil; lowlands to ca. 1000 m. ADULT (**2a**): upperparts medium gray, crown and nape grayish cinnamon; forehead, lores, and chin black; throat, breast, and undertail-coverts pale cinnamon; flanks pale gray, belly white; wings and tail blackish edged gray. SUBADULT (**2b**): similar but lores dusky, chest buff-yellow. *p. 43*

3 *S. melanopis* BLACK-FACED TANAGER. South America, lowlands to ca. 2000 m. ADULT (**3a**): upperparts dark gray; underparts lighter, palest on belly; forehead, sides of head, throat, and upper breast black. SUBADULT (**3b**): upperparts dark yellowish olive-green; below pale olive-yellow, lightest on chin and belly; eye-ring pale yellow; wings and tail blackish edged yellowish olive-green. *p. 45*

4 *Neothraupis fasciata* WHITE-BANDED TANAGER. Brazilian tablelands and e Bolivia to ca. 1000 m. ADULT (**4a**): upperparts medium gray; wings and tail brownish; wing-coverts black and white, forming a wing-bar; mask through lores and ear-coverts black; chin and throat white; underparts light gray, becoming white on belly. SUBADULT (**4b**): pattern similar; browns replace black and gray. *p. 46*

5 *Cypsnagra hirundinacea* WHITE-RUMPED TANAGER. Lowlands and tablelands of Brazil, s Suriname, and e Bolivia. ADULT: NORTHERN FORM (*pallidigula* **5a**): upperparts, wings, and tail black; rump white; wing-edgings and wing-coverts partially edged white; short supercilium buffy; throat and breast pale buffy cinnamon, remaining underparts white. SOUTHERN FORM (*hirundinacea* **5c**): similar but lacks supercilium; chin and throat amber; breast, flanks, and undertail-coverts pale cinnamon. SUBADULT (e.g., *hirundinacea* **5b**): pale echo of same pattern; brown replaces black. *p. 48*

6 *Conothraupis speculigera* BLACK-AND-WHITE TANAGER. Local and apparently nomadic in Peru and w Ecuador. ADULT MALE (**6a**): black; rump and flanks medium gray; wing-spot and belly white. ADULT FEMALE (**6b**): upperparts olive-yellow; eye-ring yellow; underparts pale yellow, dusky on chest and flanks. SUBADULT MALE (**6c**): like female but less yellow, underparts heavily streaked dusky. *p. 50*

7 *Conothraupis mesoleuca* CONE-BILLED TANAGER. Known from a single specimen from Mato Grosso, Brazil, a male. Similar to Black-and-white Tanager (**6a**) but smaller, flanks and rump black. *p. 51*

Plate 2 *Lamprospiza, Cissopis, Chlorornis, Compsothraupis, Sericossypha*

LAMPROSPIZA–SERICOSSPHYA
Five monotypic genera of distinctive and easily recognizable species, although some species might be taken as icterids or corvids.

8 *Lamprospiza melanoleuca* RED-BILLED PIED TANAGER. Amazonia. ADULT MALE (**8a**): upperparts and breast glossy blue black extending in bands to sides; remaining underparts and underwing-coverts white; bill red. ADULT FEMALE (**8b**): resembles male but back, rump, and uppertail-coverts gray, underparts faintly tinged cinnamon. SUBADULT MALE: similar to female but bill blackish; back mottled gray and black; wing-coverts tipped white. *p. 51*

9 *Cissopis leveriana* MAGPIE TANAGER. W Venezuela, Amazonia, and se Brazil; lowlands to ca. 1800 m. Glossy blue black foreparts meet white posterior parts in an irregular line; wings black, some coverts and secondaries edged white; tail black, long, graduated, and spotted white; irides yellow. *p. 53*

10 *Chlorornis riefferii* GRASS-GREEN TANAGER. Andes, Colombia–Bolivia; range centered at 2000–2700 m. NORTHERN END OF RANGE (*riefferii* **10b**): bright green (shining Parrot Green no. 160); lesser coverts lighter (Apple Green); bill and legs flame scarlet; loral area, ear-coverts, chin, center of belly, and undertail-coverts chestnut. SOUTHERN END OF RANGE (*boliviana* **10a**): similar but green is lighter and brighter; chestnut mask extends to forehead and upper throat. Adults of other races are intermediate. SUBADULT: duller, bill brown. *p. 55*

11 *Compsothraupis loricata* SCARLET-THROATED TANAGER. Ne Brazil. Black; feathers edged shiny blue black; bill long, rather icteridlike; tail long; legs heavy. MALE (**11a**): throat and upper breast scarlet; bases of back and flank feathers white (rarely visible). FEMALE (**11b**): throat and upper breast black. SUBADULT MALE: lacks scarlet patch and glossy metallic sheen of adult male. *p. 56*

12 *Sericossypha albocristata* WHITE-CAPPED TANAGER. Andes, extreme w Venezuela–c Peru; 1600–3200 m. Black; plushy crown and lores white; legs heavy. ADULT MALE (**12b**): throat and upper breast scarlet. ADULT FEMALE (**12a**): throat and upper breast deep carmine suffused black. SUBADULT: throat black. *p. 56*

Plate 3 *Nesospingus, Chlorospingus* (part 1)

NESOSPINGUS **13** *N. speculiferus* PUERTO RICAN TANAGER. Puerto Rico. ADULT: upperparts, wings, and tail olive-brown, head darker; wing-spot white; underparts white streaked brown, especially across lower breast; posterior underparts tinged brown. SUBADULT: see text. *p. 58*

CHLOROSPINGUS (Plates 3–4) Humid mountain slopes. Bills stubby. Except as noted, upperparts olive-green, wings edged pale olive-yellow, underwing-coverts white. Sexes alike.

14 *C. ophthalmicus* COMMON BUSH-TANAGER. Mountains, Mexico–n Argentina; mostly 1000–2500 m. Plumage highly variable (see text, Table 4). Breast band yellow or yellow olive (except *cinereocephalus*). SUBSPECIES WITH WHITE POST-OCULAR SPOTS: head colors vary among shades of brown or gray; lightly spotted throat varies from yellow brown through cinnamon to almost white; *ophthalmicus* (**14f**) and *albifrons* (**14e**) exemplify dark-eyed races (Mexico–w Panama, Bolivia–Argentina); *jacqueti* (**14d**) exemplifies pale-eyed races (Venezuela–n Colombia). SUBSPECIES WITHOUT WHITE POST-OCULAR SPOT: pale-throated races (e.g., *flavopectus* **14b**) occur from most of c Colombia through Ecuador and Peru; races with blackish heads and heavily spotted throats (e.g., *nigriceps* **14c**) occur in parts of Colombia; and a race in c Peru (*cinereocephalus* **14a**) has a pale gray throat and chest. *p. 60*

15 *C. tacarcunae* TACARCUNA BUSH-TANAGER. Parts of c and e Panama and adjacent Colombia; 800–1500 m. Throat and breast dull yellow; sides, flanks, and undertail-coverts olive-yellow; center of belly white; irides pale; no post-ocular spot. *p. 63*

16 *C. inornatus* PIRRE BUSH-TANAGER. E Panama; 800–1550 m. Crown and ocular area dark gray; throat yellow; underparts olive-yellow, darkest on sides, palest on belly; irides creamy white. *p. 64*

17 *C. punctulatus* DOTTED BUSH-TANAGER. Wc Panama; 850–1400 m. Throat heavily spotted; now considered a race of Common Bush-Tanager (**14**). *p. 64*

18 *C. semifuscus* DUSKY BUSH-TANAGER. Pacific Colombia and Ecuador; 900–2500 m. Irides pale; small white post-ocular spot sometimes present. NORTHERN PORTION OF RANGE (*livingstoni* **18b**): head dark gray; underparts medium gray; hint of olive-green breast band; flanks and undertail-coverts olive-green. SOUTHERN PORTION OF RANGE (*semifuscus* **18a**): head brownish olive; throat dark buffy gray (Smoke Gray); breast band, flanks, and undertail-coverts yellowish olive-green, belly pale gray. *p. 65*

19 *C. zeledoni* ZELEDON'S BUSH-TANAGER. Costa Rica. Now considered a color morph of Sooty-capped Bush-Tanager (**20**). *p. 66*

20 *C. pileatus* SOOTY-CAPPED BUSH-TANAGER. Costa Rica and w Panama; 1500 m to treeline. Head blackish gray with long white supercilium; throat white spotted blackish gray; breast band, flanks, and undertail-coverts olive-yellow; belly pale gray. *p. 66*

21 *C. parvirostris* YELLOW-WHISKERED BUSH-TANAGER. C Colombia–Bolivia; mostly 1400–2100 m. Irides usually pale; color of sides of throat varies from orange yellow (*huallagae* **21a**) to yellow (*parvirostris* **21b**) and flares out into "whiskers"; underparts gray tinged brownish (Smoke Gray) on breast, paler on center of throat; undertail-coverts olive-yellow. *p. 67*

22 *C. flavigularis* YELLOW-THROATED BUSH-TANAGER. Lower montane elevations. Underparts gray; center of belly white; undertail-coverts olive-yellow. W PANAMA (*hypophaeus* **22a**): yellow throat; underparts tinged brown (Drab Brown). PACIFIC COLOMBIA AND ECUADOR (*marginatus* **22c**): yellow limited to sides of throat, pale irides (no range overlap with **21**). E COLOMBIA–BOLIVIA (*flavigularis* **22b**): throat yellow (Spectrum Yellow); irides yellowish brown or dark. *p. 68*

Plate 4 *Chlorospingus* (part 2), *Cnemoscopus*, *Hemispingus* (part 1)

CHLOROSPINGUS (part 2)

23 *C. flavovirens* YELLOW-GREEN BUSH-TANAGER. Local, sw Colombia, nw Ecuador; ca. 1000 m. Upperparts olive-green; ocular area blackish; ear-coverts dusky; underparts yellow olive, throat yellowish; center of belly and undertail-coverts buffy yellow. *p. 69*

24 *C. canigularis* ASHY-THROATED BUSH-TANAGER. Mostly lower montane elevations. Underparts pale gray, broad band across breast yellow; posterior flanks yellowish olive-green; undertail-coverts yellow tinged olive. CARIBBEAN COSTA RICA (*olivaceiceps* **24b**): head greenish olive. N ANDES (e.g., *conspicillatus* **24a**): head medium gray, sometimes tinged brown. E ECUADOR AND PERU (*signatus* **24c**): head dark gray; post-ocular streak white. *p. 70*

CNEMOSCOPUS **25** *C. rubrirostris* GRAY-HOODED BUSH-TANAGER. Andes; mostly 2100–2900 m. Hood gray, throat paler; upperparts yellowish olive-green; underparts yellow, flanks tinged olive. N PERU NORTHWARD (*rubrirostris* **25a**): bill and legs reddish. TO THE SOUTH (*chrysogaster* **25b**): smaller, bill and legs brown. *p. 71*

HEMISPINGUS (Plates 4–5) Mid to high Andean elevations. Species on this plate have upperparts yellowish olive-green unless noted.

26 *H. atropileus* BLACK-CAPPED HEMISPINGUS. Possibly two species. *p. 73*

26-1 *H. atropileus* (*atropileus* subspecies group) BLACK-CAPPED HEMISPINGUS. Usually over 2400 m. Long supercilium whitish. ADULT: W VENEZUELA–ECUADOR (*atropileus* **26c**): crown, nape, and area through eye blackish brown; throat and breast yellow to buffy orange-yellow; underparts yellow to yellowish olive-green. PERU (*auricularis* **26b**): blackish areas on head deeper and more extensive; throat typically more orange yellow. SUBADULT (e.g., *auricularis* **26a**): duller, head tinged olive. *p. 73*

26-2 *H. atropileus* (*calophrys* subspecies group) ORANGE-BROWED HEMISPINGUS. S Peru–nw Bolivia; near treeline. ADULT (**26d**): similar to **26-1**, but broad supercilium and cheeks deep orange-yellow buff; blackish area through eye narrow. SUBADULT (**26e**): duller, head tinged olive. *p. 74*

27 *H. parodii* PARODI'S HEMISPINGUS. Cuzco, Peru, near treeline. Bill robust; head blackish olive-green (**27b**) or olive-green (**27a**); supercilium, throat, and upper breast deep buff-yellow (**27b**) or yellow tinged olive (**27a**); underparts yellowish olive-green to yellow. *p. 75*

28 *H. superciliaris* SUPERCILIARIED HEMISPINGUS. Mostly over 2500 m. Supercilium short and narrow (width variable); bill relatively thin; underparts yellow, olive-yellow on sides (except **28d**). COLOMBIA–PERU and S PERU–BOLIVIA (e.g., *urubambae* **28c**): supercilium white; forehead, lores, and ear-coverts blackish (depth of color variable); crown greenish olive. VENEZUELA (*chrysophrys* **28b**): supercilium yellow. C PERU (e.g., *leucogaster* **28d**): upperparts and head medium-dark gray tinged olive; throat and breast pale to light gray; belly white; undertail-coverts lightly tinged cinnamon. SUBADULT (**28a**): less contrast on head; breast and sides more olive. *p. 75*

29 *H. reyi* GRAY-CAPPED HEMISPINGUS. Venezuela. Crown medium gray; upperparts deep yellowish olive-green; underparts yellow tinged buff, becoming yellowish olive-green posteriorly. *p. 77*

30 *H. frontalis* OLEAGINOUS HEMISPINGUS. Mostly 1500–2500 m. COASTAL C VENEZUELA (*hanieli* **30a**): upperparts olive-green, wings and tail edged pale cinnamon; supercilium and throat pale yellow ochre, underparts yellow ochre tinged olive-green on sides; undertail-coverts cinnamon. VENEZUELA IN NE AND ANDES (e.g., *iteratus* **30c**): upperparts more olive than **30a**, supercilium and throat more yellow orange. COLOMBIA SOUTH (e.g., *frontalis* **30b**): weak supercilium pale yellow; throat and upper breast pale orange yellow becoming buff posteriorly and tinged greenish olive on sides and flanks. *p. 77*

CHLOROSPINGUS

CNEMOSCOPUS

HEMISPINGUS

Plate 5 *Hemispingus* (part 2), *Pyrrhocoma*, *Thlypopsis* (part 1)

HEMISPINGUS (part 2)

31 *H. melanotis* BLACK-EARED HEMISPINGUS. Andes; middle elevations. Sides of head black or blackish; upperparts gray, tinged olive in some races; breast and undertail-coverts cinnamon to cinnamon-rufous. ADULT: EXTREME W VENEZUELA–ECUADOR EAST OF ANDES (*melanotis* **31a**): crown gray; supercilium narrow and usually short; belly very pale. SW COLOMBIA AND NW ECUADOR (*ochraceus* **31d**): no supercilium; underparts dull brown. PERU NORTH OF NORTHERN PERUVIAN LOW (e.g., *piurae* **31e**): crown black; supercilium long and bold; underparts tawny. C PERU (*berlepschi* **31b**): no supercilium; tawny breast contrasts with pale cinnamon belly. S PERU AND NW BOLIVIA (*castaneicollis* **31c**): supercilium thin; chin black; flanks tinged olive; center of belly pale. SUBADULT (e.g., *piurae* **31f**): pale version of adult. *p. 78*

32 *H. goeringi* SLATY-BACKED HEMISPINGUS. Venezuelan Andes; above 2600 m. Upperparts dark gray; crown, nape, and ear-coverts black; long supercilium white; underparts pale tawny; tarsi long. *p. 79*

33 *H. rufosuperciliaris* RUFOUS-BROWED HEMISPINGUS. Local, Peru; above 2600 m. Crown, nape, and ear-coverts black; long supercilium tawny; upperparts and undertail-coverts slaty; remaining underparts tawny; tarsi long. *p. 79*

34 *H. verticalis* BLACK-HEADED HEMISPINGUS. Extreme w Venezuela–n Peru; usually above 2500 m. ADULT: gray, lighter below; center of belly and undertail-coverts drab-gray; hood black with a light brown (light Drab) median crown-stripe; irides pale; bill thin. SUBADULT: throat gray. *p 80*

35 *H. xanthophthalmus* DRAB HEMISPINGUS. Nc Peru–nw Bolivia; usually above 2500 m. Upperparts olive-brown; underparts pale gray becoming white on belly; undertail-coverts drab-gray; irides pale; bill thin. *p. 81*

36 *H. trifasciatus* THREE-STRIPED HEMISPINGUS. C Peru–c Bolivia; near treeline. Head black with long supercilium buffy white; median crown-stripe and upperparts ochraceous olive-green; underparts buffy, palest on belly; bill thin. *p. 82*

PYRRHOCOMA **37** *P. ruficeps* CHESTNUT-HEADED TANAGER. Se Brazil and adjoining Paraguay and Argentina; lowlands to 1200 m. Bill stout. MALE (**37a**): medium gray; hood chestnut; mask black. FEMALE (**37b**): grayish olive, paler below; center of belly whitish; hood clay color; throat dingy. *p. 83*

THLYPOPSIS Gray or olive-gray upperparts contrast with orange tawny, tawny, or chestnut crowns that extend into hoods in some species. Crown olive or suffused olive in subadult plumages. Sexes alike.

38 *T. fulviceps* FULVOUS-HEADED TANAGER. Coastal Venezuela–ne Colombia; 800–2000 m. ADULT: upperparts medium gray; underparts light gray to white; hood tawny (e.g., *fulviceps* **38a**); hood deeper (between Amber and Chestnut) in ne Colombia (*intensa* **38c**). SUBADULT (**38b**): hood paler, tinged olive on crown. *p. 84*

39 *T. ornata* RUFOUS-CHESTED TANAGER. Sc Colombia–c Peru; mostly 2400–3000 m. ADULT (**39a**): hood and underparts pale tawny, belly white; upperparts grayish olive. SUBADULT (**39b**): paler and yellower; crown suffused grayish olive. *p. 85*

40 *T. pectoralis* BROWN-FLANKED TANAGER. Local, c Peru; 2700–3000 m. ADULT (**40a**): upperparts grayish olive; hood cinnamon-rufous, paler below; flanks light grayish-olive; belly white. SUBADULT (**40b**): similar pattern; crown olive. *p. 86*

41 *T. sordida* ORANGE-HEADED TANAGER. Ec Venezuela and lowlands east of the Andes except n and c Amazonia; mostly below 500 m. ADULT (**41a**): hood orange yellow, crown and nape tinged cinnamon-rufous; upperparts grayish horn color; underparts pale cinnamon. SUBADULT (**41b**): upperparts (to crown) grayish olive; eye-ring, throat, and breast yellow, becoming pale olive-green and white posteriorly. *p. 87*

Plate 6 *Thlypopsis* (part 2), *Hemithraupis, Chrysothlypis, Nemosia*

THLYPOPSIS (part 2)

42 *T. inornata* BUFF-BELLIED TANAGER. Local, nc Peru; 500–2000 m. ADULT (**42b**): crown deep cinnamon-rufous; upperparts deep greenish gray (Glaucous); underparts buff tinged cinnamon. SUBADULT (**42a**): upperparts grayish olive; forehead and ocular area buff-yellow tinged cinnamon; underparts yellower than adult. p. 88

43 *T. ruficeps* RUST-AND-YELLOW TANAGER. C Peru–Argentina; 1500–3300 m. ADULT (**43b**): crown and sides of head tawny; upperparts olive-green; underparts yellow tinged olive on flanks. SUBADULT (**43a**): like adult but forehead and ear-coverts buff, crown and nape like back. p. 89

HEMITHRAUPIS Mostly lowlands. Tails long; bills slender and usually yellowish. Males are distinctive. Female Guira and Rufous-headed may not be distinguishable in field. Yellow olive flanks and greater contrast between upper and underparts distinguish typical female Yellow-backed from congeners.

44 *H. guira* GUIRA TANAGER. Most of n South America. MALE (e.g., *fosteri* **44a**): upperparts olive-green, rump yellow; underparts yellow; mask black edged yellow; breast and rump suffused rufous; races vary in color intensity and in extent of yellow around mask. FEMALE (e.g., *fosteri* **44b**): upperparts yellow olive, rump yellowish; semblance of yellowish eye-ring and/or eye-stripe; underparts yellow, flanks gray; races vary in intensity of yellow in plumage. p. 90

45 *H. ruficapilla* RUFOUS-HEADED TANAGER. Se Brazil. MALE (**45a**): upperparts olive-green, rump yellow; head mostly rufous, yellow behind ear-coverts; underparts yellow, flanks gray, tinged rufous on chest. FEMALE (**45b**): similar to female Guira Tanager (**44b**). p. 92

46 *H. flavicollis* YELLOW-BACKED TANAGER. Local in South America and e Panama. TYPICAL MALE (e.g., *ornata* **46c**): upperparts black or blackish, lower back and rump yellow, wing speculum white; throat and undertail-coverts yellow; remaining underparts white mottled black. MALE IN WC AMAZONIA (*peruana* **46e**): wing-coverts yellow. MALE WEST OF ANDES (*albigularis* **46a**): center of throat white. FEMALE IN E BRAZIL (*insignis* **46d**): upperparts olive-green; underparts yellow, tinged olive on flanks. FEMALE WEST OF ANDES (*albigularis* **46b**): center of belly white, sides grayish. FEMALES OF OTHER RACES: intermediate with underparts slightly tinged yellow. p. 93

CHRYSOTHLYPIS Foothills and lowlands. Bills long and thin; tails somewhat short.

47 *C. chrysomelas* BLACK-AND-YELLOW TANAGER. MALE: COSTA RICA (*titanota* **47d**): yellow; wings, upper back, tail, and narrow eye-ring black. E PANAMA (*ocularis* **47c**): loral area black. FEMALE: COSTA RICA (*titanota* **47a**): upperparts yellowish olive-green; breast band and undertail-coverts yellowish; throat and belly white; flanks grayish. E PANAMA (*ocularis* **47b**): upperparts yellowish olive-green; underparts yellow, flanks tinged olive-green. p. 95

48 *C. salmoni* SCARLET-AND-WHITE TANAGER. Pacific Colombia–nw Ecuador. MALE (**48b**): flame scarlet; flanks white; wings and tail dusky. FEMALE (**48a**): upperparts brownish olive-green; underparts grayish white, tinged buff on throat, breast, and undertail-coverts. p. 96

NEMOSIA **49** *N. pileata* HOODED TANAGER. N South America; lowlands. Irides and legs yellow. MALE (**49a**): upperparts grayish blue, crown and sides of head and neck black, bordering underparts in a distinctive jagged line; underparts and lores white. FEMALE (**49b**): similar but lacks black on head and neck. p. 97

50 *N. rourei* CHERRY-THROATED TANAGER. Two records, se Brazil. MALE: upperparts ashy gray with bluish cast especially on wing-coverts; wings and tail black edged gray; broad mask through forehead and ear-coverts (almost touching on nape) black; underparts white; throat red. FEMALE: unknown. p. 99

Plate 7 *Phaenicophilus, Calyptophilus, Rhodinocichla, Mitrospingus, Chlorothraupis, Orthogonys*

PHAENICOPHILUS Two closely related species confined to Hispaniola and surrounding islands. Both species have forehead, ocular area, and ear-coverts black with white spots above lores and above and below eyes; nape and upper back gray; lower back, rump, wings, and tail yellowish olive-green.

51 *P. palmarum* BLACK-CROWNED PALM-TANAGER. ADULT: crown black; throat and center of breast and belly white; remaining underparts gray. SUBADULT: see text. *p. 100*

52 *P. poliocephalus* GRAY-CROWNED PALM-TANAGER. ADULT: crown gray; chin, throat, and malar stripe white; remaining underparts gray. SUBADULT: see text. *p. 100*

CALYPTOPHILUS
53 *C. frugivorus* CHAT TANAGER. Hispaniola and Gonâve I. Races vary in size and depth of color (see text; *frugivorus*, illus.). Upperparts brownish olive, flight feather edged pale brown (Fawn Color); loral spot and all or part of underwing-coverts yellow; underparts mostly white; sides, flanks, and undertail-coverts brownish. *p. 102*

RHODINOCICHLA **54** *R. rosea* ROSY THRUSH-TANAGER. Upperparts flanks, and belly dark brownish olive to olive-brown. MALE (e.g., *harterti* **54a**): supercilium pale (Ruby) red becoming white posteriorly in some races; remaining underparts pale (Ruby) red. FEMALE (**54b**): similar but red replaced by cinnamon-rufous. *p. 103*

MITROSPINGUS Dark, blackish and olive; bills long and stout, irides pale; underwing-coverts gray.

55 *M. cassinii* DUSKY-FACED TANAGER. Costa Rica–w Ecuador. Upperparts and forehead blackish gray; chin, lores, and ear-coverts black; crown yellowish; throat light gray; underparts yellowish olive-green tinged buff, yellowest on belly; undertail-coverts tinged cinnamon-rufous. *p. 105*

56 *M. oleagineus* OLIVE-BACKED TANAGER. S Venezuela and adjacent areas. ADULT: upperparts yellowish olive-green; primaries blackish edged gray; front of crown, ear-coverts, and throat medium gray; underparts yellow tinged yellowish olive-green, yellowest on belly. SUBADULT: see text. *p. 106*

CHLOROTHRAUPIS Predominantly olive; bill large and dark.

57 *C. carmioli* OLIVE TANAGER. Central America and e Andean slope; mostly lowlands. ADULT (e.g., *lutescens* **57**): upperparts olive-green; underparts olive-yellow tinged yellowish olive-green on sides and flanks; throat yellower than underparts in some races; *frenata* has paler, yellower lores. SUBADULT: clearer yellow below compared to adult. *p. 107*

58 *C. olivacea* LEMON-SPECTACLED TANAGER. North and west of Andes, e Panama–Ecuador; mostly lowlands. Upperparts dark olive-green; eye-ring, lores, and streaks on throat bright yellow; underparts dark yellowish olive-green, becoming yellowish on center of belly and undertail-coverts. Center of belly and undertail-coverts of females extensively yellow. *p. 109*

59 *C. stolzmanni* OCHRE-BREASTED TANAGER. Pacific slope, Colombia and Ecuador; mostly 400–1500 m. Head dark olive; back greenish olive; underparts ochraceous (Clay Color) tinged olive especially on sides and flanks. *p. 109*

ORTHOGONYS Bill slender compared to *Chlorothraupis*.
60 *O. chlorictus* OLIVE-GREEN TANAGER. Se Brazil; 900–1800 m. Upperparts deep yellowish olive-green; crown greenish olive; underparts yellow, tinged olive on sides and flanks. *p. 110*

Plate 8 *Eucometis, Lanio*

EUCOMETIS **61** *E. penicillata* GRAY-HEADED TANAGER. Mostly lowlands. ADULT: upperparts yellow olive. MEXICO–HONDURAS (*pallida* **61b**): head and throat dark gray; underparts pale yellow, richer yellow on chest. NICARAGUA–NW COSTS RICA (*spodocephala*): similar but underparts are deeper orange yellow. PACIFIC COSTA RICA–W PANAMA (*stictothorax*): underparts orange yellow streaked buff. C PANAMA–N SOUTH AMERICA (*cristata* and *affinis*): underparts yellow, crest long, and throat pale gray. AMAZONIA (*penicillata* **61e**): throat white; crest long with white center. BOLIVIA–SE BRAZIL (*albicollis* **61c**): head, throat, and very long crest buffy gray (Smoke Gray); throat pale. SUBADULT: lacks contrasting gray on head; (e.g., *stictothroax* **61a**) head greenish olive, throat olive-yellow; (*albicollis* **61d**) throat pale yellow. p. 112

LANIO Lowlands. No range overlap among the 4 species. Bills are long, strongly hooked, black or blackish. Males (except as noted) have black heads, wings, and tails; yellow to rufous back, rump, and underparts; and varying amounts of white on wing-coverts that is often hidden by dark scapulars. Females have brown wings and tails; tawny or tawny-tinged rumps and uppertail-coverts.

62 *L. fulvus* FULVOUS SHRIKE-TANAGER. Amazonia mostly north of Amazon River. MALE (**62a**): tawny chest patch and cinnamon posterior underparts separated by a yellower band. FEMALE (**62b**): rump and underparts cinnamon tawny, slightly paler on throat and center of belly; some females (of both subspecies) are much more greenish yellow below than illustration. p. 115

63 *L. versicolor* WHITE-WINGED SHRIKE-TANAGER. Amazonia south of Amazon River. MALE (**63a**): wing-coverts extensively white; yellow of body tinged orange; yellowish tinge to crown and throat difficult to see in field. FEMALE (**63b**): underparts cinnamon buff contrasting with yellow center of belly. p. 116

64 *L. aurantius* BLACK-THROATED SHRIKE-TANAGER. Caribbean s Mexico–c Honduras. MALE (**64a**): underparts and rump yellow, tinged orange or brownish on chest. FEMALE (**64b**): throat and upper breast light gray contrasting with olive-yellow underparts, center of belly yellow; head grayish; upper back ochraceous olive-green. p. 117

65 *L. leucothorax* WHITE-THROATED SHRIKE-TANAGER. E CARIBBEAN HONDURAS–COSTA RICA (*leucothorax*): MALE (**65c**): throat white. FEMALE (**65d**): throat pale (Drab) brown; underparts cinnamon yellow, center of belly yellow; upper back reddish brown (Amber). PACIFIC C COSTA RICA–W PANAMA (*melanopygius* and *reversus*): MALE (**65a**): throat buffy, rump and posterior underparts black. FEMALE (**65b**): like female *leucothorax* but throat brownish gray or gray. The race in Caribbean w Panama (*ictus*) is intermediate (both sexes) between *leucothorax* and *melanopygius*. p. 118

EUCOMETIS

LANIO

Plate 9 *Creurgops, Heterospingus, Tachyphonus* (part 1)

CREURGOPS Bill rather heavy. Andes; centered at ca. 2000 m elevation.

66 *C. verticalis* RUFOUS-CRESTED TANAGER. Extreme w Venezuela–c Peru. FEMALE (**66a**): upperparts medium gray; underparts cinnamon tawny. MALE (**66b**): appears similar to female except when rufous crest is exposed in excitement. SUBADULT: see text. *p. 119*

67 *C. dentata* SLATY TANAGER. S Peru–c Bolivia. ADULT MALE (**67b**): gray; underparts slightly paler and barred whitish on belly; crown and nape chestnut. ADULT FEMALE (**67a**): upperparts dark gray; partial supercilium white; underparts tawny except chin, center of belly, and undertail-coverts white. SUBADULT (**67c**): resembles adult female; supercilium weaker and underparts paler and barred grayish. *p. 120*

HETEROSPINGUS

68 *H. xanthopygius* SULPHUR-RUMPED TANAGER. Lowlands west of Andes. Gray or black; bill rather heavy, long, and hooked; lower back and rump yellow (usually hidden when perched); sides at base of wing (often partially exposed while perched) and underwing-coverts white. Considered 2 species by A.O.U. *Check-list*.

68-1 *H. xanthopygius* (*rubrifrons* subspecies group) SULPHUR-RUMPED TANAGER. Costa Rica and Panama. Sexes alike (**68d**); upperparts dark gray; underparts lighter tinged yellow; uppertail- and undertail-coverts mixed gray and yellow. *p. 121*

68-2 *H. xanthopygius* (*xanthopygius* subspecies group) SCARLET-BROWED TANAGER. EXTREME E PANAMA EASTWARD ACROSS N COLOMBIA (*xanthopygius*): MALE (**68b**): blackish gray with tuft behind eye mostly red (Spectrum Red); lesser coverts yellow. FEMALE (**68c**): upperparts dark gray; underparts paler. PACIFIC COAST SOUTH TO C ECUADOR (*berliozi*): MALE: like **68b** but almost jet black. FEMALE (**68a**): gray tinged russet. *p. 122*

TACHYPHONUS (Plates 9–10) Lowlands except as noted. Sexually dimorphic; males are black except as noted. Underwing-coverts white (except **73**). The colorful crests and white portions of lesser wing-coverts of some species are normally hidden but evident in display. Bill typically bluish black, silvery at base of lower mandible.

69 *T. cristatus* FLAME-CRESTED TANAGER. Sometimes considered 2 species as follows (see text). *p. 123*

69-1 *T. cristatus* (*cristatus* subspecies group) FLAME-CRESTED TANAGER. Most of Amazonia; e Brazil. MALE: crown patch conspicuous and red south of the Amazon (e.g., *brunneus* **69d**), but color varies north of Amazon between red and orange yellow (*intercedens* **69a**); rump and throat patch pale buff, but throat patch much reduced in some individuals in nw portions of range (**69e**). TYPICAL FEMALE (e.g., *brunneus* **69c**): reddish brown (Amber); crown tinged chestnut; throat and belly pale; narrow eye-ring buffy. FEMALE, NC SOUTH AMERICA (*intercedens* **69b**): olive above, yellow buff tinged olive below. *p. 123*

69-2 *T. cristatus* (*nattereri* subspecies group) NATTERER'S TANAGER. Mato Grosso. Known from a single male. No throat patch; crown orange-rufous; lesser and median wing-coverts white; rump patch indistinct (**69f**). *p. 125*

70 *T. rufiventer* YELLOW-CRESTED TANAGER. E Peru, adjacent Brazil, nw Bolivia. MALE (**70a**): crest yellow; rump and underparts buffy, breast cinnamon-rufous but depth of color is variable as is extent of black band across breast. FEMALE (**70b**): head gray; upperparts yellowish olive-green; throat pale buff; underparts yellow, color deepens posteriorly. *p. 125*

71 *T. surinamus* FULVOUS-CRESTED TANAGER. Amazonia. MALE (e.g., *insignis* **71b**; *napensis* **71c**): crest often hidden; posterior flanks cinnamon-rufous; pectoral tufts (not always visible) white to rufous; rump pale buff or cinnamon-rufous (see text). FEMALE (e.g., *insignis* **71a**, *brevipes* **71d**): head gray, ocular area buffy yellow, throat whitish; upperparts olive; underparts buffy or brownish (see text), undertail-coverts ochre. *p. 126*

CREURGOPS

HETEROSPINGUS

TACHYPHONUS

Plate 10 *Tachyphonus* (part 2), *Trichothraupis*

TACHYPHONUS (part 2)

72 *T. luctuosus* WHITE-SHOULDERED TANAGER. Lowlands and lower montane slopes in Andes. ADULT MALE: white-wing coverts always visible; white patch is most extensive west of Andes north to c Panama (*panamensis* **72d**); white patch is smaller in Amazonia (e.g., *luctuosus* **72b**) and Trinidad as well as in the region from Caribbean Honduras to c Panama where some individuals have a concealed yellow crown and in sw Costa Rica and adjacent Panama (*nitidissimus* **72a**) where crown is orange and cinnamon-rufous in display. ADULT FEMALE: Upperparts olive or yellow-green; underparts yellow, tinged olive on chest and flanks. C PANAMA SOUTHWARD (e.g., *panamensis* **72e**): crown and sides of head gray, throat and upper breast white, forming a hood. HONDURAS–W PANAMA (e.g., *axillaris* **72c**): crown and sides of head brownish olive, throat yellowish. SUBADULT (e.g., *panamensis* **72f**): crown and sides of head olive, eye-ring whitish, throat yellow olive, wings edged buffy yellow. *p. 128*

73 *T. delatrii* TAWNY-CRESTED TANAGER. E Central America, nw South America. MALE (**73b**): black; exposed crest orange (sometimes cinnamon or yellow). FEMALE (**73a**): olive brown, paler and tinged ochre (Clay Color) on foreparts, blackish posteriorly. *p. 130*

74 *T. coronatus* RUBY-CROWNED TANAGER. Se Brazil region. MALE: usually appears all black (**74b**); in display, raises crest and shows small white interscapular patch (**74a**). FEMALE (**74c**): upperparts reddish brown (Amber), head grayer; underparts cinnamon (some individuals do not show as much contrast as illustration); chin whitish; lores and thin eye-ring paler than crown; breast and flanks streaked dusky. *p. 131*

75 *T. rufus* WHITE-LINED TANAGER. Costa Rica–n Argentina except se Brazil region. MALE: often appears all black (**75b**); in display, shows long white lesser coverts (**75a**); underwing-coverts like **74**. FEMALE: reddish brown; individual plumages vary from deep Russet and Tawny (**75c**) to pale Antique Brown and Cinnamon (**75d**); extent of dusky streaking on underparts also variable. *p. 133*

76. *T. phoenicius* RED-SHOULDERED TANAGER. Locally distributed around Amazonia. MALE: usually appears all black (**76b**); in display (**76a**), lesser coverts red (or red and white); underwing-coverts like **74**. FEMALE (**76c**): very drab; upperparts olive-brown; underparts buffy gray (Smoke Gray); throat and belly white tinged buff; sides of head blackish. *p. 135*

TRICHOTHRAUPIS

77. *T. melanops* BLACK-GOGGLED TANAGER. E Andean slopes from Peru south and se Brazil region. Underwing pattern distinctive. MALE: upperparts deep grayish olive; forehead and ocular area black; wings and tail black tinged reddish brown (Burnt Umber); underparts pale buff, becoming buff on undertail-coverts; orange yellow crown may be hidden (**77b**) or displayed (**77a**). FEMALE (**77c**): upperparts brownish olive, more or less tinged buff on crown; wings dark brown (Fuscous); underparts pale cinnamon. *p. 136*

TACHYPHONUS

TRICHOTHRAUPIS

Plate 11 *Habia*

HABIA Bill strong; tail long, round, and often held open. Plumages blended; males are red, brown, or sooty with red crests of varying lengths. Some females similar to males, others citrine or brown.

78 *H. rubica* RED-CROWNED ANT-TANAGER. Mexico–se Brazil. TYPICAL MALE (e.g., *rubica* **78b**, with crest raised): upperparts brownish red, underparts paler; crest scarlet edged black (may be folded into a black line) and bill blackish. Races vary in brightness of red on throat (*coccinea* **78d**, ne Colombia and w Venezuela, no overlap with **79**, has reddest throat) and in intensity of underparts (*rosea* **78f**, wc Mexico, is palest). TYPICAL FEMALE (e.g., *bahiae* **78e**): upperparts olive-brown or cinnamon-brown; underparts paler (Antique Brown), throat ochraceous (Clay Color); northernmost races have an orange yellow crest (often concealed) which is reduced or absent in many South American races. SC BRAZIL (*hesterna* **78a**): underparts almost white except for cinnamon undertail-coverts; Amazonian races are intermediate in paleness of underparts. COSTA RICA AND PANAMA (*vinacea* **78c**): yellowish olive-green tinged brown with a pale olive-yellow throat. *p. 139*

79 *H. fuscicauda* RED-THROATED ANT-TANAGER. Mexico–n Colombia. MALES: Scarlet crown often concealed. DARK FORM (*fuscicauda* **79c**): upperparts, chin, and flanks dark brown (Fuscous) tinged red; throat flame scarlet; upper breast reddish brown (deep Ferruginous); underparts sooty, tinged scarlet. BRIGHT FORM (*insularis* **79d**): throat and upper breast pale scarlet; undertail-coverts pale flame scarlet; remaining plumage sooty scarlet, palest on belly. FEMALE: BROWN FORM (*salvini* **79a**): brown (mostly Raw Umber), darker above; contrasting buff-yellow throat. PALE FORM (*willisi* **79b**): upperparts brownish olive; underparts dingy olive-yellow, brownest on flanks; throat bright yellow. *p. 142*

80 *H. atrimaxillaris* BLACK-CHEEKED ANT-TANAGER. Sw Costa Rica. ADULT MALE (**80a**): upperparts blackish gray, tinged reddish brown; chin, lores, and area under ear-coverts blackish gray; center of throat pale scarlet; underparts light to medium gray, tinged pale scarlet; crest flame scarlet, often only a thin line or concealed. FEMALE AND SUBADULT MALE (**80b**): duller; underparts tinged pale orange; no scarlet on crown. *p. 144*

81 *H. gutturalis* SOOTY ANT-TANAGER. N. Colombia. ADULT MALE (**81b**): blackish gray, tinged brown; blackest on head and palest on belly; broad scarlet crest with black feather tips displayed often (as shown) or flattened back; throat rosy scarlet. SUBADULT FEMALE (**81a**): duller; crest shorter and less red; throat pink mixed with pale gray. *p. 145*

82 *H. cristata* CRESTED ANT-TANAGER. W Colombia. ADULT (**82b**): long silky crest scarlet, usually folded into a line and spike; head dusky scarlet; throat flame scarlet; upperparts brick red, wings brown; underparts gray tinged red, grayest on flanks. SUBADULT (**82a**): head cinnamon-rufous; upperparts brown (Russet); underparts cinnamon; tinged rufous throughout. *p. 146*

HABIA

Plate 12 *Piranga* (part 1)

PIRANGA Bill rather stout; sexually dimorphic; males are red or have red in plumage; females mostly yellowish olive-green. Juveniles are streaked above and below in *bidentata, flava, olivacea, rubra*, and *ludoviciana*.

83 *P. bidentata* FLAME-COLORED TANAGER. Mexico–w Panama; highlands. ADULT MALE: mostly red (*sanguinolenta* **83c**; *citrea* is similar) or orange (*flammea* **83d**; *bidentata* is similar), posterior underparts palest; back streaked dusky; ear-coverts blackish; median and greater coverts and tertials tipped whitish; outertail feathers with white patches. ADULT FEMALE: pattern similar but buffy yellow and yellow, tinged olive on head and flanks (*bidentata* **83b**); other races are slightly more orange or buffy (*sanguinolenta* is deepest in color). SUBADULT MALE (e.g., *citrea* **83a**): pattern similar; foreparts often orange, crown tinged olive; posterior underparts yellow (compare Western Tanager **88**). *p. 148*

84 *P. flava* HEPATIC TANAGER. More than one species may be involved (see text). *p. 149*

84-1 *P. flava* (*hepatica* subspecies group) NORTHERN HEPATIC-TANAGER. Se USA–n Nicaragua. MALE (e.g., *hepatica* **84a**): typically dull dusky scarlet (brightest on foreparts); ear-coverts grayish. FEMALE: similar to **84e**, but grayish ear-coverts more apparent. *p. 149*

84-2 *P. flava* (*lutea* subspecies group) HIGHLAND HEPATIC-TANAGER. Highlands and Andes, Costa Rica–nw Bolivia. MALE: deeper red than **84-1** (almost maroon in *haemalea* **84d**); throat and breast contrastingly paler. Toothed bill is typically blackish, but is pale horn with blackish base in some races, making separation from Summer Tanager (**85**) more difficult. FEMALE (e.g., *faceta* **84e**): typically yellowish olive-green above, olive-yellow below becoming yellow on throat and center of belly. *p. 150*

84-3 *P. flava* (*flava* subspecies group) LOWLAND HEPATIC-TANAGER. MALE (e.g., *macconnelli* **84c**): orange red, lacks gray ear-coverts; in n Argentina region, upperparts tinged dusky (Brick Red). FEMALE: similar to **84e**; some races (e.g., *saira* **84b**) are mostly bright yellow below, deep yellow around bill; in n Argentina region, upperparts deep olive-gray. *p. 152*

85 *P. rubra* SUMMER TANAGER. Breeds in USA and n Mexico, winters to nw South America. MALE: rosy red (underparts Geranium Pink, upperparts tinged dusky); bill horn, often appearing yellowish; eastern race (*rubra* **85a**) is illustrated; western race (*cooperi*) is paler and larger. FEMALE (color varies substantially, extremes are illustrated): WESTERN RACE (*cooperi* **85c**): pale yellow tinged pale (Drab) brown. EASTERN RACE (*rubra*): patchy orange yellow (**85b**) to deep buff (almost cinnamon) and buffy olive (**85d**). *p. 154*

86 *P. roseogularis* ROSE-THROATED TANAGER. Se Mexico, Belize, and ne Guatemala. MALE (**86b**): upperparts olive-brown; underparts buffy gray (Smoke Gray); crown scarlet; wings, tail, throat, and undertail-coverts reddish. FEMALE (**86a**): pattern similar; crown, wings, and tail tinged olive-yellow; throat and undertail-coverts pale yellow. *p. 157*

87 *P. olivacea* SCARLET TANAGER. Breeds in se Canada and e USA; winters in n South America. Except for alternate plumage of male, upperparts yellowish olive-green, underparts olive-yellow. MALE IN BASIC PLUMAGE (**87b**): wings and tail black. FEMALE (**87c**): wings and tail olive-brown edged yellowish olive-green; underparts becoming yellow on belly and undertail-coverts. SUBADULT MALE (**87a**): resembles female but often has yellow spots on greater coverts and tertials (compare Western Tanager **88**); sometimes scapulars are black. MALE IN ALTERNATE PLUMAGE (**87d**): scarlet; wings and tail black. *p. 157*

PIRANGA

Plate 13 *Piranga* (part 2), *Calochaetes*, *Ramphocelus* (part 1)

PIRANGA (part 2)

88 *P. ludoviciana* WESTERN TANAGER. W North America, wintering to w Panama. MALE IN BOREAL SUMMER (**88c**): head scarlet, becoming yellow posteriorly; rump and underparts yellow; back, wings, and tail black; middle wing-coverts yellow and tips of greater wing-coverts whitish. MALE IN BOREAL WINTER: pattern similar but extent of red on head highly variable; some individuals (**88a**), possibly first year birds, are much duller. FEMALE, YELLOW MORPH (**88b**): dull version of male with 2 yellowish wing-bars; back olive green contrasting with yellowish crown, nape, and rump; underparts yellow tinged olive on sides; red around bill variable. FEMALE, GRAY MORPH (**88d**): lacks yellow except on belly and undertail-coverts; lacks contrasting upperparts. p. 160

89 *P. leucoptera* WHITE-WINGED TANAGER. Highlands; c Mexico–c Bolivia. ADULT MALE, MIDDLE AMERICA (e.g., *latifasciata* **89b**): scarlet; forehead, lores, eye-ring, chin, wings, and tail black; width of 2 white wing-bars variable. ADULT MALE, SOUTH AMERICA (e.g., *venezuelae* **89a**): black mask restricted to lores and ocular area. FEMALE (e.g., *venezuelae* **89d**): patterns similar to respective males but dark gray replaces black, upperparts yellowish olive-green, and underparts yellow. SUBADULT MALE (e.g., *latifasciata* **89c**); scarlet replaced by orange. p. 162

90 *P. erythrocephala* RED-HEADED TANAGER. Pacific slope of Mexico; highlands. MALE (**90b**): head pale scarlet (Geranium Pink) with black lores and eye-ring; upperparts yellowish olive-green; underparts yellow, tinged olive on sides and flanks. FEMALE (**90a**): upperparts yellowish olive-green becoming buff on forehead; lores blackish; ear-coverts gray; throat and upper breast bright yellow becoming pale yellow on lower breast and buffy gray (Smoke Gray) on flanks; belly and undertail-coverts buffy. p. 164

91 *P. rubriceps* RED-HOODED TANAGER. Local in Andes, Colombia–c Peru. ADULT MALE (**91b**): hood red, dusky on lores and ear-coverts, scarlet on throat and upper breast; upperparts yellowish olive-green becoming yellow on rump; underparts and lesser and median wing-coverts yellow; wings and tail black. ADULT FEMALE (**91c**): similar but hood more restricted. SUBADULT (possibly juvenile) (**91a**): head orange; throat and breast olive-yellow. p. 164

CALOCHAETES **92** *C. coccineus* VERMILION TANAGER. E Andean slope, c Colombia–c Peru. Shiny red with black bill, lores, ocular area, throat, upper breast, wings and (short) tail. p. 165

RAMPHOCELUS (Plates 13–14) Base of lower mandible exposed and shining white (except **93**); bills of females have less contrast. Males black and red (or yellow); females duller in most species.

93 *R. sanguinolentus* CRIMSON-COLLARED TANAGER. Gulf-Caribbean lowlands, s Mexico–c Panama; locally on Pacific slope. ADULT (**93a**): black with crimson on the central crown, nape, sides of neck, breast, upper- and undertail-coverts, and underwing-coverts; bill bluish white. SUBADULT (**93b**): blackish brown with rufous red feathers distributed patchily where adult is red. p. 167

94 *R. nigrogularis* MASKED CRIMSON TANAGER. Amazonian lowlands. MALE (**94a**): black with bright red on the central crown, nape, sides of head, breast, sides, flanks, rump and uppertail-coverts (patchily on undertail-coverts); underwing-coverts orange. FEMALE (**94b**): slightly duller than male; patch on center of belly smaller and dark reddish brown. p. 168

Plate 14 *Ramphocelus* (part 2)

95 *R. dimidiatus* CRIMSON-BACKED TANAGER. Panama, Colombia, and Venezuela north of the Andes. MALE (**95b**): blackish red (Carmine) becoming clear red posteriorally; center of belly, thighs, wings, and tail black. FEMALE (**95a**): head reddish brown (Burnt Umber) becoming redder on back and bright red (mixture of Flame Scarlet and Geranium Pink) posteriorly; wings and tail blackish brown. *p. 169*

96 *R. melanogaster* HUALLAGA TANAGER. C Peru (mainly Huallaga Valley). MALE (**96b**): compared to **95b**, black band on the center of the belly broader and back blacker. FEMALE (**96a**): pale red area around bill; otherwise like **95a**. *p. 171*

97 *R. carbo* SILVER-BEAKED TANAGER. Generally east of the Andes to sc Brazil. ADULT MALE (**97c**): black tinged crimson, becoming deep crimson on throat and breast; wings and tail brownish black (Sepia). FEMALE: Varies regionally between dark and light races and intermediates. DARK RACES (e.g., *carbo* **97a**): grayish brown (Fuscous); belly and rump paler and tinged scarlet. LIGHT RACES (e.g., *connectens* **97b**): upperparts (except rump) and chin brown (between Raw and Burnt Umber); underparts and rump pale tawny. Some intermediates are rosy rufous below. SUBADULT MALE: resembles female but underparts extensively tinged scarlet. *p. 171*

98 *R. bresilius* BRAZILIAN TANAGER. East coast of Brazil. MALE (**98b**): upperparts carmine red; rump and underparts red (Spectrum Red); wings and tail blackish. FEMALE (**98a**): upperparts fuscous, tinged reddish on forehead and lower back, becoming red (Spectrum Red) on uppertail-coverts; chin and throat ochraceous brown (between Drab and Clay Color), becoming reddish brown (Ferruginous) on breast and redder on undertail-coverts; wings and tail dark grayish-brown. *p. 173*

99 *R. passerinii* SCARLET-RUMPED TANAGER. Mexico–w Panama. MALE (**99b**): velvet black with lower back, rump, and uppertail-coverts scarlet. FEMALE ON PACIFIC SLOPE (*costaricensis* **99c**): head olive-brown becoming paler (Drab) on throat; upper back olive buff; lower back, rump, and uppertail-coverts dusky orange; band across chest orange; remaining underparts olive-yellow. FEMALE ON CARIBBEAN SLOPE (*passerinii* **99a**): patterned like **99c**; lower back, rump, uppertail-coverts, and chest band olive buff. *p. 175*

100 *R. flammigerus* FLAME-RUMPED TANAGER. Sometimes considered 2 species. Intermediates occur where ranges meet. *p. 176*

100-1 *R. flammigerus* (*icteronotus* subspecies group) LEMON-RUMPED TANAGER. Lowlands of Panama, Colombia, and Ecuador on the Pacific slope and Cauca Valley, Colombia. MALE (**100a**): velvet black, with yellow lower back, rump, and uppertail-coverts. FEMALE (**100d**): upperparts, wings, and tail grayish olive to grayish brown; lower back, rump, and uppertail-coverts pale yellow; underparts straw yellow, yellowest on breast. *p. 176*

100-2 *R. flammigerus* (*flammigerus* subspecies group) FLAME-RUMPED TANAGER. Higher Colombian elevations in W and C Andes. MALE (**100b**): lower back, rump, and uppertail-coverts scarlet. FEMALE (**100c**): upperparts, wings, and tail blackish brown; lower back, rump, and uppertail-coverts flame scarlet; underparts yellow with breast band flame scarlet and undertail-coverts tinged flame scarlet. *p. 178*

RAMPHOCELUS

Plate 15 *Spindalis, Thraupis* (part 1)

SPINDALIS 101 *S. zena* STRIPE-HEADED TANAGER. Caribbean islands. Three subspecies groups (see text). Males have striped black and white heads, contrasting black and white wing patterns, and yellow breasts that become white on the belly and undertail-coverts. Females differ among subspecies groups but show some of male's wing pattern. *p. 178*

101-1 *S. zena* (*zena* subspecies group) WESTERN STRIPE-HEADED TANAGER. MALE (e.g., *zena* **101d**): band behind nape narrow; back varies from black (*zena*) to blackish olive-green (*townsendi*) to olive-green (remaining races); yellow on throat is broader and rufous band across upper breast lacking on *salvini* and *pretrei*. FEMALE (e.g., *zena* **101c**): olive-brown, paler below; *salvini* and *pretrei* have white superciliaries and moustachial stripes which are also present but less apparent in *benedicti*. *p. 179*

101-2 *S. zena* (*dominicensis* subspecies group) EASTERN STRIPE-HEADED TANAGER. MALE (e.g., *dominicensis* **101a**): upper back orange yellow; male of *portoricensis* has narrow cinnamon-rufous band on upper back and only a hint of rufous on throat. FEMALE (e.g., *dominicensis* **101b**): streaked below, rump yellowish; female of *portoricensis* is whiter below with a white moustachial streak. *p. 180*

101-3 *S. zena* (*nigricephala* subspecies group) JAMAICAN STRIPE-HEADED TANAGER. MALE (**101f**): large size, back yellow olive, breast orange yellow. FEMALE (**101e**): throat gray, tinged orange on chest. *p. 181*

THRAUPIS (Plates 15–16) Rather sleek, wings somewhat long and pointed, tails medium-sized and nearly square. Plumages are typically blended with different shades of blue.

102 *T. episcopus* BLUE-GRAY TANAGER. From c Mexico to s edge of Amazonia. ADULT: blue gray; head and underparts typically paler and bluer than back; color of lesser and median coverts highly variable (e.g., *cana* **102a** and *major* **102b**). SUBADULT (e.g., *major* **102c**): gray, tinged blue; lacks contrasting head and wing-coverts. *p. 183*

103 *T. sayaca* SAYACA TANAGER. Now usually considered 2 species. *p. 186*

103-1 *T. sayaca* (*sayaca* subspecies group) SAYACA TANAGER. S edge Amazonia–n Argentina. ADULT (e.g., *sayaca* **103-1**): grayer than **102**; little contrast between crown and back; wing-coverts greenish blue (see text for nw Bolivia). SUBADULT: like **102c**. *p. 186*

103-2 *T. sayaca* (*glaucocolpa* subspecies group) GLAUCOUS TANAGER. Caribbean Venezuela and Colombia. ADULT (**103-2b**): crown and back greenish gray (Glaucous); throat smoke gray; undertail-coverts white; flanks bright blue; wing-spot dark. SUBADULT (**103-2a**): similar but buffy. *p. 188*

104 *T. cyanoptera* AZURE-SHOULDERED TANAGER. Se Brazil. Larger and heavier-billed than congeners. ADULT (**104**): wing-coverts bright blue-violet (Smalt Blue); upperparts dusky turquoise blue or green; underparts paler with buffy on belly and undertail-coverts. SUBADULT: upperparts more greenish blue and underparts buffier (Smoke Gray) than adult. *p. 188*

105 *T. ornata* GOLDEN-CHEVRONED TANAGER. Se Brazil. Lesser and median coverts yellow; crown blue contrasting with plumbeous back; breast and sides violaceous; throat, belly, and undertail-coverts smoke gray; thinner bill than congeners. *p. 190*

106 *T. abbas* YELLOW-WINGED TANAGER. Mexico–Nicaragua. Blackish and yellow wing pattern perched and in flight; head, throat, breast, and lesser and median wing-coverts pale violet; back blackish olive-green; rump grayish olive; belly lime green. *p. 191*

107 *T. palmarum* PALM TANAGER. Nicaragua–s Brazil. Individuals vary by subspecies, sex, and age in darkness of color and extent of violaceous tone to plumage; extremes are illustrated. DARK-PLUMAGED INDIVIDUALS (e.g., *melanoptera* male **107b**): grayish olive, tinged violet on upperparts (except crown) and breast; pale smoke gray wing pattern perched and in flight. LIGHT-PLUMAGED INDIVIDUALS (e.g., *palmarum* female **107a**): yellowish olive-gray, most yellow on crown and belly; back dusky; wing pattern similar but with less contrast. *p. 192*

SPINDALIS

THRAUPIS

Plate 16 *Thraupis* (part 2), *Cyanicterus*, *Buthraupis* (part 1)

THRAUPIS (part 2)

108 *T. cyanocephala* BLUE-CAPPED TANAGER. Mountains, Trinidad–Bolivia. Underwing-coverts and thighs typically yellow. ECUADOR–BOLIVIA (*cyanocephala* **108c**): crown and nape blue; lores and ear-coverts black; upperparts, flanks, and undertail-coverts yellowish olive-green; remaining underparts gray. COLOMBIA AND VENEZUELAN ANDES: similar but throat and breast tinged blue merging into the gray belly (or ending in a sharp line in *margaritae*). C COASTAL VENEZUELA (*olivicyanea* **108b**): underparts (except flanks and undertail-coverts) blue. NE VENEZUELA AND TRINIDAD (e.g., *subcinerea* **108a**): underparts gray with a pale gray moustachial stripe. *p. 194*

109 *T. bonariensis* BLUE-AND-YELLOW TANAGER. Andes, Ecuador–Bolivia to lowlands of n Argentina. MALES: head blue, area around bill black; wings and tail black with blue edgings, underparts and rump yellow orange (intensity varies by race); back olive (ne Bolivia northward, *darwinii* **109d**) or black (other races, e.g., *bonariensis* **109e**). FEMALES AND SUBADULT MALES: grayish olive, wings and tail blue gray; highly variable. NORTHERN RACE (*darwinii* **109c**): usually tinged blue on head suggesting pattern of male, but some individuals resemble **109a**. SOUTHERN RACES: underparts vary from warm buff (**109a**) to whitish with a hint of yellow band across breast (**109b**). *p. 195*

CYANICTERUS **110** *C. cyanicterus* BLUE-BACKED TANAGER. Guiana highlands and nc Amazonia. Bill heavy, somewhat curved; irides orange. MALE (**110a**): upperparts, throat, and upper breast blue; tail and wings edged greenish blue, lesser and median coverts blue; underparts golden yellow. FEMALE (**110b**): crown, nape, back, and rump greenish blue; forehead, short supercilium, and ear-coverts dull yellow; throat and breast buff; remaining underparts bright yellow, tinged bluish on flanks. *p. 197*

BUTHRAUPIS (Plates 16–17) Chunky birds in 2 size groups. On this plate are smaller species (formerly in genus *Bangsia*) of n Andes and e Central America whose plumages are black, blue black, or dark green (Leaf Green) with varying amounts of yellow. Most with orange yellow crescent on upper breast.

111 *B. arcaei* BLUE-AND-GOLD TANAGER. Foothills. PANAMA (*caeruleigularis* **111a**): upperparts, throat, and most of sides and flanks dull violaceous blue to blackish; remaining underparts yellow to buffy yellow; irides red. COSTA RICA (*arcaei* **111b**): sides and flanks mostly yellow. *p. 199*

112 *B. melanochlamys* BLACK-AND-GOLD TANAGER. Columbia; local in nc and w Andes; ca. 1400 m. Upperparts, throat, sides, and flanks black; wing-coverts and uppertail-coverts blue (Cerulean); remaining underparts golden yellow, tinged orange on breast. *p. 200*

113 *B. rothschildi* GOLDEN-CHESTED TANAGER. Pacific slope, c Colombia–nw Ecuador; 150–1050 m. Black tinged blue violet; center of breast orange yellow; undertail-coverts and underwing-coverts yellow. *p. 201*

114 *B. edwardsi* MOSS-BACKED TANAGER. Pacific slope, wc Colombia–nw Ecuador; 1050–2100 m. Head violet blue; crown, lores, and throat blackish; upperparts dark green (Leaf Green); wings and tail edged turquoise green; underparts yellow green (Bunting Green); center of upper breast yellow. *p. 201*

115 *B. aureocincta* GOLD-RINGED TANAGER. Pacific slope, wc Colombia. MALE (**115a**): similar to preceding species but blackish green on head, throat, and flanks; yellow lines encircle ear-coverts. FEMALE (**115b**): paler version of male; black on head replaced by olive-green. The few females in collections may be subadults. *p. 202*

Plate 17 *Buthraupis* (part 2), *Wetmorethraupis*

BUTHRAUPIS (part 2) This plate includes the larger *Buthraupis* species, stocky birds with strong tarsi; restricted to the Andes.

116 *B. montana* HOODED MOUNTAIN-TANAGER. Mostly 2000–3500 m. W VENEZUELA–S PERU (e.g., *cucullata* **116b**); head and throat black; irides red; upperparts vary from dull blue black (Indigo) to blue violet (Smalt Blue); underparts golden yellow edged blue violet at rear of flanks; thighs black. NW BOLIVIA (*montana* **116a**): nape silvery; upperparts blue violet (Smalt Blue) tinged silver; lower mandible pinkish. *p. 203*

117 *B. eximia* BLACK-CHESTED MOUNTAIN-TANAGER. 2800–3400 m. W VENEZUELA AND E ANDES SOUTH TO CUNDINAMARCA, COLOMBIA (*eximia* **117b**): crown, nape, and rump blue violet (Smalt Blue); ear-coverts, throat, and upper breast black; back dark green (Leaf Green); wings and tail black edged green, coverts blue; underparts yellow (Spectrum Yellow) tinged buff. REMAINDER OF COLOMBIA SOUTH TO N PERU (e.g., *chloronota* **117a**): similar with rump green (mixed with a few blue feathers in northern race). *p. 204*

118 *B. aureodorsalis* GOLDEN-BACKED MOUNTAIN-TANAGER. Peru south of the Northern Peruvian Low; 3150–3500 m. Head, upper back, and breast black except for blue violet (Smalt Blue) crown; wings and tail black; vent and undertail-coverts reddish brown (Burnt Umber); remainder of plumage golden yellow with reddish brown spots on sides and belly. *p. 205*

119 *B. wetmorei* MASKED MOUNTAIN-TANAGER. Local in sc Colombia, Ecuador, and extreme n Peru; 2900–3650 m. Ocular area, ear-coverts, and throat black forming a mask; upperparts yellowish olive-green except edge around mask and rump yellow; wings and tail black with blue wing-bars; breast and belly yellow tinged buff, becoming yellowish olive-green on sides, flanks, vent, and undertail-coverts. *p. 206*

WETMORETHRAUPIS
120 *W. sterrhopteron* ORANGE-THROATED TANAGER. E Andean slope in extreme n Peru; ca. 600–800 m. Head, back, chin, sides, wings, and tail black; wing-coverts, tertials, and secondaries edged violet blue (Smalt Blue); throat and breast orange (Chrome Orange) suffused with white; remaining underparts pale yellow ochre (Chamois). *p. 206*

BUTHRAUPIS

WETMORETHRAUPIS

Plate 18 *Anisognathus, Stephanophorus*

ANISOGNATHUS Dark upperparts contrast with brilliant underparts and head spots or patches; blue violet wing-coverts; bills rather strong; tails somewhat long. Widespread in the Andes.

121 *A. lacrymosus* LACRIMOSE MOUNTAIN-TANAGER. Mostly above 2500 m; often considered 2 species. *p. 207*

121-1 *A. lacrymosus* (*lacrymosus* subspecies group) LACRIMOSE MOUNTAIN-TANAGER. W Venezuela–c Peru. PERIJÁ MOUNTAINS (*pallididorsalis* **121b**): crown and back greenish gray (Glaucous); remainder of head olive-yellow with yellow spots below eye and behind ear-coverts; rump and lesser and median coverts blue; wings and tail edged pale grayish-blue; underparts yellow tinged yellow ochre especially on breast; thighs blackish. SW COLOMBIA ON E SIDE OF W ANDES (*intensus* **121c**): like **121b** but head and back blackish; underparts tawny buff, touched with black on sides and flanks. IN REMAINDER OF RANGE: *melanops* resembles *intensus* but upperparts bluer, underparts golden yellow; *tamae* is closer to *pallididorsalis* than to *intensus*; *olivaceiceps, palpebrosus, caerulescens*, and *lacrymosus* are somewhat paler than *intensus* in their upperparts and yellower than *intensus* in their underparts; *lacrymosus* differs further by having only a single yellow spot below eye. *p. 207*

121-2 *A. lacrymosus* (*melanogenys* subspecies group) SANTA MARTA MOUNTAIN-TANAGER (**121a**). Crown and nape blue violet (Smalt Blue); sides of head black with a yellow spot below eye; back and rump blue black (Indigo); wings and tail edged pale blue, coverts blue; underparts between yellow and orange yellow, sides with black markings. *p. 208*

122 *A. igniventris* SCARLET-BELLIED MOUNTAIN-TANAGER. Mostly 2600 m to treeline. C ANDES, COLOMBIA, ECUADOR, AND N PERU NORTH OF NORTHERN PERUVIAN LOW (*erythrotus* **122a**): black except crescent behind ear-coverts, breast, flanks, and anterior belly scarlet; rump and wing-coverts blue (Ultramarine). C PERU–C BOLIVIA: (*igniventris* **122b**): similar but crescent and underparts orange red (between Chrome Orange and Flame Scarlet). NC PERU (*ignicrissus*): intermediate in color with undertail-coverts mixed black and red. EXTREME W VENEZUELA AND E ANDES, COLOMBIA (*lunulatus*): like *erythrotus* but undertail-coverts mixed black and red. SUBADULT: red is replaced by brownish orange (Burnt Orange). *p. 209*

123 *A. flavinuchus* BLUE-WINGED MOUNTAIN-TANAGER. Coastal range of Venezuela and Andes from extreme w Venezuela to Bolivia; mostly 1400–2400 m. Head, upperparts (except as noted), wings, and tail black; lesser and median coverts violet blue (Smalt Blue); wing- and tail-edgings turquoise blue to green (except violet blue in *cyanopterus*) center of crown and nape and underparts golden yellow. EXTREME W VENEZUELA AND E ANDES, COLOMBIA (*victorini* **123a**): back dark green (Leaf Green); rump lighter (Bunting Green); wing-edgings turquoise. EXTREME S PERU–C BOLIVIA (*flavinuchus* **123b**): back black; rump blue violet (Smalt Blue). REMAINING RACES: intermediate; backs and rumps are various combinations of black, greenish black, and dark green (Leaf Green). *p. 210*

124 *A. notabilis* BLACK-CHINNED MOUNTAIN-TANAGER. Pacific slope, sw Colombia and Ecuador; 900–2200 m. Head, chin, and nape black with small orange yellow patch at rear of crown; upperparts olive-yellow, palest on rump; wing-coverts and wing-edgings blue violet; underparts orange yellow tinged buff. *p. 212*

STEPHANOPHORUS

125 *S. diadematus* DIADEMED TANAGER. Se Brazil, adjoining Paraguay, Uruguay, and ne Argentina. ADULT (**125a**): blue violet (Smalt Blue) suffused black; crown patch red (Spectrum Red) and white; edges of crown patch and lesser and median coverts blue (Spectrum Blue). Often appears dull black in the field but raises white crest regularly. SUBADULT (**125b**): grayer with hint of white crown patch. *p. 212*

Plate 19 *Iridosornis, Dubusia, Delothraupis, Pipraeidea*

IRIDOSORNIS Medium-sized, somewhat stubby bills, long tails, and often appearing chubby and rounded. Blue of back, wings, and tail appears black in some lights.

126 *I. porphyrocephala* PURPLISH-MANTLED TANAGER. Mainly Pacific Colombia and Ecuador 1500–2200 m. ADULT (**126b**): head blue black, blackish on lores and ear-coverts, becoming blue on back and blue green on rump; wing-coverts and wing- and tail-edgings turquoise green; throat yellow to orange yellow; band across breast blue black; underparts dusky turquoise blue becoming pale buff on center of belly; undertail-coverts brown (Russet). SUBADULT, possibly juvenile (**126a**): pattern similar but dull and grayish. *p. 214*

127 *I. analis* YELLOW-THROATED TANAGER. E Andean slopes, s Colombia–s Peru; mostly 1600–2250 m. Similar to **126**, but breast and belly pale cinnamon tinged dusky on sides and flanks, undertail-coverts cinnamon-rufous, and upperparts more greenish. *p. 215*

128 *I. jelskii* GOLDEN-COLLARED TANAGER. E Andean slope, c Peru–c Bolivia; near treeline. Lores, ocular area, and throat black; crown mixed black and yellow becoming yellow ochre on sides of neck; back blue violet (Smalt Blue) tinged tawny on rump; wings and tail edged light blue (Cerulean Blue); underparts tawny, tinged dusky on breast. *p. 215*

129 *I. rufivertex* GOLDEN-CROWNED TANAGER. Mostly 2600 m to treeline. Often considered 2 species. *p. 216*

129-1 *I. rufivertex* (*rufivertex* subspecies group) GOLDEN-CROWNED TANAGER. EXTREME W VENEZUELA–n Peru (e.g., *ignicapillus* **129b**): crown orange yellow; remainder of head, throat, and upper back black; body blue violet becoming dusky on belly; wing-coverts and tertials light blue (Cerulean Blue); vent and undertail-coverts tawny (mostly blue violet in *caeruleoventris*). *p. 216*

129-2 *I. rufivertex* (*reinhardti* subspecies group) YELLOW-SCARFED TANAGER. C PERU (**129a**): similar to **129b** but with a broad yellow band across nape and ear-coverts and undertail-coverts blue. *p. 217*

DUBUSIA **130** *D. taeniata* BUFF-BREASTED MOUNTAIN-TANAGER. Mostly 2500 m to treeline. W VENEZUELA–N PERU (*taeniata* **130a**): head, upper back, and upper breast black with lines of bluish white that start at forehead and form a supercilium; lower back and rump dusky blue-violet; broad band across breast pale buff; belly and flanks deep buffy yellow becoming dusky blue-violet posteriorally; undertail-coverts pale buff. SANTA MARTA MOUNTAINS, COLOMBIA (*carrikeri* **130c**): similar to **130a** but smaller with a deeper buff breast that extends through throat and spottily through chin. C PERU (*stictocephala* **130b**): like **130a** but entire crown and nape streaked bluish white; back paler, and buff breast band narrower. *p. 218*

DELOTHRAUPIS **131** *D. castaneoventris* CHESTNUT-BELLIED MOUNTAIN-TANAGER. E Andean slope, c Peru–c Bolivia; 2200 m to treeline. Crown and upperparts pale blue-violet tinged blackish (clear along supercilium); mask and short malar stripe black; underparts brown (between Tawny and Cinnamon-Rufous). *p. 219*

PIPRAEIDEA **132** *P. melanonota* FAWN-BREASTED TANAGER. SC BRAZIL–N ARGENTINA (*melanonota*): lowlands to 2000 m. MALE (**132b**): crown, nape, lesser coverts, and rump light blue violet; back blackish blue-violet (Smalt Blue); face mask black; underparts pale cinnamon becoming cinnamon on breast; wings and tail edged blue. FEMALE (**132a**): similar but duller with upperparts suffused dark brown. MOUNTAINS, VENEZUELA–N ARGENTINA (*venezuelensis*): similar to **132a** and **132b** but underparts paler; backs slightly darker, and irides bright red. *p. 220*

IRIDOSORNIS

126a 126b

127

128

129a 129b

DUBUSIA

130a 130b 130c

DELOTHRAUPIS

131

PIPRAEIDEA

132a 132b

Plate 20 *Euphonia* (part 1)

EUPHONIA (Plates 20–22) Small; tails short and bills stubby. Except as noted, males have upperparts, head, throat, and upper breast blue black or purplish black (appearing black in the field) and remaining underparts yellow. Except as noted, upperparts of females are yellowish olive-green to greenish olive. Underwing-coverts are white. Subadult males typically resemble females or combine male and female plumage features. Found in lowlands except as noted.

133 *E. jamaica* JAMAICAN EUPHONIA. Jamaica. Heavy bill. MALE (**133b**): upperparts medium gray tinged blue; underparts paler, tinged buff; posterior flanks and center of belly yellow; undertail-coverts buffy white. FEMALE (**133a**): head like that of male; remaining upperparts yellowish olive (Citrine); underparts buffy gray; belly and undertail-coverts pale buff. *p. 224*

134 *E. plumbea* PLUMBEOUS EUPHONIA. Nc South America. MALE (**134b**): upperparts and throat dark blue gray; underparts golden yellow, sides and flanks touched gray. FEMALE (**134a**): head and upper back blue gray; throat pale olive-gray; belly and undertail-coverts yellow. *p. 225*

135 *E. affinis* SCRUB EUPHONIA. Males have large white tail spots. E MEXICO–W COSTA RICA (*affinis*): MALE (**135d**): yellow cap typically extends to rear edge of eye. FEMALE (**135c**): forehead yellowish; crown and nape tinged medium gray; underparts dingy olive-yellow becoming yellow on center of belly and undertail-coverts. In ec Mexico (*olmecorum*) female is decidedly paler. W MEXICO (*godmani*): MALE (**135b**): undertail-coverts white. FEMALE (**135a**): forehead yellower than **135c**; center of belly and undertail-coverts white. *p. 226*

136 *E. luteicapilla* YELLOW-CROWNED EUPHONIA. Nicaragua–e Panama. MALE (**136b**): yellow cap extends to nape; tail lacks white spots. FEMALE (**136a**): underparts olive-yellow becoming yellow on chin, center of belly, and undertail-coverts. *p. 228*

137 *E. chlorotica* PURPLE-THROATED EUPHONIA. South America east of Andes (except n edge). MALE (e.g., *serrirostris* **137c**): yellow cap extends to rear edge of eye. FEMALE (e.g., *serrirostris* **137b**): underparts dusky yellow except lower breast pale gray and center of belly white. SUBADULT MALE (e.g., *chlorotica* **137a**): upperparts olive-green; underparts olive-yellow, clearest yellow on belly and undertail-coverts. *p. 229*

138 *E. trinitatis* TRINIDAD EUPHONIA. Nc South America and Trinidad. MALE (**138b**): yellow cap extends beyond eye. FEMALE (**138a**): like **137b** but slightly less grayish. SUBADULT MALE: similar to **137a**. *p. 230*

139 *E. concinna* VELVET-FRONTED EUPHONIA. C Colombia. MALE (**139b**): forehead blue black; yellow cap small; underparts tinged deep cinnamon on flanks and belly; no white tail-spots. FEMALE (**139a**): head olive-gray; forehead and short supercilium yellowish; underparts buffy yellow tinged olive, becoming yellow on center of belly. *p. 232*

140 *E. saturata* ORANGE-CROWNED EUPHONIA. Pacific Colombia and Ecuador. MALE (**140b**): orange yellow cap extends to nape; underparts orange yellow tinged reddish brown (Amber). FEMALE (**140a**): underparts yellowish olive-green, yellowest on belly. *p. 232*

141 *E. finschi* FINSCH'S EUPHONIA. Nc South America. MALE (**141b**): orange yellow cap extends to rear edge of eye; lower breast and sides orange yellow becoming tinged with reddish brown on flanks, belly, and undertail-coverts. FEMALE (**141a**): underparts yellowish olive-green becoming yellow on center of belly. *p. 233*

EUPHONIA

Plate 21 *Euphonia* (part 2)

142 *E. violacea* VIOLACEOUS EUPHONIA. Se Venezuela–n Argentina. MALE (**142a**): orange yellow cap extends to center of eye; throat buffy orange-yellow; underparts orange yellow; large white tail spots. FEMALE (**142b**): forehead yellowish; underparts bright yellowish olive-green becoming yellow on center of belly. *p. 233*

143 *E. laniirostris* THICK-BILLED EUPHONIA. From e Costa Rica through w South America to c Mato Grosso, Brazil. MALE: yellow cap extends past eye; color of underparts (including throat) varies from yellow (*hypoxantha* **143c**) to orange yellow tinged buff (*melanura* **143b**); white tail spots except for *melanura*. FEMALE (e.g., *hypoxantha* **143a**): similar to **142b**; depth of color variable; *melanura* most dusky. *p. 236*

144 *E. hirundinacea* YELLOW-THROATED EUPHONIA. Middle America. MALE (**144c**): yellow cap extends to center of eye; underparts (including throat) yellow to orange yellow. FEMALE (**144b**): underparts pale gray with olive-yellow sides, flanks, and undertail-coverts. SUBADULT MALE (**144a**): at one stage has head color of adult male and upperparts of female. *p. 238*

145 *E. chalybea* GREEN-CHINNED EUPHONIA. Ec South America. Very thick bill. MALE (**145b**): upperparts tinged blue green; very small forehead patch yellow; chin dark; underparts yellow. FEMALE (**145a**): underparts buffy gray (Smoke Gray) with chin, sides, flanks, and undertail-coverts olive-yellow. *p. 239*

146 *E. musica* BLUE-HOODED EUPHONIA. Crown and nape light blue extending to behind ear-coverts. Often considered 3 species. *p. 241*

146-1 *E. musica* (*elegantissima* subspecies group) BLUE-HOODED EUPHONIA. Middle America (e.g., *elegantissima*). MALE (**146d**): forehead and underparts orange yellow heavily tinged reddish brown (Amber). FEMALE (**146c**): forehead like male; underparts olive-yellow; throat cinnamon. *p. 241*

146-2 *E. musica* (*aureata* subspecies group) GOLDEN-RUMPED EUPHONIA. South America (e.g., *aureata*). MALE (**146f**): forehead and throat black; rump and underparts orange yellow variably tinged buff. FEMALE (**146e**): forehead buff; underparts olive-yellow, yellowest on belly. *p. 242*

146-3 *E. musica* (*musica* subspecies group) ANTILLEAN EUPHONIA. Caribbean region (e.g. *sclateri*). MALE (**146b**): rump, forehead, throat, and underparts orange yellow tinged buff (in Lesser Antilles, males resemble females). FEMALE (**146a**): forehead orange yellow; underparts olive-yellow becoming yellow on throat. *p. 243*

147 *E. fulvicrissa* FULVOUS-VENTED EUPHONIA. C Panama–Pacific slope Ecuador. MALE (**147b**): yellow cap extends to rear edge of eye; underparts golden yellow becoming cinnamon along the midpoint and on undertail-coverts; white tail spots except in sw Colombia and nw Ecuador. FEMALE (**147a**): upperparts shining bluish green; forehead reddish brown (Amber); underparts olive-yellow becoming cinnamon on center of belly and undertail-coverts. *p. 245*

148 *E. imitans* SPOT-CROWNED EUPHONIA. Pacific slope, c Costa Rica–w Panama. MALE (**148b**): yellow cap, spotted black, extends just past eye; blue black throat extends to lower breast; white tail spots. FEMALE (**148a**): upperparts bluish green becoming yellowish on uppertail-coverts; forehead chestnut; underparts greenish yellow (Citrine), becoming yellower on chin and tawny buff on center of belly and undertail-coverts. *p. 246*

149 *E. gouldi* OLIVE-BACKED EUPHONIA. Gulf-Caribbean slope, s Mexico–w Panama. MALE (**149b**): upperparts shining bluish green; yellow cap extends to center of eye; ear-coverts, throat, breast, and barrings on flanks yellowish olive-green; center of belly and undertail-coverts tawny; white tail spots absent or very small. FEMALE (**149a**): similar to male but forehead reddish brown (Burnt Umber), underparts yellower, and tawny restricted to undertail-coverts. *p. 247*

EUPHONIA

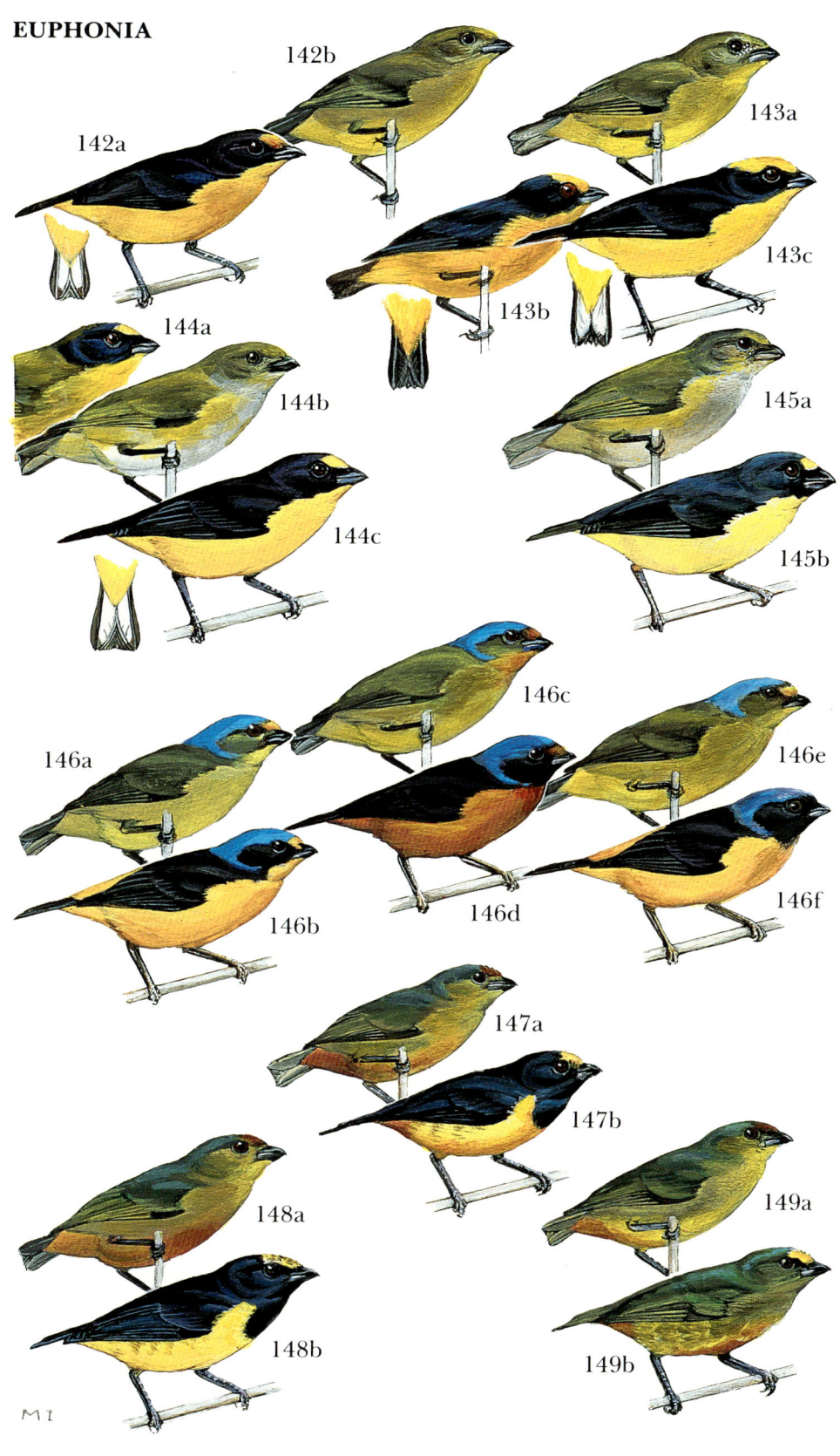

Plate 22 *Euphonia* (part 3)

150 *E. chrysopasta* WHITE-LORED EUPHONIA. Amazonia and nearby areas. MALE (**150b**): lores and chin white; upperparts shining bluish green, becoming gray on nape and yellowish on forehead and rump; earcoverts, sides, flanks, and bars on breast yellowish olive-green; remaining underparts yellow. FEMALE (**150a**): head and upperparts like male; underparts light gray tinged buff, becoming white on belly; sides and flanks partially olive-yellow; undertail-coverts yellow. *p. 247*

151 *E. mesochrysa* BRONZE-GREEN EUPHONIA. Sc Colombia and e Andean slope–c Bolivia; mostly 1000–2150 m. MALE (**151b**): upperparts shining bluish green tinged gray on nape; forehead yellow; throat, sides, and flanks yellowish olive (Citrine); center of breast, belly, and undertail-coverts deep buffy yellow. FEMALE (**151a**): similar to male but slightly paler and more yellowish; lacks yellow forehead; center of lower breast and belly pale gray. *p. 249*

152 *E. minuta* WHITE-VENTED EUPHONIA. Mexico–Amazonian Brazil. MALE (e.g. *humilis* **152b**): cap to center of eye (restricted to forehead in *minuta*) and breast orange yellow (yellow in *minuta*) becoming yellow on belly and white on center of belly and undertail-coverts. FEMALE (**152a**): chin, breast, and flanks olive-yellow; throat pale gray; center of belly white; undertail-coverts pale gray. *p. 250*

153 *E. anneae* TAWNY-CAPPED EUPHONIA. Costa Rica–extreme nw Colombia; mostly 600–1500 m. MALE (**153b**): rufous chestnut crown extends to nape; underparts buffy yellow; undertail-coverts white. FEMALE (**153a**): forehead rufous; nape plumbeous; throat and breast pale gray becoming yellow ochre (tinged pink) on belly and undertail-coverts and olive-yellow to yellow on sides and flanks. *p. 252*

154 *E. xanthogaster* ORANGE-BELLIED EUPHONIA. E Panama and South America–se Brazil; to ca. 2300 m. MOST RACES (e.g., *chocoensis*): MALE (**154a**): cap extends to beyond eye; underparts buffy orange-yellow; white tail spots. FEMALE (**154b**): forehead yellow; nape gray; underparts buffy gray becoming yellowish green on flanks. COASTAL MOUNTAINS OF VENEZUELA AND N AND S ENDS OF RANGE IN ANDES (e.g., *exsul*): MALE (**154d**): crown rufous and lower breast and undertail-coverts rufescent. FEMALE (**154c**): like **154a** but forehead rufous, center of belly dark pinkish buff, undertail-coverts cinnamon. *p. 252*

155 *E. rufiventris* RUFOUS-BELLIED EUPHONIA. W Amazonia. MALE (**155b**): blue black extends to lower breast; sides orange yellow; underparts orange yellow tinged tawny; no crown patch or white tail-spots. FEMALE (**155a**): underparts light gray tinged buff; chin, sides, and flanks olive-yellow; undertail-coverts orange buff. *p. 254*

156 *E. pectoralis* CHESTNUT-BELLIED EUPHONIA. Se Brazil and adjoining areas. MALE (**156b**): blue black extends to lower breast; sides yellow; underparts chestnut; no crown patch or white tail-spots. FEMALE (**156a**): crown medium gray; breast and center of belly light gray; chin, sides, and flanks olive-yellow; rear edge of flanks and undertail-coverts cinnamon-rufous. *p. 256*

157 *E. cayennensis* GOLDEN-SIDED EUPHONIA. W Amazonia. MALE (**157b**): blue black; sides orange yellow; no crown patch or white tail-spots. FEMALE (**157a**): underparts light gray tinged buff; chin, sides, and flanks olive-yellow. *p. 257*

EUPHONIA

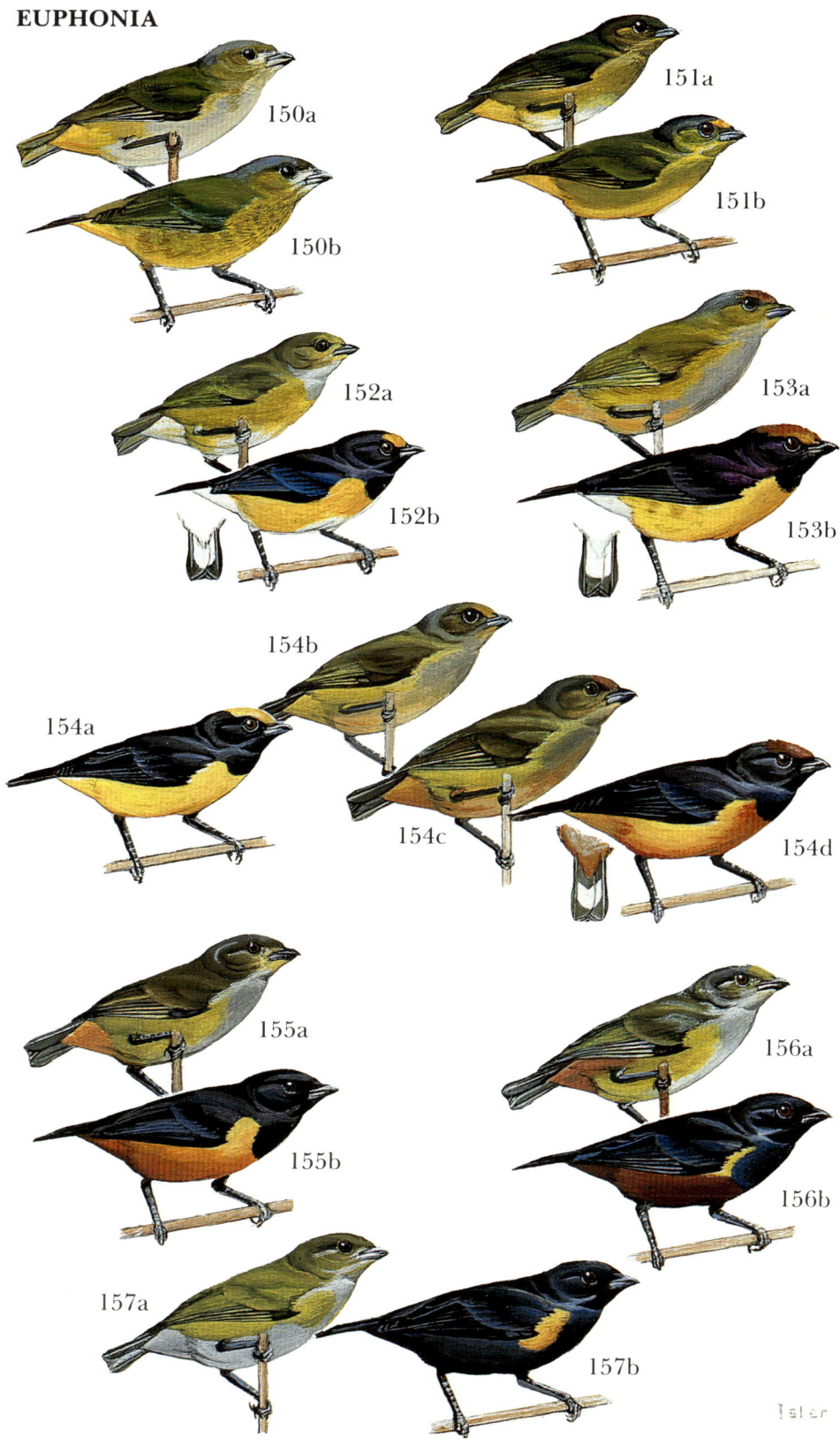

Plate 23 *Chlorophonia, Chlorochrysa*

CHLOROPHONIA Chunky birds with stubby bills and short tails. Adult males are bright green (Parrot Green) except as noted. Females are more yellow-green and show less contrast. Subadult males resemble females (together they typically outnumber adult males in the field).

158 *C. flavirostris* YELLOW-COLLARED CHLOROPHONIA. Local, e Panama–nw Ecuador; 400–1900 m. Bill and legs yellow orange; irides and narrow eye-ring pale yellow. MALE (**158b**): yellow collar around base of nape joins yellow underparts; variable chestnut band between yellow and green of breast; flanks green; rump yellow. FEMALE (**158a**): yellow-green, becoming yellow on center of lower breast and belly. *p. 259*

159 *C. cyanea* BLUE-NAPED CHLOROPHONIA. N South America–n Argentina; mostly below 2000 m. MALE: underparts yellow; narrow eye-ring blue; some races (e.g., *psittacina* **159a**) have forehead yellow, back dusky green, and neck band and rump turquoise blue whereas other races (e.g., *cyanea* **159c**) back and wing-covert as well as rump blue (see text). FEMALE (e.g., *psittacina* **159b**): foreparts like that of mate; upperparts dusky green, rump blue in *psittacina*; underparts dull greenish yellow. *p. 259*

160 *C. pyrrhophrys* CHESTNUT-BREASTED CHLOROPHONIA. Andes, Venezuela–c Peru; ca. 1500–3000 m. MALE (**160b**): crown and nape violet blue (Smalt Blue); supercilium and forehead black and green; rump and underparts bright yellow with dark brown (Russet) on center of breast and belly and on undertail-coverts; narrow black band between green and yellow of breast. FEMALE (**160a**): green; crown and nape blue bordered chestnut; underparts greenish yellow, yellowest on belly. *p. 261*

161 *C. occipitalis* BLUE-CROWNED CHLOROPHONIA. Middle America; mountains; often considered 2 species. *p. 262*

161-1 *C. occipitalis* (*occipitalis* subspecies group) BLUE-CROWNED CHLOROPHONIA. Mexico–n Nicaragua. MALE (**161c**): underparts except flanks yellow separated from breast by a black line; hindcrown cerulean blue. FEMALE (**161b**): underparts yellow green, yellowest through middle of belly; crown patch like male but duller. *p. 262*

161-2 *C. occipitalis* (*callophrys* subspecies group) GOLDEN-BROWED CHLOROPHONIA. Costa Rica–w Panama. MALE (**161a**): similar to **161c** but forehead and supercilium golden yellow; hindcrown blue violet (Campanula); neck band cerulean blue. FEMALE: like **161b**, but hindcrown dull blue-violet. *p. 263*

CHLOROCHRYSA Small, acrobatic tanagers with strong legs. Brilliant, glistening green except for color patches as noted.

162 *C. phoenicotis* GLISTENING-GREEN TANAGER. Mostly Pacific slope, Colombia–nw Ecuador; 700–2200 m. ADULT (**162**): small patch on ear-coverts shining blue gray and orange; lesser wing-coverts shining gray; blackish underwing. SUBADULT: see text. *p. 265*

163 *C. calliparaea* ORANGE-EARED TANAGER. Mostly e Andean slope, Colombia–Bolivia; 900–2000 m. MALE: NORTHERN FORM (*bourcieri* **163c**): crown patch and rump band orange; throat black; sides of neck burnt orange; tinged blue green (Turquoise Green) on belly, lower back, uppertail coverts, and foreparts of head. SOUTHERN FORM (*fulgentissima* **163a**): similar but throat and strip through center of underparts blue violet (Smalt Blue). FEMALE (*bourcieri* **163b**): same pattern but duller. *p. 265*

164 *C. nitidissima* MULTICOLORED TANAGER. W Colombia; 1400–2000 m. MALE (**164b**): forehead and sides of head yellow, tinged cinnamon around bill and on throat; lower ear-coverts black and chestnut; back lemon yellow; rump and underparts blue (Cerulean to Cobalt Blue) becoming blackish on center of lower breast and belly. FEMALE (**164a**): duller; patch on lower ear-coverts brown; rump and underparts green. *p. 266*

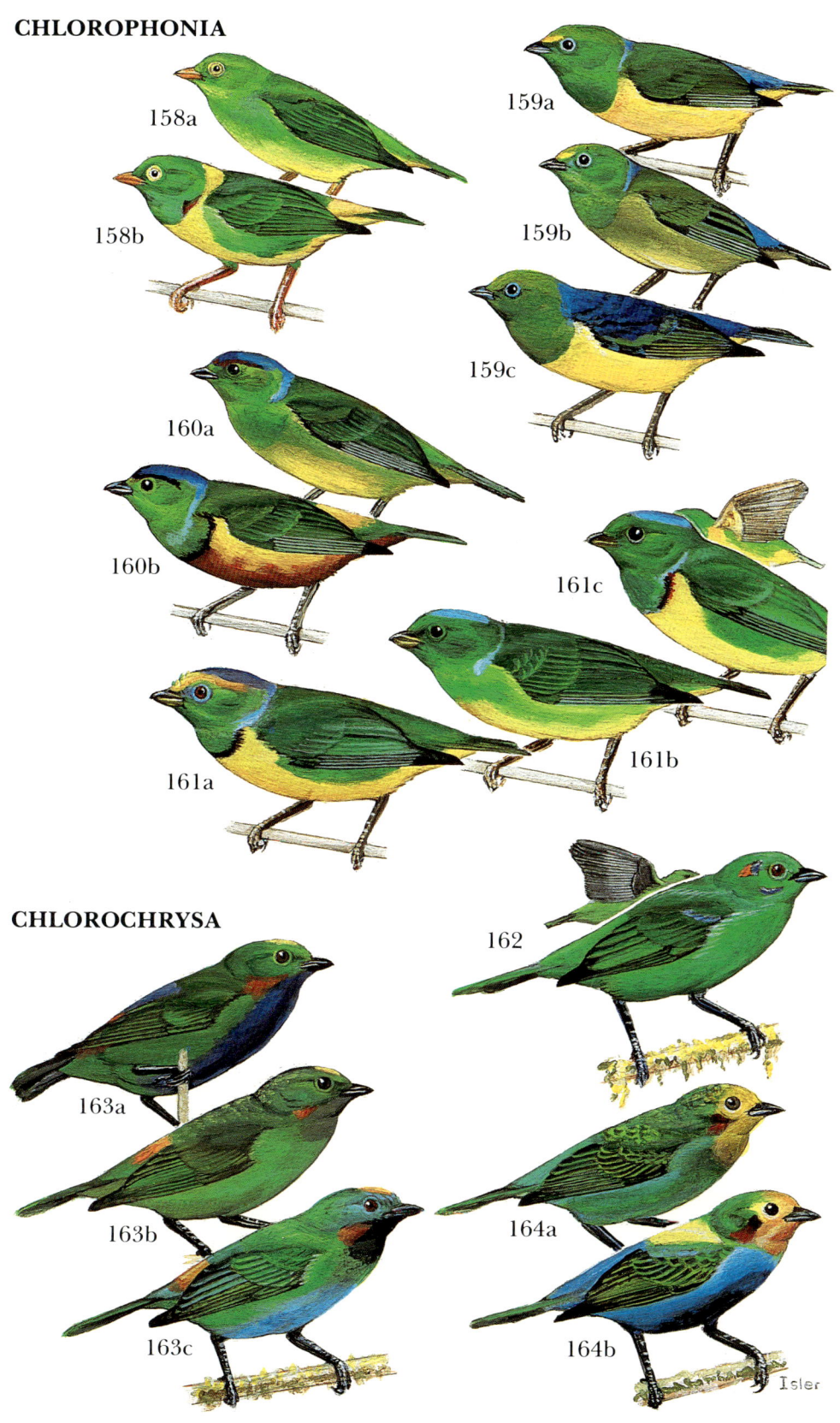

Plate 24 *Tangara* (part 1)

TANGARA (Plates 24–28) Nearly all species are boldly marked and only selected features are described. Wings and tail are blackish, edged blue or green unless noted. Common characteristics are given for well-marked species groups (see genus account in text). *pp. 267ff.*

165 *T. inornata* PLAIN-COLORED TANAGER. Costa Rica–n and w Colombia; primarily lowlands. Mostly gray; blue lesser coverts are usually concealed. SOUTHERN FORM (*inornata* **165a**): upperparts medium gray; underparts paler, becoming white on belly; wings and tail edged gray, area around bill and through eye blackish. NORTHERN FORM (*rava* **165b**): tinged buff, especially on posterior underparts. *p. 272*

166 *T. cabanisi* AZURE-RUMPED TANAGER. Pacific slope, s Mexico and adjacent Guatemala; 600–1700 m. Greenish blue with blackish spots (variable) on foreparts; head grayish blue, area around bill blackish; upperparts pale turquoise-blue, back tinged green; underparts pale blue-green, becoming white on belly. *p. 273*

167 *T. palmeri* GRAY-AND-GOLD TANAGER. Pacific slope, e Panama–n Ecuador; mostly 300–1100 m. Upperparts and wing- and tail-edgings light gray; underparts pale gray to white; small face mask black; blackish spots across back and breast mixed with silvery green on back and buffy yellow on breast. *p. 274*

168 *T. mexicana* TURQUOISE TANAGER. East of the Andes; lowlands. Nape, back, and area around bill black. REPRESENTATIVE RACES: *T. m. boliviana* (**168b**): mostly blue violet spotted black especially on upper breast and flanks; belly, undertail-coverts, and underwing-coverts yellow. *T. m. mexicana* (**168c**): underparts pale yellow; lesser coverts turquoise. *T. m. brasiliensis* (**168a**): pattern similar but grayish blue with white underparts. *p. 275*

SPECIES GROUP 3 (**169–171**) Unmistakable multicolored patterns that include red or orange rump; black around bill, eye-ring, and back; green or blue green head; and blue on underparts.

169 *T. chilensis* PARADISE TANAGER. Mostly Amazonia. Crown and ear-coverts yellow-green; nape, upper back, vent, and undertail-coverts black; throat violet. REPRESENTATIVE RACES: *T. c. chilensis* (**169a**): lower back and rump scarlet. *T. c. paradisea* (**169b**): lower back flame scarlet, rump orange yellow. *p. 277*

170 *T. fastuosa* SEVEN-COLORED TANAGER. Ne Brazil. Blue green (Cyan) of head extends to upper back; lower back, rump, and edge of tertials orange; small throat patch black. *p. 279*

171 *T. seledon* GREEN-HEADED TANAGER. Ec South America. ADULT (**171a**): yellow green band behind nape extends into black of throat and upper breast; rump orange, uppertail-coverts yellow green. SUBADULT (**171b**): dull version of adult. *p. 280*

172 *T. cyanocephala* RED-NECKED TANAGER. E South America. MALE (e.g., *cyanocephala* **172a**): green (shining Apple Green); area around bill and back black; crown and throat blue violet; ring around nape, ear-coverts, and lower chin red (deepest in *cyanocephala*); wing-coverts orange in *cyanocephala* only. FEMALE (e.g., *cearensis* **172b**): similar but back streaked dull black and green. *p. 282*

173 *T. desmaresti* BRASSY-BREASTED TANAGER. Se Brazil; mainly higher elevations. Mostly green, nape and back streaked black; area around bill and small throat patch black; lesser coverts, chin, and breast orange yellow; belly and undertail-coverts yellow. *p. 283*

174 *T. cyanoventris* GILT-EDGED TANAGER. Se Brazil. Head and upperparts orange yellow and yellow green, nape and back streaked black; small throat patch black; breast and sides pale turquoise green, becoming green (Apple Green) posteriorly. *p. 283*

TANGARA

Plate 25 *Tangara* (part 2)

SPECIES GROUP 5 (**175–182**) Back striped black (except **182**).

175 *T. johannae* BLUE-WHISKERED TANAGER. Pacific lowlands, Colombia–Ecuador. Green (Chartreuse); forehead, sides of head, and throat black, malar stripe turquoise blue; rump yellow. *p. 285*

176 *T. schrankii* GREEN-AND-GOLD TANAGER. Mostly Amazonian lowlands. ADULT MALE: green (Lime Green); crown, rump, center of breast and belly yellow; chin, forehead, and square patch behind eye black. FEMALE AND SUBADULT MALE: duller, see text. *p. 286*

177 *T. florida* EMERALD TANAGER. Costa Rica–sw Colombia; 300–1200 m. ADULT MALE: green (Lime Green); crown, rump, and center of posterior underparts yellow; square patch behind eye black. FEMALE AND SUBADULT MALE: duller, see text. *p. 287*

178 *T. arthus* GOLDEN TANAGER. Venezuela–n Bolivia; centered 1000–1500 m. Yellow ochre, becoming orange yellow to yellowish cinnamon on head; patch behind eye black. REPRESENTATIVE RACES: *T. a. arthus* (**178b**): underparts brown (Burnt Umber) and yellow. *T. a. aurulenta* (**178c**): underparts yellow ochre. *T. a. sophiae* (**178a**): throat chestnut. *p. 289*

179 *T. icterocephala* SILVER-THROATED TANAGER. Costa Rica–Pacific Ecuador; mostly 600–1600 m. ADULT (**179b**): golden yellow; wing-and tail-edgings yellow-green; throat gray (Pearl Gray) tinged green; long black malar stripe. SUBADULT (**179a**): pattern similar but tinged dusky; center of belly yellow. *p. 290*

180 *T. xanthocephala* SAFFRON-CROWNED TANAGER. Andes; mostly 1500–2600 m. Green (Emerald Green to Pistachio); small mask, throat, and upper back black; belly and undertail-coverts pale cinnamon. NORTHERN FORM (*venusta* **180a**): crown and ear-coverts orange yellow to yellow. SOUTHERN FORM (*lamprotis* **180b**): crown and nape orange; ear-coverts yellow. C Peru form is intermediate. *p. 291*

181 *T. chrysotis* GOLDEN-EARED TANAGER. Local in Andes, c Colombia–c Bolivia (elevation varies); shining green (Lime Green); forehead and supercilium shining yellow-green tinged buff; ear-coverts clay color amidst black head patches; belly and undertail-coverts deep cinnamon. *p. 292*

182 *T. parzudakii* FLAME-FACED TANAGER. W Venezuela–Peru; 1500–2500 m. Back and head patches black; underparts and rump opalescent green (Pistachio) and pale cinnamon. *T. p. parzudakii* (**182b**): head flame scarlet and orange yellow. *T. p. lunigera* (**182a**): Pacific Colombia–Ecuador. Head orange. *p. 293*

SPECIES GROUP 6 (**183–187**) Green (except **187**) with dark spots.

183 *T. xanthogastra* YELLOW-BELLIED TANAGER. Lowlands in w Amazonia, to 1800 m in s Venezuela. Belly and undertail-coverts bright yellow; wings and tail edged pale turquoise green. *p. 294*

184 *T. punctata* SPOTTED TANAGER. Lowlands to 1600 m in s Venezuela and e Amazonia; 700–1700 m, e Andean slope, Ecuador–Bolivia. Head tinged turquoise; belly white; wings and tail edged green (Apple Green). *p. 295*

185 *T. guttata* SPECKLED TANAGER. E Middle and n South America; 700–1500 m. ADULT MALE (**185a**): supercilium yellow (orange yellow in some races); lores black; underparts (except flanks) white becoming yellowish posteriorly; wings and tail edged pale bluish green. SUBADULT FEMALE (**185b**); duller. *p. 297*

186 *T. varia* DOTTED TANAGER. Lowlands, s Venezuela and c Amazonia. MALE: green (Apple Green), including most of underparts; spots faint; wings and tail edged turquoise green. FEMALE: wings not as blue; belly yellower; spots very faint or absent. *p. 299*

187 *T. rufigula* RUFOUS-THROATED TANAGER. Pacific Colombia and Ecuador, 400–2100 m. Head brownish black, throat deep cinnamon; back, wings, and tail brownish black with pale yellow-ochre to yellow-green edges; rump yellow-green; breast and sides pale yellow-green (Pistachio) spotted brownish black; belly white; undertail-coverts pale cinnamon. *p. 300*

TANGARA

Plate 26 *Tangara* (part 3)

SPECIES GROUP 7 (**188–189, 195**). The Bay-headed and Rufous-winged Tanagers are bright blue or green with distinctive brown heads (except female Rufous-winged). The Rufous-cheeked Tanager (**195**) may be related.

188 *T. gyrola* BAY-HEADED TANAGER. Costa Rica–Amazonia; elevations vary by race as does plumage. REPRESENTATIVE ADULT MALES: *T. g. bangsi* (**188a**): head chestnut bordered on nape by yellow line; upperparts shining green except rump turquoise blue and lesser coverts yellow; underparts turquoise blue becoming green posteriorly. *T. g. albertinae* (**188c**): similar but lacks nape line, back yellow green; lesser coverts cinnamon-rufous. *T. g. viridissima* (**188b**): similar to *bangsi* but rump and underparts green. FEMALE: resembles male but is sometimes duller. SUBADULT (e.g., *deleticia* **188d**): green; a hint of rufous on the head; also a hint of blue on underparts of races in which adults are blue below. *p. 301*

189 *T. lavinia* RUFOUS-WINGED TANAGER. Central America and Pacific slope nw South America; mostly foothills. MALE (e.g., *dalmasi* **189a**): like **188** but lower nape and back extensively yellow; wing-coverts and flight feathers cinnamon-rufous; underparts green with varying amounts of blue on chin, throat, and belly. FEMALE (e.g., *dalmasi* **189b**): duller; head green (sometimes partially chestnut); back tinged yellow; cinnamon-rufous wing-edgings more limited than in male. SUBADULT: see text. *p. 303*

SPECIES GROUP 8 (**190–194, 242**) Plumages tend to be shiny and to change color (esp. among buff, green, blue, or violet) according to the light angle. Black mask through lores and ear-coverts (except **192** and **193**, which may be conspecific).

190 *T. cayana* BURNISHED-BUFF TANAGER. N SOUTH AMERICA EAST OF ANDES (e.g., *cayana*): MALE (**190b**): shiny yellow buff tinged violet on throat and upper breast; crown cinnamon-rufous; mask black; wings and tail edged blue green. FEMALE (**190a**): similar but duller and tinged green; throat whitish. SE BRAZIL (*chloroptera*): MALE (**190d**): black of mask extends through throat to center of breast and belly; crown like back. FEMALE (**190c**): tinged pale olive-green. C BRAZIL: races intermediate in plumage. *p. 304*

191 *T. cucullata* LESSER ANTILLEAN TANAGER. GRENADA (*cucullata*): MALE (**191b**): buffy tinged gold on upperparts and violet on underparts; black mask; crown blackish chestnut; wings and tail edged blue green. FEMALE (**191c**): duller, tinged green; crown chestnut. ST. VINCENT (*versicolor*): MALE (**191a**): larger and more brightly colored. FEMALE: larger but similar to **191c**. *p. 306*

192 *T. peruviana* BLACK-BACKED TANAGER. Se Brazil. MALE (**192b**): head chestnut; back black; rump and wing-coverts yellow buff; wing- and tail-edgings and underparts blue green; vent and undertail-coverts pale reddish brown (Amber). FEMALE (**192a**): head pale chestnut; upperparts grayish olive; underparts pale silvery green becoming buff posteriorly. *p. 306*

193 *T. preciosa* CHESTNUT-BACKED TANAGER. Se Brazil. MALE (**193b**): similar to **192b** but back chestnut. FEMALE (**193a**): similar to **192a**. *p. 308*

194 *T. vitriolina* SCRUB TANAGER. Colombia and Ecuador north and west of Andes. Resembles female Burnished-buff Tanager (**190a**) but deeper green or violet, depending on light, center of belly and undertail-coverts pale buff. *p. 309*

195 *T. rufigenis* RUFOUS-CHEEKED TANAGER. N Venezuela. Blue green, greener below; chin and ear-coverts rufous; flight feathers edged cinnamon; center of belly and undertail-coverts pale buff to cinnamon. *p. 310*

TANGARA

Plate 27 *Tangara* (part 4)

196 *T. ruficervix* GOLDEN-NAPED TANAGER. Andes, Colombia–c Bolivia. Face mask black; underparts buffy white becoming cinnamon posteriorly. COLOMBIA–C PERU (e.g., *ruficervix* **196a**): turquoise blue, spotted dusky especially on back; patches of silvery blue violet on crown and cinnamon on nape. C PERU–C BOLIVIA (e.g., *inca* **196b**): foreparts mostly blue violet; hindparts mostly turquoise blue; nape patch cinnamon-rufous. *p. 310*

197 *T. labradorides* METALLIC-GREEN TANAGER. Andes, Colombia–n Peru. Shining silvery green to blue; forehead and supercilium shining buff; face mask, nape, scapulars, and greater coverts black; center of belly to undertail-coverts pale gray and cinnamon. *p. 311*

198 *T. cyanotis* BLUE-BROWED TANAGER. Andes. COLOMBIA–S PERU (*lutleyi* **198a**): head and back black with broad supercilium shining green to blue; wing-coverts, rump, and underparts shining silvery turquoise-green to blue except center of belly to undertail-coverts pale cinnamon to cinnamon. BOLIVIA (*cyanotis* **198b**): similar but ear-coverts and back dusky blue. *p. 312*

SPECIES GROUP 10 (**199–201**) Similarly patterned; black backs and breasts contrast with lighter hoods; small black masks around bill and eyes.

199 *T. cyanicollis* BLUE-NECKED TANAGER. Andes, Venezuela–c Bolivia and lowlands south of Amazonia. ADULT (e.g., *granadensis* **199b** and *cyanopygia* **199c**): hood blue, throat sometimes violet; wing-coverts, wing-edgings, and rump turquoise to greenish straw; posterior underparts black, violet, or blue. SUBADULT (**199a**): brownish gray; hint of adult colors especially on ear-coverts and wing-edgings. *p. 313*

200 *T. larvata* GOLDEN-HOODED TANAGER. Middle America and Pacific slope, Colombia–Ecuador. ADULT (e.g., *centralis* **200a**): hood sulphur yellow; mask bordered violet and blue; rump, wing-coverts, and flanks blue violet to turquoise blue; center of belly to undertail-coverts white to pale cinnamon. SUBADULT (**200b**): head, lower back, rump, and wing- and tail-edgings green; upper back medium gray; hint of mask; underparts paler, tinged cinnamon posteriorly. *p. 314*

201 *T. nigrocincta* MASKED TANAGER. Patchily distributed east of Andes to c Brazil and Bolivia. ADULT (**201a**): hood pale blue-violet (Lavender Blue); rump, coverts, wing- and tail-edgings, and flanks turquoise blue and green; center of belly to undertail-coverts white. SUBADULT (**201b**): duller; lower breast to flanks medium gray. *p. 317*

202 *T. dowii* SPANGLE-CHEEKED TANAGER. Mountains; considered 2 species by A.O.U. Check-list.

202-1 *T. dowii* (*dowii* subspecies group) SPANGLE-CHEEKED TANAGER. Costa Rica–w Panama. Upperparts, throat, and upper breast blackish spangled with blue green and straw yellow; nape patch cinnamon-rufous; rump shining bluish green; posterior underparts cinnamon (**202a**). *p. 317*

202-2 *T. dowii* (*fucosa* subspecies group) GREEN-NAPED TANAGER. E Panama. Similar to **202a**, but nape spots bluish green, throat spangles blue, sides and flanks more extensively spotted dusky and bluish green, and center of underparts more buffy (**202b**). *p. 318*

203 *T. nigroviridis* BERYL-SPANGLED TANAGER. Muntains, n Venezuela–Bolivia. Black, spotted more or less with straw color, silvery green, and blue; mask and back black; rump turquoise blue. *p. 319*

204 *T. vassorii* BLUE-AND-BLACK TANAGER. Andes, Venezuela–Bolivia. ADULT: SOUTH TO N PERU (*vassorii* **204a**): violaceous blue; wings, tail, and lores black. BOLIVIA AND S PERU (*atrocoerulea* **204b**): similar but paler (Flaxflower Blue); back black; head and underparts mottled blackish; nape tinged straw color. SUBADULT (*vassorii* **204c**): gray tinged blue; lores, wings, and tail blackish. *p. 320*

TANGARA

Plate 28 *Tangara* (part 5)

SPECIES GROUP 12 (**205–209**) Males have black caps or black heads that are dusky in females. Pale pointed feathers overlie black or dusky feather bases, giving a somewhat spotted appearance (**205–207** and female **208**). Underwing-coverts white (except **207** male). Mostly 1500–2200 m.

205 *T. heinei* BLACK-CAPPED TANAGER. Venezuela–n Ecuador. ADULT MALE (**205b**): silvery blue; crown and nape black; ear-coverts, throat, and breast with pointed green (Paris Green) feathers. ADULT FEMALE (**205a**): crown and nape dusky green; pointed (pale Paris Green) feathers on throat and breast; remaining upperparts and flanks mostly bright yellow green. SUBADULT: duller with less contrast than female. *p. 321*

206 *T. viridicollis* SILVERY-BACKED TANAGER. S Ecuador–s Peru. MALE (e.g., *viridicollis* **206b**): black; upperparts, sides, and flanks silvery blue-gray (silvery Opaline Green in *fulvigula*); ear-coverts and throat with pointed orange yellow feathers. FEMALE (e.g., *viridicollis* **206a**): crown and nape buffy brown (Raw Umber) becoming buffy on ear-coverts and throat; upperparts yellow green; underparts green and gray. *p. 322*

207 *Tangara argyrofenges* STRAW-BACKED TANAGER. Locally, n Peru–c Bolivia. MALE (e.g., *argyrofenges* **207b**): crown, nape, underparts, wings, and tail edgings black (edgings green in subadult male); ear-coverts, throat, and upper breast shiny blue-green; back, rump, sides, and flanks shiny buff-yellow (silvery yellow in *caeruleigularis*). FEMALE (e.g., *caeruleigularis* **207a**): crown and nape dusky green; cheeks, throat, and breast opaline green; upperparts and sides dusky yellow; remaining underparts gray; wings and tail edged green (Peacock Green). *p. 322*

208 *Tangara cyanoptera* BLACK-HEADED TANAGER. MALE: N COLOMBIA, AND N VENEZUELA (*cyanoptera* **208c**): shiny straw-yellow tinged green; head and throat black; wings and tail black edged blue violet (Smalt Blue). S VENEZUELA (*whitelyi* **208a**): similar but silvery blue-green; dusky feather bases very evident; wing- and tail-edgings black. FEMALE (e.g., *cyanoptera* **208b**; *whitelyi* similar but darker): crown, nape, and ear-coverts dusky blue; back and rump shining deep yellow-green; wings and tail edged green; throat and breast white over dusky blue; posterior underparts pale yellow suffused green. *p. 323*

209 *Tangara pulcherrima* GOLDEN-COLLARED HONEYCREEPER. C Colombia–c Peru. Bill thin and pointed. MALE (e.g., *pulcherrima* **209b**): throat and upperparts black with thin collar yellow orange and straw yellow on center of back and rump, wings and tail edged blue; underparts straw yellow, tinged olive on sides; center of belly and undertail-coverts white tinged cream. FEMALE (e.g., *pulcherrima* **209a**): head and upperparts olive-green with rump yellowish and semblance of a nuchal collar; underparts resemble those of male. *p. 324*

SPECIES GROUP 13 (**210–211**) Black and blue violet or blue, often appearing dark except for shining straw-yellow and chestnut patches; underwing-coverts white. Lowlands east of Andes.

210 *Tangara velia* OPAL-RUMPED TANAGER. AMAZONIA (e.g., *iridina* **210b**): upperparts mostly black; underparts mostly deep blue violet (Smalt Blue); center of belly and undertail-coverts chestnut; rump shining straw-yellow tinged green. E COASTAL BRAZIL (*cyanomelaena* **210a**): similar but area between forehead and crown straw yellow; lower breast, sides, and flanks silvery blue. *p. 325*

211 *Tangara callophrys* OPAL-CROWNED TANAGER. E Amazonia. Resembles **210** but broad forehead and supercilium straw yellow; center of belly and undertail-coverts black. *p. 327*

TANGARA

Plate 29 *Dacnis*

DACNIS Most with conical pointed bills, short tails. Males are distinctive (although **216** and **218** are similar); their blue coloring often appears blue green; wings and tails are black edged with their body color (except **214**). Head and underpart colors distinguish drab females. Typically encountered in lowlands (except **215**).

212 *D. albiventris* WHITE-BELLIED DACNIS. Amazonia; local and scarce. Bill short. MALE (**212b**): deep blue-violet; mask black; belly and undertail-coverts white. FEMALE (**212a**): upperparts yellowish olive-green, brightest on rump; underparts paler; throat whitish; belly yellow. *p. 327*

213 *D. lineata* BLACK-FACED DACNIS. Irides yellow. WEST AND NORTH OF ANDES (e.g., *egregia*): MALE (**213c**): blue green; mask and back black; center of belly, undertail-coverts, and underwing-coverts yellow. FEMALE (**213d**): upperparts greenish olive; underparts paler; belly and undertail-coverts yellow. AMAZONIA (*lineata*): MALE (**213b**): turquoise blue; belly and undertail-coverts white. FEMALE (**213a**): belly and undertail-coverts white tinged yellow. *p. 328*

214 *D. flaviventer* YELLOW-BELLIED DACNIS. Amazonia. Irides red. MALE (**214b**): black and yellow pattern distinctive; appears yellow olive in some lights; crown green (Parrot Green no. 260) appearing brownish at times. FEMALE (**214a**): upperparts olive-green; underparts yellowish white, mottled dusky on breast and sides and becoming buffy on undertail-coverts. *p. 330*

215 *D. hartlaubi* TURQUOISE DACNIS. Colombia; very local. Irides yellowish; bill heavier than congeners. MALE (**215a**): resembles **213** except throat patch black and underparts entirely turquoise. FEMALE (**215b**): upperparts olive-brown, greater coverts and secondaries edged tawny buff; underparts grayish buff, yellowish white on center of belly and undertail-coverts. *p. 331*

216 *D. nigripes* BLACK-LEGGED DACNIS. Se Brazil. Tail short. MALE (**216b**): like male of **218** (ranges overlap) but legs black, patches of black on throat and mantle smaller. FEMALE (**216a**): like female of **217** (no range overlap) but throat buffy white. *p. 333*

217 *D. venusta* SCARLET-THIGHED DACNIS. Costa Rica–nw Ecuador. ADULT MALE (**217c**): black; crown, nape, sides of head, center of upper back, scapulars, lower back, and rump blue; scarlet thighs often hidden. FEMALE (**217b**): upperparts dusky blue-green, brightest on ear-coverts, scapulars, and rump; underparts buffy gray-brown, tinged cinnamon on belly and undertail-coverts. SUBADULT MALE (**217a**): similar to female; throat black. *p. 333*

218 *D. cayana* BLUE DACNIS. Nicaragua–se Brazil. Legs pinkish. MALE: typically blue (e.g., *paraguayensis* **218e**), some races (e.g., *coerebicolor* **218b**) are bluish violet; forehead, lores, throat, and back black. FEMALE: green, paler below; throat gray; crown and ear-coverts blue (e.g., *paraguayensis* **218d**) or blue violet (e.g., *coerebicolor* **218a**) corresponding to color of male. SUBADULT (e.g., *napaea* **218c**): resembles female but blue of head more restricted, yellower below. *p. 334*

219 *D. viguieri* VIRIDIAN DACNIS. E Panama, nw Colombia. Irides yellow. MALE (**219b**): turquoise green (Cyan); wing-coverts and secondaries yellowish olive-green; upper back and primaries black. FEMALE (**219a**): upperparts olive-green tinged blue; lores blackish; primaries blackish edged green; underparts pale olive-green tinged yellow on belly and undertail-coverts. *p. 336*

220 *D. berlepschi* SCARLET-BREASTED DACNIS. Sw Colombia, nw Ecuador. Irides yellow. MALE (**220a**): deep blue (Ultramarine), streaked silvery blue on back and becoming silvery blue on rump; lower breast scarlet; belly straw yellow; undertail-coverts whitish. FEMALE (**220b**): olive-brown; underparts paler with a rosy band across lower breast and becoming straw yellow on belly and undertail-coverts. *p. 337*

DACNIS

Plate 30 *Chlorophanes, Cyanerpes, Xenodacnis, Oreomanes, Diglossa* (part 1)

CHLOROPHANES 221 *C. spiza* GREEN HONEYCREEPER. Mostly lowlands; s Mexico–se Brazil. Bill slightly curved and yellowish below. MALE: shining green (e.g., *arguta* **221a**) to turquoise (e.g., *caerulescens* **221c**); head black; irides red. FEMALE (**221b**): green (Apple Green); upperparts dusky; some races tinged straw yellow on throat and center of belly; underwing-coverts whitish. p. 337

CYANERPES Primarily lowlands. Bills curved; tails short. Males blue or blue violet (Smalt Blue); wings and tails black. Females greenish, streaked below. Except for **225**, underwing-coverts of males are blackish, those of females white tinged yellow.

222 *C. nitidus* SHORT-BILLED HONEYCREEPER. S Venezuela and w Amazonia. Bill short; legs pink. MALE (**222a**): blue (Spectrum Blue); black throat extends to lower breast. FEMALE (**222b**): head (incl. ear-coverts) and back green (Parrot Green no. 260); underparts pale cream color, streaked green. p. 340

223 *C. lucidus* SHINING HONEYCREEPER. Middle America. MALE (**223a**): blue violet, becoming blue on head; black throat extends to center of breast; legs yellow. FEMALE (**223b**): upperparts and flanks shining green; head grayish blue, streaked buffy on ear-coverts; throat, center of belly, and undertail-coverts buffy; breast streaked blue; legs greenish yellow. p. 342

224 *C. caeruleus* PURPLE HONEYCREEPER. N South America. MALE (**224a**): like **223a** but head blue violet, black throat patch smaller and squarer. FEMALE (**224b**): like **223b** but lores buff, cheeks and throat buffy, and breast streaked green. p. 343

225 *C. cyaneus* RED-LEGGED HONEYCREEPER. Sc Mexico–n Bolivia and coastal Brazil. Underwing-coverts yellow; legs red (male) or reddish; bill length highly variable. MALE IN ALTERNATE PLUMAGE (e.g., *eximius* **225a**): blue violet (Smalt Blue); back black; crown turquoise; no throat patch. MALE IN BASIC PLUMAGE (e.g., *pacificus* **225b**): upperparts olive green; eyebrow white; underparts dull yellowish white streaked olive-green; wings and tail black. FEMALE (e.g., *gemmeus* **225c**): similar but with grayish olive wings and tail. p. 344

XENODACNIS **226** *X. parina* TIT-LIKE DACNIS. Andes, s Ecuador and Peru. Bill very stubby. ADULT MALE: SOUTHERN FORM (*parina* **226a**): deep blue becoming blue gray on posterior underparts. NORTHERN FORM (*bella* **226c**): larger, streaked light blue. FEMALE: SOUTHERN FORM (*parina* **226b**): crown blue; upperparts buffy brownish olive, tinged blue on rump and wing-coverts; underparts pale cinnamon-rufous, center of belly buffy white. NORTHERN FORM (*bella* **226d**): larger; blue of crown more restricted; tinged blue throughout. SUBADULT MALE (e.g., *bella* **226e**): upperparts bluish olive-brown; underparts mixed blue and pale cinnamon-rufous. p. 347

OREOMANES **227** *O. fraseri* GIANT CONEBILL. Central Andes. Long pointed bill; upperparts blue gray; underparts chestnut; chestnut, black, and white head and throat pattern is variable (e.g., **227a**, **227b**). p. 348

DIGLOSSA (Plates 30–32) Flowerpiercers. Montane, mostly Andean; hooked, upturned bills (least obvious in **237**). Plumages typically black and gray with tawny to buff (**228–234**, Plates 30–31) or blue (**235–238**, Plate 32).

228 *D. baritula* SLATY FLOWERPIERCER. Often considered 3 species. p. 351

228-1 *D. baritula* (*baritula* subspecies group) CINNAMON-BELLIED FLOWERPIERCER. Mexico–Honduras. ADULT MALE (e.g., *montana* **228f**): head blackish; upperparts plumbeous; underparts tawny; throat gray (tawny in *baritula*). FEMALE: resembles **228d** but underparts tinged cinnamon. SUBADULT (**228e**) like female but darker. p. 352

228-2 *D. baritula* (*plumbea* subspecies group) SLATY FLOWERPIERCER. Costa Rica and Panama. MALE (**228c**): upperparts blackish gray; underparts dark slate gray, paler on center of belly. FEMALE (**228d**): upperparts deep grayish-olive; underparts lighter and faintly streaked buffy; belly buffy white; undertail-coverts pale cinnamon. p. 353

228-3 *D. baritula* (*sittoides* subspecies group) RUSTY FLOWERPIERCER. South America. MALE (**228b**): upperparts plumbeous; underparts pale cinnamon. FEMALE: typically resembles **228d**, but some races are paler, yellower below (e.g., *dorbignyi* **228a**). p. 354

Plate 31 *Diglossa* (part 2)

229 *D. lafresnayii* GLOSSY FLOWERPIERCER. High Andean elevations. Now generally considered 3 species. *p. 355*

229-1 *D. lafresnayii* (*gloriosissima* subspecies group) CHESTNUT-BELLIED FLOWERPIERCER. Local, w Colombia. ADULT (**229a**): black; posterior underparts reddish brown (between Amber and Chestnut); lesser and median coverts and uppertail-coverts blue gray. *p. 356*

229-2 *D. lafresnayii* (*lafresnayii* subspecies group) GLOSSY FLOWERPIERCER. Venezuela–Northern Peruvian Low. ADULT (**229b**): black; lesser and median coverts blue gray. SUBADULT (**229c**): brownish-black, hint of patch on wing coverts. *p. 356*

229-3 *D. lafresnayii* (*mystacalis* subspecies group) MOUSTACHED FLOWERPIERCER. Northern Peruvian Low–Bolivia. ADULT (e.g., *unicincta* **229e**, *mystacalis* **229g**): black; vent and undertail-coverts tawny brown; moustachial stripe white, buffy, or tawny brown; breast band whitish, brown, or absent. SUBADULT (e.g., *unicincta* **229d**, *mystacalis* **229f**): blackish brown, underparts spotted whitish; spotty moustachial stripe; undertail-coverts reddish brown. *p. 357*

230 *D. carbonaria* CARBONATED FLOWERPIERCER. High Andean elevations. Now generally considered 4 species. *p. 358*

230-1 *D. carbonaria* (*humeralis* subspecies group) BLACK FLOWERPIERCER. Extreme w Venezuela–Northern Peruvian Low except parts of n Colombia. ADULT: black; lesser and median coverts and uppertail-coverts blue gray (*humeralis* **230g**), or only tail-coverts blue gray (*nocticolor*), or all black (*aterrima* **230h**). SUBADULT: some are brownish black without blue gray patches and extremely similar to subadult Glossy Flowerpiercer (**229c**). *p. 358*

230-2 *D. carbonaria* (*brunneiventris* subspecies group) BLACK-THROATED FLOWERPIERCER. N Colombia and Northern Peruvian Low–nw Bolivia. ADULT (**230d**): upperparts and throat black; moustachial stripe and underparts rufous (Antique Brown); rump, lesser and median coverts, sides, and flanks light gray. SUBADULT (*brunneiventris* **230b**, *vuilleumieri* **230c**): blackish brown; whitish moustachial stripe; underparts pale cream color or pale cinnamon-rufous, streaked blackish brown. *p. 359*

230-3 *D. carbonaria* (*carbonaria* subspecies group) GRAY-BELLIED FLOWERPIERCER. Nc Bolivia. ADULT (**230a**): black; uppertail-coverts medium gray; lesser coverts and belly light gray; undertail-coverts tawny brown. SUBADULT (**230e**): upperparts dark gray tinged buff (Smoke Gray); throat medium gray, streaked and becoming cream color on belly; undertail-coverts cinnamon. *p. 360*

230-4 *D. carbonaria* (*gloriosa* subspecies group) MERIDA FLOWERPIERCER. Venezuelan Andes. ADULT (**230f**): black; lower breast, center of belly, and undertail-coverts brown (Russet); short supercilium and lesser and median coverts light gray; lower rump medium gray. SUBADULT: resembles cinnamon-rufous subadult of Black-throated Flowerpiercer (**230c**). *p. 362*

231 *D. venezuelensis* VENEZUELAN FLOWERPIERCER. Ne Venezuela. Sides at base of wings and underwing-coverts white. MALE (**231a**): otherwise black. FEMALE (**231b**): upperparts dark brownish gray; underparts gray; head tinged yellowish olive, becoming buffy on throat. *p. 362*

232 *D. albilatera* WHITE-SIDED FLOWERPIERCER. Nc Venezuela–sc Peru. Sides at base of wings and underwing-coverts white. MALE (**232a**): otherwise black. FEMALE (**232b**): upperparts olive tinged cinnamon; underparts cinnamon, palest on center of belly, tinged olive on sides and flanks. SUBADULT MALE: resembles adult, but tinged buff on underparts, especially center of belly. *p. 363*

233 *D. duidae* SCALED FLOWERPIERCER. Amazonas, Venezuela. Upperparts, throat, and upper breast blackish gray; scaled light gray on lower breast, becoming light gray on belly and barred on undertail-coverts. *p. 364*

234 *D. major* GREATER FLOWERPIERCER. Bolivar, Venezuela. Dark to medium gray with fine, light blue gray streaks (extent varies by race); face mask black; moustachial streak pale gray (variable); undertail-coverts brown (Tawny to Antique Brown). *p. 364*

DIGLOSSA

Plate 32 *Diglossa* (part 3), *Euneornis, Tersina, Nephelornis, Tangara* (addendum)

DIGLOSSA (part 3)

235 *D. indigotica* INDIGO FLOWERPIERCER. Pacific slope, Colombia–n Ecuador; 700–2200m. Irides red; head dark blue (Indigo Blue no. 173) becoming blue on body; wing- and tail-edgings blue green (Turquoise Green); tail short; bill clearly upturned and hooked. *p. 365*

236 *D. glauca* DEEP-BLUE FLOWERPIERCER. E Andean slope, s Colombia–n Bolivia, 1400–2300 m. Irides golden yellow; plumage blue black, wing- and tail-edgings paler; lores and short forehead blackish; tail longer and bill heavier than **235**. *p. 366*

237 *D. caerulescens* BLUISH FLOWERPIERCER. C Venezuela–n Bolivia; mostly 2000–2600 m. ADULT: bluish gray (Plumbeous); slightly paler below, lightest on belly; forehead and lores blackish; races vary in intensity of blue coloration and extent of white on belly (e.g., *caerulescens* **237a**, *saturata* **237b**); bill long and relatively straight; irides dull red. SUBADULT: similar with yellow base to bill. *p. 367*

238 *D. cyanea* MASKED FLOWERPIERCER. C Venezuela–c Bolivia; mostly 2100–3200 m. ADULT (e.g., *cyanea* **238b**): blue, palest on crown, coverts, and wing- and tail-edgings; irides bright red; mask black; bill long and straight, but more noticeably hooked than Bluish Flowerpiercer (**237**). SUBADULT (**238a**): grayer, irides dark; semblance of black mask; base of bill yellow. *p. 368*

EUNEORNIS **239** *E. campestris* ORANGEQUIT. Jamaica. MALE (**239a**): grayish blue, throat reddish brown (Amber); lores blackish. FEMALE (**239b**): upperparts brownish olive becoming paler (Fawn Color) on wings; underparts grayish olive tinged cinnamon on posterior underparts; throat and belly streaked pale buffy. *p. 369*

TERSINA **240**. *T. viridis* SWALLOW-TANAGER. E Panama and n and c South America; mostly below 1200 m. Bill wide and flat. MALE (**240b**): blue to green depending on the light; forehead, ocular area, and throat black; belly and undertail-coverts white; flanks barred black. FEMALE (**240a**): green (Parrot Green); underparts barred green and pale yellow; center of belly pale yellow; forehead, lores, and throat buffy white (Smoke Gray). *p. 370*

NEPHELORNIS **241**. *N. oneilli* PARDUSCO. C Peru, timber line. ADULT (**241a**): upperparts olive-brown, flight feathers and greater coverts edged cinnamon; throat pale buff; the buffy tone extending to behind ear-coverts; underparts mixed cinnamon-brown and cinnamon and becoming browner (Antique Brown) on sides and flanks. SUBADULT (**241b**): browner, especially on throat and underparts. *p. 372*

TANGARA (Addendum, related to species on Plate 26)
242. *T. meyerdeschauenseei* GREEN-CAPPED TANAGER. Puno, Peru; 2000–2200 m. MALE (**242a**); crown greenish straw; supercilium blue green; forehead, lores, and eye-ring black; ear-coverts blue green (Turquoise Green); upperparts bluish green mixed with straw color especially on rump; underparts buff tinged blue especially on breast; undertail-coverts pale buff; wings and tail edged blue green. FEMALE (**242b**): duller; crown more straw color; back green; underparts tinged green. *p. 373*

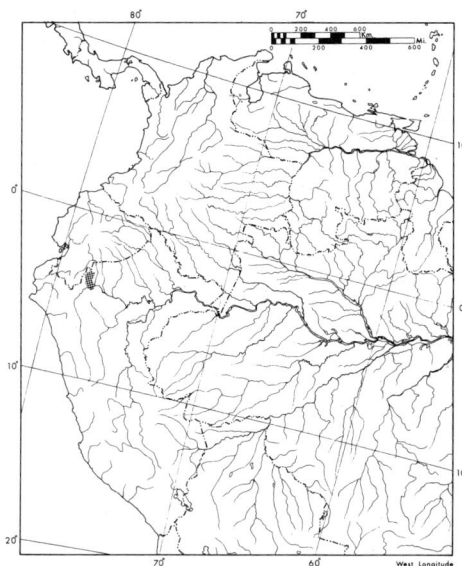

Wetmorethraupis sterrhopteron

very similar in appearance and were formerly placed in a separate genus, *Compsocoma*.

Table 18 The *Anisognathus* Mountain-Tanagers

121	*A. lacrymosus*	Lacrimose Mountain-Tanager
121-1	*lacrymosus* subspecies group.	Lacrimose Mountain-Tanager
121-2	*melanogenys* subspecies group.	Santa Marta Mountain-Tanager
122	*A. igniventris*	Scarlet-bellied Mountain-Tanager
123	*A. flavinuchus*	Blue-winged Mountain-Tanager
124	*A. notabilis*	Black-chinned Mountain-Tanager

branches (O'Neill 1969). Stomach contents (1): seeds and pulp of fruit and a beetle.

Vocalizations

Repeats a deliberate *in-chee-tooch* (O'Neill 1969). Call is a penetrating *seet* (Parker *in litt.*).

Breeding

No information.

Sources

Primary Lowery and O'Neill 1964; O'Neill *in litt.*; O'Neill 1969; Parker *in litt.* **Weights (n = 3):** LSUMZ data. **Stomach contents** LSUMZ data. **Vocalizations** O'Neill 1969.

ANISOGNATHUS

Anisognathus Mountain-Tanagers (Table 18) are restricted to the Andes and the coastal range of Venezuela. As a group, *Anisognathus* species do not seem to share any especially distinctive behavioral attributes, although *Anisognathus* may be more frugivorous than most tanagers. The Lacrimose and Scarlet-bellied live at somewhat higher elevations than the Blue-winged and Black-chinned. The latter two species are

Anisognathus lacrymosus 121
Lacrimose Mountain-Tanager

The mountain-tanager of the Santa Marta Mountains of Colombia, considered a subspecies (*melanogenys*) of the Lacrimose Mountain-Tanager by the *Peters Check-list*, is thought to be a distinct species by many authors (e.g., Meyer de Schauensee 1970).

Anisognathus lacrymosus (*lacrymosus* subspecies group **121-1**)
Lacrimose Mountain-Tanager
Plate 18

Length 16–17 cm (6½–7 in.). Weight 31 g (25.0–38.0 g). Eight subspecies. Some individuals of the nominate race have a trace of the yellow post-auricular spot (Remsen *in litt.*).

Geographic Range

A. l. melanops: the Andes of VENEZUELA in Trujillo, Mérida, and Táchira east of the Western Venezuelan Low. *A. l. tamae*: the Andes west of the Western Venezuelan Low in Táchira, VENEZUELA, and nc COLOMBIA in s Norte de Santander and n Boyacá. *A. l. pallididorsalis*: the Perijá Mountains. *A. l. olivaceiceps*: the W Andes in Antioquia and the C Andes south to Quindío and Tolima, COLOMBIA. *A. l. intensus*: sw COLOMBIA on the e slope of the W Andes in Valle and Cauca. *A. l. palpebrosus* and *caerulescens*: from Cauca and Huila, COLOMBIA, south through the Andes of s COLOMBIA and ECUADOR to Piura and

ANISOGNATHUS

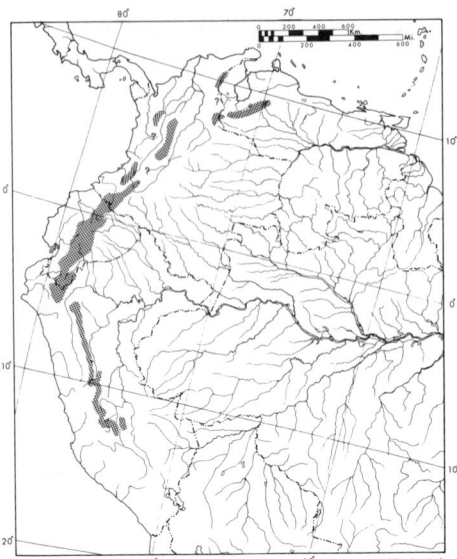

Anisognathus lacrymosus (*lacrymosus* subspecies group)

Cajamarca, PERU, north of the Northern Peruvian Low (specimens collected further south were probably misidentified). *A. l. lacrymosus*: the e slope of the Andes south of the Northern Peruvian Low from Amazonas (LSUMZ) to Ayacucho (Weske 1972) and extreme n Cuzco, (Weske 1972), PERU.

Elevational Range

Generally from 2100 m (1800 m in Venezuela) to treeline (as high as 3800 m). Mostly above 2600 m in Colombia (Hilty and Brown 1986).

Habitat and Behavior

Inhabits humid elfin forest, montane forest with stunted trees, forest edge, and scrubby hillsides near forest. Also occurs in *Polylepis* woodlands and bamboo thickets. Encountered mostly in pairs, sometimes in groups of 3–4 individuals. Travels independently or with mixed-species flocks. Members of a pair frequently perch and fly close together. Appears to move about widely, traveling some distance between foraging sites.

Typically forages in tall shrubs and thickets but often goes higher to the subcanopy. Appears to eat mostly berries and fruit including those of melastomes and *Schefflera*. In Peru, sits quietly near the ends of branches in fruiting shrubs, leans down or stretches up to pluck fruit. Often begins insect-foraging near the base of a shrub or the lower limbs of a tree and moves upward and then hops out into foliage, sometimes out so far that its perch bends with the bird's weight. Hops and peers deliberately; picks insects off leaves, leaf stems, and lichens on bark; occasionally sallies to air for flying insects. Stomach contents: vegetable matter (15); animal matter (1); both (1). Contents included fruit pulp, seeds, and insects.

Vocalizations

Song in Peru: series of 2–6 phrases consisting of sharp forceful squeaky notes centered at a High pitch. Typical phrases are *CHUCK-zit-it*, *SWICK-id-dee-it-it*, and *swick-id-DIT*; frequently the same phrase is repeated. Pauses between series are variable and long (often 1 min.); may utter a soft High-pitched *see* or *swee* during pauses. Sings at dawn from favored perches atop small trees or tall shrubs; usually changes perches every 1–2 min.; vibrates tail while singing (Isler data). The Blue-capped Tanager, *Thraupis cyanocephala* **108**, has a similar song. Calls in Peru: a High-pitched soft *tss-it* and individual notes of the song, e.g., a High-pitched *swick* (Parker, LNS).

Breeding

In Colombia, Silliman found a nest in May (Hilty and Brown 1986).

Sources

Primary Hilty and Brown 1986; Isler data; LSUMZ data; Parker data; Taczanowski 1884b. **Weights (n = 80):** LSUMZ data; Weske 1972. **Stomach contents** LSUMZ data. **Vocalizations** LNS recordings by Isler (3), Parker (7). **Breeding dates** Hilty and Brown 1986.

Anisognathus lacrymosus (*melanogenys* subspecies group **121-2**)
Santa Marta Mountain-Tanager
Plate 18

Length 18 cm (7 in.). Weight 41 g (1 male). Monotypic if specifically distinct. Also known as the Black-cheeked Mountain-Tanager.

Geographic Range

Santa Marta Mountains, COLOMBIA.

Elevational Range

1600–3200 m (Hilty and Brown 1986); populations shift to lower elevations during the

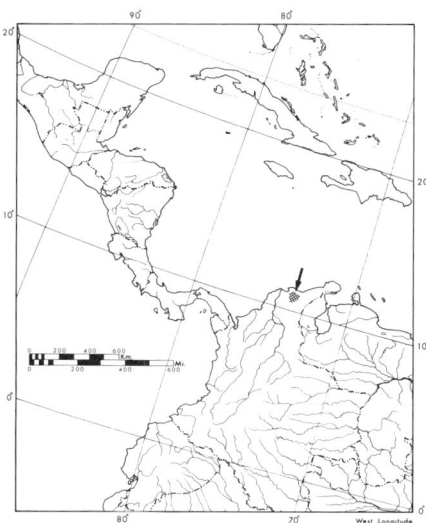

Anisognathus lacrymosus (*melanogenys* subspecies group)

wet season June–September (T. B. Johnson in Hilty and Brown 1986).

Habitat and Behavior

Inhabits mossy forest edge, second-growth woodland, and overgrown pastures, less frequently inside forest. Travels in pairs or groups of up to 6 individuals; often with mixed-species flocks; an important nuclear species (Moynihan 1979). Usually conspicuous. Hops along branches and in foliage from 2 m above the ground to the subcanopy, less often to the canopy; often in fruiting shrubs and trees (T. B. Johnson in Hilty and Brown 1986).

Vocalizations

Calls a weak chirping note (Todd and Carriker 1922).

Breeding

Observed in October building an open cup nest 14 m above the ground (T. B. Johnson in Hilty and Brown 1986).

Sources

Primary Hilty and Brown 1986; Todd and Carriker 1922. **Weights (n = 1)** LSUMZ data. **Nests and breeding dates** Hilty and Brown 1986.

Anisognathus igniventris **122**
Scarlet-bellied Mountain-Tanager
Plate 18

Length 16 cm (6½ in.). Weight 34 g (21.5–41.0 g). Four subspecies.

Geographic Range

A. i. lunulatus: west of the Western Venezuelan Low from Táchira, VENEZUELA, and Norte de Santander, COLOMBIA, through the E Andes to Cundinamarca, COLOMBIA. *A. i. erythrotus*: the C Andes in Caldas, Cauca, and Huila, COLOMBIA; both slopes from Nariño, COLOMBIA, through ECUADOR to n PERU north of the Northern Peruvian Low (to the Río Chamaya in the w range). *A. i. ignicrissus*: PERU south of the Northern Peruvian Low in c Cajamarca (LSUMZ) south of the Río Chamaya in the w range and from s Amazonas to Huánuco (LSUMZ) in the e range. *A. i. igniventris*: the e Andean slope from Junín (LSUMZ), PERU, to Santa Cruz (Remsen, Traylor, and Parkes in press), BOLIVIA.

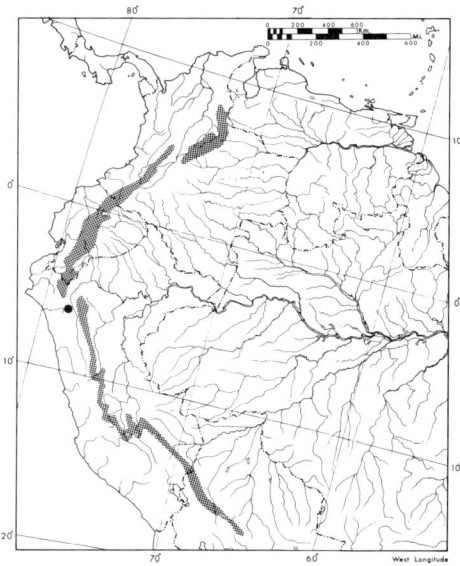

Anisognathus igniventris

Elevational Range

Ca. 2600 m to treeline (as high as 3600 m Graves 1983); rarely descends to 2250 m.

Habitat and Behavior

Habitat preferences appear to differ somewhat by region. In the north (*lunulatus* and *erythrotus*), occurs mostly outside of forest in thickets, shrubs, and low trees on scrubby hillsides and in clearings and other disturbed areas, in remnant patches of woodland, and at páramo edge; occasionally occurs in elfin and montane forest (Hilty *in litt.*). In the south (*ignicrissus* and *igniventris*), often occurs inside elfin and montane forest as well as in thickets and shrubby forest edge.

Encountered mostly in pairs or in small groups of 3–8 individuals, rarely singly or in larger aggregations. Travels alone or with other species; said to be nuclear in mixed-species flocks (Moynihan 1979). In Colombia (*erythrotus*), slips quietly along hedgerows, bounding from the interior of one dense thicket or tree to the next with short undulating flight (Hilty and Brown 1986). In Huánuco, Peru (*ignicrissus*), moved quickly through the forest canopy and subcanopy when with mixed-species flocks, but when independent of flocks, tended to remain within a small area for long periods (Isler data).

In Peru and Bolivia, forages at all levels in trees and bushes. Median foraging height in Bolivia (Remsen data) was about 6 m above the ground (42 obs.), mostly in the upper one-third of trees (33 obs.). Appears to eat mostly fruit; also eats centers and/or petals of melastome flowers (Isler data). Typically picks fruit without acrobatics; sometimes leans down, reaches out, or clings to the sides of fruit clusters to pluck a berry, returning to a stable perch to eat. Swallows some fruits whole and rolls others around in its bill to remove the skin. In Peru, typically ate 1 or 2 fruits from a cluster of berries and then moved on to the next cluster (Isler data). In Bolivia, obtained insects from leaves (3 obs.) by reaching under, hanging down, and sallying; also sallied to air 2 m (Remsen data). Stomach contents: vegetable matter (41); animal matter (1); both (2). Contents included fruit pulp, seeds, leaves, buds, and insects.

Vocalizations

Calls (in Peru): a faint High-pitched sputtering *pss-tit* (Isler, LNS). When agitated: repeats a lower-pitched *chuck* note. Also utters a *whit* or *whip* that is musical from a distance (Parker data). Song: In Peru (*ignicrissus*), a loud 4–5 sec. burst of rapidly delivered complex notes centered at a Moderate pitch. The song begins with a rattle of harsh notes and gradually shifts (with slightly declining volume) into a rhythmic rolling of rising and falling squeaky notes. During the day, the burst of song is usually given only once between long periods of silence, but at dawn may be repeated after pauses of 12 sec. to 2 min. In Colombia (*erythrotus*) a similar pattern and pitch but less harsh, somewhat tinkling and almost bell-like. During the day, songs are typically delivered from concealment, but at dawn, songs may also be delivered from tree tops.

Breeding

In Peru, vigorously defends a territory (Parker data). In Colombia, nests have been found in trees and thickets (Olivares 1969); 2 eggs (believed to be of this species) are pale greenish white with small reddish brown and violet gray spots, especially at the large end (Ogilvie-Grant 1912).

Sources

Primary Hilty and Brown 1986; Isler data; LSUMZ data; Parker data; Peters and Griswold 1943; Remsen data; Remsen 1985. **Weights (n = 98)** LSUMZ data; Weske 1972. **Stomach contents** Foster data; LSUMZ data. **Vocalizations** LNS recordings by Isler (2), Parker (2); recordings by R. A. Rowlett (1), Whitney (1); Hilty and Brown 1986. **Nest and eggs** Ogilvie-Grant 1912; Olivares 1969.

Anisognathus flavinuchus 123
Blue-winged Mountain-Tanager
Plate 18

Length 16–17 cm (6½ in.). Weight 42 g (33.0–56.0 g). Nine subspecies.

Geographic Range

A. f. venezuelanus: n VENEZUELA in the littoral sector of the coastal range from Yaracuy to Miranda. *A. f. viridorsalis*: interior sector of the coastal range along the Aragua-Miranda boundary, VENEZUELA. *A. f. victorini*: sw VENEZUELA in Táchira west of the Western Venezuelan Low; COLOMBIA locally in the E Andes from Santander south to the head of the Magdalena Valley in Huila. *A. f. antioquiae*: COLOMBIA on the n slope of the W Andes; both slopes of the C Andes in Antioquia and the e slope in Tolima. *A. f. cyanopterus*: the w slope of the C Andes, COLOMBIA, from Caldas south; the s part of the W Andes in Valle and Cauca; the w slope from Nariño, COLOMBIA, south to Bolívar, ECUADOR (north of the Río Chimbo). *A. f. baezae*: the e slope from Nariño, COLOMBIA, to Tungurahua, ECUADOR. *A. f. alamoris*: the w slope from Azuay to Loja, ECUADOR. *A. f. somptuosus*: the e slope from Morona-Santiago, ECUADOR, to Ayacucho (Schulenberg and Plenge 1980) and nw Cuzco (Cordillera Vilcabamba, Weske 1972), PERU. *A. f. flavinuchus*: the e slope from Puno, PERU, to Santa Cruz, BOLIVIA.

Elevational Range

In Venezuela, 900–2100 m (mostly at higher elevations); further south, from 1400 m (locally from 1200 m) to 2300 m. Occasionally strays higher.

Habitat and Behavior

Inhabits montane forest; also encountered at forest edge and in second-growth woodland. May occur at higher elevations when congeners are not present (cp. Terborgh and Weske 1975). Encountered in pairs and family groups of 3–6 individuals, sometimes in larger groups of up to 10 or more. Travels independently or with mixed-species flocks. In mixed flocks, the Blue-winged Mountain-Tanager tends to be erratic and restless, often making side forays (cp. Moynihan 1979:135). Surprisingly quick and active for its size (Hilty data).

Forages inside forest, primarily from midheights to the canopy. Sometimes descends to shrubbery in the understory and at forest edge (Parker data). In Valle, Colombia, median height was about 12 m off the ground (Hilty data, 25 obs.). Stomach contents: vegetable matter (10); vegetable and animal matter (2). Contents included fruit pulp, seeds, and insects.

In Valle, Colombia: Typically took *Miconia* berries without acrobatics; occasionally used quick agile movements, such as lunging forward into a hanging position. Hung down to take *Cecropia* fruit. Swallowed some fruits whole and rolled others around in its bill to remove the skin. Searched for insects nimbly and rapidly. Hopped along slim branches (appeared to avoid those thickly covered with moss), inspecting foliage, moss clumps, and branch surfaces. Frequently stretched or hung to pick at green leaves or to probe dead-leaf clusters; pulled off curled dead leaves and held them against a branch with a foot to extract prey. Occasionally hovered or sallied to air. (Hilty data.) In Peru, hopped along mossy epiphyte-laden branches away from leaves, searching moss and bark; also fed on large melastome fruits (Parker data).

Vocalizations

Calls: a thin High-pitched *tic* or *tic-it*, singly or in a ticking series. The song in Bolivia is a

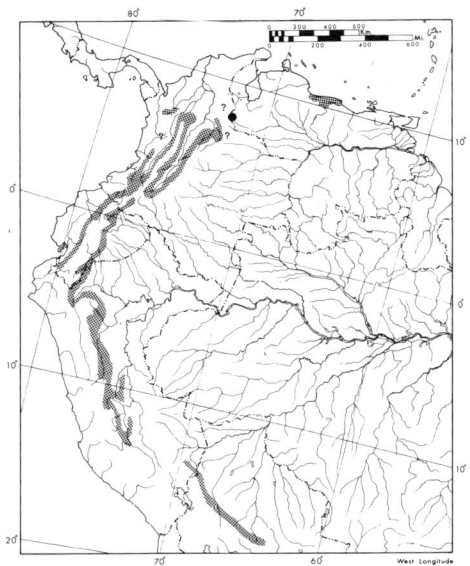

Anisognathus flavinuchus

gradually exploding series of whistled notes, *too-too tyoo-towoo-towoo too-WIT too-WIT too-WIT*, that begins softly and Low-pitched, then becomes louder and higher-pitched, and ends with very loud forceful Moderate-pitched notes; 3–4 sec. long; given throughout the day. Also given in flight as the tanager rises 30–45 m above its perch with wings beating shallowly and then drops to a new perch or returns to the original one (Parker data). In a duet, the *tic* call notes are extended to *tsick* and are increased in volume and speed of delivery while dropping in pitch to squeals and whistled notes of the song before rising in pitch and subsiding to High-pitched *tic* notes once again. It is noteworthy that the elaborate songs and duetting have been heard only in Bolivia and that the song in the northern portion of the range south to Peru may be limited to a ticking series of call notes.

Breeding

In captivity, a cup nest, made of coarse grass and lined with finer grass, was situated in a tree (Norgaard-Olesen 1973).

Sources

Primary Hilty data; Hilty and Brown 1986; LSUMZ data; Parker data; Remsen data; Schäfer and Phelps 1954. **Weights (n = 53)** LSUMZ data; Miller 1963; Weske 1972. **Stomach contents** LSUMZ data. **Vocalizations** LNS recordings by Parker (3), Schwartz (1), van den Berg (1); recording by R. A. Rowlett (1); Hilty and Brown 1986. **Nests** Norgaard-Olesen 1973.

Anisognathus notabilis   **124**
Black-chinned Mountain-Tanager
Plate 18

Length 18 cm (7 in.). Monotypic.

Geographic Range

The Pacific slope from Risaralda, COLOMBIA, southward to El Oro (sight, Aug. 1980—Ridgely) and w Loja, ECUADOR.

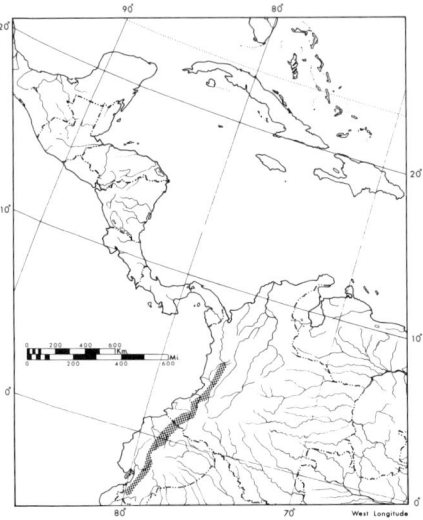

Anisognathus notabilis

Elevational Range

900–2200 m; once to 300 m in w Nariño (Hilty and Brown 1986).

Habitat and Behavior

Inhabits wet mossy forest and forest edge. Often encountered in groups of up to 5–6 individuals (Hilty and Brown 1986); also singly and in pairs. Sits rather upright for a time and then moves rapidly along branches, peering at foliage and searching for fruit (Hilty and Brown 1986).

Vocalizations

Utters high thin *tic* notes (Hilty and Brown 1986).

Breeding

No information.

Sources

Primary Hilty and Brown 1986; Ridgely *in litt.*

STEPHANOPHORUS

The relationships of this monotypic genus are very uncertain. While it is often placed near *Anisognathus*, presumably because of plumage similarities, its vocalizations, habitat, and behavior seem more like those of *Trichothraupis* and related genera.

Stephanophorus diadematus   **125**
Diademed Tanager
Plate 18

Length 19 cm (7½ in.). Weight 38 g (2 males, 35.0 and 41.5 g). Monotypic.

Geographic Range

From Rio de Janeiro, se Minas Gerais, São Paulo, and Paraná, BRAZIL, and e Alto Paraná, PARAGUAY, southward through se BRAZIL, URUGUAY, and ne ARGENTINA (Misiones, Corrientes, extreme ne Santa Fe, and Entre Ríos) to n Buenos Aires, ARGENTINA.

Elevational Range

From sea level to 2400 m (Mt. Itatiaia, Brazil). Restricted to mountainous regions in Rio de Janeiro (Sick 1985).

Habitat and Behavior

Inhabits *Araucaria* forest, dense low forests atop mountains, woodlands (often in swampy places), tall bushes in marshes, river-edge vegetation, and gardens and parks. Encountered in pairs and singly. Frequently assembles in small groups with other species at fruiting trees; sometimes follows mixed-species flocks (Parker *in litt.*). Rests often on tops of bushes or trees; when alarmed drops into heavy cover (Wetmore 1926). Appears to be rather sedentary.

Forages mostly from mid to upper levels of trees (Belton *in litt.*); also in thickets and low dense vegetation. Besides fruit, also eats flowers, buds, and insects. In Brazil, appeared to glean leaves (Parker data) and is fond of sweet secretions of plant lice (Sick 1985). Stomach contents (1): moyé berries (probably *Schinus* sp). In Rio Grande do Sul, reported eating 9 species of fruit including those of *Ficus*, persimmons (*Diospyros kaki*), and papaya (see Voss and Sander 1980, 1981).

Stephanophorus diadematus

Vocalizations

Call: a soft High-pitched *chewp chewp*; other calls are described by Sick (1985) as *quatt* and *pitz*. Sings from bare limbs or leafy tree tops in the canopy. Dawn song: a regularly delivered (every 3–4 sec.) 2–3 sec. warble, e.g., *tio turri weri tweee*; Low- to Moderate-pitched; the second and third notes are lower pitched than the first and fourth (Belton, LNS). Day song: consists of mellow warbled notes, centered at a Moderate pitch, and given in 2–5 sec.; not unlike the song of some *Piranga* tanagers, but generally more rapidly delivered and fluid; repeated after pauses of 10–14 sec.; typically ends on an emphatic up-beat note in Rio Grande do Sul, Brazil. A counter song (probably of the female) consists of a sliding Low- to Moderate-pitched whistle followed by 2 softer short Low-pitched whistles (Belton, LNS). During incubation, the male sings chattering disconnected notes uttered in a very low tone (Sclater and Hudson 1888) which are often repeated for hours (Hudson 1870).

Breeding

Builds a shallow nest 3–4 m off the ground in trees and shrubs. Eggs (4) are white or bluish white, spotted deep red or purplish gray; some eggs have black scrawls. (Also see Ogilvie-Grant 1912.) Breeding dates: Brazil (Rio Grande do Sul) Oct.

Sources

Primary Belton 1985; Descourtilz 1852; Frisch and Frisch 1964; Holt 1928; Parker data; Sclater and Hudson 1888; Sick 1985; Wetmore 1926; Vigil 1973. **Weights (n = 2)** Belton 1985; Sick 1985. **Stomach contents** Aplin 1894. **Vocalizations** LNS recordings by Belton (4), Parker (6); Belton 1985; Wetmore 1926. **Nests, eggs, and breeding dates** Frisch and Frisch 1964; Ogilvie-Grant 1912; Santos 1948; Sclater and Hudson 1888; USNM.

IRIDOSORNIS

The strikingly beautiful *Iridosornis* species (Table 19) are confined to the Andes. These tanagers typically forage from near the ground to just below midheights. They live in pairs and small groups and forage both with and apart from mixed-species flocks. All species seem to eat fruit, especially small berries, and insects. Their vocalizations are somewhat subdued, and the species inhabiting lower elevations tend to remain inconspicuous in dense vegetation.

The lower elevation (1600–2200 m) species, the Purplish-mantled and Yellow-throated Tanagers, form a superspecies and are thought by some authors (e.g., Zimmer 1944) to be conspecific; their habitat, behavior, and vocalizations appear identical. The remaining *Iridosornis* species live at higher elevations. The Golden-collared is found only near treeline where it gleans thin branches and leaves, whereas the sympatric Yellow-scarfed Tanager ranges from treeline down to lower elevations (2050 m) and forages for insects mostly in moss.

Table 19 The *Iridosornis* Tanagers

126	*I. porphyrocephala*		Purplish-mantled Tanager
127	*I. analis*		Yellow-throated Tanager
128	*I. jelskii*		Golden-collared Tanager
129	*I. rufivertex*		Golden-crowned Tanager
	129-1	*rufivertex* subspecies group	Golden-crowned Tanager
	129-2	*reinhardti* subspecies group	Yellow-scarfed Tanager

Iridosornis porphyrocephala **126**
Purplish-mantled Tanager
Plate 19

Length 14 cm (5½ in.). Monotypic.

Geographic Range

COLOMBIA on the entire Pacific slope, locally on the e slope of the W Andes (near low passes), and the C Andes in Antioquia (no recent records); Pacific slope of ECUADOR in Imbabura and Loja (probably this slope).

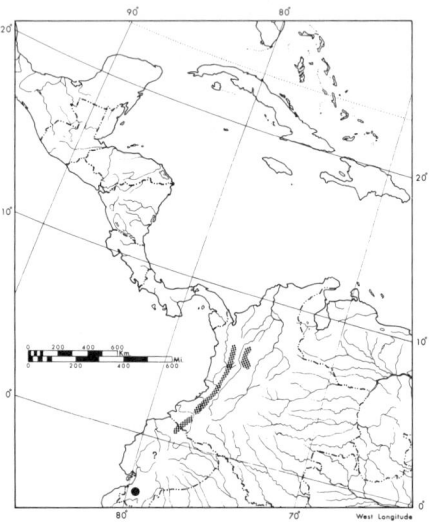

Iridosornis porphyrocephala

Elevational Range

Mostly 1500–2200 m; in Colombia, recorded down to 750 m in Cauca and up to 2700 m in Antioquia (Hilty and Brown 1986).

Habitat and Behavior

Inhabits mossy forest and second-growth woodland, also forest edge; occasionally occurs in less humid areas. Single birds, pairs, or families follow mixed-species flocks or travel alone. Often keeps hidden within lower growth shrubbery. Forages 2–10 m above the ground. Hops and peers in foliage for insects. Eats berries, but does not assemble in fruiting trees with other frugivores. (Hilty and Brown 1986.)

Vocalizations

Calls: utters High-pitched slightly raspy *tsit* notes that sometimes run into a trill. Also delivers a buzzy downscale *seeeer*, mostly High-pitched, repeated every 3 sec., that is probably a song; sings in an upright position with head thrown back while perched at a normal foraging height.

Breeding

No information.

Sources

Primary Hilty and Brown 1986. **Vocalizations** recordings by Whitney (2); Hilty and Brown 1986.

Iridosornis analis 127
Yellow-throated Tanager
Plate 19

Length 15 cm (6 in.). Weight 26 g (20.0–29.0 g). Monotypic.

Geographic Range

The e Andean slopes from Napo, ECUADOR, through ECUADOR (Ridgely *in litt.*) and PERU to e Puno (LSUMZ). Sight record (probably this species) from w Putumayo, COLOMBIA (Hilty and Brown 1986).

Elevational Range

Mostly 1600–2250 m; found as high as 2600 m (LSUMZ data) and as low as 1130 m (Terborgh and Weske 1975).

Habitat and Behavior

Inhabits dense humid montane forest, especially with thick undergrowth; also occurs in thickets and second growth at forest edge. In San Martín, Peru, also found in a depauperate sandy-soil forest (O'Neill *in litt.*). Pairs and small groups of 3 or more individuals typically travel with mixed-species flocks. Joins feeding aggregations at fruiting trees. Forages from the undergrowth to the canopy, but most often below midheights. Observed in trees, searching moss on lower branches near the trunk (Parker data). Stomach contents: vegetable matter (3); animal matter (6); both (4). Contents included fruit, seeds, and insects.

Vocalizations

Utters a squeezed out downward-inflected *tseeeer*, going from High to Moderate pitch, that is repeated after 2–13 sec., probably a song (Parker, LNS).

Breeding

No information.

Sources

Primary LSUMZ data; Parker data; Taczanowski 1884b. **Weights (n = 63)** LSUMZ data; Weske 1972. **Vocalizations** LNS recording by Parker (1); Taczanowski 1884b.

Iridosornis jelskii 128
Golden-collared Tanager
Plate 19

Length 14 cm (5½ in.). Weight 20 g (16.0–26.0 g). Two subspecies.

Geographic Range

I. j. jelskii: the e Andean slope from La Libertad (LSUMZ) and San Martín (LSUMZ) southward to Junín, PERU. *I. j. bolivianus*: Cuzco, PERU, southward to La Paz, BOLIVIA.

Elevational Range

3000–3350 m depending on location of treeline.

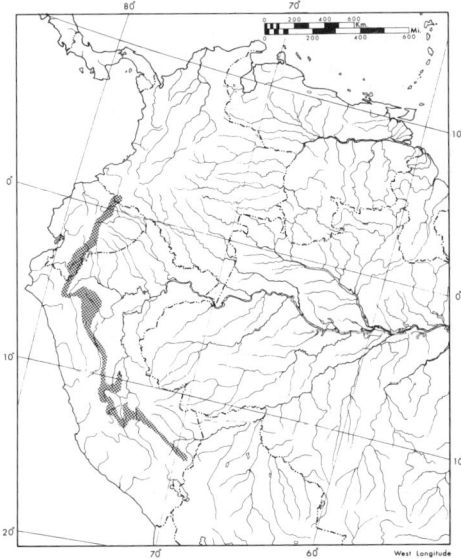

Iridosornis analis

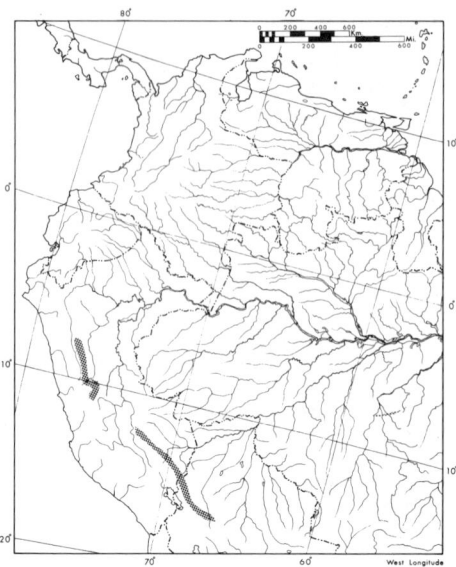

Iridosornis jelskii

1984; Tallman 1974. **Weights (n=45)** LSUMZ data. **Stomach contents** LSUMZ data. **Vocalizations** LNS recording by Isler (1).

Iridosornis rufivertex **129**
Golden-crowned Tanager

The *reinhardti* subspecies of the Golden-crowned (as defined by the *Peters Check-list*) occurs south of the Northern Peruvian Low and is considered to be specifically distinct by most authors (e.g., Meyer de Schauensee 1970). The habitat and behavior of *reinhardti* differs from that of the *rufivertex* subspecies group of the Golden-crowned Tanager.

Iridosornis rufivertex
(*rufivertex* subspecies group **129-1**)
Golden-crowned Tanager
Plate 19

Length 15 cm (6 in.). Weight 23 g (18.0–27.9 g). Four subspecies.

Geographic Range

I. r. caeruleoventris: Antioquia, COLOMBIA at the n ends of the W and C Andes.
I. r. rufivertex, ignicapillus, and *subsimilis*: Táchira, VENEZUELA, west of the Western Venezuelan Low southward locally in the E Andes in Norte de Santander, Santander, and Cundinamarca, COLOMBIA; the Andes from Huila and Cauca, COLOMBIA, southward through ECUADOR (both slopes) to n PERU north of the Northern Peruvian Low near the Piura-Cajamarca border (Parker et al. 1985).

Elevational Range

2600 m to treeline (as high as 3800 m); recorded as low as 2300 m in Colombia (Hilty and Brown 1986).

Habitat and Behavior

Inhabits shrubby growth in elfin forest and at forest edge. Occurs in isolated patches of low trees and shrubs near treeline. Found less often in taller forest at lower elevations (Parker et al. 1985). Encountered in pairs and groups of 3–4 individuals, sometimes singly. Usually accompanies mixed-species flocks; may be a nuclear species (Moynihan 1979). Peers and skulks in dense vegetation. Flies rapidly across open spaces and dives

Habitat and Behavior

Inhabits low trees, shrubs, and bamboo in elfin forest and at forest edge at or near treeline. Often in small isolated patches of woody vegetation, occasionally in tall trees. Encountered mostly in pairs, sometimes singly or in small groups. Typically travels with mixed-species flocks. Forages from the ground to midheights of low trees, sometimes higher, but most often at or just above eye level. Perches upright, leans down, or hovers to pick small fruits. Searches for insects along slender, bare and moss-covered branches less than 1.5 cm in diam.; gleans small leaves mostly near the ends of branches. Stomach contents: vegetable matter (24); animal matter (4); both (5). Contents included berries, seeds, fruit, and insects.

Vocalizations

Utters very soft High-pitched calls such as *seep* and *cheep* (Isler, LNS). Also rapidly delivers series of 2–5 notes, sounding like *ti-ti-ti-ti* (Isler data).

Breeding

No information.

Sources

Primary Isler data; LSUMZ data; Parker data; Parker and O'Neill 1980; Remsen data; Remsen

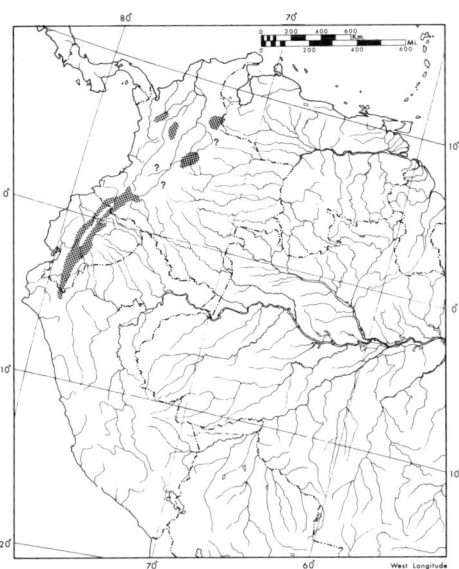

Iridosornis rufivertex (*rufivertex* subspecies group)

quickly into the center of thickets; typically forages 0.5–5 m above the ground (Hilty and Brown 1986). Takes various small fruits and gleans leaves (Parker et al. 1985). Stomach contents: vegetable matter (1); animal matter (1); both (1). Contents included seeds and insects.

Vocalizations

Calls: High- to Very-high-pitched short *tsit* notes (Whitney recording). Occasionally utters a high, thin *seeeep* (Hilty and Brown 1986).

Breeding

No information.

Sources

Primary Goodfellow 1901; Hilty and Brown 1986; LSUMZ data; Parker et al. 1985. **Weights (n = 14)** LSUMZ data. **Stomach contents** LSUMZ data. **Vocalizations** recording by Whitney (1); Hilty and Brown 1986.

Iridosornis rufivertex (*reinhardti* subspecies group 129-2) Yellow-scarfed Tanager
Plate 19

Length 14 cm (5½ in.). Weight 24 g (19.5–28.0 g). Monotypic if specifically distinct.

Geographic Range

PERU on the e Andean slope south of the Northern Peruvian Low from Amazonas to Ayacucho (Parker and O'Neill 1980) and Cuzco (Cordillera Vilcabamba, Weske 1972).

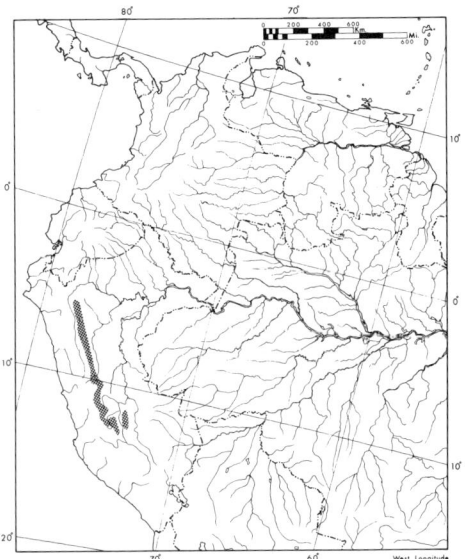

Iridosornis rufivertex (*reinhardti* subspecies group)

Elevational Range

2050 m to treeline (as high as 3500 m); mostly 2600–3050 m.

Habitat and Behavior

Inhabits trees and shrubs in montane and elfin forest, at forest edge, and on scrubby hillsides near forest. Encountered in groups of 3–5 individuals, less often in pairs. Usually accompanies mixed-species flocks, but also regularly travels alone. Moves through interiors of trees and shrubs quickly and actively with fluttery, heavy flight; jumps up from branch to branch, sometimes leaping almost a meter. At times, appears to tumble down branches to lower limbs. Forages from just above the ground to the canopy of small trees. Seems to prefer small berries. Often hops along moss-covered limbs and leaning tree trunks, probing and picking at moss. Pokes into hanging clumps of moss. Also comes down to the ground to probe moss-covered terrestrial surfaces such as large rocks and exposed roots. Sometimes reaches out or hangs down to glean tiny leaves and bare branches. Stomach contents: vegetable matter (6); animal matter (1); both (3). Contents included fruit, seeds, and insects.

Vocalizations

No information.

Breeding

No information.

Sources

Primary Isler data; LSUMZ data; Parker data; Terborgh 1971; Vuilleumier 1970. **Weights** (n = 73) LSUMZ data; Weske 1972. **Stomach contents** LSUMZ data.

DUBUSIA and DELOTHRAUPIS

The Buff-breasted Mountain-Tanager, *Dubusia taeniata* **130,** and the Chestnut-bellied Mountain-Tanager, *Delothraupis castaneoventris* **131,** are both placed in the genus *Dubusia* by some authors (e.g., Meyer de Schauensee 1970). Although their ranges overlap extensively in c Peru, the range of the Buff-breasted extends to the north of the region of sympatry, that of the Chestnut-bellied to the south. Both species live at high Andean elevations. In Peru, they are often found in the same elfin and montane forests; the Buff-breasted usually is encountered close to the ground in dense vegetation, whereas the Chestnut-bellied mostly forages inside the crowns of tall trees.

The quality, pitch, and duration of the songs of the two species are extremely similar and yet so different from songs of other tanagers as to support including these species in the same genus. Where they are sympatric, the song of the Chestnut-bellied consists of two notes and that of the Buff-breasted includes three notes, but north of the range overlap, the Buff-breasted's song is typically only two notes.

Dubusia taeniata **130**
Buff-breasted Mountain-Tanager
Plate 19

Length 20 cm (8 in.). Weight 37 g (31.0–45.0 g). Three subspecies.

Geographic Range

D. t. taeniata: w VENEZUELA in the Andes of Trujillo, Mérida, and Táchira; the Perijá Mountains; the E and C Andes and the s end of the W Andes (Cauca) in COLOMBIA southward through ECUADOR (both slopes) and n PERU (both slopes) to Piura and n Cajamarca north of the Northern Peruvian Low (LSUMZ). *D. t. carrikeri*: the Santa Marta Mountains, COLOMBIA. *D. t. stictocephala*: PERU on the e Andean slope south of the Northern Peruvian Low from Amazonas to Cuzco (n end of the Cordillera Vilcanota, LSUMZ).

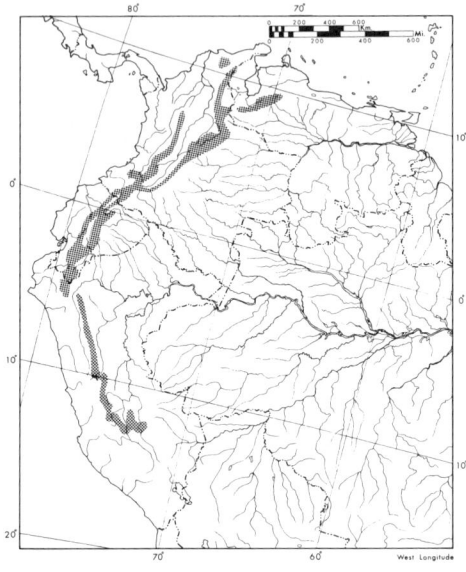

Dubusia taeniata

Elevational Range

2000 m to treeline (as high as 3600 m); mostly above 2500 m.

Habitat and Behavior

Inhabits low dense vegetation, including bamboo thickets and shrubby tangles in humid montane and elfin forest and at forest edge. Also occurs in *Polylepis* woodland and occasionally in isolated patches of brush and second growth. Single birds or pairs are encountered alone or with mixed-species flocks. In Colombia, apparently travels over large areas (Hilty and Brown 1986). Usually stays concealed within low dense foliage. More often heard than seen, but occasionally sits atop a bush and looks around (Hilty and Brown 1986).

Typically forages within thickets, shrubs, and foliage of small trees. Occasionally visits fruiting trees. In Peru, hopped along larger limbs, scanning upper surfaces and bending under limbs to inspect mosses, bark, and especially lichens; also searched moss on steep banks (Parker data). Stomach contents: animal and vegetable matter (3). Contents included fruit, seeds, and insects.

Vocalizations

Song in Venezuela, Colombia, and Ecuador: 2 whistled notes, the first slurs downward then upward and the second (slightly lower in pitch) slides downward, *peeoueee paaaay*; Moderate-pitched, about 2 sec. long. In Peru: similar, but has 3 notes, *peeouee peeoueee paaaay*, the first note slightly higher in pitch than the second; intervals between songs are about 3–7 sec. long (Parker, LNS). Goodfellow (1901) heard it utter a loud chattering noise.

Breeding

No information.

Sources

Primary Hilty and Brown 1986; LSUMZ data; Meyer de Schauensee and Phelps 1978; Parker data; Parker and O'Neill 1980. **Weights (n = 30)** LSUMZ data; Weske 1972. **Stomach contents** LSUMZ data. **Vocalizations** LNS recordings by Parker (3), Schwartz (6); recording by R. A. Rowlett (1); Hilty and Brown 1986.

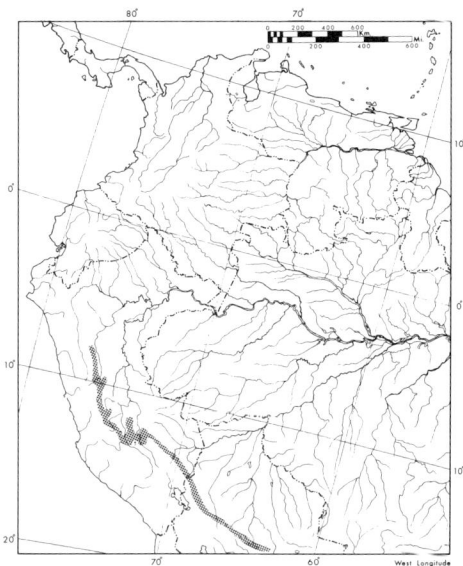

Delothraupis castaneoventris

Delothraupis castaneoventris 131
Chestnut-bellied Mountain-Tanager
Plate 19

Length 15 cm (6 in.). Weight 28 g (24.6–33.0 g). Two subspecies; differences are of dubious validity (Remsen 1984).

Geographic Range

The e slope of the Andes from the se corner of La Libertad (Remsen 1984), PERU, southward to w Santa Cruz (sight observations and tape recordings—Parker and R. A. Rowlett), BOLIVIA.

Elevational Range

From 2200 m to treeline, as high as 3500 m (Remsen 1984).

Habitat and Behavior

Inhabits montane and elfin forest and forest edge; also occurs in isolated patches of forest near treeline. Encountered in pairs or singly; rarely in small groups of 3–4 individuals. Typically travels with mixed-species flocks of small insectivores in forest canopy. Moves slowly within a tree, but in order to keep pace with the flock, does not stay long in a single tree. Usually forages just beneath the crowns of tall trees but occasionally descends to small trees and shrubs, coming close to the ground at forest edge (Parker data). In Bolivia, median foraging height was about 10 m above the ground, and average distance to the top of the canopy was 2.5 m (Remsen data, 13 obs.).

Picks berries while perched. Typically searches for insects while moving along moss-covered branches and limbs that are about 1.5–5 cm in diam. Hops slowly and deliberately along a branch, occasionally jumping to another branch. Peers at moss, leaves, and bromeliads. Primarily picks insects from moss; leans head-down or hangs upside down to probe mossy undersides of branches. Also takes insects from leaf tops, reaches up to obtain prey from undersides of leaves, and picks at petioles. At one location, observed sallying to air to obtain small flying insects (George 1964).

Vocalizations

Song: 2 Moderate-pitched, sweetly whistled notes, *peeee pay-aay*, the first higher-pitched than the second; together the notes take about 1.5 sec. and are repeated after a 4–5 sec. pause. In Bolivia, the phrase is sometimes extended to 3 notes, *peeee pee pay*. Sits upright while singing; often repeats the phrase for long periods.

Breeding

No information.

Sources

Primary Isler data; LSUMZ data; Parker data; Parker and O'Neill 1980; Remsen data; Remsen 1984, 1985. **Weights (n = 27)** LSUMZ data; Weske 1972. **Stomach contents** LSUMZ data; Taczanowski 1884b. **Vocalizations** LNS recordings by Isler (3), Parker (4); recordings by R. A. Rowlett (2).

PIPRAEIDEA

Although located near *Dubusia* in the *Peters Check-list*, the Fawn-breasted Tanager is often placed between the euphonias and the *Tangara* tanagers (e.g., see Meyer de Schauensee and Phelps 1978).

Pipraeidea melanonota   **132**
Fawn-breasted Tanager
Plate 19

Length 14 cm (5½ in.). Weight 21 g (18.0–25.2 g). Two subspecies.

Geographic Range

P. m. venezuelensis: VENEZUELA in Sucre, the coastal range from Distrito Federal to Carabobo, nw Lara, c Mérida, n Amazonas, and sw Bolívar along the Brazil border (possibly in adjacent BRAZIL); COLOMBIA locally in the Andes in Norte de Santander and from Boyacá, Quindío, Tolima, and Valle southward; both Andean slopes in ECUADOR; and PERU on the w Andean slope to Lima (Plenge 1974) and on the e slope through PERU and BOLIVIA to nw ARGENTINA (Jujuy, Salta, and Tucumán). *P. m. melanonota*: c Mato Grosso, BRAZIL, and possibly adjoining BOLIVIA; s Bahia and e Minas Gerais southward through the coastal states of BRAZIL to c Rio Grande do Sul (Belton 1985), thence northwest through Misiones, ARGENTINA, to Paraguarí and Canendiya (Ridgely *in litt.*), PARAGUAY; disjunctly in Colonia, Florida, and Maldonado, URUGUAY (Gore and Gepp 1978) and n Buenos Aires, ARGENTINA.

Elevational Range

P. m. venezuelensis: mostly 1500–2500 m; locally higher, to 3250 m in Bolivia (LSUMZ), and lower, to 900 m in Venezuela and Colombia, 350 m in Bolivia (Bond and Meyer de Schauensee 1942), and 500 m in Tucumán, Argentina. *P. m. melanonota*: sea level to 2050 m on Mt. Itatiaia, Brazil (Holt 1928).

Habitat and Behavior

P. m. venezuelensis: inhabits semiopen habitats such as second growth, bushy pastures, cultivated areas, gardens, and forest edge; also occurs in woodlands in s Peru and Bolivia. Scarce in many regions, but may be expanding range in Colombia as deforestation occurs (Hilty 1977). *P. m. melanonota*: lives in forest and woodland; also occurs in riparian habitats (incl. restinga), occasionally in semiopen environments. Scarce and possibly a seasonal migrant in Uruguay.

Encountered in pairs and singly. Appears to travel over wide areas in search of food. Flight is swift. Rarely with mixed-species flocks but often joins large feeding aggregations at fruiting trees. Usually forages in the canopy when inside forest but hunts for food at all levels of trees and shrubs outside forest; seen feeding in tall herbaceous plants in Colombia (Munves 1975).

Often peers about, searching for insects (Brown and Neto 1976) and sallies to air (Hilty and Brown 1986). Hunted for hairy caterpillars in Rio Grande do Sul, Brazil (Voss 1977). In Argentina, scanned bark and the undersides of branches (4 cm in diam.) and inspected a bromeliad (Parker data). In Brazil, observed feeding on melastome fruits (Willis 1966c), said to favor the berries of *Asparagus sprengeri* (Santos 1948), and eats buds and flowers (Sick 1985). In São Paulo, Brazil, observed to take up residence seasonally at colonies of ithomiines butterflies. Descended to low vegetation where the butterflies roosted on twigs; peered about from exposed horizontal perches to locate prey; sallied 1–3 m to snatch a butterfly and continued to a horizontal branch; consumed the abdominal contents (presumably the exterior body is toxic), sometimes holding the body by a foot; and dropped the remains before searching for the next victim. (Brown and Neto 1976.) Stomach contents: vegetable matter (6); vegetable and animal matter (4). Contents included berries, fruit pulp, seeds, and larvae. Also observed to take moths (Collins and Watson 1983).

Pipraeidea melanonota

Vocalizations

Song: a simple series of strong monotonic High-pitched *see* notes delivered in 2–3 sec. regardless of the number of notes within a series. Some series have as few as 4 and others as many as 11 individual notes, a few are given so rapidly the series becomes an insectlike trill. Repeats the series after pauses of 2–3 sec. Usually sings from the crowns of tall trees. A second song type, suggesting a subsong of thrushes, is more varied with an element of mimicry (Sick 1985).

Breeding

In Peru, a pair was observed building a nest 15 m up in a tree at the edge of a clearing. Both birds flew into and under an epiphyte clump, taking moss picked from limbs of lower trees (Parker data). In Brazil, a nest, built of grassy material and moss, was situated 20 m up among ferns and epiphytes on a horizontal reach of a tree trunk (Belton 1985). Breeding dates: Colombia March. Brazil (Rio Grande do Sul) Sept and Oct.

Sources

Primary Belton 1985; Hilty 1977; Hilty and Brown 1986; LSUMZ data; Miller 1963; Mitchell 1957; Parker data; Sick and Pabst 1968; Schäfer and Phelps 1954; Sick 1985; Taczanowski 1884b. **Weights (n = 14)** Belton 1985; LSUMZ data; Miller 1963; Weske 1972. **Stomach contents** Goodfellow 1901; LSUMZ data; Olivares 1969;

Taczanowski 1884b. **Vocalizations** LNS recordings by Belton (6), Parker (7), Schwartz (7); Belton 1985; Sick 1985. **Nests and breeding dates** Belton 1985; Gertler in Hilty and Brown 1986; Parker data.

EUPHONIA

In addition to their small size, euphonias (Table 20) have two outstanding attributes that are shared only with the chlorophonias in the tanager assemblage. First, their stomachs appear to be specially adapted for eating fruits such as mistletoe berries, and second, they build domed nests with side entrances.

Euphonias are noted for dispersing seeds of parasitic mistletoe to new hosts. After breaking and discarding the skin of mistletoe berries, euphonias swallow the insides whole, and while they derive nourishment from the pulp, the gelatinous mass containing mistletoe seeds travels rapidly through their simplified digestive systems. Their intestines may hold as many as twenty berries at one time (see Wetmore 1927). When the euphonias excrete a portion of the sticky mass on a branch, a new mistletoe plant may be born. It is a mistake, however, to characterize all euphonias as mistletoe specialists; of the three species for which numerous feeding observations exist (the Violaceous, Fulvous-vented, and Orange-bellied), mistletoe accounts for only a small percentage of feeding observations.

Euphonias usually place their globular nests in crannies or other protected places such as amidst profusions of epiphytic plants growing on tree limbs, on steep banks in nooks surrounded by dense vegetation, and in hollows in tree stumps. Four species have been discovered occupying abandoned pensile nests of flycatchers (Tyrannidae). Only females incubate, but both sexes feed their young by regurgitation. Males of many euphonias breed in the subadult plumage which typically appears to be retained for a year.

The twenty-five euphonia species are quite similar in pattern as may be seen in Plates 20–22. In a number of cases, however, similar species replace each other geographically and appear to constitute a superspecies. The plumage similarities of these apparent superspecies are often accompanied by common habitat preferences, feeding behaviors, and vocalizations that sometimes extend to other possibly closely-related species. Consequently, eight species groups (three of which only include one species) and five superspecies are suggested in Table 20.

Species group 1

The relationship of the Jamaican Euphonia to other euphonia species is very uncertain, and until recently the Jamaican was placed in the monotypic genus *Pyrrhuphonia*. It appears that the Jamaican Euphonia evolved in its current location (Pregill and Olson 1981). In plumage, it most closely resembles the Plumbeous Euphonia of the next species group.

Species group 2

The Scrub, Yellow-crowned, Purple-throated, and Trinidad Euphonias appear to constitute a superspecies and mostly inhabit lowland forest borders, including river-edge situations, and patches of trees and shrubs in semiopen areas. They also live in woodland, especially the more open varieties. The males of the four species are yellow and blue black, with only minor plumage differences; the females are slightly more dissimilar (see Plate 20). These species may often be located in the field by their call note, a clear Moderate-pitched whistle, *bee*, that may be doubled or tripled or delivered with varying inflections. Their songs are also similar and consist of rapid twittering or squeaky phrases, delivered in a few seconds and repeated after a short pause.

Except possibly for the Trinidad Euphonia on the island of Trinidad (cp. Snow and Snow 1971), these euphonias seem to be mostly frugivorous. Some species, especially the Purple-throated, migrate seasonally from regions where fruit is available only part of the year. All four species have been noted foraging for insects on thin bare branches or twigs.

These four species appear to be allopatric except for the presumed sympatry of the Purple-throated and Trinidad Euphonias in southern Venezuela. This is not clearly established, however, and if their ranges do not overlap, the Purple-throated and Trinidad may be conspecific.

The Plumbeous Euphonia appears to be related to the aforementioned euphonias. The Plumbeous delivers the *bee* calls of the four preceding species and also has a similar song. Apparently a specialist of habitats resulting from poor soil conditions, the Plumbeous is sympatric with the Purple-throated Euphonia in northern South America where

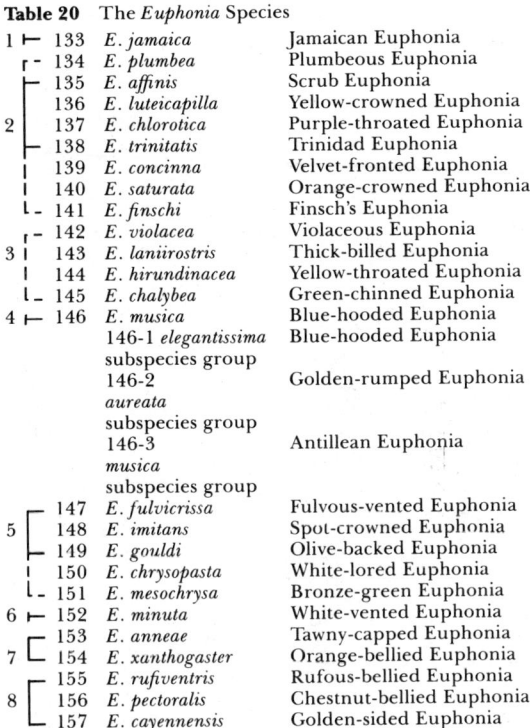

Table 20 The *Euphonia* Species

1	⊢	133 *E. jamaica*	Jamaican Euphonia
	⌈ -	134 *E. plumbea*	Plumbeous Euphonia
	⌈	135 *E. affinis*	Scrub Euphonia
	⊢	136 *E. luteicapilla*	Yellow-crowned Euphonia
2		137 *E. chlorotica*	Purple-throated Euphonia
	⊢	138 *E. trinitatis*	Trinidad Euphonia
		139 *E. concinna*	Velvet-fronted Euphonia
		140 *E. saturata*	Orange-crowned Euphonia
	⌊ -	141 *E. finschi*	Finsch's Euphonia
	⌈ -	142 *E. violacea*	Violaceous Euphonia
3		143 *E. laniirostris*	Thick-billed Euphonia
		144 *E. hirundinacea*	Yellow-throated Euphonia
	⌊ -	145 *E. chalybea*	Green-chinned Euphonia
4	⊢	146 *E. musica*	Blue-hooded Euphonia
		146-1 *elegantissima* subspecies group	Blue-hooded Euphonia
		146-2 *aureata* subspecies group	Golden-rumped Euphonia
		146-3 *musica* subspecies group	Antillean Euphonia
	⌈	147 *E. fulvicrissa*	Fulvous-vented Euphonia
5		148 *E. imitans*	Spot-crowned Euphonia
	⌊	149 *E. gouldi*	Olive-backed Euphonia
		150 *E. chrysopasta*	White-lored Euphonia
	⌊ -	151 *E. mesochrysa*	Bronze-green Euphonia
6	⊢	152 *E. minuta*	White-vented Euphonia
7	⌈	153 *E. anneae*	Tawny-capped Euphonia
	⌊	154 *E. xanthogaster*	Orange-bellied Euphonia
	⌈	155 *E. rufiventris*	Rufous-bellied Euphonia
8		156 *E. pectoralis*	Chestnut-bellied Euphonia
	⌊	157 *E. cayennensis*	Golden-sided Euphonia

Note: Numbers and brackets to the left of the table refer to suggested superspecies (solid lines) and species groups (solid plus dotted lines) discussed in the genus account.

the gray plumage of the Plumbeous sets it apart.

Other candidates for inclusion in species group 2 are the Velvet-fronted, Orange-crowned, and Finsch's Euphonias. None is well known, and we have no record of their vocalizations. The Velvet-fronted and Orange-crowned are allopatric with the other species of this group, and the ranges of the Trinidad and the Velvet-fronted seem to abut in the Magdalena Valley of Colombia, suggesting they are replacement species. The range of Finsch's Euphonia overlaps those of both the Purple-throated and Plumbeous.

Species Group 3

The Violaceous, Thick-billed, and Yellow-throated Euphonias prefer open woodlands, and also inhabit second growth, forest edge, and wooded river habitats. Plumages of the males are very similar as are those of the female Violaceous and Thick-billed Euphonias (see Plate 21). Fruit seems to be their source of nourishment almost exclusively; insect-searching has rarely been observed for these species.

Vocal mimicry is an outstanding feature of the three species. The Violaceous and Thick-billed incorporate the call notes, especially alarm calls, of many birds into their own calls and songs. The Yellow-throated also mimics, but its range of notes does not seem as broad as its close relatives. In addition to appropriating calls, all three euphonias occasionally take over nests of other species, especially pensile nests of flycatchers.

The ranges of the Yellow-throated and Thick-billed Euphonias seem to abut without overlap in Costa Rica, but field work is needed to determine whether the two species are sympatric in western Panama (see Wetmore, Pasquier, and Olson 1984). The Thick-billed and Violaceous also appear to be mostly allopatric with a small range overlap along both sides of the Amazon River in central Brazil. Further work may show that these three species should be considered a superspecies.

A fourth species is tentatively suggested

for inclusion in this group. The male Green-chinned Euphonia is patterned like the males of the preceding three species except for the green coloration and dark chin, and the female most resembles the female Yellow-throated Euphonia. The Green-chinned is most often encountered in forest. Its vocalizations do not appear to be imitative, but they are not well known. The range of the Green-chinned is almost entirely overlapped by that of the Violaceous Euphonia and the two species are often seen together in mixed-species flocks.

Species group 4

The Blue-hooded Euphonia is the only member of this species group. A single species in the *Peters Check-list*, the Blue-hooded is treated as three species in the *A.O.U. Check-list*. The Blue-hooded Euphonia lives in mountains in most parts of its range, and its principal food appears to be mistletoe berries.

Species group 5

The allopatric Fulvous-vented, Spot-crowned, and Olive-backed Euphonias occur west and north of the Andes (to Mexico) and primarily inhabit forest canopy, although they often descend to midheights or lower at forest edge. These three species eat fruit and insects without appearing to favor either. They travel mostly in pairs and are encountered with mixed-species flocks in the canopy. All three deliver a burry short rattle, *tr-r-r-r*, that is highly characteristic of the group. This note can often be heard in the forest canopy when these tiny birds are hidden by foliage. Songs of the Spot-crowned and Olive-backed Euphonias are also similar, but the only other vocalization recorded of the Fulvous-vented, aside from the burry rattle, is an upward-inflected *wheet*.

The shining blue green upperparts of the females of the foregoing species and of the male Olive-backed Euphonia are also found on two species that range east of the Andes in South America, the White-lored and Bronze-green Euphonias, and similarities in vocalizations are also noteworthy. The White-lored emits the *tr-r-r-r* notes of the Olive-backed, Spot-crowned, and Fulvous-vented Euphonias, and the White-vented commonly delivers a *wheet* note that is similar to that of the Fulvous-vented. The songs of the White-lored and Bronze-green are not especially similar, however, to those of the species living west of the Andes. The White-lored lives mostly along edges of Amazonian forest and the Bronze-green inhabits the canopy of montane forest on the eastern slope of the Andes.

Species group 6

The White-vented Euphonia does not have any obviously close relatives and consequently has been placed in a variety of taxonomic positions by different authors. The White-vented occurs on both sides of the Andes, lives mainly high in trees, and appears to be primarily insectivorous although it is often observed taking mistletoe.

Species group 7

The Tawny-capped and Orange-bellied Euphonias appear to constitute a superspecies that is widely distributed in forested regions from Costa Rica to southeastern Brazil both in lowlands and mountains. These species are often found at midheights in forest, although the preferred foraging height of the Orange-bellied appears to vary regionally, and the Tawny-capped is primarily encountered below midheights. The two species appear to eat mostly fruit. Their songs include a large variety of phrases, some of which may be imitative, that are often given in repetitive series; their most common call is a burry *dee-dee-dee*.

Species group 8

The Rufous-bellied, Chestnut-bellied, and Golden-sided Euphonias have ranges that neatly replace one another east of the Andes, and the three species share obvious commonalities in appearance, behavior, and voice. These euphonias are typical species of forest canopy and are frequently observed in mixed-species flocks. Their calls are nearly identical, a raspy insectlike *bzzz-bzzz-bzzz-bzzz*. Because they usually remain high off the ground in forest canopy, their behaviors are not well known despite their abundance.

Euphonia jamaica 133
Jamaican Euphonia
Plate 20

Length 11 cm (4½ in.). Weight 17 g. Monotypic.

Geographic Range

JAMAICA.

Elevational Range

At all elevations.

Habitat and Behavior

Encountered in open woodland, forest edge, orchards, and trees around houses and gar-

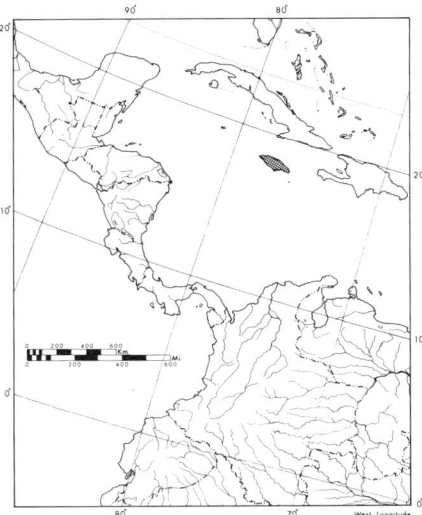

Euphonia jamaica

dens. Appears to undertake seasonal movements around the island (Jeffrey-Smith 1956). Sometimes joins large feeding aggregations, but may drive other species from favorite trees when fruit is ripening. Roosts in large groups in tree crowns. Generally sluggish in its movements.

Forages in the canopy of fruiting trees. Eats a variety of fruit including those of *Ficus*, *Cecropia*, and *Dunalia* (Cruz 1981), mistletoe berries, guava, and young shoots and fruit of the "cho-cho" vine. Hops about busily picking fruit from any position: upright, head-down, or hanging (Gosse 1847). Damages fruit in gardens and orchards.

Vocalizations

Song is sweet and musical; often repeats the same note, ending with a higher-pitched note, e.g., *chu chu chu chu chwit* (Gosse 1847). Also delivers a soft prolonged chuckling warble of a single note, sometimes sounding like the plaintive mewing of a kitten. Call notes include hummingbirdlike chirps and a long *tweee*; other notes are harsh and chattery.

Breeding

The domed nest with side entrance, made of a mixture of grass, stems, and vegetable down and lined with grass, is often concealed in Spanish moss (*Tillandsia* sp) in trees and may be at almost any height above the ground. Both sexes seem to build the nest (see Gosse 1847). Eggs (3–4) are white, marked with lavender, purplish red, or reddish brown, especially at the large end. Breeding dates: Feb–May.

Sources

Primary Bond 1961; Cruz 1974; Gosse 1847; Jeffrey-Smith 1956; Taylor 1955. **Weights (n = 3)** Cruz 1974. **Vocalizations** Bond 1961; Danforth 1928; Gosse 1847. **Nests, eggs and breeding dates** Bond 1961; Field 1894; Gosse 1847; Jeffrey-Smith 1956; March 1863; Ogilvie-Grant 1912; USNM.

Euphonia plumbea 134
Plumbeous Euphonia
Plate 20

Length 9 cm (3½ in.). Weight 9 g (8.8–9.5 g). Monotypic.

Geographic Range

The upper reaches of the Rio Negro in Amazonas, BRAZIL, ne Guainía (sight, Hilty and Brown 1986), COLOMBIA, and south of the Río Ventuari in Amazonas, VENEZUELA, eastward through c and s Bolívar, VENEZUELA, and c GUYANA to SURINAME and adjacent BRAZIL in Amapá (Meyer de Schauensee 1966). Specimens reported to be from Manaus, Amazonas, Brazil (Pelzeln 1869) may have come from upriver.

Elevational Range

From near sea level to ca. 1000 m.

Habitat and Behavior

Encountered in savanna woodlands, scrubby woodland, forest edge, and the edges of granite plates in highlands (Hilty *in litt.*). Sometimes joins other euphonias (Haverschmidt 1972). In Suriname, forages in savanna bushes (Haverschmidt 1968, 1972). Also seen high in trees at forest edge (Ridgely *in litt.*). Stomach contents: berries.

Vocalizations

Call: a Moderate-pitched whistled *bee bee* or *bee bee wheet*, given slowly or rapidly, and sometimes alternating fast and slow. Call is similar to that of the Trinidad Euphonia, *E. trinitatis* **138**, but higher, sharper, and with rising inflection (Schwartz, LNS). Also a short soft *wit* while foraging. Song: In Venezuela, repeats *WEET sweet-a-swee-swee*, the first note whistled at a Moderate pitch, and the last notes (Moderate- to High-pitched) rapidly jumbled together; pauses are short; sometimes alternates song and call; sings

Euphonia plumbea

from tops of tall trees (Schwartz, LNS). In Guyana, Snyder (1966) describes song as a high scraping *witchay-chewit* . . . *witchay-chewit* or *weetu-chit*.

Breeding

No information.

Sources

Primary Haverschmidt 1968, 1972; Meyer de Schauensee and Phelps 1978; Snyder 1966. **Weights (n = 3)** Haverschmidt 1968; Sick 1985. **Stomach contents** Haverschmidt 1968. **Vocalizations** LNS recordings by T. H. Davis (1), Schwartz (6); Snyder 1966.

Euphonia affinis **135**
Scrub Euphonia
Plate 20

Length 9 cm (3½ in.). Weight 10 g (8.5–12.8 g). Three subspecies including one (*olmecorum*) described since 1970 (Dickerman 1981). Yellow crown of the male sometimes extends beyond the eye (see Dickey and van Rossem 1938). Some individuals from Guerrero, Mexico, are intermediate between *godmani* (illus.) and the nominate race (illus.); Dickerman 1981.

Geographic Range

E. a. godmani: the Pacific slope of MEXICO from se Sonora to c Guerrero. *E. a. olmecorum*: the Gulf slope from s Tamaulipas and e San Luis Potosí to n Chiapas, MEXICO. *E. a. affinis*: the Gulf-Caribbean slope from the Yucatán Peninsula (incl. Cozumel I.) through BELIZE and GUATEMALA to Atlántida, HONDURAS, and the Pacific slope from extreme w Oaxaca, MEXICO, southeastward through GUATEMALA, EL SALVADOR, HONDURAS, and NICARAGUA to Guanacaste, COSTA RICA (possibly further east, see Slud 1964).

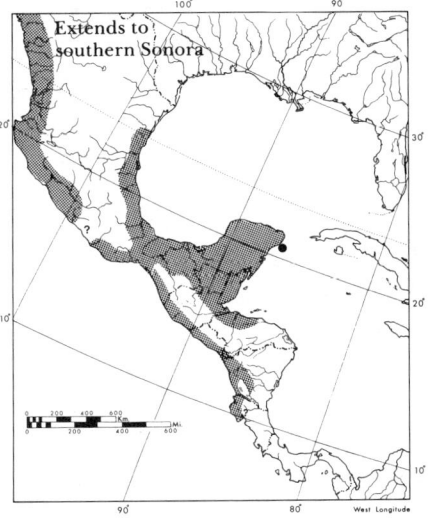

Euphonia affinis

Elevational Range

From sea level to 2250 m; generally below 1000 m.

Habitat and Behavior

Lives in both semiarid and humid regions. Prefers semiopen areas with low dense growth and patches of trees, such as dry forest and forest edge, second growth, scrub, and cultivated lands. In humid regions, frequents gallery forest, open woodland, forest edge and clearings, and gardens. Seldom in the forest canopy. Travels in pairs and small groups; at times in company with the Yellow-throated Euphonia, *E. hirundinacea* **144**. Often flies long distances in the open. Rests in the tops of bare or dead trees, especially in the early morning. Sidles along branches shifting its tail from side to side (Slud 1964).

Typically forages in bushes and low trees in semiopen areas and in the crowns of trees in tall open woodland. Appears to be primarily frugivorous; favors mistletoe berries and other small fruits, especially those of *Ficus*; also eats fruits of *Neea* of the family Nyctaginaceae (see Kantak 1979). Visits orange trees where the fruit has been drilled by woodpeckers (Dickey and Van Rossem 1938) and reported to feed on ripe plantains until it was so full it could not fly (Boucard 1883). In Costa Rica, searched the undersides of bare branches, presumably for insects; observed with a large grasshopper in its bill (Slud 1980). Stomach contents: vegetable matter (10). Contents were mostly mistletoe berries.

Vocalizations

Calls are Moderate-pitched and vary by locality and/or individually. One type of call is a whistled *bee-bee*, often tripled, or sometimes turned into a wistful *wheeee*. A second type is *whit-it-it-it* which is sometimes shortened to 3 notes or speeded up into 4–6 notes delivered in less than 1 sec.; a variant recorded in sw Chiapas, Mexico, is *whee-didee*, the last note slightly higher in pitch (Whitney recording). Calls, apparently initiated by the male, are given frequently, but with irregular pauses, by both sexes. The song is a weak twitter, e.g., *wheetidy-titity-witity-titity*, High- to Moderate-pitched.

Breeding

One collected female carried 3 eggs (Rowley 1966). Eggs, all from Mexico, are uniformly colored pale greenish-blue (Ogilvie-Grant 1912). Breeding dates: Mexico May.

Sources

Primary Andrle 1967; Dickey and Van Rossem 1938; Edwards 1972; Rand and Traylor 1954; Salvin and Godman 1879–1904; Slud 1964, 1980; Smithe 1966; Sutton 1951a, 1951b; Wetmore 1944. **Weights (n=28)** Klaas 1968; LSUMZ data; Paynter 1955; Russell 1964; Smithe 1966. **Stomach contents** Davis 1960; Dickey and van Rossem 1938; Wetmore 1944. **Vocalizations** LNS recordings by Thurber (3); recordings by Whitney (4); Davis 1972; Slud 1964, 1980. **Nests, eggs, and breeding dates** Ogilvie-Grant 1912; Rowley 1966.

Euphonia luteicapilla 136
Yellow-crowned Euphonia
Plate 20

Length 9 cm (3½ in.). Weight 13 g (11.4–14.5 g). Monotypic. Males breed in subadult plumage which resembles that of female except for some black feathers on upperparts.

Geographic Range

The Caribbean slope from n NICARAGUA through COSTA RICA to Bocas del Toro, PANAMA, and in the region of the Panama Canal; on the Pacific slope from Guanacaste, COSTA RICA (absent from the dry nw), to c Darién, PANAMA (Olson 1981a). Possible sight record in e HONDURAS (Howell in Monroe 1968).

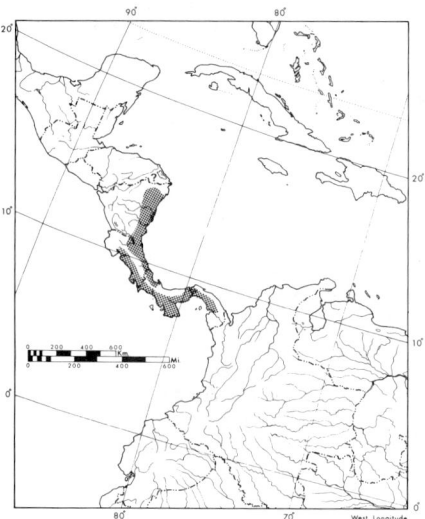

Euphonia luteicapilla

Elevational Range

Lowlands, rarely above 900 m; once as high as 1600 m in Panama (Wetmore, Pasquier, and Olson 1984).

Habitat and Behavior

Inhabits semiopen areas with scattered trees in humid regions; also open scrub in dry regions in Panama. Frequents trees in pastures, cultivated lands, neglected clearings, partially deforested areas, along roadsides and streams, and in savannas, second growth, open woodland, and forest edge. Also occurs in the canopy of deciduous forest and occasionally in humid forest in Costa Rica, but seldom penetrates far into forest. In Costa Rica, numbers varied seasonally, perhaps reflecting elevational movement (Skutch 1954).

Travels in pairs, singly, and in small groups of 3–4 individuals. Roams restlessly and appears to wander over wide areas (Skutch 1954). Joins feeding aggregations at fruiting trees. Usually forages high in trees, searching mostly for mistletoe berries but also for other small fruits. Examines leafless twigs (Slud 1964). Occasionally comes to feeding shelves to eat bananas (Skutch 1954).

Vocalizations

Call: 2–3 Moderate-pitched whistles, *bee-bee-bee*, varying in speed but rapid, delivered in about 1 sec. Both males and females call often. Song: a rapid *pit diTREEa-twiddledee bee bee*; the introductory note is High-pitched, the twitter that follows has a peculiar twang and is Moderate- to High-pitched, and the *bee* ending (sounds like the call) is sometimes omitted; about 2–3 sec. long with 1–3 sec. pauses (Morton, LNS). Sings from the tops of small trees and shrubs; song sounds thin at a distance.

Breeding

In Costa Rica, nests are built inside nooks and crannies and sheltered crotches, e.g., ascending shoots atop stumps, clusters of thick leathery leaves in trees, and matted roots of epiphytes. Nests have been found in agricultural country and at forest edge, most often built at around 2 m (range 1–30 m) above the ground. Together, the pair selects the nest site and builds the nest. The small domed structure with narrow round side entrance is constructed with fine stems, petioles, and other fibers, dead leaves, and moss and is lined with dry grass or strips of leaves. (Skutch 1954.) In Panama, a bulky open cup was once found in a partly rotted out woodpecker hole in a fence post (Wetmore, Pasquier, and Olson 1984). Eggs (2–4, usually 3), laid on consecutive days, are white, heavily mottled all over with brown. In Costa Rica, the female incubates alone for 13–14 days attended closely by her mate. Both parents come to the nest together to feed the nestlings by regurgitation. Nestling period is 22–24 days. Two or more broods may be reared in a season. (Skutch 1954.) Breeding dates Costa Rica Jan and March–July. Panama March.

Sources

Primary Carriker 1910; Ridgely 1976; Skutch 1954; Slud 1964. **Weights (n = 5)** Hartman 1955; Strauch 1977. **Vocalizations** LNS recordings by Morton (3), Parker (1); recordings by Whitney (2); Slud 1964; Skutch 1954. **Nests, eggs, and breeding dates** Skutch 1954; Wetmore, Pasquier, and Olson 1984.

Euphonia chlorotica 137
Purple-throated Euphonia
Plate 20

Length 9–10 cm (3½–4 in.). Weight 11 g (8.0–14.3 g); apparently varies by subspecies. Five subspecies: the nominate race has a more extensive crown patch, almost midway in size between the remaining subspecies (illus.) and the crown of the Trinidad Euphonia, *E. trinitatis* 138.

Geographic Range

E. c. cynophora: s Táchira, VENEZUELA, south to Meta, COLOMBIA, and thence east to n Amazonas and nw Bolívar (east to the Río Caura), VENEZUELA (specimen reported for n Brazil should be reexamined). *Remaining subspecies*: extreme se Bolívar, VENEZUELA, southeastward through THE GUIANAS; in a band along the Amazon River from extreme se Amazonas, COLOMBIA, eastward through Amazonas and Pará, BRAZIL; east of the Andes from Cajamarca, Amazonas, and Loreto, PERU, southward through PERU, BOLIVIA, and n ARGENTINA to La Rioja, Córdoba, and n Buenos Aires, ARGENTINA, and eastward through Mato Grosso, BRAZIL, and PARAGUAY to e BRAZIL (except s Rio Grande do Sul).

Elevational Range

Sea level to 900 m in the Venezuelan tepuis, to ca. 1200 m along the Andes, and to ca. 2000 m in s Bolivia.

Habitat and Behavior

In heavily forested regions of Amazonia, confined to low-lying forest (incl. *varzea* forest) and river-edge habitats. Elsewhere, encountered in humid to arid regions in open woodland, gallery forest, forest edge and clearings, mangroves and other swamps, thorn woodland, second growth, scrub (incl. caatinga and cactus scrub), matorral, savanna, and scattered trees in pastures, plantations, parks, and gardens. Does not penetrate far inside humid forest. Appears to migrate seasonally out of dry Andean valleys (Stolzmann in Taczanowski 1884b) and away from Espírito Santo, Brazil (Sick 1985).

Pairs, less often individuals or family groups, frequently travel with mixed-species flocks; often with other euphonias in Amazonia. Moves over wide areas, at least in some regions. Active and vociferous while foraging. Forages in the tops of the tallest trees; lower at forest borders and in scrub. Often feeds on mistletoe berries but also eats other fruits including persimmons, and those of *Ficus* and cactus which is favored in dry regions. Sometimes hovers to pick *Rhipsalis* fruits (Sick 1985). Methodically examines tree branches (Dorst 1957b). Stomach contents (10): vegetable matter, including fruit and seeds.

In Paraguay when eating 7–10 mm fruit of *Allophyllus edulis*: Typically perched alongside a fruit cluster and ate one fruit after another. Usually bit at a fruit, often taking 10–15 bites, and left the seed hanging. Sometimes plucked fruit and held it against its perch to peck off pieces. Often rolled the pulp around in its bill before swallowing it. (Foster data.)

Vocalizations

In se Brazil: Song is a rapid jumbled series of notes that are dominated by High-pitched squeals and squeaks but also include Low-pitched harsh notes; usually 2 sec. (to 4 sec.) long. Call: a whistled *bee bee* usually 2 or 3 (sometimes 1 or 4) notes; typically Moderate-pitched but occasionally somewhat higher. Sometimes alternates song and call. Agitated calls: 1–4 whistled upward-inflected *wheeet*s; 3–6 rapid even *dee* notes; a clear Moderate-pitched *TI-a TI-a*; and harsh flat machine-gun phrases centered at Moderate pitch, e.g., *chid-d-d-d-d-d-d*. (Belton, LNS.)

Breeding

In Paraguay, a domed nest, composed of fibers and dry leaves and lined with fine fibers, was placed among 4 vertical twigs in the crown of a tall tree. The circular side entrance was roofed over by dense rhizomes and fibers growing above the nest. The nest also had a false entrance, unconnected with the interior, atop the sphere. (Bertoni 1904.)

In captivity: Both sexes built the nest together, the male more industriously. One male completed a second nest without the female's help and used it as a dormitory while the female incubated. The female incubated alone for about 15 days, attended

230 EUPHONIA

Euphonia chlorotica

closely by her mate. Eggs (3–5) were grayish white, marked with reddish-brown and gray. Both parents came together to feed the young regurgitated food, the male usually feeding first. A second brood was hatched but not successfully reared. (Ingels 1971a; Ingels, Maroy, and Norgaard-Olesen 1976.) Breeding dates: Paraguay Nov.

Sources

Primary Bertoni 1904; Descourtilz 1852; Dorst 1957b; Foster data; Hilty and Brown 1986; LSUMZ data; Remsen 1976; Snethlage 1913; Snethlage 1927–1928; Taczanowski 1884b; Terborgh and Weske 1969; Willis 1977. **Weights (n=16)** Belton 1985; LSUMZ data; Sick 1985. **Stomach contents** Beebe 1909; Foster data; LSUMZ data. **Vocalizations** LNS recordings by Belton (11); Belton 1985; Sick 1985; Taczanowski 1884b. **Nests, eggs, and breeding dates** Bertoni 1904; Ingels 1971a; Ingels, Maroy, and Norgaard-Olesen 1976.

Euphonia trinitatis **138**
Trinidad Euphonia
Plate 20

Length 10 cm (4 in.). Weight 11 g (8.8–14.0 g). Monotypic.

Geographic Range

The lower and middle Magdalena Valley in COLOMBIA from e Antioquia northward

Euphonia trinitatis

to Atlántico, thence eastward along the Caribbean slope through COLOMBIA and VENEZUELA to Sucre and Delta Amacuro and southward in VENEZUELA to n Amazonas and c Bolívar; TRINIDAD.

Elevational Range

Lowlands mostly below 600 m; to 1100 m in Colombia (Hilty and Brown 1986) and 850 m in Venezuela (Schäfer and Phelps 1954).

Habitat and Behavior

Primarily inhabits dry open woodland, forest and woodland edge, and second growth; also encountered in scrub, savanna with patches of trees, gallery forest, and shade trees in agricultural and residential areas. Travels in pairs, often in small groups, occasionally in groups of 6–10 individuals. At one location, a dozen or so individuals roosted together (Darlington 1931). Only occasionally associates with mixed-species flocks.

Usually forages from midheights to the canopy. Eats insects and berries including those of mistletoe. In Trinidad, searched for insects on the undersides of twigs less than 7 mm in diam. by using the diagonal-lean method. (Snow and Snow 1971, 12 obs.).

Vocalizations

Call: 1–4 unforceful Moderate-pitched whistles, typically *bee-bee*, almost always given on an even pitch. Notes vary in length so that the entire phrase, whether 1 or 4 notes, is given in about 1 sec. Calls often. Call-song: a variety of whistled notes, like the call note, are repeated at regular 3 sec. intervals; notes contain 1–3 syllables. Song: a jumble of scratchy notes (mostly Moderate- and High-pitched) usually without emphasis; phrases last about 1.5 sec. and are repeated irregularly at intervals of up to 10 sec. Sometimes alternates songs and calls.

Breeding

In courtship display, both sexes flick wings and turn from side to side, frequently bowing low, the male showing his bright crown (ffrench 1973). Nests have been found 1.4–12 m off the ground in trees. The flattened ball-shaped nest with side entrance is constructed mostly of grasses and placed amid twigs on the end of a horizontal branch. Eggs (3–4) are pale cream or white, marked with shades of brown. Both sexes build the nest and feed the young, but only the female incubates. Breeding dates: Colombia April. Venezuela April. Trinidad Feb–April.

Sources

Primary Darlington 1931; ffrench 1973; Friedmann and Smith 1950; Hilty and Brown 1986; Snow and Snow 1971; Thomas 1979. **Weights (n = 4)** Snow and Snow 1971; Thomas 1982. **Vocalizations** LNS recordings by Parker (2), Schwartz (15). **Nests, eggs, and breeding dates** Allen 1905; Belcher and Smooker 1937; Cherrie 1916; ffrench 1973; Thomas data.

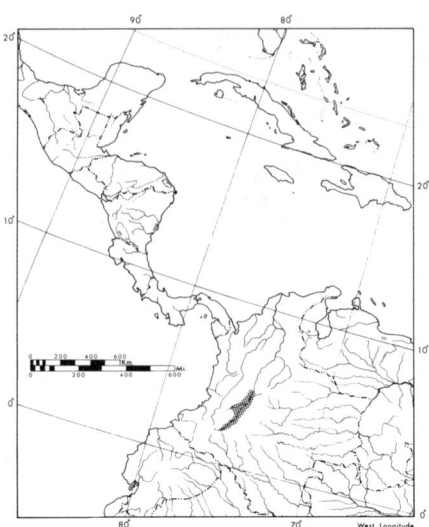

Euphonia concinna

Euphonia concinna **139**
Velvet-fronted Euphonia
Plate 20

Length 9 cm (3½ in.). Weight 10 g (9.0–12.0 g). Monotypic.

Geographic Range

COLOMBIA in the upper Magdalena Valley from n Tolima southward to c Huila (USNM); one report from the w slope of the C Andes in Valle (Hilty and Brown 1986).

Elevational Range

200–1000 m; up to 1800 m in Cundinamarca (Hilty and Brown 1986).

Habitat and Behavior

Inhabits dry open woodland, hedgerows, and trees bordering streams. Eats small fruits, especially of parasitic plants (Olivares 1969).

Vocalizations

Miller (1947) heard one singing a warbler-like song from high in a tree.

Breeding

No information.

Sources

Primary Hilty and Brown 1986; Miller 1947; Olivares 1969. **Weights (n = 3)** Miller 1947.

Euphonia saturata **140**
Orange-crowned Euphonia
Plate 20

Length 10 cm (4 in.). Monotypic.

Geographic Range

The e slope of the W Andes in Valle, COLOMBIA, and the Pacific slope from Valle southward through sw COLOMBIA and w ECUADOR to extreme nw PERU in Tumbes.

Elevational Range

700–1300 m in Colombia (Hilty and Brown 1986); sea level to 1000 m in Ecuador.

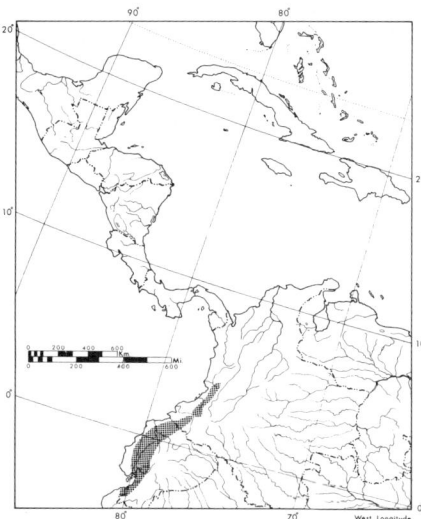

Euphonia saturata

Habitat and Behavior

In the northern portion of its range, inhabits humid forest edge, broken forest on steep hillsides (Hilty *in litt.*), trees in clearings and agricultural areas, tall second growth, woodlots, and parks; in arid areas, favors open riparian woodland and scattered tall trees (Hilty *in litt.*). In the southern portion of its range, occurs in dry habitats in sc Ecuador (Ridgely *in litt.*) and tall deciduous forest in Tumbes, Peru (Parker *in litt.*). Encountered in pairs or singly; independent of other species or, especially in forested regions, with mixed-species flocks of other tanagers. Forages from mid to upper levels of trees.

Vocalizations

Call is a high *pee-deet*, reminiscent of the Trinidad Euphonia, *E. trinitatis* **138** (Hilty and Brown 1986).

Breeding

No information.

Sources

Primary Hilty and Brown 1986; Hilty *in litt.*; Isler data. **Vocalizations** Hilty and Brown 1986.

Euphonia finschi 141
Finsch's Euphonia
Plate 20

Length 9 cm (3½ in.). Weight 10–11 g. Monotypic.

Geographic Range

Extreme se Bolívar, VENEZUELA, and extreme ne Roraima, BRAZIL, eastward through c GUYANA and n SURINAME to n FRENCH GUIANA.

Elevational Range

Lowlands; one record at ca. 1200 m in Venezuela (Meyer de Schauensee and Phelps 1978).

Habitat and Behavior

Encountered in shrubby forest edge, savannas, open woodlands, second growth, and river-edge habitats. Pairs or small groups move quickly from tree to tree. Reported to eat small fruits, including mistletoe berries.

Vocalizations

Call is low and sibilant (Young 1929).

Breeding

No information.

Sources

Primary Davis 1980; Haverschmidt 1968; Penard and Penard 1910; Young 1929. **Weights (n = ?)** Haverschmidt 1968.

Euphonia violacea 142
Violaceous Euphonia
Plate 21

Length 10 cm (4 in.). Weight 15 g (12.5–17.0 g). Three subspecies. White inner webs of tail feathers help separate this species from the black-tailed race of the Thick-billed Euphonia, *E. laniirostris* **143**, where their ranges abut or overlap near the Amazon River.

Geographic Range

VENEZUELA in n Amazonas, Bolívar, Delta Amacuro, e Monagas, and e Sucre; TRINIDAD AND TOBAGO (ffrench 1973); THE GUIANAS; and BRAZIL north of the Amazon River from nc Roraima (Pinto 1966) and extreme e Amazonas eastward to Amapá

Euphonia finschi

and south of the Amazon River from e Amazonas (lower Rio Madeira) eastward to Maranhão; thence southward inland through Piauí, Goiás, Minas Gerais, São Paulo, and Paraná to Paraguarí and Itapúa, PARAGUAY, and Misiones, ARGENTINA; and the coastal states of BRAZIL from Paraíba southward to n Rio Grande do Sul.

Elevational Range

Lowlands; to 1100 m in Venezuela.

Habitat and Behavior

Inhabits open woodlands, low-lying (incl. *varzea*) and gallery forest, forest edge and clearings, and tall second growth. Also occurs in isolated trees and shrubs near forest or woodland, such as in savanna, cultivated areas, and areas of human settlement. Appears to require large wooded tracts to survive in se Brazil (see Willis 1979). Moves about seasonally to favorite feeding sites (Penard and Penard 1910). Pairs, single birds, and small groups usually travel by themselves but sometimes join feeding aggregations or associate with other small tanagers (Lamm 1948). Flies swiftly from one feeding site to another, but often rests in tree tops between feeding sessions. In Brazil, roosts in dense tangles of mistletoe (*Psittacanthus* sp), several individuals to the plant (Sick 1985).

Forages at all levels in trees and shrubs. In

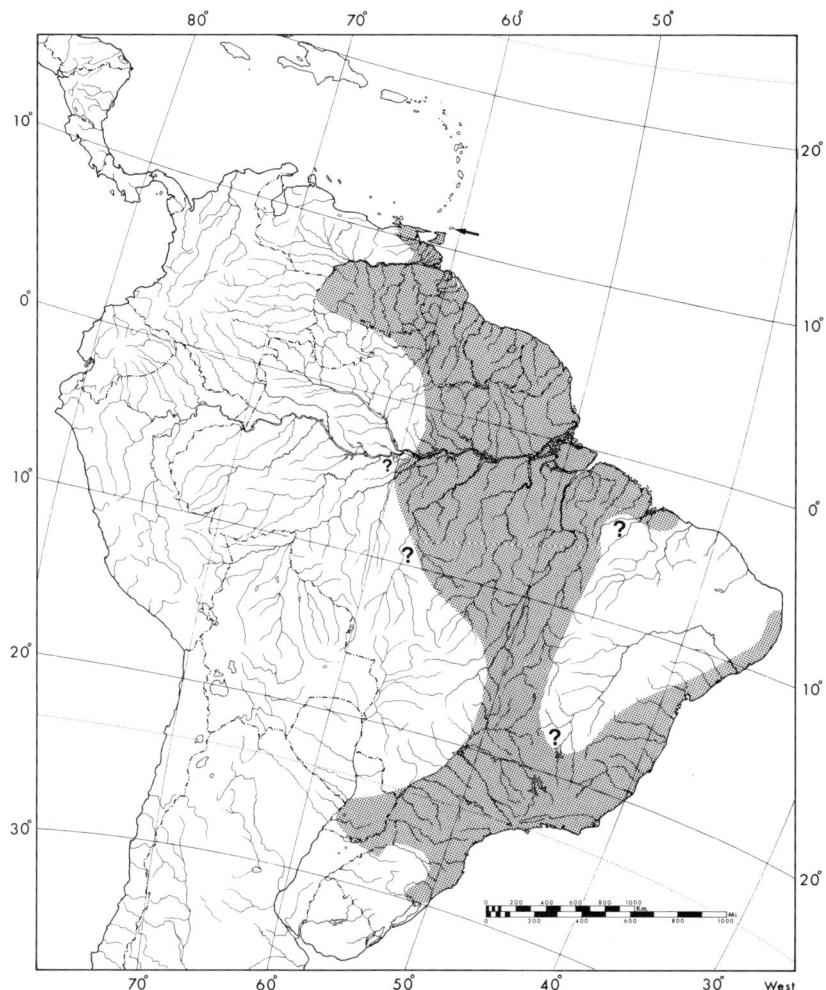

Euphonia violacea

Trinidad, the median foraging height was about 6 m off the ground and 97% of 206 observations involved fruit-eating. Of these, 62% were fruits of epiphytes and parasites, including the bromeliad *Aechmaea nudicaulis* (18% of all fruit eaten), the cactus *Rhipsalis* (16%), and mistletoe (14%). Typically hung down to take many epiphytic fruits; hovered briefly to pick *Rhipsalis* fruits that are attached to hanging stems. Swallowed some fruits whole and chewed others to remove the skin. Pecked out pieces or crushed larger fruits. Nibbled at catkins of *Piper*. (Snow and Snow 1971.) Also said to eat bananas (Bertoni 1919), and in Brazil, took nectar from the *Psittacanthus* mistletoe and extracted the bodies of terrestrial snails (Sick 1985). Stomach contents: seeds and fruit pulp.

In Paraguay when eating 7–10 mm fruit of *Allophyllus edulis*: Plucked fruit, sometimes leaning way over acrobatically, and took it to a horizontal perch. Held the fruit against a branch to peck out pieces leaving the seed, or rolled the fruit around in its bill, opening and closing its bill in tiny arcs to peel the pulp away from the seed. Sometimes impaled the fruit on its bill while peeling it. (Foster data.)

Vocalizations

Song: shifts quickly among clear pleasant-sounding musical notes, e.g., *di-sweet!* or *peeep!*, short trills, and raspy, thin, unpleasant phrases such as *chi-chi* or *tzer*; typically, song elements are distinct (not jumbled together) and many are imitative of other species (see Snow 1974, Sick 1985); elements vary widely in pitch, are given rapidly (more than 1 note/sec.) without pause, and may continue for a minute or two without stopping. The call-song is also heard often and consists of song elements delivered slowly, 1 element/4–5 sec. Sings frequently, sometimes from concealment. Alarm calls: a loud, somewhat harsh, Moderate-pitched *che-ep* and a loud chatter or rattle.

Breeding

Builds a ball-shaped domed nest with side entrance made with dead leaves, grass, rootlets, and moss and lined with ferns and grass. Nests are usually well protected, often hidden between leaves of tree orchids, in niches among epiphytes or vines on tree trunks, or on the ground among leaves on roadside banks in forest. Appropriates unused nests of other species such as the Rusty-margined Flycatcher, *Myiozetetes cayanensis* (Snethlage 1935).

Eggs (3–5, usually 4) are dull white to pinkish-white, marked with shades of bright or dark red, mostly at the large end. Females incubate alone, but both parents feed the young; the nestling period is 21 days (Ricklefs 1976). Sometimes uses the same nest to raise a second brood. Breeding dates: Trinidad Jan–Aug (mostly May–July). Suriname Feb, April, and Nov. Brazil (Pará) Oct.

Sources

Primary Belcher and Smooker 1937; Bertoni 1901; ffrench 1973; Haverschmidt 1955, 1968; Isler data; Novaes 1978; Snethlage 1927–1928; Snow and Snow 1971. **Weights (n = 87)** Belton 1985; Bertoni 1909; ffrench 1973; Haverschmidt 1948, 1952, 1968; Ricklefs 1968, 1976; Sick 1985; Snow and Snow 1971. **Stomach contents** Layard 1873; Moojen, Carvalho, and Lopes 1941; Novaes 1969. **Vocalizations** LNS recordings by Belton (1), T. H. Davis (4), Isler (1), Parker (1), D. W. Snow (1), Ward (1); Sick 1985. **Nests, eggs, and breeding dates** Belcher and Smooker 1937; Bertoni 1919; ffrench 1973; Haverschmidt 1955, 1968; Herklots 1961; Pinto 1953.

Euphonia laniirostris 143
Thick-billed Euphonia
Plate 21

Length 10 cm (4 in.). Weight 15 g (13.0–16.5 g). Five subspecies; all races except *melanura* (illus.) have white spots on the undertail; a few individuals of *melanura* collected along the Rio Madeira in c Brazil have a hint of white on the undertail (Zimmer 1943a). Subadult male breeds in a plumage that is intermediate between those of male and female.

Geographic Range

E. l. crassirostris: along the Pacific slope from e Puntarenas, COSTA RICA (records elsewhere probably represent wanderers, Slud 1964), and along the Caribbean slope from Coclé, PANAMA, eastward through PANAMA (possibly absent from sw Darién); n COLOMBIA north of the Andes (incl. the Magdalena and Cauca Valleys) south along the base of the Andes to s Chocó on the Pacific slope; n VENEZUELA east to c Sucre and south in the llanos north of the Orinoco River (see Thomas 1979) to n Boyacá and Arauca, COLOMBIA. *E. l. hypoxantha*: the Pacific slope from Esmeraldas, ECUADOR, southward to s Cajamarca, PERU. *E. l. melanura*: from extreme e Vichada westward to Meta, COLOMBIA, thence southward along the e base of the Andes through ECUADOR and PERU to San Martín and n Ucayali, PERU, and Acre (Novaes 1957), BRAZIL, and eastward through Amazonas (except se portion), BRAZIL, to w Pará along the Amazon River. *E. l. zopholega* and *laniirostris*: east of the Andes from Junín, PERU, to Santa Cruz, BOLIVIA, eastward to se Amazonas and c Mato Grosso, BRAZIL.

Elevational Range

Sea level to 1200 m in Panama, 1900 m in Venezuela, 2200 m in Colombia, and 1800 m in Peru.

Habitat and Behavior

Outside of Amazonia, prefers open woodlands, second growth, broken forest edge, and gallery forest. In Amazonia, inhabits edges of low-lying forest (incl. *varzea* forest and matorral). Also occurs in shaded plantations and occasionally penetrates adjoining dense forest. In some areas, found in shade trees in cultivated areas and town gardens.

Mostly pairs, sometimes small groups or individuals, travel by themselves or with

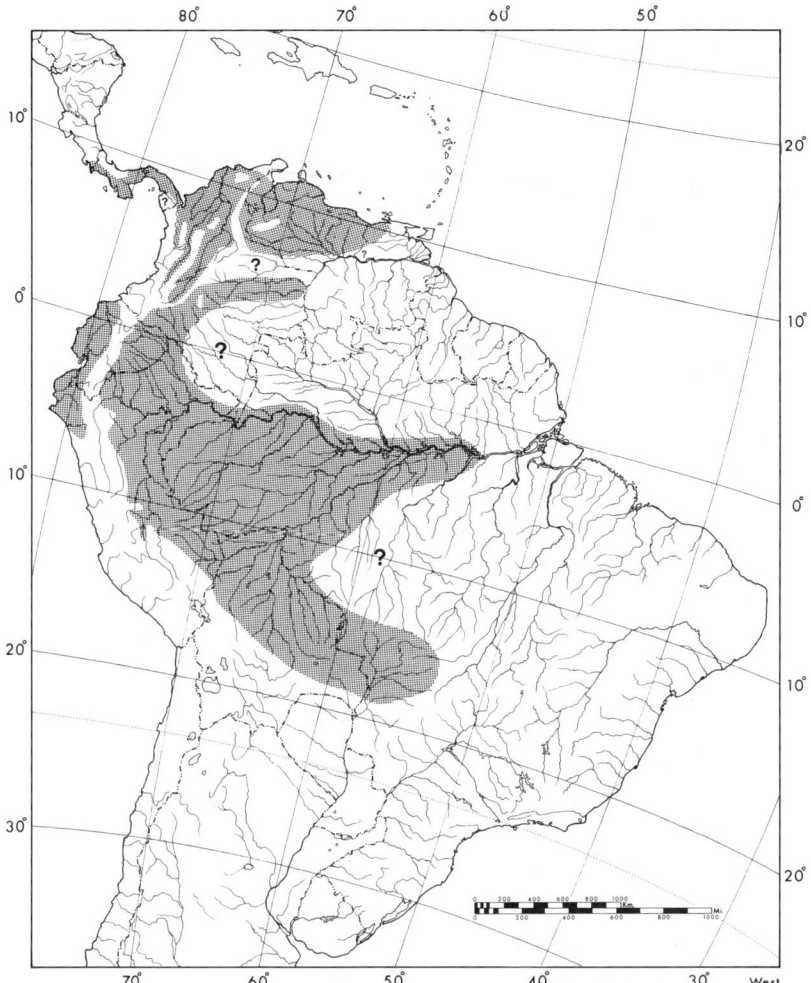

Euphonia laniirostris

mixed-species flocks, including flocks of other euphonias. Regularly rests on exposed dead tree branches. Searches for small fruits, especially mistletoe berries, primarily from midheights to crowns of trees. Eats some fruit by mandibulation, dropping the skin when pulp is gone (LSUMZ data). In Colombia, said to eat fruits of *Aiphanes* and *Sapium* (Borrero 1955). Stomach contents (5): vegetable matter, including fruit and seeds.

Vocalizations

Notes used in vocalizations are often loud, penetrating, and Moderate-pitched but otherwise variable: a downward-inflected *chwee!*, *tweer!*, a whistled *whee-et?* or *wheet-wheet!*, an upward-inflected *beeee*, a hoarse *wee*, a drawn out *chweéyoo*, and a *phweee-oó-ee*, given by the female at the nest after eggs hatch (Barnard 1954). Notes often imitate other species with great fidelity to the original (see Morton 1976 and Remsen 1976). Morton observed mimicry being used by pairs at the nest to provoke mobbing of intruders as well as by individuals sitting inactively high in trees. Song: notes are delivered without pause and are often imitative; usually varies from loud and harsh to soft and pleasant phrases. Vocalizations typically differ from note to note except in call-songs in which the same type of note is delivered regularly, typically 1 phrase/3 sec., some-

Breeding

Constructs a domed nest with side entrance that sometimes has a small overhang. Nests are made of fine twigs, fibers, and leaves and lined with dry grass; reused nests were found to be lined with strips of dried *Heliconia* or banana leaves. Nests are usually built on or within 3 m of the ground, generally well hidden in small cavities in roadside banks, hollowed out fence posts, and plant baskets hanging on houses. In Venezuela, a nest was tucked beside an orchid plant growing in the crotch of a tree trunk 15 m above the ground (Thomas data). Also in Venezuela, a pair appropriated the chamber of an unused nest of a Great Kiskadee, *Pitangus sulphuratus*, that had been built atop a thornbird's nest 6 m off the ground (Skutch 1969).

Both sexes build the nest together. One female, however, removed and then rewove all her mate's contributions (Barnard 1954). Eggs (2–5, usually 4), laid on consecutive days, are white or pinkish-white, speckled and streaked brown, especially at the large end. Incubation lasts 14–16 days and the nestling period is 18–21 days (2 nests). Both parents feed the young; parents may tear off the nest's roof when young are ready to fly (see Barnard 1954). Two, possibly 3, broods are raised in a season. One nest was used in 2 successive years. At one location in Panama, 9 nests were built in the same season in hanging baskets surrounding a single house; eggs were hatched successfully at 3 of these nests; nests were visited by helpers as well as parents, but feeding of nestlings by helpers was not confirmed (Johnson and Washington *in litt.*). In captivity, the female incubated alone; spiders were the only live food given to the young which were fed by regurgitation (Roles 1971). Breeding dates: Panama March, April, and June–Sept. Venezuela April and Aug. Colombia Jan and Dec.

Sources

Primary Barnard 1954; Friedmann and Smith 1955; Hilty and Brown 1986; LSUMZ data; Moynihan 1962c; Munves 1975; Remsen 1976; Ridgely 1976; Slud 1964; Todd and Carriker 1922. **Weights (n=28)** LSUMZ data; Ricklefs 1976; Strauch 1977; Thomas 1982; Weske 1972. **Stomach contents** Brosset 1964; Friedmann and Smith 1955; LSUMZ data; Olivares 1963. **Vocalizations** LNS recordings by Emanuel (1), Morton (1), Parker (4), Schwartz (8), van den Berg (1); Barnard 1954; Morton 1976; Remsen 1976; Ridgely 1976; Eisenmann in Slud 1964. **Nests, eggs, and breeding dates** Barnard 1954; Beebe 1909; Bond 1943; Borrero 1955; Friedmann and Smith 1955; Johnson and Washington *in litt.*; Skutch 1969; Thomas data; Todd and Carriker 1922; Willis and Eisenmann 1979; Wyatt 1871.

Euphonia hirundinacea 144
Yellow-throated Euphonia
Plate 21

Length 10 cm (4 in.). Weight 14 g (11.6–17.8 g). Two subspecies. Males apparently breed in subadult plumage (Dickey and van Rossem 1938).

Geographic Range

From San Luis Potosí (*A.O.U. Check-list*), s Tamaulipas, Puebla, n Oaxaca, and Chiapas, MEXICO, southeastward (incl. the Yucatán Peninsula) through BELIZE; both slopes in GUATEMALA and HONDURAS; EL SALVADOR; NICARAGUA (distribution unclear); COSTA RICA on the Pacific slope in Guanacaste (scarce or absent on the Pacific slope farther south) east through the central plateau to the Carribean slope; and w PANAMA in w Chiriquí (see Wetmore, Pasquier, and Olson 1984).

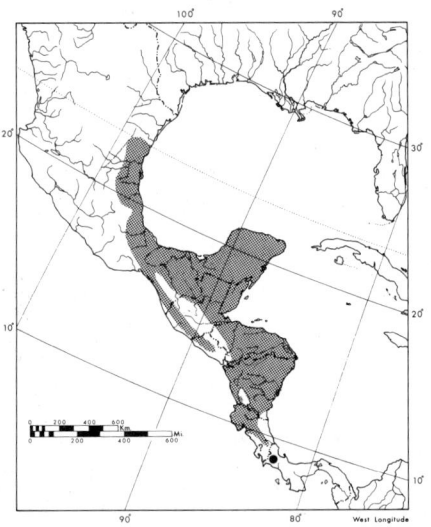

Euphonia hirundinacea

Elevational Range

Lowlands and lower montane elevations to ca. 2100 m but mostly below 1200 m; confined to plateau and hill country in El Salvador and c Costa Rica; confined to foothills (900–1200 m) in Panama.

Habitat and Behavior

Inhabits humid and dry regions. Prefers forest edge, open woodland, second growth, shaded plantations, gallery forest, and forest in ravines. Penetrates heavy forest near the edge and wanders to tall trees in nearby cultivated areas and gardens. Scarce within large areas of humid forest, extensively deforested regions, and regions of pine forest. Moves about seasonally. Small groups or pairs actively wander over wide areas in search of food; sometimes observed with Scrub Tanagers, *E. affinis* **135.** Flight is somewhat undulating. Perches quietly between feeding sessions.

Forages from mid to upper levels of trees. Bounds along from one clump of mistletoe to another, gluttonously eating the berries (Sutton 1951b). Also partial to *Ficus* fruits; in one study, took figs of *Ficus padifolia* (Moraceae) almost exclusively in preference to fruits of four species of trees of other families (Kantak 1979, 322 obs.). Swallows some fruits whole and expresses juice with its bill from other fruits. Also said to feed on ripe bananas (Richmond 1893). In apparent insect-searching, observed working through leaves and small branches of trees and over seed heads of palms (Wetmore 1943) and investigating moss clumps and epiphytes (Edwards 1972). Seen catching an insect and feeding it to its fledgling (Eaton and Edwards 1948). Stomach contents: mistletoe berries.

Vocalizations

Song: rapidly goes back and forth between shrill High-pitched and squeaky Moderate-pitched notes. Some notes are imitative of other birds, but its notes appear to be less diverse than those of the closely related Violaceous, *E. violacea* **142,** and Thick-billed, *E. laniirostris* **143,** Euphonias. Call-song: a variety of phrases, including imitative notes and twitters, that are delivered at about 1 phrase/2 sec. While nest building, the male sometimes utters a fine metallic *pink pink* (Skutch 1954).

Breeding

Both sexes work together to build a domed nest with side entrance using fine tendrils and other bits of vegetation and dried grass for the lining. Nest sites are usually below eye level but sometimes as high as 15 m above the ground (Sutton, Lea, and Edwards 1950). Nests have been found in holes in the banks of streams and roadsides (some of the holes were possibly excavated by swallows, Cherrie 1892), on top of fence posts, on tree trunks, branches, and palm fronds, and hidden in epiphytes or clumps of moss. In Belize, one pair occupied a suspended nest of the Royal Flycatcher, *Onychorhynchus coronatus*, that was located in dense forest over a stream (Peck in Russell 1964).

Eggs (usually 5) are white, lightly spotted umber and sometimes blotched brown at the large end. The female incubates alone, often attended by her mate. On returning to the nest after a recess, the pair races to the entrance, the female always winning and the male darting by, never alighting on or near the nest. At one nest, the incubation period was 16 days, and nestlings fledged after 17 days, possibly prematurely (Skutch 1954). Breeding dates: Mexico May and Aug. Belize June. Guatemala March–May. Costa Rica May.

Sources

Primary Andrle 1967; Cherrie 1892; Dickey and van Rossem 1938; Edwards 1972; Monroe 1968; Russell 1964; Skutch 1954; Slud 1964; Smithe 1966; Sutton 1951a; Sutton, Lea, and Edwards 1950; Wetmore 1943. **Weights (n = 50)** Klaas 1968; LSUMZ data; Russell 1964; Smithe 1966. **Stomach contents** Dickey and van Rossem 1938. **Vocalizations** LNS recording by L. I. Davis; recordings by R. A. Rowlett (4), Whitney (2); Davis 1972; Skutch 1954; Slud 1964; Sutton, Lea, and Edwards 1950. **Nests, eggs, and breeding dates** Andrle 1967; Cherrie 1892; Eaton and Edwards 1948; Russell 1964; Skutch 1954; Smithe 1966; Sutton, Lea, and Edwards 1950.

Euphonia chalybea 145
Green-chinned Euphonia
Plate 21

Length 11 cm (4½ in.). Weight 19 g (18.0–20.0 g). Monotypic. First year males resemble females (Bertoni 1901). Also known as the Green-throated Euphonia.

Geographic Range

The coastal region of se BRAZIL from Rio de Janeiro southward to c Rio Grande do Sul, thence westward through se BRAZIL and Misiones, ARGENTINA, to e PARAGUAY (Alto Paraná and Guairá).

Elevational Range

Lowlands.

Euphonia chalybea

Habitat and Behavior

Inhabits forest and woodland, edges, and overgrown plantations; also wanders to nearby isolated trees. Encountered in pairs and family groups. Joins feeding aggregations and occasionally accompanies mixed-species flocks. Restless but sometimes sits quietly on a branch and looks around. Forages in trees and shrubs mostly for small fruits and possibly nectar. Said to favor epiphytic fruits, including those of *Rhipsalis* cactus (Voss and Sander 1981); also eats pokeberries and fruits of *Abutilon* (Descourtilz 1852). Searches branches for insects including caterpillars and spiders (Bertoni 1901).

Vocalizations

Song: a series of fluid, yet squeaky and raspy, warbling notes that go between Moderate and High pitch; typically 5 sec. (1–7 sec.) long with pauses of about 5 sec. Sings frequently in the morning from leafy tree tops. Also utters a short series, *chik chik chik chik chik*; Moderate-pitched; delivered in about 1 sec. with much longer pauses between series. Said to have a strong sonorous metallic call (Bertoni 1901).

Breeding

In Paraguay, a nest was placed inside a compact group of orchids growing in an isolated tree near a house; it appeared to have a side entrance (Bertoni 1901). In Brazil, a nest was similarly placed in epiphytes on a large limb 15 m off the ground, built of plant stems and bits of leaves (Parker *in litt.*). Eggs (thought to be of this species) are yellowish with red brown spots (Nehrkorn 1899). Breeding dates: Brazil (Paraná) Oct.

Sources

Primary Belton 1985; Bertoni 1901; Descourtilz 1852; Sick 1985. **Weights (n=4)** Belton 1985; Bertoni 1901. **Vocalizations** LNS recordings by Belton (2); Belton 1985; Bertoni 1901. **Nests, eggs, and breeding dates** Bertoni 1901; Nehrkorn 1899; Parker *in litt.*

Euphonia musica 146
Blue-hooded Euphonia

The single species of the *Peters Check-list* is considered by the *A.O.U. Check-list* to be three species which we treat as three subspecies groups in the following accounts. The limited data available do not suggest any major differences in behavior or vocalizations among the three subspecies groups.

Euphonia musica (*elegantissima* subspecies group 146-1)
Blue-hooded Euphonia
Plate 21

Length 10 cm (4 in.). Weight 15 g (13.1–17.0 g). Three subspecies: the southernmost subspecies (*vincens*) is probably invalid (see Wetmore, Pasquier, and Olson 1984).

Geographic Range

From extreme se Sonora, sw Chihuahua, w Durango, Jalisco, Guanajuato, San Luis Potosí, c Nuevo León, and sw Tamaulipas, MEXICO, southward locally through GUATEMALA, BELIZE, HONDURAS, EL SALVADOR, NICARAGUA, AND COSTA RICA to Chiriquí and Veraguas, PANAMA.

Elevational Range

Primarily 1000–2500 m, but recorded from near sea level to 3050 m in Panama, seems most common at 1050–1500 m (Wetmore, Pasquier, and Olson 1984). Appears to wander to lowlands after the breeding season.

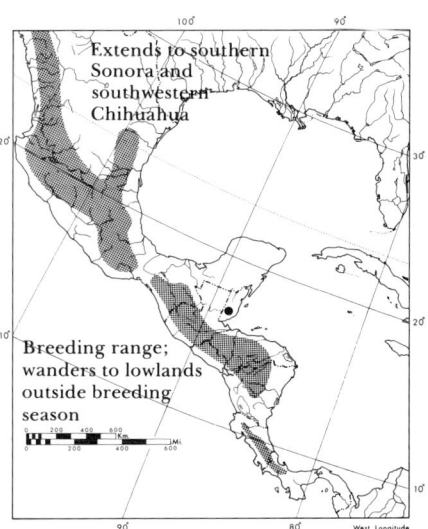

Euphonia musica (*elegantissima* subspecies group)

Habitat and Behavior

Frequents mistletoe-covered trees, especially oak trees in the northern portion of its range, in a variety of habitats such as pine-oak woodland, oak scrub, open second growth, forest and woodland edge, shaded plantations, and scattered trees in open areas near forest; not often found inside forest. Apparently retreats in winter from extreme n parts of its range (van Rossem 1945).

Encountered in pairs or small groups of up to 9 (Schaldach 1963) individuals, sometimes singly. Flies in goldfinchlike dips (Slud 1964). Travels long distances in search of food. Greedily feeds on mistletoe berries, but occasionally eats other small fruits. Quietly forages at mistletoe clumps or inside foliage in the canopy of a tall tree where it may remain for some time.

Vocalizations

Principal calls: *chup*, a plaintive Moderate-pitched *chee*, and a downward-inflected loud *chew*. Song is a chittering series (ca. 4–8 sec. long) of Moderate-pitched notes underlaid with soft Low-pitched *chup* notes (possibly a duet); connects the series with *chup*s or loud *teek*s so that there is hardly a pause. Sings (sometimes from concealment) from the tops of tall trees.

Breeding

Builds a domed nest made chiefly of moss and Spanish moss, often placed within or atop moss clumps. A small entrance hole leads through the loosely built outer structure to a pouch-shaped lining inside. In Panama, a male and female built a nest together in a tree fork 18 m above the ground; the female always preceded the male to the nest (Ridgely in Wetmore, Pasquier, and Olson 1984). In Mexico, a nest was found among heavy foliage of a fallen branch lodged 6 m up in an oak tree; another was located 4.5 m up in the crown of a tree. Eggs are creamy white, sparingly or thickly sprinkled with brownish or purplish spots, especially at the large end. Breeding dates: Mexico May. Panama March and May. Costa Rica May.

Sources

Primary Baepler 1962; Binford 1968; Carriker 1910; Dickey and van Rossem 1938; Edwards 1972; Land 1970; Monroe 1968; Rand and Traylor 1954; Ridgely 1976; Robbins and Heed 1951; Slud 1964. **Weights (n = 28)** LSUMZ data. **Vocalizations** LNS recordings by Morton (1), van den Berg (1); recording by Whitney (1); Peterson and Chalif 1973; Ridgely 1976; Slud 1964. **Nests, eggs, and breeding dates** Blake 1956; Carriker 1910; Ogilvie-Grant 1912; Robbins and Heed 1951; Wetmore, Pasquier, and Olson 1984.

Euphonia musica
(*aureata* subspecies group   146-2)
Golden-rumped Euphonia
Plate 21

Length 11 cm (4½ in.). Weight 16 g (15.1 and 16.1 g). Three subspecies.

Geographic Range

TRINIDAD; SURINAME w through GUYANA (probably) to e Bolívar, VENEZUELA (once in lowlands of Pará, BRAZIL); the coastal range and Andes of VENEZUELA from Sucre to Táchira; the Perijá Mountains; COLOMBIA locally in all 3 Andean ranges; both slopes in ECUADOR; along the w slope of the Andes in nw PERU southward to c Cajamarca; along the e slope of the Andes southward through PERU and BOLIVIA to Tucumán (sight record on Cordoba-San Luis border, Casares 1944), ARGENTINA; s(?) Bahia, s Goiás, and s Mato Grosso, BRAZIL, southward through e PARAGUAY, to e Chaco, Corrientes, and Misiones, ARGENTINA (once in Entre Ríos), and c Rio Grande do Sul, BRAZIL.

Elevational Range

In the Andean portion of range, primarily 1000–2000 m; also (perhaps seasonally) higher to 2600 m or lower to 300 m (Parker *in litt.*). Lowlands in se Brazil and neighboring areas.

Habitat and Behavior

Inhabits woodlands, forest edge, and tall second growth. Also occurs in areas of human habitation, shaded plantations, scrub (especially in s portion of range), and humid montane forest. Pairs or groups of 3–8 individuals usually travel together but occasionally wander with mixed-species flocks. Sometimes moves actively within trees, bounding from branch to branch. May fly long distances in search of food; flight is direct (Ginés et al. 1951). Forages mostly in the tops of trees but sometimes descends to thickets. Primarily eats small fruits, especially mistletoe berries; also cactus fruits (Descourtilz 1852). Occasionally seen searching for insects in tree foliage. Stomach contents (1): fruit pulp.

Vocalizations

Song: twittering squeaky High-pitched notes underlaid with Moderate-pitched *cheep*s or *chup*s and chittering sounds; up to 10 sec. long with pauses of 1–22 sec. Longer pauses are sometimes filled with hard sharp Moderate-pitched *tic* or *teek* and soft *chup* notes. Sings from concealment in the tops of trees. Call: a plaintive whistle, Low- to Moderate-pitched, *tweeer* or *teeer*. Sometimes mixes song and call.

Breeding

In Trinidad, a domed nest with side entrance, placed about 2 m above the ground in the outer branches of a small tree at forest edge, contained 2 pale cream eggs, marked pale reddish brown and black, forming a cap at the large end (Belcher and Smooker 1937). Three eggs from Venezuela were uniformly greenish white (Ogilvie-Grant 1912). Breeding dates: Colombia April and May. Trinidad July. Brazil (Rio Grande do Sul) Jan.

Sources

Primary Belcher and Smooker 1937; Descourtilz 1852; ffrench 1973; Ginés et al. 1951; Hilty and Brown 1986; Lönnberg and Rendahl 1922; Meyer de Schauensee and Phelps 1978; Parker data; Santos 1948. **Weights (n = 2)** Miller 1963. **Stomach contents** LSUMZ data. **Vocalizations** LNS recordings by T. H. Davis (2), Parker (5), Schwartz (8); Sick 1985. **Nest, eggs, and breed-

Euphonia musica (*aureata* subspecies group)

ing dates Belcher and Smooker 1937; Belton 1985; Gertler and Gniadek in Hilty and Brown 1986.

Euphonia musica
(*musica* subspecies group **146-3**)
Antillean Euphonia
Plate 21

Length 10 cm (4 in.). Weight 13 g (12.4–14.4 g). Three subspecies: *sclateri* is illustrated. Underparts of males of *musica* are ochraceous yellow and the chin and throat are dark violet. Females of all three subspecies are similar, and males of *flavifrons* resemble females.

Geographic Range

E. m. musica: HISPANIOLA and Gonâve Island. *E. m. sclateri*: PUERTO RICO.
E. m. flavifrons: LESSER ANTILLES in Barbuda, Antigua, Montserrat, Guadeloupe, Dominica, Martinique, St. Lucia, St. Vincent, and Grenada; casual in Saba, St Barthélemy, Terre-de-haut and Bequia; no recent reports from Barbuda, Montserrat, St. Vincent, and Grenada (Bond 1982).

Euphonia musica (*musica* subspecies group)

Elevational Range

Prefers mountains (up to the summits) but wanders to lowlands.

Habitat and Behavior

Inhabits humid and dry forest, forest edge, and shaded plantations; also occurs where mistletoe is found in arid scrub. Numbers are declining on some islands. Pairs and small groups of up to 12 individuals actively travel from one tree to another. Flight is bounding (Wetmore 1927). Flits about in tree tops staying hidden within dense foliage and mistletoe clumps. Stomach contents (51): vegetable matter including several species of mistletoe, 2–20 seeds per stomach. Also reported (1): seeds of small fruits. In St. Vincent (where there are no recent records), said to have eaten the fruit of the loblolly tree and buds of the silk-cotton tree (Clark 1905). In Puerto Rico, Leck (1972a) suspected it ate *Cecropia* fruits.

Vocalizations

While foraging, utters a plaintive whistle variously described as *ee-oo*, *whee*, or *wheur*; also a scolding *chit-it* or a hard metallic *chi-chink*, and a soft *tuc-tuc*. Both sexes utter the whistle followed by a rapidly repeated double note that forms a rapid chattering twitter, given while perched or flying. From exposed branches, sings a trilling tinkling *tuc-tuc-tuc* etc, punctuated with explosive whistles; sometimes sings for 20 min. at a time.

Breeding

Builds a domed nest with side entrance. On St. Vincent, a nest was made of moss and rootlets with an inner cup of dried grass and plant shreds; it was situated 9 m above the ground attached to a vine growing against the trunk of a forest palm. In Puerto Rico, a nest was found between thickly growing shoots of a mango tree. Eggs (4) are white, marked reddish brown, especially in a heavy wreath about the large end. Breeding dates: Puerto Rico Jan–July. St Lucia April.

Sources

Primary Biaggi 1970; Bond 1928a, 1928b, 1961; Clark 1905; Dod 1978; Diamond 1973; Raffaele 1983; Wetmore 1927; Wetmore and Swales 1931. **Weights (n = 6)** Olson and Angle 1977. **Stomach contents** Bowdish 1903; Wetmore 1927. **Vocalizations** Bond 1928a, 1928b; Clark 1905; Dod 1978; Raffaele 1983; Reynard 1982; Wetmore 1927; Wetmore and Swales 1931. **Nests, eggs, and breeding dates** Bond 1941; Gundlach 1878; Raffaele 1983.

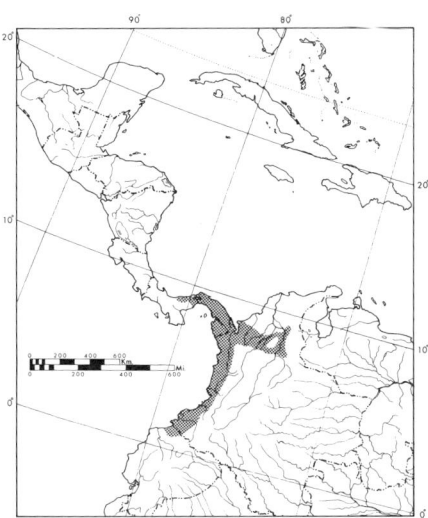

Euphonia fulvicrissa

Euphonia fulvicrissa 147
Fulvous-vented Euphonia
Plate 21

Length 9 cm (3½ in.). Weight 11 g (10.1–13.0 g). Three subspecies.

Geographic Range

Both slopes in PANAMA from c PANAMA (Coclé and Colón on the Caribbean, w Panamá province on the Pacific) eastward to Chocó, COLOMBIA, and along the n base of the Andes to the n end of the E Andes in Norte de Santander (USNM) and the middle Magdalena Valley in Antioquia, COLOMBIA, and southward along the Pacific coast from Chocó, COLOMBIA, to Esmeraldas, ECUADOR. Nineteenth-century records from Costa Rica (see Slud 1964) and w Panama are questionable.

Elevational Range

Lowlands and foothills; in Colombia, to 1000 m, usually below 500 m (Hilty and Brown 1986).

Habitat and Behavior

Inhabits forest, forest edge, and trees in forest clearings; also occurs in tall second growth. Usually encountered in pairs, sometimes in small groups, or singly. Often travels with mixed-species flocks in forest (Hilty and Brown 1986). Forages actively in tree tops but regularly comes lower to fruiting trees and shrubs at borders and in clearings. On Barro Colorado I., Panama, foraging height is mostly 10–25 m above the ground; typically takes fruits less than 5 mm in diam.; and eats small arthropods (Willis 1980). In Panama, primarily took catkins of *Piper* and fruits of *Lantana*; also ate fruits of *Hamelia*, *Cecropia*, and mistletoe (Leck 1971b). Observed eating arillate fruits of *Lindackeria* (Greenberg 1981b).

Vocalizations

Call: a short dull burry Low- to Moderate-pitched rattle, *tr-r-r-r*, given singly, doubled, or tripled; often given regularly with pauses of about 2 sec. (a song?). Also a Moderate- to High-pitched upward-inflected whistle, *wheet*, repeated after pauses averaging 3.5 sec.

Breeding

In Panama in December, a male and female brought fibrous material to a chambered nest in thick hanging moss 12 m above the ground (Ridgely in Wetmore, Pasquier, and Olson 1984).

Sources

Primary Greenberg *in litt.*; Haffer 1975; Hilty and Brown 1986; Leck 1971a, 1971b; Moynihan 1962c; Ridgely 1976; Wetmore, Pasquier, and Olson 1984; Willis and Eisenmann 1979.

Weights (n = 9) Leck 1975; LSUMZ data; Willis 1980; Strauch 1977. **Vocalizations** LNS recordings by van den Berg (2); recording by Whitney (1); Ridgely 1976. **Nests and breeding dates** Wetmore, Pasquier, and Olson 1984.

Euphonia imitans 148
Spot-crowned Euphonia
Plate 21

Length 10 cm (4 in.). Monotypic.

Geographic Range

Pacific slope from San José Province, COSTA RICA, eastward to w Chiriquí, PANAMA.

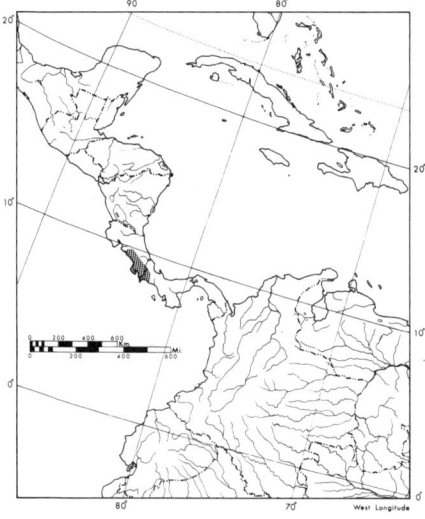

Euphonia imitans

Elevational Range

Lowlands and foothills to ca. 1350 m.

Habitat and Behavior

Inhabits humid forest and forest edge; occasionally wanders to adjacent areas with scattered trees. Encountered in pairs or alone, rarely in groups of 3 individuals. Rests and roosts in pockets of moss or epiphytes on tree branches. Forages at all heights (mostly in the canopy) for fruit, insects, and possibly nectar.

In Costa Rica, eats a variety of fruit including those of melastomes and epiphytes, green spikes of *Piper*, and at least 2 species of arillate fruits. Squeezes or bites out pulp of some berries, then drops the tough skin. Clings to large fruits (e.g., guava) pecking out small pieces; sometimes retrieves fallen fragments from the ground. Searches for insects and larvae on mossy branches and among dead leaves caught in vine tangles. Drinks nectar or rainwater from tiny blossoms; also seems to squeeze flowers in its bill to press out nectar. Sometimes comes to feeding tables for bananas. (Skutch 1972.)

Vocalizations

Call: a rattling *tr-r-r-r*, sometimes doubled. Also a Moderate- to High-pitched *whe-d-d-d-SIP*, given like a machine-gun burst, delivered regularly, about every 3 sec., possibly a song. Song: typically repeats a phrase 5–8 times, and then abruptly shifts to another phrase; most phrases are dry and chaffy but some are clear; song is centered at a Moderate pitch (Whitney recording). Song is given by the male from a tree and sometimes maintained for 15–30 min. When disturbed at the nest, emits a throaty rattle interspersed with other notes (Skutch 1972).

Breeding

In Costa Rica, male and female together build their domed nest among ferns, moss clumps, or epiphytes on mossy trunks or limbs. Materials used are green moss, rootlets, and ferns, and narrow strips of bark and/or fine vegetable fibers for the lining. Nests are located near forest edge, placed 2–7.5 m above the ground (8 nests) or above a brook or river (2 nests). The side entrance is sometimes shielded by a small roof projection. Eggs (3, sometimes 2), laid on consecutive days, are white or pinkish white, sparingly marked with brown, more thickly at the large end. The female incubates alone, but her mate is often nearby. On leaving the nest, the female habitually drops like a dead weight, almost to the ground, before flying upward. After a recess, the pair races to the nest, the male veering at the last minute to allow the female to enter alone. Incubation period (one nest): 18 days. Breeding dates: Costa Rica March–May. (Skutch 1972.)

Sources

Primary Skutch 1972; Slud 1964. **Vocalizations** recordings by Whitney (4); Skutch 1972; Slud 1964; Wetmore, Pasquier, and Olson 1984. **Nests, eggs, and breeding dates** Skutch 1972.

Euphonia gouldi 149
Olive-backed Euphonia
Plate 21

Length 9–10 cm (3½–4 in.). Weight 14 g (10.9–16.0 g). Two subspecies.

Geographic Range

The Gulf-Caribbean slope from c Veracruz, n Oaxaca, Chiapas, Tabasco, and s Quintana Roo (one record), MEXICO, southeastward through GUATEMALA, BELIZE (except the ne corner), HONDURAS, NICARAGUA, and COSTA RICA (spills over to the Pacific slope in Guanacaste, Slud 1964), to nw Veraguas, PANAMA.

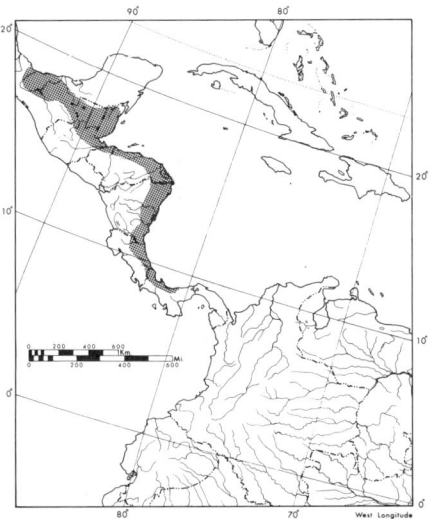

Euphonia gouldi

Elevational Range

Sea level to ca. 500 m but occasionally goes higher, reaching its limit in Guatemala at 1200 m.

Habitat and Behavior

Prefers forest interiors; also inhabits forest edge, tall second growth, and adjacent plantations and clearings with scattered trees. Encountered in pairs and small groups, rarely singly. Often accompanies mixed-species flocks. Forages most often from mid to upper levels of forest, but also seeks food in low trees and tall shrubs at forest edge and occasionally in thick forest understory. Picks fruit from a perched position, rarely in flight (Moermond and Denslow 1985). Swallows small fruit (e.g., *Miconia* berries; Land 1963) whole, but sometimes takes pieces from larger fruits (Moermond and Denslow 1985). Birds studied in captivity ate a variety of small-seeded fleshy fruits and in experiments, exhibited preferences for one fruit over another based on ripeness, accessibility, and fruit type (see Moermond and Denslow 1983). Stomach contents (4): small-seeded fruits.

Vocalizations

Calls: a rattling *tr-r-r-r*, sometimes doubled or tripled. Also gives a burry Moderate-pitched *dee-dee-dee* and repeats a Moderate-pitched *CHOO-wi-sit?* (possibly a song). Song: various combinations of short notes, some dry or chaffy and others clear, delivered for some time without pause. Spreads and wags tail from side to side while singing (Hilty *in litt.*).

Breeding

Builds a domed nest with side entrance, placed from 15 cm to 4.5 m above the ground. The nest may be incorporated into natural hanging growth or may be suspended from vines, branches, or rootlets (Russell 1964). Two to four eggs form a clutch (Willis in Smithe 1966). Breeding date: Belize May.

Sources

Primary Carriker 1910; Howell 1957; Land 1970; Monroe 1968; Russell 1964; Slud 1964; Smithe 1966. **Weights (n = 20)** LSUMZ data; Russell 1964; Smithe 1966; Strauch 1977. **Stomach contents** Tashian 1952. **Vocalizations** LNS recording by Parker (1); recordings by Whitney (2); Slud 1964. **Nests, eggs, and breeding dates** Edwards 1972; Russell 1964; Smithe 1966.

Euphonia chrysopasta 150
White-lored Euphonia
Plate 22

Length 10 cm (4 in.). Weight 14 g (11.0–16.2 g). Two subspecies. Also known as the Golden-bellied Euphonia.

Geographic Range

East of the Andes from w Meta, Guianía, and e Vichada, COLOMBIA, southward through e ECUADOR and e PERU to Santa Cruz, BOLIVIA; eastward north of the Amazon River through s COLOMBIA and

Euphonia chrysopasta

BRAZIL to s VENEZUELA (Amazonas to c Bolívar), THE GUIANAS (no records for GUYANA, but likely to occur), and Amapá, BRAZIL; and eastward south of the Amazon River to e Amazonas, extreme nw Mato Grosso, and Rondônia, BRAZIL.

Elevational Range

Lowlands to ca. 1000 m; occasionally as high as 1300 m (Gyldenstolpe 1945b).

Habitat and Behavior

Inhabits edge of humid terra firma and lowlying (incl. *varzea*) forest and second-growth woodland. Also occurs inside terra firma forest, in tall trees of shaded plantations, and in isolated trees in forest clearings. Pairs often accompany mixed-species flocks of other small tanagers but seldom travel with other euphonias. Forages mostly in the canopy but comes lower, especially at forest edge. Eats fruit and insects; searches on branches and in foliage (Willis 1977). Seen at mistletoe and *Cecropia* catkins (Parker data). Stomach contents (1): seeds.

Vocalizations

Calls: a burry or kissing Moderate-pitched *chit!* or *cheet*; a slightly upward-inflected Moderate-pitched whistle, *wheet*; and a Lowpitched *whert*; notes are sometimes doubled or call notes may be combined. Call-song: call notes or phrases are delivered at about 20/min. Song: energetic phrases, *si-si-WILL-*

ow or *si-si-WRILL*; notes are rapid and High-pitched, leading into a rich Moderate- to Low-pitched, warble; 1.5 sec. phrases are delivered at about 20 phrases/min. Sings loudly from tree tops. Spreads and wags tail from side to side while singing in a manner similar to that of the Olive-backed Euphonia, *E. gouldi* **149,** of Central America (Hilty *in litt.*). In one recording, one member of a pair sang the song while the other uttered soft Low-pitched mewing notes.

Breeding

In Peru, 2 domed nests with side entrances, made of yellowish plant material, grasses, mosses, and strips of leaves, were placed among long black spines of palm tree trunks, 5 and 8 m above the ground; built by both sexes (Parker data). In Ecuador, a pair built a nest with side entrance 10 m up in epiphytes (Hilty and Brown 1986). Breeding dates: Ecuador Aug. Peru Aug and Sept.

Sources

Primary Hilty and Brown 1986; O'Neill 1974; Pearson 1969, 1975c; Willis 1977. **Weights (n = 11)** Dick, McGillivray, and Brooks 1984; LSUMZ data; Pearson 1971; Sick 1985. **Stomach contents** LSUMZ data. **Vocalizations** LNS recordings by T. H. Davis (1), Parker (8), Schwartz (2), van den Berg (2). **Nests and breeding dates** Hilty and Brown 1986; Parker data.

Euphonia mesochrysa 151
Bronze-green Euphonia
Plate 22

Length 10 cm (4 in.). Weight 13 g (12.0–15.0 g). Three subspecies.

Geographic Range

E. m. mesochrysa: COLOMBIA on the e slope of the C Andes at the head of the Magdalena Valley in Huila, the e slope of the E Andes in Meta and w Caquetá (sight, Hilty and Brown 1986); the e slope of the Andes in Napo and Morona-Santiago, ECUADOR. *E. m. media* and *tavarae*: e Andean slope from Cajamarca and Amazonas, PERU, to extreme w Santa Cruz (Remsen, Traylor, and Parkes in press), BOLIVIA. A lowland record from Loreto, Peru, is probably erroneous.

Elevational Range

Typically ca. 1000–2150 m; occasionally wanders lower (to ca. 600 m) in hill forest. The Loreto record was at ca. 150 m.

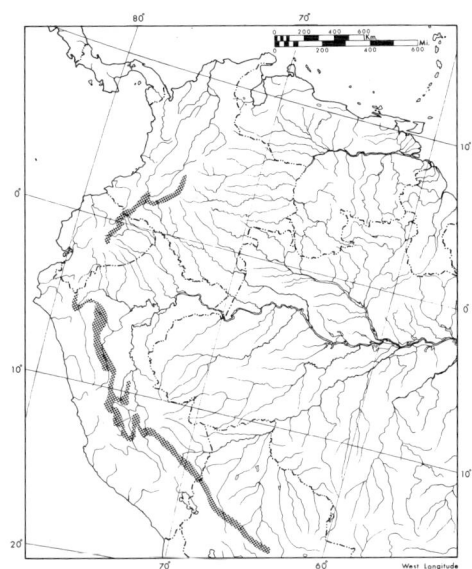

Euphonia mesochrysa

Habitat and Behavior

Inhabits humid forest; also occurs at forest edge and in isolated trees near forest. Travels regularly with mixed-species flocks, especially with *Tangara* tanagers (Parker *in litt.*). Forages mostly in the canopy; searches small clumps of mosses, lichens, and other epiphytes on branches and large limbs, occasionally on tree trunks; frequently observed at mistletoe clumps and *Miconia* berries; also seen at *Cecropia* catkins (Parker data). Squeezed fruit before eating (LSUMZ data). Stomach contents (2): fruit.

Vocalizations

Calls: a soft burry *tr-r-r-r-r*, sometimes doubled or tripled and shortened , e.g., *tr-r-r-r tr-r-r*; Moderate-pitched. Also a sweeter Moderate- to High-pitched *chip* that sometimes is doubled, tripled, or extended to a chitter. Song: *whurt tr-r-r tr-r-r tr-r-r tr-r-r*, the first note whistled and Low-pitched; 2 sec. long with 4–8 sec. pauses; often overlaid with *chip* notes, possibly a duet. (Parker, LNS.) Song and calls have a ventriloquial quality (Parker *in litt.*).

Breeding

No information.

Sources

Primary Hilty and Brown 1986; LSUMZ data; Parker data; Parker, Parker, and Plenge 1982;

Taczanowski 1884b. **Weights (n = 9)** LSUMZ data. **Stomach contents** LSUMZ data. **Vocalizations** LNS recordings by Parker (3).

Euphonia minuta 152
White-vented Euphonia
Plate 22

Length 9 cm (3½ in.). Weight 10 g (7.9–11.5 g). Two subspecies. Subadult male is yellowish green above; forehead yellow; throat violet blue; underparts yellow, becoming greenish yellow on sides (Wetmore, Pasquier, and Olson 1984). May breed in subadult plumage.

Geographic Range

E. m. humilis: scattered records on the Gulf-Caribbean slope from se MEXICO (Palenque, Chiapas) through c GUATEMALA (Cobán) and BELIZE (2 locations) to NICARAGUA (Chontales); the Caribbean slope from COSTA RICA through PANAMA (locally) to n Antioquia, COLOMBIA, thence eastward along the n slope of the Andes to the Magdalena Valley in e Antioquia; and along the Pacific slope from sw COSTA RICA eastward to Veraguas, PANAMA (Ridgely 1976), and from c Panamá province eastward through PANAMA to COLOMBIA and thence southward to Pichincha, ECUADOR. *E. m. minuta*: east of the Andes in s Táchira, VENEZUELA, and from Meta and Vaupés, COLOMBIA, southward through e ECUADOR and e PERU to Santa Cruz, BOLIVIA, and eastward through VENEZUELA (Amazonas, se Bolívar, Delta Amacuro, and e Sucre) to THE GUIANAS, thence southward through Amazonian BRAZIL to s Amazonas and c and e Pará. A single record from e Mato Grosso, BRAZIL (Fry 1970).

Elevational Range

Generally below 500 m; recorded to 1500 m.

Habitat and Behavior

Inhabits humid forest and woodland and forest edge. Also occurs in tall trees in forest clearings, shaded plantations, and tall second growth. Appears to wander over large areas after the breeding season. Pairs and small groups of 3–6, rarely up to a dozen, individuals usually travel by themselves, but regularly accompany mixed-species flocks, especially flocks of other euphonias. In s Peru, sometimes joined permanent canopy flocks, but occurred at a lower population density than the core species of the flocks (Munn 1985). Also joins feeding aggregations. Habitually stretches or half-spreads its tail and wags it slowly from side to side displaying white tail-spots.

Forages in the canopy from midheights to the crowns of tall emergent trees; descends lower at forest edge and in isolated trees, but rarely goes below 10 m off the ground. Eats mistletoe berries and other small fruits, insects, and spiders. Appears to take more insects than most euphonias (Skutch 1972). Searches for insects along slender dead twigs less than 1 cm in diam. by sidling sideways or by hopping, alternating directions, and bending over to examine undersides; leans head-down to investigate undersides of thicker, mossy or lichen-encrusted branches; also picks prey from foliage (Skutch 1972). Stomach contents (2): vegetable matter, including fruit.

Vocalizations

Song: consists of rapid phrases that typically begin with emphatic notes, e.g., *CHEER-a-wee-wee*, *CHEE-da-dee*, or *CHIT-a-wee-wichee-da-dee*; Moderate- and High-pitched; separated by 2–6 sec. pauses; changes phrases or repeats the same phrase up to about 10 times. Calls: a Moderate-pitched *wee-chup* and thin sharp notes such as *peet* (Hilty and Brown 1986). Both sexes call constantly while nest-building (Skutch 1972).

Breeding

In Costa Rica: Both sexes build the domed nest with side entrance; materials used included fibrous rootlets, green or brown moss, liverworts, living ferns, seed plumes, fine fibers for the lining, and cobweb. Nests are concealed in dense vegetation among epiphytic plants growing on tree branches 4.5–6 m above the ground, at or near forest edge. Eggs (usually 3) are white, heavily marked with brown. The female incubates for 15–17 days. After a recess, a pair races to the nest, the female entering alone; the male hovers or alights briefly before flying away. Both parents feed the nestlings by regurgitation. The young fledge after 17–21 days, when they can fly fairly well. (Skutch 1972.) Breeding dates: Costa Rica March–Aug.

Sources

Primary Carriker 1910; Hilty and Brown 1986; Remsen 1976; Ridgely 1976; Skutch 1972, 1976; Slud 1964; Willis 1977. **Weights (n = 13)** Fry 1970; Haverschmidt 1968; LSUMZ data; Strauch 1977; Willis 1980. **Stomach contents** LSUMZ

EUPHONIA 251

Euphonia minuta

data; Pinto 1953. **Vocalizations** LNS recordings by Parker (1), Schwartz (2); recordings by Whitney (2); Hilty and Brown 1986; Peterson and Chalif 1973; Slud 1964. **Nests, eggs, and breeding dates** Skutch 1972.

Euphonia anneae 153
Tawny-capped Euphonia
Plate 22

Length 11 cm (4 in.). Weight 15 g (15.0 and 15.4 g). Two subspecies.

Geographic Range

The Caribbean slope in COSTA RICA from Alajuela southeastward; locally on both slopes in PANAMA; and extreme nw COLOMBIA in foothills west of the Gulf of Urabá, Chocó (see Haffer 1975).

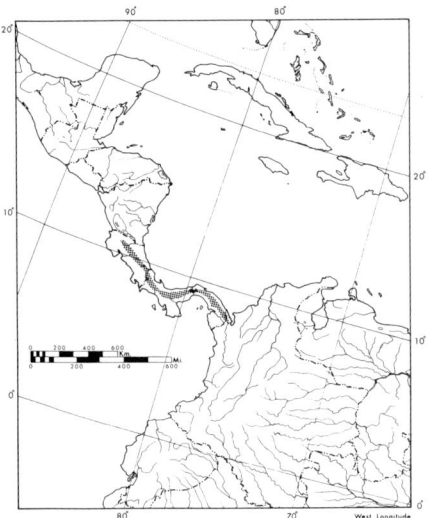

Euphonia anneae

Elevational Range

Mostly 600–1500 m, extremes 50–2100 m; extremes possibly represent post-breeding wandering (Slud 1964).

Habitat and Behavior

Inhabits dense forest and forest edge; also occurs in second-growth woodland. Encountered in pairs, small groups, or singly. Travels alone or with other tanagers, especially *Tangara* species, but associations with other species may be brief (Moynihan 1962c). Forages low in trees, usually within 7 m of the ground (Ridgely 1976). Feeds extensively on mistletoe berries within forest, less often on *Miconia* berries at forest edge (Wetmore, Pasquier, and Olson 1984).

Vocalizations

Song: Usually repeats a note or phrase 2–4 times, then switches to a different note or phrase; typical phrases (Moderate- and/or High-pitched) include a whistled *whee whee whee* or *wheer wheer*, a nasal *nah-a-a-ak*, a whining upward-inflected *eeeenk*, a squeezed out *seeet*, and a variety of other sputtering phrases that may be imitative; sings from about 6 m up in trees (Whitney *in litt.*). Call: a Moderate-pitched burry *dee-dee-dee*; phrases from the song may also be used as calls.

Breeding

In Panama in March, a collected female was ready to lay her eggs (Wetmore, Pasquier, and Olson 1984).

Sources

Primary Carriker 1910; Haffer 1975; Ridgely 1976; Slud 1964; Wetmore, Pasquier, and Olson 1984. **Weights (n = 2)** Strauch 1977. **Vocalizations** recordings by R. A. Rowlett (1), Whitney (3); Slud 1964. **Breeding dates** Wetmore, Pasquier, and Olson 1984.

Euphonia xanthogaster 154
Orange-bellied Euphonia
Plate 22

Length 9–11 cm (3½–4½ in.). Weight 13 g (9.0–16.0 g). Eleven subspecies including two described since 1970, *badissima* and *oressinoma* (Olson 1981a). Three subspecies, *exsul* (illus.), *badissima*, and *ruficeps*, have chestnut or rufous crowns (foreheads in females) and are more rufescent below than other subspecies. Colors of crowns and underparts of remaining subspecies vary somewhat from pure yellow to yellow tinged ochraceous or slightly rufescent. Crowns of subspecies in s Peru become darker clinally towards Bolivia.

Geographic Range

E. x. exsul and *badissima*: VENEZUELA in the coastal ranges from Distrito Federal to Carabobo and the Andes from Lara westward; the Perijá Mountains; COLOMBIA locally on the e slope of the E Andes from Norte de Santander to Boyacá (see Olson

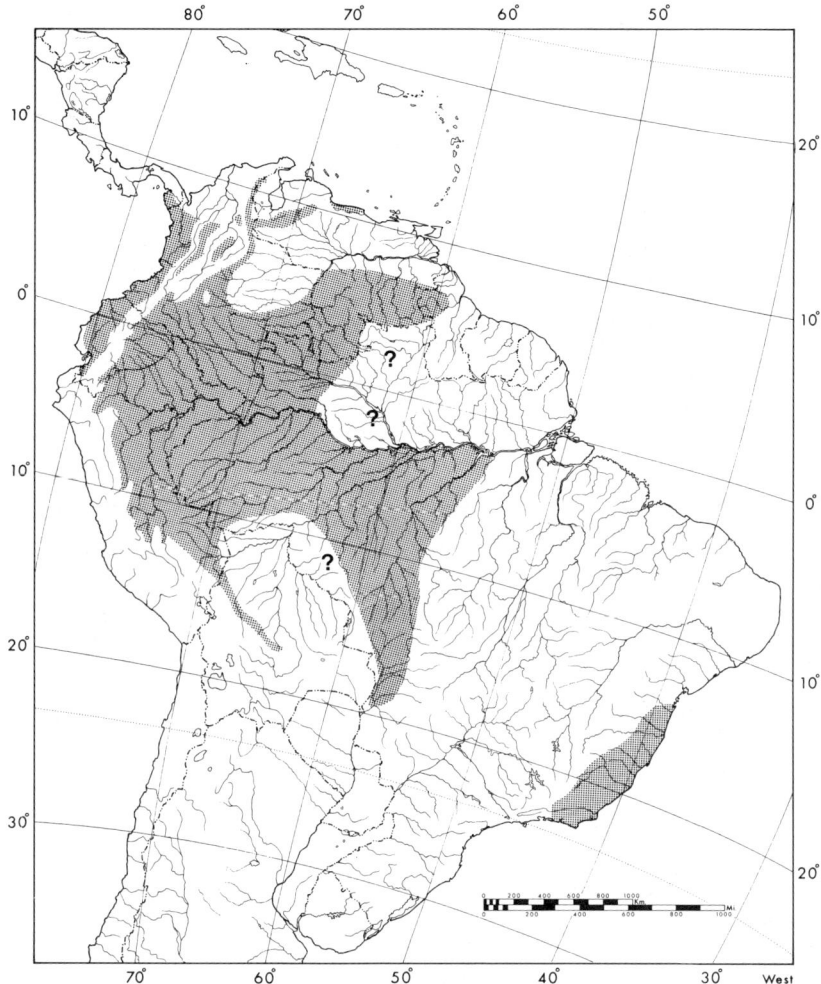

Euphonia xanthogaster

1981a for intergrades). *E. x. chocoensis*, *oressinoma*, and *quitensis*: the Pacific coast from e Darién (south and west of Río Tuira, Olson 1981a), PANAMA, southward through w COLOMBIA and w ECUADOR to Tumbes, PERU (Wiedenfeld, Schulenberg, and Robbins 1985); COLOMBIA on both slopes along the Cauca Valley, and the w slope of the E Andes from Magdalena to Boyacá. *E. x. dilutior*, *cyanonota*, *brunneifrons*, and *brevirostris*: the head of the Magdalena Valley in Huila (Olson 1981a); east of the Andes from Cundinamarca, COLOMBIA, southward through e ECUADOR and e PERU to Puno, and eastward north of the Amazon River through COLOMBIA and w Amazonas, BRAZIL, to s VENEZUELA (Amazonas and s Bolívar) and adjacent w GUYANA, and eastward south of the Amazon through Acre, Rondônia, and Amazonas, BRAZIL, to c Pará and wc Mato Grosso. *E. x. ruficeps*: La Paz and Cochabamba, BOLIVIA. *E. x. xanthogaster*: e BRAZIL from Bahia southward to Rio de Janeiro.

Elevational Range

Lowlands and mountains near sea level to 2600 m; rarely above 2300 m. Confined to higher elevations in some regions. In Venezuela (*exsul*), 350–2250 m, mostly 900–1500 m in coastal ranges; in the Perijá Mountains and the n end of the E Andes of

Colombia (*badissima*), ca. 650–1400 m; in Panama (*oressinoma*), 500–1550 m; and in Bolivia (*ruficeps*), 1000–2150 m.

Habitat and Behavior

In the mountains, frequents forest, forest edge, and clearings; also occurs in second growth. In lowlands, inhabits humid terra firma and low-lying (incl. *varzea*) forest, forest edge, and clearings; also found in tall second growth and shaded coffee plantations. Encountered singly, in pairs, and in small groups of 3–6 individuals. Joins feeding aggregations and occasionally follows mixed-species flocks of other tanagers, especially *Tangara* species and other euphonias; at times joins canopy or understory flocks of insectivorous birds.

In Valle, Colombia (at 1050 m): Foraged from low in bushes to the tops of the tallest trees but mostly in the crowns of low trees in tall forest; median foraging height was about 4.5 m above the ground (295 obs.). Ate over 40 species of fruit (89% of all feeding records). Favored melastome fruits (56% of all fruit eaten), especially *Miconia* berries (73% of all melastomes). Also ate fruiting spikes of arums (11%), fruits of epiphytes and mistletoe (10%), and *Cecropia* catkins (8%). Typically perched on branches or twigs, occasionally hovered, to take small (3–8 mm) fruits; clung to fruiting spikes; and picked at capsules of large fruits. Ate flowers (6% of all feeding records) incl. catkinlike flower buds of arums and flowers of the melastome *Topobea brachyura*. Caught insects (5% of all feeding records) mostly in the air, either by sallies or flutter-pursuits. Occasionally picked insects and/or spiders from spider webs or stretched up to pick insects off leaf surfaces and petioles. (Hilty data.)

Foraging observations from Peru and Bolivia (Parker and Remsen data) are consistent with these data from Colombia except median foraging height was about 9 m above the ground (Remsen data, 31 obs.). Stomach contents (5): vegetable matter, including mistletoe berries and *Ficus* fruits.

Vocalizations

Call: a distinctive, buzzy, somewhat complaining, Moderate-pitched *dee* given singly or in a series of 2–4 (mostly 3) notes. Also *zhurr-deet*, a gravelly *chee-chee*, and *zhurr dit-dit-dit* that seem to be agitated calls. In one type of song, utters *wheet-wheet* and *ta-weee ta-weee* alone or in combination with call notes; delivered at about 1 phrase every 1–2 sec.; sometimes phrases run together in a continuous finchlike warble. In what may be purely a dawn song, alternates 2 types of loud, clear, pleasant whistles: *wheet wheet wheet*, the second 2 notes lower in pitch than the first, and *wheet wheet wheet wheer*, stepping down the scale with the last note slurred; Moderate- to Low-pitched. Often sings from high in a tall tree.

Breeding

Builds a domed mossy ball with side entrance a few meters above the ground (7 nests, Hilty and Brown 1986). Eggs (4) are cream color with dark spots (Phelps 1954). Breeding dates: Colombia Nov–April.

Sources

Primary Haffer 1975; Hilty data; Hilty and Brown 1986; Morton 1979; Munn and Terborgh 1979; Olivares 1969; Parker data; Remsen data; Remsen 1976; Schäfer and Phelps 1954; Terborgh and Weske 1969; Wetmore 1939. **Weights (n = 107)** LSUMZ data; Miller 1963; Weske 1972. **Stomach contents** Foster data; LSUMZ data; Wetmore 1939. **Vocalizations** LNS recordings by Parker (6), Schwartz (13), van den Berg (2); Hilty and Brown 1986; Sick 1985. **Nests, eggs, and breeding dates** Hilty and Brown 1986; Miller 1963; Phelps 1954.

Euphonia rufiventris 155
Rufous-bellied Euphonia
Plate 22

Length 10 cm (4 in.). Weight 14 g (13.0–18.0 g). Monotypic.

Geographic Range

East of the Andes from s Meta and e Guianía, COLOMBIA, southward through e ECUADOR and e PERU to Santa Cruz, BOLIVIA, and eastward to VENEZUELA (Amazonas and Bolívar) and in BRAZIL north of the Amazon River to the Rio Negro in c Amazonas and south of the Amazon to c Pará and wc Mato Grosso (Willis 1976).

Elevational Range

Lowlands to 1100 m; mostly below ca. 500 m.

Habitat and Behavior

Inhabits humid terra firma and low-lying (incl. *varzea*) forest. Also occurs at forest edge, in second-growth woodland, and in shaded plantations. Single birds and pairs regularly follow large mixed-species flocks in the canopy; seldom joins other euphonias at forest edge. Forages from midheights to

Euphonia rufiventris

the canopy in forest; occasionally descends to fruiting trees and tall shrubs at forest edge. Eats fruit, including those of epiphytes and mistletoe; often seen in or around epiphytes (Remsen *in litt.*). Stomach contents (4): vegetable matter, including fruit pulp and *Cecropia* seeds.

Vocalizations

Call: a raspy, insectlike, *bzzz-bzzz-bzzz-bzzz*; Moderate-pitched; the number of notes vary (3–6) as well as the speed of delivery. Possible song: 2 female-plumaged birds, atop a 30 m tree, sang what appeared to be a duet; one bird delivered a series of Moderate-pitched *zeeet* notes while the other sang *zit-zit*, *wit-wit*, *what-eeeee*; the *zit-zit* is High-pitched, the *wit-wit* is a Low-Pitched whistle, and the *what-eeeee* is a Moderate- to High-pitched whistle. The sequence lasted about 2–3 sec. and was repeated without pause for several minutes. While singing, the 2 birds rapidly turned one way and then another, flicking their tails from side to side. (Parker, LNS.)

Breeding

No information.

Sources

Primary Hilty and Brown 1986; Isler data; LSUMZ data; Meyer de Schauensee and Phelps 1978; Parker, Parker, and Plenge 1982; O'Neill 1974; Pearson 1977; Terborgh and Weske 1969.

Weights (n = 10) LSUMZ data. **Stomach contents** LSUMZ data; Schubart, Aguirre, and Sick 1965. **Vocalizations** LNS recordings by Parker (3), Schwartz (1); recording by R. A. Rowlett (1).

Euphonia pectoralis 156
Chestnut-bellied Euphonia
Plate 22

Length 11 cm (4½ in.). Weight 16 g (15.0–16.5 g). Monotypic.

Geographic Range

Se BRAZIL from s Bahia southward to c Rio Grande do Sul (Belton 1985) and inland to e Mato Grosso (Sick 1985), s Goiás, w São Paulo, and Paraná, and through Misiones, ARGENTINA, to Alto Paraná and Paraguarí, se PARAGUAY.

Elevational Range

Sea level to 1550 m.

Habitat and Behavior

Encountered within forest and at forest edge; also occurs in second growth. Not found in 3 remnant woodlots in se Brazil studied by Willis (1979). Seems to wander seasonally and may migrate elevationally in part of range. Pairs or single birds usually travel alone. In Brazil, pairs also form single-species groups that join mixed-species flocks for short periods (Davis 1946). Joins feeding aggregations in fruiting trees. Very lively and seems to be always in motion, especially in the early morning; rests quietly at times on bare branches.

Forages from mid to upper levels of trees; mostly in the canopy. Takes small fruits including those of melastomes, epiphytes, cacti, *Cecropia*, palms, and *Solanum*. Also eats small insects that hide in the crevices of bark. Visits flowers to take nectar and/or insects. Observed clinging to hummingbird feeders to obtain sugar water (Sick 1985).

Vocalizations

Call: 3–5 raspy, insectlike, Moderate-pitched notes, *bzzz-bzzz-bzzz*, given in less than a sec.; usually pauses 3–4 sec. before uttering the series again. Song includes imitations of calls of other species (Sick 1985).

Breeding

Builds a dome-shaped nest of mosses and ferns. Nests have been found concealed on the side of a tree trunk suspended from roots of an epiphytic fern, amid epiphytes on a large limb about 2 m off the ground among branches of a bush, and in indentations (2 nests) on the sides of steep banks. One of the nests contained 3 eggs. Breeding dates: Brazil (Rio de Janeiro) Jan. Paraguay Aug.

Sources

Primary Belton 1985; Bertoni 1901, 1919; Descourtilz 1852; Davis 1945b, 1946; Holt 1928; Parker data; Sick 1985; Willis 1979. **Weights (n = 4)** Belton 1985; Sick 1985. **Vocalizations** LNS recordings by Belton (2) and Parker (3); Sick 1985. **Nests and breeding dates** Bertoni 1919; Parker *in litt.*; Snethlage and Schreiner 1929.

Euphonia cayennensis 157
Golden-sided Euphonia
Plate 22

Length 11 cm (4 in.). Weight 15–16 g. Monotypic.

Geographic Range

VENEZUELA in ne Bolívar (El Palmar, Schwartz, LNS recording) and se Bolívar (Cerro Auyán-tepuí and Mt. Roraima, Gilliard 1941); THE GUIANAS; BRAZIL north of the Amazon River from Amapá west to e Amazonas (east of the Rio Negro) and south of the Amazon in ne Pará and w Maranhão.

Elevational Range

Sea level to 1100 m (Cerro Auyán-tepuí, Venezuela).

Habitat and Behavior

Inhabits interiors of terra firma and lowlying forest; also occurs in savanna forest, forest edge, second growth, and shaded plantations. Encountered in small groups. Occurs sporadically in mixed-species flocks (Willis 1977). Habitually wags its tail from side to side (Sick 1985). Forages in the upper levels (15–50 m off the ground) of trees. Appears to eat both fruit and insects. Stomach contents (2): seeds. Additional stomach contents included berries.

Vocalizations

Call: 3–6 raspy, insectlike, Moderate-pitched notes, *bzzz-bzzz-bzzz*, sometimes given very fast (6 in less than 1 sec.) and sometimes more slowly (3 in 1–1.5 sec.). Calls of fe-

Euphonia pectoralis

males are softer and buzzier (T. H. Davis *in litt.*). Possible duet: a Moderate-pitched, sibilant, flat (sometimes upward-rising), short whistle and a shorter *tu* which may be repeated quickly in pairs or triplets; delivered along with the burry notes in no particular sequence. In captivity, raises feathers of crown, throat, and lower breast while singing (Ingels 1975).

Breeding

In Brazil, a dome-shaped nest with small entrance, made of moss and root fibers and lined with fine vegetable fibers, was placed about 1 m above the ground. Also used abandoned flycatcher nests in two instances: one was a nest of an Ochre-bellied Flycatcher, *Pipromorpha oleaginea*, that was located inside forest, the other was a nest of a *Myiozetetes* species that was placed about 1 m up in a fruit tree in second growth (Snethlage 1935). In the latter nest, a female was observed incubating. Eggs (3–5) are whitish, sparingly spotted red. Breeding dates: Brazil (Pará) Nov.

Sources

Primary Haverschmidt 1968; Novaes 1970; Pinto 1953; Snyder 1966; Willis 1977. **Weights (n = ?)** Haverschmidt 1968. **Stomach contents** Beebe 1916; Haverschmidt 1968; Layard 1873. **Vocalizations** LNS recordings by Bierregaard (1), T. H. Davis (4), Schwartz (3); Snyder 1966. **Nests, eggs, and breeding dates** Pinto 1953; Snethlage 1935.

Euphonia cayennensis

CHLOROPHONIA

Chlorophonias (Table 21) are closely related to euphonias. Like euphonias, their digestive systems are adapted to a frugivorous diet (see *Euphonia* genus account), and chlorophonias also build globular domed nests that are typically well hidden in vegetation. As with at least some euphonias, pairs of Golden-browed Chlorophonias race to their nest in a distraction display, and both parents feed regurgitated food to nestlings. Chlorophonias differ from euphonias in their bright green coloration and in details of feather structure, and they also have a stockier appearance.

Table 21 The *Chlorophonia* Species

158	*C. flavirostris*	Yellow-collared Chlorophonia
159	*C. cyanea*	Blue-naped Chlorophonia
160	*C. pyrrhophrys*	Chestnut-breasted Chlorophonia
161	*C. occipitalis*	Blue-crowned Chlorophonia
161-1	*occipitalis* subspecies group	Blue-crowned Chlorophonia
161-2	*callophrys* subspecies group	Golden-browed Chlorophonia

Chlorophonias are found from central Mexico to southeastern Brazil, mostly in highlands. We know of no undisturbed forest location where two species occur together, but Hilty (*in litt.*) has found Yellow-collared and Chestnut-breasted Chlorophonias less than 400 m apart in a disturbed area in Valle, Colombia. Primarily forest inhabitants, chlorophonias travel at times to nearby trees in clearings and plantations. They are typically encountered in small groups and pair off in the breeding season. Chlorophonias forage mostly for small fruits high in trees.

Although their coloration and sluggish movements make them hard to spot high in the canopy, chlorophonias often may be located by their songs and calls. Most species repeat a distinctive plaintive whistle and deliver nasal yaps.

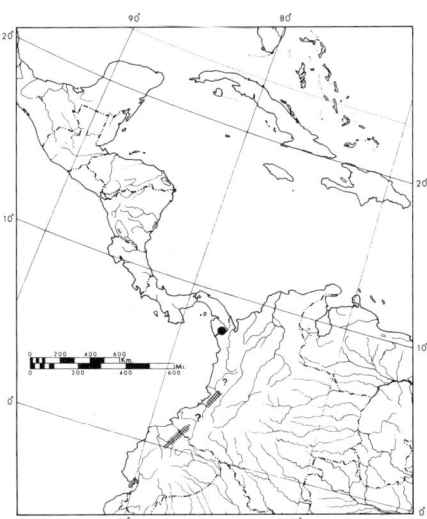

Chlorophonia flavirostris

Chlorophonia flavirostris 158
Yellow-collared Chlorophonia
Plate 23

Length 10 cm (4 in.). Weight 11 g (1 male). Monotypic. Adult males are a minority in flocks, suggesting that the subadult male plumage (resembling the female) is retained for some time.

Geographic Range

Once in extreme e Darién, PANAMA (Capparella in press); COLOMBIA on the Pacific slope of the Andes in Valle (Hilty and Brown 1986) and s Nariño; nw ECUADOR in Esmeraldas (Ridgely 1980) and Pichincha.

Elevational Range

100–1900 m (Hilty and Brown 1986).

Habitat and Behavior

Inhabits wet forest on steep slopes; also occurs at forest edge and in second growth. Pairs and groups of 3–7 individuals travel alone or with mixed-species flocks. In Colombia, seasonally forms larger single-species flocks of up to 30, rarely 80, individuals (Hilty 1977). Joins feeding aggregations.

In Valle, Colombia: Foraged mostly in the crowns of tall trees; median height was about 14 m off the ground. Ate over 9 species of fruit, especially *Ficus* fruit (40% of all fruit eaten) and *Miconia* berries (37%). Typically perched on a branch or twig to take fruit, sometimes on the fruit itself (*Schefflera* sp), and occasionally snatched a berry in flight. Moved deliberately while foraging for insects; hopped from branch to branch in an erratic fashion; and hung from petioles to inspect the undersides of large leaves. Observed capturing insects only twice. (Hilty data, 82 obs.) Stomach contents (1): fluid.

Vocalizations

Most common call is a soft Moderate-pitched *pek*. Flight call is a plaintive high thin whistle, *peeeeeeee*. Also delivers a slow High-pitched rattling buzz followed by one to several soft Moderate-pitched whistles, possibly a song.

Breeding

No information.

Sources

Primary Hilty data; Hilty and Brown 1986; Ingels 1979. **Weight (n = 1)** LSUMZ data. **Stomach contents** LSUMZ data. **Vocalizations** recording by R. A. Rowlett (1); Hilty and Brown 1986; Parker data.

Chlorophonia cyanea 159
Blue-naped Chlorophonia
Plate 23

Length 11 cm (4 in.). Weight 14 g (11.0–15.0 g). Seven subspecies: males and females of *frontalis, minuscula,* and *roraimae* are like *psittacina* (illus.) except male *roraimae* has a blue-tinged back. Males of *intensa* and *longi-*

pennis resemble *cyanea* (illus.); females of the latter 3 races also like *psittacina* but lack yellow foreheads. Males breed in subadult plumage resembling females; males in adult plumage constitute a notably small proportion of the population.

Geographic Range

C. c. roraimae: s VENEZUELA (Amazonas and Bolívar), adjacent BRAZIL, and c GUYANA. *C. c. minuscula*: the coastal range in VENEZUELA from Anzoátegui to e Sucre. *C. c. frontalis*: mountains of VENEZUELA from Distrito Federal to Falcón and nw Lara. *C. c. psittacina*: Santa Marta Mountains, COLOMBIA. *C. c. intensa*: the Pacific slope of the Andes south to Valle, COLOMBIA. *C. c. longipennis*: the Perijá Mountains; the Andes from s Lara to Táchira (east of the Western Venezuelan Low), VENEZUELA; E Andes in Cundinamarca and locally in the C Andes from Antioquia (USNM) south to Huila, COLOMBIA; e slope of the Andes from Napo (Pearson 1972), ECUADOR, southward through PERU to w Santa Cruz, BOLIVIA. *C. c. cyanea*: se BRAZIL from s Bahia southward to n Rio Grande do Sul and westward through Misiones, ARGENTINA, to c PARAGUAY east of Río Paraguay (Short 1975).

Elevational Range

500–1800 m in s Venezuela, 700–2500 m in n Venezuela; in Colombia, 600–2100 m, usually above 1400 m in the Andes; from 250 m (Parker *in litt.*) to 2100 m in Ecuador, Peru, and Bolivia; mostly 900–1500 m in Peru (Parker, Parker, and Plenge 1982)—appears to wander seasonally to lower elevations (Ridgely *in litt.*); down to near sea level in se Brazil.

Habitat and Behavior

Inhabits humid terra firma and montane forests, especially forest edge. Also occurs in trees in forest clearings, second-growth woodland, shaded plantations, and gardens (se Brazil). Family groups and pairs occasionally associate with mixed-species flocks. Joins feeding aggregations at fruiting trees. Inconspicuous; moves deliberately through vegetation. Often discovered through vocalizations.

Forages from midheights to the canopy, but usually stays in the tops of trees. Eats small fruits, including those of melastomes, and mistletoe berries; also insects. In Bolivia, picked 3–4 mm fruits; gleaned insects from mossy limbs (25 cm in diam.); and sallied to foliage (Remsen data, 7 obs.). Stomach contents (5): vegetable matter, including fruit and seeds (incl. mistletoe seeds).

In Paraguay when eating 7–10 mm fruit of *Allophyllus edulis*: Typically stayed inside tree crowns. Mostly reached or leaned over to pluck a fruit and carried it to a horizontal branch. Perching horizontally, the bird manipulated the fruit in its bill, apparently to soften it or break the skin, then held it against the branch to peck off pieces. Sometimes perched on a branch near fruit and reached up to take bites without plucking it. Never seen eating the seed. (Foster data.)

Vocalizations

Calls: nasal Moderate-pitched *ek* or *enk* notes. In an apparent song, call notes are delivered rapidly and mixed with lower-pitched *chew* notes and a rapid *didle-itle-itle*. In addition, delivers a plaintive downward-inflected whistle *teeeu*, Moderate- to Low-pitched, sometimes repeated in a regular pattern, a possible song.

Breeding

In Colombia, 2 domed nests with side entrances were made of grasses and rootlets and placed in crevices in overhanging cliffs; a third was built in a small cavity in a vertical bank; all were located near forest (Todd and Carriker 1922). In Paraguay, pouch-shaped nests were hidden among mosses and ferns growing on heavy tree trunks (Bertoni 1919). Eggs (3) are pure white, covered with fine chestnut speckles, more thickly at the large end. Both parents fed fledglings by stuffing fruit down their throats (Foster data). Breeding dates: Colombia Jan, May, and June.

Sources

Primary Bertoni 1901, 1919; Foster data; Hilty and Brown 1986; Meyer de Schauensee and Phelps 1978; Parker data; Remsen data; Sick 1985; Todd and Carriker 1922. **Weights (n = 13)** Belton 1985; LSUMZ data; Miller 1963; Sick 1985. **Stomach contents** Foster data; LSUMZ data; Wetmore 1939. **Vocalizations** LNS recordings by Emanuel (1), Parker (4), Schwartz (3); recording by Whitney (1); Hilty and Brown 1986. **Nests, eggs, and breeding dates** Bertoni 1919; Euler 1900; Gniadek in Hilty and Brown 1986; Santos 1948; Todd and Carriker 1922.

Chlorophonia cyanea

Chlorophonia pyrrhophrys 160
Chestnut-breasted Chlorophonia
Plate 23

Length 12 cm (5 in.). Weight 17 g (16.0–18.0 g). Monotypic.

Geographic Range

The Andes from Trujillo, VENEZUELA, to Norte de Santander, COLOMBIA; the Perijá Mountains; locally through the C and W Andes of COLOMBIA, south on the e slope of the Andes to Napo, ECUADOR, and the w slope to Pichincha (Ridgely *in litt.*), ECUADOR; PERU on the e slope near the Piura-Cajamarca border (Parker et al. 1985); and locally from Amazonas (LSUMZ) southward to Huánuco (LSUMZ).

Elevational Range

1800–3300 m in Venezuela, 1400–2700 m in Colombia, ca. 1900 m in Ecuador, and 2100–2650 m in Peru.

Habitat and Behavior

Inhabits tall humid montane forest (also elfin forest in Venezuela), tall second growth, forest edge, and adjoining areas with scattered trees. Encountered mostly in pairs,

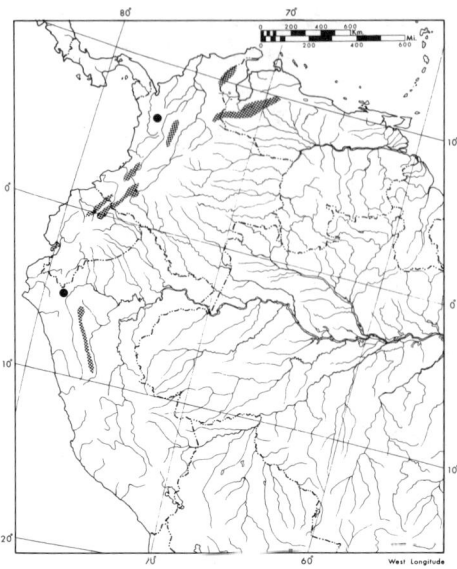

Chlorophonia pyrrhophrys

also singly, and at times, forms single-species flocks. Occasionally travels with mixed-species flocks and readily joins feeding aggregations at fruiting trees. Forages from midheights to the canopy for fruit, including mistletoe berries.

Vocalizations

Song: an irregular rambling series of nasal notes often sounding like *eeh, eeeah, uhh*; Low- to Moderate-pitched; sometimes the notes have a mewing quality; delivered from high in trees. Call: *ta-KEE!* or *KEEE!*, sharper and more forceful than the song, yet a little mournful; Moderate-pitched.

Breeding

In Venezuela, Ridgely (*in litt.*) found a pair building a nest in a hollow halfway up the face of a dripping-wet 15 m high roadcut at forest edge; both sexes were rapidly bringing in tendrils and other fibers, presumably for the nest lining. Breeding dates: Venezuela March.

Sources

Primary Hilty and Brown 1986; LSUMZ data; Meyer de Schauensee and Phelps 1978; Moynihan 1979; Parker data; Ridgely *in litt.* **Weights (n = 5)** LSUMZ data; Miller 1963. **Vocalizations** LNS recordings by Schwartz (4); recording by Whitney (1). **Nests and breeding dates** Ridgely *in litt.*

Chlorophonia occipitalis **161**
Blue-crowned Chlorophonia

This Middle American chlorophonia is considered a single species in the *Peters Check-list*, but its two subspecies are recognized as specifically distinct by the *A.O.U. Check-list*. Their behavior and vocalizations appear to be similar.

Chlorophonia occipitalis
(*occipitalis* subspecies group **161-1**)
Blue-crowned Chlorophonia
Plate 23

Length 13 cm (5 in.). Weight 26 g (25.0–27.5 g). Monotypic if specifically distinct. Subadult males resemble adult females (Dickey and van Rossem 1938).

Geographic Range

Veracruz, MEXICO, and from e Oaxaca and Chiapas, MEXICO, southeastward through GUATEMALA, EL SALVADOR, and HONDURAS to nc NICARAGUA.

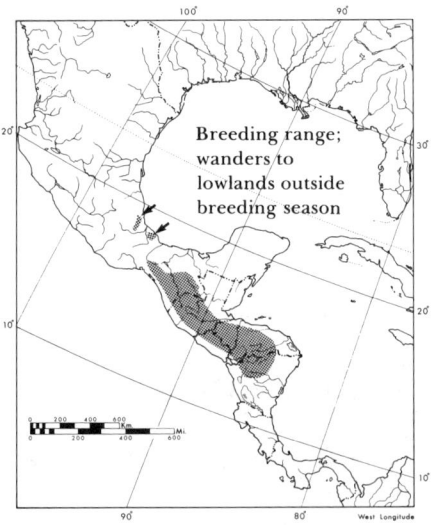

Chlorophonia occipitalis (*occipitalis* subspecies group)

Elevational Range

500–2500 m; mostly 1000–2000 m. Descends nearly to sea level during winter months (Monroe 1968).

Habitat and Behavior

Primarily inhabits dense broad-leafed forest and forest edge; also occurs in shaded coffee plantations and tree-studded clearings near forest. Encountered mostly in small groups, also in pairs and singly. Joins feeding aggregations at fruiting trees. Typically forages in the canopy of tall trees for mistletoe berries and other small fruits. Searches for insects on mossy branches (Parker *in litt.*).

Vocalizations

Calls (Low-pitched) are a barked nasal *enk* or *enk-it* and a plaintive downward-inflected whistle *eeeeeee*, sometimes preceeded by *whit* notes. Song consists of liquid phrases like *turdle-dee* and scratchy *chup* or *dit* notes (possibly a duet); Low- or Moderate-pitched. (Whitney recordings.)

Breeding

In Mexico, a nest was found about 3 m above the ground completely concealed in a clump of bromeliads attached to a perpendicular vine hanging from an oak tree. The domed nest with side entrance was built of strips of bark, mosses, and epiphytic stalks and lined with fine fibers. Both sexes brought nesting material. Eggs (3) were white, marked reddish, especially around the large end. (Rowley 1984.) A similar egg with pale brown markings was described by Nehrkorn (1899). In captivity, 5 eggs formed a clutch; incubation took 15 days; the nestling period was 21 days; both parents fed the young by regurgitation; live spiders were the only food accepted by the parents (see Gourlay 1974). Breeding dates: Mexico April.

Sources

Primary Alvarez del Toro 1964; Andrle 1967; Dickey and Van Rossem 1938; Land 1970; Lowery and Dahlquest 1951; Monroe 1968; Rowley 1984. **Weights (n = 5)** LSUMZ data. **Stomach contents** Dickey and van Rossem 1938. **Vocalizations** recordings by Whitney (3). **Nests, eggs, and breeding dates** Gourlay 1974; Nehrkorn 1899; Rowley 1984.

Chlorophonia occipitalis
(*callophrys* subspecies group 161-2)
Golden-browed Chlorophonia
Plate 23

Length 13 cm (5½ in.). Weight 24 g (23.8 and 24.1 g). Monotypic if specifically distinct. Subadult males resemble females and do not seem to attain adult plumage for 2–3 years (Carriker 1910); breeds in subadult plumage.

Geographic Range

Both slopes from Guanacaste (Cordillera de Tilarán), COSTA RICA, southeastward to Chiriquí and Veraguas, PANAMA.

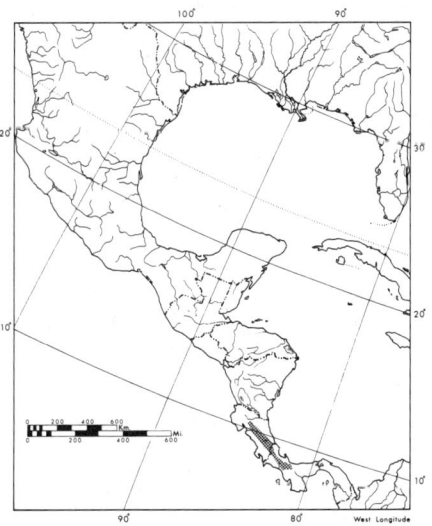

Chlorophonia occipitalis (*callophrys* subspecies group)

Elevational Range

From 750 m (mostly above 1500 m) to treeline; descends lower seasonally.

Habitat and Behavior

Inhabits forest, forest edge, and clearings with scattered trees. Encountered in groups of 3–12 individuals and in pairs during the breeding season. Travels independently or (occasionally) with other canopy species; casually with understory flocks (Powell 1979). Apparently follows set rounds; crosses openings directly from one site to another in rapid dipping flight (Slud 1964). Usually forages high in forest trees; occasionally comes down to isolated tall shrubs. Lingers in trees containing large numbers of small fruits. Eats a variety of small fruits, including those of *Ficus, Marcgravia,* and the Loranthaceae (see Wheelwright et al. 1984), and may take insects. Hops along branches, scanning undersides; flutters among leaves, or hovers at fruiting clusters; slowly squeezes berries with its bill to drink the juice, then drops the remains (Slud 1964). Contorts its body comically when voiding sticky waste (Slud 1964).

Vocalizations

Calls: a conversational stream of nasal notes suggesting the yapping of a small dog, *enk-enk-enk* (Low-pitched); sometimes mixed with a nasal *enk-it* or rapid *it-UCK* (Low- to Moderate-pitched). Also a mournful downward-inflected Low-pitched whistle, *eeeeee* or *eeeeou* sometimes doubled, typically repeated at irregular intervals.

Breeding

In Costa Rica: Domed nests with side entrances, composed of mosses, slender rootlets, and cobweb, are built 10.5–30 m off the ground in isolated trees in forest clearings. Both sexes build the nest which is typically hidden among mosses or epiphytes (one nest was built between a heavy bare limb and the tree trunk). Three eggs form a clutch. The female incubates alone, often accompanied by her mate. After a recess, they race to the nest, the male always losing. The male sometimes regurgitates food for the female as she is about to fly to the nest. The nestling period is 23–25 days, and both parents feed the young by regurgitation. May raise a second brood within 2 weeks after fledging of the first. (Skutch 1953, 1954.) Breeding dates: Costa Rica March–July. Panama March.

Sources

Primary Buskirk 1976; Carriker 1910; Ridgely 1976; Skutch 1954; Slud 1964. **Weights (n = 2)** Hartman 1955; LSUMZ data. **Vocalizations** LNS recordings by Parker (2), van den Berg (4); Ridgely 1976; Skutch 1954; Slud 1964. **Nests, eggs, and breeding dates** Skutch 1954; Wetmore, Pasquier, and Olson 1984.

CHLOROCHRYSA

The small size and green colors of *Chlorochrysa* tanagers (Table 22) tend to blend into foliage, and even after they depart the leaves to forage along moss-covered limbs, *Chlorochrysa* hop so quickly that protracted observation is difficult. Most of the relatively small body of knowledge of *Chlorochrysa* species is derived from Hilty's work in Valle, Colombia, where both the Glistening-green and Multicolored Tanagers occur.

Table 22 The *Chlorochrysa* Tanagers

162 *C. phoenicotis*	Glistening-green Tanager
163 *C. calliparaea*	Orange-eared Tanager
164 *C. nitidissima*	Multicolored Tanager

Chlorochrysa species are distinguished by long thin bills, strong tarsi, and patches of distinctive feathers, located behind the ear opening, that are enlarged near the end like a club (see Innes 1979). Club-shaped feathers, most developed in the Orange-eared Tanager, are also found on some species of the genus *Tangara* and on the Green Honeycreeper, *Chlorophanes spiza* **221,** and help link these genera taxonomically (see Miller 1919 and Storer 1969).

Chlorochrysa tanagers inhabit Andean slopes from Colombia to Bolivia, their vertical range centered at about 1200–1800 m. The three species are essentially allopatric. On the Pacific slope in sw Colombia where two species are found, the Multicolored Tanager occurs at higher elevations than the Glistening-green.

Chlorochrysa species primarily eat insects, especially small larvae, that they glean off the undersides of leaves. These tanagers employ a wide variety of acrobatic techniques to reach leaf bottoms. Most often they hang upside down from a twig, petiole, or from the leaf itself, and they also stretch upright to reach the undersides of leaves overhead. The strong tarsi that allow them to hang from leaf surfaces also move them quickly across moss and epiphyte-laden branches where they poke into vegetation. Additionally, *Chlorochrysa* eat fruit, although amounts apparently differ by species.

All three species typically travel in pairs, often with mixed-species flocks; the Multicolored seems to be less gregarious than its congeners. Notes of *Chlorochrysa* species are lisping or wheezy.

Chlorochrysa phoenicotis 162
Glistening-green Tanager
Plate 23

Length 13 cm (5 in.). Weight 22 g (1 male). Monotypic. Subadults (possible juveniles) are dull green and lack gray patches (USNM).

Geographic Range

One record from the w slope of the C Andes in Antioquia (USNM), COLOMBIA; the Pacific slope from Risaralda, COLOMBIA, to Pichincha, ECUADOR; and one record from Guayas (sight, Aug 1980—Ridgely), ECUADOR.

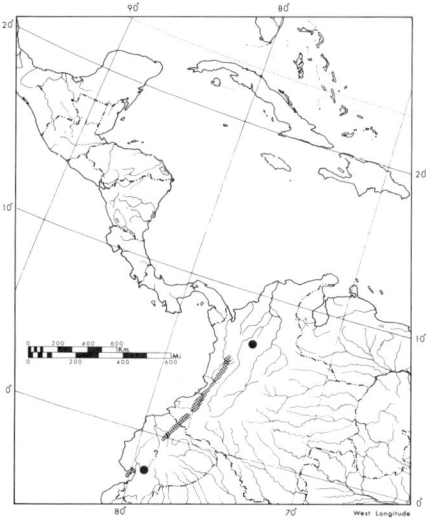

Chlorochrysa phoenicotis

Elevational Range

700–2200 m; usually above 1000 m (Hilty and Brown 1986).

Habitat and Behavior

Favors the interior of wet montane forest; occasionally occurs at forest edge or in tall second growth. Single birds, pairs, and family groups typically travel with mixed-species flocks and join feeding aggregations at fruiting trees.

In Valle, Colombia: Usually foraged in upperparts of the understory and in the canopy of small trees but also occurred in the canopy of tall trees; median foraging height was 9 m above the ground (63 obs.). Hunted mostly for insects (62% of all foraging records), including caterpillars. Searched actively and acrobatically, primarily on the undersides of leaves in outer foliage. Hopped rapidly along slender branches stopping at twigs to inspect leaf surfaces and petioles. Clung upside down to tiny twigs, vines, and the leaves themselves to inspect leaf undersides. Hung from palm fruits or "ran up the ladder" of palm fronds searching for insects. While perched upright, often twisted or turned to look up under leaves, reaching up or out to snatch prey. Sometimes scooted along inner branches poking into moss clumps, bromeliads, vine tangles, and hanging dead leaves. Also ate fruit (38% of all foraging records). Favored melastome fruits (91% of all fruit eaten), especially *Miconia* berries. Perched on twigs or branches to pluck fruit; swallowed small berries whole. (Hilty data.)

Vocalizations

Most common call is a high lisping 3–4 noted *czee, czee, czee*, sometimes becoming *ee-see-seez-seez*, weak but distinctive (Hilty and Brown 1986).

Breeding

In Colombia, a cup nest was found hollowed in moss on the side of a limb at mid levels (Hilty and Brown 1986). Breeding dates: Colombia April–June.

Sources

Primary Hilty data; Hilty and Brown 1986. **Weights (n = 1)** LSUMZ data. **Vocalizations** Hilty and Brown 1986. **Nests and breeding dates** Hilty and Brown 1986.

Chlorochrysa calliparaea 163
Orange-eared Tanager
Plate 23

Length 12 cm (5 in.). Weight 17 g (14.9–21.5 g). Three subspecies: *calliparaea* resembles *bourcieri* (illus.) but is deeper blue (nearly Cobalt) below.

Geographic Range

C. c. bourcieri: w slope of the E Andes in COLOMBIA in Cundinamarca, the head of the Magdalena Valley in Huila, and the e slope of the Andes from Caquetá, COLOMBIA, southward through ECUADOR and n PERU to Huánuco, PERU. *C. c. calliparaea*: e Andean slope from Pasco to n Ayacucho, PERU, (LSUMZ). *C. c. fulgentissima*:

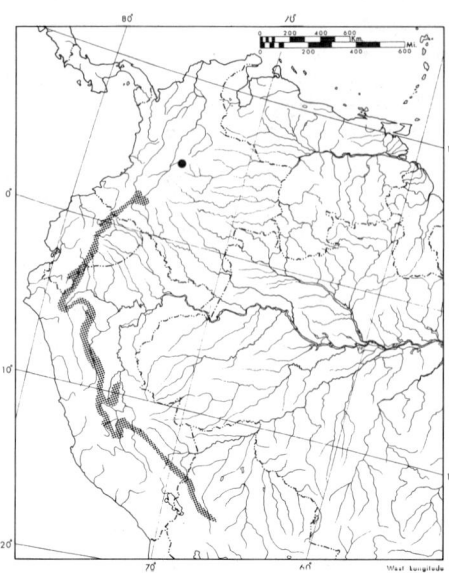

Chlorochrysa calliparaea

e Andean slope from Cuzco, PERU, to nw Cochabamba, BOLIVIA.

Elevational Range

900–2000 m, mostly 1200–1700 m; 1600–1800 m in the Magdalena Valley, Colombia (Hilty and Brown 1986).

Habitat and Behavior

Inhabits humid mossy montane forest and forest edge; also occurs in second growth. Pairs and single birds typically travel with mixed-species flocks. Forages mostly in the canopy and subcanopy. Hops along, hangs from, or clings to mossy limbs and trunks to probe moss and inspect parasitic plants. Hangs or reaches out to glean insects from leaves in dense outer foliage. Occasionally seen in fruiting *Miconia*. In Bolivia, picked small (3 mm) fruits (Remsen data). Stomach contents: vegetable matter (7); animal matter (1); both (1). Contents included fruit, seeds, and 6 caterpillars (5 were larger than 20 mm).

Vocalizations

Utters a high-pitched wheezy *seeep* (Hilty and Brown 1986).

Breeding

No information.

Sources

Primary Goodfellow 1901; Hilty and Brown 1986; LSUMZ data; Parker data; Remsen data; Terborgh and Weske 1975; Zimmer 1930. **Weights (n = 18)** LSUMZ data. **Stomach contents** LSUMZ data. **Vocalizations** Hilty and Brown 1986.

Chlorochrysa nitidissima **164**
Multicolored Tanager
Plate 23

Length 12 cm (5 in.). Weight 19 g (17.3–21.6 g). Monotypic.

Geographic Range

COLOMBIA locally on both slopes of the W Andes from Risaralda and extreme s Antioquia south to c Cauca, the w slope of the C Andes in Quindío, and the e slope of the C Andes in Caldas near the Antioquia border (USNM).

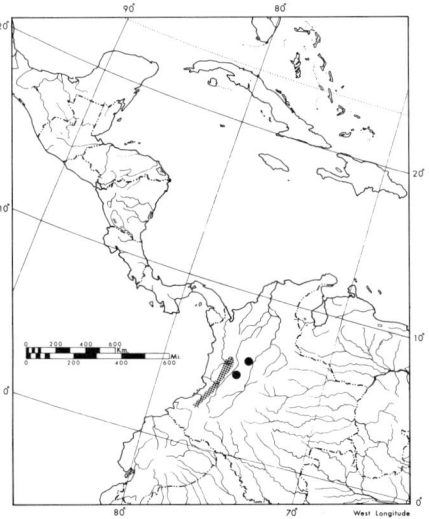

Chlorochrysa nitidissima

Elevational Range

1400–2000 m; descends to 900 m on the Pacific slope in Cauca (Hilty and Brown 1986).

Habitat and Behavior

Inhabits the interior of humid and wet montane forest; occasionally occurs at forest edge or in tall second growth. Mostly pairs, less often single birds, and sometimes family groups travel independently or with mixed-species flocks. Joins feeding aggregations in fruiting trees. May be threatened by habitat destruction (Hilty 1985).

In Valle, Colombia: Foraged from mid to upper levels of forest, mostly in the crowns of trees; median foraging height was about 10 m off the ground (50 obs.); rarely descended below 4.5 m. Primarily searched for insects (87% of all foraging records), particularly small larvae; also took hairy caterpillars. Typically clung from leaves in outer foliage to glean leaf undersides; sometimes flew directly from one leaf perch to another. Hung from the tips of palm leaflets or "climbed the ladder" of palm fronds. Also reached up to glean leaf undersides; peered along outer limbs; and hung from moss clumps, branches, or vines to probe moss, fruit clumps, and dead leaves. Ate arillate fruit (*Tovomita* sp) and pecked at green 10–12 mm berries. (Hilty data.) Feeds on flower clusters and on small *Ficus* fruits (Miller 1963).

Vocalizations

Call: one to several wheezy *ceeet* notes similar to *C. calliparaea* (Hilty and Brown 1986).

Breeding

In Colombia, stub-tailed fledglings were observed in November. (Hilty and Brown 1986).

Sources

Primary Hilty data; Hilty and Brown 1986; Miller 1963. **Weights (n = 8)** Miller 1963. **Vocalizations** Hilty and Brown 1986. **Breeding dates** Hilty and Brown 1986.

TANGARA

Tangara includes more species than any other genus of purely neotropical birds: forty-seven in the *Peters Check-list*. Up to ten species may occur in the same Andean region, and one of the joys of nature study in the Neotropics is the discovery of fruiting shrubs adorned with the contrasting colors of many different species of these feathered jewels. The sheer number of *Tangara* species can make them difficult to grasp, however, and in this section we suggest 13 species groups (Table 23) that were derived from an examination of their ranges, appearance, behaviors (especially foraging behaviors), vocalizations, and nest sites.

Most *Tangara* species have a limited geographic range, and the Andean species tend to have fairly narrow elevational ranges. Only two species, the Speckled and Bay-headed Tanagers, are distributed widely to both the east and the west of the Andes. Many *Tangara* appear to replace one another geographically.

Tangara species are also compartmentalized by differences in habitat preferences. Most are forest-based, living high in the canopy within forest and descending at forest edge to fruiting shrubs, but about ten species primarily inhabit shrubs and trees in semiopen situations and rarely venture into forest. The handful of *Tangara* (e.g., Lesser Antillean Tanager) that are widespread in both forest and semiopen areas are found in regions where few tanagers of any kind occur.

Of eleven species whose foraging behavior has been studied year-round, fruit accounted for between 53 and 86 percent of all feeding observations, and small berries, especially those of melastomes, were taken most often. *Tangara* typically perch alongside fruit clusters to pick berries and swallow them whole. *Cecropia* fruits, a favorite at clearings, are often nibbled while the bird hangs down from the catkin. Although we cannot discern major groupings of *Tangara* based on fruit-eating, some species appear to peck pieces out of large pulpy or encapsulated fruits much more often than others.

Perhaps most important, in regions where a number of species are sympatric, *Tangara* tanagers employ specialized insect-foraging techniques. Some seek insects on foliage; others on branches. Of those that search branches, some forage primarily on twigs near branch extremities, others on large limbs near the trunk; some on the tops of branches, others on the undersides; and some search mossy branches while others prefer bare branches. Similar specializations occur among species that seek insects on leaves. Only a few *Tangara* species employ aerial insect-foraging techniques extensively.

Until recently, the songs of *Tangara* tana-

Table 23 The *Tangara* Tanagers

Group	No.	Species	Common Name
1	165	T. inornata	Plain-colored Tanager
1	168	T. mexicana	Turquoise Tanager
2	166	T. cabanisi	Azure-rumped Tanager
2	167	T. palmeri	Gray-and-gold Tanager
	169	T. chilensis	Paradise Tanager
3	170	T. fastuosa	Seven-colored Tanager
	171	T. seledon	Green-headed Tanager
	172	T. cyanocephala	Red-necked Tanager
4	173	T. desmaresti	Brassy-breasted Tanager
	174	T. cyanoventris	Gilt-edged Tanager
	175	T. johannae	Blue-whiskered Tanager
	176	T. schrankii	Green-and-gold Tanager
	177	T. florida	Emerald Tanager
5	178	T. arthus	Golden Tanager
	179	T. icterocephala	Silver-throated Tanager
	180	T. xanthocephala	Saffron-crowned Tanager
	181	T. chrysotis	Golden-eared Tanager
	182	T. parzudakii	Flame-faced Tanager
	183	T. xanthogastra	Yellow-bellied Tanager
	184	T. punctata	Spotted Tanager
6	185	T. guttata	Speckled Tanager
	186	T. varia	Dotted Tanager
	187	T. rufigula	Rufous-throated Tanager
	188	T. gyrola	Bay-headed Tanager
7	189	T. lavinia	Rufous-winged Tanager
	195	T. rufigenis	Rufous-cheeked Tanager
	190	T. cayana	Burnished-buff Tanager
	191	T. cucullata	Lesser Antillean Tanager
8	192	T. peruviana	Black-backed Tanager
	193	T. preciosa	Chestnut-backed Tanager
	194	T. vitriolina	Scrub Tanager
	242	T. meyerdeschauenseei	Green-capped Tanager
	196	T. ruficervix	Golden-naped Tanager
9	197	T. labradorides	Metallic-green Tanager
	198	T. cyanotis	Blue-browed Tanager
	199	T. cyanicollis	Blue-necked Tanager
10	200	T. larvata	Golden-hooded Tanager
	201	T. nigrocincta	Masked Tanager
	202	T. dowii	Spangle-cheeked Tanager
11		202-1 dowii subspecies group	Spangle-cheeked Tanager
		202-2 fucosa subspecies group	Green-naped Tanager
	203	T. nigroviridis	Beryl-spangled Tanager
	204	T. vassorii	Blue-and-black Tanager
	205	T. heinei	Black-capped Tanager
	206	T. viridicollis	Silvery-backed Tanager
12	207	T. argyrofenges	Straw-backed Tanager
	208	T. cyanoptera	Black-headed Tanager
	209	T. pulcherrima	Yellow-collared Honeycreeper
	210	T. velia	Opal-rumped Tanager
13	211	T. callophrys	Opal-crowned Tanager

Notes: Numbers and brackets to the left of the table refer to superspecies (solid lines) and species groups (dotted lines) discussed in the genus account. If considered specifically distinct, the subspecies groups of *T. dowii* would constitute a superspecies. Species 168 and 195 have been shifted on the table from the taxonomic order of the *Peters Check-list* (which is followed in the text) and species 242 inserted in order to facilitate use of the table.

gers were essentially unknown, but recordists such as Theodore A. Parker III and Paul Schwartz have discovered *Tangara* vocalizations that may shed additional light on the relationships among species. *Tangara* tanagers in some species groups deliver a rhythmic repetition of call notes in their songs, whereas species in other groups have complex and distinctive vocalizations.

As Skutch (1976) has noted, *Tangara* species are not very obvious when nesting, partly because they do not deliver loud advertising songs from obvious exposed perches and also because of the rarity of attention-gathering territorial border disputes. Nests of fewer than half the *Tangara* species have been found, and they are typically well concealed. Nests of some species are hidden within dense clusters of leaves in shrubs and the outer branches of trees; many other *Tangara* place their nests in mossy tangles on limbs; and a few in the crannies of trees. Females typically build the cup nest alone, although they are attended closely by the male who may bring nesting materials. Two eggs usually form a clutch, and they are whitish (sometimes tinged with color) and speckled brown or lavender, especially about the large end. The incubation period is most often 13–14 days, the nestling period 15–16 days. The young are fed insects and fruit by both parents. While some species (e.g., Silver-throated Tanagers) may be exceptions, fledglings stay with their parents for a considerable length of time. Helpers at the nest have been observed for three species. Various species have hybridized in captivity (see Ingels 1971b, Merry 1971).

A brief summary follows of the characteristics of each of the thirteen species groups suggested in Table 23.

Species Group 1

Plain-colored and Turquoise Tanagers differ from most *Tangara* in that they live in tightly knit groups of 4–6 individuals whose ties persist into the breeding season when nonbreeding individuals have been observed to help feed nestlings. Turquoise Tanagers are rarely joined by other species, but the activities of Plain-colored Tanagers tend to attract other species. The Plain-colored lives to the west and the Turquoise to the east of the Andes. Both species mostly occur in semiopen areas within forested regions. Insects are usually gleaned from thin bare branches in the crowns of trees. The quality of vocalizations of the two species are similar: High-pitched notes that are sometimes given so rapidly that they merge into a twitter.

Species Group 2

The Azure-rumped and Gray-and-gold Tanagers are alike in appearance, habitat preference, and voice. Both species combine thin *chit* notes with sweet rising *sweeet* notes in their calls. Other *Tangara* that deliver similar vocalizations are found in species group 3. The Azure-rumped and Gray-and-gold Tanagers live in the forest canopy and forest edge, occasionally traveling to isolated trees in clearings. In Valle, Colombia, Hilty found that the Gray-and-gold obtains about four-fifths of its insect prey in aerial sallies, and although the Azure-rumped also sallies for insects, it appears to be more of a generalist, perhaps as a result of the lack of competition from other *Tangara* species (see Hilty and Simon 1977).

Species Group 3

The Paradise, Seven-colored, and Green-headed Tanagers are quite similar in plumage pattern and occupy nonoverlapping ranges east of the Andes. The Paradise and Green-headed Tanagers share a number of attributes of behavior and voice; the Seven-colored is poorly known.

Paradise and Green-headed Tanagers live in the forest canopy, but venture into scattered trees and shrubs in nearby clearings where they forage closer to the ground. Typically, they travel in groups of 4–10 individuals, probably a pair and their last two broods, and are encountered independently and with mixed-species flocks. Paradise and Green-headed Tanagers are often observed eating fruit although they also spend much time hopping along branches, searching for insects under their perches or on nearby substrates. Their calls incorporate distinctive combinations of High-pitched sweet notes and Moderate-pitched sharp notes.

Species Group 4

This group consists of three species of eastern Brazil of uncertain affinities. The poorly known Red-necked Tanager might be better placed with species of the preceding group. The Red-necked lives in small groups and its call resembles those of the Paradise and Green-headed Tanagers.

The Brassy-breasted and Gilt-edged Tanagers are closely related to each other and have hybridized (Bond 1947). These species have different but overlapping geographic and elevational ranges, and in the extensive area of overlap, they associate often. Their behaviors and vocalizations appear to be similar. Like the Red-necked Tanager, they may be related to species of the preceding group or, as suggested by their striped backs, to the following group.

Species Group 5

Striped backs distinguish this forest-based group with one exception: the Flame-faced Tanager has a black back. No other *Tangara* have striped backs except the Brassy-breasted and Gilt-edged Tanagers (species group 4). The outstanding behavioral feature of species group 5 tanagers is the insect-foraging behavior of six of the eight species: the Blue-whiskered, Emerald, Golden, Silver-throated, Saffron-crowned, and Flame-faced Tanagers. These species mostly search for insects underneath mossy branches, examining the moss with the diagonal-lean foraging method. Previously unpublished data gathered by Steven Hilty in the moss-laden forests on the Pacific slope of the Andes in Colombia, where all six species occur, indicate that the six species tend either to live at different elevations or to forage on branches of different sizes (perhaps reflecting their preferences for foraging within different parts of trees).

Of the two remaining species, the Golden-eared Tanager forages for insects mostly on the uppersides of branches (both bare and mossy), and the Green-and-gold lives in lowland Amazonia where it seems to take insects from leaves as often as branches.

Like most species in the genus, the striped-backed *Tangara* tanagers eat a great deal of fruit and travel with mixed-species flocks. Except for that of the Green-and-gold Tanager, nests have usually been found on mossy limbs, sometimes burrowed into the moss itself.

Species Group 6

Species in this group have a distinctive speckled appearance and probably share a number of other attributes (based on many observations for the Speckled and Rufous-throated Tanagers and on some for the Spotted and Yellow-bellied Tanagers). These species are largely allopatric, although four of the five occur in the Guiana Highlands of southern Venezuela where two or three members of the group are sometimes seen together.

These *Tangara* primarily live in the forest canopy but descend closer to the ground at forest edge to forage in fruiting shrubs. They pick fruit from a perched position or sidle down twigs to pick berries head-down at the ends of branches. Insects are sought in leaves at the very tops of the crowns of tall trees. Here, species of this group typically glean top and bottom leaf surfaces acrobatically, hanging upside down, stretching and contorting their bodies, and sometimes walking and hopping on the leaves to find prey. They (especially the Rufous-throated) also hover to pick insects off outer foliage and sally to air.

Species in this group are usually found in pairs or small parties that perhaps consist of a pair and their recent offspring. Although they are encountered with mixed-species flocks, some observations suggest that members of this group are peripheral species, joining and leaving the flocks frequently. The speckled *Tangara* tanagers have similar calls: a high-pitched *tic* or *chip* given singly, delivered in a twittering or chipping series, or accelerated into trills that appear to be their songs.

Species Group 7

The Bay-headed and Rufous-winged Tanagers are extremely close in appearance and behavior; the Rufous-cheeked is endemic to n Venezuela, is poorly known, and is tentatively placed in this group.

The Bay-headed and Rufous-winged Tanagers mostly inhabit forests but also venture to nearby tree-studded clearings. These two species eat a wide variety of fruit and take insects mostly from the undersides of slender branches using the diagonal-lean method. Where the Bay-headed and Rufous-winged Tanagers are sympatric, the Bay-headed is found mainly above 500 m and the Rufous-winged below that elevation. Although the demarcation line is not sharp and the two species sometimes occur in the same flocks, the general pattern suggests that the two species are competitors (see Haffer 1967a, 1975).

Not much is known of the Rufous-cheeked Tanager, but aspects of its appearance (e.g., general coloration, rufous wing edgings) and ecology (forest-based, foraging mostly in large trees) suggest that the Rufous-cheeked Tanager might belong in this species group, or alternatively in species group 9.

Species Group 8

Most members of this group inhabit semi-open areas, especially pastures and other agricultural areas containing hedgerows and isolated clumps of trees. They also inhabit savanna, scrubby forest edge, parks and gardens, gallery forest, and low second growth. The Lesser Antillean Tanager is found in a wide variety of habitats, including forests, which appears to reflect the paucity of other tanagers in its range.

Given their physical similarity (see Plate

26) and limited sympatry, considerable uncertainty exists as to how many species are involved in this group. The Scrub Tanager may be conspecific with the Burnished-buff. Alternatively, forms of the Burnished-buff Tanager north and south of the Amazon River may be specifically distinct. The Black-backed and Chestnut-backed Tanagers are thought by some (e.g., Sick 1985) to be a single polymorphic species. In addition, the newly described Green-capped Tanager, *Tangara meyerdeschauenseei* **242**, fits into this species group.

In south-central Brazil, ranges of the Burnished-buff and Chestnut-backed Tanagers overlap. Hybrids, known as "Arnault's Tanager," are believed to result from matings of these two species (Bond 1951, Ingels 1971b).

Feeding habits of tanagers in this group are poorly known, but these *Tangara* appear to be mainly frugivorous (the Scrub Tanager may be an exception). Several of the species travel seasonally over large regions and appear locally as favorite fruits ripen. As might be expected of birds living primarily in semiopen areas, these *Tangara* tanagers are rarely found with mixed-species flocks. They travel alone, in pairs, or in small groups, probably families, that forage over large areas, flying directly from one group of trees and shrubs to another. These tanagers nest in isolated trees or shrubs; two eggs are typical.

Species Group 9

This group consists of three species of which there is only limited knowledge. They are blue or blue green (looking silvery green in some light) with cinnamon buff undertail-coverts and white or cinnamon buff bellies, and they inhabit Andean forests, mostly from 1400 to 2000 m in elevation. Like most *Tangara*, these tanagers typically live in pairs or small groups, presumably families, and are often encountered with mixed-species flocks, especially with other *Tangara* species. Members of this group forage from tops of shrubs to the forest canopy for insects and fruit. The inadequate data indicate that the Golden-naped often goes to the air for insects; the Metallic-green gleans leaves; and the Blue-browed searches thin bare branches.

Species Group 10

The three species of this group have blue or golden hoods, contrasting black mantles and breasts, and black lores that extend around the eye in a mask. They are considered a superspecies by the *A.O.U. Check-list*. The very similar Golden-hooded and Masked Tanagers were formerly considered conspecific; they are primarily lowland species whose ranges are separated by the Andes where they generally occur at lower elevations than the Blue-necked Tanager. The Blue-necked Tanager is also found in lowlands southeast of Amazonia.

Members of this species group generally inhabit semiopen areas and occupy isolated pockets of trees and shrubs in clearings, forest edge, and second growth; the Masked Tanager occurs in the forest canopy in Amazonia. Living in pairs or small groups, they often travel between dispersed food sources and only occasionally follow mixed-species flocks. Their vocalizations include notes like *tic* or *chit* that are repeated in ticking series, and distinctive wheezy or complaining notes. The Golden-hooded and Blue-necked Tanagers appear to be primarily frugivorous; they typically capture insects in flight through sallies to air or leaves or by hover-gleaning foliage. The Masked Tanager's insect-foraging behavior is essentially unrecorded.

Species Group 11

The species in this weakly-defined group live mostly at elevations over 1500 m in Central America and the Andes. The three species have similar blue and black posterior upperparts and small black masks, and although the Blue-and-black lacks the pale spangles of the other species, one of its subspecies is spotted. The Blue-and-black Tanager lives at higher elevations in the Andes than any other *Tangara* and is the only *Tangara* encountered near treeline.

Members of this group live in small groups that travel alone or with mixed-species flocks. Although all three species may be seen foraging from the undergrowth to the canopy, the Spangle-cheeked and Beryl-spangled Tanagers tend to remain at midheights in the vegetation and the Blue-and-black Tanager mostly in the canopy when in montane forest. When insect-foraging, tanagers in this group hop along branches quickly, gleaning twigs and slim branches, peering at leaves, and probing moss.

Species Group 12

Although the plumages of males and females of many *Tangara* species differ in minor ways, this species group exhibits the most pronounced sexual dimorphism. Males of the Black-capped, Silvery-backed, and Straw-backed Tanagers are patterned similarly with green or gold ear-coverts and throats that contrast with black crowns and napes and black or blue gray chests. The male Black-headed Tanager and Golden-collared Honeycreeper appear black hooded and are extensively opalescent below. Females of all five species have dusky caps that contrast with green backs and also have pointed feathers on the throat and chest that produce a speckled appearance (least evident in the Golden-collared Honeycreeper). The Golden-collared Honeycreeper formerly constituted the monotypic genus *Iridophanes*, but because of plumage similarities (see Storer 1969) it was placed alongside the Black-headed Tanager in the *Peters Check-list*.

All five species are found in South American mountains, mostly at about 1500–2000 m in elevation, although lower in Venezuela. They are primarily encountered at forest edge but are not well known. Most foraging observations have been in fruiting shrubs and trees, but two species have been observed searching for insects on the undersides of thin branches.

In northern Colombia and Venezuela, where both the Black-headed and Black-capped Tanagers occur, each species seems to be scarce at elevations or locations where the other is common (see Schäfer and Phelps 1954 and Todd and Carriker 1922). It appears that the Black-capped, Silvery-backed, and Straw-backed Tanagers are nearly allopatric and they may constitute a superspecies; an additional member of this group has been collected on Pico Sira in Huánuco, Peru (Graves and Weske in prep.).

Species Group 13

The Opal-rumped Tanager and the Opal-crowned Tanager formerly constituted the genus *Tanagrella*. They are essentially blue below and black above with an opal rump. The Opal-rumped and Opal-crowned Tanagers are typically found in the upper levels of forest, foraging for small fruits and seeking insects while hopping along large branches. The range of the Opal-crowned appears to fall entirely within the range of the Opal-rumped Tanager, and the two species occur together in mixed-species flocks (Munn 1985).

Tangara inornata **165**
Plain-colored Tanager
Plate 24

Length 12 cm (5 in.). Weight 18 g (16.4–19.1 g). Three subspecies: *inornata* and *rava* are illustrated; *languens* most resembles *inornata*. Subadults have pale buff on belly and undertail-coverts.

Geographic Range

T. i. rava: the Caribbean slope from Heredia, COSTA RICA, to Colón and Coclé, PANAMA. *T. i. languens*: from Colón and Coclé, PANAMA, on the Caribbean slope and w Panamá province, PANAMA, on the Pacific slope eastward to n Chocó, COLOMBIA, and thence southward along the Pacific coast to nw Valle (sight, Pujals *fide* Brown *in litt.*). *T. i. inornata*: COLOMBIA along the n base of the Andes from w Antioquia to the Magdalena Valley and south in the Magdalena Valley to Cundinamarca (Olivares 1969).

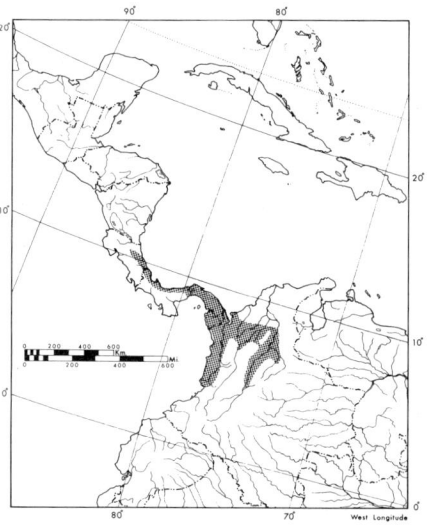

Tangara inornata

Elevational Range

Lowlands; less numerous in foothills. Mostly from sea level to 200 m, as high as ca. 400 m in Costa Rica (Stiles 1983); sea level to ca. 800 m in Panama and to ca. 1000 m in Colombia; once at ca. 2000 m in Cundinamarca, Colombia (Olivares 1969).

Habitat and Behavior

Inhabits semiopen areas within wooded regions. Frequents forest and woodland edges (especially abutting water), woodland, tree-studded cleared areas adjacent to forest, second growth, gallery forest, and shaded cacao plantations; occasionally found in forest canopy. Lives in pairs or in groups of 4–6 individuals. Outside the breeding season, 2 or 3 groups may flock together. Groups typically travel apart from other birds, but movements and call notes often attract other species. Moves in an extremely restless, active, and noisy manner, flicking wings and tail often. Periodically stops to rest quietly, often on leafless perches. Numbers vary seasonally in c Panama, suggesting regional movements (see Karr 1977 and Greenberg 1981c).

Forages mostly in the crowns of trees but comes lower for fruit. In Panama, takes a wide variety of 3–5 mm fruits, including those of *Tetracera*, *Lantana*, and *Hamelia* and catkins of *Cecropia* (Leck 1971b). Seems to have a decided preference for *Cecropia* fruit and usually perches on the catkins to eat them.

Gleans small insects from undersides of (mostly) bare twigs and branches using the diagonal-lean method. Upon alighting, lowers its head immediately to scan the branch and then moves with quick hops (Slud 1964). Occasionally flutter-pursues escaping prey or sits in the open making short sallies for flying insects. Stomach contents (1): small fruit seeds.

Vocalizations

Calls: utters a series of High-pitched sibilant *tst* and *jeet* notes producing a sound of light pleasant quality; individuals of a foraging group call in rapid succession; sometimes calls are given so rapidly that individual notes are barely distinguishable. Occasionally the basic call note is relieved by a Moderate-pitched kissing note; also delivers a *tsrrr* when flying off (Eisenmann 1952). Song: a series of about 15 notes delivered in about 2.5 sec. with pauses of equal duration; each series begins with a few rapid sibilant *tsst* notes, like the call note, but slows rather than accelerates (Morton, LNS).

Breeding

In Costa Rica, Slud (1964) observed 3 individuals chasing one another in possible courtship flights among semi-isolated large trees in a clearing: "Fluttering smoothly and slowly while continuously 'ticking,' they were weaving about the leafy branches along established aerial pathways at a fair height from the ground."

In Panama, 3 cup nests were built about 9 m up in densely foliaged crowns of fruit trees growing in a clearing. Nests were made of viny fibers and covered with moss. The female constructed one nest, attended closely by her mate who carried nesting material but never added it to the nest. Eggs (2) are whitish and speckled. At one nest, 2 nestlings were fed by 4 adults that came in a flock. (Skutch 1954, 1976.) Also in Panama, Wetmore watched a nest being constructed on a small, nearly horizontal branch 20 m off the ground. Breeding dates: Panama Feb–May and Aug.

Sources

Primary Hilty and Brown 1986; Leck 1971a, 1971b, 1972c; Moynihan 1962c; Ridgely 1976; Skutch 1954; Slud 1964; Wetmore, Pasquier, and Olson 1984. **Weights (n = 13)** Leck 1975; Ricklefs 1976; Strauch 1977; Willis 1980. **Stomach contents** Hallinan 1924. **Vocalizations** LNS recordings by Morton (2), Parker (1); Eisenmann 1952. **Nests, eggs, and breeding dates** Skutch 1954; Wetmore, Pasquier, and Olson 1984; Willis and Eisenmann 1979.

Tangara cabanisi 166
Azure-rumped Tanager
Plate 24

Length 14 cm (5½ in.). Monotypic. The subadult plumage is duller than the adult plumage.

Geographic Range

S MEXICO in s Chiapas (Sierra Madre) and adjacent region of w GUATEMALA.

Elevational Range

Ca. 600–1700 m, mostly above 1200 m.

Habitat and Behavior

Inhabits tall humid forest canopy; also occurs at forest edge and in the vicinity of cacao plantations. Encountered in pairs, also singly and in small groups; 16 individuals were once seen together. Occasionally travels with mixed-species flocks. Actively darts about the tree tops and frequently flies back and forth across clearings, but sometimes rests quietly in the tops of large trees.

In Chiapas, Mexico: Ate fruit (incl. *Ficus* and melastome fruits) and insects. Foraged mostly in tree tops but also came lower to fruiting shrubs (once on the ground at the

274 TANGARA

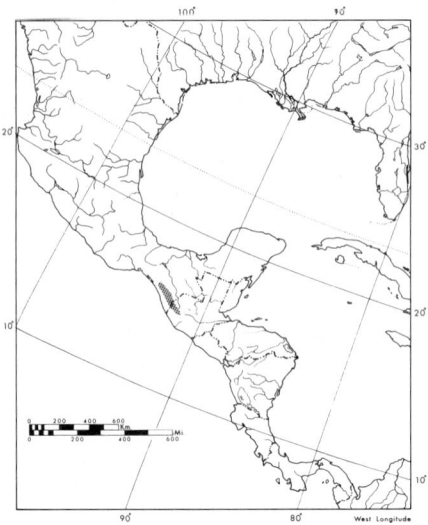

Tangara cabanisi

base of a melastome shrub). Used a variety of methods to obtain insects. Frequently searched for prey in the canopy among leaf axils and on the undersides of outer branches using the diagonal-lean foraging technique. Also examined mossy branches less than 5 cm in diam. Made short clumsy aerial sallies above the canopy from exposed perches. (Hilty and Simon 1977.)

Vocalizations

Calls: buzzy High-pitched tittering notes, *bzzz bzzz bzzz zeezah*, given by members of a pair while chasing around the top of a tree. Calls given prior, during, or immediately after flight: an upward-inflected *seeee*, a rapid *chi-di-di-dit* and other High-pitched notes (also see Hilty and Simon 1977). Song: a High-pitched *seeeawit*, inflected downward and then upward, often followed by *chi-di-di*; phrases are delivered in rapid succession. The songs appeared to be delivered from favored bare-branch perches at the very top of tall trees; sings for several minutes on a perch, then moves to the next one; singing posture is nearly upright with head tipped back slightly. (Whitney recordings.)

Breeding

In Chiapas, Mexico, Whitney (*in litt.*) found a mossy cup nest placed about 12 m above the ground in the fork of a large limb (ca. 1.5 m from the end of a 6 m long branch) in an enormous *Ficus* tree that overhung a canyon. One bird, presumably the female, would sit on the nest for about 15 min. and then leave to forage with its mate, who remained nearby, for about 10–15 min. Breeding dates: Mexico April.

Sources

Primary Alvarez del Toro 1964; Brodkorb 1939; Hilty and Simon 1977; Whitney *in litt.* **Vocalizations:** recordings by Whitney (3); Hilty and Simon 1977. **Nests and breeding dates** Whitney *in litt.*

Tangara palmeri **167**
Gray-and-gold Tanager
Plate 24

Length 15 cm (6 in.). Weight 32 g (30.0 g; 32.6 g, average of 9). Monotypic. Juvenile lacks breast band (Wetmore, Pasquier, and Olson 1984).

Geographic Range

From mountains of extreme e Darién, PANAMA, southward along the Pacific slope through COLOMBIA (Haffer 1975) to Pichincha, ECUADOR.

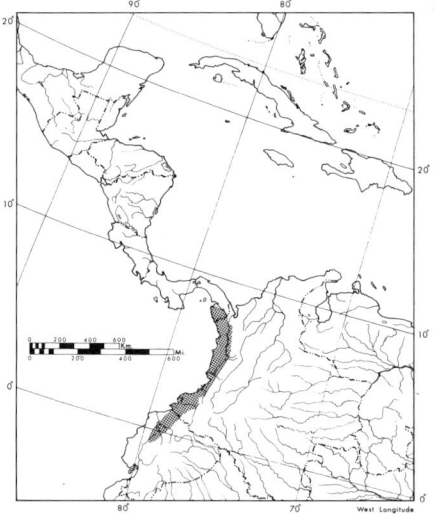

Tangara palmeri

Elevational Range

Lowlands to 1100 m; mostly above 300 m in Colombia (Hilty and Brown 1986).

Habitat and Behavior

Inhabits very wet forest, often on steep hillsides, and forest edge; occasionally wanders to second growth or scattered trees in clearings adjacent to forest (Hilty data). Generally lives in pairs or groups of 3–8 individuals. Noisy, active, and excitable. Although followed at times by mixed-species flocks, moves so rapidly it sometimes leaves other species behind (Hilty and Brown 1986). Observed in mixed-flocks about half the time (Hilty data). Joins feeding aggregations at fruiting trees.

In Valle, Colombia: Generally foraged from mid to upper levels of forest in the crowns of midsized to tall trees; very rarely descended below 3 m off the ground, rarely in fruiting shrubs. Median foraging height was about 12 m (450 obs.). Ate over 32 species of fruit (80% of 541 obs.). Favored *Miconia* berries (40% of all fruit eaten), *Cecropia* catkins (35%), and *Ficus* fruits (7%). Typically perched on a twig or branch to take small fruits; rarely snatched a berry in flight. Swallowed small berries whole and squeezed out juice or pecked pieces from large fruits. Perched on petioles or hung upside down from catkins to nibble *Cecropia* fruits. Primarily caught insects by aerial sallies (82% of 106 insect-foraging obs.). Often perched near flowers that attract insects and circled out short distances from exposed branches on tree tops, usually landing on a new perch. Also sallied to foliage, and least often, hopped along bare or mossy branches, reaching to pick insects off substrates. (Hilty data.) Stomach contents (2): vegetable and animal matter. One stomach contained 98% seeds (incl. seeds of *Bourreria*) and the wing of a beetle; the other held 40% bee parts, 30% seeds (Ehretiaceae), a pit, and bits of fruit skin.

Vocalizations

Delivers a variety of calls and staccato notes, most commonly a High-pitched thin *chit chup sweeeee*, last note rising. Also gives these notes singly; greets or flies off with a rapid excited series of *chit*s, *sweet*s, and other notes.

Breeding

Mossy cup nests are placed 30–35 m off the ground on heavy moss-covered branches in tall trees (Hilty in litt.). One individual was seen taking insects to its nest (Hilty data). Breeding dates: Colombia Dec–Feb, July, and Aug.

Sources

Primary Hilty data; Hilty and Brown 1986; Lehmann 1957; Ridgely 1976. **Weight (n = 10)** Hilty and Simon 1977; LSUMZ data. **Stomach contents** Wetmore, Pasquier, and Olson 1984. **Vocalizations** LNS recording by Parker (1); Hilty and Brown 1986; Robbins, Parker, and Allen 1985. **Nests and breeding dates** Hilty *in litt.*; Hilty and Brown 1986.

Tangara mexicana 168
Turquoise Tanager
Plate 24

T. m. brasiliensis: length 14 cm (5½ in.); weight 26 g. *Remaining races*: length 12 cm (5 in.); weight 20 g (17.0–23.5 g). Five subspecies: *mexicana*, *boliviana*, and *brasiliensis* are illustrated; *media* most resembles *mexicana*, and *vieilloti* most resembles *boliviana*. The population in Amazonian Brazil east of the Rio Negro and Rio Madeira is intermediate in plumage between *mexicana* and *boliviana*.

Geographic Range

T. m. vieilloti: TRINIDAD. *T. m. media*: VENEZUELA from e Sucre southward through Delta Amacuro to se Bolívar and thence westward though n Bolívar to n Amazonas and adjacent COLOMBIA in e Vichada. *T. m. mexicana*: THE GUIANAS and Amapá, BRAZIL (Novaes 1978). *T. m. boliviana*: the Amazon Basin from COLOMBIA in w Meta and the Río Guaviare southward through e ECUADOR and e PERU to Santa Cruz, BOLIVIA, and eastward in BRAZIL to the Rio Negro and Rio Madeira. *T. m. mexicana* x *boliviana* (sometimes referred to as *T. m lateralis*): Amazonian BRAZIL east of the Rio Negro and Rio Madeira to Pará, extreme w Goiás (sight, Ridgely *fide* Brown *in litt.*), and c Mato Grosso. *T. m. brasiliensis*: coastal BRAZIL from extreme s Bahia southward to Rio de Janeiro.

Elevational Range

Lowlands mostly below 500 m; to ca. 1000 m in Venezuela and Peru.

Habitat and Behavior

Lives in trees in a wide variety of semiopen habitats: forest and woodland edge, tree-studded clearings, tall second growth, shaded plantations, and parks and gardens. Also found inside *varzea* forest, open woodland, and ribbons of gallery forest that

Tangara mexicana

weave through sc Brazilian savannas. In densely forested regions, favors edges of rivers and oxbow lakes (Hilty *in litt.*) and may benefit when forests are disturbed (Willis 1977).

Highly social intraspecifically. Lives in close-knit groups of 3–7, sometimes up to 10, individuals that typically remain apart from mixed-species flocks, but join feeding aggregations at fruiting trees. In s Peru, is a transient in permanent mixed-species canopy flocks and joins temporary tanager flocks (Munn 1985). Travels restlessly through tree tops and across open spaces. Individuals follow each other closely, calling continually in flight; several together make a twittering sound. Active while foraging but perches quietly atop tall trees between feeding sessions.

In Trinidad: Foraged at all levels except on the ground; showed some preference for higher levels when searching for insects. Foraged for insects (47% of 433 feeding records) about as often as fruit (53%). Took 26 species of fruit favoring *Miconia* berries (31% of all fruit-eating obs.); also ate fruits of *Cecropia* (13%), *Ficus* (10%), and *Ilex* (8%). Perched to pick fruit and berries; swallowed small fruits whole and mashed or pecked pieces out of larger ones. Typically sought insects on undersides of (frequently dead) branches, mostly 1.3 cm in diam. or less (91% of 201 insect-foraging records). Also searched foliage and flower and seed heads;

and aerial sallied. (Snow and Snow 1971.)
   Foraging observations from Peru (Parker and Remsen data) are generally consistent with these data from Trinidad; insect searching has been noted most frequently; usually searches for insects on bare branches in crowns of tall (20–30 m) trees; sometimes descending to midheights. In se Brazil, favored buds of the pea family (Leguminosae) as well as melastome berries; also ate guava fruits and bananas (Descourtilz 1852); ate *Cecropia* and tore off pieces of ripe orange (Sick 1985). Stomach contents: vegetable matter (3); animal matter (1). Contents included fruit and small insects. Additional stomach contents included mistletoe berries.

Vocalizations

Outside of se Brazil, utters thin, Highpitched *tic* notes that are often rapidly repeated or trilled. In se Brazil (*brasiliensis*), delivers notes that are high-pitched and strident, a repeated *tzri, tsic* (rendered in Portuguese), like the squeak of a bat (Sick 1985).

Breeding

During the breeding season in Trinidad, pairs apparently break away from their foraging flock to build their nest and to incubate, but rejoin flocks when eggs hatch. At 2 nests, young were attended and fed by all members of the foraging flock from the time they hatched until independence. (Snow and Collins 1962.)
   The female, attended closely by her mate, builds the deep cup nest, constructed of moss and fibers and covered with lichens and leaves. In Trinidad, 2 nests were built 6 and 7.5 m off the ground, one in the upright fork of a mango tree (Belcher and Smooker 1937). In Suriname, said to place its nest on tree branches usually at great heights (Haverschmidt 1968). In se Brazil, one nest was set in the fork of 4 branches in the crown of a dense shrub (Weid 1830). Selected the highest and best concealed site in a large aviary (Ingels 1974b). Eggs (2–3) are usually grayish, marked with white or green and brown or purple. In the aviary, the incubation period was 12–14 days; both parents appeared to feed the young (Ingels 1974b). Breeding dates: Colombia Feb and Oct. Trinidad April–Oct. Suriname Feb–April and Aug. Brazil (Pará) Nov.

Sources

Primary Descourtilz 1852; Haverschmidt 1968; Hilty and Brown 1986; Isler data; Novaes 1973; Pearson 1969, 1975a; Snow and Snow 1971; Snow and Collins 1962; Terborgh and Weske 1969; Willis 1977. **Weights** (*brasiliensis* n = ?; remaining races n = 35): Dick, McGillivray, and Brooks 1984; ffrench 1973; Haverschmidt 1948, 1968; LSUMZ data; Pearson 1971; Sick 1985; Snow and Snow 1971. **Stomach contents** Beebe 1909; Haverschmidt 1968; LSUMZ data; Pelzeln 1869. **Vocalizations** LNS recordings by Bierregaard (2); Isler (1); Hilty and Brown 1986; Sick 1985. **Nests, eggs, and breeding dates** Belcher and Smooker 1937; ffrench 1973; Hilty and Brown 1986; Ingels 1974b; Pinto 1953; Remsen *in litt.*; Wied 1830.

Tangara chilensis **169**
Paradise Tanager
Plate 24

Length 12–13 cm (5–5½ in.). Weight (*paradisea*) 17 g (16.0–17.0 g); (*chlorocorys* and *chilensis*) 23 g (17.0–27.0 g). Four subspecies: *chilensis* and *paradisea* are illustrated; *chlorocorys* resembles *chilensis* and *coelicolor* resembles *paradisea*. Colors, especially of lower backs and rumps, are less intense in subadult plumages.

Geographic Range

T. c. coelicolor and *paradisea*: from Meta and Vaupés, COLOMBIA, and nw BRAZIL from the upper Rio Negro eastward through s VENEZUELA (Bolívar and Amazonas) and THE GUIANAS (except coastal region) to BRAZIL north of the Amazon River from e Amazonas (Manaus area) to Amapá. *T. c. chlorocorys* and *chilensis*: east of the Andes from Caquetá and Amazonas, COLOMBIA, southward through ECUADOR and PERU to Santa Cruz, BOLIVIA, and eastward through sw Amazonas and Rondônia, BRAZIL, to extreme se Amazonas and wc Mato Grosso (Willis 1976).

Elevational Range

Lowlands to ca. 1100 m; locally to 1400 m.

Habitat and Behavior

In lowlands, inhabits the canopy of terra firma and low-lying (incl. *varzea*) forest and second-growth woodland; also frequently encountered at forest edge, in shaded plantations, and in clearings with scattered trees. Occurs locally in scrubby forest with poor soil conditions on lower Andean slopes in Peru (O'Neill *in litt.*). Highly gregarious. Groups of 3–15, mostly 5–10, individuals travel independently, but are often encountered in company with other birds. Appears to be the leader of temporary tanager flocks (see Munn 1985), but seems to move in and

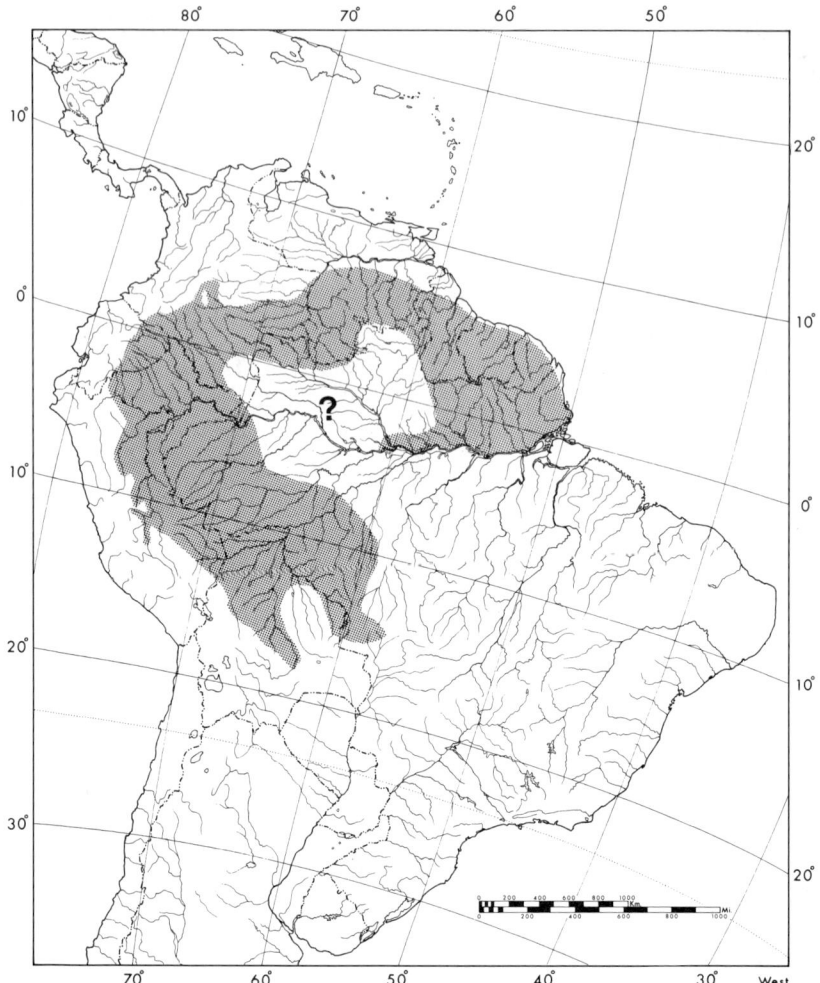

Tangara chilensis

out of canopy mixed-species flocks rapidly (Parker *in litt.*). Joins feeding aggregations at fruiting trees. Observed bathing in water collected in *Cecropia* leaves (O'Neill *in litt.*).

Within forest, forages primarily in the upper canopy (25–50 m above the ground), rarely under 12 m. Feeds lower in fruiting trees and tall shrubs at forest edge and in clearings. Observed eating melastome fruits including *Miconia* (Parker *in litt.*) and fruits of *Aralia* (Descourtilz 1852). Hops along bare branches, looking underneath; also peers into bromeliads and nearby foliage. In Peru, all of 13 insect-foraging observations involved leaning down to glean the undersides of branches and lianas 2.5 cm or less in diam.; in one instance, a fleeing insect was pursued (Remsen data). Stomach contents: vegetable matter (10); animal matter (1); both (1). Contents included fruit pulp and insects. Additional stomach contents included seeds, fly larvae, short-horned grasshoppers, and spiders.

Vocalizations

Utters a sharp Moderate-pitched *chak* and a High-pitched thin upward-inflected *zeee*; each may be given alone or repeated; or the 2 types of notes may be given together, e.g., *chak zeee*, *chak zee-a-zee*, or *zeee chak-chak-chak*. Dawn song: the phrase *chak-zeee* given regularly, about 1 phrase/2 sec. (Parker, LNS). Also delivers a thin High-pitched *sizit* given

Tangara fastuosa

singly or in rapid chipping series (which may be a song); also uttered when taking flight.

Breeding

Two eggs from Guyana (said to be of this species) are white or greenish white, marked lilac and purplish red, especially around the large end (Ogilvie-Grant 1912).

Sources

Primary Hilty and Brown 1986; Munn 1985; O'Neill 1974; Parker data; Parker, Parker, and Plenge 1982; Pearson 1971; Sick 1985; Taczanowski 1884b; Terborgh and Weske 1969; Willis 1977. **Weights** (*paradisea* n = 4; remaining races n = 17): Dick, McGillivray, and Brooks 1984; LSUMZ data; Pearson 1971. **Stomach contents** Foster data; Haverschmidt 1968; LSUMZ data; Taczanowski 1884b. **Vocalizations** LNS recordings by Bierregaard (1), Munn (1), Parker (6), van den Berg (2); Hilty and Brown 1986; Sick 1985. **Eggs** Ogilvie-Grant 1912.

Tangara fastuosa   **170**
Seven-colored Tanager
Plate 24

Length 13 cm (5 in.). Monotypic.

Geographic Range

Ne BRAZIL in Pernambuco and Alagoas.

Elevational Range

Lowlands to at least 850 m (LSUMZ data).

Habitat and Behavior

Inhabits forest (incl. *varzea* forest) and bushy second growth. Associates with mixed-species flocks. Seen in the topmost branches of a large tree (Forbes 1881). Often trapped as a cage bird, and its existence may be threatened. "Pugnacious" in the aviary (Ingels 1974a), and in captivity, performed anting (Whitaker 1957). Stomach contents (1): vegetable matter.

Vocalizations

Delivered *it-it-it-it* (rendered in Portuguese) in a dispute between males (Sick 1985).

Breeding

No information.

Sources

Primary Forbes 1881; Lamm 1948; Sick 1985.
Stomach contents LSUMZ data.

Tangara seledon   **171**
Green-headed Tanager
Plate 24

Length 13 cm (5 in.). Weight 18 g (16.0 and 20.0 g). Monotypic. Individuals in subadult plumage are encountered often; probably breeds in subadult plumage.

Geographic Range

Coastal regions in se BRAZIL from c Bahia (sight, Ridgely *fide* Brown *in litt.*) southward to extreme ne Rio Grande do Sul (Belton 1974, 1985) and inland from Paraná and Santa Catarina, BRAZIL, through Misiones, ARGENTINA, to Canendiyu (sight, Ridgely *fide* Brown *in litt.*), Alto Paraná and Itapúa (Foster data), PARAGUAY.

Elevational Range

Lowlands to ca. 900 m (Mt. Itatiaia); more abundant at low elevations.

Habitat and Behavior

Inhabits forest, second growth, forest edge, plantations, parks, and fruit trees in cultivated areas and near village houses. May move seasonally between forest and semi-open areas. Absent from remnant woodlots studied in São Paulo state (Willis 1979). Lives in family groups and larger single-species flocks of 6–12, occasionally up to 20, individuals. Flocks are encountered alone or in association with other tanagers. Hops actively among branches and frequently flies from tree to tree.

Forages from midheights to the canopy (ca. 9–25 m up) in the forest (Parker data), lower at edges and in fruit trees around houses, plantations, and orchards. Eats cultivated fruits such as oranges, bananas, and figs as well as wild fruits and berries, including those *Hamelia, Urtica*, and bromeliads. Comes to feeding trays for papaya. Typically searches for insects by hopping along slender to medium-sized bare branches. Versatile and acrobatic, getting into a variety of postures to look for insects including caterpillars and other larvae. Gleans leaves and branch surfaces and examines bark, lichens, or crevices that might be hiding prey. Stomach contents: vegetable matter (5); animal matter (1). Contents included fruit and ants.

In Paraguay when eating 7–10 mm fruits of *Allophyllus edulis*: Fed mostly inside crowns of trees. Remained in a tree for 2 min. or less on a typical visit. Perched and reached out to pluck fruits. While sometimes swallowed whole, fruits were more often manipulated with the bill to remove seeds or perhaps to soften pulp. Occasionally placed fruit against a branch to eat it. (Foster data.)

Vocalizations

Calls: a High-pitched *zweet*, slightly upward-inflected and slightly buzzy; sometimes shortened and followed by Moderate-pitched notes, e.g., *ZWEE-dit, ZWEE-dit-see*, or *ZWEE-di-di-di-dit*, or by a short twittering. Dawn song: repeats without pause *SIT sir ZWEET*, the last note like the call; delivered at a rate of about 90 notes/min. One individual sang from the crown of a 10 m high tree, turning from side to side while perched diagonally with bill pointed toward the ground. (Parker, LNS.)

Breeding

Builds a compact cup nest made of grass and leaves and lined with soft material, e.g., corn tassels or feathers. Hides it within dense foliage of trees or shrubs, in bromeliads on tree trunks (once, ca. 10 m up), among epiphytic orchids that cover tree limbs, or 2–3 m up in banana trees between the trunk and leaf stalks or among hanging green bananas. Both sexes collect nesting materials and build the nest.

Eggs (3, once 2) are white or flesh, marked with various shades of brown or dark gray, especially at the large end. Al-

Tangara seledon

though the young are said to develop quite rapidly in the wild (Bertoni 1901), in captivity, the incubation period was 17 days, the young left the nest after 30–35 days, and fledglings were fed by parents for 75 days (Norgaard-Olesen 1973). At one nest (in the wild), only the female fed the nestlings while the male stood guard nearby. In the aviary for the first few days after hatching, the female fed the nestlings with food fed to her by the male. In the wild, usually rears a second brood, often in a second nest (Vigil 1973); fledglings from both broods accompany their parents throughout most of their first year. Breeding dates: Brazil (Rio de Janeiro) Nov, Dec, and Feb. Paraguay Nov and Dec.

Sources

Primary Bertoni 1901; Descourtilz 1852; Euler 1900; Foster data; Mitchell 1957; Parker data; Sick 1985; Vigil 1973; Weid 1830. **Weights (n = 3)** Bertoni 1901; Sick 1985. **Stomach contents** Foster data; Hempel 1949. **Vocalizations** LNS recordings by Parker (4); Goeldi 1894; Snethlage and Schreiner 1929. **Nests, eggs, and breeding dates** Bertoni 1901; Euler 1867; Goeldi 1894; Nehrkorn 1899; Parker data; Snethlage and Schreiner 1929; Vigil 1973.

Tangara cyanocephala 172
Red-necked Tanager
Plate 24

Length 13 cm (5 in.). Three subspecies: primarily vary in head colors and extent of throat patch, but plumage pattern is consistent. Subadult lacks red on head (Sick 1985).

Geographic Range

T. c. cearensis: Ceará, Brazil. *T. c. corallina*: coastal region of BRAZIL in Pernambuco and Alagoas, possibly southward to nw Bahia. *T. c. cyanocephala*: coastal region of BRAZIL from Espírito Santo southward to ne Rio Grande do Sul; individual records from Canendiyu (sight, Aug 1977—Ridgely), PARAGUAY, and Misiones, ARGENTINA; said to occur in Alto Paraná, PARAGUAY (Bertoni in Zotta 1940).

Elevational Range

Lowlands and foothills to at least 1000 m.

Habitat and Behavior

Forest-based; inhabits forest and forest edge, woodlands, fruiting shrubs in abandoned fields, parks, and scrub (caatinga in the northern portion of its range). Typically lives in small groups of 4 or more individuals that travel alone or with other species, especially other *Tangara* tanagers in the southern portion of its range. Davis (1946) believed it remained in mixed-species flocks only for short periods of time, but Mitchell (1957) thought it might be a nuclear species. Forages at the tops of fruiting trees and lower in berry bushes. Said to favor fruits of pokeweed (*Phytolacca* sp), melastomes, *Urtica*, and myrtle (Descourtilz 1852).

Vocalizations

Frequently utters short High-pitched call notes, including a piercing *seet!* and a soft *sip* randomly delivered but at times speeded up into a short trill (possibly the song).

Breeding

In captivity: Built a deep cup nest made exclusively of grass that was placed 1.8 m above the ground. Eggs (3) were whitish with brown spots, mostly at the large end. The female incubated alone for 12–13 days, but both parents fed the young. The young left the nest after 15 days and were fed by the parents for an additional 3½ weeks. (Norgaard-Olesen 1973.)

Sources

Primary Davis 1945b, 1946; Descourtilz 1852; Forbes 1881; Hamilton 1871; Lamm 1948; Mitchell 1957; Olrog 1959; Parker data; Pinto 1954; Sick and Pabst 1968; Sick 1985. **Vocalizations** LNS recordings by Parker (1); Descourtilz 1852; Sick 1985. **Nests and eggs** Norgaard-Olesen 1973.

Tangara desmaresti 173
Brassy-breasted Tanager
Plate 24

Length 13 cm (5 in.). Weight 19 g (1 male). Monotypic.

Geographic Range

Coastal se BRAZIL from Espírito Santo (Sick 1985) southward to Paraná and westward to Minas Gerais (Sick 1985).

Elevational Range

Mountains to 2200 m; mostly 800–1800 m.

Habitat and Behavior

Inhabits forest, forest edge, second growth, and plantations. Appears to be partially migratory in Espírito Santo (Sick 1985). Encountered in pairs, families, and groups of 6–12 individuals (Parker data). Frequently joins mixed-species flocks, but perhaps only for short periods of time (Davis 1946). Constantly on the move, fluttering from branch to branch. Observed anting (Sick 1985).

Forages for fruit and insects primarily in the crowns of trees. Very agile while insect-foraging; often hops along slender branches within foliage near the ends of limbs; seems to prefer small-leaved trees. Of 41 observations, gleaned leaves while perched (16), sallied to foliage (8) or to air (7), and scanned and picked at lichens and mosses (8); occasionally worked along using the diagonal-lean method (Parker data). Stomach contents (1): vegetable matter. Said to favor fruits including those of melastomes, *Urtica*, and myrtle (Descourtilz 1852).

Vocalizations

Call note, probably flock contact: a High-pitched, thin but emphatic *tseee* or abrupt *tsit!*, occasionally repeated rapidly in a short series. Also emits a gravelly Moderate-pitched chittering. (Parker, LNS.) Groups come together at times in noisy congregations (Sick 1985).

Tangara cyanocephala

Breeding

The cup nest is deep, well-lined, and typically placed at the tip of a branch, for example in an araucaria tree (Sick 1985). In captivity: In courtship display, raised bill and feathers, vibrated wings, and appeared to beg for food. The nest was built by the female, but the male brought nesting material. Eggs (3) were whitish, speckled with fine gray spots. The female, occasionally fed by the male, incubated the eggs alone for 12–13 days. (Steinbacher 1938.)

Sources

Primary Davis 1945b, 1946; Descourtilz 1852; Holt 1928; Parker data; Pinto 1951; Sick 1985. **Weights (n = 1)** LSUMZ data. **Stomach contents** Hempel 1949. **Vocalizations** LNS recordings by Parker (3). **Nests and eggs** Sick 1985; Steinbacher 1938.

Tangara cyanoventris 174
Gilt-edged Tanager
Plate 24

Length 13 cm (5 in.). Weight 20 g. Monotypic.

Geographic Range

Se BRAZIL from s Bahia (one record from n Bahia), Espírito Santo, and s Minas Gerais southward to São Paulo.

Tangara desmaresti

Elevational Range

Lowlands to at least 1200 m; mostly 500–1000 m.

Habitat and Behavior

Inhabits forest, tall second growth, and reverted clearings. Encountered in pairs and groups of up to 8 or more individuals; occurs in mixed-species flocks. Several members of a group appeared to be anting (Sick 1957a). Forages from midheights to the canopy, also in low bushes; searches for insects by gleaning small leaves and looking under slender branches; occasionally probes curled green leaves; observed in fruiting melastomes (Parker data). Also said to eat fruit of *Urtica* (Descourtilz 1852).

Vocalizations

Abrupt notes, given singly or in a series, include a High-pitched *tsit* or *seet!* that sometimes drops into a Moderate-pitched chittering or churring and a *chip* or *chup* that sometimes turns into a short burst of similar churring. (Parker, LNS.)

Breeding

In Rio de Janeiro, a pair, building a nest 12 m off the ground in the fork of a tree, appeared to be lining the nest with bamboo strips (Parker data). Young birds of a previ-

Tangara cyanoventris

ous brood have been observed helping at the nest (Sick 1985). Breeding dates: Rio de Janeiro Nov.

Sources

Primary Erickson and Mumford 1976; Holt 1928; Mitchell 1957; Parker data; Pinto 1951; Sick 1985; Wied 1830. **Weights** (n = 1?) Sick 1985. **Vocalizations** LNS recording by Parker (1). **Nests and breeding dates** Parker data.

Tangara johannae **175**
Blue-whiskered Tanager
Plate 25

Length 13 cm (5 in.). Monotypic.

Geographic Range

The Pacific slope from w Antioquia (Mutatá, Haffer 1975) and c Chocó, COLOMBIA, southward to Pichincha (Ridgely *in litt.*), ECUADOR; one record from Los Ríos (ANSP), ECUADOR.

Elevational Range

Lowlands to 700 m (Hilty and Brown 1986).

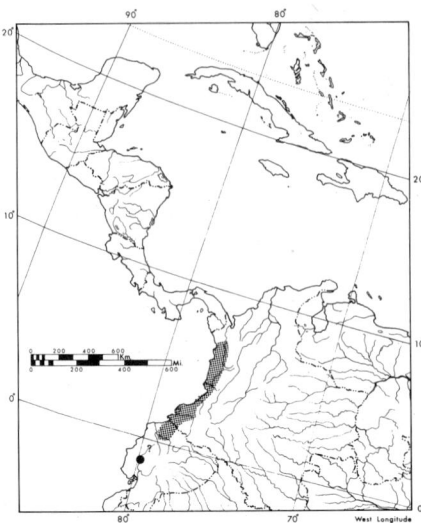

Tangara johannae

having the crown green (Parrot Green) spotted black and the rump green slightly suffused yellow.

Geographic Range

T. s. schrankii: east of the Andes from Caquetá and Vaupés, COLOMBIA, southward through e ECUADOR, e PERU, and BOLIVIA along the base of the Andes to w Santa Cruz (Remsen, Traylor, and Parkes in press), and eastward south of the Amazon River through Acre and Amazonas, BRAZIL, to extreme e Amazonas and the vicinity of the Rio Aripuaná in extreme nw Mato Grosso (Novaes 1976). *T. s. venezuelana*: s VENEZUELA in e Amazonas and s Bolívar.

Elevational Range

Lowlands to ca. 1200 m, as high as 1650 m in Peru (LSUMZ); 300–900 m in Venezuela (Meyer de Schauensee and Phelps 1978).

Habitat and Behavior

Inhabits humid terra firma and low-lying (incl. *varzea*) forest and forest edge; wanders to tall trees in nearby coffee plantations and clearings. Typically encountered in pairs and groups of up to 8 individuals that travel through the canopy with mixed-species flocks; occurs as a transient in permanent canopy flocks and associates with temporary tanager flocks (Munn 1985). Also regularly joins insectivorous understory flocks, following them through the upper understory (Munn and Terborgh 1979).

Forages mostly from mid to upper levels of trees (generally above 8 m off the ground) but sometimes comes lower. In Bolivia, usually hunted for insects in dense foliage on outer limbs; picked prey from leaves (18 obs.), primarily off undersides with acrobatic maneuvers (9), without acrobatics (7), or by hovering (2); also sallied to air and hung to glean a branch (Remsen data). In Peru, of 6 insect-foraging observations, gleaned the undersides of slim branches (3), hung to glean the undersides of very large leaves (2), and once gleaned the upperside of a leaf stem (Remsen data). Also in Peru, gleaned dead branches (Isler data, 3 obs.) and hover-gleaned the tip of a palm frond (Parker data). Occasionally searches dead leaves (Remsen and Parker 1984). Stomach contents: vegetable matter (14); animal matter (2); both (1). Contents included fruit, seeds, and insects.

Vocalizations

No information.

Habitat and Behavior

Within wet forest, encountered in areas of forest regrowth around landslides, road edges, and slashed clearings (Hilty *in litt.*). Rather scarce; seems to occur at low population densities. Travels with mixed-species flocks and exploits fruiting trees (Haffer 1975). Takes insects from slender branches using the diagonal-lean method (Hilty and Brown 1986).

Vocalizations

Call note: a shrill buzzy high-pitched *tzzeee* (Hilty and Brown 1986).

Breeding

In Colombia in January, a cup nest was found on a high mossy limb (Hilty and Brown 1986).

Sources

Primary Haffer 1967b, 1975; Hilty and Brown 1986. **Vocalizations** Hilty and Brown 1986. **Nests and breeding dates** Hilty and Brown 1986.

Tangara schrankii **176**
Green-and-gold Tanager
Plate 25

Length 12 cm (4½ in.). Weight 19 g (14.0–23.0 g). Two subspecies. Female and subadult male differ from adult male (illus.) in

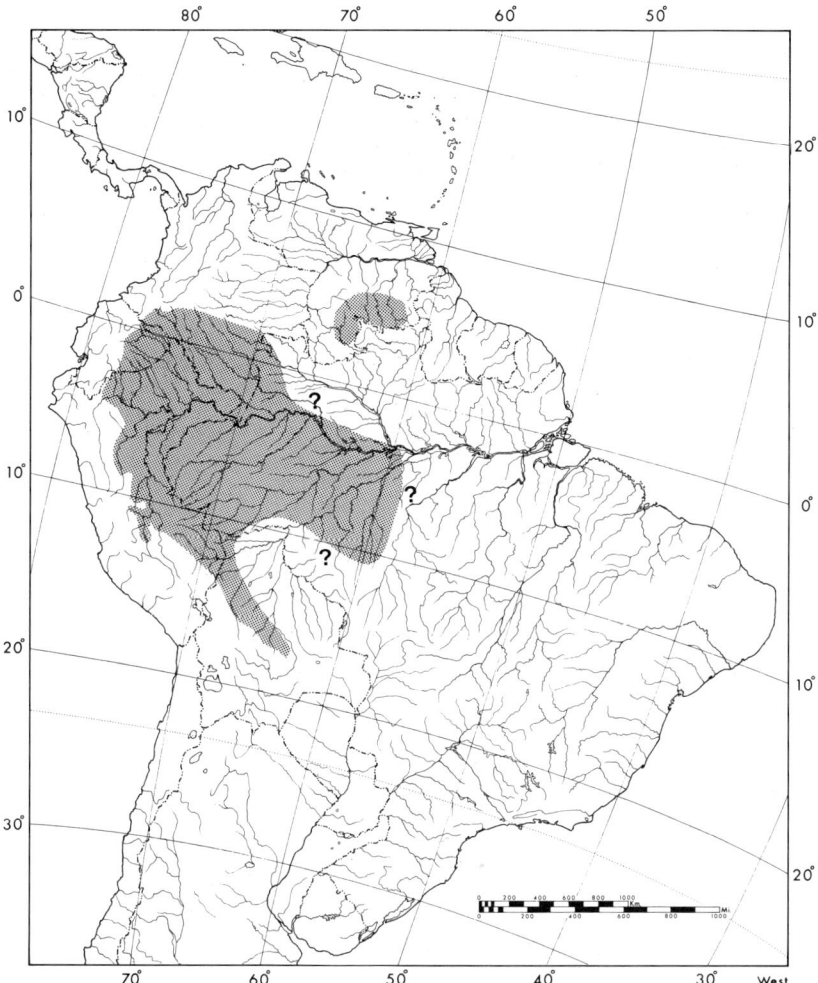

Tangara schrankii

Breeding

In Peru, Schulenberg found a cup nest 2 m off the ground at the base of the first frond of a small palm tree; the nest contained 2 nestlings (LSUMZ data).

Sources

Primary Hilty and Brown 1986; Isler data; Munn and Terborgh 1979; Novaes 1957; Parker data; Parker, Parker, and Plenge 1982; Pearson 1975a; Remsen data; Terborgh and Weske 1969, 1975. **Weights (n = 35)** LSUMZ data; Weske 1972. **Stomach contents** Foster data; LSUMZ data. **Nests** LSUMZ data (Schulenberg).

Tangara florida 177
Emerald Tanager
Plate 25

Length 12 cm (4½ in.). Weight 18 g (16.5–18.5 g). Two subspecies: differences appear to be invalid (Wetmore, Pasquier, and Olson 1984). Plumages of females and subadult males differ from the adult male (illus.) by being duller and by having crowns green and belly less yellow. Subadult males retain this plumage through the first breeding season (Carriker 1910).

Geographic Range

The Caribbean slope in COSTA RICA from s Alajuela (nw side of Volcán Poás) to n Limón (Río Reventazón) and probably southward along the Talamanca Cordillera (Slud 1964); PANAMA on the entire Caribbean slope and on the Pacific slope from c Panamá province (Cerro Azul, USNM) eastward through Darién; on the Pacific slope from s Chocó, COLOMBIA, southward to Esmeraldas (Ridgely *in litt.*) and Pichincha (sight, Ridgely 1980), ECUADOR.

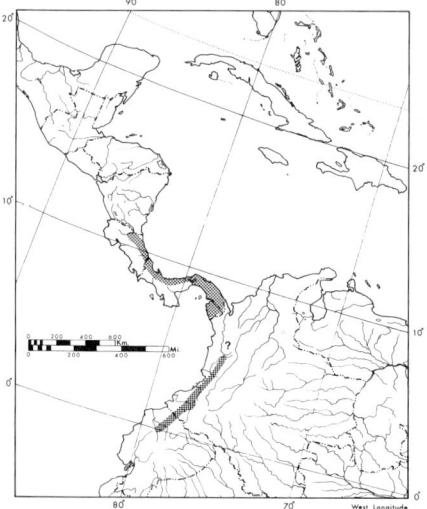

Tangara florida

Elevational Range

Foothills and lower slopes, mostly ca. 500–900 m, as high as 1200 m in Costa Rica and Panama and as low as 100 m in Colombia.

Habitat and Behavior

Inhabits mossy forest and forest edge, sometimes encountered in second growth; rarely strays to isolated fruiting trees or shrubs in open areas adjacent to forest. Single birds, pairs, and small groups of 3–7 individuals typically travel with mixed-species flocks; often seen with the Silver-throated Tanager, *T. icterocephala* **179**. In Costa Rica, may move about seasonally (Slud 1964).

In Valle, Colombia: Typically foraged in the crowns of trees and tall shrubs, but recorded from the undergrowth to the canopy. Median foraging height was about 9 m off the ground. Primarily ate fruit (71% of 468 obs.); over 29 species were taken. Typically perched on twigs or branches and plucked *Miconia* berries (66% of all fruit eaten). Perched on petioles or hung from catkins to take *Cecropia* fruits (10%); also hung from twigs or petioles next to berry clumps such as those of *Ilex* (7%). Ate flowers or flower buds from the melastome *Topobea brachyura* (1% of all feeding records). (Hilty data.)

Also in Valle, habitually hunted for insects in moss in the crowns of trees; foraged well away from the tree trunk but rarely out into foliage. About 95% of 116 observations were on moss-covered rather than bare branches. Typically used the diagonal-lean method to examine mossy undersides of branches mostly 1.3–2.5 cm in diam. (73 out of 97 obs.). Also hung upside down from branches or moss to inspect large hanging moss clumps and moss-filled crotches as well as branch undersides. Occasionally poked head or bill into holes in the moss or tore the moss loose to uncover insects. (Hilty data.)

Observed once at an army ant swarm (*Labidus* sp) foraging 0.3–2.4 m over the swarm (Hilty 1974). Stomach contents (2): seeds and fruit.

Vocalizations

Delivers a sharp *tsit* or a raspy, penetrating *jree* or *dzreee*; repeated randomly or sometimes accelerated into a twitter, possibly when interacting aggressively; Moderate- to High-pitched. Probable song: burry High-pitched *zeeeeeee* notes repeated regularly with 3 sec. pauses and continued for 2–3 min.; sang from a branch about 8 m off the ground on the outer edge of a tree overlooking a deep valley; perched rather upright with head tilted back slightly (Whitney recording).

Breeding

In Colombia, 2 mossy cup nests were found on epiphyte- and moss-covered limbs 8 and 12 m above the ground (Hilty and Brown 1986); one nest contained 2 nestlings. In Costa Rica, a similar nest was found that appeared to be little more than a burrow into heavy moss on a limb, but another nest was a ball of moss with a cup inside that had been built about 1.5 m off the ground in a 3 m high sapling in a clearing surrounded by forest; insects were brought to the latter nest by one adult (Whitney *in litt.*). In Colombia, a pair was seen carrying insects and berries to their nest (Hilty data). Breeding dates: Costa Rica March; Colombia Jan–April.

Sources

Primary Carriker 1910; Hilty data; Hilty and Brown 1986; Ridgely 1976; Slud 1964. **Weights (n = 2)** LSUMZ data. **Stomach contents** LSUMZ data. **Vocalizations** LNS recordings by Parker (2); recording by Whitney (1); Hilty and Brown 1986; Slud 1964. **Nests and breeding dates** Hilty and Brown 1986; Whitney *in litt.*

Tangara arthus 178
Golden Tanager
Plate 25

Length 13 cm (5½ in.). Weight 22 g (18.7–27.5 g). Nine subspecies with obvious differences: *arthus, aurulenta,* and *sophiae* are illustrated; *sclateri* is tinged brown (Antique Brown) throughout underparts; *palmitae* and *occidentalis* resemble *aurulenta; goodsoni, aequatorialis,* and *pulchra* are intermediate between *aurulenta* and *sophiae* in that some (but not all) individuals have a brownish (Tawny) tinge on the throat. *T. a. arthus* of Venezuela may be specifically distinct (Wetmore 1939).

Geographic Range

T. a. arthus: VENEZUELA in the coastal ranges from Miranda and Guárico (Morton 1979) westward to Falcón and nw Lara, and in the Andes from c Lara to Táchira.
T. a. sclateri: COLOMBIA on the w slope of the E Andes in Santander, on the e slope of the E Andes in Boyacá, and in the Macarena Mountains in Meta. *T. a. aurulenta, palmitae,* and *occidentalis*: the Perijá Mountains and all 3 Andean ranges in COLOMBIA except where *sclateri* occurs. *T. a. goodsoni, aequatorialis,* and *pulchra*: ECUADOR on both slopes and the e slope of the Andes in PERU south to Ayacucho (? subspecies, Weske 1972).
T. a. sophiae: e slope of the Andes from Cuzco, PERU, to Cochabamba, BOLIVIA.

Elevational Range

700–2500 m; most numerous 1000–1500 m.

Habitat and Behavior

Inhabits interior of mossy forest and shrubby forest edge; also occurs in second growth and occasionally wanders to isolated trees in clearings near forest. Pairs or single birds, sometimes small groups of up to 5 or 6 individuals, typically accompany mixed-species flocks, especially flocks of other *Tangara* species. In Venezuela (*arthus*), observed in larger groups of up to 30 individuals (Schäfer and Phelps 1954).

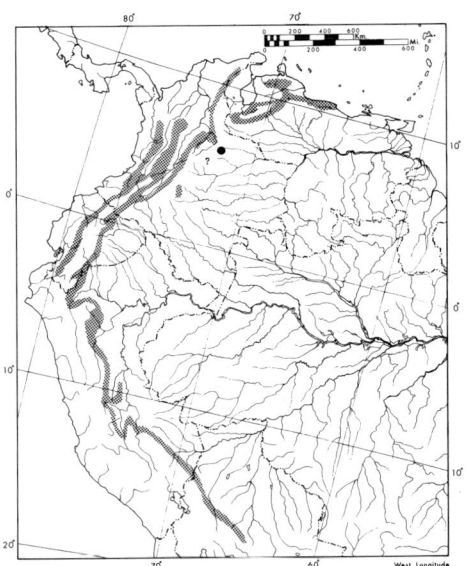

Tangara arthus

In Valle, Colombia: Foraged in the crowns of trees of various heights. Median foraging height was about 10 m off the ground; rarely descended below 3 m. Ate fruit about half the time (57% of 307 obs.); over 22 species were taken. Favored melastome fruits (59% of all fruit eaten), especially *Miconia* berries (89% of all melastomes). Also ate fruits of *Ilex* (13%), *Cecropia* (12%), and *Ficus* (8%). Perched on twigs or branches to pick berries and reached down from petioles to eat *Cecropia* catkins. Occasionally clung to or hung from petioles and fruit clusters to peck pieces out of larger fruits. Ate flowers or parts of flowers from the melastome *Topobea brachyura* (2% of all feeding records). (Hilty data.)

Also in Valle, typically hunted for insects on mossy branches within tree crowns. Moved quickly from branch to branch but hopped slowly along a branch. Used the diagonal-lean or head-down method to deliberately examine the undersides of branches and limbs; 76 of 102 observations were on branches 1.3–5 cm in diam. Searched bare branches only 16% of the time. Occasionally hung from vines, branches, or moss to inspect moss-covered tree trunks or hanging moss clumps. Foraged at times in foliage but only examined twigs and moss and ignored leaves. (Hilty data.)

Foraging observations obtained elsewhere in Colombia, Peru, and Bolivia appear consistent with the data from Valle, Colombia.

Stomach contents: vegetable matter (8); animal and vegetable matter (1). Contents included fruit, seeds, and insects.

Vocalizations

In Venezuela, delivers several varieties of abrupt staccato Moderate-pitched phrases such as *CHID-it, CHID-id-id-it*, or *CHID-id-id-it chup*; usually pausing 2–6 sec. between phrases; during longer pauses (20 or more sec.) utters single sharp Moderate- to High-pitched *tsick* notes (Schwartz, LNS). In Colombia and Bolivia, calls include a penetrating High-pitched *seeeet* and a short *tsk*.

Breeding

In captivity (*aurulenta*): Displays were performed by the male before nest-building and by the female when feeding the young. In display, head is thrown back, wings drooped, and tail slightly raised, accompanied by shriller and shriller cries ending with a trailing note. The male offered nesting material during the nuptial display. Both sexes carried nesting material but only the female built the nest. Eggs (1–2), laid on consecutive days, were white, slightly tinged pink with reddish brown spots that coalesced at the large end. Incubation (14–15 days) was carried out by the female alone. Except for several unsuccessful attempts by the male, the young were fed by the female. During the second rearing, the male frequently perched near the nest to guard it from intruders. (Ciarpaglini 1971.) Breeding dates: Colombia July, Sept, and Oct. Venezuela March.

Sources

Primary Hilty data; Hilty and Brown 1986; Parker data; LSUMZ data; Miller 1963; Remsen data; Ridgely and Gaulin 1980; Wetmore 1939. **Weights (n = 21)** LSUMZ data; Miller 1963; Thomas 1982; Weske 1972. **Stomach contents** LSUMZ data. **Vocalizations** LNS recordings by Schwartz (5); recording by R. A. Rowlett (1); Hilty and Brown 1986. **Eggs and breeding dates** Ciarpaglini 1971; Hilty and Brown 1986; Thomas data.

Tangara icterocephala **179**
Silver-throated Tanager
Plate 25

Length 13 cm (5 in.). Weight 22 g (17.7–24.7 g). Three subspecies: *frantzii* closely resembles *icterocephala* (illus.) but is slightly more dusky; *oresbia* is even more dusky, especially on the throat. Subadult plumage (illus.) is retained through the first breeding season (Carriker 1910).

Geographic Range

T. i. frantzii: both slopes from Guanacaste and Alajuela, COSTA RICA, to Veraguas, PANAMA (Wetmore, Pasquier, and Olson 1984). *T. i. oresbia*: Coclé and w Panamá province, PANAMA. *T. i. icterocephala*: the nw end of the C Andes in Antioquia (USNM), COLOMBIA, and the Pacific slope in e Darién, PANAMA, and from Antioquia, COLOMBIA, southward through COLOMBIA and ECUADOR to Loja.

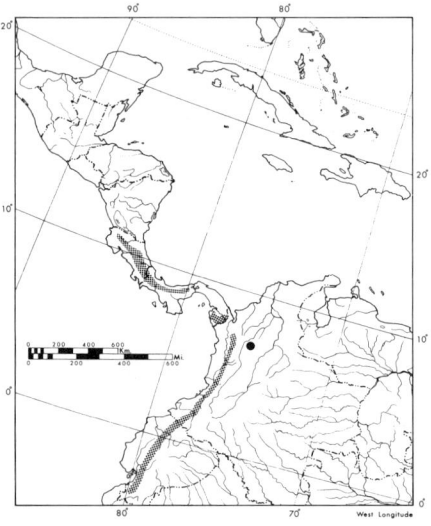

Tangara icterocephala

Elevational Range

Ca. 600–1600 m; occasionally ranges to near sea level or up to 2300 m, especially after the breeding season.

Habitat and Behavior

Inhabits mossy forest and forest edge; also occurs in tall second growth. In Costa Rica, often roams to fruiting trees and shrubs growing in clearings bordered by forest, but in Colombia, rarely strays from forest. Lives alone or in pairs, but is attracted to gatherings of other species and typically accompanies canopy mixed-species flocks or joins feeding aggregations. Many, often 12 or more, Silver-throated Tanagers may occur in the same mixed-species flock. Occasionally travels with montane understory flocks. Very active and restless.

In Valle, Colombia: Foraged mostly in tree and shrub crowns of various heights (78% of 523 obs.). Median foraging height was 8.5 m off the ground (706 obs.); rarely foraged below 3 m. Ate over 32 species of fruit (80% of 758 obs.). Favored melastome fruits (55% of all fruit eaten), especially *Miconia* berries (88% of all melastomes). Typically perched on twigs or branches to pluck small fruits. Perched on, hung upside down from, or clung to petioles, leaves, or catkins to nibble *Cecropia* fruit (21% of all fruit eaten). Rarely clung to larger fruits or berries to peck out pieces, snatched a berry in flight, or ate a flower bud. (Hilty data.)

Also in Valle, hunted for insects (147 obs.) in the outer parts of trees, chiefly on the undersides of thin moss-covered branches 1.3 cm or less in diam. Hopped quickly from branch to branch, but moved in spurts along a branch, stopping to peer deliberately under one side and then the other. Mostly used this diagonal-lean foraging method but also hung or clung to moss clumps, ferns, vines, and stems to obtain prey. Sometimes dug into moss clumps or inspected bromeliads; occasionally searched vines, hanging dead twigs, and bare branches; and rarely hovered or sallied to foliage or branches. (Hilty data.)

The less comprehensive foraging observations available for Costa Rica are generally consistent with data from Colombia; may forage closer to the ground in Costa Rica. Eats fruits of melastomes (Wheelwright et al. 1984) and also commonly takes arillate fruits of the epiphytic vine, *Souroubea guianensis* (Skutch 1980). Stomach contents (3): vegetable matter, including fruit and *Cecropia* seeds.

Hilty (1974) once came across 10 of these tanagers foraging 0.3–2.4 m above an army ant swarm. Avoiding the larger antbirds, several individuals lunged after prey while others appeared to ignore the escaping insects.

Vocalizations

While foraging and in flight, frequently utters distinctive harsh buzzy flat Moderate-pitched *jjeut* or a High-pitched, insectlike *bzeeet*, slightly upward-inflected; also a High-pitched *tic*. Notes may be paired but are not run into series.

Breeding

In Costa Rica: Probably nests often in forest, but the nests (13) discovered were all located in isolated trees growing in dooryards, pastures, or above mountain streams 1.8–10.7 m off the ground. These were bulky cups of mostly moss and leaves and bound with cobweb and were usually hidden on mossy branches among foliage. Females constructed the nests alone, but males sometimes brought material and helped shape the nest. At all nests, females were attended and often fed by their mates. Eggs (2), usually laid on consecutive days, were dull white or grayish, rather heavily mottled all over with brown concentrated on the large end. Only the female incubated; at one nest the incubation period was 14 days. Both parents fed the nestlings. The young appeared to separate from their parents as soon as they could take care of themselves. (Skutch 1954.) Breeding dates: Costa Rica March–Sept. Panama Feb. Colombia Feb, April, and Oct.

Sources

Primary Buskirk 1976; Carriker 1910; Hilty data; Hilty and Brown 1986; Moynihan 1962c; Powell 1979; Ridgely 1976; Skutch 1954; Slud 1964. **Weights (n = 61)** Hartman 1955; Hartman and Brownell 1961; LSUMZ data; Oniki 1972; Strauch 1977. **Stomach contents** LSUMZ data; Salvin and Godman 1879–1904. **Vocalizations** LNS recordings by Morton (1); Parker (1), van den Berg (2); recording by Whitney (1); Hilty and Brown 1986; Skutch 1954; Slud 1964. **Nests, eggs, and breeding dates** Hilty and Brown 1986; Skutch 1954; Wetmore, Pasquier, and Olson 1984.

Tangara xanthocephala 180
Saffron-crowned Tanager
Plate 25

Length 13 cm (5 in.). Weight 19 g (15.0–23.6 g). Three subspecies: *venusta* and *lamprotis* are illustrated; *xanthocephala* is intermediate.

Geographic Range

T. x. venusta: the Andes of VENEZUELA from s Lara to Táchira; the Perijá Mountains; COLOMBIA in all 3 Andean ranges (locally in the E Andes and on the Amazonian slope) and the Macarena Mountains; both slopes in ECUADOR; and the e Andean slope in PERU from Cajamarca to n Pasco. *T. x. xanthocephala*: the e Andean slope in s Pasco and n Junín (Chanchamayo region), PERU. *T. x. lamprotis*: the e Andean slope from Ayacucho (LSUMZ) and Cuzco,

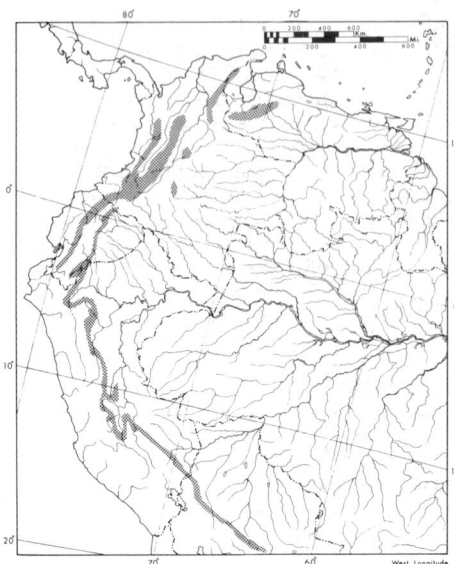

Tangara xanthocephala

PERU, to w Santa Cruz (Remsen, Traylor, and Parkes in press), BOLIVIA.

Elevational Range

1100–2600 m (one record at 3150 m in Colombia); most numerous above 1500 m.

Habitat and Behavior

Inhabits forest, especially forest edge, and tall second growth; also occurs in shaded plantations and scattered trees in open areas near forest. Pairs and groups of 3–10 individuals generally travel with other canopy birds, especially other *Tangara* species.

Forages for fruit at all heights (Remsen and Hilty data, 25 obs.). Eats mostly small (<5 mm, Remsen data) fruits including *Miconia* berries and other melastomes, *Cecropia* fruits, and mulberries (*Morus* spp). Normally picks fruit while perched upright. The most frugivorous *Tangara* found at one location in Huila, Colombia (Ridgely and Gaulin 1980). Searches for insects high in trees, sometimes lower at forest edge. Inspects slender mossy branches (median diam. ca. 2.5 cm, Remsen and Hilty data, 37 obs.) with the diagonal-lean or head-down method; reaches into mossy clumps on the undersides of branches; sometimes pokes its entire head into moss. Also hops along slender bare or sparsely moss-covered outer branches gleaning branch surfaces, twigs, and occasionally leaves. Stomach contents: vegetable matter (13); vegetable and animal matter (2). Contents included fruit pulp, berries, seeds, and insects.

Vocalizations

Call note (*venusta*): a crisp High-pitched *chit* or *tsit* repeated at short intervals (Parker, LNS).

Breeding

In s Peru, a nest containing 2 eggs was found 12 m above the ground in a clump of moss hanging from the underside of the lowest branch of a 20 m tree about 0.7 m from the trunk (Schulenberg, LSUMZ data). Breeding dates: Colombia March. Peru Nov.

Sources

Primary Hilty data; Hilty and Brown 1986; LSUMZ data; Miller 1963; Parker data; Remsen data; Ridgely and Gaulin 1980; Terborgh and Weske 1975. **Weights (n = 33)** LSUMZ data; Miller 1963. **Stomach contents** LSUMZ data. **Vocalizations** LNS recording by Parker (1). **Nests and breeding dates** LSUMZ data (Schulenberg); Miller 1963.

Tangara chrysotis   181
Golden-eared Tanager
Plate 25

Length 14 cm (5½ in.). Weight 24 g (23.0–25.5 g). Monotypic.

Geographic Range

Upper Magdalena Valley in Huila, COLOMBIA; the e slope of the Andes from w Caquetá, COLOMBIA, southward through ECUADOR and PERU (locally) to Cochabamba, BOLIVIA (see Remsen 1984).

Elevational Range

Recent Peruvian and Bolivian records are in a narrow band ca. 1150–1750 m, but 19th-century records are 760–2100 m (see Remsen 1984). Sight records to 2400 m in Huila, Colombia (Ridgely and Gaulin 1980).

Habitat and Behavior

Inhabits montane forest and forest edge. Appears to occur at low population densities in most parts of its range; perhaps most common in e Ecuador (Ridgely *in litt.*). Usually encountered in pairs or singly, occasionally in a group of 3–4 individuals (Parker *in litt.*). Typically travels with large tanager flocks, especially *Tangara* species. Joins feeding aggregations at fruiting trees. In captiv-

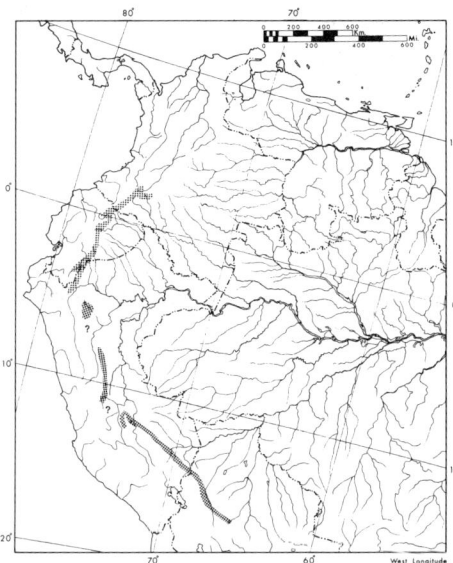

Tangara chrysotis

ity: Ear-covert displays were used most frequently in competitive disputes over food. In display, the head was raised until the bill was almost vertical; the tail may also be raised forming a right angle with the bill. Displayed at close range (0.3 m) and only to birds of its own size. (Ingels 1974c.)

Usually forages from midheights to the crowns of trees. Foraging height in Bolivia was about 10–30 m above the ground and the median height to the top of the canopy was about 1.5 m (Remsen data, 16 obs.). Eats small fruits, especially melastome berries; also *Morus* mulberries (Ridgely and Gaulin 1980). In Peru and Bolivia: Typically hops and creeps somewhat sluggishly along bare or moss-covered branches (2.5–7.6 cm in diam., Remsen data) gleaning insects without acrobatics from moss and bark on upper surfaces; occasionally uses the diagonal-lean method to obtain prey from branch undersides. Also searches dead leaves (Remsen and Parker 1984), and gleans leaves (Parker and Parker 1982). In captivity, searched the vegetation for spiders, moths, and small grasshoppers (Ingels 1974c). Stomach contents (1): small worms and plant material.

Vocalizations

Call note: *tsuck*, lower-pitched than that of most other *Tangara* species (Remsen 1984). In captivity, males sang a hissing piping song or a series of high-pitched rattling notes while raising their ear-coverts.

Breeding

No information.

Sources

Primary Hilty and Brown 1986; Ingels 1974c; LSUMZ data; Norgaard-Olesen 1973; Parker data; Parker and Parker 1982; Remsen data; Remsen 1984; Ridgely and Gaulin 1980; Weske 1972. **Weights (n=4)** LSUMZ data. **Stomach contents** LSUMZ data. **Vocalizations** Ingels 1974c; Norgaard-Olesen 1973; Remsen 1984.

Tangara parzudakii 182
Flame-faced Tanager
Plate 25

Length 14–15 cm (5½–6 in.). Weight (*parzudakii* and *urubambae*) 28 g (25.0–31.0 g). Three subspecies: *parzudakii* and *lunigera* are illustrated; *urubambae* looks like *parzudakii*. Subadult plumage of *parzudakii* differs from the adult in having ear-coverts and forehead orange yellow mixed with blackish and underparts less iridescent green.

Geographic Range

T. p. parzudakii and *urubambae*: sw Táchira, VENEZUELA (west of the Western Venezuelan Low); the w slope of the E Andes in Cundinamarca and the head of the Magdalena Valley in Huila, COLOMBIA; and the e slope of the Andes from Caquetá (sight, Hilty and Brown 1986) and w Putumayo, COLOMBIA, through ECUADOR and PERU to Ayacucho (LSUMZ) and Cuzco. *T. p. lunigera*: the Pacific slope from Risaralda, COLOMBIA, southward through COLOMBIA and ECUADOR to El Oro.

Elevational Range

1000–2600 m; rarely to 700 m on the Pacific slope in Cauca, Colombia. Most numerous above 1500 m.

Habitat and Behavior

Inhabits montane forest and forest edge; also occurs in second growth. Pairs, groups of 3–7 individuals, and single birds travel by themselves or with mixed-species flocks. Sometimes perches quietly for long periods (10–15 min.) in tree tops, looking all around and calling occasionally.

Forages for small fruits and insects mostly in upper levels of forest but also lower in shrubbery along forest edge and in the understory. Reported to eat the fruits of melastomes (incl. the larger fruits) and *Cecropia*.

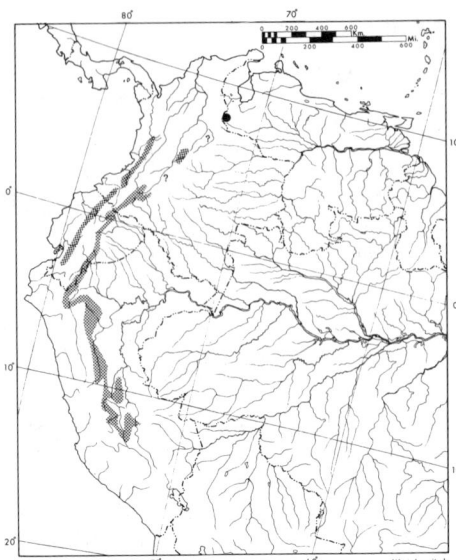

Tangara parzudakii

Tangara xanthogastra 183
Yellow-bellied Tanager
Plate 25

Length 11 cm (4½ in.). Weight 15 g (13.0–18.0 g). Two subspecies.

Geographic Range

T. x. xanthogastra: Bolívar and Amazonas, VENEZUELA (below 750 m); east of the Andes from w Meta and Vaupés, COLOMBIA, southward through e ECUADOR and e PERU, and along the base of the Andes to Cochabamba (Remsen and Ridgely 1980), BOLIVIA; and eastward to c Amazonas, BRAZIL (north of the Amazon River to the upper Rio Negro and the Rio Solimões and south of the Amazon to the middle Rio Juruá and upper Rio Purus). *T. x. phelpsi*: tepuis and mountains of Amazonas and Bolívar, VENEZUELA, above 1000 m.

Elevational Range

T. x. xanthogastra: lowlands and lower slopes to 1350 m (LSUMZ); mostly below 1000 m; 300–750 m in Venezuela. *T. x. phelpsi*: 1000–1800 m.

Habitat and Behavior

T. x. xanthogastra inhabits terra firma and low-lying forest, forest edge, and second growth, and *phelpsi* occurs in montane forest on Venezuelan tepuis. The Yellow-bellied Tanager travels with canopy birds, especially other *Tangara* species, and joins feeding aggregations. Forages mostly in crowns of trees from mid to upper levels of forest. Observed eating melastome fruit, foraging on *Cecropia* catkins and in mistletoe, and searching for insects on leaves and slender branches (Parker data). In Bolivia, picked insects from undersides of leaves by leaning down, reaching up, and hovering (Remsen data, 4 obs.). Stomach contents: vegetable matter (9); animal matter (4). Contents included fruit and caterpillars (one measured 4 cm).

Sometimes hangs upside down from petioles or leaves to pull tiny fruits from *Cecropia* catkins, then perches upright to eat them. Searches slowly and deliberately for insects on moss- or lichen-covered branches inside tree crowns using the diagonal-lean or head-down methods; frequently hangs completely upside down, sometimes for 5 sec. or more, to inspect mossy undersides. Probes into moss clumps; rarely gleans leaves in outer foliage. Stomach contents (8): vegetable matter, including fruit and seeds.

Vocalizations

Call and possible song: sharp High-pitched *chit!* notes that sometimes run into a short twittering trill. Also utters *seeet* notes (Hilty and Brown 1986).

Breeding

Courtship feeding was observed (Ridgely and Gaulin 1980). A pair fed berries to fledglings (Isler data).

Sources

Primary Hilty data; Hilty and Brown 1986; Isler data; LSUMZ data; Parker data; Ridgely and Gaulin 1980. **Weights (n = 21)** LSUMZ data. **Stomach contents** LSUMZ data. **Vocalizations** LNS recordings by Isler (1), Parker (1); Hilty and Brown 1986.

Vocalizations

No information.

Breeding

No information.

Sources

Primary Hilty and Brown 1986; LSUMZ data; Meyer de Schauensee and Phelps 1978; O'Neill 1974; Parker data; Pearson 1969; Remsen data;

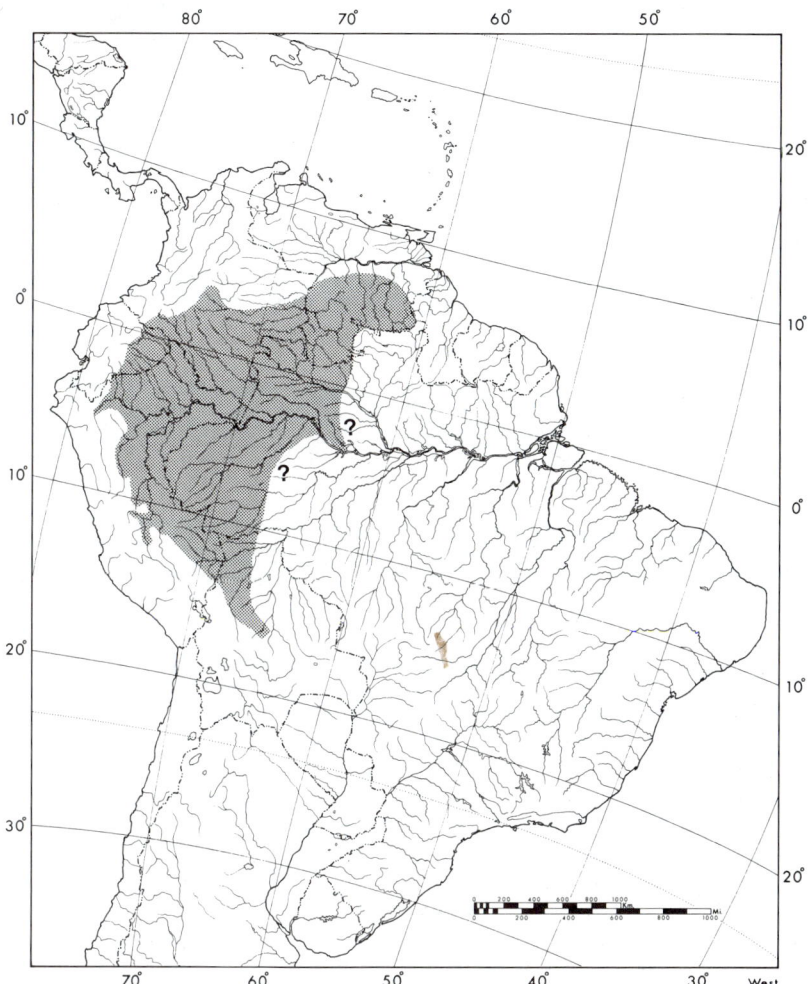

Tangara xanthogastra

Remsen and Ridgely 1980. **Weights (n=17)** LSUMZ data; Pearson 1971. **Stomach contents** Foster data; LSUMZ data.

Tangara punctata 184
Spotted Tanager
Plate 25

Length 11–12 cm (4½–5 in.). Weight 15 g (13.0–17.0 g). Five subspecies.

Geographic Range

T. p. punctata: s VENEZUELA in Bolívar and Amazonas, THE GUIANAS, BRAZIL north of the Amazon River from Amapá westward to the Rio Negro in Amazonas and south of the Amazon in Pará. *T. e. zamorae, perenensis, annectens,* and *punctulata*: the e slope of the Andes from Napo (USNM), ECUADOR, southward through PERU to Cochabamba, BOLIVIA.

Elevational Range

T. p. punctata: from sea level to 1600 m. *Remaining races*: ca. 700–1700 m in foothills and lower Andean slopes.

Habitat and Behavior

Inhabits forest (particularly mossy forest in the Andes, terra firma forest in e Amazonia,

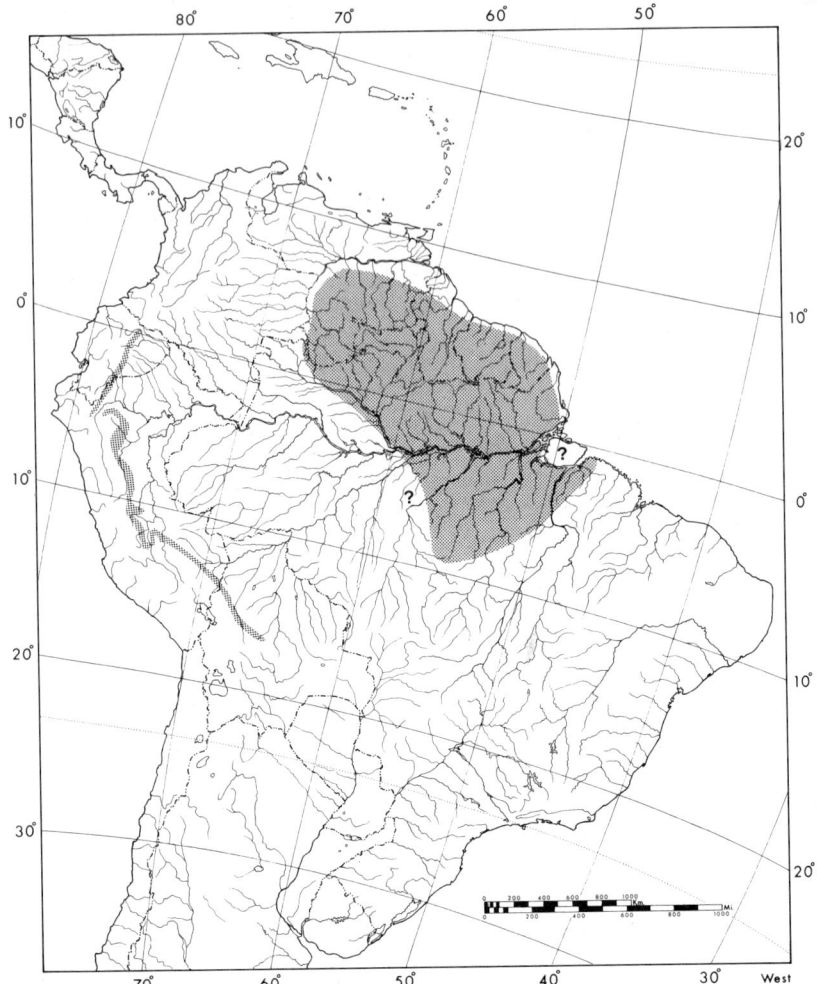

Tangara punctata

and savanna forest in Suriname), forest edge, and nearby second growth. Also occurs in shaded plantations and tree-studded clearings. Said to move about seasonally in n Brazil (Descourtilz 1852). Encountered singly, in pairs, and in small groups of 2–4 individuals; once up to 8 individuals were seen with a large mixed-species flock (Parker data). Travels independently or with other canopy tanagers. Occurs only sporadically with mixed-species flocks in the Manaus area, Brazil (Willis 1977). Joins feeding aggregations at fruiting trees. Perches in the open at times to rest and preen (Beebe 1916).

Forages mostly in the crowns (15–50 m off the ground) of forest trees; only comes lower to obtain fruits (e.g., melastomes) in small trees and tall shrubs. Walks and hops on tops of leaves and along twigs at the very ends of limbs searching small-leaved foliage and flowers (Parker data). Also searches larger leaves (up to 10 x 18 cm) picking prey off top (2 obs.) and bottom (2 obs.) surfaces (Remsen data). Stomach contents: vegetable matter (4); animal matter (1). Contents included fruit pulp, seeds, berries, and a snout beetle.

Vocalizations

Delivers a High-pitched, somewhat dry *chip* in a rapidly repeated staccato manner, then shifts into an evenly pitched, chipping trill (Venezuela) that sometimes has a soft whistled quality (Bolivia); the trill (1–2 sec.

duration) sometimes trails off slightly at the end. (Parker, LNS.)

Breeding

No information.

Sources

Primary Beebe 1916; Haverschmidt 1968; LSUMZ data; Meyer de Schauensee and Phelps 1978; Parker data; Remsen data; Willis 1977. **Weights (n = 17)** Dick, McGillivray, and Brooks 1984; Haverschmidt 1948, 1968; LSUMZ data. **Stomach contents** LSUMZ data; Haverschmidt 1968; Schubart, Aguirre, and Sick 1965. **Vocalizations** LNS recordings by Parker (2).

Tangara guttata   **185**
Speckled Tanager
Plate 25

Length 12 cm (4½ in.). Weight 18 g (15.0–20.5 g). Six subspecies: *tolimae* resembles *bogotensis* (illus.); *eusticta*, *chrysophrys*, *guttata*, and especially *trinitatis* are more yellow on sides of head.

Geographic Range

T. g. eusticta: the Caribbean slope from s Alajuela, COSTA RICA, eastward to e San Blas, PANAMA; and the Pacific slope from San José province, COSTA RICA, locally eastward to e Darién, PANAMA. *T. g. tolimae*: the C Andes in COLOMBIA south to n Tolima (e slope). *T. g. bogotensis*: the E Andes in COLOMBIA from extreme n Norte de Santander (USNM) south to Cundinamarca on the w slope and (perhaps locally) to w Caquetá (sight, Hilty and Brown 1986) on the e slope; the Macarena Mountains; the Perijá Mountains; and the Andes of VENEZUELA from Táchira to s Lara. *T. g. chrysophrys*: VENEZUELA in Falcón (Sierra de San Luis), the coastal range from Yaracuy to Sucre, w and sw Bolívar, and Amazonas south to adjacent BRAZIL (Sierra de Curupira). *T. g. guttata*: VENEZUELA in se Bolívar. *T. g. trinitatis*: TRINIDAD.

Elevational Range

300–2000 m; mostly 700–1500 m; 300–500 m on the Caribbean slope in Panama (Wetmore, Pasquier, and Olson 1984).

Habitat and Behavior

Inhabits forest, forest edge, second growth, trees and shrubs in clearings, and shaded plantations; also occurs in areas of human habitation. In Trinidad, lives mostly inside forest; only 11% of Snow and Snow's (1971) feeding records were in nonforest habitats. In n Venezuela, scarce in forest (Schäfer and Phelps 1954).

Lives in pairs, families, and small groups of up to 6 individuals (to 8 in Trinidad); rarely solitary. Typically accompanies other small birds, especially other *Tangara* species. In Panama, probably not closely integrated in mixed-species flocks (Moynihan 1962c). Joins feeding aggregations at fruiting trees. Very active; constantly on the move. In Costa Rica, appears to roam over a wide area each day in search of food (Skutch 1954). A pair was observed anting (Skutch 1977).

Forages mostly in the canopy but descends to shrubs bearing fruit. In Trinidad, rarely dropped below 3.5 m off the ground; of 96 foraging observations, 74% involved fruit-eating (14 spp) and 26% insect-searching. Plucked small fruits, especially *Miconia* berries (53% of all fruit eaten), from a perched position and swallowed them whole. Also favored fruits of the families Euphorbiaceae and Ulmaceae (together, 36% of all fruit eaten). Took fruit from the ends of slender twigs by edging down the branch head downward. (Snow and Snow 1971.) In Costa Rica, ate 6 species of arillate fruits, especially *Souroubea guianensis* and *Dipterodendron elegans*; swallowed some whole, seed and all, or pecked pieces of aril out of fruits that were too large to swallow or were still attached to capsules (Skutch 1980). Observed eating seeds of *Lantana* (Thomas data). Came to feeding shelves for bananas (Skutch 1954).

Hunts for spiders and insects, including caterpillars, in dense outer foliage. Uses acrobatic maneuvers, but moves deliberately. Typically searches the undersides of leaves (92% of the Snows' insect-foraging obs.) by looking up from a perch, clinging to slender twigs head-down, or hanging upside down from leaves. Also investigates curled dead leaves by hanging head-down. Rarely searches bare branches and tree trunks or sallies to air for insects. Stomach contents: vegetable matter (2); vegetable and animal matter (1). Contents included fruit (incl. *Amaranthus* and *Solanum*) and a beetle.

Vocalizations

Call: a short, clear, High-pitched *tit* or *chit* (sometimes *tit-a-chit*), somewhat bell-like. In another vocalization, call notes are repeated with increasing frequency, becoming almost a trill before ending abruptly; quality is me-

Tangara guttata

tallic and lacking liquidity; delivered chiefly when taking flight (Skutch 1954).

Breeding

In Costa Rica, 5 nests were found 3–7.6 m up among the foliage of isolated trees (4 nests) and in a tall bush. Both sexes constructed the compact open cup, mostly made of leaves and rootlets. Two eggs, laid on consecutive days, were white, marked with brown, especially at the large end. (Other eggs collected in Costa Rica and Venezuela are white to grayish, marked with brown, gray, and purplish red.) Females incubated alone, but mates usually remained nearby; males fed their mates frequently during incubation and nest building. The incubation period was 13 days (2 nests) and the young fledged after 15 days. Both parents fed insects and berries to the nestlings. At one nest, Skutch (1961) observed a third adult attending nestlings; sometimes parents and helper came together to feed the nestlings or the helper came alone. One family group was still together the year following fledging. (Skutch 1954.) Breeding dates: Costa Rica April–June. Panama March. Trinidad Jan, June, and July.

Sources

Primary ffrench 1973; Hilty and Brown 1986; Meyer de Schauensee and Phelps 1978; Ridgely 1976; Schäfer and Phelps 1954; Skutch 1954; Slud 1964; Snow and Snow 1971. **Weights**

Tangara varia

(n = 22) ffrench 1973. **Stomach contents** LSUMZ data; Goldman in Wetmore, Pasquier, and Olson 1984. **Vocalizations** recording by R. A. Rowlett (1); Skutch 1954; Slud 1964. **Nests, eggs, and breeding dates** ffrench 1973; Ginés et al. 1951; Nehrkorn 1899; Ogilvie-Grant 1912; Skutch 1954; Wetmore, Pasquier, and Olson 1984.

Tangara varia **186**
Dotted Tanager
Plate 25

Length 11 cm (4 in.). Weight 10 g. Monotypic.

Geographic Range

VENEZUELA in Amazonas and s Bolívar and in BRAZIL along the Rio Negro and lower Rio Tapajós; 19th-century records from FRENCH GUIANA (type locality) and SURINAME.

Elevational Range

Lowlands below 300 m.

Habitat and Behavior

In Venezuela, inhabits clearings along rivers in rain forest (Meyer de Schauensee and Phelps 1978). In Brazil, scarce; lives in tall forest of tablelands and hillsides, forest edge, clearings, and plantations. Travels regularly with mixed-species flocks. Forages from midlevels to crowns of trees (15–50 m off the ground). Searches branches and foliage for insects and fruit. (Willis 1977.)

Vocalizations

No information.

Breeding

No information.

Sources

Primary Willis 1977. **Weights (n = 1)** Sick 1985.

Tangara rufigula 187
Rufous-throated Tanager
Plate 25

Length 12 cm (4½ in.). Weight 19 g (1 female). Monotypic.

Geographic Range

The Pacific slope from Risaralda, COLOMBIA (below Cerro Tatamá) south to El Oro, ECUADOR (Chapman 1926).

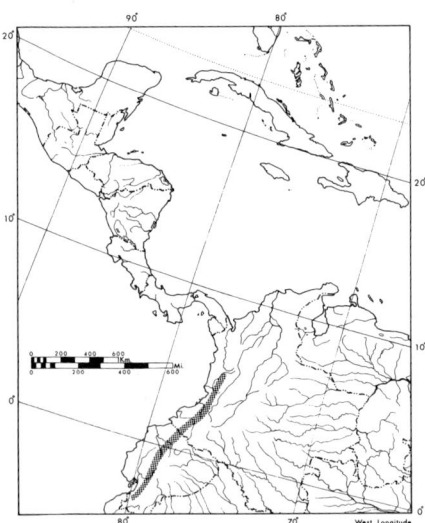

Tangara rufigula

Elevational Range

400–2100 m.

Habitat and Behavior

Inhabits lower montane forest, favoring edges of broken or irregular forest and small openings on steep slopes. Also occurs in forest canopy and second growth. Encountered in pairs and small compact groups of 3–6 individuals, rarely singly. Travels independently or with mixed-species flocks and frequently joins feeding aggregations at fruiting trees. Actively darts about tree crowns in outer foliage, hopping from branch to branch, scampering along twigs and branches, or fluttering among leaves. When resting, often perches in open tree tops.

In Valle, Colombia: Foraged mostly in the crowns of shrubs and trees of various heights. Median foraging height (1100 obs.) was about 9 m off the ground; rarely descended below 3 m (5%). Hunted for fruit at lower levels (median height 8.5 m) than for insects (median height 13.7 m). Ate over 24 species of fruit and berries (73% of 1212 obs.). About two-thirds of all fruit taken were *Miconia* berries; frequently ate green as well as ripe berries. Also favored *Cecropia* catkins (7%) and fruit contained in split open capsules or pods (8%). To obtain fruit, typically perched on twigs or branches but also hung from twigs, leaves, or catkins. Mostly swallowed small fruits whole; rarely pecked at or mashed larger fruits or carried fruit capsules to limbs to pick out contents. Ate pieces of flowers and buds (4% of all feeding records), especially buds of the melastome *Topobea brachyura* (67% of all flowers eaten). Often inspected and pecked at old seed or dried flower heads, possibly looking for insects. (Hilty data.)

Also in Valle, Colombia: Mostly searched for insects on top and bottom leaf surfaces at the ends of twigs in tree crowns. Acrobatic; especially fond of inspecting leaves by extending legs and stretching out neck to peer over upper leaf surfaces or by hanging upside down from twigs or petioles to look at undersides. Often hunted over large leaves, sometimes walking on tree top leaves. Frequently sallied to air (26% of all insect-foraging) or sallied to or hovered at leaf surfaces (10%). Sometimes searched upper surfaces of (mostly bare) branches by slanting body forward as if to fly, squatting slightly, and cocking head from side to side. Inspected spider webs for insects. Visible prey included caterpillars and other larvae and flying termites. (Hilty data.)

Vocalizations

Utters excited bursts of ticking and twittering *tic-ti-ti-ti-ti* . . . , especially as one or several closely follow each other across clearings (Hilty and Brown 1986).

Breeding

In Colombia, two moss cups were found 10 and 18 m above the ground; one was in a hanging epiphyte (Hilty and Brown 1986). Hilty (data) observed a male feeding an insect to a female. Breeding dates: Colombia Aug and Sept.

Sources

Primary Hilty data; Hilty and Brown 1986. **Weights (n = 1)** LSUMZ data. **Vocalizations** Hilty and Brown 1986. **Nests and breeding dates** Hilty and Brown 1986.

Tangara gyrola 188
Bay-headed Tanager
Plate 26

Length 12 cm (5 in.). Weight 21 g (17.5–26.5 g). The nine subspecies differ in color combinations of underparts (green to blue), rumps (green to blue), lesser coverts (green, golden yellow, or cinnamon-rufous) and the widths of golden bands between nape and upper back. Colors of individuals sometimes vary within a subspecies. In their underparts, *toddi* resembles *viridissima* (illus.); *gyrola* is green below with a blue area on the center of the breast and upper belly; and the remaining subspecies most resemble *bangsi* (illus.). More than one species may be involved (see *A.O.U. Check-list*).

Geographic Range

T. g. bangsi and *deleticia*: both slopes from s Alajuela and San José provinces, COSTA RICA, southeastward through PANAMA; the Andean region of COLOMBIA southward to n Nariño and eastward to the w slope of the E Andes. *T. g. nupera*: Pacific slope from s Nariño, COLOMBIA, through ECUADOR to Tumbes, PERU (Wiedenfeld, Schulenberg, and Robbins 1985). *T. g. toddi* and *viridissima*: the Santa Marta and Perijá Mountains and the e slope of the E Andes southward to Boyacá, COLOMBIA, and eastward through VENEZUELA in the Andes and along the coastal ranges to TRINIDAD. *T. g. gyrola*: c Amazonas and c and s Bolívar, VENEZUELA, and adjacent Roraima, BRAZIL, eastward to THE GUIANAS and sc Amapá, BRAZIL (Novaes 1978). *T. g. catharinae*: e slope of the Andes from Meta (incl. the Macarena Mountains), COLOMBIA, southward through ECUADOR and PERU to w Santa Cruz (Remsen, Traylor, and Parkes in press), BOLIVIA; extending into Amazonia in se PERU. *T. g. parva* and *albertinae*: sw Amazonas, VENEZUELA, nw Amazonas, BRAZIL, and adjacent COLOMBIA (e Guianía, e Vaupés, and se Amazonas), and extreme n Loreto, PERU, southward and eastward through BRAZIL south of the Amazon River to wc Mato Grosso (Willis 1976a), s Pará (Pinto and Camargo 1957), and e Pará (Belém area).

Elevational Range

T. g. bangsi and *deleticia*: ca. 500–1600 m, descending to lowlands on the Pacific slope of Costa Rica (Slud 1964) and adjacent Panama, in the region of the Panama Canal (Ridgely 1976), and in n Colombia; as high as 2100 m along the Pacific slope in Colombia (Hilty and Brown 1986). *T. g. nupera*: lowlands. *T. g. toddi*, *viridissima*, and *gyrola*: from sea level to ca. 1800 m; more abundant in highlands. *T. g. catherinae*: ca. 300–1600 m. *T. g. parva* and *albertinae*: lowlands.

Habitat and Behavior

Inhabits montane and low-lying (incl. *varzea*) forest. Also occurs (and nests) in nearby tree-studded clearings, shaded coffee plantations, and second growth. In c Panama, moves about seasonally, apparently in response to the availability of fruit (Karr 1977). Lives in pairs, singly, or in family groups. Frequently accompanies mixed-species flocks of other small canopy species. Joins feeding aggregations at fruiting trees. Skutch (1954) observed an individual roosting alone every night for a month at the same spot: 15 cm off the ground on a horizontal thorn near the center of a tree in a clearing.

Typically forages high in tree crowns within forest; lower at forest edge. Most feeding records in Trinidad (Snow and Snow 1971) and Valle, Colombia (Hilty data) were at heights of over 7.5 m from the ground; rarely foraged below 3 m. Median foraging height in Colombia was 12.2 m. Fruit constituted 70% of 564 observations in Trinidad and 60% of 188 observations in Colombia; a combined total of 43 fruit species were recorded at the two sites.

Favors fruits of *Miconia*, *Cecropia*, and *Ficus*. Eats fruits from pods and capsules of at least 7 species of arillate fruits, especially from the epiphytic vine, *Souroubea guianensis* (Skutch 1980). Typically perches upright on twigs or branches to obtain small fruits which are swallowed whole; occasionally hovers or snatches berries in flight. Rarely

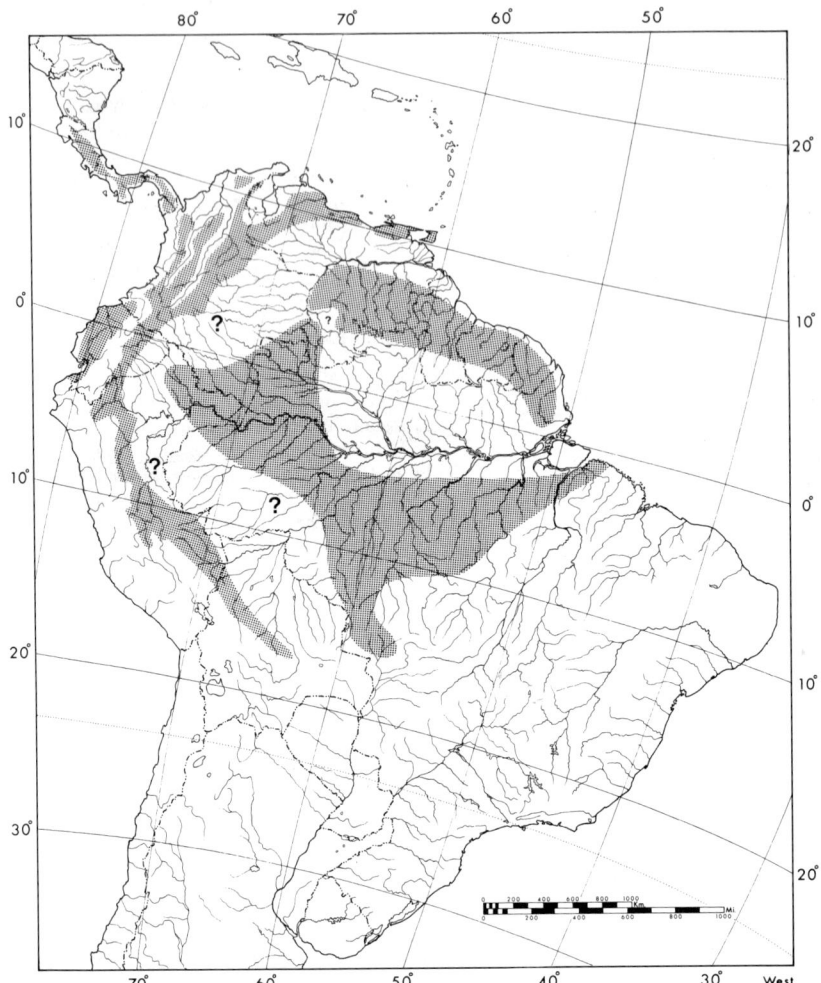

Tangara gyrola

pecks pieces out of large fruits. Hangs from petioles or clings to catkins to eat *Cecropia* fruit. Also plucks tiny white protein corpuscles from bases of *Cecropia* leaf petioles (Skutch 1954), and eats flower buds of the melastome *Topobea brachyura* (3% of all Hilty's feeding records).

Searches for insects almost entirely on branches (ca. 90% of the Snows' and Hilty's insect-foraging records), typically on bare or lightly moss-covered branches 5 cm or less in diameter (see Table 24). Primarily gleans branch undersides using the diagonal-lean method. In Trinidad, many records were in trees with a new flush of foliage. In Colombia, foraged on both live and dead branches usually well away from tree trunks. Occasionally searches moss, flower heads, and seed stalks; pokes into hanging dead leaves; clings to tree trunks to search bark; or hangs from vines and branches to probe lichens and hanging moss. Rarely sallies or flutter-pursues flying insects. Stomach contents: vegetable matter (10); vegetable and animal matter (2). Contents included fruit, large seeds, and insects (incl. a coleopteran).

Vocalizations

Calls: A short scratchy High-pitched (sometimes lower) *tssit*; a buzzy *seeaaweee*, middle part slurred lower; and a coarse *shree* often heard in flight (Hilty and Brown 1986). Also twitters in flight (ffrench 1973). **Song:** In

Table 24 Percentage of Insect-foraging Records by Branch Size for the Bay-headed Tanager at Two Locations

Branch Size	Trinidad (145 obs.)	Colombia (43 obs.)
<1.3 cm	6%	32%
1.3 cm	30	28
2.5 cm	32	28
5 cm	23	10
>5 cm	10	2

Sources: Snow and Snow 1971; Hilty data.

Trinidad, consists of 5 notes, the last 2 lower in pitch, *seee, seee, seee, tsou tsooy* (ffrench 1973). In Costa Rica, 4–6 notes descending in pitch, delivered with a distinctive whining twang (Skutch 1954).

Breeding

In Costa Rica, out of 8 nests, all but one were concealed in dense foliage. Most were 4.5–5.5 m up in isolated trees in clearings near forest; one was 7.6 m off the ground in a vine tangle at forest edge; another 2.7 m up in a sparsely branched tree at the edge of a cliff. (Skutch 1954.) In Trinidad, nests were found 2.4–4.6 m up in crowns of small trees and saplings; also in a small shrub. All nests were open cups constructed mostly of moss.

In Costa Rica: Females build the nest by themselves; mates usually remain out of sight. Sometimes males bring nesting material to the female during early construction stages or sing in a nearby tree. Two eggs, laid on consecutive days, are whitish, lightly sprinkled with brown, mostly around the large end. Females incubate for 13–14 days; males are generally inattentive during incubation. Both parents feed the young who utter loud shrill cries when receiving food. Nestling period is 15–16 days. One pair successfully reared a second brood and possibly a third. (Skutch 1954.) Breeding dates: Costa Rica Feb–Oct. Trinidad Jan–Aug. Panama March and April.

Sources

Primary Hilty data; LSUMZ data; Parker data; Remsen data; Skutch 1954; Slud 1964; Snow and Snow 1971. **Weights (n = 168)** ffrench 1973; Hartman and Brownell 1961; LSUMZ data; Miller 1963; Strauch 1977. **Stomach contents** LSUMZ data; Wetmore, Pasquier, and Olson 1984. **Vocalizations** LNS recordings by L. I. Davis (1), Morton (1), Parker (2); recordings by Isler (2); ffrench 1973; Hilty and Brown 1986; Skutch 1954; Slud 1964. **Nests, eggs, and breeding dates** Belcher and Smooker 1937; ffrench 1973; Skutch 1954; Wetmore, Pasquier, and Olson 1984.

Tangara lavinia 189
Rufous-winged Tanager
Plate 26

Length 12 cm (5 in.). Three subspecies: males vary most noticeably in the extent to which blue replaces green in the underparts. Subadult plumage resembles the subadult plumage of the Bay-headed Tanager, *T. gyrola* **188**, but usually shows a trace of rufous on the wings; often encountered in subadult plumage (Ridgely *in litt.*).

Geographic Range

T. l. cara and *dalmasi*: the Caribbean slope from extreme e GUATEMALA (Puerto Barrios region) southward through HONDURAS, NICARAGUA, and COSTA RICA to San Blas (Ridgely 1976), PANAMA; locally on the Pacific slope from Chiriquí to e Panamá province, PANAMA (Wetmore, Pasquier, and Olson 1984). *T. l. lavinia*: from e Darién, PANAMA, southward along the Pacific slope through COLOMBIA (incl. I. Gorgona, Ridgely *in litt.*) to Esmeraldas, ECUADOR.

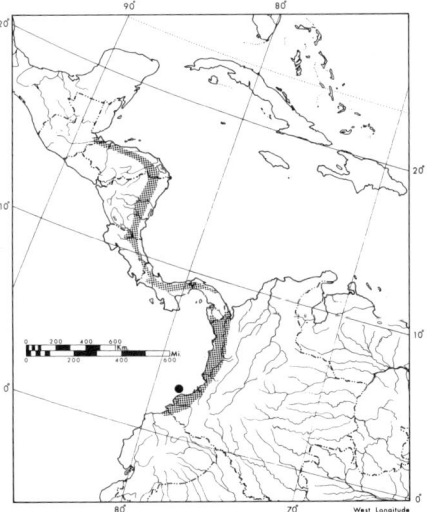

Tangara lavinia

Elevational Range

Lowlands to 750 m from Guatemala to Nicaragua; mostly ca. 400–800 m in Costa Rica, occasionally descending lower; in foothills (ca. 500–1000 m) in Panama (Ridgely *in litt.*); mostly below 500 m in Colombia, sightings to 1000 m (Hilty and Brown 1986).

Habitat and Behavior

Inhabits forest and forest edge; also occurs in tall second growth and clearings with scattered trees near forest. Single birds, pairs, and small groups typically travel with mixed-species flocks; may be independent of other species more often in Costa Rica (Slud 1964). Forages from about 3 m above the ground to the crowns of tall trees, perhaps most often in the canopy. In Valle, Colombia: Ate fruit, including those of *Ficus*, *Cecropia*, and melastomes. Searched for insects on dead branches, both bare and moss-covered, using the diagonal-lean method; seemed to prefer tips of slender branches less than 1.3 cm in diam. that slanted slightly upward. (Hilty data.)

Vocalizations

Calls in Costa Rica: a weak *tst* or sharp *tswist*, a *see'ts-ts-ts-ts-ts*, a sharp *tsreet tsreet tsreet*, and an *er-err'* that sounds like a creaking hinge. Possible song in Costa Rica: a patterned, soft *see'tsir tsi'rtsir tsi'rtsir*. (Slud 1964.) Flight call in Colombia: a hummingbirdlike, staccato *deet-a-deet-a* and *deet deet deet*; High- to Moderate-pitched (Whitney recording).

Breeding

In Valle, Colombia, Hilty observed a nest being built in July (Hilty and Brown 1986).

Sources

Primary Carriker 1910; Haffer 1975; Hilty data; Salvin and Godman 1879–1904; Slud 1964. **Stomach contents** Hallinan 1924. **Vocalizations** recording by Whitney (1); Slud 1964. **Breeding dates** Hilty and Brown 1986.

Tangara cayana **190**
Burnished-buff Tanager
Plate 26

Length 13–14 cm (5–5½ in.). Weight 18 g (15.2–22.5 g). Seven subspecies; *cayana* (illus.) and *chloroptera* (illus.) represent extremes; *fulvescens* resembles *chloroptera*; the male of *huberi* is like *chloroptera* but black of underparts is duller and the flanks and undertail-coverts are colored like *cayana*; the female of *huberi* resembles *chloroptera* but wings and tail are bluish; *flava*, *sincipitalis*, and *margaritae* are even closer to *chloroptera*, but the males still tend towards *cayana* in color. The underwing-coverts of *flava* and *fulvescens* are buffy white, blackish in *chloroptera*, and intermediate in the remaining subspecies.

Geographic Range

T. c. fulvescens and *cayana*: COLOMBIA east of the Andes south to s Meta and ec Vaupés; VENEZUELA (except s Amazonas); THE GUIANAS; and BRAZIL north of the Amazon River in n Roraima, Amapá, and ne Pará and south of the Amazon at the confluence of the Rio Tapajos and Amazon River (Pará). Also locally elsewhere in Amazonia in s Pará, BRAZIL, (Pinto and Camargo 1957); along the Rio Madeira in c Amazonas, BRAZIL; El Beni, BOLIVIA (Gyldenstolpe 1945b); and Madre de Dios (LSUMZ) and San Martín, PERU (specimens from Puno, Peru, refer to *Tangara meyerdeschauenseei* **242**). *T. c. huberi*: Ilha Maranjó, Pará, BRAZIL. *T. c. flava*, *sincipitalis*, and *margaritae*: BRAZIL from Maranhão, se Pará, and w Mato Grosso eastward to the coast and southward to Goiás and s Bahia. *T. c. chloroptera*: from Minas Gerais, BRAZIL, southward to se BRAZIL (c São Paulo and w Paraná), PARAGUAY (east of the Río Paraguay), and adjacent ARGENTINA in Misiones (along the Río Paraná).

Elevational Range

Lowlands and foothills to ca. 1500 m; in Venezuela, found as high as 2500 m north of the Orinoco River and 1800 m in the tepuis (Meyer de Schauensee and Phelps 1978); to ca. 1000 m in Rio de Janeiro, Brazil (Parker *in litt.*).

Habitat and Behavior

Inhabits semiopen areas in dry regions. Frequents isolated trees and shrubs in savannas, pastures, cultivated lands, and gardens; scrub; open woodland; gallery forest; second growth; forest and woodland edge; and palm groves. Moves about seasonally among areas where fruit is ripening. Lives in pairs and small groups, presumably families; encountered once in an aggregation of 15 individuals at a blossoming tree (Mitchell 1957). Sometimes joins other species at fruiting trees or accompanies mixed-species flocks at forest edge. Travels long distances across open areas between scattered groups of shrubs and/or trees.

Forages from low in bushes to tree tops. Stomach contents: vegetable matter (18); animal matter (1). Contents included berries, fruit, seeds (incl. those of *Michaelia champaca*, *Schinus*, guava, and *Eriobotrya japonica*), and wasps. Additional stomach contents in-

Tangara cayana

cluded mistletoe berries. Said to eat commercially grown fruits such as papayas and bananas and is sometimes a pest to farmers. Also captures termites (Mitchell 1957) and eats *Cecropia* and palm fruits. In c Brazil, seeks fruits of *Hamelia* in the family Rubiaceae (Sick 1985). Comes to feeding tables; seen feeding at a fruit bowl in a hotel dining room (Haverschmidt 1970).

Vocalizations

In Venezuela: Calls are a squeaky Moderate- to High-pitched *tsweek* or abrupt *tsit*. Song: the 2 call notes alternate and then accelerate into a rapidly delivered series of High-pitched *sizza* notes that sometimes approaches a trill; a series lasts about 3–5 sec. In Brazil, call is rendered in Portuguese as a sharp whistled *sii* (Sick 1985).

Breeding

Builds an open cup nest, composed of rootlets, leaves, and grass and lined with fine roots, placed on foliaged branches 1.5–2.5 m above the ground in isolated low trees. Eggs (2) are whitish, pale blue or lavender, or brownish white, marked with brown, especially about the large end (cp. Ogilvie-Grant 1912). Breeding dates: Venezuela Jan, April, and May. Suriname Jan–April, July, and Nov. Brazil (Mato Grosso) Oct and Nov.

Sources

Primary Descourtilz 1982; Erickson and Mumford 1976; Forbes 1881; Friedmann and Smith 1950; Fry 1970; Ginés et al. 1951; Haverschmidt 1968; Hilty and Brown 1986; LSUMZ data; Schäfer and Phelps 1954; Snethlage 1927–1928. **Weights (n = 30)** Contreras 1979; Fry 1970; Haverschmidt 1952, 1968; LSUMZ data; Thomas 1982, data. **Stomach contents** Friedmann and Smith 1950; Haverschmidt 1968; LSUMZ data; Moojen, Carvalho, and Lopes 1941; Schubart, Aguirre, and Sick 1965. **Vocalizations** LNS recordings by Kellogg and Schwartz (1), Schwartz (3); Snyder 1966. **Nests, eggs, and breeding dates** Allen 1891; Cherrie 1916; Haverschmidt 1955, 1968, 1975; Ogilvie-Grant 1912; Ramo and Busto 1984; Santos 1948.

Tangara cucullata 191
Lesser Antillean Tanager
Plate 26

Length 14–15 cm (5½–6 in.). Two subspecies: both are illustrated. Formerly known as the Hooded Tanager.

Geographical Range

T. c. cucullata: GRENADA. *T. c. versicolor*: ST. VINCENT.

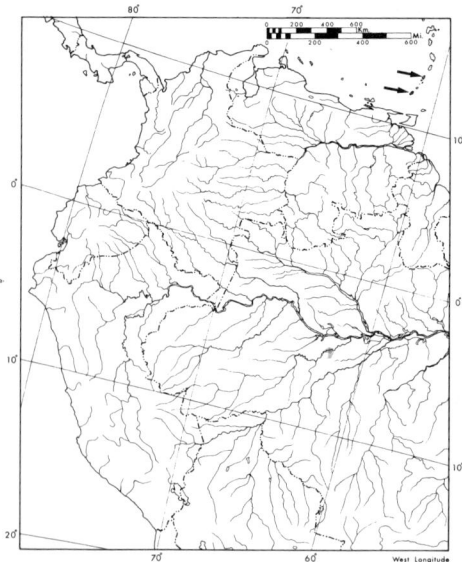

Tangara cucullata

Elevational Range

At all island elevations, but appears to be more common in highlands than lowlands on St. Vincent.

Habitat and Behavior

On Grenada, occurs in a variety of habitats with woody plants including lowland arid scrub, humid forest, forest edge, cultivated areas, and montane thickets. On St. Vincent, inhabits montane rain forest, second growth, lowland forest, and cultivated areas with trees. Strong, robust, and bold. Forages from low in bushes to tree tops. Eats a variety of fruits including figs and mangoes, but said to be partial to sour-sop (probably *Annona* sp). Takes insects off leaves and sallies to air (Lack and Lack 1973).

Vocalizations

Song: a series of clear whistled notes, increasing in volume, and ending abruptly; introduced by a squeaky sound that suggests the song of the Palm Tanager, *Thraupis palmarum* **107** (Clark 1905). Bond (1961) describes the voice as *weet-weet-weet-wit-wit-wit-wit*. Call note is a characteristic *chirp* (Clark 1905).

Breeding

Builds an open cup nest, composed mostly of leaves, situated on a forked branch 1.8–6 m above the ground in a tree or bush; often builds near houses. Robs materials from nests of other birds (Wells 1886). Eggs (2) are white or bluish, marked with shades of brown and gray, sometimes in a ring around the large end. Breeding dates: Grenada May.

Sources

Primary Bond 1928b; Clark 1905; Devas 1954; Lack and Lack 1973; Lack et al. 1973; Wells 1886. **Vocalizations** Bond 1961; Clark 1905. **Nests, eggs, and breeding dates** Bond 1928b, 1961; Clark 1905; Ogilvie-Grant 1912; Wells 1886.

Tangara peruviana 192
Black-backed Tanager
Plate 26

Length 15 cm (6 in.). Monotypic. Considered conspecific with the Chestnut-backed Tanager, *T. preciosa* **193**, by Sick (1985).

Tangara peruviana

Geographic Range

Coastal regions of se BRAZIL from Rio de Janeiro southward to Santa Catarina.

Elevational Range

Lowlands to ca. 600 m (Ridgely *in litt.*).

Habitat and Behavior

Lives in trees and shrubs in semiopen areas including hedgerows and small trees bordering pastures, thick vegetation along streams, shrubby woodland edge, and tangles near ocean beaches. Does not penetrate heavy forest. Encountered in pairs, also alone or in small groups. Active, but perches quietly at times atop small trees and shrubs, especially at sunset. Moves about seasonally in search of food. Eats berries and fruit including those of *Schinus* species (Descourtilz 1852). Fond of sweet excretions of plant lice (Sick 1985).

Vocalizations

Sick (1985) describes the song (presumably of this form) as reminiscent of the Sayaca Tanager, *Thraupis sayaca* **103-1**. As that song is a series of squeaky notes, the description differs substantially from a song described and recorded for the Chestnut-backed Tanager, *T. preciosa* **193**, which is possibly conspecific.

Tangara preciosa

Breeding

Occasionally occupies the remains of a bulky nest of the Monk Parakeet, *Myiopsitta monachus* (Sick 1985).

Sources

Primary Descourtilz 1852; Novaes 1950; Sick 1968, 1985; Wied 1830. **Nests** Sick 1985.

Tangara preciosa **193**
Chestnut-backed Tanager
Plate 26

Length 15 cm (6 in.). Weight 23 g (22.0–24.0 g). Monotypic. Considered conspecific with the Black-backed Tanager, *T. peruviana* **192**, by Sick (1985).

Geographic Range

Se BRAZIL from extreme n São Paulo southward to Rio Grande do Sul; URUGUAY; ne ARGENTINA in Buenos Aires (Olrog 1963), Entre Rios, Corrientes, and Misiones; and se PARAGUAY (east of the Río Paraguay).

Elevational Range

Lowlands to ca. 1000 m (Ridgely *in litt.*).

Habitat and Behavior

Inhabits trees and thickets at the edge of forest, especially where *Araucaria* trees are present; also occurs in patches of woodland, gardens, and orchards in open country. Moves about seasonally, apparently occupying different regions with regularity. Encountered in pairs and in mixed-species flocks. Feeds on ripe oranges through holes made by other birds. Observed eating fruits of the peppertree (*Schinus* sp) and *Eriobotrya* loquats (Voss and Sander 1980, 1981). Searches for insects in tree foliage (Parker data).

Vocalizations

Song: 4–5 moderately sustained, Highpitched, lisping, identical notes *seeeee seeeee seeeee seeeee seeeee* (Belton 1985; Belton, LNS). Call note: a squeaky *zeeek!* or *zurk* (female; Parker, LNS).

Breeding

In Rio Grande do Sul, Brazil, a nest (not visible) was located about 10 m up among thick fronds in the pompon of an araucaria tree (Thomas in Belton 1985). Breeding dates: Brazil (Rio Grande do Sul) Dec.

Sources

Primary Belton 1985; Berlepsh and Ihering 1885; Cuello and Gertenstein 1962; Gore and Gepp 1978; Parker data; Santos 1948; Sick 1985. **Weights (n = 3)** Belton 1985. **Vocalizations** LNS recordings by Belton (1), Parker (1); Belton 1985. **Nests and breeding dates** Belton 1985.

Tangara vitriolina **194**
Scrub Tanager
Plate 26

Length 14 cm (5½ in.). Weight 23 g (18.4–26.8 g). Monotypic.

Geographic Range

Interior Andean valleys of COLOMBIA from Antioquia and Norte de Santander southward and the Pacific slope from Antioquia, COLOMBIA, southward to Pichincha, ECUADOR.

Elevational Range

300–2400 m (LSUMZ); mostly at higher elevations.

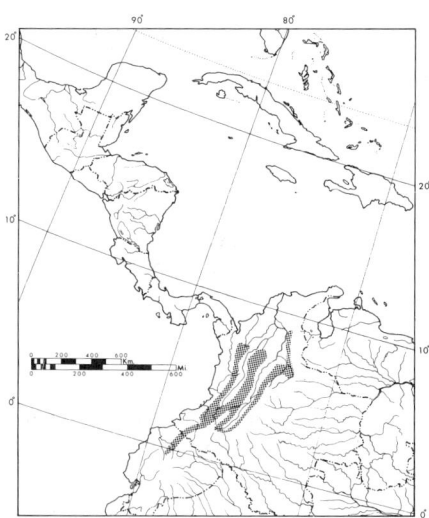

Tangara vitriolina

Habitat and Behavior

Lives in scattered trees and shrubs in semiarid country; is extending range as forest is cleared in wetter regions (Hilty and Brown 1986). Inhabits scrub, hedgerows, and isolated trees in cultivated areas and overgrown pastures; also occurs in scrub in broken forest or open woodland, at forest edge, and around human habitations. Lives singly and in pairs; joins feeding aggregations at fruiting trees. Peers about somewhat like a vireo (Hilty and Brown 1986). Forages from low in bushes to tops of tall trees. Hunts mostly for insects (Hilty and Brown 1986) by searching leaves, epiphytes, flowers, and seed heads. Also eats fruit, including melastome berries. Stomach contents (1): insects.

Vocalizations

Utters shrill buzzy *ziit* notes (Hilty and Brown 1986).

Breeding

Appeared to defend a nesting territory against wrens (Miller 1947). Builds an open cup nest constructed mostly of moss and lined with fine fibers. Eggs (2) are white, sometimes tinged blue, green, or cream and heavily marked with lilac and/or brown, especially about the large end.

Sources

Primary Hilty data; Hilty 1977; Hilty and Brown 1986; Miller 1947, 1963; Munves 1975; Olivares 1969; Willis 1966c. **Weights (n = 15)** LSUMZ data; Miller 1947, 1963. **Stomach contents** LSUMZ data. **Vocalizations** Hilty and Brown 1986. **Nests and eggs** Nehrkorn 1899; Ogilvie-Grant 1912; Olivares 1969; Sclater and Salvin 1879.

Breeding

No information.

Sources

Primary Meyer de Schauensee and Phelps 1978; Schäfer and Phelps 1954; Wetmore 1939.

Tangara rufigenis 195
Rufous-cheeked Tanager
Plate 26

Length 12 cm (5 in.). Monotypic.

Geographic Range

Coastal mountains of n VENEZUELA from Distrito Federal and Aragua westward to nc Lara.

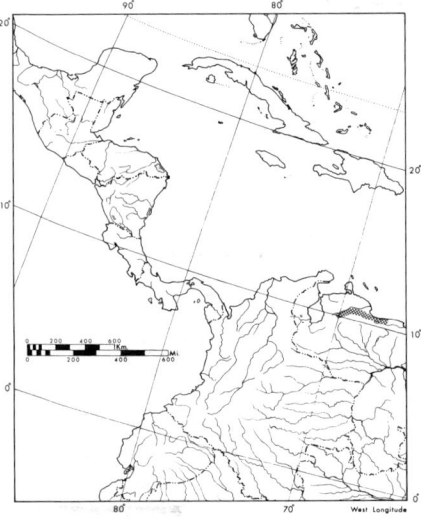

Tangara rufigenis

Elevational Range

900–1400 m, as high as 2050 m.

Habitat and Behavior

Inhabits montane forest; also occurs at forest edge. Encountered in pairs and groups of up to 8 individuals. Frequently travels in mixed-species flocks. Forages primarily from mid to upper levels of trees. Works quickly through the limbs of large trees and eats berries (Wetmore 1939).

Vocalizations

No information.

Tangara ruficervix 196
Golden-naped Tanager
Plate 27

Length 13 cm (5 in.). Weight 19 g (16.0–22.2 g). Six subspecies: *leucotis*, *taylori*, and *amabilis* resemble *ruficervix* (illus.); *inca* resembles *fulvicervix* (illus.); more than one species may be involved. Compared to those of males, the nape patches of females of northern subspecies are narrower and lack black borders. Subadult plumage (*fulvicervix*, possibly juvenal): crown and nape gray (Dark Neutral Gray) with a slight turquoise tinge; paler (Light Neutral Gray) below, palest on the belly; wings and tail like adult but paler (LSUMZ).

Geographic Range

T. r. ruficervix, *leucotis*, *taylori*, and *amabilis*: COLOMBIA on both slopes of the W and C Andes and the w slope of the E Andes from Cundinamarca southward; both slopes of the Andes from Cauca and Huila, COLOMBIA, southward through ECUADOR (south to El Oro on the w slope); and the e slope in PERU south to Huánuco. *T. r. inca* and *fulvicervix*: e Andean slope from Junín, PERU, southward to Cochabamba, BOLIVIA.

Elevational Range

1100–2400 m; seemingly most numerous above 1500 m.

Habitat and Behavior

Inhabits forest edge, second growth, and isolated trees and bushes in clearings and pastures; also occurs inside montane forest but usually found near openings (Hilty and Brown 1986). Encountered in pairs; also singly and in small groups of 3–5 individuals. Typically accompanies mixed-species flocks, especially other *Tangara* species.

Forages mostly 5–25 m off the ground in the crowns of tall shrubs and trees, often in fruiting or flowering trees. Median foraging height in Valle, Colombia, was about 12 m above the ground (Hilty data, 13 obs.). Picks small fruits, including those from mela-

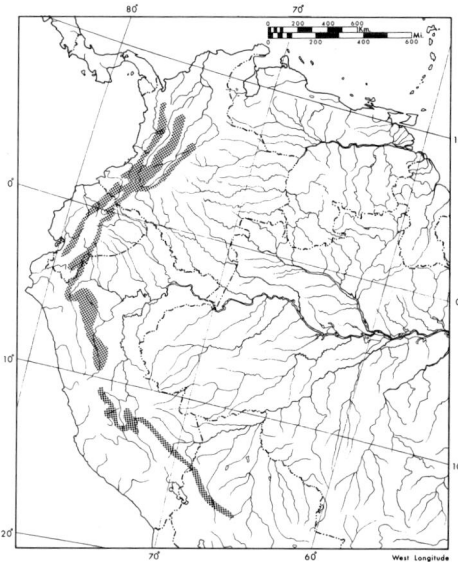

Tangara ruficervix

stomes, *Ficus*, and *Morus*; probes and nibbles at *Cecropia* catkins. Sallies to air and searches in the canopy for insects. In Valle, observed hovering and sallying to foliage (Hilty data). Stomach contents: vegetable matter (1); vegetable and animal matter (1). Contents included fruit pulp, seeds, berries, and insects.

Vocalizations

No information.

Breeding

In captivity: Extremely belligerent when forming pairs; battles were often short and violent in the aviary. Nest was flimsy; incubation lasted about 14 days; and young stayed in the nest for nearly 3 weeks. Some food appeared to be fed to nestlings by regurgitation. (Murray 1970.) Two eggs form a clutch both in the wild (Miller 1963) and in captivity. Breeding dates: Colombia Feb and April.

Sources

Primary Hilty and Brown 1986; Miller 1963; Murray 1970; Parker data; Remsen data; Ridgely and Gaulin 1980; Weske 1972. **Weights (n = 15)** LSUMZ data; Miller 1963; Weske 1972. **Stomach contents** LSUMZ data. **Eggs and breeding dates** Gniadek in Hilty and Brown 1986; Miller 1963; Murray 1970.

Tangara labradorides 197
Metallic-green Tanager
Plate 27

Length 12 cm (5 in.). Weight 15 g (13.0–16.4 g). Two subspecies.

Geographic Range

COLOMBIA in the W and C Andes, both slopes of the E Andes in Cundinamarca, the head of the Magdalena Valley in Huila; the Pacific slope from Nariño, COLOMBIA, south to Pichincha, ECUADOR; and the e Andean slope from Zamora-Chinchipe, ECUADOR (sight, Ridgely 1980) to n San Martín, PERU (Bond 1955; LSUMZ).

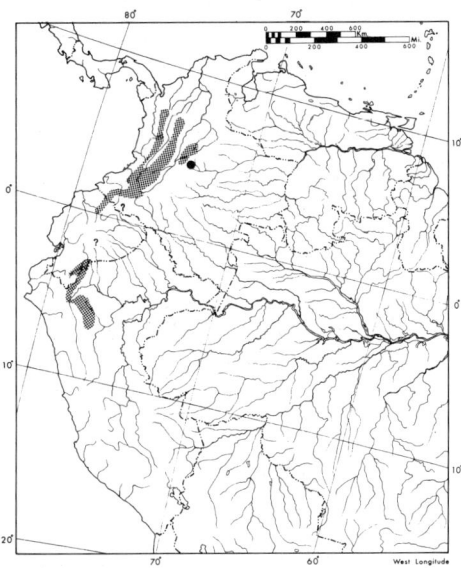

Tangara labradorides

Elevational Range

From 1300 m (900 m on the Pacific slope in Cauca, Colombia) to 2750 m; mostly 1400–2000 m.

Habitat and Behavior

Encountered at forest edge; also occurs in second-growth woodland, humid forest, and nearby bushy or tree-studded clearings. Pairs and small groups of 3–5 individuals, sometimes single birds, usually accompany mixed-species flocks, especially other *Tangara* species. Moves actively through outer foliage.

Forages from shrubs and other low growth to the crowns of large trees. In Valle, Colombia: Median foraging height was about 9 m off the ground (59 obs.); foraged lower for fruit than for insects; 68% of the observations involved insect-searching. Typically gleaned outer leaves by hopping rapidly along slender branches to the tips and inspecting top and bottom leaf surfaces for grubs and other insects; occasionally hung down or flutter-pursued insects attempting to escape. All but two observations involved leaf searching; once peered at tips of twigs head-down and once sallied to air. Perched on twigs to pluck small fruits including *Miconia* berries and other melastome fruits; nibbled at *Cecropia* catkins. Swallowed small fruits whole and bit chunks out of larger ones. (Hilty data.) Other foraging observations are consistent with this data from Valle, Colombia. In captivity, insects were the only food eaten (Ingels 1974b).

Vocalizations

Calls: a Moderate-pitched coarse *jitt*, a High-pitched squeaky *eeek*, and a wheeze. Utters a ticking twitter in flight.

Breeding

In Colombia, a nest was observed in July and stub-tailed young were seen in June, August, and November (Gniadek in Hilty and Brown 1986).

Sources

Primary Hilty data; Hilty and Brown 1986; Parker data; Ridgely and Gaulin 1980; Willis 1966c. **Weights (n = 14)** LSUMZ data; Miller 1963. **Vocalizations** recording by R. A. Rowlett (1); Hilty and Brown 1986; Miller 1963. **Breeding dates** Hilty and Brown 1986.

Tangara cyanotis 198
Blue-browed Tanager
Plate 27

Length 12 cm (5 in.). Weight 15 g (12.5–17.0 g). Two subspecies: both are illustrated.

Geographic Range

T. c. lutleyi: the head of the Magdalena Valley in Huila, COLOMBIA, and the e slope of the Andes from w Putumayo (sight, Hilty and Brown 1986), COLOMBIA, southward through ECUADOR and PERU to Cuzco. *T. c. cyanotis*: e Andean slope in La Paz and Cochabamba, BOLIVIA.

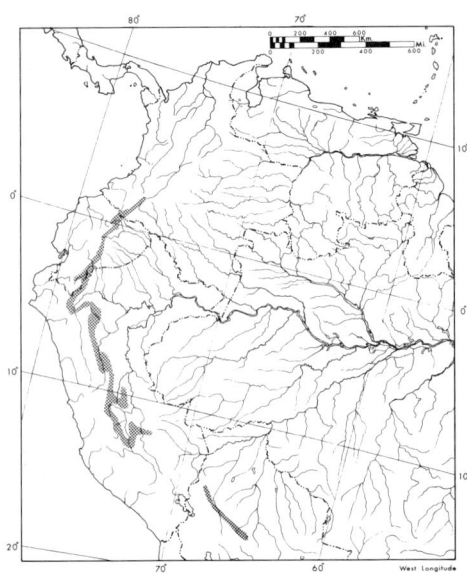

Tangara cyanotis

Elevational Range

1300–2200 m.

Habitat and Behavior

Inhabits montane forest, forest edge, wooded ravines, and second growth. Encountered in pairs or singly, rarely in small groups of 3–4 individuals. Travels independently or with mixed-species flocks, often with other canopy tanagers. In Bolivia: Foraged at heights of 3–24 m up in crowns of shrubs and trees; median height was about 7 m and median distance to the canopy was about 1.5 m (16 obs.). Sat upright (6 obs.) or hung (1) to pluck fruit and berries; picked insects off branch (3) and leaf (1) tops; and leaned down to obtain prey from branch undersides (4) and moss (1). (Remsen data.) In Peru, searched for insects in the canopy, for fruit (e.g., melastomes) in shrubs; mostly examined undersides of bare or sparsely moss-covered branches (1–4 cm in diam.) using the diagonal-lean method; also gleaned the undersides of small leaves (Parker data). Stomach contents (19): vegetable matter, including fruit pulp and seeds.

Vocalizations

No information.

Breeding

No information.

Sources

Primary Hilty and Brown 1986; LSUMZ data; Parker data; Remsen data; Taczanowski 1884b. **Weights (n = 12)** LSUMZ data.

Tangara cyanicollis 199
Blue-necked Tanager
Plate 27

Length 12 cm (5 in.). Weight 17 g (14.0–18.8 g). Seven subspecies: *caeruleocephala* and *cyanopygia* are illustrated; other subspecies vary in the amount of purple on throat and underparts and whether the rump color tends toward blue, silvery green, or straw yellow. *T. c. hannahiae* and *melanogaster* have black or nearly all black underparts.

Geographic Range

T. c. hannahiae: COLOMBIA on the e slope of the E Andes in Norte de Santander, the Perijá Mountains, and VENEZUELA in the Andes of Zulia, Táchira, Mérida, and w Barinas and mountains from w Lara eastward through Yaracuy and Carabobo to n Guárico (Meyer de Schauensee and Phelps 1978). *T. c. granadensis*: COLOMBIA on both slopes of the C and W Andes from Antioquia (USNM) south to Cauca and Huila; both this subspecies and *caeruleocephala* and intermediates occur on the w slope of the E Andes. *T. c. caeruleocephala*: COLOMBIA on the e slope of the E Andes from e Cundinamarca southward through e ECUADOR to La Libertad and San Martín, PERU. *T. c. cyanopygia*: the entire Pacific slope of ECUADOR. *T. c. cyanicollis*: e Andean slope from Huánuco, PERU, south to Cochabamba, BOLIVIA. *T. c. melanogaster*: BRAZIL in the n half of Mato Grosso (Sick 1955, Fry 1970) and s Pará (Sick 1957a, Novaes 1960). *T. c. albotibialis*: known only from Veadeiros, Goiás, BRAZIL.

Elevational Range

300–2400 m; usually above 1000 m in the Andes.

Habitat and Behavior

Inhabits semiopen areas; often found in isolated trees and bushes. In the Andes, occurs at forest edge and in clearings with scattered trees, second growth, plantations, and inhabited areas; occasionally found inside forest and open woodland. In Brazil (*melanogaster* and *albotibialis*), lives in palm groves in gallery forest, in dry forest, and in scrub (cerrado). Encountered mostly in pairs, also alone and in family groups. Usually travels in single-species flocks which may join feeding aggregations at fruiting trees and shrubs or follow mixed-species flocks at forest edge. Rests in trees between feeding sessions. Observed anting (Sick 1957a).

In Valle, Colombia (138 obs.): Foraged mostly in the crowns of bushes and small trees; median foraging height was about 8 m off the ground; rarely went above 15 m (6%). Ate fruit (86% of all obs.), insects (13%), and flower buds (1%). Took over 24 species of fruit, favoring *Miconia* berries (51% of all fruit eaten) and *Cecropia* catkins (19%). Perched upright on twigs or branches to pick berries which it swallowed whole; rarely pecked pieces out of larger fruit. Hung from leaves, petioles, or catkins to eat *Cecropia* fruits. Insects were mostly captured by sallies to air (10 obs.) and leaves (3); also searched flower heads and a fruiting stalk of a palm. (Hilty data.)

In Peru, foraged in canopy foliage and on bare limbs, twice on lichen covered branches but not seen in mossy situations (Parker data). In Bolivia, sallied to the underside of a leaf (Remsen data). Stomach contents: vegetable matter (9); vegetable and animal matter (1). Contents included fruit, berries, seeds, and insects.

Vocalizations

Often noisy while foraging. Utters a complaining Moderate-pitched *che* and a High-pitched *seet*. Gives notes singly or repeats the *che* in rapid series that may end with a louder *chep* or *seep*. Also *zibít zibít* (rendered in Portuguese), reminiscent of a *Carduelis* siskin (Sick 1985).

Breeding

In Colombia, a mossy cup nest was found at moderate height in a tree in a clearing (Hilty and Brown 1986). One clutch contained 2 eggs (Miller 1963). In captivity, eggs (2) were white with brown spots, incubation took about 15 days, the nestling period was approximately 20 days, and fledglings became independent after 3 weeks (Norgaard-Olesen 1973). Breeding dates: Colombia Feb and July.

Sources

Primary Fry 1970; Hilty data; Hilty and Brown 1986; Olivares 1969; Parker data; Remsen data; Sick 1985; Willis 1966c. **Weights (n = 19)** Fry 1970; LSUMZ data; Miller 1963; Sick 1985. **Stomach contents** Brosset 1964; LSUMZ data; Olivares 1963; Schubart, Aguirre, and Sick

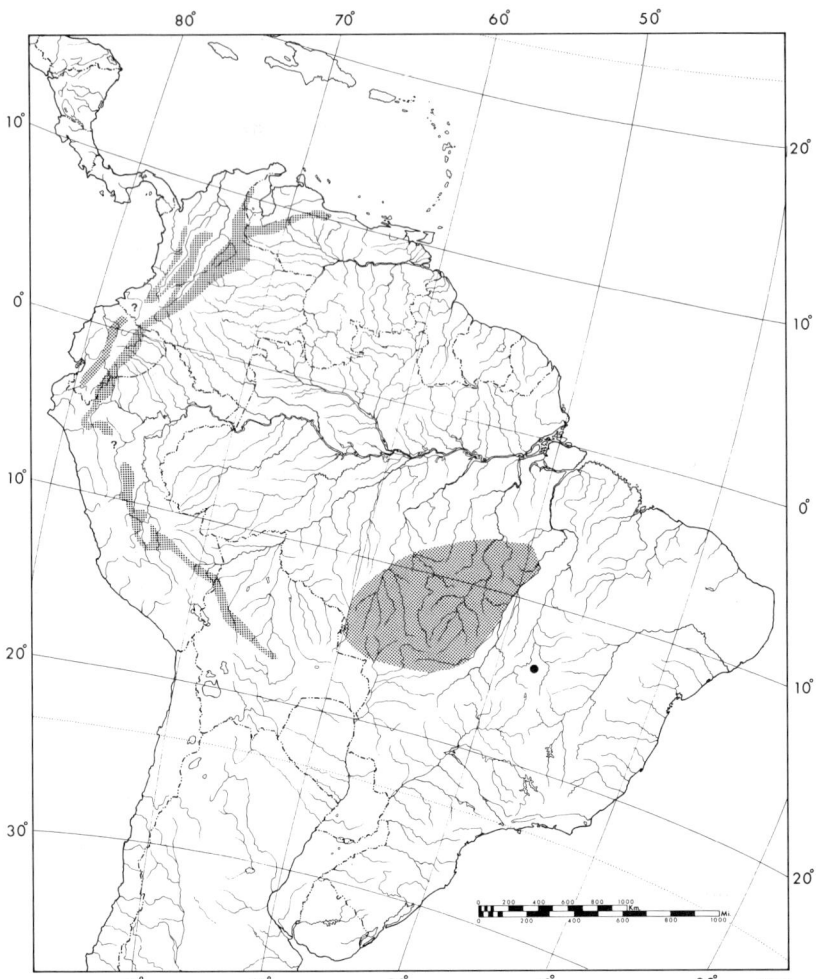

Tangara cyanicollis

1965. **Vocalizations** LNS recording by Schwartz (1); Parker data; Sick 1985. **Nests, eggs, and breeding dates** Hilty and Brown 1986; Miller 1963; Norgaard-Olesen 1973; Sick 1957b.

Tangara larvata **200**
Golden-hooded Tanager
Plate 27

Length 12 cm (5 in.). Weight 20 g (17.1–23.9 g). Four subspecies: colors vary clinally with the northernmost subspecies having the richest colors and the southernmost subspecies the palest. Also known as the Golden-masked Tanager.

Geographic Range

The Gulf-Caribbean slope from s MEXICO (n Oaxaca, Tabasco, and n Chiapas) southward through CENTRAL AMERICA to Córdoba, COLOMBIA, thence eastward in COLOMBIA along the n slope of the Andes to the Magdalena Valley, and thence southward to n Tolima; and on the Pacific slope from San José province, COSTA RICA, eastward to Veraguas (Wetmore, Pasquier, and Olson 1984), PANAMA, and from Panamá province eastward and southward through COLOMBIA to Manabí, ECUADOR.

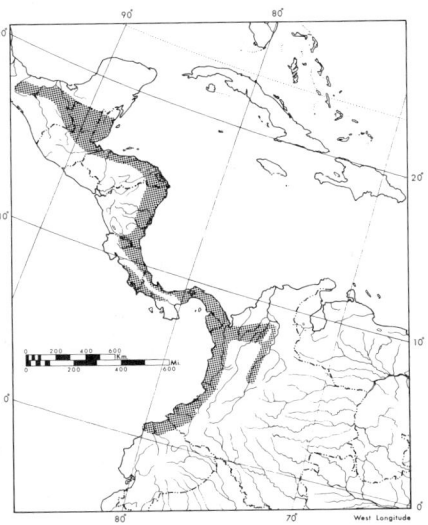

Tangara larvata

Elevational Range

Lowlands and foothills from sea level to ca. 750 m from Mexico to Nicaragua, to 1500 m in Costa Rica and Panama (usually below 1200 m), to 1800 m (usually below 1100 m) in Colombia, and to ca. 1000 m in Ecuador.

Habitat and Behavior

Inhabits forest edge, clearings with scattered trees and bushes, plantations, second growth, open woodland, and trees near houses; occasionally occurs inside forest. Encountered in pairs or small groups (probably families), rarely alone. Flies between scattered clumps of vegetation; sometimes wanders over large areas. Most often in single-species groups but sometimes joins feeding aggregations at fruiting trees or follows mixed-species flocks at forest edge or in the canopy. Active and restless; hops and flits among branches, cocking head and peering around. Rests in tree tops at times (Hilty and Brown 1986). Roosts in dense foliage in pairs, family groups, and larger groups of up to 16 individuals (Skutch 1954).

Generally forages at midheights or lower in nonforest habitats, but usually stays in the canopy when inside forest. On Barro Colorado I., Panama, typically foraged at 5–25 m above the ground (Willis 1980). In Valle, Colombia: Generally foraged lower for fruit than for insects; median foraging height was 13.7 m off the ground; 12% of the records were below 3 m. Mostly observed at fruit (64% of 180 obs.). Ate over 19 species of fruit, especially those from melastomes (62% of all fruit eaten); also favored fruits of *Cecropia* (13%) and *Ficus* (10%). Usually perched on twigs or branches to pluck berries but sometimes hung from larger fruits to remove pieces; clung to catkins to peck at *Cecropia* fruits. Also pecked at flower stalks, possibly eating petals. (Hilty data.) In Costa Rica, occasionally took fruit in flight (Moermond and Denslow 1985). In Panama, ate 3 mm berries and peeled the edible pericarp off small green mistletoe berries and dropped the seed (Leck 1971b, 1972c). In Costa Rica, observed to eat 5 species of arillate fruits (Skutch 1980); came to feeding tables for bananas only when natural food was scarce (Skutch 1954).

In Valle, Colombia: Often captured insects, including termites, that were in flight (73% of 52 insect-foraging obs.). Primarily made aerial sallies, frequently short sallies of 0.5 m or less, and sometimes stretched up to snatch flying insects without leaving its perch. Also hovered and sallied to leaves and pecked prey off thin branches, petioles, and flower heads. (Hilty data.) Observations of insect-foraging behavior from other locations are consistent with the foregoing. Stomach contents (1): seeds and plant matter.

Vocalizations

Utters a sharp dry or buzzy Moderate- to High-pitched *dzit* or *tsip*, which is repeated in strings or accelerated into trills of clearer metallic *tik*s or *tsick*s that probably form its song. Also a single wheezy twang, *nyaaa*. Pairs give call notes often, including during flight.

Breeding

Builds its nest most often in the crotch of a leafy tree or bush, less often in dense vegetation near the end of a branch; heights range 1.5–15 m off the ground (Skutch 1954). Other sites were in a hole about 25 m up in the top of a dead tree trunk, among fruits of a banana stalk, in a dry maize plant, and in an abandoned nest of an oropendola (*Zarhynchus wagleri*). Pairs construct the nest together. The compact open cup is made of fine brown fibers, strips of dead leaves, and cobweb and lined with black fibrous material. Two eggs, laid on consecutive days, are dull white or pale gray, thickly flecked with brown, especially at the large end. The female incubates alone for 13–15 days, often accompanied and sometimes fed by her mate. The parents usually come to the nest together with food concealed in their bills to feed nestlings. Individuals in subadult and adult plumages have been observed helping mated pairs feed their nestlings, and one pair tolerated help by a Tropical Gnatcatcher, *Polioptila plumbea*. Nestling period is 14–16 days, at which point the young can fly quite well. Two, sometimes three, broods are reared in a season. (Skutch 1954, 1961, 1976.)

In captivity: The nesting cycle and behavior was similar to the foregoing (see Ingels 1971a and Miller 1973). Ingels also observed a courtship display in which the pair perched next to each other and, with their heads and tails stretched slightly, bowed deeply, calling loudly each time they returned to the upright position. Only insects were fed to nestlings for the first 10–14 days. Breeding dates: Costa Rica Feb–Sept. Panama Feb–Aug. Colombia Jan–May.

Sources

Primary Eisenmann 1957, 1961; Hilty data; Hilty and Brown 1986; Howell 1957; Leck 1971b; Monroe 1968; Ridgely 1976; Russell 1964; Skutch 1954; Slud 1964; Smithe 1966. **Weights (n = 35)** Hartman 1955; Hartman and Brownell 1961; LSUMZ data; Russell 1964; Smithe 1966; Strauch 1977; Willis 1980. **Stomach contents** LSUMZ data. **Vocalizations** LNS recordings by Morton (1), Parker (2), van den Berg (1); recording by Whitney (1); Eisenmann 1957; Skutch 1954; Slud 1964. **Nests, eggs, and breeding dates** Eisenmann 1957; Hilty and Brown 1986; Ingels 1971a; Skutch 1954; Salvin and Godman 1879–1904; Wetmore, Pasquier, and Olson 1984.

Tangara nigrocincta   **201**
Masked Tanager
Plate 27

Length 12 cm (5 in.). Weight 17 g (15.0–17.8 g). Monotypic. Also known as the Black-banded Tanager.

Geographic Range

N GUYANA; from s Bolívar and Amazonas, VENEZUELA, and e Vichada and w Meta, COLOMBIA, southward locally through e COLOMBIA (Hilty and Brown 1986), e ECUADOR, and e PERU to w Santa Cruz (Remsen, Traylor, and Parkes in press), BOLIVIA; and eastward in w BRAZIL north of the Amazon River to the upper Rio Negro and w Roraima (Novaes 1965) and south of the Amazon to c Pará (Roth *fide* Brown *in litt.*) and w Mato Grosso (Willis 1976a).

Elevational Range

Lowlands and foothills to 1400 m. Most often 300–900 m.

Habitat and Behavior

Inhabits terra firma and low-lying (incl. *varzea*) forest in humid lowlands; elsewhere, occurs in open forest and second-growth woodland, forest and woodland edge, trees and bushes in clearings, and shaded plantations. Encountered in pairs and small (family?) groups. Travels alone, is transitory in mixed-species flocks (both permanent canopy flocks and temporary tanager flocks; see Munn 1985), and joins feeding aggregations at fruiting trees and shrubs. Forages in the canopy of forest trees but comes lower in isolated trees and shrubs outside forest. In Peru, once seen hanging to pick an insect off the top of a leaf in the canopy about 25 m above the ground (Remsen data). Stomach contents (5): fruit pulp and seeds.

Vocalizations

Utters High-pitched *tsit* or *chit* notes in various ways; sometimes single notes are repeated or accelerated into a short trill, *tsit tsit-it-it-it-it* or given in a brief rapid series ending with 3 wheezy Moderate-pitched *cheou* notes. Song(?) consists of 3 High-pitched wheezy *tseeee* notes, as if whistled through the teeth, the last note slurred downward to a Moderate pitch; delivered in about 3 sec., repeated after a pause sprinkled with several *tsit* notes. (Schwartz, LNS.)

Breeding

In captivity, became very aggressive during the breeding season; built a cup nest; eggs (2) were white, heavily spotted brown; the female incubated alone for 13 days; and young left the nest after 17 days (Norgaard-Olesen 1973).

Sources

Primary Hilty and Brown 1986; O'Neill and Pearson 1974; Parker data; Remsen and Ridgely 1980; Terborgh and Weske 1969, 1975. **Weights (n = 8)** LSUMZ data. **Stomach contents** Foster data; LSUMZ data. **Vocalizations** LNS recording by Schwartz (1). **Eggs** Norgaard-Olesen 1973.

Tangara dowii   **202**
Spangle-cheeked Tanager

Consists of two subspecies according to the *Peters Check-list* that are considered specifically distinct by the *A.O.U. Check-list*. Although the two subspecies are separated by about a 400 km gap, their habitats, foraging behavior (Ridgely *in litt.*), and calls appear to be quite similar.

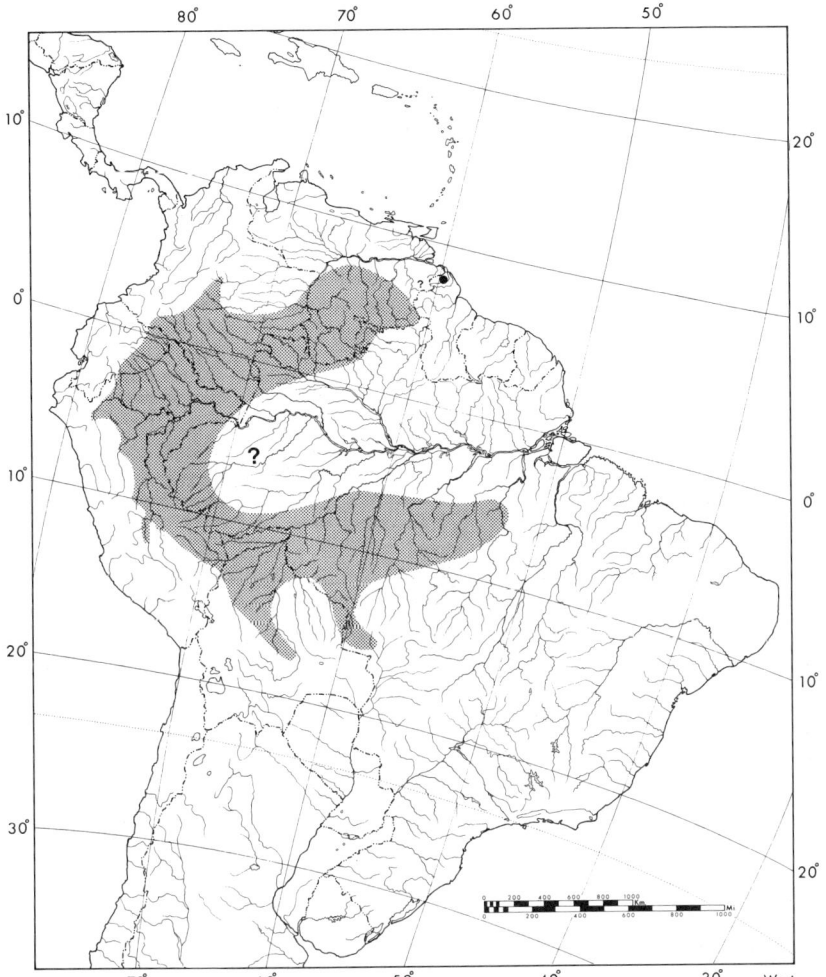

Tangara nigrocincta

Tangara dowii
(*dowii* subspecies group   **202-1**)
Spangle-cheeked Tanager
Plate 27

Length 12 cm (5 in.). Monotypic if specifically distinct.

Geographic Range

From e Guanacaste and s Alajuela (Cordillera de Tilarán), COSTA RICA, eastward to Veraguas, PANAMA.

Elevational Range

1100–3200 m; mostly 1600–2700 m (Stiles 1983); wanders lower.

Habitat and Behavior

Inhabits humid montane forest, forest edge, and adjacent tree-studded clearings. Generally encountered in small groups of up to 6 or more individuals; sometimes in pairs. Not territorial outside the breeding season (Buskirk 1976). Travels alone or occasionally in company with other species, especially the Common Bush-Tanager, *Chlorospingus ophthalmicus* **14**. Appears to migrate to higher elevations in the boreal winter (Wolf 1976). Flies swiftly and directly from one

318   TANGARA

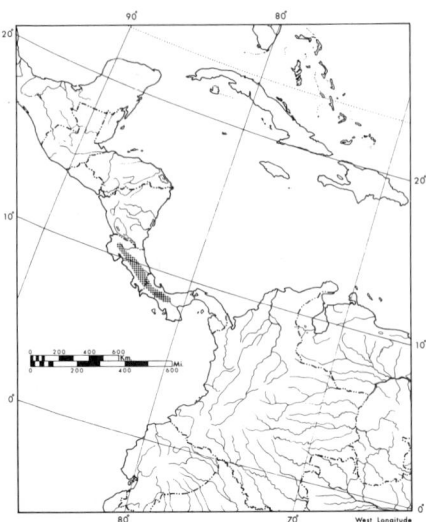

Tangara dowii (*dowii* subspecies group)

Tangara dowii
(*fucosa* subspecies group   202-2)
Green-naped Tanager
Plate 27

Length 12 cm (4½ in.). Weight 21 g (18.0–23.0 g). Monotypic if specifically distinct.

Geographic Range

PANAMA in e Darién on Cerro Pirre and Cerro Malí.

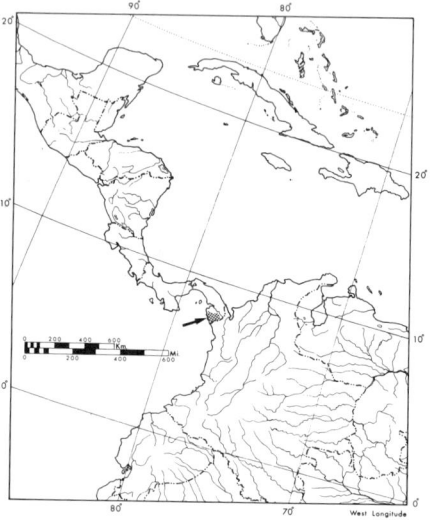

Tangara dowii (*fucosa* subspecies group)

Elevational Range

Mostly above 1400 m; once at 550 m (Wetmore, Pasquier, and Olson 1984).

Habitat and Behavior

Groups of 3–4 individuals travel alone or with mixed-species flocks that often include the Pirre Bush-Tanager, *Chlorospingus inornatus* **16**. Observed taking berries of *Miconia* and an epiphytic vine and foraging in the crowns of trees in elfin forest, gleaning small leaves and mosses on slender branches (Robbins, Parker, and Allen 1985). Stomach contents (3): fruit.

Vocalizations

Calls: High-pitched simple *tsit* notes or a more squealing *tseet*, given alone or rapidly in various combinations of 2–4 notes. Some-

foraging area to another. Darts from branch to branch, seldom spending much time at one site (Slud 1964). Forages from the understory to midheights in trees. Eats fruit and insects. Climbs and hops among branches examining foliage; also peers myopically at sides and undersides of its perch (Slud 1964). Observed taking fruits of *Gaiadendron* (Wolf 1976) and of melastomes (4 spp) and *Urera* of the family Urticaceae (Wheelwright et al. 1984).

Vocalizations

Utters short High-pitched metallic *tsit!* notes, sometimes longer, more piercing *tseet* notes; given alone, in combinations, or in twitters.

Breeding

No information.

Sources

Primary Buskirk 1976; Powell 1979; Ridgely 1976; Slud 1964; Stiles and Hespenheide 1972. **Vocalizations** LNS recording by Parker (1); recording by Whitney (1); Slud 1964.

times 5 or more *tseet* or *tsit* notes are strung together rapidly. (Parker, LNS.)

Breeding

No information.

Sources

Primary LSUMZ data; Parker data; Robbins, Parker, and Allen 1985. **Weights (n = 7)** LSUMZ data. **Stomach contents** LSUMZ data. **Vocalizations** LNS recordings by Parker (2); Robbins, Parker, and Allen 1985.

Tangara nigroviridis 203
Beryl-spangled Tanager
Plate 27

Length 12 cm (5 in.). Weight 17 g (14.0–19.5 g). Three subspecies.

Geographic Range

VENEZUELA in the coastal range from Miranda west to Carabobo and the Andes from s Lara southwest to Táchira; the Perijá Mountains; COLOMBIA in all 3 Andean ranges and the Macarena Mountains; southward on the w slope of the Andes through ECUADOR to Loja; and southward on the e Andean slope through ECUADOR, PERU, and nw BOLIVIA to Cochabamba.

Elevational Range

900–3000 m; most numerous 1500–2400 m.

Habitat and Behavior

Inhabits forest edge, second growth, and trees in clearings near forest; also occurs inside forest, especially at openings. Travels in pairs and groups of up to 15 individuals, rarely alone. Frequently accompanies mixed-species flocks and joins feeding aggregations at fruiting trees. In Valle, Colombia, hops very rapidly, almost runs, along thin branches, then stops and stays 3–5 sec. at a perch before moving on (Hilty data).

Forages mostly at heights of 2–9 m off the ground; also occurs in tree crowns and near the ground in plants and ferns (Hilty data). Picks small fruits, especially *Miconia* berries and other melastome fruits (15% of 92 obs.). In Valle, Colombia: 85% of 92 observations involved insect-foraging; typically searched for insects head-down (over 50% of insect-foraging obs.). In slightly over half the observations, gleaned the undersides of thin twigs and slender branches less than 1.3 cm in diam. that were bare or patchily covered with moss. Also peered at leaves, poked into hanging moss clumps, and searched tiny epiphytes, stream-side ferns, thin vines, and once even a barbed wire fence. Often stretched up, reached out, or hung down to pick prey off substrates. (Hilty data.) Stomach contents: vegetable matter (7); vegetable and animal matter (1). Contents included fruit pulp, seeds, and coleopterans.

Vocalizations

No information.

Breeding

Eggs are creamy white or pale green, thickly marked with brown and lilac, especially at the large end.

Sources

Primary Hilty data; Hilty and Brown 1986; LSUMZ data; Parker data; Remsen data; Ridgely and Gaulin 1980; Willis 1966c. **Weights (n = 34)** LSUMZ data; Miller 1963. **Stomach contents** LSUMZ data. **Eggs** Ogilvie-Grant 1912; Sclater and Salvin 1879.

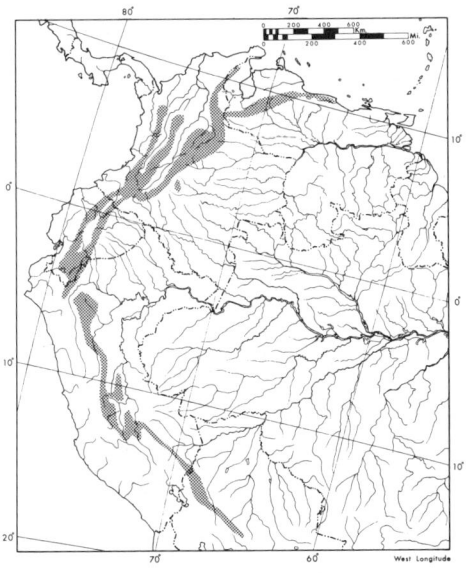

Tangara nigroviridis

Tangara vassorii 204
Blue-and-black Tanager
Plate 27

Length 13 cm (5 in.). Weight 18 g (15.0–21.0 g). Three subspecies: *vassorii* and *atrocoerulea* are illustrated; *branickii* resembles nominate race except top and sides of head are tinged gray (Smoke Gray). Subadults of all 3 races are gray.

Geographic Range

T. v. vassorii: the Andes in VENEZUELA (Trujillo, Mérida, and Táchira), COLOMBIA, ECUADOR, and PERU (both slopes, Parker et al. 1985) north of the Northern Peruvian Low in Piura and Cajamarca. *T. v. branickii*: south and east of the Northern Peruvian Low in Amazonas and La Libertad, PERU. *T. v. atrocoerulea*: the e slope of the Andes from Huánuco, PERU, to w Santa Cruz (Remsen, Traylor, and Parkes in press), BOLIVIA.

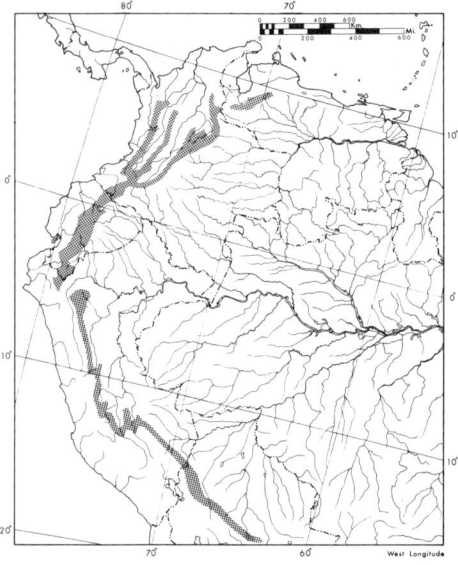

Tangara vassorii

Elevational Range

Mostly 2400–3500 m (treeline); sometimes lower, as low as 1300 m in Bolivia (Parker data). In Colombia, may move to lower elevations seasonally (Ridgely and Gaulin 1980).

Habitat and Behavior

Inhabits humid montane and elfin forest, forest edge, second growth, shrubs and trees in forest clearings, and patches of woody growth at treeline. Lives mostly in pairs and small groups of 3–6 individuals (sometimes up to 15 or more), rarely alone. Usually accompanies mixed-species flocks and sometimes joins feeding aggregations at fruiting trees. Spritely; hops quickly along branches and flutters through foliage; rarely spends much time in one tree.

Forages from low in bushes to the tallest tree crowns; typically stays high in trees within forest. Especially fond of *Miconia* and other melastome fruits. In Huánuco, Peru: Perched on twigs or branches and leaned down or reached out to snap up berries in a rapid motion, then sat upright, quietly looking around while mandibulating the berry. Typically searched for insects by hopping along slender (less than 2 cm in diam.) moss-covered branches and peering around (16 obs.). Used the diagonal-lean method to take prey off branch undersides, gleaned top and bottom leaf surfaces, probed clumps of moss, and examined small bromeliads. Also hung upside down to inspect leaves, petioles, and bunches of dead twigs. (Isler data.) Stomach contents: vegetable matter (14); vegetable and animal matter (3). Contents included fruit pulp, seeds, berries, and insects. Additional stomach contents included seeds of melastome fruits.

Vocalizations

Calls: a very thin High-pitched but emphatic *tsit!*, sometimes given in a rapid ticking series, especially as individuals take flight; also a slightly lower *swit!*, sometimes *swit! swit! swit!* or a harder *SWIT-it*. Silliman (in Hilty and Brown 1986) describes the song as consisting of a series of high-pitched "wheedly" notes, starting slowly, and ending in a trill.

Breeding

In Colombia, nests (2) were found in June (Gniadek in Hilty and Brown 1986).

Sources

Primary Hilty data; Hilty and Brown 1986; Isler data; Parker data; Parker and O'Neill 1980; Remsen data; Taczanowski 1884b; Terborgh and Weske 1975. **Weights (n=63)** LSUMZ data. **Stomach contents** Goodfellow 1901; LSUMZ data; Taczanowski 1884b. **Vocalizations** LNS recordings by Isler (2), Parker (1), Schwartz (2); Hilty and Brown 1986. **Breeding dates** Hilty and Brown 1986.

Tangara heinei 205
Black-capped Tanager
Plate 28

Length 13 cm (5 in.). Weight 21 g (19.8–22.8 g). Monotypic.

Geographic Range

The coastal ranges of VENEZUELA from Distrito Federal and n Guárico (Meyer de Schauensee and Phelps 1978) westward to Yaracuy and on Cerro El Cerron at the juncture of Falcón, Zulia, and Lara; the Andes of VENEZUELA from Lara southwestward to Táchira; the Perijá Mountains; COLOMBIA in the Santa Marta Mountains and all 3 Andean ranges (apparently locally distributed in the E Andes); southward on the Pacific slope to Pichincha (sight, Ridgely 1980), ECUADOR, and on the e slope to Napo, ECUADOR.

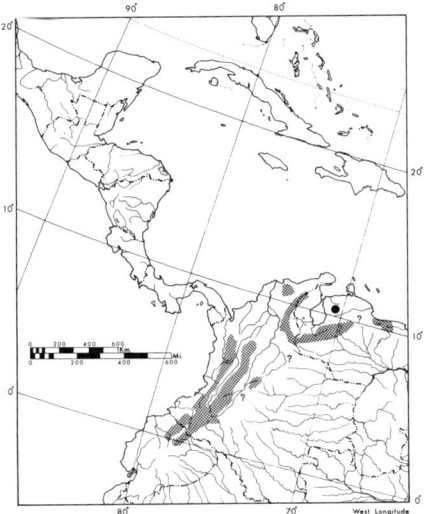

Tangara heinei

Elevational Range

1000–2700 m; mostly 1500–2200 m in the Andes; lower in the Santa Marta Mountains and coastal ranges of Venezuela.

Habitat and Behavior

Encountered at humid forest edge and in natural openings within forest, partially logged forest, tall second growth, and patches of shrubs and trees near forest. Single birds, pairs, and family groups often travel by themselves but may join other species at fruiting trees or follow mixed-species flocks at forest edge. Forages for fruit and insects from low in bushes to the crowns of tall trees; most often from midheights to tops of trees. In Valle, Colombia: Perched on twigs to pick *Miconia* berries and other melastome fruits and searched for insects primarily near tree trunks on moss-covered or bare branches mostly less than 2.5 cm in diam. or on vines and lianas (29 obs.). Hopped along branches using the diagonal-lean method but did not lean over very far; picked prey off top and sides of branches. Occasionally clung to tree trunks or hung from vines. (Hilty data.)

Vocalizations

Calls: utters 2 kinds of nasal and scratchy *zheet* notes, one High-pitched and the other more nasal and Moderate-pitched; also an occasional clear High-pitched *tsit*. Song: variable; typically starts out with a few *zheets* on the same pitch, then alternates between the 2 types of *zheet* calls while increasing in tempo and loudness, and ends in a scratchy wheedling which is repeated 3–5 times; lasts 6–12 sec.; pauses between outbursts are irregular in length and contain call notes. (Schwartz, LNS.)

Breeding

Two nests: one was a grassy cup decorated with moss placed 2.3 m above the ground (Hilty and Brown 1986), and the other was built in a sparsely leaved shrub (1 m high) growing on a steep moss-covered slope (Ewert 1975). At the latter nest, only the female gathered nesting material, but both male and female molded material into the nest. Eggs are pale greenish white or dull blue, heavily marked brown and (sometimes) lilac gray, especially at the large end. Breeding dates: Venezuela May. Colombia Jan, April, and Aug.

Sources

Primary Hilty data; Hilty and Brown 1986; Schäfer and Phelps 1954; Todd and Carriker 1922; Willis 1966c. **Weights (n = 4)** Miller 1963. **Vocalizations** LNS recording by Schwartz (1). **Nests, eggs, and breeding dates** Hilty and Brown 1986; Ewert 1975; Ogilvie-Grant (1912); Sclater and Salvin 1879.

Tangara viridicollis 206
Silvery-backed Tanager
Plate 28

Length 13 cm (5 in.). Weight 21 g (18.1–24.0 g). Two subspecies. Also known as the Silvery Tanager.

Geographic Range

T. v. fulvigula: Azuay, El Oro, and Loja, ECUADOR (possibly confined to the w slope), and n PERU north and west of the Northern Peruvian Low (south to Lambayeque and Cajamarca). *T. v. viridicollis*: the e Andean slope south and east of the Northern Peruvian Low from Amazonas to s Puno (not yet recorded in Ayacucho), PERU.

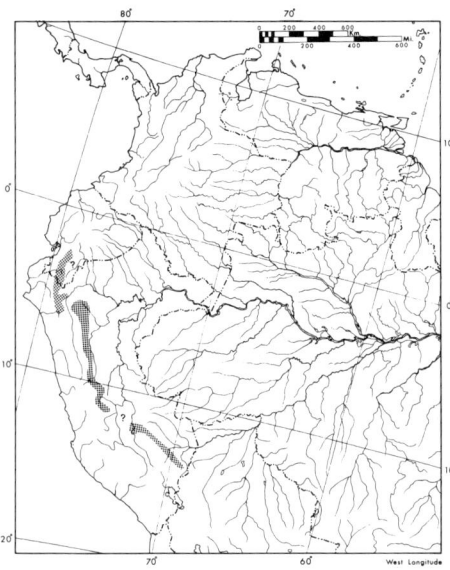

Tangara viridicollis

Elevational Range

1450–3050 m; most common 1500–2000 m.

Habitat and Behavior

Frequents forest edge, second growth, and wooded ravines; usually found near forest edge when inside forest (Parker data); also occurs in isolated trees and bushes away from forest (Stolzmann in Tacznowski 1884b). Encountered in pairs and small groups of 3–5 individuals. Travels alone or with mixed-species flocks. Forages from the tops of tall trees to low bushes, even on the ground (Stolzmann *ibid*). Visits fruiting melastomes. Eats coffee berries and is said to do much damage to the plants (Stolzmann *ibid*). Stomach contents: vegetable matter (1); animal matter (2); both (1). Contents included seeds and spiders.

Vocalizations

Stolzmann (*ibid*) reports the call is distinctive and not as thin as other *Tangara* species.

Breeding

No information.

Sources

Primary LSUMZ data; Parker data; Taczanowski 1884b. **Weights** (n = 23) LSUMZ data. **Stomach contents** LSUMZ data.

Tangara argyrofenges 207
Straw-backed Tanager
Plate 28

Length 13 cm (5 in.). Weight 19 g (18.0–20.0 g). Two subspecies. Subadult has greenish edgings to flight feathers and a dusky cream back. Also known as the Green-throated Tanager.

Geographic Range

T. a. caeruleigularis: e Andean slope in Amazonas, San Martín, and Junín (FMNH), PERU. *T. a. argyrofenges*: La Paz, Cochabamba, and w Santa Cruz, BOLIVIA.

Elevational Range

1350–1700 m in Peru and 1200–2700 m (centered at 1600–1900 m) in Bolivia.

Habitat and Behavior

Inhabits humid montane forest and forest edge and clearings. Encountered in pairs (Parker data). In Peru, accompanies mixed-species flocks and forages high in trees (Stolzmann in Tacznowski 1884b). Apparently eats both fruit and insects. Observed foraging at *Cecropia* catkins and searching leaves, bark, and slender branches (Parker data). Stomach contents (1): small berries.

Vocalizations

No information.

Breeding

No information.

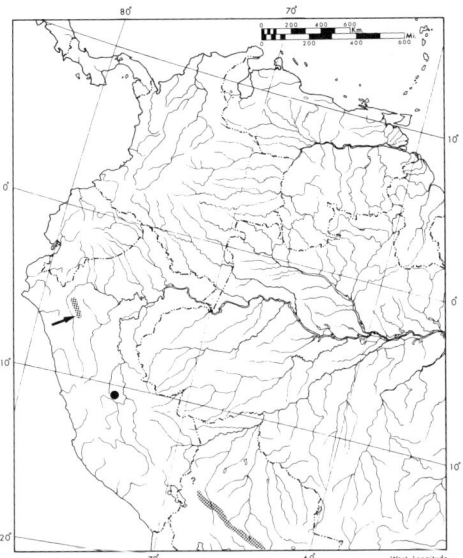

Tangara argyrofenges

Tangara cyanoptera

Sources

Primary LSUMZ data; Parker data; Parker, Parker, and Plenge 1982; Taczanowski 1884b.
Weights (n = 5) LSUMZ data. **Stomach contents** Niethammer 1956.

Tangara cyanoptera   **208**
Black-headed Tanager
Plate 28

T. c. cyanoptera: length 13 cm (5 in.); weight 18 g (1 female). *T. c. whitelyi*: length 14 cm (5½ in.); weight 23 g (21.5–24.5 g). Two subspecies.

Geographic Range

T. c. cyanoptera: n COLOMBIA on both slopes of the E Andes in Norte de Santander and in the Santa Marta Mountains; the Perijá Mountains; and n VENEZUELA in the Andes from Táchira to Lara and mountains and foothills from Falcón east to Sucre and Monagas. *T. c. whitelyi*: tepuis in s VENEZUELA (Amazonas and Bolívar) and adjacent BRAZIL and GUYANA (Mt. Twekquay).

Elevational Range

600–2000 m in Colombia, 450–2200 m in n Venezuela, and 1100–2250 m in the tepuis.

Habitat and Behavior

Inhabits second growth and forest edge; also occurs in wooded ravines and open woodland. Typically encountered in pairs, sometimes in (family?) groups of 3–5 individuals or singly. Usually travels independently, but sometimes follows mixed-species flocks. Hops and flutters on outer branches and in foliage (Hilty and Brown 1986). Forages from mid to upper levels of trees, sometimes lower. Observed eating berries (Thomas data), melastome fruits, and *Cecropia* catkins (Parker data). Also forages for insects, mostly on twigs or in foliage; seldom peers underneath branches using the diagonal-lean method (Hilty *in litt.*), but *whitelyi* was observed employing this method on a partly moss-covered branch 10 cm in diam. (O'Neill data).

Vocalizations

Call: a slightly quivering lisping High-pitched *djeet*. Song(?): repeats a 1–2 sec. Moderate- to High-pitched piercing quivering squeal given without inflection; has something of the quality of running a fingernail across a blackboard, but slightly musical; irregularly utters call notes between phrases.

Breeding

Eggs are white, marked with shades of brown and gray.

TANGARA

Sources

Primary Gilliard 1959; Hilty and Brown 1986; Meyer de Schauensee and Phelps 1978; Schäfer and Phelps 1954. **Weights** (*cyanoptera* n = 1; *whitelyi* n = 6): Foster data; Thomas 1982. **Vocalizations** LNS recordings by Parker (1), Schwartz (1). **Eggs** Nehrkorn 1899; Ogilvie-Grant 1912.

Tangara pulcherrima 209
Golden-collared Honeycreeper
Plate 28

Length 11 cm (4½ in.). Weight 15 g (14.0–16.0 g). Two subspecies. Subadult male resembles female but irides brown rather than red and base of mandible silvery rather than yellow (LSUMZ). Often placed in the monotypic genus *Iridophanes*.

Geographic Range

T. p. pulcherrima: the head of the Magdalena Valley in Huila (sight, Hilty and Brown 1986), COLOMBIA, and along the e slope of the Andes from w Caquetá (sight, Hilty and Brown 1986), COLOMBIA, southward through ECUADOR and PERU to s Cuzco. *T. p. aureinucha*: the Pacific slope from Valle (Hilty 1977), COLOMBIA, southward to Pichincha, ECUADOR.

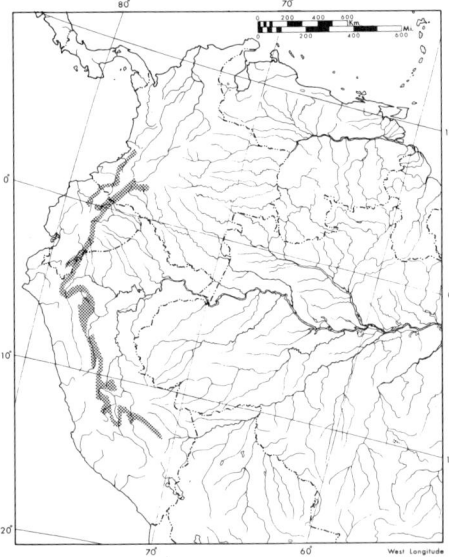

Tangara pulcherrima

Elevational Range

1000–2150 m (LSUMZ); mostly 1300–1600 m on e slope of Ecuador (Ridgely in Hilty and Brown 1986).

Habitat and Behavior

Inhabits humid forest, forest edge and openings, second-growth woodland, and tree-studded clearings. Encountered singly, in pairs, and in groups of 3–9 individuals. Travels apart from or with mixed-species flocks. Flies in a swift flutter (Ingels 1974a). Forages from mid to upper levels. Visits fruiting shrubs and trees, including those of *Miconia* (O'Neill pers. comm.) and *Cecropia*; probes *Cecropia* catkins and other flowers, possibly taking nectar and/or insects (Parker data). Stomach contents (4): vegetable matter, including fruit, seeds, and flower petals. In captivity, eats fruit, insects, and nectar (McEwen 1979).

Vocalizations

Call: a high lisping buzzy *czee*, sometimes doubled (Hilty and Brown 1986). In captivity: Male and female constantly called to one another. During egg-laying, the male slowly repeated 2 notes, 1 high and 1 low, at regular intervals for about an hour. (McEwen 1979.)

Breeding

In captivity: Prenuptial feeding by the male was frequently observed. Three cup-shaped nests were constructed by the male, and one nest was built in a nest box by the female, but the male and female never built a nest together. The male repeatedly flew at his mate at high speeds, apparently in courtship. Two eggs, laid on consecutive days in the female's nest, were pale bluish gray with rust-colored streaks converging to form a solid patch at the large end. Only the female incubated. The male defended the nest area from other birds in the aviary and frequently fed his mate on and off the nest. Both parents fed the young; only live flies and spiders were given to the nestlings. The nestling period was 17 days. (McEwen 1979.) In the wild, observed feeding *Miconia* berries to a fledgling (Hilty 1977).

Sources

Primary Hilty 1977; Hilty and Brown 1986; LSUMZ data; McEwen 1979; Parker data. **Weights (n = 6)** LSUMZ data. **Stomach contents** LSUMZ data. **Vocalizations** Hilty and Brown 1986. **Eggs** McEwen 1979.

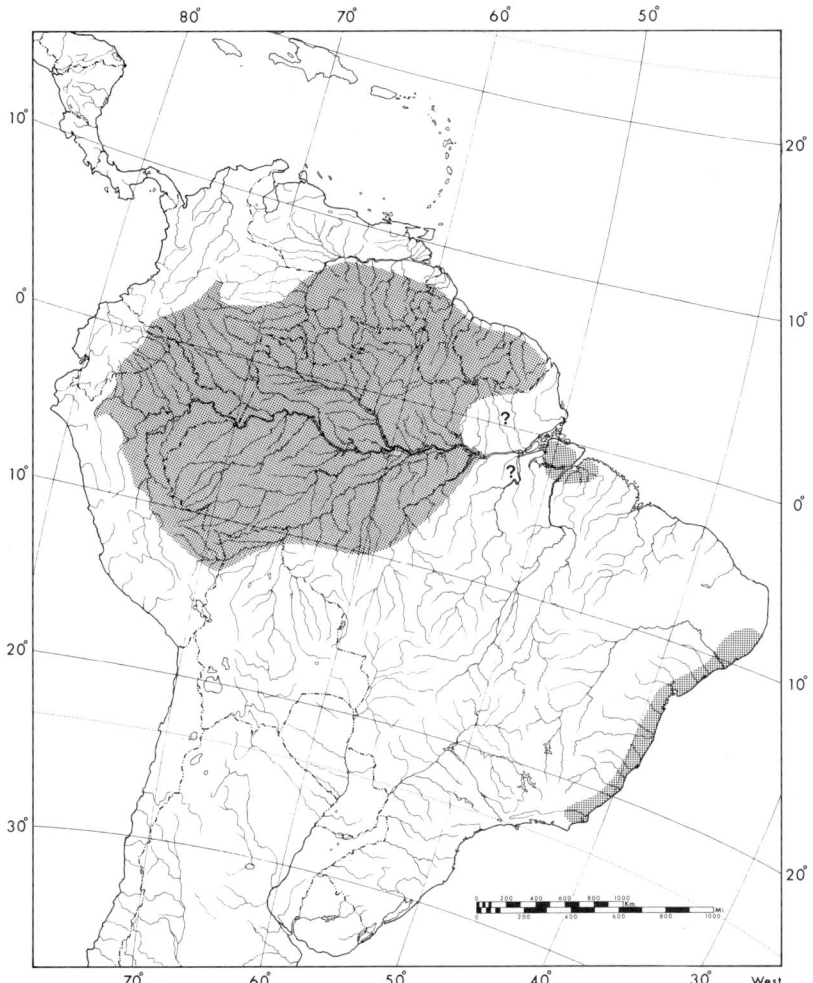

Tangara velia

Tangara velia 210
Opal-rumped Tanager
Plate 28

Length 12–14 cm (4½–5½ in.). Weight (*iridina*) 21 g (19.0–23.0 g). Four subspecies: *velia* resembles *iridina*; *signata* also resembles *velia* except the posterior edges of the forehead are silvery as in *cyanomelaena*.

Geographic Range

T. v. velia: THE GUIANAS and BRAZIL north of the Amazon River in Pará and Amazonas west to the lower Rio Negro. *T. v. iridina*: s VENEZUELA in Bolívar (Río Caura valley east to the Gran Sabana) and Amazonas; east of the Andes in COLOMBIA from nw Meta, s Meta, s Vichada (along the Río Guaviare), and e Vichada (Hilty and Brown 1986) southward through e ECUADOR and e PERU to extreme n BOLIVIA in El Beni (Remsen and Ridgely 1980), and in w Amazonian BRAZIL eastward to e Amazonas (Rio Negro), w Pará (lower Rio Tapajós), and extreme nw Mato Grosso (Rio Aripuana, sight, Roth *fide* Brown *in litt.*). *T. v. signata*: ne BRAZIL in ne Pará. *T. v. cyanomelaena*: the coastal region in e BRAZIL from Pernambuco south to Rio de Janeiro.

Elevational Range

Lowlands to 500 m in Colombia, 1000 m in Peru, and 1200 m in Venezuela; mostly below 500 m.

Habitat and Behavior

Inhabits terra firma and low-lying forest and forest edge; also occurs in second-growth woodland, shaded plantations, and clearings with scattered tall trees. Pairs and small groups, sometimes larger flocks of up to 15 individuals, travel alone or accompany mixed-species flocks (both permanent canopy flocks and temporary tanager flocks; see Munn 1985). Usually forages in the upper levels of forest, mostly in the crowns of tall trees, but also in the subcanopy; occasionally descends to fruiting shrubs at forest edge. Eats fruit, especially small fruits and berries, and insects. Hops along bare limbs and large (e.g., 5 cm in diam.) branches, inspecting the sides and undersides using the diagonal-lean method. Also clings to trunk surfaces and inspects epiphytes. Stomach contents (4): vegetable matter, including fruit pulp, berries, and seeds.

Vocalizations

Call: a High-pitched *tsst* repeated randomly or rapidly in twos and threes. Also utters a high-pitched twitter during flight (Isler data).

Tangara callophrys

Breeding

Eggs are grayish white, thickly dotted with darker shades of gray.

Sources

Primary Haverschmidt 1968; Hilty and Brown 1986; LSUMZ data; Parker data; Pearson 1971; Remsen and Ridgely 1980; Willis 1977. **Weights (n = 11)** LSUMZ data; Pearson 1971; Sick 1985. **Stomach contents** Haverschmidt 1968; LSUMZ data; Pinto 1953. **Vocalizations** LNS recordings by Bierregaard (1), Parker (1); Isler data. **Eggs** Nehrkorn 1899; Penard and Penard 1910.

Tangara callophrys **211**
Opal-crowned Tanager
Plate 28

Length 14 cm (5½ in.). Weight 22 g (21.0–24.0 g). Monotypic.

Geographic Range

Upper Amazonia from se COLOMBIA (w Caquetá and Putumayo) southward through e ECUADOR and e PERU (to Puno) and eastward in BRAZIL to w Amazonas (east of the border with COLOMBIA along the Amazon River, the middle Rio Juruá, and middle Rio Purus).

Elevational Range

Lowlands to 1000 m in Andean foothills.

Habitat and Behavior

Inhabits terra firma and low-lying forest, forest edge, and shaded plantations in or near forest. Pairs and small groups of up to 7 individuals travel independently or accompany mixed-species flocks (both permanent canopy flocks and temporary tanager flocks; see Munn 1985). Joins feeding aggregations at fruiting trees. Forages for fruit and insects in forest tree tops, lower at forest edge. Hops along large limbs using the diagonal-lean method to obtain prey. Stomach contents (3): fruit.

Vocalizations

Call: a high-pitched *zit*, usually repeated quickly 2–4 times; resembles call note of the Turquoise Tanager, *T. mexicana* **168** (Hilty and Brown 1986).

Breeding

No information.

Sources

Primary Goodfellow 1901; Hilty and Brown 1986; Munn 1985; O'Neill 1974; Parker data; Pearson 1972; Terborgh and Weske 1969. **Weights (n = 4)** LSUMZ data. **Stomach contents** LSUMZ data. **Vocalizations** Hilty and Brown 1986.

DACNIS

Dacnis species (Table 25) live primarily in the canopy, and five (the White-bellied, Turquoise, Black-legged, Viridian, and Scarlet-breasted) of the nine species are extremely scarce or local. Consequently, the natural histories of *Dacnis* species, on the whole, are poorly known. All are lowland species except for the Turquoise Dacnis. *Dacnis* are mostly encountered in pairs, traveling independently or associating with mixed-species flocks. The Blue Dacnis is most widespread and has been observed in Panama to specialize in locating insect prey by spotting damaged leaves. This behavior, however, has not been observed for any other *Dacnis* species. Storer (1969) describes how the Blue Dacnis may have evolved from the *Tangara* tanagers. *Dacnis* was formerly placed in the family Coerebidae.

Table 25 The *Dacnis* Species

212	*D. albiventris*	White-bellied Dacnis
213	*D. lineata*	Black-faced Dacnis
214	*D. flaviventer*	Yellow-bellied Dacnis
215	*D. hartlaubi*	Turquoise Dacnis
216	*D. nigripes*	Black-legged Dacnis
217	*D. venusta*	Scarlet-thighed Dacnis
218	*D. cayana*	Blue Dacnis
219	*D. viguieri*	Viridian Dacnis
220	*D. berlepschi*	Scarlet-breasted Dacnis

Dacnis albiventris **212**
White-bellied Dacnis
Plate 29

Length 10 cm (4 in.). Weight 11 g (11.0 and 11.5 g). Monotypic.

Geographic Range

Locally within the range shown on the map in Amazonas, VENEZUELA; Meta and w Putumayo, COLOMBIA; Napo and Pastaza, ECUADOR; Loreto and Ucayali, PERU; and Pará, BRAZIL on the Rio Cururú (Sick 1960).

DACNIS

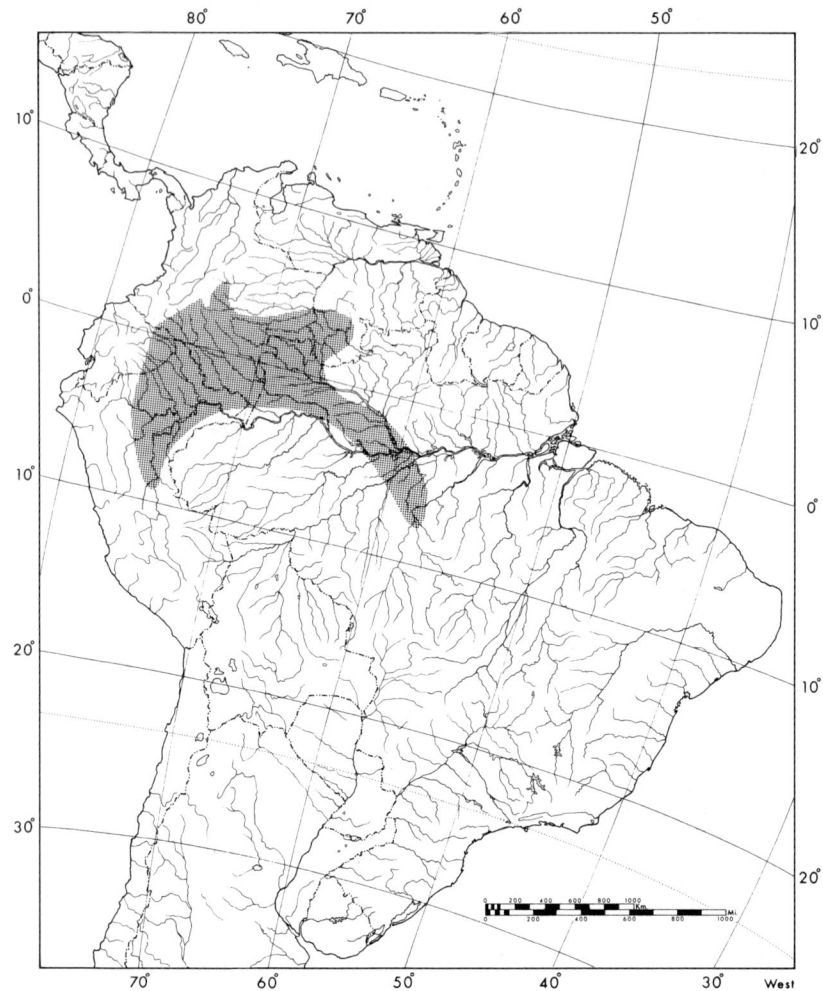

Dacnis albiventris

Elevational Range

Lowlands to 400 m.

Habitat and Behavior

Encountered in forest and in trees and shrubs at lake edges and in pastures (O'Neill and Pearson 1974). Forages in the canopy. In Brazil, observed once at about 9 m off the ground in the canopy of gallery forest associating with a mixed-species flock (Sick 1960). Scarce and/or local.

Vocalizations

No information.

Breeding

No information.

Sources

Primary Hilty and Brown 1986; Meyer de Schauensee and Phelps 1978; O'Neill and Pearson 1974; Sick 1960. **Weights (n = 2)** Sick 1960.

Dacnis lineata **213**
Black-faced Dacnis
Plate 29

Length 11 cm (4½ in.). Weight 11 g (9.5–13.0 g). Three subspecies: *lineata* and *egregia*

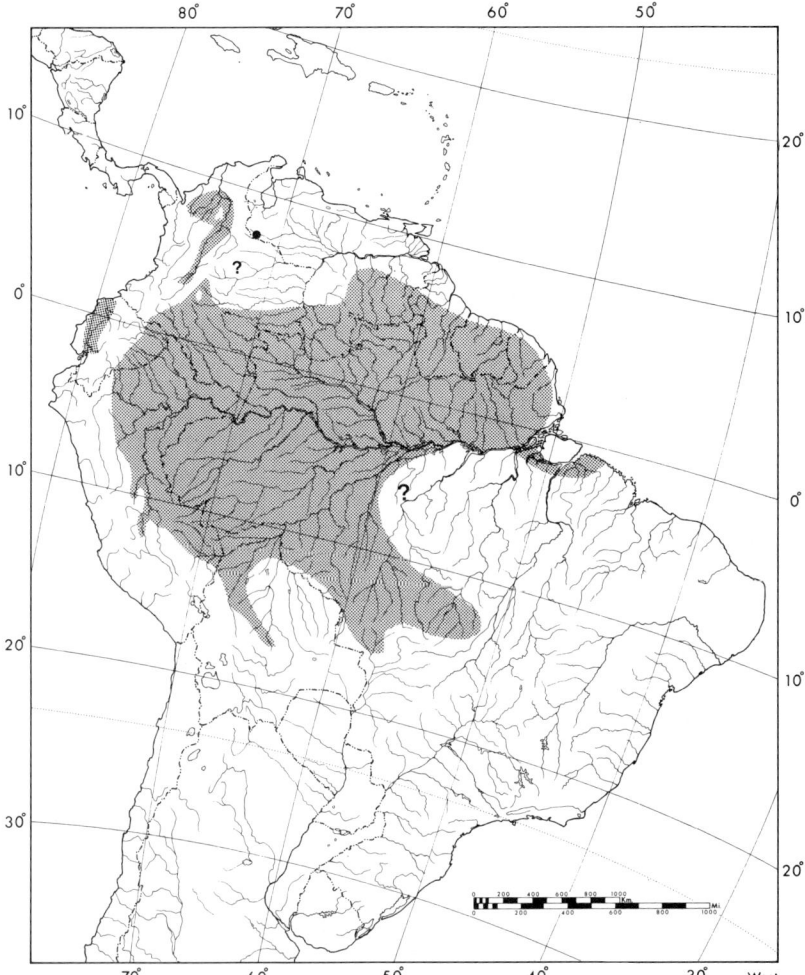

Dacnis lineata

are illustrated; *aequatorialis* resembles *egregia*. Subadult plumage, resembling female plumage, may be retained for some time (see Haverschmidt 1968).

Geographic Range

D. l. egregia: COLOMBIA from Antioquia (lower Cauca Valley) east to Santander and south to s Tolima (middle and upper Magdalena Valley). *D. l. aequatorialis*: Pacific slope in w ECUADOR from Esmeraldas south to Guayas. *D. l. lineata*: THE GUIANAS; Amazonas (south of the Río Ventuari) and Bolívar (except ne), VENEZUELA; the e base of the Andes in Táchira, VENEZUELA, and from w Meta and se Guainía, COLOMBIA, southward east of the Andes through ECUADOR and PERU to El Beni and Cochabamba, BOLIVIA; and eastward through Amazonia to wc and ec Mato Grosso (Willis 1976a, Fry 1970), Pará (unknown south of the Amazon River except in the Belém region), and Amapá (Novaes 1978), BRAZIL.

Elevational Range

Lowlands to 1350 m (mostly below 1100 m).

Habitat and Behavior

Inhabits terra firma and low-lying (incl. *varzea*) forest, forest edge (incl. savanna and gallery forest edge), tall second growth, and scattered trees in forest clearings and plantations. Encountered mostly in pairs and small groups of up to 8 individuals; also singly. Typically encountered with mixed-species flocks; associates for short periods with permanent canopy flocks (Munn 1985); joins temporary tanager flocks and feeding aggregations. In Brazil, up to 20 individuals were observed at one time in a fruiting tree (Beebe 1916). Actively flits through canopy foliage.

Forages primarily 10–50 m above the ground in the crowns of trees, occasionally descends lower, but not normally to low fruiting shrubs (Parker data). Searches for insects in dense foliage at the tips of branches and in vine tangles. Frequently hangs to take prey from leaves. In Bolivia, also reached up or out, leaned down, and hovered to obtain insects from leaf undersides; took 8 mm fruits without acrobatics (Remsen data). In Peru, observed eating melastome berries while perched (Remsen data) and plucking *Cecropia* fruits in flight (Parker data). Stomach contents: vegetable matter (17); vegetable and animal matter (2). Contents included fruit, seeds, berries, and insects.

Vocalizations

No information.

Breeding

No information.

Sources

Primary Beebe 1916; Haverschmidt 1968; Hilty and Brown 1986; LSUMZ data; Munn 1985; Novaes 1969; Parker data; Remsen data; Terborgh and Weske 1975; Willis 1977. **Weights (n=20)** Dick, McGillivray, and Brooks 1984; Fry 1970; Haverschmidt 1968; LSUMZ data. **Stomach contents** Brosset 1964; Foster data; Haverschmidt 1968; LSUMZ data; Schubart, Aguirre, and Sick 1965.

Dacnis flaviventer 214
Yellow-bellied Dacnis
Plate 29

Length 11 cm (4½ in.). Weight 13 g (12.0–14.0 g). Monotypic.

Geographic Range

VENEZUELA in Amazonas (Río Ventuari region) and Bolívar (the lower Río Caura to the upper Río Paragua); east of the Andes from w Caquetá and Vaupés, COLOMBIA, southward through e ECUADOR and e PERU (except foothill regions) to w Santa Cruz (Remsen, Traylor, and Parkes in press), BOLIVIA; and eastward through Amazonian BRAZIL to the n half of Mato Grosso and to sc and wc Pará (not recorded from Roraima).

Elevational Range

Lowlands to 450 m.

Habitat and Behavior

Inhabits the edges of low-lying forest (incl. *varzea* forest), especially along rivers and on river islands; also occurs in terra firma forest, tall second growth, and isolated trees near forest. Scarce over much of its range. Typically encountered in pairs; also in small groups; observed occasionally in groups (feeding aggregations?) of up to 10–15 individuals (Ridgely *in litt.*). Travels independently and sometimes is transient in mixed-species flocks (both permanent canopy flocks and temporary tanager flocks; see Munn 1985). Forages from midheights to the crowns of tall trees; occasionally descends lower at forest edge (Ridgely *in litt.*). In Peru, observed picking insects off small new leaves 15 m off the ground (5 m from the canopy) at the edge of a treefall (Remsen data). Stomach contents: vegetable matter (2); animal matter (6); both (1). Contents included fruit, homopterans, and caterpillars.

Vocalizations

Calls: a High-pitched short *zeet* and a buzzy, coarse, Moderate- to High-pitched *zrreet*; delivers notes often.

Breeding

No information.

Sources

Primary Hilty and Brown 1986; LSUMZ data; Munn 1985; Parker data; Snethlage 1913; Taczanowski 1884a. **Weights (n=3)** LSUMZ data. **Stomach contents** LSUMZ data; Schubart, Aguirre, and Sick 1965. **Vocalizations** LNS recordings by Parker (2); Hilty and Brown 1986.

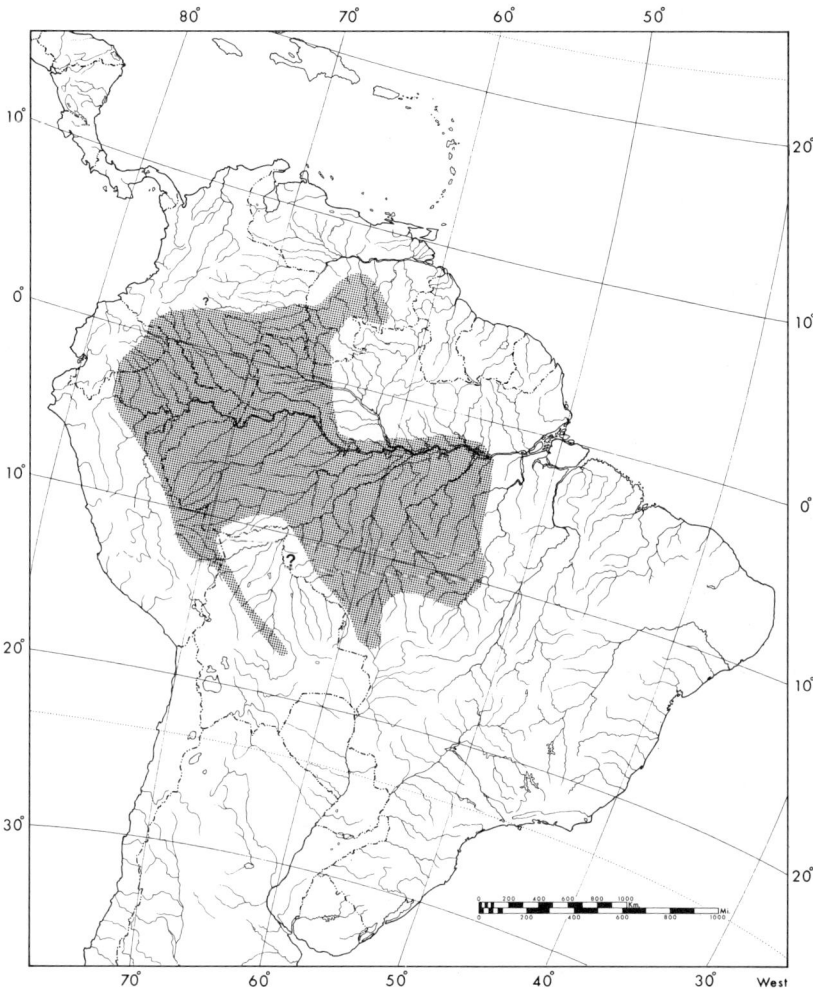

Dacnis flaviventer

Dacnis hartlaubi 215
Turquoise Dacnis
Plate 29

Length 11 cm (4½ in.). Monotypic. Also known as the Turquoise Dacnis-Tanager. Formerly placed in the monotypic genus *Pseudodacnis*.

Geographic Range

COLOMBIA on the Pacific slope in Valle, the w slope of the C Andes in Quindío, and the w slope of the E Andes in Cundinamarca (Río Bogotá valley).

Elevational Range

300–1700 m on Pacific slope, ca. 1500 m in Quindío, and 1700–2200 m in Cundinamarca.

Habitat and Behavior

Inhabits humid forest edge and nearby isolated trees. Local and scarce; may be endangered (Hilty 1985). In Valle, a single male was seen perching quietly on a high exposed bare limb and then following a mixed-species flock in the forest subcanopy; hopped sluggishly on a mossy branch and inspected a bromeliad; movements suggested a *Tangara* tanager (Hilty and Brown 1986). Stomach contents (1): fruit.

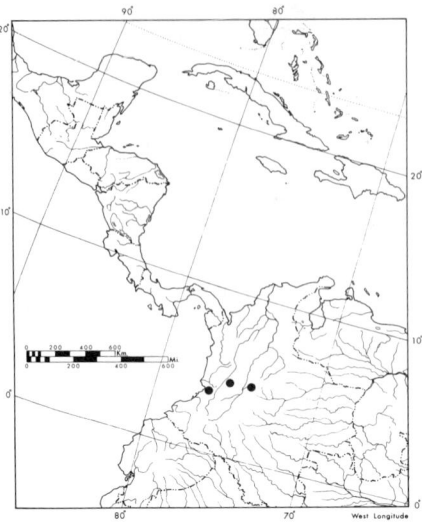

Dacnis hartlaubi

Vocalizations

No information.

Breeding

No information.

Sources

Primary Hilty and Brown 1986; Munves 1975. **Stomach contents** Hilty and Brown 1986.

Dacnis nigripes 216
Black-legged Dacnis
Plate 29

Length 11 cm (4 in.). Weight 14 g (11–15.5 g). Monotypic. Subadult male plumage (resembling that of female) appears to be retained for the first year (Gonzaga 1983).

Geographic Range

Se BRAZIL in the coastal region from c Espírito Santo (Gonzaga 1983) southward to Santa Catarina; a single record from Lagoa Santa, c Minas Gerais, may be an error in specimen labeling (Gonzaga *in litt.*).

Elevational Range

Lowlands to ca. 850 m.

Habitat and Behavior

Scarce and local; apparently moves seasonally among portions of its range. In the state of Rio de Janeiro, where found from April to August, encountered in forest clearings and second-growth edge. Observed in the early morning in small groups; by midmorning joined large mixed-species flocks of tanagers, becards, and other small birds. Was encountered in some years but not in others, possibly the result of irregular wandering in search of favorite foods. Often seen foraging among flowers of *Mabea brasiliensis* (Euphorbiaceae) from which they took nectar and small insects. Stomach contents (6): animal and vegetable matter, including *Miconia* berries, dry seeds of *Xylopia*, other unidentified fruits, coleopterans, dipterans, hymenopterans, and small caterpillars. (Gonzaga 1983.)

Vocalizations

Said to call frequently.

Breeding

No information.

Sources

Primary Gonzaga 1983. **Weights (n = 10)** Gonzaga 1983. **Stomach contents** Gonzaga 1983.

Dacnis venusta 217
Scarlet-thighed Dacnis
Plate 29

Length 12 cm (4½ in.). Weight 16 g (15.0–17.1 g). Two subspecies; males differ in the extent to which blackish underparts are tinged green. Males possibly breed in subadult plumage (see Wetmore, Pasquier, and Olson 1984).

Geographic Range

The Pacific slope from Guanacaste (Cordillera de Guanacaste), COSTA RICA, eastward through PANAMA, then southward through COLOMBIA to n Guayas (Ridgely *in litt.*), ECUADOR; the Caribbean slope from Alajuela, COSTA RICA, eastward through PANAMA to Antioquia, COLOMBIA, and along the n base of the Andes eastward to the middle Magdalena Valley.

Elevational Range

In Costa Rica and Panama, from sea level to 1650 m, mostly 600–1400 m; appears to de-

Dacnis nigripes

scend to lowlands primarily outside the breeding season. In Colombia, from sea level to 700 m, mostly 150–600 m; wanders to 1100 m (Hilty and Brown 1986).

Habitat and Behavior

Inhabits forest and forest edge, open woodland, shaded plantations, and nearby isolated trees in clearings; occasionally wanders far from woodland in search of food (Skutch 1962b). Usually encountered in small groups, sometimes pairs, singly, or in large groups of up to 15 or more individuals. Occasionally associates with mixed-species flocks in the canopy. Active and restless.

Forages in the canopy within forest and from low in shrubbery to tree tops elsewhere; in Costa Rica, usually above 6–9 m off the ground (Slud 1964). Appears to feed mostly on small (3–8 mm) fruits, especially those of *Miconia* and other melastomes. Also observed taking fruits of *Sapium* and *Dendropanax* (Wheelright et al. 1984), *Cecropia* catkins (Parker data), and flower stems of *Pourouma* (Wetmore, Pasquier, and Olson 1984). Stomach contents (2): vegetable matter, including fruit pulp and figs. Five additional stomach contents contained no more than 30% insect matter.

Vocalizations

Calls: a metallic *urp*, *zirp*, *rit*, or *wurt* and a buzzy *wuzt* or *rezt*. A female defending her

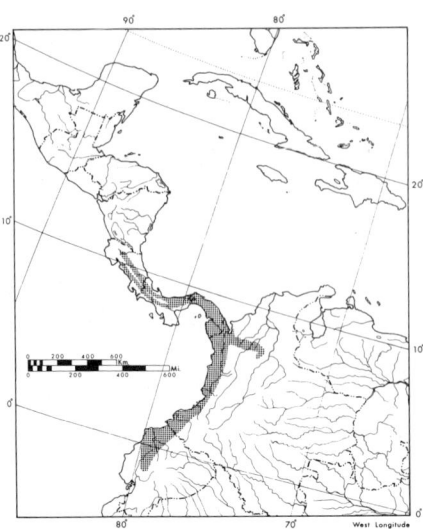

Dacnis venusta

young uttered a low nasal cry (Skutch 1962b). Excited individuals called a low nasal *wheu wheu* with a curious metallic tone (Wetmore, Pasquier, and Olson 1984).

Breeding

In Costa Rica, one nest was discovered 15 m up in the crown of a tree growing in a bushy pasture; the exceedingly frail open bowl, composed of course materials (e.g., rootlets) and camouflaged with living ferns, was slung between 2 outer branchlets hidden among a parasitic vine and dense foliage (Skutch 1962b). Another nest was found in an open grove of slender second-growth trees (Skutch 1967b). At the first nest, the female vigorously defended her young from other birds in the area; the 2 nestlings were fed primarily by the female. Breeding dates: Costa Rica May.

Sources

Primary Buskirk 1976; Carriker 1910; Greenberg 1981c; Hilty and Brown 1986; Ridgely 1976; Skutch 1962b; Slud 1964; Wetmore, Pasquier, and Olson 1984. **Weights** Greenberg and Gradwohl 1980; Hartman and Brownell 1961; LSUMZ data; Strauch 1977. **Stomach contents** LSUMZ data; Goldman in Wetmore, Pasquier, and Olson 1984. **Vocalizations** LNS recording by Parker (1); recording by R. A. Rowlett (1); Slud 1964. **Nests and breeding dates** Skutch 1962b, 1967b.

Dacnis cayana **218**
Blue Dacnis
Plate 29

Length 11–12 cm (4½–5 in.). Weight (*paraguayensis*) 15 g (?–17.8 g); (*remaining subspecies*) 13 g (10.0–15.5 g). Eight subspecies: *paraguayensis* and *coerebicolor* are illustrated; *callaina, ultramarina, cayana,* and *glaucogularis* resemble *paraguayensis*. Although slightly less purple, *napaea* and *baudoana* resemble *coerebicolor*.

Geographic Range

D. c. callaina and *ultramarina*: the Caribbean slope from extreme e HONDURAS (sight, March 1979—Ridgely) southeastward through NICARAGUA, COSTA RICA, and PANAMA to San Blas; the Pacific slope from San José, COSTA RICA, eastward through PANAMA to nw Chocó, COLOMBIA. *D. c. baudoana, coerebicolor,* and *napaea*: COLOMBIA north and west of the Andes (except nw Chocó) southward to Guayas, ECUADOR. *D. c. cayana, glaucogularis,* and *paraguayensis*: VENEZUELA (apparently except Falcón region), TRINIDAD, and THE GUIANAS southward east of the Andes through COLOMBIA, ECUADOR, PERU, and BRAZIL to Santa Cruz, BOLIVIA, Mato Grosso, BRAZIL, se PARAGUAY (east of the Río Paraguay), Misiones, ARGENTINA and n Rio Grande do Sul, BRAZIL (Belton 1985).

Elevational Range

Mostly from sea level to ca. 750 m; also higher, to 1000 m in Panama, to ca. 1200–1400 m in South America, and as high as 1650 m in Bolivia (LSUMZ).

Habitat and Behavior

Widely distributed in dry as well as humid regions. Appears to favor woodlands, young forest, open forests (e.g., savanna and gallery forests), forest edge, second growth, shaded plantations, and trees and shrubs in semiopen areas. Also found in the canopy of terra firma and low-lying (incl. *varzea*) forest to an uncertain extent. Moves about seasonally. Usually encountered in pairs or small groups; sometimes solitary; rarely seen in larger groups of up to 12 individuals. In c Panama, the average group size was 3.02 (Greenberg and Gradwohl 1985, 58 obs.). Often travels with mixed-species flocks; joins feeding aggregations at fruiting trees. Observed anting in captivity (Skutch 1962b).

Forages mostly in tree tops; height varies

Dacnis cayana

with the height of the vegetation; usually above 5 m off the ground. In Trinidad, foraged somewhat higher when insect-searching than when fruit-eating (Snow and Snow 1971). In Peru, foraged higher when with mixed-species flocks (mean: 26 m) than when alone (mean: 14 m); Pearson 1971. Of 267 observations in Trinidad, 49% were insect-searching, 44% fruit-eating, and 7% at flowers (Snow and Snow 1971). Of 105 observations in Panama, 64% were insects and 36% plant material (Greenberg 1984). Stomach contents: vegetable matter (17); animal matter (7); both (4). Contents included fruit, seeds, hymenopteran pupae, dung beetles, orthopterans, and spiders.

Typically takes insects from leaves, using acrobatic motions. Perches on twigs or petioles and leans over, hangs upside down, or stretches up to take prey off leaf undersides. Also occasionally examines stems and slender branches, probes flowers and bromeliads, or lunges or sallies for insects. In Panama, did not search methodically by hopping along branches, but appeared to fly directly between brown areas of leaf damage that seemed to be used as a clue to insect location; often these leaves were partially curled (Greenberg and Gradwohl 1980). Used its sharp bill to probe and extract hidden grubs (24 of 25 large prey items, Greenberg 1981a). When attacking insects on leaves, prey were taken from leaf tops 70% of the time, from bottoms 30% of the time

(Greenberg 1984, 65 obs.). In Trinidad, 69% of insect-searching was on foliage, 13% branches and twigs, 12% flowers and seed heads, and 6% sallies to air (Snow and Snow 1971, 130 obs.).

Eats a variety of fruits and often takes nectar. Usually picks berries while perched upright but also leans over acrobatically; clings upside down to feed on *Cecropia* catkins and other fruits. Swallows small fruits whole and mashes or bites pieces out of larger ones. To take nectar and/or insects from flowers, perches on a twig behind the flower and bends over to push its bill inside the stamen; comes to feeding tables for bananas when natural food is scarce (Skutch 1962b). In Trinidad, took 26 species of fruit, especially *Miconia* berries (39% of all fruit eaten) and fruits of the families Euphorbiaceae (24%) and Ulmaceae (10%). In Costa Rica, Skutch (1962b) found it was also fond of arillate fruit (*Clusia* sp). In Panama, Beehler (1980) saw Blue Dacnis take nectar from flowers of *Luehea seemanii* (Tiliaceae). In Brazil, Mitchell (1957) thought it partial to large flower heads of mango trees and a *Ficus*. In Paraguay, ate 7–10 mm fruits of *Allophyllus edulis* by perching near fruit and leaning over to take bites, leaving the seed hanging; occasionally plucked fruit and rolled it around in its bill dropping the seed; sometimes held the fruit against its perch to peck out pieces (Foster data).

Vocalizations

Calls: a High-pitched *tsit* or *snt* and a harsh Moderate- to High-pitched *chit* or *chid-it*. During nest building, a male repeated a slight weak lisping note over and over for about a minute (Skutch 1962b).

Breeding

Mitchell (1957) observed males in courtship display moving restlessly from branch to branch and posturing, i.e., standing tall and bowing. Engages in nuptial feeding (Skutch 1976). The nest is usually a deep cup (almost a pouch), composed of fine fibers and seed down compactly matted (illus., Ihering 1900). In Costa Rica, two nests were built in trees, 5.5 and 7.6 m above the ground in clustered outer foliage; one was suspended between two leafy twigs. The female built alone, accompanied by her mate who vigorously guarded against intruders. (Skutch 1962b.) In Panama, a nest, made of plant fibers, was suspended between 2 branches 13 m up in a tree (Ridgely *in litt.*).

Eggs (2–3) are whitish or greenish white, marked with dull gray, most heavily in a wreath at the large end. The female incubates alone, occasionally fed by her mate. Nestling period is about 13 days. Both parents feed fledglings, apparently dividing the brood between them. In Costa Rica, one pair of nestlings were fed by an adult male in addition to the parents (Skutch 1962b). Breeding dates: Trinidad March, June, and July. Brazil (Pará and Mato Grosso) Dec. Costa Rica May.

Sources

Primary Greenberg 1984; Greenberg and Gradwohl 1980; Hilty and Brown 1986; Mitchell 1957; Parker data; Ridgely 1976; Skutch 1962b; Slud 1964; Snow and Snow 1971; Terborgh and Weske 1969. **Weights** (*paraguayensis* n = 16; remaining subspecies n = 61): Belton 1985; Dick, McGillivray, and Brooks 1984; ffrench 1973; Fry 1970; Greenberg 1984; Gonzaga 1983; Greenberg and Gradwohl 1980; Haverschmidt 1948, 1968; LSUMZ data; Pearson 1971; Sick 1958; Strauch 1977. **Stomach contents** Beebe 1909; Foster data; Layard 1873; Moojen, Carvalho, and Lopes 1941; Novaes 1973; Pinto 1953; Schubart, Aguirre, and Sick 1965. **Vocalizations** LNS recordings by L. I. Davis (1), Morton (1); Slud 1964. **Nests, eggs, and breeding dates** Allen 1891; ffrench 1973; Ihering 1900; Pinto 1953; Ridgely *in litt.*; Skutch 1962b.

Dacnis viguieri **219**
Viridian Dacnis
Plate 29

Length 10 cm (4 in.). Monotypic. Subadult males resemble females.

Geographic Range

Extreme se PANAMA (Darién) and extreme nw COLOMBIA (Chocó, Antioquia, and Córdoba).

Elevational Range

Lowlands to 600 m.

Habitat and Behavior

Encountered in the canopy of humid and dry forest and at forest edge. Also said to occur in scrub (Meyer de Schauensee 1964).

Vocalizations

No information.

Breeding

No information.

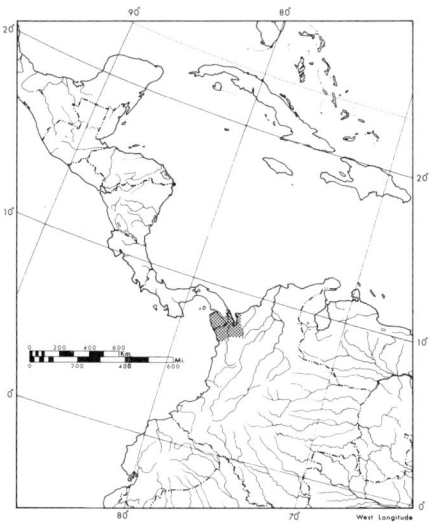

Dacnis viguieri

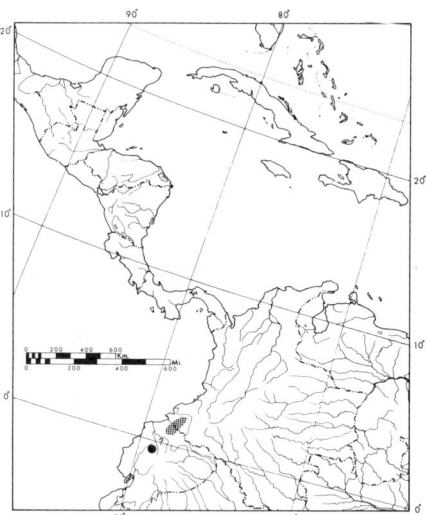

Dacnis berlepschi

Sources

Primary Haffer 1975; Hilty and Brown 1986; Meyer de Schauensee 1964; Wetmore, Pasquier, and Olson 1984.

Dacnis berlepschi **220**
Scarlet-breasted Dacnis
Plate 29

Length 12 cm (5 in.). Monotypic.

Geographic Range

Pacific slope in sw Nariño, COLOMBIA, and nw Esmeraldas, Imbabura, and n Los Ríos (sight, Greenfield *fide* Ridgely *in litt.*), ECUADOR.

Elevational Range

200–800 m; sight record in Colombia at 1200 m (Hilty and Brown 1986).

Habitat and Behavior

Encountered at wet forest edge and in tall second growth. Scarce and/or local.

Vocalizations

No information.

Breeding

No information.

Sources

Primary Hartert 1901; Hilty and Brown 1986.

CHLOROPHANES

This monotypic genus was formerly placed in the family Coeribidae. Storer (1969) portrayed its possible evolution from *Tangara*. A specimen originally described as *Chlorophanes purpurascens* is apparently a hybrid between the Green Honeycreeper and the Blue Dacnis, *Dacnis cayana* **218,** or the Red-legged Honeycreeper, *Cyanerpes cyaneus* **225** (see Auber 1974).

Chlorophanes spiza **221**
Green Honeycreeper
Plate 30

Length 13 cm (5 in.). Weight 19 g (14.0–23.0 g). Seven subspecies: *arguta* and *caerulescens* are illustrated; *guatemalensis*, *exsul*, and *axillaris* resemble *arguta*; *subtropicalis* resembles *caerulescens*; and *spiza* is intermediate between *arguta* and *caerulescens*. Subadult males resemble females and possibly retain this plumage for some time.

Geographic Range

C. s. guatemalensis, *arguta*, and *exsul*: on the Gulf-Caribbean slope from s MEXICO (ne Oaxaca, n Chiapas, and w Campeche) and on the Pacific slope from Guanacaste, COSTA RICA, southward through CEN-

TRAL AMERICA (except arid districts) to nw COLOMBIA (n Chocó and w Antioquia), thence southward along the Pacific coast through COLOMBIA and ECUADOR to extreme nw PERU (Tumbes). *C. s. subtropicalis, spiza,* and *caerulescens*: THE GUIANAS; TRINIDAD; VENEZUELA in Bolívar, Amazonas, the coastal region from Sucre west to Carabobo, and the Andes in Barinas (s slope), Mérida, and Táchira; the Perijá Mountains; COLOMBIA on the slopes of the Andes (except the Pacific slope) and from w Meta and Guainía south; e ECUADOR; e PERU; e BOLIVIA south to Santa Cruz; and BRAZIL north of the Amazon River and south of the Amazon to c Mato Grosso, e Pará, and c Maranhão. *C. s. axillaris*: coastal BRAZIL from Pernambuco south to Santa Catarina.

Elevational Range

From sea level to 1400 m (to ca. 1600 m in Bolivia and 2300 m in Colombia); mostly at lower elevations.

Habitat and Behavior

Encountered in flowering and fruiting trees in or near forest (terra firma, low-lying, gallery, and river island forests). Frequents forest edge and openings, tree-studded clearings, plantations and other areas of cultivation with trees, and second-growth woodland. Forages mostly in tree tops but descends to shrubs at forest edge and occasionally to the understory. Sedentary when food is abundant, but travels over wide areas at other times in search of new food sources.

Typically found in pairs, also in family groups or singly. Restless; often nervously jerks or flicks one or both wings. Sporadically accompanies mixed-species flocks, perhaps more regularly at certain seasons or locations (e.g., s Peru; see Munn 1985). Joins feeding aggregations but is very aggressive and frequently drives away other species. Sometimes seizes small birds with its bill and hangs on viciously (Skutch 1962b). In Panama, during 4 days of observation, a pair was seen to defend a portion of a flowering tree, apparently a feeding territory (see Beehler 1980).

In Trinidad, foraged primarily above 8 m off the ground and for insects mostly above 15 m; of 191 feeding observations, 63% were fruit-eating, 22% were at flowers, and 15% insect-searching (Snow and Snow 1971). *Miconia* berries constituted about half of all fruit-eating observations both in Trinidad (172 obs.) and in Valle, Colombia (33 obs., Hilty data). In Trinidad, took 22 species of fruit including fruits of the families Ulmaceae (20%) and Euphorbiaceae (12%). In Costa Rica, favored arils of *Clusia*, took fruits of *Cecropia* when succulent food was scarce, and visited feeding tables to eat bananas and to sip juice from oranges (Skutch 1962b). In Brazil, feeds on racemes of *Lasiacis* grass, berries of *Rhipsalis* cacti, and fruits of many species (see Sick 1985).

Mostly takes fruit while perched; sometimes hangs upside down from leaves or from *Cecropia* catkins (Hilty data). In Central America, observed to obtain about one-fourth of its fruit in flight (Moermond and Denslow 1985); in Peru, seen to make short sallies (Remsen data). In Trinidad: Swallowed most fruits whole; rarely pulled pieces from or chewed at large ones. In 55% of 33 insect-catching observations, perched among flowers, mainly tree flowers with long stamens, and darted about catching small insects attracted to the flowers, usually snapping them up in flight. Occasionally took nectar from these same flowers. Also searched for insects in foliage (14%), on branches and twigs (10%), and aerial sallied (20%). (Snow and Snow 1971.) Stomach contents: vegetable matter (23); animal matter (4); both (8). Contents included fruit pulp, berries, seeds (incl. seeds of *Miconia* and *Cecropia* and a berrylike grass seed), dipterans, and hymenopterans. Also observed to take moths (Collins and Watson 1983).

Vocalizations

Calls: strong and weak single *tsips* or *chips* given singly or in a hummingbirdlike chipping (Slud 1964), a loud strident *tswee tswee* (Peterson and Chalif 1973), a High-pitched *pseet* (Parker, LNS), and a short nasal grunt *uhr* given by the male (Eisenmann 1952). Probable song in Costa Rica: repeats a scratchy *tst tst CHIT* followed by a rapid chittering of *tst* notes; High-pitched; delivered (1 obs.) from 6 m up in a bare tree at forest edge (Whitney recording).

Breeding

In Costa Rica: The male occasionally seizes the female with his bill, but it is unclear whether this behavior is sexually motivated. Nests (5) were found only in trees standing in clearings near forest, but females repeatedly took nesting material into the woods. The shallow cup nests, resembling bunches of dead leaves, were placed 3–10.7 m above the ground in the fork of a sapling, among clustered outer foliage of a dense tree crown, and between leafy shoots on a horizonal branch. The female built alone, usually accompanied by her mate. Eggs (2) were white with brown spots, forming a wreath at

CHLOROPHANES 339

Chlorophanes spiza

the large end. One female incubated alone for about 13 days and both parents fed nestlings. (Skutch 1962b.) In Trinidad, a nest was built far out on a spray of big timber bamboo (Belcher and Smooker 1937). In Colombia, a male feigned injury by perching and clinging in the foliage with wings fluttering, probably in defense of young (Miller 1963). Breeding dates: Costa Rica April–June. Panama July. Trinidad May–July.

Sources

Primary Hilty data; Hilty and Brown 1986; Howell 1957; Moynihan 1962c; Novaes 1969; Parker data; Schäfer and Phelps 1954; Skutch 1962b; Slud 1964; Snow and Snow 1971. **Weights (n = 108)** Burton 1975; Dick, McGillivray, and Brooks 1984; ffrench 1973; Fry 1970; Hartman and Brownell 1961; Haverschmidt 1968; LSUMZ data; Miller 1963; Strauch 1977; Weske 1972. **Stomach contents** Foster data; LSUMZ data; Olivares and Hernandez 1962; Schubart, Aguirre, and Sick 1965. **Vocalizations** LNS recording by Parker (1); recording by Whitney (1); Eisenmann 1952; Peterson and Chalif 1973; Slud 1964. **Nests, eggs, and breeding dates** Belcher and Smooker 1937; Eisenmann 1952; Skutch 1962b.

CYANERPES

The brilliance and curved bills of male *Cyanerpes* honeycreepers (Table 26) create an appearance that cannot help but satisfy one's expectations of a tropical bird. Females are also attractive but more subtly colored. Wings of *Cyanerpes* honeycreepers are relatively long; tails and tarsi short. Storer (1969) described how *Cyanerpes* may be derived from the same stock as *Tangara* tanagers; formerly they were considered part of the family Coerebidae.

Table 26 The *Cyanerpes* Honeycreepers

222	*C. nitidus*	Short-billed Honeycreeper
223	*C. lucidus*	Shining Honeycreeper
224	*C. caeruleus*	Purple Honeycreeper
225	*C. cyaneus*	Red-legged Honeycreeper

Cyanerpes species actively dart and flutter high in trees, pausing only periodically to rest. They travel in pairs or single-species groups that at times join mixed-species flocks. Only the Short-billed Honeycreeper seems to occur in mixed-species flocks most of the time, but the Short-billed is very poorly known.

The three longer-billed *Cyanerpes* species consume fruit, insects, and nectar in special ways. Narrow curved bills enable them to extract nutritious arils through cracks in slowly opening seed pods before heavier billed birds can reach into the tough husks. In addition, *Cyanerpes* use their curved bills to reach tiny insects hiding beneath thin branches, twigs, and vines. These honeycreepers, especially the Red-legged, also take insects on the wing, often by waiting around fragrant flowers. The degree to which flowers are tapped for nectar varies greatly among species as well as seasonally. The three long-billed species appear to travel long distances seasonally in search of favorite fruiting and flowering trees.

Voices of *Cyanerpes* species are thin and weak. The songs of two species consist of call notes repeated regularly and monotonously. The Red-legged Honeycreeper also has a soft but more varied nuptial song.

Nests of *Cyanerpes* have been found from about eye level to 14 m above the ground. The female alone builds a shallow cup so thin-walled that eggs can be seen through it. The female incubates the eggs for between 12 and 13 days, and nestlings leave the nest after about 14 days. The male attends the female during the entire nesting period and helps feed the young.

The Red-legged Honeycreeper ranges further north and south than its congeners, reflecting its tendency to occupy more open, drier habitats. The Shining and Purple Honeycreepers are essentially parapatric replacing each other near the Panama-Colombia border (see Haffer 1975 and Wetmore, Pasquier, and Olson 1984), and appear to differ little in habitat or behavior. While three species (the Short-billed, Purple, and Red-legged) occur in Amazonia, we have not identified any locations where all three have been encountered.

Cyanerpes nitidus 222
Short-billed Honeycreeper
Plate 30

Length 9 cm (3½ in.). Weight 9 g (8.0–10.2 g, all with moderate to heavy fat). Monotypic.

Geographic Range

VENEZUELA in Amazonas and nw and c Bolívar; east of the Andes from se Guainía, Vaupés, and Caquetá, COLOMBIA, southward through e ECUADOR and ne PERU to Pasco and eastward through

Cyanerpes nitidus

BRAZIL north of the Amazon River to e Amazonas and south of the Amazon to n Rondônia (LSUMZ) and extreme nw Mato Grosso (Rio Aripuaná). One record from Amapá, BRAZIL (Novaes 1978).

Elevational Range

Lowlands to ca. 500 m.

Habitat and Behavior

Inhabits terra firma forest and forest edge. Also occurs in low-lying forest. Typically travels with mixed-species flocks; sometimes joins feeding aggregations. Forages 15–30 m above the ground in the canopy, often in fruiting trees; searches for insects on branches and in foliage (Willis 1977). Stomach contents (3): vegetable matter, including fruit and seeds.

Vocalizations

No information.

Breeding

No information.

Sources

Primary Hilty and Brown 1986; LSUMZ data; Willis 1977. **Weights (n = 5)** LSUMZ data. **Stomach contents** LSUMZ data.

Cyanerpes lucidus 223
Shining Honeycreeper
Plate 30

Length 10 cm (4 in.). Weight 11 g (extremes not reported). Two subspecies.

Geographic Range

The Gulf-Caribbean slope (apparently restricted to foothills) from s MEXICO (e Chiapas) through nc GUATEMALA to nw Honduras (Atlántida); locally in BELIZE (Cockscomb Mountains) and NICARAGUA; the entire Caribbean slope of COSTA RICA and PANAMA and on the Pacific slope from San José, COSTA RICA, through PANAMA to just inside the Colombian border in extreme nw Chocó.

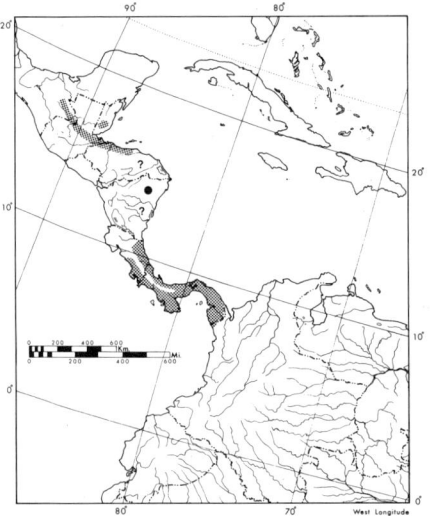

Cyanerpes lucidus

Elevational Range

From sea level to 1200 m; in Panama, to 1600 m; most common in foothills, ca. 500–1000 m (Ridgely *in litt.*).

Habitat and Behavior

Inhabits epiphyte-burdened forest and forest edge and openings; also occurs in areas with scattered trees near forest. Moves about seasonally (see Greenberg 1981c). Encountered in pairs or small family groups, occasionally singly or in large groups. Travels independently or associates with mixed-species flocks, especially other honeycreepers. Joins feeding aggregations at flowering or fruiting trees. In Costa Rica: Somewhat aggressive; often displaces Red-legged Honeycreepers, *C. cyaneus* **225,** from food sources, and on occasion, the two species battle physically. Displays aggression by spreading wings; also by prominently showing yellow legs. (Skutch 1972.) Actively flits about the foliage, but at times perches quietly on exposed branches in tree tops (Slud l964).

Generally forages high in tall forest trees, but occasionally comes lower to small trees and shrubs. Of 16 observations in Panama, 44% were fruit-eating, 37% insect-searching, and 19% at flowers (Greenberg 1981c). Eats a variety of fruit, but favors arils surrounding the seeds of a number of trees, shrubs, and vines, especially those of *Clusia* (Skutch 1972). Extracts the seeds with its long slender bill through narrow slits of newly opening pods and swallows the seeds whole. Also fond of a plumlike fruit, *Spondias edulis*. Comes to feeding tables for bananas, especially during rainy periods.

To procure nectar or possibly small insects, perches behind and above flowers and leans forward to insert its bill into blossoms. Also obtains insects and spiders by gleaning thin vines or leafless twigs while perched, or by hanging in various positions. Sometimes employs the diagonal-lean method on thicker branches or hovers to inspect tree scars and knotholes. Occasionally sallies for flying insects and probes small curled dead leaves.

Vocalizations

Calls: a single sharp High- to Very-high-pitched *tsip*, *pssst*, or *tsik* that sometimes runs into a trill; a high cricketlike *zee zee* (Russell 1964); and a slightly rattling *tsrrrp* (Eisenmann in Wetmore, Pasquier, and Olson 1984). Possible song: a monotonous repetition of one slight note, delivered at 1 note/sec. for about 15 min. (Skutch 1972).

Breeding

In Costa Rica: A nest was found about 6 m off the ground in tall timber bamboo at forest edge. The slightly built shallow cup, composed of slender dark strands, was attached by its rim with cobweb to thin horizontal terminal twigs and well hidden in foliage. The female constructed the nest alone but was accompanied by her mate. Two eggs were laid on consecutive days and incubated by the female for a period of 12–13 days. Both parents fed nestlings, the female slightly more often. Food appeared to consist chiefly of insects at first, but as nestlings grew older, the parents brought red objects thought to be *Clusia* seeds; also possibly berries. Nestling period was 13 or 14 days. (Skutch 1972.) In Panama, an individual was seen carrying nesting material into a mass of epiphytes in a tree over a river (Wetmore, Pasquier, and Olson 1984). Breeding dates: Costa Rica June. Panama Jan.

Sources

Primary Beehler 1980; Cherrie 1892; Edwards 1972; Moynihan 1962c; Russell 1964; Skutch 1972; Slud 1964; Wetmore, Pasquier, and Olson 1984. **Weights (n = 5)** Hartman and Brownell 1961. **Vocalizations** LNS recordings by Morton (2), Parker (1); Skutch 1972; Slud 1964; Wetmore, Pasquier, and Olson 1984. **Nests, eggs, and breeding dates** Skutch 1972; Wetmore, Pasquier, and Olson 1984.

Cyanerpes caeruleus **224**
Purple Honeycreeper
Plate 30

Length 10 cm (4 in.). Weight 12 g (7.8–14.0 g). Five subspecies.

Geographic Range

The Pacific slope from extreme se Darién, PANAMA, south through COLOMBIA and ECUADOR along the base of the Andes to Guayas; along the n base of the Andes in COLOMBIA from Chocó eastward to the Magdalena Valley, thence south in the Magdalena Valley to Tolima; from the Santa Marta region and the e slope of the Andes in Boyacá, COLOMBIA, eastward through n VENEZUELA on the e side of the Perijá Mountains and both sides of the Andes; the coastal ranges from Carabobo to Sucre, VENEZUELA; TRINIDAD; east of the Andes from s Meta, Vaupés, and Guainía, COLOMBIA, eastward through s VENEZUELA (Amazonas, Bolívar, and north through Delta Amacuro to Sucre), THE GUIANAS, and ec BRAZIL to n Maranhão; southward east of the Andes through ECUADOR and PERU to Santa Cruz, BOLIVIA, and Amazonian BRAZIL to wc Mato Grosso (Willis 1976a) and se Pará.

Elevational Range

Most numerous below 800 m but ranges to 1950 m on Andean slopes and 1800 m in the Venezuelan tepuis.

Habitat and Behavior

Inhabits humid regions and (perhaps seasonally) wetter portions of dry regions. Favors flowering trees in terra firma and low-lying (incl. *varzea*) forest, forest edge, and tree-studded clearings; also occurs in tall second growth, plantations, and gardens. Moves about seasonally in many parts of its range. Usually lives in pairs or small family groups, sometimes in larger groups of 10 or more individuals or singly. Travels alone or accompanies mixed-species flocks; joins feeding aggregations at flowering and fruiting trees.

Typically forages in tree tops. In Trinidad: Foraged primarily above 8 m but descended lower, occasionally to the ground where it fed on fallen fruits. Searched at higher levels for insects than for fruit. Of 237 feeding observations, 40% were insect-searching, 31% fruit-eating, and 29% at flowers (proportions of nectar, fruit, and insects varied seasonally). Ate a limited variety of fruits (12 spp). Favored fruit of *Trema micrantha* (35% of all fruit eaten), *Clusia* (18%), and the family Euphorbiaceae (18%). Swallowed small fruits and berries whole, squeezed and crushed larger ones, and pecked pieces off soft arillate fruits. Drank nectar and occasionally pierced ripe oranges with its bill. (Snow and Snow 1971.)

Also in Trinidad, insect-foraging was 63% on branches and twigs, 17% in foliage, 15% in aerial sallies, and 5% on flower and seed heads (94 insect-searching obs.). Primarily hung down to glean insects off the undersides of fine twigs 0.6–1.3 cm in diam., often dead twigs on an otherwise healthy tree. Sometimes preyed on tiny spiders, and if one attempted to escape by descending on a thread, the honeycreeper fluttered after it. (Snow and Snow 1971.)

Scattered observations from other localities appear consistent with the Snows' data from Trinidad. Stomach contents: vegetable matter (4); animal matter (1); both (1). Contents included flowers, seeds (incl. seeds of an orchid), fruit, and insects. Additional stomach contents included spiders.

Vocalizations

Call: a High-pitched lisping *zzree*.

Breeding

In Trinidad, a small cup nest was set in the hollow of a stump less than 2 m above the ground (ffrench 1973). In Brazil, 2 nests were 2 m and 3 m above the ground, the latter placed on the end of a branch (Pinto 1953). Eggs (2) are white, blotched with

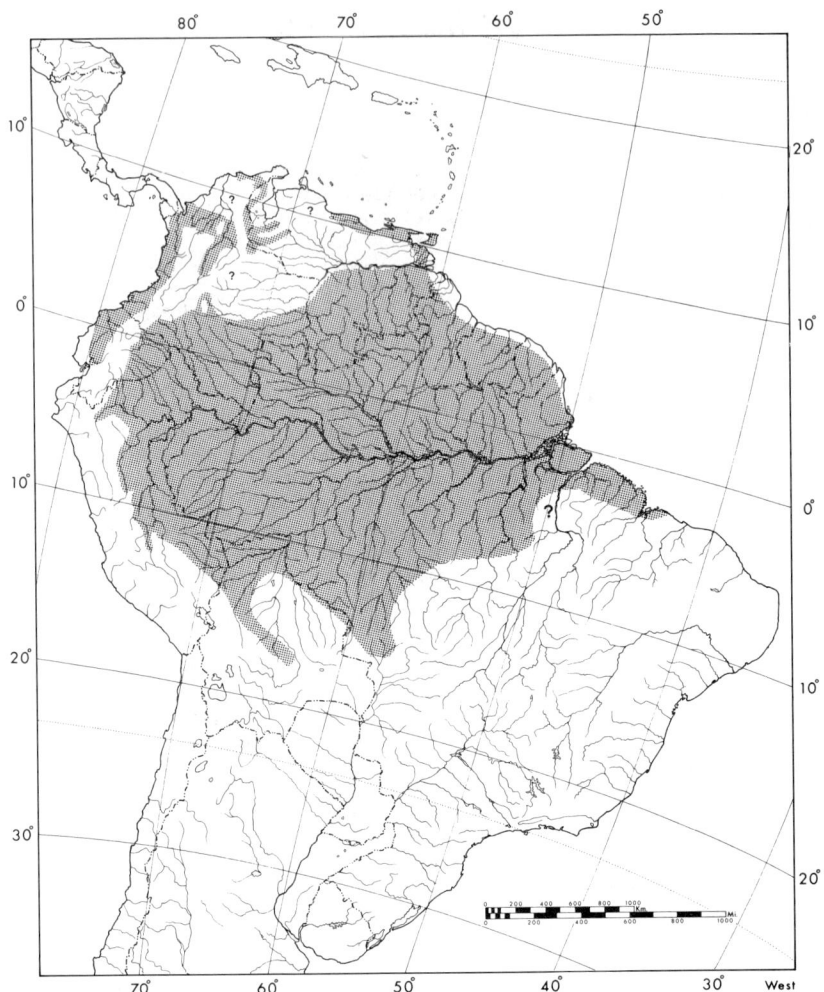

Cyanerpes caeruleus

dark vinaceous chocolate spots and ashy stains. Both parents feed nestlings (ffrench 1973). In captivity, the female incubated alone while the male fluttered about nearby (Bond 1971). Breeding dates: Trinidad April and June. Brazil (Pará) Oct and Dec.

Sources

Primary ffrench 1973; Hilty and Brown 1986; Novaes 1973; Schäfer and Phelps 1954; Snow and Snow 1971; Terborgh and Weske 1975. **Weights (n = 53)** ffrench 1973 (males only); Haverschmidt 1952, 1968; LSUMZ data. **Stomach contents** Beebe 1909; Haverschmidt 1968; LSUMZ data; Olivares and Hernandez 1962; Schubart, Aguirre, and Sick 1965. **Vocalizations** LNS recordings by T. H. Davis (1), Parker (1);

Hilty and Brown 1986. **Nests, eggs, and breeding dates** Belcher and Smooker 1937; Bond 1971; ffrench 1973; Pinto 1953.

Cyanerpes cyaneus **225**
Red-legged Honeycreeper
Plate 30

Length 12 cm (5 in.). Weight 14 g (11.0–18.3 g). Eleven subspecies, including the recently described *holti* (Parkes 1977). In the field, subspecies vary noticeably in size and especially in bill length (see illus.). The body (but not the wing and tail) feathers of the male are molted twice a year into distinct basic and alternate plumages. Subadult males resemble females for a short time (see Dickey and van Rossem 1938), and the bills of subadults (even after separation from parents) are shorter than that of adults (Sick 1985).

Geographic Range

C. c. carneipes: Oriente, CUBA (probably introduced); one record on JAMAICA (an escape?); s MEXICO from se San Luis Potosí, Veracruz, Puebla, and Oaxaca (incl. Cozumel I.) through both slopes of CENTRAL AMERICA (incl. Coiba and the Pearl Is., PANAMA) to extreme e PANAMA and Córdoba (Río Sinu), COLOMBIA. *C. c. pacificus*: west of the Andes from c Chocó, COLOMBIA, to Manabí, ECUADOR. *C. c. gigas*: Gorgona I. off Cauca, COLOMBIA.
C. c. gemmeus and *eximius*: along the w base of the E Andes from Santander, COLOMBIA, north to the Santa Marta region and the Perijá Mountains; VENEZUELA along the bases of the Perijá Mountains and the Andes, coastal ranges (except driest areas) from Falcón eastward to Sucre, and on Margarita I. *C. c. tobagensis*: TOBAGO. *C. c. cyaneus, brevipes, dispar,* and *violaceus*: TRINIDAD; the e base of the Andes and the Macarena Mountains in Meta, COLOMBIA; from e Vaupés and e Guianía, COLOMBIA, Bolívar and e Monagas, VENEZUELA, and THE GUIANAS southward through BRAZIL to Maranhão, Goiás, and c Mato Grosso, and westward to PERU south of the Río Marañón and east of the Andes and n BOLIVIA (south to La Paz, Cochabamba, and Santa Cruz). *C. c. holti*: coastal BRAZIL from Pernambuco southward to s Rio de Janeiro (Sick 1985).

Elevational Range

From sea level to 2000 m; mostly below 1200 m.

Habitat and Behavior

Typically encountered in flowering trees at forest edge and in tall second growth, open woodland, and semiopen situations where trees are not too low or too far apart; especially favors flowering shade trees of coffee plantations and areas of human habitation. Also inhabits savanna forest, gallery woodland, and occasionally occurs in the canopy of terra firma and low-lying forest. Migrates seasonally in conjunction with the flowering and fruiting of favored trees.

Typically seen in groups of 5–15 individuals, sometimes in larger aggregations of up to 100; pairs split off during the breeding season. Travels apart from or with mixed-species flocks; may contribute to mixed-species flock formation (Moynihan 1962c). Quarrelsome but normally limits hostilities to posturing, calls, and an occasional pursuit. Disputes are often between females. Contestants face each other, bow up and down, turn from side to side, flit wings outward and upward, and repeat a nasal *chaa*. Or they may stare motionless except for flitting wings, with bills pointed skyward (Skutch 1954, 1962b).

Intensely active; crisscrosses and flutters about through foliage. Flight between trees is rapid and direct. Occasionally stops and perches for long periods on bare branches high in trees. Bathes in foliage after a rain by flapping around in wet leaves or splashing in water-filled bracts of bromeliads.

Typically forages from midheights to tree tops, occasionally descends lower. In Trinidad: Searched at higher levels for insects than for fruit; of 125 observations, 44% involved insect-searching, 44% fruit-eating, and 12% were at flowers (proportions of insects, fruit, and flowers varied seasonally). Favored *Miconia* berries (33% of all fruit eaten) and fruits with fleshy arils. Arillate fruits from a vine and 3 trees, none of which was taken by any other tanager, constituted 35% of fruit-eating observations. (Snow and Snow 1971.)

Hangs upside down or hovers to extract arils from newly opening pods and clings to or hangs from foliage to obtain small fruits. Feeds on oranges or other large pulpy fruits through holes made by larger birds. Comes to feeding tables for bananas; slices off pieces of banana with a sideways scissorlike action of the bill. When insect-searching, creeps along limbs using the diagonal-lean method to glean the undersides of slender branches and twigs less than 1.3 cm in diam. or stretches neck up to pick prey off leaves (in Trinidad, usually searched leaf tops). Flutters at the tips of slender branches and hovers to glean leaves or to snap up insects coming to flowers; also aerial sallies (in Trinidad, 40% of insect prey were taken in flight by hovers, sallies, etc.). Inspects curled dead leaves and clings to rough tree bark to examine crevices.

When feeding at flowers, clings beside blossoms and inserts its bill inside to obtain nectar and/or to capture small insects. In captivity, drank artificial nectar with a rapid pumping action without lifting its head (Gibson 1979). Stomach contents: vegetable matter (8); animal matter (2); both (2). Contents

Cyanerpes cyaneus

included berries, fruit, seeds (incl. seeds of *Miconia*), flies, beetles (incl. snout beetles), caterpillars, hymenopterans (incl. ants and ichneumons), and spiders. Additional stomach contents included nectar and chalcid hymenoptera.

Vocalizations

Calls: utters 2 types of notes, a short weak High-pitched *tsip*, *tsst*, or *zzee* and a nasal mewing Moderate-pitched *dzey* or *chaa* given randomly. Dawn song: monotonously repeats, sometimes for 20 min. or more, one of the two types of call notes with pauses of

1–4 sec. Possible courtship song: a barely audible melodic warble sung by the male in the presence of a female; heard by Skutch (1962b) in the wild and described by Gibson (1979) in the aviary as a short note whistled twice, a longer ascending note, and a rapid double note whistled 5 times.

Breeding

In captivity, mating was interspersed with chasing and fighting to the extent that the pair often rolled on the ground (Gibson 1979). In the wild, nests are usually placed less than 5 m (range 2–14 m) up in isolated bushes or trees in pastures or gardens, or at the edge of tall thickets. The shallow small thin-walled hemispherical cup, made of wiry fibrous rootlets and slender stems, is attached with spider web to a branch crotch in dense outer foliage. Sometimes steals materials from nests of other birds. Females build alone, usually attended closely by their mates. Eggs (2–3, mostly 2), laid on consecutive days, are white or bluish, speckled with brown, especially in a wreath at the large end. In Costa Rica, females incubate for 12–13 days and the nestling period is 14 days (Skutch 1954). Although females take most of the responsibility, both sexes feed young. Nestlings are brought fruit primarily, but insects are also given and seemed a necessity in the aviary (Gibson 1979). In Brazil, the interval between nest completion and fledging was 22 days and a pair may have had a second brood (Carvalho 1958). Breeding dates: Mexico May. Costa Rica April–June. Panama Feb. Trinidad March, June, and July. Brazil (Pará) Sept and Dec; (Mato Grosso) Oct.

Sources

Primary Dickey and Van Rossem 1938; Gibson 1979; Haverschmidt 1968; Pinto 1953; Schäfer and Phelps 1954; Skutch 1954, 1962b; Slud 1964; Snow and Snow 1971; Todd and Carriker 1922; Wetmore, Pasquier, and Olson 1984. **Weights (n = 86)** Dick, McGillivray, and Brooks 1984; ffrench 1973; Hartman and Brownell 1961; Haverschmidt 1948, 1952, 1968; Klaas 1968; LSUMZ data; McDiarmid, Ricklefs, and Foster 1977; Paynter 1955; Ricklefs 1976; Russell 1964; Strauch 1977; Tashian 1953. **Stomach contents** Beebe 1909, 1916; Haverschmidt 1968; LSUMZ data; Pinto 1953; Tashian 1952; Wetmore, Pasquier, and Olson 1984. **Vocalizations** LNS recordings by L. I. Davis (1), T. H. Davis (2), Schwartz (2); recording by Whitney (1); Skutch 1954; Eisenmann in Wetmore, Pasquier, and Olson 1984. **Nests, eggs, and breeding dates** Allen 1891; Alvarez del Toro 1952; Bond 1961; Carvalho 1958; ffrench 1973; Pinto 1953; Skutch 1954; Willis and Eisenmann 1979.

XENODACNIS

Monotypic, *Xenodacnis* lives high in the Andes of extreme southern Ecuador and Peru in habitats containing shrubs of the genus *Gynoxis*. Its taxonomic affinities are uncertain, but *Xenodacnis* appears to fit between the tanager and wood-warbler (Parulinae) assemblages.

Xenodacnis parina 226
Tit-like Dacnis
Plate 30

X. p. bella and *petersi*: length 13 cm (5 in.); weight of males 17 g (15.4–18.5 g), females 15 g (11.5–17.5 g). *X. p. parina*: length 11 cm (4½ in.); weight of males 12 g (11.0–12.0 g), females 11 g (10.0–12.0 g); weights include specimens with moderate or heavy fat. Three subspecies: *bella* and *parina* are illustrated; *petersi* resembles *bella*.

Geographic Range

X. p. bella: sc ECUADOR in nw Azuay (sight, probably this subspecies, Ridgely 1980) and nc PERU in extreme s Amazonas and La Libertad (LSUMZ) east of the Río Marañón. *X. p. petersi*: on the w Andean slope of c PERU in Ancash, Huánuco (west of the Río Marañón, Short and Morony 1969), and Lima. *X. p. parina*: s PERU on the e Andean slope in Junín, Ayacucho, Apurímac (LSUMZ), and Cuzco, and the w Andean slope in Arequipa (George 1964).

Elevational Range

From 3000 m to above treeline.

Habitat and Behavior

Inhabits patches of woody plants at or above treeline, including treeline forest edge and *Polylepis* woodland. Appears to be confined to areas where shrubs of *Gynoxys* (Compositae) are present (Parker and O'Neill 1980). Usually encountered in pairs or singly but occurs locally (esp. *petersi*) at very high densities; in Ancash, dozens of individuals have been found in an area of *Gynoxys* less than a hectare in size; within such aggregations, individuals attempt to defend small feeding territories (Parker *in litt.*). Darts from one clump of trees or bushes to another; makes an audible flapping of the wings as it takes to flight (Parker data).

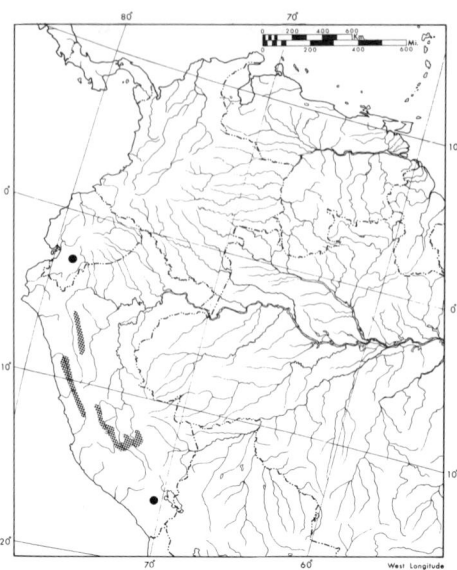

Xenodacnis parina

with simultaneous notes, and then the female ends the duet with a series of raspy notes. (Parker, LNS.)

Breeding

In Ancash, Peru: When nesting, apparently defends a territory of about 100 m along treeline. In May, an excited pair acted as though they were protecting a nest (which could not be found) in the root system of a *Gynoxys* shrub. Flightless juveniles were fed insects. (Parker data.)

Sources

Primary George 1964; Koepcke 1970; LSUMZ data; Parker data; Parker and O'Neill 1980; Ridgely 1980; Short and Morony 1969. **Weights** (*petersi* and *bella* males n = 9, females n = 11; *parina* males n = 6, females n = 5): LSUMZ data; Short and Morony 1969; Weske 1972. **Stomach contents** LSUMZ data. **Vocalizations** LNS recordings by Parker (10); Koepcke 1970. **Breeding dates** Parker data.

In e Peru: Forages mostly in low shrubs and small trees but also in the crowns (9–12 m off the ground) of small-leaved trees. Primarily gleans undersides of leaves, especially along the central veins of *Gynoxys* shrubs. Seen to feed on aphidlike insects (homopterans) and sugary droplets secreted either by the insects or the leaves; both liquid and crystalline droplets are consumed; droplets are present throughout the year. Sometimes gleans the trunk and branches of *Gynoxys* and also bark and leaves of other vegetation, especially *Polylepis*. Probes flowers of mistletoe (*Tristerix* spp) in search of nectar and/or insects. (Parker data.) Reported to feed on fine plant parts and flowers (Koepcke 1970), and nectar was observed on head and breast feathers of collected birds (Parker data). Stomach contents (14): insects, including caterpillars.

Vocalizations

Calls: a scratchy Moderate-pitched *jeeup* sometimes extended into a chitter of hissing notes. Song: a rapid series, e.g., *whit whit whit whit whit whit zweet zweet zweet*; the first notes are whistles, liquid and Low-pitched, the *zweet* notes are Moderate- to High-pitched. The number of notes and their quality and accenting are variable; song is very loud for so small a bird. Sometimes the *whit* note is simply repeated, especially by female-plumaged birds, and at times, this series is harsh and scratchy. In a duet, the male introduces the song, the female joins in

OREOMANES

The single species is restricted to *Polylepis* woodlands of the high Andes where it often probes for insects under bark. It is probably related to conebills of the genus *Conirostrum*. *Conirostrum* species are considered wood-warblers (Parulinae) by the *Peters Check-list* but part of the tanager assemblage by the *A.O.U. Check-list*. A hybrid between *Oreomanes fraseri* and *Conirostrum ferrugineiventre* has been collected in Peru (see Schulenberg 1985).

Oreomanes fraseri **227**
Giant Conebill
Plate 30

Length 15 cm (6 in.). Weight 25 g (22.0–27.0 g). Three subspecies are recognized in the *Peters Check-list*, but Vuilleumier (1984b) concluded that the geographic variation is minor, partly clinal and partly checkerboard, and does not warrant recognition of subspecies.

Geographic Range

The Andes from Nariño, COLOMBIA, southward through ECUADOR to Loja? (location unclear); from Ancash to Tacna,

Oreomanes fraseri

PERU, in the w cordilleras; and in the e cordilleras from Cuzco, PERU, to Cochabamba and Potosí, BOLIVIA, (see Vuilleumier 1984b).

Elevational Range

Recorded 2700–4850 m, mostly 3500–4200 m (Vuilleumier 1984b).

Habitat and Behavior

Inhabits islands of *Polylepis* (Rosaceae) woodland at or above treeline. Found in small copses as well as large stands of *Polylepis* trees. Encountered in pairs, singly, or in small (probably family) groups of 3–5 individuals. Usually independent, but occasionally associates with other species. In Peru: Travels from one stand of *Polylepis* trees to another, generally remaining in one stand of trees for at least 10 min. Moves slowly and deliberately from one plant to its neighbor, not making long flights within the *Polylepis* stand. Pairs remain close together. Sometimes can be detected by the sound of bark being peeled off trees. (Parker data.)

In Peru: Forages for insects from near the ground to tops of trees, at times up to 12 m above the ground. Primarily searches for insects under the bark of *Polylepis* trees and usually on the trunk or large limbs; seen to extract small larvae from under the bark. Inserts and opens its bill under the bark to separate the layers. Also tugs or flakes off loose bark, often with neck far outstretched, sometimes reaching around or under 5–8 cm limbs. To probe bark on tree trunks, sometimes clings upside down or climbs with legs spread out. Some individuals gradually hitch up a tree to where smaller limbs branch out, then fly down to near the base of a different tree. Others seem to prefer leafless tangles in the canopy and occasionally work out to foliage to glean leaves. In addition to probing *Polylepis* bark, picks at moss and lichens, systematically gleans aphids and sugary secretions from the undersides of *Gynoxys* leaves (once observed picking 5 aphids from under a single leaf), and probes flowers of epiphytic mistletoe (*Tristerix* spp) in *Polylepis* trees. (Parker data.) Collected birds (LSUMZ) were stained with pollen. Stomach contents (12): insects, including caterpillars, beetles, and a small moth.

Vocalizations

Calls include a Moderate-pitched *keek!* or *eek!* (Parker, LNS), a *seep* in flight (Parker data), and a high-pitched plaintive *ssit ssit ssit* or *sseet sseet sseet* (George 1964). Parker (data) heard a whispy series of whistles and *cheep*s and a choppy series, *whit-ti-which-chip-ti-whit-ti*, etc sounding like a *Conirostrum* species (Parulinae).

Breeding

No information.

Sources

Primary Hilty and Brown 1986; George 1964; Johnson 1967; LSUMZ data; Parker data; Parker and O'Neill 1980; Vuilleumier 1984b. **Weights (n = 25)** LSUMZ data; Vuilleumier 1984b. **Stomach contents** LSUMZ data. **Vocalizations** LNS recording by Parker (1); George 1964; Johnson 1967; Parker data.

DIGLOSSA

Diglossa flowerpiercers (Table 27) have received substantial attention from ornithologists over the years. Some *Diglossa* species exhibit a curious feeding behavior in which they hold tubular flower corollas with their hooked upper mandibles, pierce the corollas with their pointed lower mandible, and extract nectar and possibly insects with their tongues (see Skutch 1954; Moynihan 1963). This behavior has caused flowerpiercers to

Table 27 The *Diglossa* Flowerpiercers

	⌐ 228	*D. baritula*	Slaty Flowerpiercer
		228-1 *baritula* subspecies group	Cinnamon-bellied Flowerpiercer
		228-2 *plumbea* subspecies group	Slaty Flowerpiercer
		228-3 *sittoides* subspecies group	Rusty Flowerpiercer
1	⊢ 231	*D. venezuelensis*	Venezuelan Flowerpiercer
	⌐ 232	*D. albilatera*	White-sided Flowerpiercer
	⌐ 229	*D. lafresnayii*	Glossy Flowerpiercer
		229-1 *gloriosissima* subspecies group	Chestnut-bellied Flowerpiercer
		229-2 *lafresnayii* subspecies group	Glossy Flowerpiercer
		229-3 *mystacalis* subspecies group	Moustached Flowerpiercer
2	230	*D. carbonaria*	Carbonated Flowerpiercer
		230-1 *humeralis* subspecies group	Black Flowerpiercer
		230-2 *brunneiventris* subspecies group	Black-throated Flowerpiercer
		230-3 *carbonaria* subspecies group	Gray-bellied Flowerpiercer
		230-4 *gloriosa* subspecies group	Merida Flowerpiercer
	⌐ 233	*D. duidae*	Scaled Flowerpiercer
3	⌐ 234	*D. major*	Greater Flowerpiercer
	⌐ 235	*D. indigotica*	Indigo Flowerpiercer
	236	*D. glauca*	Deep-blue Flowerpiercer
4	237	*D. caerulescens*	Bluish Flowerpiercer
	⌐ 238	*D. cyanea*	Masked Flowerpiercer

Notes: Numbers and brackets to the left of the table refer to superspecies (solid lines) and species groups (solid plus dotted lines) defined by Vuilleumier (1969). If considered specifically distinct, the subspecies groups of *D. baritula*, *D. lafresnayii*, and *D. carbonaria* would each constitute a superspecies. Species 231 and 232 have been shifted on the table from the taxonomic order of the *Peters Check-list* (which is followed in the text) in order to facilitate identification of species groups defined by Vuilleumier.

be labeled as "nectar thieves," but in some situations, flowerpiercers may play an important role in pollination (see Graves 1982b).

Another reason for the interest in flowerpiercers is that they often take part in intense competitive interactions, not only intraspecifically and with other flowerpiercer species but also with species of other groups, such as hummingbirds (Trochilidae) and conebills (Parulinae). See Colwell (1973), Moynihan (1963, 1979), and Snow and Snow (1980).

Finally, ornithologists have found that the Glossy and Carbonated Flowerpiercers provide outstanding examples of speciation in progress; see Zimmer (1929b), Vuilleumier (1969), and Graves (1982a). Although each is classified as a single species in the *Peters Check-list*, the Glossy and Carbonated as well as the Slaty Flowerpiercers are subdivided into subspecies groups in this book so that the natural histories of the subspecies groups may be compared.

At a higher taxonomic level, Vuilleumier (1969) divided *Diglossa* into four species groups (bracketed in Table 27) on the basis of physical characteristics, and members of each of these species groups also seem to share some distinct attributes of morphology (also see Bock 1985), habitat preferences, social behavior, and feeding behavior.

Species group 1

The members of species group 1, termed the *albilatera* Species-group by Vuilleumier, are the only sexually dimorphic *Diglossa* species. The Slaty and White-sided Flowerpiercers are usually encountered at flowering shrubs where they puncture flowers for nectar. Both species are small in size and adept at hiding inside flowering thickets when aggressive competitive hummingbirds approach. The Slaty and White-sided pick insects, their only other recorded food, from leaves and twigs, and the Slaty also snaps up insects in aerial sallies. The Slaty and White-sided are often encountered in pairs. The Venezuelan is considered by Vuilleumier (1969) to form a superspecies with the White-sided, but the Venezuelan has not been studied sufficiently to know whether its behavior is similar to that of the White-sided.

Species group 2

Compared to members of the first species group, the Glossy and Carbonated Flowerpiercers of species group 2 are not as likely to hide from competitors. On the contrary, they are extremely aggressive towards other species and towards conspecifics to the extent that Glossy and Carbonated Flowerpiercers typically live alone and form pairs only while breeding. Moreover, compared to the Slaty and White-sided, the Glossy and Carbonated usually forage more widely in shrubs and trees, seeking insects as well as nectar. The Carbonated tends to occupy more open habitats than the Glossy Flowerpiercer which is usually confined to areas of high rainfall and dense vegetation, especially in Peru. The third member of this species group, the Scaled Flowerpiercer, is poorly known.

Species group 3

The Greater Flowerpiercer was placed by Vuilleumier in its own species group because it exhibits physical characteristics of both the previous species group and the one that follows. The Greater gleans leaves at branch tips and has not yet been reported to pierce flowers. It has been encountered alone and in pairs that vocalize in duets.

Species group 4

Those *Diglossa* species, often called the blue flowerpiercers, whose bills are least modified and that rarely, if ever, pierce flowers are included in species group 4. The blue flowerpiercers typically forage for insects and fruit from midheights to the canopy, mostly in forest. Moreover, the blue flowerpiercers often join and follow mixed-species flocks in distinct contrast to the independence of members of the first two species groups.

Diglossa baritula **228**
Slaty Flowerpiercer

If a single species, as treated in the *Peters Check-list*, the Slaty Flowerpiercer occupies mountains from Mexico to Argentina and has the widest range of any *Diglossa* species. Other authors (Vuilleumier 1969; A.O.U. Check-list) consider the Slaty Flowerpiercer to be a superspecies comprising three allospecies. We have treated these forms as subspecies groups and have provided separate accounts for each, but major differences in their behaviors do not emerge from the available information (also see Wetmore, Pasquier, and Olson 1984). The subspecies groups are separated by range gaps in Nicaragua and in Panama.

Diglossa baritula
(*baritula* subspecies group **228-1**)
Cinnamon-bellied Flowerpiercer
Plate 30

Length 11 cm (4 in.). Weight 8 g (6.0–9.4 g). Three subspecies: *baritula* has cinnamon-rufous extending up from the breast through the center of the throat; *parva* resembles *montana*.

Geographic Range

D. b. baritula: s MEXICO from Jalisco, Guanajuato, Hidalgo, and Veracruz south to Oaxaca. *D. b. montana* and *parva*: extreme s MEXICO (Chiapas), GUATEMALA, EL SALVADOR, and HONDURAS.

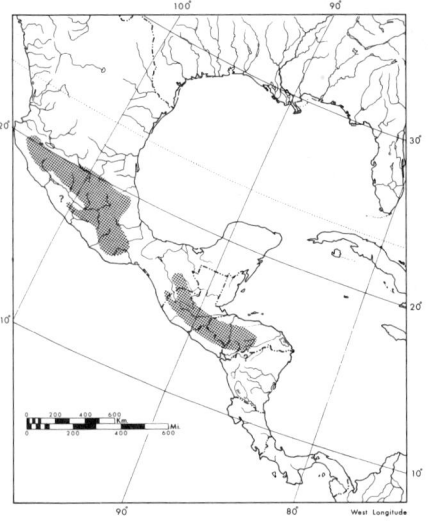

Diglossa baritula (*baritula* subspecies group)

Elevational Range

1500–3350 m.

Habitat and Behavior

Frequents flowering shrubs and plants in shrubby openings and bushy clearings in pine-oak, fir, and cypress forests; forest edge; and areas near forest, e.g., overgrown pastures, cultivation, and gardens. Lives singly, in pairs, or in small family groups; occasionally found in large parties of 6–10 individuals. Alertly and actively flits among blossoms and foliage. Flies neither high nor far, usually remaining within a small area where there are plenty of flowers (Skutch 1954). Moves up and down mountain slopes seasonally, however, between areas where favorite plants are in bloom.

Forages for nectar and insects from herbaceous flowers near the ground to tree tops. Works actively through flowers spending only about one sec. at each blossom (Skutch 1954). Clings to flower stalks and punctures bases of corollas to obtain nectar. Perches among low bushes and makes short sallies of no more than a few meters to snatch flying insects.

Vocalizations

Call: weak lisping *tsip tsip* (Skutch 1954). Song: a rapid, somewhat squeaky *sweez sweez sweez sweez SWIT-swee-see-see-see*; starts High-pitched, then drops to a Moderate Pitch; sometimes the end is cut off; 2–3 sec. long and repeated after 3–4 sec.; occasionally given while foraging. A territorial dawn song sung by a male was similar but delivered more rapidly and sweetly, at a higher pitch, and dropping slightly at the end. Males generally sing from low in bushes, but one sang from the topmost twig of a tall dead tree (Skutch 1954). Singing bouts may last for 13 min. or more. Both male and female sing (Skutch 1954).

Breeding

In Guatemala: Nested when nectar-producing flowers were most abundant despite chilling winds and frosty nights. A pair defended a nesting territory against a female flowerpiercer but not against her fledgling. One nest was 1.2 m above the ground placed between 2 cypress saplings growing close together, and another was 1.5 m up in a shrub standing in a bushy pasture. One of these nests, a deep open cup made of dead leaves, pine needles, and fine rootlets, contained 2 bright blue eggs, heavily spotted brown on the large end. The female incubated alone but was often visited by her mate. Both parents (more often the male in early stages) fed the young by regurgitation; food appeared to be insects. (Skutch 1954.) Breeding dates: Guatemala Nov–Jan.

Sources

Primary Dickey and van Rossem 1938; Edwards 1972; Monroe 1968; Newman 1954; Peterson and Chalif 1973; Schaldach 1963; Skutch 1954; Wetmore 1941. **Weights (n = 11)** LSUMZ data. **Vocalizations** LNS recordings by Thurber (2); Edwards 1972; Skutch 1954. **Nests, eggs, and breeding dates** Skutch 1954.

Diglossa baritula
(*plumbea* subspecies group 228-2)
Slaty Flowerpiercer
Plate 30

Length 11 cm (4 in.). Weight 10 g (9.3–10.1 g). Two subspecies: doubtfully distinct (Wetmore, Pasquier, and Olson 1984). Subadults resemble females but upperparts are slightly grayer and underparts paler, marked with pinkish buff (Wetmore, Pasquier, and Olson 1984). Albinistic individuals are seen occasionally.

Geographic Range

D. b. plumbea: from c Guanacaste, COSTA RICA, southeastward to Chiriquí, PANAMA. *D. b. veraguensis*: the Pacific slope in Veraguas, PANAMA.

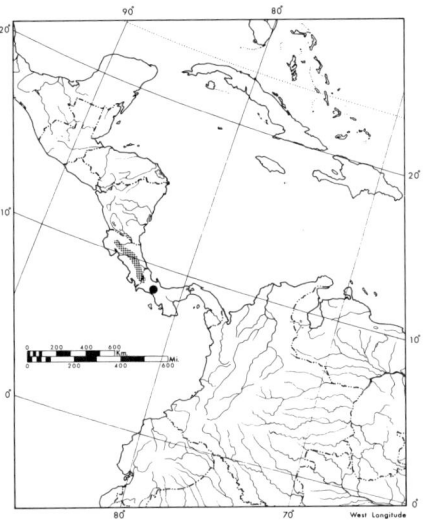

Diglossa baritula (*plumbea* subspecies group)

Elevational Range

In Costa Rica, mostly between 2000 m and treeline, as low as 1200 m seasonally. In Panama, mostly above 1500 m.

Habitat and Behavior

Inhabits areas where flowering shrubs abound, especially forest openings and shrubby clearings, forest edge, montane scrub, and tree-studded or overgrown pastures. Lives singly, in pairs, or in small family groups which rarely come together at a single site. Hops rapidly from flower to flower, seldom flying more than a few feet; appears to use regular foraging routes (Wolf 1976). Very active and flicks wings often. In Costa Rica, breeding pairs defended a feeding territory against conspecifics. When attacked by competitive Green Violet-ear hummingbirds, *Colibri thalassinus*, the Flowerpiercers escaped by hopping into foliage too dense for hummingbirds to follow and generally foraged low and inside the shrubs, whereas hummingbirds were more active on the upper and outer parts of shrubs. (Colwell et al. 1974.)

Typically forages low in the vegetation, feeding on a variety of flowers. Perches near a flower on a branch or flower stalk and punctures the base of the corolla with its lower mandible, extracting nectar with its tongue. Captures flying insects by making short sallies from low shrubbery. Stomach contents (1): 26 insects of at least 19 species, including flies (10 spp), beetles (4 spp), small wasps, leaf hoppers, and a moth larva.

Vocalizations

Song: In Costa Rica, a fast thin *sweezee sweezee sweezee sweezee zee zee*; High-pitched; delivered in a little over 1 sec. and repeated after a 3 sec. pause. One male sang a weak high-pitched trilled song over and over while his mate was nest-building (Skutch 1954). In Panama, described as a fast thin squeaky high twitter, *sweézee seézee tzeedeéa dzeedzeé* lasting about 2 sec.; given from a vine 2 m off the ground (Eisenmann in Wetmore, Pasquier, and Olson 1984).

Breeding

In Costa Rica: Six nests were found in a pasture bordered on 3 sides by forest. Two were 1.2 and 2.7 m up in clumps of small thorny palms, one supported between upright stems and the other between basal leaflets of a frond. The remaining 4 nests were placed 0.4–0.9 m above the ground in tussocks of tall coarse pasture grass. The female built alone while the male stayed out of sight. Nests were bulky open cups made of dried and shrivelled small leaves, dried pine needles, and fine rootlets and lined with rootlets and moss. Two eggs, laid on consecutive days, were light blue, finely speckled with brown, especially in a wreath at the large end. At one nest, the incubation period was 14 days. The young were fed with regurgitated food delivered by both parents. The nestling period was about 16 days. (Skutch 1954.) Breeding dates: Costa Rica Feb, March, July, and Aug.

Sources

Primary Colwell et al. 1974; Ridgely 1976; Skutch 1954; Slud 1964; Wetmore, Pasquier, and Olson 1984; Wolf 1976. **Weights (n = 3)** LSUMZ data; Strauch 1977. **Stomach contents** Stiles and Hespenheide 1972. **Vocalizations** LNS recordings by Parker (3); recording by Whitney (1); Skutch 1954; Slud 1964. **Nests, eggs, and breeding dates** Skutch 1954.

Diglossa baritula (*sittoides* subspecies group   228-3) Rusty Flowerpiercer
Plate 30

Length 11 cm (4 in.). Weight 9 g (7.0–10.7 g). Six subspecies: plumages tend to vary within subspecies as well as between subspecies. Males differ most noticeably in amount of blackish on forehead and sides of head, and females vary in the depth of yellow and clarity of streaking of underparts. Some subadult males are nearly identical to females, others have cinnamon tinged underparts, and still others are duskier on breast and flanks than females (see Zimmer 1942b). May breed in subadult plumage.

Geographic Range

D. b. mandeli: Sucre, VENEZUELA. *D. b. hyperythra*: coastal range from Miranda to Yaracuy, VENEZUELA, and the Santa Marta Mountains, COLOMBIA. *D. b. coelestis*: the Perijá Mountains. *D. b. dorbignyi* and *decorata*: Cerro El Cerrón in extreme nw Lara and the Andes from s Lara to Táchira, VENEZUELA, through COLOMBIA (locally in the E Andes in Norte de Santander and Cundinamarca) and ECUADOR to sc PERU (in the w cordillera south to Lima and on the e slope south to Cuzco). *D. b. sittoides*: La Paz, BOLIVIA, southward to nw ARGENTINA (Salta, Jujuy, and Tucumán).

Elevational Range

From ca. 1500 m to treeline; scarce above 2500 m in some regions; wanders down to sea level in coastal Peru (sight, Lima, May 1977—Graves).

Habitat and Behavior

Inhabits flowering trees and shrubs on cutover slopes and at forest and woodland edge. Often lives in flowering ornamentals planted about settlements. Also occurs in open woodland, montane scrub, and hedgerows along roads. Very unusual within dense montane forest.

Usually lives alone or in pairs, much less often in small groups; incidental in mixed-species flocks. Extremely active and quick moving. Often harassed by larger flowerpiercers and by hummingbirds. Spends much time dodging repeated attacks by competitors; escapes by fleeing into dense thickets or foliage but emerges to feed on exposed flowers when adversaries depart. At times, however, persists in feeding despite the presence of competitors, and in some localities is able to maintain a feeding territory (see Moynihan 1979).

Forages for nectar and insects, mostly on flowering shrubs and trees, from the ground (Plenge 1974) to as high as 12 m in trees (Remsen data). Pierces flowers at bases of corollas, often leaning down from its perch. Appears to inspect flowers as if to decide which contain nectar (Parker data). Sallies to air and apparently gleans insects from flowers. Stomach contents (4): insects.

Vocalizations

Call note: a loud sharp *cheek* (Parker data). Apparently delivers at least 2 types of songs, one mostly twittering and the other containing pure trills, but the song containing trills may not be given in all regions (Moynihan 1979).

Breeding

Builds a very deep cup nest. Eggs (2) are gray to blue with indefinite gray spots, mostly on the large end (Nehrkorn 1899; also see Ogilvie-Grant 1912).

Sources

Primary Hilty and Brown 1986; Moynihan 1979; Parker data; Remsen data; Taczanowski 1884a. **Weights (n = 13)** LSUMZ data; Miller 1963. **Stomach contents** LSUMZ data. **Nests and eggs** Nehrkorn 1899; Ogilvie-Grant 1912; Phelps 1954.

Diglossa lafresnayii   229
Glossy Flowerpiercer

Distributed in isolated populations near treeline in the Andes, forms of the Glossy Flowerpiercer have been treated either as subspecies of a single species (*Peters Check-list*) or as allospecies of a superspecies (Vuilleumier 1969). Within the framework of the *Peters Check-list*, this book provides natural history information for three subspecies

Diglossa baritula (*sittoides* subspecies group)

groups equivalent to the allospecies of Vuilleumier.

The first subspecies group contains a single form, *gloriosissima*, that is restricted to the Western Andes of Colombia; if considered a species, its English name would be Chestnut-bellied Flowerpiercer. The second subspecies group also contains a single form, *lafresnayii*, that occupies the remaining Andes in Venezuela, Colombia, Ecuador, and Peru south to the Northern Peruvian Low; its English name would be Glossy Flowerpiercer. The third, the *mystacalis* subspecies group, includes the four remaining subspecies that occur south of the Northern Peruvian Low to northwest Bolivia; its English name would be Moustached Flowerpiercer.

The northern form, the Glossy Flowerpiercer, appears to occupy more open habitats than the southern races constituting the Moustached, and differences can be heard in their songs. Both flowerpiercers deliver lengthy vocalizations in which each note differs from the last. However, notes in songs of the Glossy are twittering and variable in delivery rate compared to the heavy notes of the Moustached. Whether these differences have biological significance is unclear. We have no record of the song of the Chestnut-bellied.

Diglossa lafresnayii
(*gloriosissima* subspecies group **229–1**)
Chestnut-bellied Flowerpiercer
Plate 31

Length 14 cm (5½ in.). Monotypic if specifically distinct.

Geographic Range

The n end of the W Andes in Antioquia and the s end in Cauca west of Popayán, COLOMBIA.

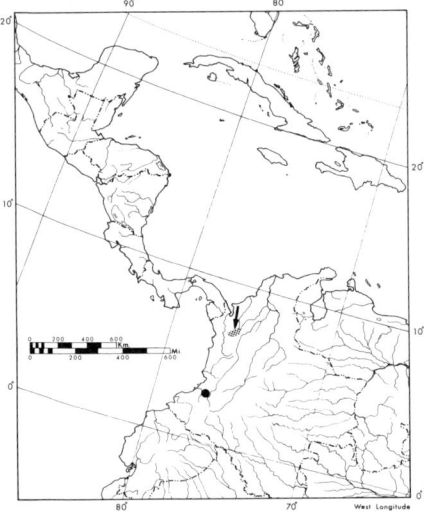

Diglossa lafresnayii (*gloriosissima* subspecies group)

Elevational Range

At or near treeline, 3150–3800 m.

Habitat and Behavior

Inhabits scrub and elfin forest borders. Local and apparently scarce. In Antioquia: Individuals appeared to maintain territories separate from the sympatric form of the Carbonated Flowerpiercer, *D. carbonaria* **230**; no overt fighting was seen nor overlap of singing; only one species sang at a time. Observed feeding on flowers. (Moynihan 1979.)

Vocalizations

No information.

Breeding

No information.

Sources

Primary Hilty and Brown 1985; Moynihan 1979.

Diglossa lafresnayii
(*lafresnayii* subspecies group **229–2**)
Glossy Flowerpiercer
Plate 31

Length 14 cm (5½ in.). Weight 16 g (13.1–19.0 g). Monotypic if specifically distinct.

Geographic Range

The Andes from Trujillo, VENEZUELA, to Norte de Santander, COLOMBIA; COLOMBIA in the E Andes in Cundinamarca and the C Andes from s Antioquia to Quindío and Tolima; and from e Cauca and Huila, COLOMBIA, southward through ECUADOR to Cajamarca, PERU, north of the Northern Peruvian Low.

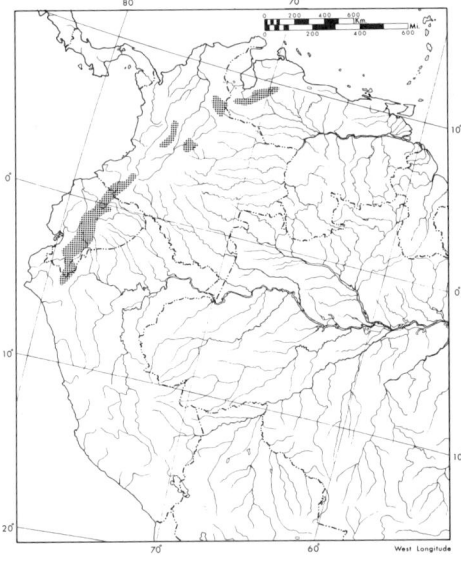

Diglossa lafresnayii (*lafresnayii* subspecies group)

Elevational Range

From 2000 m to treeline; most often within 500 m of treeline.

Habitat and Behavior

Inhabits dense patches of shrubs and small trees at páramo and puna edge. Also occurs in scrub, at montane forest edge, and on bushy slopes at lower elevations. In Ecuador, favors humid areas (Moynihan 1979). Solitary; rarely observed with mixed-species flocks. Often remains within dense shrubbery, darting out occasionally to feed. Crosses open spaces quickly before diving into cover (Silliman in Hilty and Brown 1985). Birds in subadult plumage are more apt to remain inside thickets than adults (Moynihan 1963).

Staunchly defends a feeding territory against conspecifics and in some localities against other nectarivorous species as well (see Moynihan 1963, 1979). Usually wins combatative encounters with other species. Forages low in vegetation, but sometimes goes higher in flowering trees. Captures insects by probing leaf bases, leaf clusters, and crevices in bark (Moynihan 1963); also makes aerial sallies (Hilty and Brown 1985). Obtains nectar by piercing corollas. Stomach contents: vegetable matter (1); animal matter (9). Contents included beetles and other insect remains.

Vocalizations

Calls: *chip* or *chut* (Parker data). Song: a long series (may go on for minutes) of single and double notes, some thin and High-pitched, others stronger and Moderate-pitched, given at the rate of 4–6 notes or doublets/sec.; becomes somewhat louder and softer in turn, sometimes speeding up in the louder portions. Overall quality, while somewhat musical, is that of a twitter that stumbles along. Sings while perched at favorite stations, often at tops of shrubs, near territorial centers. Both males and females appear to sing (Moynihan 1963).

Breeding

Pair bonds seem to be brief (Moynihan 1979).

Sources

Primary Hilty and Brown 1985; Moynihan 1963, 1979; Vuilleumier and Ewert 1978. **Weights (n=29)** LSUMZ data; Vuilleumier and Ewert 1978. **Stomach contents** LSUMZ data; Vuilleumier and Ewert 1978. **Vocalizations** LNS recordings by Gulledge (1), Parker (7), Schwartz (4); recordings by Whitney (2); Parker data.

Diglossa lafresnayii (*mystacalis* subspecies group 229–3) Moustached Flowerpiercer
Plate 31

Length 14 cm (5½ in.). Weight 16 g (12.0–19.2 g). Four subspecies. Adult plumages: *pectoralis* differs from *unicincta* (illus.) in having a white or brownish white breast band, and *albilinea* differs from *mystacalis* (illus.) in having a pale buffy moustachial stripe. Subadult plumages: *pectoralis* resembles *unicincta*; *albilinea* resembles *mystacalis* with pale moustachial stripe. Juveniles leave the nest before fully grown.

Geographic Range

D. l. unicincta: e Andean slope from Amazonas (south of the Northern Peruvian Low) to Huánuco (west of the Río Huallaga, LSUMZ), PERU. *D. l. pectoralis*: Huánuco (east of the Río Huallaga), Pasco (LSUMZ), and Junín, PERU. *D. l. albilinea*: Ayacucho (LSUMZ), Cuzco, and Puno, PERU. *D. l. mystacalis*: La Paz and Cochabamba (Remsen, Traylor, and Parkes in press), BOLIVIA.

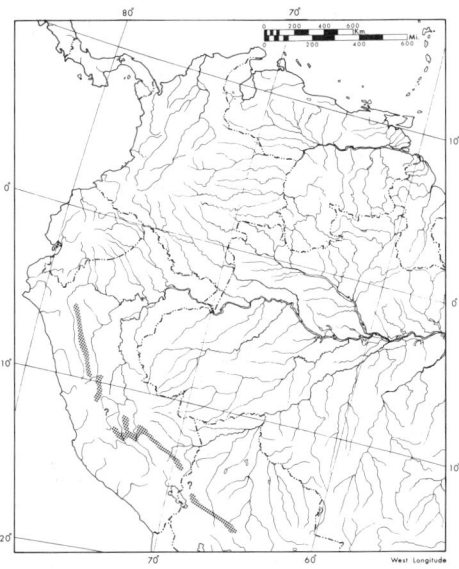

Diglossa lafresnayii (*mystacalis* subspecies group)

Elevational Range

2500–3600 m (Graves 1983); most common near treeline.

Habitat and Behavior

Inhabits elfin forest and patches of scrubby thickets surrounded by puna grassland. Also occurs in contiguous montane forest and forest edge, *Polylepis* woodland, bamboo thickets, and scrub on steep hillsides. Usually solitary except while breeding; occurs only incidently in mixed-species flocks. Highly territorial; not only drives away conspecifics but other species as well. The extent that territory is shared with other species may vary over the year (see Moynihan 1979). Moves rapidly inside vegetation; typically stays hidden and is much more often heard than seen.

Usually forages close to the ground; in Bolivia, the median foraging height was about 1.7 m off the ground (Remsen data, 9 obs.). Typically gleans the undersides of small leaves and leaf stems somewhat acrobatically by stretching up, reaching out, hanging, or leaning down to pick prey off substrates. Obtains nectar by piercing the bases of flowers. Also observed probing small flowers (Ericaceae) head-on like a hummingbird (Isler data). Stomach contents (60): insects, including flies.

Vocalizations

Song: a series of rather strong and stilted, but sweet, Moderate-pitched notes that rise and fall in pitch erratically; delivered at the rate of 4–5 notes/sec. and continued for some time, often for 2–5 minutes. Song is similar to that of the Citrine Warbler, *Basileuterus luteoviridis*, which lives in the same habitat but, unlike the warbler, the song of the *Diglossa* remains at a relatively even volume from start to finish.

Breeding

Three cup nests of moss from La Libertad, Peru, were located as follows: about 1.2 m off the ground on the side of a rock under a fern; behind a bush and about 0.3 m off the ground, supported by a dying fern and a tuft of grass; and about 1 m up in a small shrub. Each nest contained 2 eggs, blue or bluish green, marked with brownish gray, concentrated in a wreath at the large end. (LSUMZ data, Robbins and Schulenberg.) Breeding dates: Peru Sept.

Sources

Primary Isler data; LSUMZ data; Moynihan 1979; Remsen data. **Weights (n = 76)** LSUMZ data; Weske 1972. **Stomach contents** LSUMZ data. **Vocalizations** LNS recordings by Isler (2), Parker (2). **Nests, eggs, and breeding dates** LSUMZ data.

Diglossa carbonaria 230
Carbonated Flowerpiercer

Although our format requires us to follow the *Peters Check-list* and to treat the Carbonated Flowerpiercer as a single species, Graves (1982a) showed that well-marked subspecies came into contact and concluded that *Diglossa carbonaria* constituted four allospecies. Consequently, we have prepared natural history accounts of four equivalent subspecies groups. The first, the *humeralis* subspecies group, ranges from extreme nw Venezuela to Cajamarca, Peru, north of the Northern Peruvian Low (except for the northern end of the C and W Andes in Colombia). The *brunneiventris* subspecies group has two disjunct populations; one occurs in the northern end of the C and W Andes in Colombia and the other from the Northern Peruvian Low southward to La Paz, Bolivia. The third, the *carbonaria* subspecies group, consists of a single subspecies that ranges from La Paz to Chuquisaca, Bolivia. The final subspecies, the *gloriosa* subspecies group, occurs in the Venezuelan Andes east of the Western Venezuelan Low.

Descriptions of the habitat and behavior of the four subspecies groups are quite limited, and no major differences among them are apparent. Voice recordings are available only for the Black-throated Flowerpiercer.

Diglossa carbonaria
(*humeralis* subspecies group 230–1)
Black Flowerpiercer
Plate 31

Length 13–14 cm (5–5½ in.). Weight 12 g (9.6–14.3 g). Three subspecies: *humeralis* and *aterrima* are illustrated; *nocticolor* is all black with dark gray rump (difficult to observe in the field). Some individuals of all subspecies have faint gray barring on flanks, uppertail-coverts, undertail-coverts, and lower belly; some individuals of the *humeralis* subspecies have chestnut undertail-coverts or a pale supercilium (Graves 1982a). Subadult females of the *aterrima* subspecies are grayish brown, indistinctly streaked dusky. May breed in subadult plumage (Moynihan 1963).

Geographic Range

D. c. nocticolor: Santa Marta Mountains, COLOMBIA, and the Perijá Mountains.

D. c. humeralis: Táchira, VENEZUELA, west of the Western Venezuelan Low, and the E Andes from Norte de Santander to Cundinamarca, COLOMBIA. *D. c. aterrima:* the C Andes from extreme se Antioquia (USNM) southward and the W Andes in Cauca (Cerro Munchique area), COLOMBIA; the Andes from Nariño, COLOMBIA, through ECUADOR and nw PERU to the Northern Peruvian Low (south to between Cuterdo and Chota in c Cajamarca, see Graves 1982a).

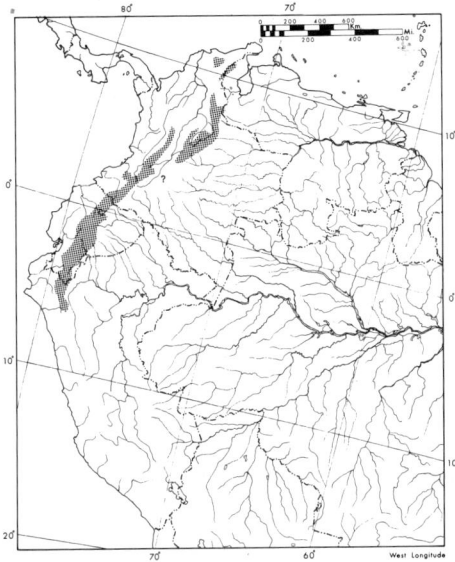

Diglossa carbonaria (humeralis subspecies group)

Elevational Range

From ca. 2200 m to treeline.

Habitat and Behavior

Inhabits dense and often fairly tall thickets and shrubs, mostly in areas with scattered trees and at forest edge. Also occurs in *Polylepis*-forested ravines, hedgerows along fields, and other semiopen situations, including parks and gardens around human habitations. Occasionally wanders to within montane forest. Solitary and highly aggressive; attacks immediately, without singing or displaying. Hostile towards conspecifics, and individuals maintain territories thoughout the nonbreeding season. Battles often with other species of flowerpiercers, conebills, and hummingbirds. Participates only incidentally in mixed-species flocks. Keeps distant from other species when with feeding aggregations at bountifully flowering shrubs or trees (see Moynihan 1963, 1979). Extremely active; flits about, but also stays in the interior of thickets for long periods, presumably to rest and preen. Birds in subadult plumage tend to remain inside shrubbery more than adults (Moynihan 1963).

Usually forages in shrubs and low trees but ascends to the tops of eucalyptus trees (Moynihan 1979). Furtively works through shrubs seeking flowers; not able or willing to pierce some types of blossoms (see Snow and Snow 1980). In Peru, entered flowers directly as well as pierced bases of flowers of a *Tristerix* mistletoe (see Graves 1982b). Probes for insects on leaf bases and in bark (Moynihan 1963) and aerial sallies (Jelski in Taczanowski 1884a). In Colombia, seen eating flower petals (Todd and Carriker 1922). In an urban garden in Ecuador, systematically searched leaves and plants for insects and flew through open windows and doors to hunt about rooms for spiders (Goodfellow 1901). Stomach contents (7): parts of small insects.

Vocalizations

Song is described as a rapid twitter (Moynihan 1979). Both males and females sing often.

Breeding

When nesting, pairs maintain a territory and are extremely hostile towards other pairs of the same species. Pair bonds seem to be brief (Moynihan 1963). In Ecuador, a rootlet and moss cup nest was suspended from thorns on the edges of a swordlike aloe leaf 0.8 m above the ground; two eggs were blue, speckled with red (Goodfellow 1901). Breeding dates: Ecuador Nov.

Sources

Primary Goodfellow 1901; Graves 1982a; Hilty and Brown 1986; Moynihan 1963, 1979; Taczanowski 1884a. **Weights (n=45)** LSUMZ data. **Stomach contents** LSUMZ data. **Nests, eggs, and breeding dates** Goodfellow 1901.

Diglossa carbonaria (*brunneiventris* subspecies group 230-2)
Black-throated Flowerpiercer
Plate 31

Length 13 cm (5½ in.). Weight 12 g (9.8–15.0 g). Two subspecies including *vuilleumieri*, described by Graves (1980). In Peru, plumages of individuals vary, especially in the extent of gray on flanks and in the completeness of the malar stripe and supercilium (see Zimmer 1930). In the field, the gray of the flanks, which extends to underwing-coverts, is very apparent.

Geographic Range

Two widely separated populations. *D. c. vuilleumieri* (Graves 1980): n ends of the C and W Andes in Antioquia, COLOMBIA.
D. c. brunneiventris: from the the Northern Peruvian Low in c Cajamarca (south of Cutervo, see Graves 1982a), PERU, southward in the w cordillera of the Andes to Tarapacá, CHILE (Johnson 1967) and southward on the e slope to La Paz, BOLIVIA (east of La Paz city; see Graves 1982a).

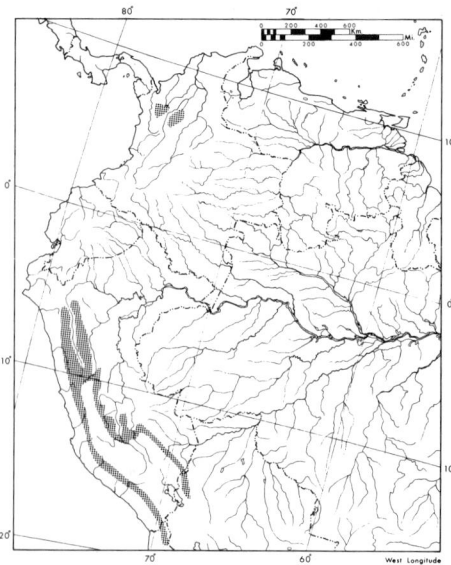

Diglossa carbonaria (*brunneiventris* subspecies group)

Elevational Range

From ca. 2000 m to treeline.

Habitat and Behavior

Occurs in rather dry as well as humid regions, but is often found near watercourses or in ravines in dry regions. Inhabits scrub, forest borders, and open woodland. Abundant in some areas and scarce or absent in others; in w Peru, may shift habitats seasonally (see Koepcke 1958). Lives alone or in pairs. Sprightly and constantly on the move. Individuals are aggressive towards each other and towards other flowerpiercer species; maintains a territory year-round (see Moynihan 1979). Not normally in mixed-species flocks, except possibly in Colombia (Moynihan 1979) where it may be endangered (Hilty 1985).

Forages from near the ground to tree tops. Searches for nectar and insects among flowers and at the tips of branches; clings in various attitudes including upside down. In Peru, pierced the bases as well as directly entered flowers of a *Tristerix* mistletoe (see Graves 1982b). The bill often remains open after piercing flowers (Parker data). In Peru during the rainy season, often foraged on the ground near treeline; tilted head and peered to spot prey on the ground; hopped or fluttered from place to place; often remained on the ground for some time before flying up to shrubs (Isler data). Stomach contents (8): insects.

Vocalizations

Song: 1 sec. flashes of Moderate- to High-pitched twittering; intervals between these bursts are uneven in length, perhaps most often 10–20 sec. At times, when intervals are short, thin barely audible Moderate-pitched notes, given at the rate of 10–15 notes/sec., may connect the song phrases. (Parker, LNS.) Sings from tops of shrubs within its territory (Koepcke 1958).

Breeding

Makes courtship flights (Koepcke 1958).

Sources

Primary Isler data; Koepcke 1958; LSUMZ data; Moynihan 1979; Parker data; Taczanowski 1884a. **Weights (n = 72)** LSUMZ data; Weske 1972. **Stomach contents** Koepcke 1958; LSUMZ data. **Vocalizations** LNS recordings by Parker (3).

Diglossa carbonaria
(*carbonaria* subspecies group **230-3**)
Gray-bellied Flowerpiercer
Plate 31

Length 13 cm (5½ in.). Weight 11 g (9.0–14.8 g). Monotypic if specifically distinct. Underwing-coverts gray like flanks. Throughout its range, a few individuals in adult plumage have some characteristics of the *brunneiventris* subspecies group **230-2**: a

Diglossa carbonaria (*carbonaria* subspecies group)

rufous malar, a supercilium, and/or belly feathers with rufous edgings (see Graves 1982a). Juvenal plumage resembles that of the subadult *D. c. brunneiventris* (illus.) but it is not quite as streaked or contrasting (LSUMZ); subadult plumage illustrated is an older bird (skull 90% ossified).

Geographic Range

BOLIVIA from La Paz (City of La Paz, see Graves 1982a) southeast to Santa Cruz and Chuquisaca.

Elevational Range

From ca. 2250 m to treeline.

Habitat and Behavior

Lives in dry as well as humid environments. Inhabits elfin forest shrubbery; also occurs in second growth. Behaves aggressively towards other species (Moynihan 1979). Leans down, hangs, or reaches up to flowers (Remsen data), and stands on flower heads while feeding (Parker data). Sallies for flying insects from tops of bushes (Sclater 1875). Stomach contents (23): insect parts.

Vocalizations

No information.

Breeding

No information.

Sources

Primary Graves 1982a; Moynihan 1979; Parker data; Remsen data; Sclater 1875; Vuillemier 1969. **Weights (n = 22)** LSUMZ data. **Stomach contents** LSUMZ data.

Diglossa carbonaria (*gloriosa* subspecies group 230-4) Merida Flowerpiercer Plate 31

Length 12 cm (5 in.). Weight 11 g (11.0 and 11.5 g). Monotypic if specifically distinct. Underwing-coverts dark gray. Many individuals in adult plumage have traces of a rufous malar stripe (Graves 1982a). Subadult plumage resembles that of *D. carbonaria vuilleumieri* **230-2** (illus.).

Geographic Range

The Andes from Táchira (east of the Western Venezuelan Low) to Trujillo, VENEZUELA.

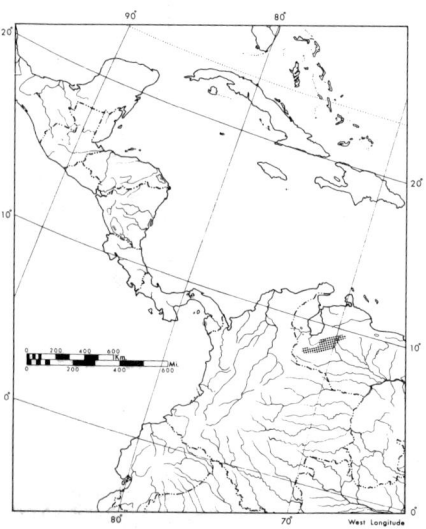

Diglossa carbonaria (*gloriosa* subspecies group)

Elevational Range

From 2500 m to treeline.

Habitat and Behavior

Inhabits semiopen scrub and forest edge; occasionally occurs in elfin forest. Encountered in isolated bushes and eucalyptus trees at lower elevations. Individuals are aggressive towards conspecifics. Actively flits around foliage and feeds at flowers (Moynihan 1979).

Vocalizations

Call is reported to be a long thin trill (Meyer de Schauensee and Phelps 1978). Gives flight songs apparently in territorial defense (Vuilleumier and Ewert 1978).

Breeding

In Mérida: Song and flight pursuit suggested that a pair was courting. A nest that was probably of this species was in a clump of grass atop a 1.2 m embankment. The deep cup of grass and moss was only slightly protected by a few blades of grass. Breeding dates: April. (Vuilleumier and Ewert 1978.)

Sources

Primary Meyer de Schauensee and Phelps 1978; Moynihan 1979; Vuilleumier and Ewert 1978. **Weights (n = 2)** Vuilleumier and Ewert 1978. **Nests and breeding dates** Vuilleumier and Ewert 1978.

Diglossa venezuelensis 231 Venezuelan Flowerpiercer Plate 31

Length 14 cm (5½ in.). Monotypic. Subadult males are duller and browner than adult males.

Geographic Range

VENEZUELA in w Sucre and nw Monagas.

Elevational Range

1600–2500 m.

Habitat and Behavior

Inhabits shrubbery in forest and at forest edge. Forages actively in the foliage at mid-heights.

Vocalizations

No information.

Breeding

No information.

Sources

Primary Meyer de Schauensee and Phelps 1978.

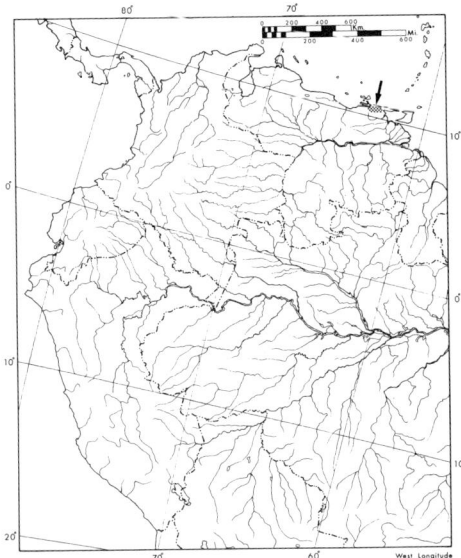
Diglossa venezuelensis

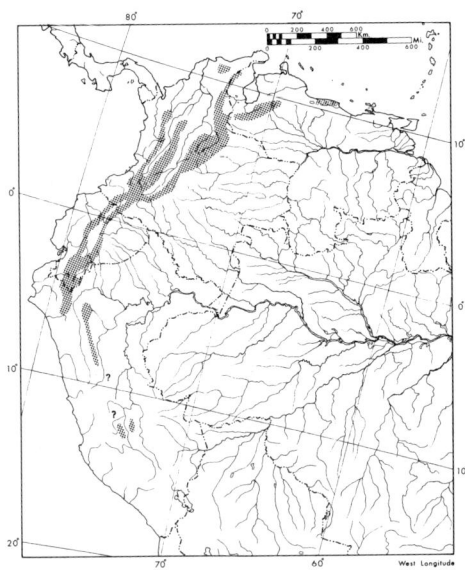
Diglossa albilatera

Diglossa albilatera 232
White-sided Flowerpiercer
Plate 31

Length 12 cm (4½ in.). Weight 10 g (8.2–12.0 g). Four subspecies. Subadult males are duller and browner than adult males.

Geographic Range

VENEZUELA in the coastal range from Aragua to Miranda and the Andes in Trujillo, Mérida, and Táchira; the Perijá Mountains; COLOMBIA in the Santa Marta Mountains and all 3 Andean ranges southward through ECUADOR to Lambayeque and Cajamarca (LSUMZ), PERU, in the w cordillera and (locally?) to Ayacucho and extreme nw Cuzco (Weske 1972), PERU, on the e Andean slope.

Elevational Range

1600–3300 m; centered at ca. 1800–2400 m; sight record at 1300 m in Lambayeque, Peru (Parker data).

Habitat and Behavior

Inhabits dense shrubbery and low trees, especially those in bloom, at forest edge, on scrubby hillsides, and in second growth and the forest understory. Also occurs in parks and gardens in suburban areas. Usually encountered in pairs, sometimes singly. Occasionally joins mixed-species flocks at forest edge. Moves quickly and furtively among flowering shrubs. Both sexes frequently flick wings to expose white flank feathers. Territorial; regularly attacked by hummingbirds and stays deep within foliage when hummingbirds are present.

Forages for nectar and insects usually at midheights or lower (0.5–5 m) but may go higher in trees to reach attractive flowers (Moynihan 1979). Darts from one flower to another puncturing the bases of corollas to obtain nectar. Generally spends about 1 sec. at each blossom when competing with hummingbirds, longer at long tubular flowers too large for the bills of most hummingbirds (Snow and Snow 1980). Gleans insects from foliage and twigs. Stomach contents: vegetable matter (1); animal matter (1). Contents included plant and beetle parts.

Vocalizations

Song: a 2 sec., flat, Moderate- to High-pitched trill, sometimes harsh (Parker data) or preceded by 2 faint notes (Hilty and Brown 1986). Pauses between trills are 6–30 sec.; one individual sang regularly for over 4 min. pausing about 8 sec. between trills; another uttered short thin High-pitched *sip* notes during long pauses.

Breeding

In Ecuador, a compact open cup nest, made of moss, grass, and rootlets and lined with moss, was situated 0.8 m above the ground in the midst of a cluster of fine shoots of a bamboo growing on a bushy mountainside (Skutch 1954:434). Eggs (2) are blue or greenish blue, thickly speckled brown, especially at the large end. Breeding dates: Ecuador Oct.

Sources

Primary Hilty and Brown 1986; Moynihan 1979; Parker data; Ridgely and Gaulin 1980; Skutch 1954; Snow and Snow 1980; Todd and Carriker 1922. **Weights (n = 26)** LSUMZ data. **Stomach contents** LSUMZ data. **Vocalizations** LNS recordings by Parker (4), Schwartz (3), van den Berg (1); recording by R. A. Rowlett (1); Hilty and Brown 1986. **Nests, eggs, and breeding dates** Nehrkorn 1899; Ogilvie-Grant 1912; Sclater and Salvin 1879; Skutch 1954.

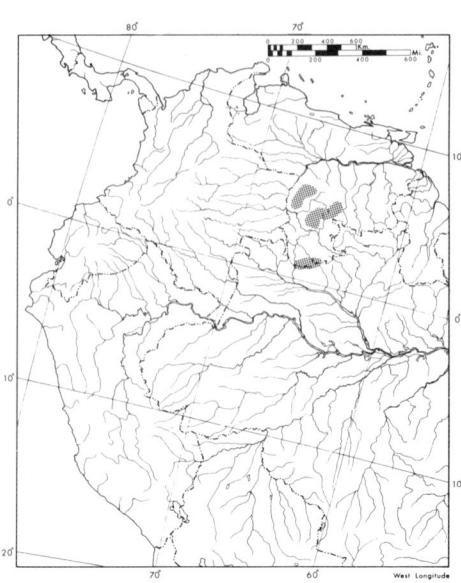

Diglossa duidae

Diglossa duidae 233
Scaled Flowerpiercer
Plate 31

Length 13 cm (5½ in.). Weight 16 g (13.8–16.5 g). Two subspecies.

Geographic Range

D. d. hitchcocki: ne Amazonas, VENEZUELA, northward to the Bolívar border. *D. d. duidae*: c and s Amazonas and adjacent sw Bolívar, VENEZUELA, and adjacent Amazonas, BRAZIL.

Elevational Range

Tepuis at 1400–2500 m; mostly at higher elevations.

Habitat and Behavior

Inhabits montane forest, low brushy forest on summits of tepuis, and low scattered trees and bushes in open country. Encountered alone or in pairs.

Vocalizations

Said to utter a short thin whistle (Meyer de Schauensee and Phelps 1978).

Breeding

No information.

Sources

Primary Chapman 1931; Meyer de Schauensee and Phelps 1978. **Weights (n = 10)** Foster data.

Diglossa major 234
Greater Flowerpiercer
Plate 31

Length 17 cm (6½ in.). Four subspecies.

Geographic Range

Tepuis in se Bolívar, VENEZUELA, and adjacent Roraima, BRAZIL.

Elevational Range

1650–2800 m.

Habitat and Behavior

Inhabits montane forest, low brushy forest on summits of tepuis, and scattered low trees and bushes in more open country. Encountered alone or in pairs foraging in dense foliage at the ends of branches (Parker data). Inspects almost every leaf for insects (Schomburgk in Chubb 1921).

Vocalizations

Song: In a duet, two birds faced each other about 15 cm apart, simultaneously flicking both wings to expose whitish underwing-coverts. One sang very thin, High-pitched *sip* or *tip* notes in a tinkling series, alternating slowing and accelerating while varying the notes slightly in pitch. The other bird

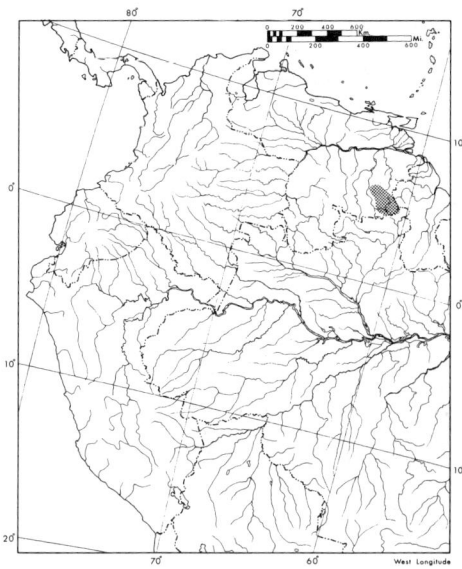

Diglossa major

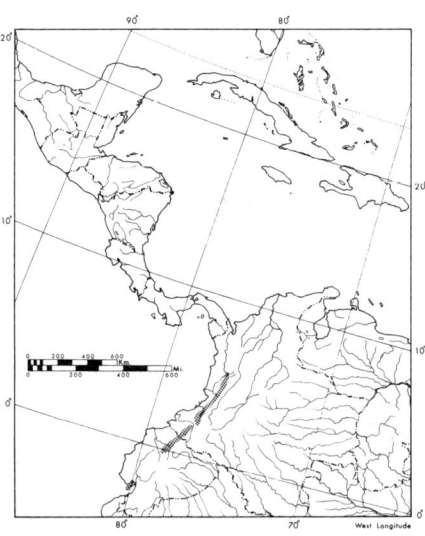

Diglossa indigotica

delivered scratchy, somewhat harsh, Moderate-pitched chatters. The pair continued the duet without pause for several minutes. (Parker, LNS.)

Breeding

Nests presumed to be of this species were open cups built of grasses and small sticks and placed among rocks, usually under an overhanging shelf; generally located 18–36 cm above the ground (Gilliard 1941).

Sources

Primary Gilliard 1941; Meyer de Schauensee and Phelps 1978; Parker data. **Vocalizations** LNS recording by Parker (1). **Nests** Gilliard 1941.

Diglossa indigotica 235
Indigo Flowerpiercer
Plate 32

Length 11 cm (4½ in.). Monotypic. Feathers of young birds are black edged dull bluish-green (Lönnberg and Rendahl 1922).

Geographic Range

The Pacific slope from Risaralda (Cerro Tatamá), COLOMBIA, southward to Pichincha, ECUADOR.

Elevational Range

700–2200 m; in Colombia, most common 1000–1400 m.

Habitat and Behavior

Inhabits wet mossy forest, forest edge, and tall second growth. Pairs or single birds typically travel with mixed-species flocks. Usually forages at midheights or higher, but descends to as low as 1.5 m above the ground (Hilty data). Behavior similar to that of the Deep-blue Flowerpiercer, *D. glauca* **236** (Hilty and Brown 1986).

Vocalizations

Occasionally utters a high thin *chip*; also *squik, squik, squik, squik*, delivered deliberately (Hilty and Brown 1986).

Breeding

In Valle, Colombia, seen carrying nesting material in June (Hilty and Brown 1986).

Sources

Primary Hilty data; Hilty and Brown 1986. **Vocalizations** Hilty and Brown 1986. **Breeding dates** Hilty and Brown 1986.

Diglossa glauca 236
Deep-blue Flowerpiercer
Plate 32

Length 12 cm (4½ in.). Weight 12 g (9.5–13.0 g). The two subspecies differ slightly in size and color. Subadult (possibly juvenal) plumage is sooty in color and base of lower mandible is yellow (Hellmayr 1935).

Geographic Range

D. g. tyrianthina: the e slope of the Andes from w Caquetá (sight, Hilty and Brown 1986) and w Putumayo (Fitzpatrick and Willard 1982), COLOMBIA, southward to Tungurahua, ECUADOR. *D. g. glauca*: the e slope of the Andes from Amazonas (LSUMZ; presumably this subspecies), southward to Cochabamba (LSUMZ; Bond and Meyer de Schauensee 1942), BOLIVIA.

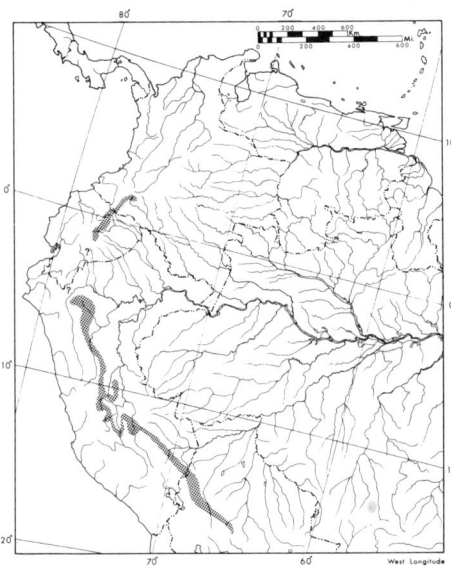

Diglossa glauca

Elevational Range

From 1000 m (1400 m in Colombia) to 2600 m (Graves 1983); mostly below 2000 m; once at 2800 m in Peru (Weske 1972).

Habitat and Behavior

Inhabits humid montane forest, especially mossy forest, and forest edge. Encountered singly or in pairs and occasionally in small groups of 3–4 individuals; once in a flock of 10 or more (Parker data). Frequently travels with mixed-species flocks; occurs regularly with Bluish and Masked Flowerpiercers, *D. caerulescens* 237 and *cyanea* 238, at elevations where they occur together in Colombia (Hilty and Brown 1986). Active and nervous; almost constantly fidgets and flicks wings (Hilty and Brown 1986).

Forages most often from midheights to the canopy within forest and at midheights at forest edge (Parker data); occasionally descends lower. In Bolivia, the median foraging height was about 9 m off the ground and about 1.5 m from the top of the canopy; mostly picked 3–4 mm fruits while perched (once in flight); occasionally picked insects off mossy branches 5 cm in diam. (Remsen data, 49 obs.). In Peru, often seen in vine tangles as well as on mossy limbs (Parker data). In Colombia, said to pierce corollas (Hilty and Brown 1986), but in Peru, rarely seen about flowers (Parker data). Stomach contents: animal matter (7); vegetable matter (4); both (2). Contents included insects and seeds.

Vocalizations

In Peru and Bolivia: Calls include a short, somewhat explosive, Moderate- to High-pitched *cheet* and a High-pitched *peet*. Song consists of High-pitched, extremely thin, squeaky, tinkling phrases of uneven notes; additional notes, resembling call notes, are sprinkled throughout phrases. In Colombia: Calls are described as a high-pitched pure tone, *keeeee*, mechanical or amphibianlike and often doubled, and a *ti-ti-dweeee*. Song a high-pitched series of thin chips and squeaks, dropping, accelerating, and very jumbled at the end. (Hilty and Brown 1986.)

Breeding

No information.

Sources

Primary Hilty and Brown 1986; LSUMZ data; Parker data; Remsen data. **Weights (n = 37)** LSUMZ data; Weske 1972. **Stomach contents** LSUMZ data. **Vocalizations** LNS recordings by Parker (2); recording by R. A. Rowlett (1); Hilty and Brown 1986.

Diglossa caerulescens **237**
Bluish Flowerpiercer
Plate 32

Length 13 cm (5 in.). Weight 13 g (10.1–16.0 g). Six subspecies; plumage extremes are illustrated.

Geographic Range

D. c. caerulescens: coastal range of VENEZUELA from Distrito Federal to Carabobo. *D. c. ginesi*: the Périja Mountains. *D. c. saturata*: the Andes in VENEZUELA (Trujillo to Táchira) and COLOMBIA (all 3 ranges) south to Caquetá on the e slope and Pichincha (ANSP), ECUADOR, on the Pacific slope. *D. c. media, pallida*, and *mentalis*: the Andes from Azuay (Meyer de Schauensee 1951) and Morona-Santiago (Ridgely 1984), ECUADOR southward through PERU (on the w cordillera south to Cajamarca) to La Paz (LSUMZ), BOLIVIA.

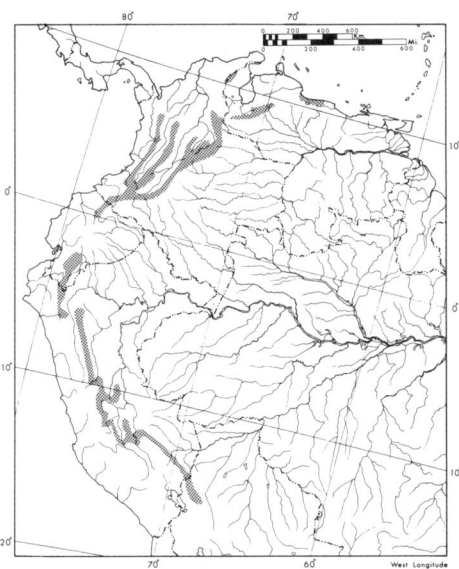

Diglossa caerulescens

Elevational Range

From 1350 m to treeline; mostly 2000–2600 m. In coastal Venezuela, descends to lower elevations seasonally (Schäfer and Phelps 1954).

Habitat and Behavior

Frequents scrubby montane forest, elfin forest, second growth, and forest edge and clearings. Often found on windswept ridges and areas of poor soil conditions. Occasionally encountered inside montane forest. Status varies substantially among parts of the Andes; apparently absent or scarce in most of Ecuador. Seems to wander over large areas seasonally. Usually encountered in pairs or singly; associates with mixed-species flocks and is often found in company with the Masked Flowerpiercer, *D. cyanea* **238**. Occurrence in flocks seems to vary regionally and/or seasonally. Restless, active, and somewhat aggressive.

Forages in the highest parts of shrubs and small trees outside of forest, from mid-heights to the canopy inside forest. In Peru, appears to feed mostly on insects which are primarily, if not solely, gleaned from leaves (Parker data). In some areas, favors *Clusia* trees (Vuilleumier in Hilty and Brown 1986). In addition to insects, takes small fruits, e.g., blackberries (*Rubus* sp) and melastome berries. At one site in Colombia, only seen to enter flowers straight-on (Snow and Snow 1980). Stomach contents: animal matter (6); vegetable matter (1); both (1). Contents included beetles and fruit.

Vocalizations

Calls: a loud Moderate-pitched *chink* and a distinctive flutelike note given in flight (Parker data). Song: High-pitched sweet notes run into a slightly lower pitched squeaky twitter or a Moderate-pitched buzzy chatter; a phrase takes about 2.5 sec. of which the twitter or chatter is about 1 sec. In one recording, phrases are repeated regularly with pauses of about 5.5 sec. (Parker, LNS).

Breeding

In Colombia, said to build an open cup nest made of grass and moss and placed in low bushes (Sclater and Salvin 1879). Eggs are greenish blue or fairly dark blue, blotched with red brown or lavender spots, mostly at the large end.

Sources

Primary Hilty and Brown 1986; Moynihan 1979; Parker data; Schäfer and Phelps 1954. **Weights (n = 27)** LSUMZ data; Weske 1972. **Stomach contents** LSUMZ data. **Vocalizations** LNS recordings by Parker (3); recording by Whitney (1). **Nests and eggs** Nehrkorn 1899; Ogilvie-Grant 1912; Sclater and Salvin 1879.

Diglossa cyanea 238
Masked Flowerpiercer
Plate 32

Length 15 cm (6 in.). Weight 17 g (12.0–22.5 g). Five subspecies.

Geographic Range

D. c. tovarensis: VENEZUELA in the coastal range in Aragua and Distrito Federal.
D. c. obscura: the Perijá mountains (only in Venezuela). *D. c. cyanea, dispar*, and *melanops*: the Andes from Trujillo, VENEZUELA, through COLOMBIA (all 3 Andean ranges), ECUADOR, PERU (in the w range south to Cajamarca), and BOLIVIA to w Santa Cruz (Remsen, Traylor, and Parkes in press).

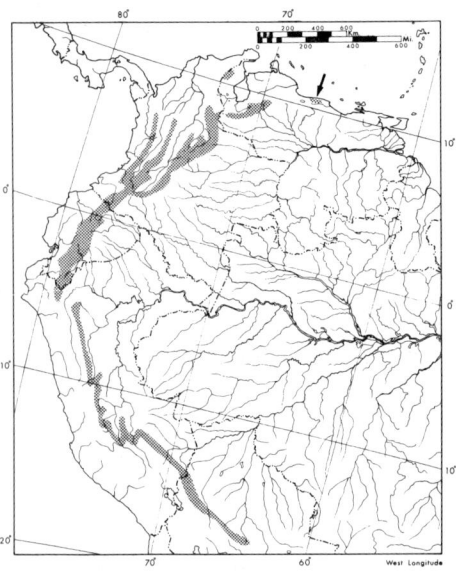

Diglossa cyanea

Elevational Range

From 1800 m (rarely 1500 m) to 3600 m. Mostly 2200–3100 m; however, the center of abundance seems to vary among different Andean locations (Moynihan 1979) and/or seasonally (Hilty and Brown 1986).

Habitat and Behavior

Inhabits montane and elfin forest, both inside forest and at forest edge. Also occurs in second growth and areas with scattered trees and bushes. Very common at some locations and relatively scarce at others. Lives in pairs or family groups of 3–4 individuals and singly. In Peru, frequently escorts mixed-species flocks for a short time, and then leaves the flock to forage alone (Isler data). Occasionally occurs in single-species aggregations of up to 30 individuals in fruiting shrubs, but is territorial for at least part of the year; sometimes aggressive towards or attacked by other species.

Forages from midheights to the canopy within forest, in the upper portions of nearby isolated trees and shrubs, and low in fruiting shrubs and patches of thickets and shrubbery; rarely descends to the ground. May remain in the same tree for considerable time, moving short distances among clusters of leaves, flitting and hopping about, and gleaning leaf surfaces. Perches atop large leaves at times. Often searches for insects in flowering and fruiting trees. Also examines bark crevices (Moynihan 1963), mossy branches, and clusters of dead flowers. Typically reaches out or leans down to pick insects off substrates; also chases insects in flight (Stolzmann in Taczanowski 1884a). Eats fruit, especially blackberries (*Rubus* spp) and melastome berries. To obtain nectar and possibly insects, places bill into flowers directly; also said to pierce tubular flower corollas (Moynihan 1963). Stomach contents: animal matter (38); vegetable matter (15); both (4). Contents included insects, seeds, and fruit.

Vocalizations

Sings throughout the day, even when foraging, for at least part of the year. Song: *pseat* or *tsick* notes accelerate into a 2–3 sec. jumble of twitters in Venezuela or an extended with 2–3 piercing drawn-out notes to a 3–4 sec. song in Peru; in s Peru, the drawn-out ending drops in pitch. Notes are High-pitched, thin, and lisping; repeated usually after a short pause. Utters soft *pseet* notes during longer pauses. When individuals become excited, some notes are strident and Moderate-pitched.

Breeding

Said to build a cup nest of grass and moss (Sclater and Salvin 1879). Eggs are pale greenish blue, spotted with red-brown and lilac, forming a cap on the large end. May breed twice a year (Moynihan 1979).

Sources

Primary Hilty and Brown 1986; Isler data; LSUMZ data; Moynihan 1963, 1979; Parker data; Remsen data. **Weights (n = 180)** LSUMZ data; Weske 1972. **Stomach contents** LSUMZ data. **Vocalizations** LNS recordings by Isler (7), Parker (5), Schwartz (6). **Nests and eggs** Nehrkorn 1899; Ogilvie-Grant 1912; Sclater and Salvin 1879.

EUNEORNIS

This monotypic genus is confined to Jamaica, and its affinities are very uncertain. *Euneornis* was placed in the subfamily Emberizinae by the *A.O.U. Check-list*.

Euneornis campestris **239**
Orangequit
Plate 32

Length 12 cm (5 in.). Weight 16 g (13.2–19.2 g). Monotypic. Subadult male resembles female.

Geographic Range

JAMAICA.

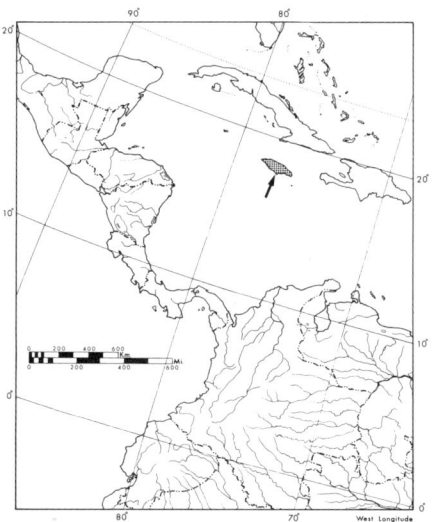

Euneornis campestris

Elevational Range

Mostly above 300 m.

Habitat and Behavior

Inhabits open woodland and woodland edge; occasionally visits orange groves and trees and shrubs around human habitations near woodland. Travels in small groups; joins feeding aggregations. Quarrelsome; drives away other species and sometimes fights viciously with conspecifics (Taylor 1955). Active and sprightly; flutters about.

Forages from high in tall trees to very low in bushes; occasionally picks up food off the ground (Jeffrey-Smith 1956). Eats various fruits and berries including *Ficus* and *Cecropia* fruit; picks fruit from a perched position (Cruz 1974). Pecks holes in ripe oranges to suck juice (Gosse 1847). Drinks nectar; gleans insects from branches and leaves (Cruz 1974). Readily comes to feeding tables for bananas and other fruit. Stomach contents: seeds from the fruit of an arumlike plant (1); insects (1).

Vocalizations

Calls: described as a shrill *swee* (Bond 1961) and a shrill sharp *chirp* (Gosse 1847); also a rapidly repeated series of harsh scolding sounds and some high-pitched *screeps* (Danforth 1928). Alarm note near a nest given by both sexes is a thin squeaking *cheep* (Jeffrey-Smith 1956).

Breeding

In display in April, after apparent copulation, a pair sat side by side about 7 cm apart facing in the same direction; the male threw back his head, opened his mandibles skywards, puffed out breast and throat feathers, and slowly swayed from side to side. The female then turned almost completely around with her head facing towards the tail of the male, crouched, partially opened her wings, and cocked her tail while the male continued to sway. Finally the female hopped away to another branch and the male resumed his normal perching position. The incident lasted 3–4 minutes. (Bray and Cawkell 1972.)

Two nests have been described: one was a rudely formed, very deep cup, made of grass and leaves, built on the fork of a horizontal branch in a bush (Gosse 1847); the other was a small shallow cup with the suggestion of a dome, located 1.5 m above ground on a slender spray near the main stem of a sapling (Jeffrey-Smith 1956). Eggs (4) are white with dull red markings that converge at the large end; the male was seen to leave the nest during incubation (Gosse 1847). Eggs are also described as pinkish white, blotched and mottled all over with brown and lilac red (Ogilvie-Grant 1912). Breeding dates: May and June.

Sources

Primary Bond 1961; Cruz 1974; Danforth 1928; Gosse 1847; Jeffrey-Smith 1956; Taylor 1955. **Weights (n = 260)** Cruz 1974; Steadman et al. 1980; Witt 1978. **Stomach contents** Danforth 1928. **Vocalizations** Bond 1961; Danforth 1928; Gosse 1847; Jeffrey-Smith 1956. **Nests, eggs, and breeding dates** Bond 1961; Gosse 1847; Jeffrey-Smith 1956; Ogilvie-Grant 1912.

TERSINA

Tersina was formerly placed in the monotypic family Tersinidae (Meyer de Schauensee 1970) or the monotypic subfamily Tersininae (*Peters Check-list*) but is relegated to tribal status within the Thraupinae by the *A.O.U. Check-list* (see Sibley 1973). The features of *Tersina* include a relatively broad flat bill (with a distinctive palate and tongue skeletal elements) and long wings. It nests in holes in earth banks and man-made structures.

Tersina viridis **240**
Swallow-Tanager
Plate 32

Length 14 cm (5½ in.). Weight 29 g (25.9–35.0 g). Three subspecies. First year male is mottled green and blue and lacks the face mask; male acquires adult plumage gradually over a 4 year period (see Schaefer 1953); breeds in subadult plumage.

Geographic Range

PANAMA in e Panamá province (sight record) and e Darién (see Wetmore, Pasquier, and Olson 1984); COLOMBIA (except in less humid regions along the Caribbean, in the upper Magdalena Valley, and in the se corner); the Perijá Mountains; VENEZUELA in the Andes, the coastal ranges from Carabobo to Sucre, and in Amazonas and Bolívar; THE GUIANAS (inland areas); TRINIDAD; ECUADOR (east of the Andes and west of the Andes to Pichincha); PERU (east of the Andes); BOLIVIA (east of the Andes south to Santa Cruz); BRAZIL (local or absent in the region along the Amazon River, in a belt along the Atlantic coast from Amapá to Rio Grande do Norte, and in s Rio Grande do Sul); ARGENTINA (Misiones); and PARAGUAY (see Short 1972).

Elevational Range

Lowlands to 1800 m; mostly 600–900 m; in n South America, possibly confined to mountainous regions when breeding and may wander erratically to lowlands at other times.

Habitat and Behavior

Inhabits open woodland, forest edge and openings, tree-studded clearings, second growth, and gallery forest and other riparian habitats. Withdraws from southern portions of its range in the austral winter (Sick and Pabst 1968). In n South America, appears to migrate elevationally (see Schaefer 1953). When not nesting, seems to move about as favorite fruits ripen. When traveling among feeding, nesting, and roosting sites, moves in somewhat dispersed groups, flying high above the canopy in a slightly undulating line. Except while nesting, typically encountered in single-species flocks of up to 12 or more individuals; in c Brazil, occurs occasionally in groups of over 100 (Negret and Negret 1981). Single-species groups aggressively discourage other species that attempt to follow them (Schaefer 1953). Very active, but then may sit quietly for some time. On breeding territories, birds of the same sex display towards each other using similar curtsy movements as employed during pair formation (see Breeding section, below).

Forages high in trees in woodland but closer to the ground in more open habitats. Eats a variety of fruits and berries; in Aragua, Venezuela, favors large pulpy fruits of the family Lauraceae, e.g., avocadoes (Schaefer 1953). Opens its bill wide to envelop large fruits and then turns and twists its bill to scrape off the fleshy pulp, letting the hard pit drop (Schaefer 1953). Fruit is normally taken from a perched position; also hovers to pluck berries (ffrench 1973). Stores fruit in an expandable throat pouch. In c Brazil, eats fruits of *Hamelia patens* (Rubiaceae); Sick 1985. Typically catches insects in aerial pursuits. Makes sallies of 3–10 m above the tree, often catching 2 or 3 insects before returning to the same perch. Proportion of fruit and insects varies seasonally (Schaefer 1953). Stomach contents: vegetable matter (12); animal matter (1); both (22). Contents included insects (mostly flying insects, e.g., flies, ants, termites, and grasshoppers; also soft beetles), seeds (incl. those of Magnoleaceae and Araliaceae), and fruit

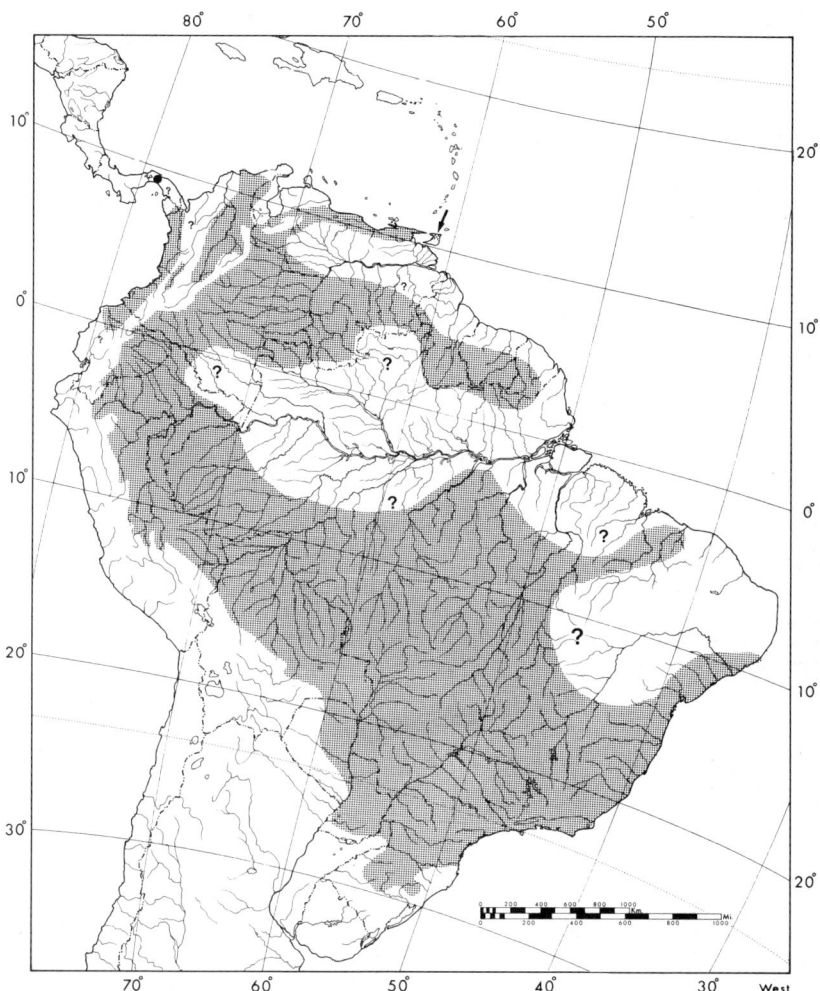

Tersina viridis

pulp (incl. avacado). Also eats moths (Collins and Watson 1983) and larvae.

Vocalizations

Songs and calls are distinctive, squeaky, and unmusical. Call: an emphatic single Moderate-pitched *tchee* or High-pitched *tsee* repeated monotonously about every 5–6 sec. Song: the call note, *tchee*, followed by a rapidly delivered shrill metallic Moderate- to High-pitched *WHEE-chy WHEE-chy WHEE-chy*. (Schwartz, LNS.) Only the males sing, always while sitting still; songs seem to have little attractive influence on females or warning effect on other males (Schaefer 1953). Schaefer also describes a very sharp *tse-it tsu-it* given by both sexes in defense of territory, 3–6 rather long nasal *tsee wee it* when fighting, and a long musical song given by subadult males.

Breeding

In Venezuela: In pair formation, two birds faced each other with feathers tightly appressed, head raised, wings hanging, and wings and tail sometimes trembling. One bird bowed low while the other drew erect, and then they reversed positions. These movements, termed the curtsy reaction, were repeated up to 100 times and were sometimes accompanied by bouncing hops and chasing.

The female initiated pair formation and the male became her constant companion; a pair often sat together for half an hour or so calling at intervals of 4–6 sec. The male formed and defended a territory against other Swallow-Tanagers and other species (e.g., swallows) competing for nesting holes. The male searched for a nest site by hovering in front of holes, sometimes flying about in spirals and circles. The female followed and chose the site. Most nests were placed in cavities made by man or by other species of birds (sometimes excavated by the Swallow-Tanager female, Todd and Carriker 1922). Sites were at the end of horizontal tunnels (5 cm to 2 m deep) 1–3 m above the ground in cliffs, earth banks, road-cuts, stone walls, or under bridges. Entrance holes were 6–10 cm in diam. when excavated in the earth; others were often much larger. The female constructed the nest alone, although the male accompanied her attentively and sometimes carried nesting material. The loose shallow cup was made of no particular material but was always lined with fine black palm fibers.

Typically 3 porcelain white eggs were laid on consecutive days by older females, every second day by younger ones. Females incubated alone for 13–17 days. During incubation males ignored their mates and seemed to change their diet from fruit to chiefly insects. Shortly before eggs hatched, the males became attentive. Both parents fed the young, the female much more than the male. Insects were mostly given to nestlings during days 1–6 and 15–20 (when feathers were sprouting); other times, their diet consisted of at least 40% fruit. Young fledged after 24 days. Males tried to induce females to attempt a second brood but were seldom successful. (Schaefer 1953.)

Nesting data from other regions are consistent with Schaefer's observations. Euler (1900) mentions occasional nesting in tree cavities. Breeding dates: Colombia Feb, May, and June. Venezuela April and May. Trinidad April–June. Brazil (Minas Gerais) Sept; (Mato Grosso) Nov; (location uncertain) Oct.

Sources

Primary Belton 1985; ffrench 1973; Negret and Negret 1981; Schaefer 1953; Todd and Carriker 1922. **Weights (n = 30)** Belton 1985; ffrench 1973; Fry 1970; LSUMZ data; Schaefer 1953; Thomas data. **Stomach contents** Berla 1944; Foster data; LSUMZ data; Moojen, Carvalho, and Lopes 1941; Schubart, Aguirre, and Sick 1965. **Vocalizations** LNS recordings by Schwartz (8); Schaefer 1953. **Nests, eggs, and breeding dates** Allen 1891; Belcher and Smooker 1937; Euler 1900; ffrench 1973; Goeldi 1894; Hilty and Brown 1986; Mitchell 1957; Schaefer 1953.

NEPHELORNIS

The single *Nephelornis* was described in 1976 as a species of uncertain affinities. One recent study (Raikow 1978) places *Nephelornis* between the tanagers and the wood-warblers (Parulinae).

Nephelornis oneilli **241**
Pardusco
Plate 32

Length 13 cm (5 in.). Weight 16 g (13.0–21.0 g). Monotypic.

Geographic Range

San Martín (LSUMZ), La Libertad (LSUMZ), and Huánuco (Lowery and Tallman 1976), PERU. In Huánuco, found to the east of the Río Huallaga (near Panao, LSUMZ) as well as to its west (Cordillera Carpish).

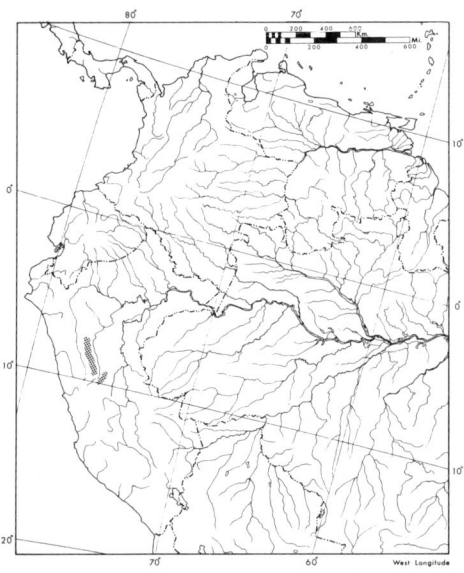

Nephelornis oneilli

Elevational Range

3000–3800 m (LSUMZ) at or near treeline.

Habitat and Behavior

Inhabits edges of isolated and semi-isolated wet elfin forest and sphagnum moss bogs with scattered low woody shrubs; sometimes occurs inside forest. Compact groups of 5–15 individuals travel independently or join mixed-species flocks, possibly for only short periods of time. Flutters and darts through foliage, rapidly skipping across twigs and leaves and occasionally bobbing its head. Rarely lingers in one shrub or tree for very long and typically perches briefly atop the vegetation and peers from side to side before flying on. Flight between patches of shrubbery is rapid and direct.

Forages mostly in low bushes with dense crowns of clustered small leaves. Also feeds in tussocks of grass, on moss-covered ground, and in tall (9 m) tree crowns at forest edge or inside forest. Typically alights in the middle of a bush and works upward and out onto limbs. Mostly jabs at surfaces with quick motions but feeds deliberately at times. Gleans leaf undersides and (less often) leaf tops and stems. Usually forages upright, though sometimes hangs head-down or stretches upward. Also probes tussocks and gleans blades of grass. Stomach contents: vegetable matter (1); animal matter (22); both (1). Contents included beetles and caterpillars. Additional stomach contents included spiders, moths, and flies.

Vocalizations

Call: members of a group constantly call *seep* and occasionally utter a soft *chip* (Isler, LNS).

Breeding

No information.

Sources

Primary Isler data; Lowery and Tallman 1976; Parker data. **Weights (n = 46)** Lowery and Tallman 1976; LSUMZ data. **Stomach contents** Lowery and Tallman 1976; LSUMZ data. **Vocalizations** LNS recording by Isler (1).

Geographic Range

Puno, PERU (head of the Río Inambari).

Elevational Range

2000–2200 m.

Habitat and Behavior

Inhabits fruiting trees and shrubs in cutover or agricultural areas, small garden plots, scrubby riparian forest, and forest edge. Seems to benefit from the clearing of forest. Encountered in pairs or singly.

Vocalizations

No information.

Breeding

No information.

Sources

Primary Schulenberg and Binford 1985. **Weights (n = 1)** LSUMZ data.

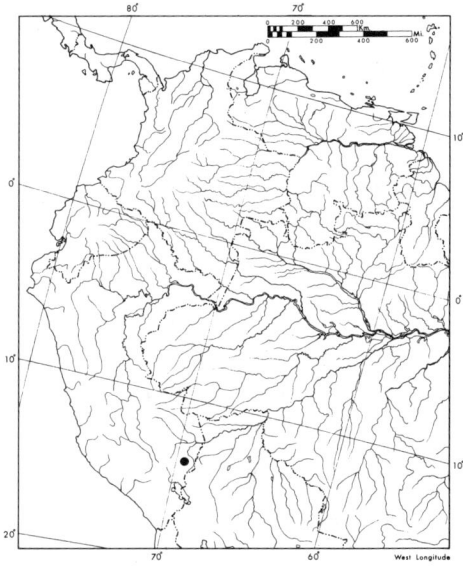

Tangara meyerdeschauenseei

Tangara meyerdeschauenseei 242
Green-capped Tanager
Plate 32

Length 14 cm (5½ in.). Weight 26 g. Monotypic. Newly described by Schulenberg and Binford (1985).

References

Airola, D. A., and R. H. Barrett. 1985. Foraging and habitat relationships of insect-gleaning birds in a Sierra Nevada mixed-conifer forest. *Condor* 87:205–216.

Alabarce, E. A., and M. M. Lucero. 1977. Observaciones sobre el paso de migraciones en el alto Pilcomayo. *Hornero* 11:410–412.

Alden, P. 1969. *Finding the birds in western Mexico*. Tucson: University of Arizona Press.

Allen, J. A. 1889. List of the birds collected in Bolivia by Dr. H. H. Rusby, with field notes by the collector. *Bull. Am. Mus. Nat. Hist.* 2:77–112.

———. 1891. On a collection of birds from Chapada, Matto Grosso, Brazil, made by Mr. Herbert H. Smith. *Bull. Am. Mus. Nat. Hist.* 3:337–380.

———. 1905. Supplementary notes on birds collected in the Santa Marta district, Colombia, by Herbert H. Smith, with descriptions of nests and eggs. *Bull. Am. Mus. Nat. Hist.* 21:275–295.

Alvarez del Toro, M. 1950. A Summer Tanager, *Piranga rubra*, annihilates a wasp nest. *Auk* 67:397.

———. 1952. Contribución al conocimiento de la oologia y nidologia de las aves chiapanecas. *Ateneo* 4:11–21.

———. 1964. *Lista de las aves de Chiapas*. Tuxtla Gutierrez, Chiapas, Mexico: Instituto de Ciencias y Artes de Chiapas.

Amadon, D. 1950. The Hawaiian Honeycreepers (Aves, Drepaniidae). *Bull. Am. Mus. Nat. Hist.* 95:155–262.

American Ornithologists' Union. 1983. *Check-list of North American Birds*, 6th ed.

Andrle, R. F. 1967. Birds of the Sierra de Tuxtla in Veracruz, Mexico. *Wilson Bull.* 79:163–187.

Aplin, O. V. 1894. On the birds of Uruguay. *Ibis* 6th Ser. 6:149–215.

Auber, L. 1974. The structure of feathers in *Chlorophanes purpurascens*. *Bull. Br. Ornithol. Club* 94:49–55.

Baepler, D. H. 1962. The avifauna of the Soloma region in Huehuetenango, Guatemala. *Condor* 64:140–153.

Baldwin, S. P., and S. C. Kendeigh. 1938. Variations in the weights of birds. *Auk* 55:416–467.

Bangs, O., and T. Barbour. 1922. Birds from Darien. *Bull. Mus. Comp. Zool. Harv. Univ.* 65:191–229.

Barbour, T. 1943. Cuban ornithology. *Mem. Nuttall Ornithol. Club* No. 9. Cambridge, Massachusetts: Nuttall Ornithol. Club.

Barlow, J. C., J. A. Dick, D. Weyer, and W. F. Young. 1972. New records of birds from British Honduras (Belize), including a Skua. *Condor* 74:486–487.

Barnard, G. C. 1954. Notes on the nesting of the Thick-billed Euphonia in the Panama Canal Zone. *Condor* 56:98–101.

Barros V., R. 1953. Algunas aves del Ecuador colectadas por German Barros Valenzuela, con notas del colector. Primera parte. *An. Acad. Chil. Cienc. Nat.* 38:155–163.

Barrows, W. B. 1883. Birds of the lower Uruguay. *Publ. Nuttall Ornithol. Club* 8:82–94.

Beebe, C. W. 1909. An ornithological reconnaissance of northeastern Venezuela. *Zoologica* (N.Y.) 1:67–114.

———. 1916. Notes on the birds of Pará, Brazil. *Zoologica* (N.Y.) 2:55–106.

Beecher, W. J. 1951. Convergence in the Coerebidae. *Wilson Bull.* 63:274–287.

Beehler, B. 1980. A comparison of avian foraging at flowering trees in Panama and New Guinea. *Wilson Bull.* 92:513–519.

Belcher, C., and G. D. Smooker. 1937. Birds of the colony of Trinidad and Tobago (in 6 parts). *Ibis* 14th Ser. 1:504–550.

Belton, W. 1973. Some additional birds for the state of Rio Grande do Sul, Brazil. *Auk* 90:94–99.

———. 1974. More new birds for Rio Grande do Sul, Brazil. *Auk* 91:429–432.

———. 1978. Supplementary list of new birds for Rio Grande do Sul, Brazil. *Auk* 96:413–415.

———. 1982. *Aves silvestres do Rio Grande do Sul*. Porto Alegre: Fund. Zoob. Rio Grande do Sul.

———. 1985. Birds of Rio Grande do Sul, Brazil. Part 2. Formicariidae through Corvidae. *Bull. Am. Mus. Nat. Hist.* 180:1–242.

Bent, A. C. 1965. Life histories of North American blackbirds, orioles, tanagers, and allies. *Bull. U.S. Nat. Mus.* 211:1-549.

Berla, H. F. 1944. Lista das aves colecionadas em Pedra Branca, Municipio de Parati, Estado do Rio de Janeiro, com algumas notas sôbre sua biologia. *Bol. Mus. Nac. Rio de J. Zool.* 18:1–24.

Berlepsch, H. von. 1887. Systematisches

Verzeichniss der von Herrn Ricardo Rohde in Paraguay gesammelten Vögel. *J. Ornithol.* 177:1-37.

Berlepsch, H. von, and H. von Ihering. 1885. Die Vögel der umgegend von Taquara do Mundo novo, Prov. Rio Grande do Sul. *Z. Gesammte Ornithol.* 97-184.

Berlioz, M. J. 1939a. A new genus and species of tanager from central Brazil. *Bull. Br. Ornithol. Club* 59:102.

———. 1939b. Etude d'une collection d'Oiseaux du Chiapas (Mexique). *Bull. Mus. Nat. Hist. Nat.* (Paris) 11:360-377.

———. 1946. Note sur une collection d'Oiseaux du Brésil Central. *Oiseau Rev. Fr. Ornithol.* 16:1-6.

Berrett, D. G. 1962. *The birds of the Mexican state of Tabasco.* Unpublished Ph.D. dissertation, Baton Rouge, Louisiana State University.

Bertoni, A. de W. 1898. Catalogo descriptivo de las aves utiles del Paraguay. *Rev. de Agronomía y Ciencas Aplicadas* (Asunción) 1:377-410, 526-539.

———. 1901. *Aves nuevas del Paraguay.* Asunción: Kraus.

———. 1904. Contribucion para el conocimiento de las aves del Paraguay. *An. Cien. Paraguayos* 3:1-10.

———. 1918. Apuntes sôbre aves del Paraguay. *Hornero* 1:188-191.

———. 1919. Apuntes sôbre aves del Paraguay. *Hornero* 1:284-287.

———. 1926. Apuntes ornitológicos. *Hornero* 3:396-401.

Biaggi, V. 1970. *Las aves de Puerto Rico.* Univ. de Puerto Rico.

Binford, L. C. 1968. *A preliminary survey of the avifauna of the Mexican state of Oaxaca.* Unpublished Ph.D. dissertation, Baton Rouge, Louisiana State University.

Blake, E. R. 1956. A collection of Panamanian nests and eggs. *Condor* 58:386-387.

Blake, E. R., and P. Hocking. 1974. Two new species of tanager from Peru. *Wilson Bull.* 86:321-324.

Bock, W. J. 1985. Is *Diglossa* (? Thraupinae) monophyletic? In Neotropical ornithology, eds. P. A. Buckley et al. *Am. Ornithol. Union Ornithol. Monogr.* 36:319-332.

Bond, J. 1928a. The distribution and habits of the birds of the Republic of Haiti. *Proc. Acad. Nat. Sci. Phila.* 80:483-521.

———. 1928b. On the birds of Dominica, St. Lucia, St. Vincent, and Barbados, B.W.I. *Proc. Acad. Nat. Sci. Phila.* 80:523-545.

———. 1929. A new tanager from the Massif de la Selle, Haiti. *Proc. Acad. Nat. Sci. Phila.* 81:473-474.

———. 1934. A new Lizard Cuckoo from the Dominican Republic with remarks on the Saona Palm Tanager. *Proc. Acad. Nat. Sci. Phila.* 85:369.

———. 1941. Nidification of the birds of Dominica, B.W.I. *Auk* 58:364-375.

———. 1943. Nidification of the passerine birds of Hispaniola. *Wilson Bull.* 55:115-125.

———. 1944. Notes on the Arrow-headed Warbler. *Wilson Bull.* 56:172-173.

———. 1947. A second specimen of *Tangara gouldi* (Sclater). *Auk* 64:128.

———. 1951. Taxonomic notes on South American birds. *Auk* 68:527-529.

———. 1955. Notes on Peruvian Coerebidae and Thraupidae. *Proc. Acad. Nat. Sci. Phila.* 107:35-55.

———. 1956. *Check-list of birds of the West Indies.* Philadelphia: Academy of Natural Sciences.

———. 1961. *Birds of the West Indies.* Boston: Houghton Mifflin.

———. 1971. *Sixteenth supplement to the check-list of birds of the West Indies (1956).* Philadelphia: Academy of Natural Sciences.

———. 1982. *Twenty-fourth supplement to the check-list of birds of the West Indies (1956).* Philadelphia: Academy of Natural Sciences.

Bond, J., and A. Dod. 1977. A new race of Chat Tanager (*Calyptophilus frugivorus*) from the Dominican Republic. *Notulae Naturae* (Philadelphia) 451:1-4.

Bond, J., and R. Meyer de Schauensee. 1942. The birds of Bolivia. Part 1. *Proc. Acad. Nat. Sci. Phila.* 94:307-391.

Borrero, J. I. 1955. Apuntes sobre aves Colombianas (No. 2). *Lozania* 9:1-15.

Boucard, A. 1883. On a collection of birds from Yucatan. *Proc. Zool. Soc. Lond.*:434-462.

Bowdish, B. S. 1903. Birds of Porto Rico. *Auk* 20:10-23.

Bray, D., and E. Cawkell. 1972. A display by Orangequits. *Gosse Bird Club Broadsheet* 18:19.

Brodkorb, P. 1939. Rediscovery of *Heleodytes chiapensis* and *Tangara cabanisi*. *Auk* 56:447-450.

Brosset, A. 1964. Les oiseaux de Pacaritambo (ouest de l'Ecuador). *Oiseau Rev. Fr. Ornithol.* 34:1-24, 112-135.

Brower, J. P., J. V. Z. Brower, and C. T. Collins. 1963. Experimental studies of mimicry. 7. Relative palatability and Müllerian mimicry among neotropical butterflies of the subfamily Heliconiinae. *Zoologica* 48:65-83.

Brown, K. S., Jr., and J. V. Neto. 1976. Predation on aposematic Ithomiine butterflies by tanagers (*Pipraeidea melanonota*). *Biotropica* 8:136-141.

Brudenell-Bruce, P. G. C. 1975. *The birds of the Bahamas.* New York: Taplinger Publishing Company.
Burton, P. J. K. 1975. Passerine bird weights from Panama and Colombia, with some notes on 'soft-part' colours. *Bull. Br. Ornithol. Club* 95:82–86.
Buskirk, W. H. 1973. Four new migrants for Costa Rica. *Condor* 75:363–6.
———. 1976. Social systems in a tropical forest avifauna. *Am. Nat.* 110:293–310.
Buskirk, W. H., G. V. N. Powell, J. F. Wittenberger, R. E. Buskirk, and T. U. Powell. 1972. Interspecific bird flocks in tropical highland Panama. *Auk* 89:612–624.
Cabanis, J. 1870. Ueber eine neue brasilische Nemosie oder Wald-Tangare, *Nemosia Rourei* nov. spec. *J. Ornithol.* 18:459–460.
Capparella, A. P. *Am. Birds*, in press.
Carriker, M. A., Jr. 1910. An annotated list of the birds of Costa Rica, including Cocos Island. *Ann. Carnegie Mus.* 6:314–915.
———. 1933a. Field notebook, April 10, 1933. *Acad. Nat. Sci. Phila.*
———. 1933b. Descriptions of new birds from Peru, with notes on other little-known species. *Proc. Acad. Nat. Sci. Phila.* 85:1–38.
———. 1934. Rediscovery of *Conothraupis speculigera* (Gould). *Auk* 51:497–499.
Carvalho, C. T. de. 1957. Notas sôbre a biologia do *Ramphocelus carbo*. *Bol. Mus. Para. Emilio Goeldi* (Zool.) 5:1–20.
———. 1958. Sôbre o ninho e os ovos de *Cyanerpes cyaneus* (Linne). *Bol. Mus. Paraense Emilio Goeldi* Nova Ser. (Zool.) 20:1–6.
Casares, J. 1944. Aves de Estanzuela (San Luis). *Hornero* 8:379–463.
Chapman, F. M. 1896. Notes on birds observed in Yucatan. *Bull. Am. Mus. Nat. Hist.* 8:271–290.
———. 1898. Notes on birds observed at Jalapa and Las Vigas, Vera Cruz, Mexico. *Bull. Am. Mus. Nat. Hist.* 10:15–43.
———. 1917. The distribution of bird-life in Colombia: A contribution to a biological survey of South America. *Bull. Am. Mus. Nat. Hist.* 36:1–729.
———. 1926. The distribution of bird-life in Ecuador: A contribution to the study of the origin of Andean bird-life. *Bull. Am. Mus. Nat. Hist.* 55:1–784.
———. 1931. The upper zonal bird-life of Mts. Roraima and Duida. *Bull Am. Mus. Nat. Hist.* 63:1–135.
Cherrie, G. K. 1892a. A preliminary list of the birds of San José, Costa Rica. *Auk* 9:21–27.
———. 1892b. Notes on Costa Rican birds. *Proc. U.S. Nat. Mus.* 14:517–537.
———. 1896. Contribution to the ornithology of San Domingo. *Field Col. Mus. Publ. 10. Ornithol. series* 1:3–26.
———. 1916. A contribution to the ornithology of the Orinoco region. *Mus. Brooklyn Inst. Arts Sci. Bull.* 2:133a–374.
Child, G. I., and S. G. Marshall. 1970. A method of estimating carcass fat and fat-free weights in migrant birds from water content of specimens. *Condor* 72:116–119.
Christy, C. 1897. Field-notes on the birds of the island of San Domingo. *Ibis* 1897:317–343.
Chubb, C. 1910. On the birds of Paraguay. Part 4. *Ibis* 9th Ser. 4:571–647.
———. 1921. *The birds of British Guiana, based on the collection of Frederick Vavasour McConnell, Camfield Place, Hatfield Herts*, Vol. 2. London: Bernard Quaritch.
Ciarpaglini, P. 1971. Notes on breeding uncommon birds at Clères in 1970. *Avic. Mag.* 77:49–57.
Clark, A. H. 1905. Birds of the southern Lesser Antilles. *Proc. Bost. Soc. Nat. Hist.* 32:203–312.
Clark, G. A., Jr. 1974. Foot-scute differences among certain North American oscines. *Wilson Bull.* 86:104–109.
Clark, H. L. 1913. Notes on the Panama Thrush-warbler. *Auk* 30:11–15.
Collins, C. T. 1972. Weights of some birds of north-central Venezuela. *Bull. Br. Ornithol. Club* 92:151–153.
Collins, C. T., and A. Watson. 1983. Field observations of bird predation on neotropical moths. *Biotropica* 15:53–60.
Colwell, R. K. 1973. Competition and coexistence in a simple tropical community. *Am. Nat.* 107:737–760.
Colwell, R. K., B. J. Betts, P. Bunnell, F. L. Carpenter, and P. Feinsinger. 1974. Competition for the nectar of *Centropogon valerii* by the hummingbird *Colibri thalassinus* and the flower-piercer *Diglossa plumbea*, and its evolutionary implications. *Condor* 76:447–484.
Connell, C. E., E. P. Odum, and H. Kale. 1960. Fat-free weights of birds. *Auk* 77:1–9.
Contreras, J. R. 1979a. Bird weights from northeastern Argentina. *Bull. Br. Ornithol. Club* 99:21–24.
———. 1979b. Avifauna Puntara. 1. Some new or little-known species for the Province San Luis. *Hist. Nat.* 1:9–12.
Cruden, R. W., and S. M. Hermann-Parker. 1977. Defense of feeding sites by Orioles and Hepatic Tanagers in Mexico. *Auk* 94:594–596.
Cruz, A. 1974. Feeding assemblages of Jamaican birds. *Condor* 76:103–107.
———. 1981. Bird activity and seed dispersal of a montane forest tree (*Dunalia arbores-*

cens) in Jamaica. *Reproductive botany* 1981:34–44 (supplement to *Biotropica*).
Cuello, J., and E. Gerzenstein. 1962. Las aves del Uruguay. *Comun. Zool. Mus. Hist. Nat. Montevideo* 93:1–191.
Danforth, S. T. 1926. An ecological study of Cartagena Lagoon, Porto Rico, with special reference to the birds. *J. Dept. Agr. Porto Rico* 10:1–136.
———. 1928. Birds observed in Jamaica during the summer of 1926. *Auk* 45:480–491.
———. 1929. Notes on the birds of Hispaniola. *Auk* 46:358–375.
———. n.d. *Puerto Rican ornithological records.* Mayagüez: College of Agriculture and Mechanic Art, Univ. of Puerto Rico.
Darlington, P. J., Jr. 1931. Notes on the birds of Río Frío (near Santa Marta), Magdalena, Colombia. *Bull. Mus. Comp. Zool. Harv. Univ.* 71:349–421.
Davidse, G., and E. Morton. 1973. Bird-mediated fruit dispersal in the tropical genus *Lasiacis* (Gramineae: Paniceae). *Biotropica* 5:162–167.
Davis, D. E. 1945a. The occurrence of the incubation-patch in some Brazilian birds. *Wilson Bull.* 57:188–190.
———. 1945b. The annual cycle of plants, mosquitoes, birds, and mammals in two Brazilian forests. *Ecol. Monogr.* 15:243–295.
———. 1946. A seasonal analysis of mixed flocks of birds in Brazil. *Ecology* 27:168–181.
Davis, J. 1960. Notes on the birds of Colima, Mexico. *Condor* 62:215–219.
Davis, L. I. 1972. *A field guide to the birds of Mexico and Central America.* Austin and London: University of Texas Press.
Davis, T. H. 1979. Additions to the birds of Suriname. *Continental Birdlife* 1:136–146.
———. 1980. An annotated checklist to the birds of Suriname. Mimeo.
Delacour, J. 1972a. Sugar-bird tanager hybrids. *Avic. Mag.* 78:48.
———. 1972b. Hybrids sugar-bird x tanager. *Avic. Mag.* 78:187–188.
Descourtilz, J. T. 1852. *Ornithologie brésilienne ou histoire des oiseaux du Brésil.* Rio de Janeiro: T. Reeves.
Devas, R. P. 1954. *Birds of Grenada, St. Vincent and the Grenadines.* B.W.I.: Yuille's Printerie Limited.
Diamond, A. W. 1973. Habitats and feeding stations of St. Lucia forest birds. *Ibis* 115:313–329.
Dick, J. A., W. B. McGillivray, and D. J. Brooks. 1984. A list of birds and their weights from Saül, French Guiana. *Wilson Bull.* 96:347–514.
Dickerman, R. W. 1981. Geographic variation in the Scrub Euphonia. *Occas. Pap. Mus. Zool. Louisiana State Univ.* 59.
Dickey, D. R., and A. J. van Rossem. 1938. The birds of El Salvador. *Field Mus. Nat. Hist. Publ. Zool. Ser.* 23:1–609.
Dinelli, L. 1918. Notas biológicas sobre las aves del noroeste de la Rep. Argentina. *Hornero* 1:57–68.
———. 1924. Notas biológicas sobre aves del noroeste de la Argentina. *Hornero* 3:253–258.
Dod, A. 1978. *Aves de la Republica Dominica.* Santo Domingo: Museo Nacional de Historia Natural.
Dorst, J. 1957a. Etude d'une collection d'oiseaux rapportée du bassin du Haut Maranon, Pérou septentrional. *Bull. Mus. Nat. Hist. Nat.* (Paris) 29:377–384.
———. 1957b. Contribution a l'étude ecologique des oiseaux du Haut Maranon. *Oiseau Rev. Fr. Ornithol.* 27:235–269.
———. 1961. Etude d'une collection d'oiseaux rapportée de la vallée de Sandia, Pérou méridional. *Bull. Mus. Nat. Hist. Nat.* (Paris) 33:563–570.
Dugand, A. 1947. Aves del Departmento del Atlántico, Colombia. *Caldasia* 4:499–648.
Dunning, J. S. 1970. *Portraits of tropical birds.* Wynnewood, Pennsylvania: Livingston Publishing Company.
———. 1982. *South American land birds, a photographic aid to identification.* Newtown Square, Pennsylvania: Harrowood Books.
Eaton, S. W., and E. P. Edwards. 1948. Notes on birds of the Gomez Farias region of Tamaulipas. *Wilson Bull.* 60:109–114.
Edwards, E. P. 1967. Nests of the Common Bush-Tanager and the Scaled Antpitta. *Condor* 69:605.
———. 1972. *A field guide to the birds of Mexico.* Sweet Briar, Virginia: Ernest P. Edwards.
Edwards, E. P. 1967. Nests of the Common Bush-Tanager and the Scaled Antpitta. *Condor* 69:605.
———. 1972. *A field guide to the birds of Mexico.* Sweet Briar, Virginia: Ernest P. Edwards.
Edwards, E. P., and R. E. Tashian. 1959. Avifauna of the Catemaco basin of southern Veracruz, Mexico. *Condor* 61:325–337.
Eisenmann, E. 1952. Annotated list of birds of Barro Colorado Island, Panama Canal Zone. *Smithson. Misc. Collect.* 117:1–62.
———. 1957. Notes on birds of the Province of Bocas del Toro, Panama. *Condor* 59:247–262.
———. 1961. Favorite foods of neotropical birds: Flying termites and *Cecropia* catkins. *Auk* 78:636–638.
———. 1962. On the systematic position of *Rhodinocichla rosea. Auk* 79:640–648.
Eisenmann, E., and H. Loftin. 1968. Birds of the Panama Canal Zone area. *Fla. Nat.* 41:57–60, 95.

Eisentraut, A. 1935. Biologische Studien im bolivianischen Chaco. VI. Beitrag zur Biologie der Vogelfauna. *Mitt. Zool. Mus.* (Berlin) 20:367–443.

Ellis, C. J. 1976. Syringal histology. 5. Thraupidae: Yellow-rumped Tanager, *Ramphocelus icteronotus* and Scarlet Tanager, *Piranga olivacea. Iowa State J. Res.* 50:357–362.

English, T. M. S. 1916. Notes on some of the birds of Grand Cayman, West Indies. *Ibis* 10th Ser. 4:17–35.

Erickson, H. T., and R. E. Mumford. 1976. Notes on birds of the Vicosa, Brazil region. *Agricultural Experiment Station Bull.* 131. West Lafayette, Indiana: Purdue University.

Euler, C. 1867. Beiträge zur Naturgeschichte der Vögel brasiliens. *J. Ornithol.* 15:177–198.

———. 1900. Descripção de ninhos e ovos das aves do Brazil. *Rev. Mus. Paulista* (São Paulo) 4:9–148.

Ewert, D. 1975. Notes on nests of four avian species from the coastal Cordillera of Venezuela. *Wilson Bull.* 87:105–107.

Faaborg, J. 1982. Avian population fluctuations during drought conditions in Puerto Rico. *Wilson Bull.* 94:20–30.

ffrench, R. P. 1973. *A guide to the birds of Trinidad and Tobago.* Wynnewood, Pennsylvania: Livingston Publishing Company.

Field, G. W. 1894. Birds of Port Henderson, Jamaica, West Indies. *Auk* 11:117–127.

Fitch, H. S., and V. R. Fitch. 1955. Observations on the Summer Tanager in northeastern Kansas. *Wilson Bull.* 67:45–54.

Fitzpatrick, J. W. 1980. Foraging behavior of neotropical tyrant flycatchers. *Condor* 82:43–57.

Fitzpatrick, J. W., and D. E. Willard. 1982. Twenty-one bird species new or little known from the Republic of Colombia. *Bull. Br. Ornithol. Club* 102:153–158.

Forbes, W. A. 1881. Eleven weeks in northeastern Brazil. *Ibis* 4th Ser. 312–362.

Foster, M. S. 1975. The overlap of molting and breeding in some tropical birds. *Condor* 77:304–314.

Foster, M. S., and N. K. Johnson. 1974. Notes on birds of Costa Rica. *Wilson Bull.* 86:58–63.

Friedmann, H. 1927. Notes on some Argentine birds. *Bull. Mus. Comp. Zool. Harv. Univ.* 68:139–236.

Friedmann, H., and F. D. Smith, Jr. 1950. A contribution to the ornithology of northeastern Venezuela. *Proc. U.S. Nat. Mus.* 100:411–538.

———. 1955. A further contribution to the ornithology of northeastern Venezuela. *Proc. U.S. Nat. Mus.* 104:463–524.

Frisch, S., and J. D. Frisch. 1964. *Aves Brasileiras.* São Paulo: Irmaos Vitale.

Fry, C. H. 1970. Ecological distribution of birds in northeastern Mato Grosso State, Brazil. *An. Acad. Bras. Cienc.* 42:275–318.

George, W. G. 1964. Rarely seen songbirds of Peru's high Andes. *Nat. Hist.* 78:26–29.

Gibson, L. 1979. Breeding and hand-rearing the Red-legged Honeycreeper. *Avic. Mag.* 85:6–15.

Gilliard, E. T. 1941. The birds of Mt. Auyan-tepui, Venezuela. *Bull. Am. Mus. Nat. Hist.* 77:439–508.

———. 1958. *Living birds of the world.* Garden City, New York: Doubleday.

———. 1959. Notes on some birds of northern Venezuela. *Am. Mus. Novit.* 1927:1–33.

Ginés, H., R. Aveledo, G. Yepez, G. Linares, and J. Poján. 1951. Avifauna. *Mem. Soc. Cienc. Nat. La Salle* 11:237–323.

Gochfeld, M., and G. Tudor. 1978. Ant-following birds in South American subtropical forests. *Wilson Bull.* 90:139–141.

Goeldi, E. A. 1894. *Aves do Brasil.* Primeira parte. Rio de Janeiro: Livraria Classica de Alves.

Gonzaga, L. P. 1983. Notas sobre *Dacnis nigripes* Pelzeln, 1856 (Aves, Coerebidae). *Iheringia Ser. Zool.* (Porto Alegre) 63:45–58.

Goodfellow, W. 1901. Results of an ornithological journey through Colombia and Ecuador. *Ibis* 8th Ser. 1:300–319.

Gore, M. E. J., and A. R. M. Gepp. 1978. *Las aves del Uruguay.* Montevideo: Mosca Hnos.

Gosse, P. H. 1847. *Birds of Jamaica.* London: John van Voorst.

Gourlay, M. P. 1974. Breeding the Blue-crowned Chlorophonia (*Chlorophonia occipitalis*). *Avic. Mag.* 80:25–28.

Graber, R. R., and J. W. Graber. 1962. Weight characteristics of birds killed in nocturnal migration. *Wilson Bull.* 74:74–88.

Gradwohl, J., and R. Greenberg. 1980. The formation of antwren flocks on Barro Colorado Island, Panamá. *Auk* 97:385–395.

Graves, G. R. 1980. A new subspecies of *Diglossa* (*carbonaria*) *brunneiventris. Bull. Br. Ornithol. Club* 100:230–232.

———. 1982a. Speciation in the Carbonated Flower-piercer (*Diglossa carbonaria*) complex of the Andes. *Condor* 84:1–14.

———. 1982b. Pollination of a *Tristerix* Mistletoe (Loranthaceae) by *Diglossa* (Aves, Thraupidae). *Biotropica* 14:316–317.

———. 1983. *Elevational correlates of intraspecific variation in plumage in Andean forest birds.* Unpublished Ph.D. Dissertation, Tallahassee, Florida State University.

———. 1985. Elevational correlates of speciation and intraspecific geographic variation in plumage in Andean forest birds. *Auk* 102:556–579.

Greenberg, R. 1981a. Dissimilar bill shapes in New World tropical and temperate forest foliage-gleaning birds. *Oecologia* 49:143–147.

———. 1981b. Frugivory in some migrant tropical forest wood warblers. *Biotropica* 13:215–223.

———. 1981c. The abundance and seasonality of forest canopy birds on Barro Colorado Island, Panama. *Biotropica* 13:241–251.

———. 1984. *The winter exploitation systems of Bay-breasted and Chestnut-sided Warblers in Panama*. Univ. Calif. Pub. Zool. 116.

Greenberg, R., and J. Gradwohl. 1980. Leaf surface specializations of birds and arthropods in a Panamanian forest. *Oecologia* 46:115–124.

———. 1985. A comparative study of the social organization of antwrens on Barro Colorado Island, Panama. In Neotropical ornithology, eds. P. A. Buckley et al. *Am. Ornithol. Union Ornithol. Monogr.* 36:845–855.

Griscom, L. 1926. The ornithological results of the Mason-Spinden expedition to Yucatán. *Am. Mus. Novit.* 235:1–19.

———. 1932. The distribution of bird-life in Guatemala. *Bull. Am. Mus. Nat. Hist.* 64:1–439.

Griscom, L., and J. C. Greenway, Jr. 1941. Birds of lower Amazonia. *Bull. Mus. Comp. Zool. Harv. Univ.* 88:83–344.

Groskin, H. 1943. Scarlet Tanagers 'anting.' *Auk* 60:55–59.

———. 1950. Additional observations and comments on "anting" by birds. *Auk* 67:201–209.

Guimarães, A. C., Jr. 1924. Ensaios sobre ornitologia. *Rev. Mus. Paulista* (São Paulo) 14:615–631.

Gundlach, J. 1855. Beiträge sur Ornithologie Cuba's. *J. Ornithol.* 3:465–480.

———. 1879. Neue Beiträge zur Ornithologie der Insel Portorico. *J. Ornithol.* 26:157–194.

———. 1882. Briefliches: zur Fortpflanzungsgeschichte des *Chlorospingus speculiferus*. *J. Ornithol.* 30:161.

Gyldenstolpe, N. 1945a. The bird fauna of rio Juruá in western Brazil. *K. Sven. Vetenskapsakad. Handl.* 22:1–338.

———. 1945b. A contribution to the ornithology of northern Bolivia. *K. Sven. Vetenskapsakad. Handl.* 23:1–300.

———. 1951. The ornithology of the rio Purus region in western Brazil. *Ark. Zool.* 2:1–320.

Haffer, J. 1967a. Interspecific competition as a possible factor in limiting the range of some trans-Andean forest birds. *Hornero* 10:438–440.

———. 1967b. On birds from the northern Chocó region, N.W.-Colombia. *Veröff. Zool. Staatssamml.* (München) 11:123–149.

———. 1975. Avifauna of northwestern Colombia, South America. *Bonn. Zool. Monogr.* 7:1–182.

Hales, H. 1896. Peculiar traits of some Scarlet Tanagers. *Auk* 13:261–263.

Hallinan, T. 1924. Notes on some Panama Canal Zone birds with special reference to their food. *Auk* 41:304–326.

Hamaher, J. I. 1936a. Summer Tanager (*Piranga rubra*) eating wasps. *Auk* 53:220–221.

———. 1936b. Summer Tanagers again destroy wasp nests. *Auk* 53:451.

Hamilton, J. F. 1871. Notes on birds from the Province of São Paulo, Brazil. *Ibis* 3rd Ser. 1:301–309.

Harrison, H. H. 1975. *A field guide to birds' nests*. Boston: Houghton Mifflin.

Hartert, E. 1898. On a collection of birds from north-western Ecuador, collected by Mr. W. F. H. Rosenberg. *Novit. Zool.* 5:477–505.

———. 1901. On some birds from north-west Ecuador. *Novit. Zool.* 8:369–371.

Hartman, F. A. 1955. Heart weight in birds. *Condor* 57:221–238.

Hartman, F. A., and K. A. Brownell. 1961. Adrenal and thyroid weights in birds. *Auk* 78:397–422.

Haverschmidt, F. 1948. Bird weights from Surinam. *Wilson Bull.* 60:230–239.

———. 1952. More bird weights from Surinam. *Wilson Bull.* 64:234–241.

———. 1954. Zur Brutbiologie von *Thraupis episcopus* in Surinam. *J. Ornithol.* 95:48–54.

———. 1955. Notes on some Surinam breeding birds. *Ardea* 43:137–144.

———. 1956. The nest and egg of *Tachyphonus phoenicius*. *Wilson Bull.* 68:322–323.

———. 1968. *Birds of Surinam*. Edinburgh: Oliver and Boyd.

———. 1970. Rufous-crowned Tanagers feeding on fruit-bowl. *Wilson Bull.* 82:228.

———. 1972. Bird records from Surinam. *Bull. Br. Ornithol. Club* 92:49–53.

———. 1975. More bird records from Surinam. *Bull Br. Ornithol. Club* 95:74–77.

Hayward, C. L. 1935. Observations on some breeding birds of Mount Timpanogos, Utah. *Wilson Bull.* 47:161–162.

Hellmayr, C. E. 1935. Catalogue of birds of the Americas. Alaudidae—Compsothlypidae. *Field Mus. Nat. Hist. Publ. Zool. Ser.* 13, Pt. 8:218–331.

———. 1936. Catalogue of birds of the Americas and the adjacent islands. Tersinidae—Thraupidae. *Field Mus. Nat. Hist. Publ. Zool. Ser.* 13, Pt. 9:1–458.

Hempel, A. 1949. Estudo da alimentação natural de aves silvestres do Brasil. *Arq. Inst. Biol.* (São Paulo) 19:237–268.

Herklots, G. A. C. 1961. *The birds of Trinidad and Tobago.* London: Collins.

Hilty, S. L. 1974. Notes on birds at swarms of army ants in the highlands of Colombia. *Wilson Bull.* 86:479–481.

———. 1977. *Chlorospingus flavovirens* rediscovered, with notes on other Pacific Colombian and Cauca Valley birds. *Auk* 94:44–49.

———. 1980. Flowering and fruiting periodicity in a premontane rain forest in Pacific Colombia. *Biotropica* 12:292–306.

———. 1985. Distributional changes in the Colombian avifauna: preliminary blue list. In Neotropical ornithology, eds. P. A. Buckley et al. *Am. Ornithol. Union Ornithol. Monogr.* 36:992–1004.

Hilty, S. L., and W. L. Brown. 1983. Range extensions of Colombian birds as indicated by the M. A. Carriker, Jr., collection at the National Museum of Natural History, Smithsonian Institution. *Bull. Br. Ornithol. Club* 103:5–17.

———. 1986. *Birds of Colombia.* Princeton: Princeton University Press.

Hilty, S. L., and D. Simon. 1977. The Azure-rumped Tanager in Mexico with comparative remarks on the Gray-and-gold Tanager. *Auk* 94:605–606.

Hilty, S. L., T. A. Parker III, and J. Silliman. 1979. Observations on Plush-capped Finches in the Andes with a description of the juvenal and immature plumages. *Wilson Bull.* 91:145–148.

Holdridge, L. R. 1967. *Life zone ecology.* San José, Costa Rica: Tropical Science Center.

Holt, E. G. 1928. An ornithological survey of the Serra do Itatiaya, Brazil. *Bull. Am. Mus. Nat. Hist.* 57:251–326.

Howell, T. R. 1957. Birds of a second-growth rain forest area of Nicaragua. *Condor* 59:73–111.

———. 1964. Birds collected in Nicaragua by Bernardo Ponsol. *Condor* 66:151–158.

———. 1965. New subspecies of birds from the lowland pine savanna of northeastern Nicaragua. *Auk* 82:438–464.

———. 1971. An ecological study of the birds of the lowland pine savanna and adjacent rain forest in northeastern Nicaragua. *Living Bird* 10:185–242.

———. 1972. Birds of the lowland pine savanna of northeastern Nicaragua. *Condor* 74:316–340.

Hoy, G. 1976. Notas nidobiológicas del noroeste Argentino. *Physis* 35:205–209.

Hubbard, J. P. 1965. The summer birds of the forests of the Mogollon Mountains, New Mexico. *Condor* 67:404–415.

———. 1967. Notes on some Chiapas birds. *Wilson Bull.* 79:236.

Huber, W. 1932. Birds collected in northeastern Nicaragua in 1922. *Proc. Acad. Nat. Sci. Phila.* 84:205–249.

Hudson, W. H. 1870. Letter from Mr. W. H. Hudson. *Proc. Zool. Soc. Lond.*:112–114.

Hutto, R. L. 1980. Winter habitat distribution of migratory land birds in western Mexico, with special reference to small foliage-gleaning insectivores. In *Migrant birds in the Neotropics: ecology, behavior, distribution, and conservation*:181–203; eds. A. Keast and E. S. Morton. Washington, D.C.: Smithsonian Institution Press.

Ihering, H. von. 1900. Catálogo critico-comparativo dos ninhos e ovos das aves do Brasil. *Rev. Mus. Paulista* (São Paulo) 4:191–300.

———. 1902. Contribuições para o conhecimento da ornithología de São Paulo. *Rev. Mus. Paulista* (São Paulo) 5:261–329.

———. 1914. Novas contribuições para a ornithología do Brazil. *Rev. Mus. Paulista* (São Paulo) 9:411–448.

Ingels, J. 1971a. Breeding Mrs. Wilson's tanagers and Purple-throated Euphonias. *Avic. Mag.* 77:11–14.

———. 1971b. Notes on the breeding of *Tangara* hybrids. *Avic. Mag.* 77:129–131.

———. 1974a. Rare tanagers imported into Belgium and the Netherlands in 1973. *Avic. Mag.* 80:20–25.

———. 1974b. The behavior and nesting of the Turquoise Tanager (*Tangara mexicana*). *Avic. Mag.* 80:168–171.

———. 1974c. The ear-covert display of the Golden-eared Tanager *Tangara chrysotis*. *Avic. Mag.* 80:109–112.

———. 1975. Rare tanagers imported into Belgium and the Netherlands during 1974. *Avic. Mag* 81:98–104.

———. 1977. Unusual nesting of the Silver-beaked Tanager *Ramphocelus carbo*. *Avic. Mag.* 83:85–87.

———. 1978. The nesting of three tanagers common in French Guiana. *Avic. Mag.* 84:105–110.

———. 1979. Remarks on specimens, holotype, description and subspecies of *Chlorophonia flavirostris* Sclater. *Bull. Br. Ornithol. Club* 99:77–80.

———. 1981. The plumages of the Blue-backed Tanager, *Cyanicterus cyanicterus*. *Le Gerfaut* 71:157–162.

Ingels, J., J. Maroy, and E. Norgaard-Olesen. 1976. Notes on establishing and breeding euphonias. *Avic. Mag.* 82:8–11.

Innes, R. C. 1979. Club-tipped feathers in some South American tanagers. *Auk* 96:808–809.

Janzen, D. H. 1973. Sweep samples of tropi-

cal foliage insects; effects of season, vegetation types, elevation, time of day, and insularity. *Ecology* 54:687–708.
Jeffrey-Smith, M. 1956. *Bird-watching in Jamaica*. Kingston, Jamaica: The Pioneer Press.
Johnson, A. W. 1967. *The birds of Chile and adjacent regions of Argentina, Bolivia and Peru*, Vol. 2. Buenos Aires: Platt Establecimientos Gráficos.
Johnson, N. K., and A. H. Brush. 1972. Analysis of polymorphism in the Sooty-capped Tanager. *Syst. Zool.* 21:245–262.
Johnson, V. R. 1964. Three winter records in the central valley of California. *Condor* 66:517–518.
Johnston, D. W. 1951. An aberrantly colored Summer Tanager. *Wilson Bull.* 63:116–117.
———. 1957. Analysis of mass bird mortality in October, 1954. *Auk* 74:447–458.
Junge, G. C. A., and G. F. Mees. 1958. The avifauna of Trinidad and Tobago. *Zool. Verh.* 37:1–172.
Kantak, G. E. 1979. Observations on some fruit-eating birds in Mexico. *Auk* 96:183–186.
———. 1981. Temporal feeding patterns of some tropical frugivores. *Condor* 83:185–187.
Karr, J. R. 1971. Ecological, behavioral, and distributional notes on some central Panama birds. *Condor* 73:107–111.
———. 1977. Ecological correlates of rarity in a tropical forest bird community. *Auk* 94:240–247.
King, W. B., and C. B. Kepler. 1970. Active anting in the Puerto Rican Tanager. *Auk* 87:376–378.
King, W. B., N. F. R. Snyder, M. Segnestam, and J. Grantham. 1979. Noteworthy ornithological records from Abaco, Bahamas. *Am. Birds* 33:746–748.
Klaas, E. E. 1968. Summer birds from the Yucatán Peninsula, Mexico. *Mus. Nat. Hist. Univ. Kans. Publ.* 17:579–611.
Koepcke, M. 1954. Corte ecológico transversal en los Andes del Perú central con especial consideración de las aves. Parte 1, costa, vertientes occidentales y región altoandina. *Mem. Mus. Hist. Nat. 'Javier Prado'* 3:1–119.
———. 1958. Die Vögel des Waldes von Zárate. *Bonn. Zool. Beitr.* 9:130–193.
———. 1961. Birds of the western slope of the Andes of Peru. *Am. Mus. Novit.* 2028:1–31.
———. 1970. *The birds of the Department of Lima, Peru*. Translated by Erma J. Fisk. Wynnewood, Pennsylvania: Livingston Publishing Company.
Lack, D., and A. Lack. 1973. Birds on Grenada. *Ibis* 115:53–59.
Lack, D., E. Lack, P. Lack, and A. Lack. 1973. Birds on St. Vincent. *Ibis* 115:46–52.
Lamm, D. W. 1948. Notes on the birds of the States of Pernambuco and Paraíba, Brazil. *Auk* 65:261–283.
Land, H. C. 1963. A tropical feeding tree. *Wilson Bull.* 75:199–200.
———. 1970. *Birds of Guatemala*. Wynnewood, Pennsylvania: Livingston Publishing Company.
Laubmann. A. 1940. *Die Vögel von Paraguay*. Stuttgart: Verlag von Strecker und Schröder.
Layard, E. L. 1873. Notes on birds observed at Pará. *Ibis* 3rd Ser. 3:374–396.
Leck, C. F. 1971a. Measurement of social attractions between tropical passerine birds. *Wilson Bull.* 83:278–283.
———. 1971b. Overlap in the diet of some neotropical birds. *Living Bird* 10:89–106.
———. 1972a. Observations of birds at *Cecropia* trees in Puerto Rico. *Wilson Bull.* 84:498–500.
———. 1972b. The impact of some North American migrants at fruiting trees in Panamá. *Auk* 89:842–850.
———. 1972c. Seasonal changes in feeding pressures of fruit- and nectar-eating birds in Panama. *Condor* 74:54–60.
———. 1975. Weights of migrants and resident birds in Panamá. *Bird-Banding* 46:201–203.
———. 1979. Avian extinctions in an isolated tropical wet-forest preserve, Ecuador. *Auk* 96:343–352.
Leck, C. F., and S. Hilty. 1968. A feeding congregation of local and migratory birds in the mountains of Panama. *Bird-Banding* 39:318.
Lehmann V., F. C. 1957. Contribuciones al estudio de la fauna de Colombia XII. *Noved. Colombianas* 3:101–156.
Ligon, J. S. 1961. *New Mexico birds and where to find them*. Albuquerque: University of New Mexico Press.
Lillo, M. 1889. Apuntes sobre la fauna de la Provincia de Tucumán. *Bol. Oficiana Quimica Tucumán* 2:76–91.
Lönnberg, E., and H. Rendahl. 1922. A contribution to the ornithology of Ecuador. *Ark. Zool.* 14:1–87.
Lowery, G. H., Jr., and W. W. Dalquest. 1951. Birds from the State of Veracruz, Mexico. *Univ. Kans. Publ. Mus. Nat. Hist.* 3:531–649.
Lowery, G. H., Jr., and J. P. O'Neill. 1964. A new genus and species of tanager from Peru. *Auk* 81:125–131.
Lowery, G. H., Jr., and D. A. Tallman. 1976. A new genus and species of nine-

primaried oscine of uncertain affinities from Peru. *Auk* 93:415–428.
March, W. T. 1863. Notes on the birds of Jamaica. *Proc. Acad. Nat. Sci. Phila.* 6:283–304.
Marcus, M. J. 1983. Additions to the avifauna of Honduras. *Auk* 100:621–629.
Marshall, J. T., Jr. 1957. Birds of pine-oak woodland in southern Arizona and adjacent Mexico. *Pacific Coast Avif. 32.* Berkeley: Cooper Ornithol. Soc.
Martin, P. S., C. R. Robins, and W. B. Heed. 1954. Birds and biogeography of the Sierra de Tamaulipas, an isolated pine-oak habitat. *Wilson Bull.* 66:38–57.
Mason, P. 1985. The nesting biology of some passerines of Buenos Aires, Argentina. In Neotropical ornithology, eds. P. A. Buckley et al. *Am. Ornithol. Union Ornithol. Monogr.* 36:954–974.
Mathews, F. S. 1904. *Field book of wild birds and their music.* New York: G. P. Putnam's Sons.
McAllister, T. H., Jr., and D. B. Marshall. 1945. Summer birds of the Fremont National Forest, Oregon. *Auk* 62:177–189.
McDiarmid, R. W., R. E. Ricklefs, and M. S. Foster. 1977. Dispersal of *Stemmadenia donnell-smithii* (Apocynaceae) by birds. *Biotropica* 9:9–25.
McEwen, A. 1979. Breeding attempt with the Golden-collared Honeycreeper in 1977 (*Tangara pulcherrima*). *Avic. Mag.* 85:141–145.
Mengel, R. M. 1963. A second probable hybrid between the Scarlet and Western Tanagers. *Wilson Bull.* 75:201–203.
Merry, O. 1971. Correspondence: *Tangara* hybrids. *Avic. Mag.* 7:230.
Meyer de Schauensee, R. 1951. Notes on Ecuadorian birds. *Notulae Naturae* (Phila.) 234:1–11.
———. 1957. *Types of birds in collection of ANSP.* Manuscript. Philadelphia: Academy of Natural Sciences.
———. 1964. *The birds of Colombia.* Narberth, Pennsylvania: Livingston Publishing Company.
———. 1966. *The species of birds of South America and their distribution.* Narbeth, Pennsylvania: Livingston Publishing Company.
———. 1970. *A guide to the birds of South America.* Wynnewood, Pennsylvania: Livingston Publishing Company.
Meyer de Schauensee, R. and W. H. Phelps, Jr. 1978. *A guide to the birds of Venezuela.* Princeton: Princeton University Press.
Miller, A. H. 1932. Observations on some breeding birds of El Salvador, Central America. *Condor* 34:8–17.
———. 1947. The tropical avifauna of the upper Magdalena Valley, Colombia. *Auk* 64:351–381.
———. 1963. Seasonal activity and ecology of the avifauna of an American equatorial cloud forest. *Univ. Calif. Publ. Zool.* 66:1–78.
Miller C., Jr., 1973. Breeding the Masked Tanager (*Tangara nigrocincta*). *Avic. Mag.* 79:165–167.
Miller, W. de W. 1919. The tanagrin genus *Procnopis* Cabanis. *Auk* 36:576–577.
Mitchell, M. H. 1957. *Observations on birds of southeastern Brazil.* Toronto: University of Toronto Press.
Moermond, T. C. 1983. Suction-drinking in tanagers Thraupidae and its relation to frugivory. *Ibis* 125:545–549.
Moermond, T. C., and J. S. Denslow. 1983. Fruit choice in neotropical birds: effects of fruit type and accessibility or selectivity. *J. Anim. Ecol.* 52:407–420.
———. 1985. Neotropical avian frugivores: patterns of behavior, morphology, and nutrition, with consequences for fruit selection. In Neotropical ornithology, eds. P. A. Buckley et al. *Am. Ornithol. Union Ornithol. Monogr.* 36:865–897.
Monroe, B. L., Jr. 1968. A distributional survey of the birds of Honduras. *Am. Ornithol. Union. Ornithol. Monogr.* 7.
Moojen, J., J. C. de Carvalho, and H. de S. Lopes. 1941. Observações sôbre o conteúdo gastrico das aves brasileiras. *Mem. Inst. Oswaldo Cruz* 36:405–444.
Moore, R. T. 1934. The Mt. Sangay labryinth and its fauna. *Auk* 51:141–156.
Moriarty, D. J. 1977. Flocking and foraging in the Scarlet-rumped Tanager. *Wilson Bull.* 89:151–153.
Morony, J. J., Jr. 1985. Systematic relations of *Sericossypha albocristata* (Thraupinae). In Neotropical ornithology, eds. P. A. Buckley et al. *Am. Ornithol. Union Ornithol. Monogr.* 36:383–389.
Morrison, A. 1948. A list of the birds observed at the hacienda Huarapa, Department of Huánuco, Peru. *Ibis* 90:126–128.
Morton, E. S. 1976. Vocal mimicry in the Thick-billed Euphonia. *Wilson Bull.* 88:485–487.
———. 1979. A comparative survey of avian social systems in northern Venezuela habitats. In *Vertebrate ecology in the northern Neotropics,* ed. J. F. Eisenberg, pp. 233–259. Washington, D.C.: Smithsonian Institution Press.
Moynihan, M. 1962a. Display patterns of tropical American 'nine-primaried' songbirds. 1. *Chlorospingus. Auk* 79:310–344.
———. 1962b. Display patterns of tropical American 'nine-primaried' songbirds. 2.

Some species of *Ramphocelus*. *Auk* 79:655–686.

———. 1962c. The organization and probable evolution of some mixed species flocks of neotropical birds. *Smithson. Misc. Collect.* 143:1–140.

———. 1963. Inter-specific relations between some Andean birds. *Ibis* 105:327–339.

———. 1966. Display patterns of tropical American 'nine-primaried' songbirds. 4. The Yellow-rumped Tanager. *Smithsonian Misc. Coll.* 149:1–34.

———. 1979. Geographic variation in social behavior and in adaptations to competition among Andean birds. *Publ. Nuttall Ornithol. Club* 18:1–162.

Munn, C. A. 1984. Birds of different feathers also flock together. *Nat. Hist.* 93:34–42.

———. 1985. Permanent canopy and understory flocks in Amazonia: species composition and population density. In Neotropical ornithology, eds. P. A. Buckley et al. *Am. Ornithol. Union Ornithol. Monogr.* 36:683–712.

Munn, C. A., and J. W. Terborgh. 1979. Multi-species territoriality in neotropical foraging flocks. *Condor* 81:338–347.

Munves, J. 1975. Birds of a highland clearing in Cundinamarca, Colombia. *Auk* 92:307–321.

Murray, H. 1970. Breeding the Fawn-naped Tanager. *Avic. Mag.* 76:243.

Naumberg, E. M. B. 1924. *Thraupis sayaca* and its allies. *Auk* 61:105–116.

———. 1930. The birds of Matto Grosso, Brazil: A report on the birds secured by the Roosevelt-Rondon Expedition. *Bull. Am. Mus. Nat. Hist.* 60:1–432.

Negret, A. J., and R. A. Negret. 1981. As aves migratorias do Distrito Federal. In *Bol. Técnico* 6. Ministério da Agricultura, Instituto Brasileiro de Desenvolvimento Florestal.

Nehrkorn, A. 1899. *Katalog der Eiersammlung*. 1st ed. Braunschweig: Harald Bruhn.

Neunteufel, A. 1953. Un ejemplo de simbiosis temporal de aves silvestres. *Hornero* 10:74–77.

Newman, R. J. 1954. *Toxostoma ocellatum* and *Diglossa baritula* in Hidalgo. *Condor* 56:361.

Niethammer, G. 1956. Zur Vogelwelt Boliviens (Teil 2: Passeres). *Bonn. Zool. Beitr.* 7:84–150.

Norgaard-Olesen, E. 1971. Correspondence: *Tangara* hybrids. *Avic. Mag.* 77:230.

———. 1973. *Tanagers*, Vol. 1. Skibby, Denmark: Skibby-Books.

———. 1974. *Tanagers*, Vol. 2. Skibby, Denmark: Skibby-Books.

Norris, R. A., and D. W. Johnson. 1958. Weights and weight variations in summer birds from Georgia and South Carolina. *Wilson Bull.* 70:114–129.

Novaes, F. C. 1950. Sôbre as aves de Sernambetiba, Distrito Federal, Brasil. *Rev. Bras. Biol.* 10:199–208.

———. 1952. Algumas adendas a ornitologia de Goias, Brasil. *Bol. Mus. Nac. Rio de J. Zool.* 117:1–7.

———. 1957. Contribuição a ornitologia do noroeste do Acre. *Bol. Mus. Para. Emilio Goeldi Nova Sér. Zool.* 9:1–30.

———. 1958. As aves e as comunidades bióticas no alto Rio Juruá, território do Acre. *Bol. Mus. Para. Emilio Goeldi Nova Sér. Zool.* 14:1–13.

———. 1959. Variação geográfica e o problema da espécie nas aves do grupo *Ramphocelus carbo*. *Bol. Mus. Para. Emilio Goeldi Nova Sér. Zool.* 22:1–63.

———. 1960. Sôbre uma coleção de aves do sudeste do Estado do Pará. *Arq. Zool.* (São Paulo) 11:133–146.

———. 1965. Notas sôbre algumas aves de Serra Parina, Território de Roraima (Brasil). *Bol. Mus. Para. Emilio Goeldi Nova Sér. Zool.* 54:1–10.

———. 1969. Análise ecológica de uma avifauna de região do rio Acará, Estado do Pará. *Bol. Mus. Para. Emilio Goeldi Nova Sér. Zool.* 69:1–52.

———. 1970. Distribuição ecológica e abundancia das aves em um trecho da mata do baixo rio Guamá (Estado do Pará). *Bol Mus. Para. Emilio Goeldi Nova Sér. Zool.* 71:1–54.

———. 1973. Aves de uma vegetação secundária na foz do Amazonas. *Bol. Mus. Para. Emilio Goeldi Nova Sér. Zool.* 21:1–88.

———. 1976. As aves do rio Aripuaná, Estados do Mato Grosso e Amazonas. *Acta Amazonica* 6:61–85.

———. 1978. Ornitologia do território do Amapá 2. *Publ. Avulsas Mus. Para. Emilio Goeldi* 29:1–75.

———. 1980. Observações sobre a avifauna do alto curso do rio Paru de Leste, Estado do Pará. *Bol. Mus. Para. Emilio Goeldi Nova Sér. Zool.* 100:1–58.

Novaes, F. C., and T. Pimentel. 1973. Observações sôbre a avifauna dos campos de Bragança, estado do Pará. *Publ. Avulsas Mus. Para. Emilio Goeldi* 20:229–246.

Ogilvie-Grant, W. R. 1912. *Catalogue of the collection of birds' eggs in the British Museum (Natural History)*, Vol. 5. London: British Museum.

Olivares, A. 1959. Cinco aves que aparentemente no habian sido registradas en Colombia. *Lozania* 12:51–56.

———. 1962. Aves de la región sur de la Sierra de la Macarena, Meta, Colombia. *Rev. Acad. Colomb. Cienc. Exactas, Fisicas Nat.* 11:305–345.

———. 1963. Notas sobre aves de los Andes Orientales en Boyacá. *Bol. Soc. Venez. Cienc. Nat.* 25:91–125.

———. 1969. *Aves de Cundinamarca*. Bogotá: Univ. Nac. Colombia.

———. 1970. Effects of the environmental changes on the avifauna of the Republic of Colombia. In *The avifauna of northern Latin America: A symposium held at the Smithsonian Institution 13–15 April 1966;* eds. H. K. Buechner and J. H. Buechner. *Smithson. Contrib. Zool.* 26:77–87.

Olivares, A., and J. Hernandez C. 1962. Aves de la comisaría del Vaupés (Colombia). *Rev. Biol. Trop. Univ. Costa Rica* 10:61–90.

Olrog, C. C. 1959. *Las aves argentinas: Una guia de campo.* Tucumán: Instituto 'Miguel Lillo.'

———1963. *Lista y distribución de las aves argentinas.* Tucumán, Argentina: Univ. Nac. Tucumán.

———. 1979. Notas ornithologicas del noroeste argentino (Aves, Passeriformes). *Neotropica* 25:125–126.

Olson, S. L. 1981a. A revision of the northern forms of *Euphonia xanthogaster* (Aves: Thraupidae). *Proc. Biol. Soc. Wash.* 94:101–106.

———. 1981b. Systematic notes on certain oscines from Panama and adjacent areas (Aves: Passeriformes). *Proc. Biol. Soc. Wash.* 94:363–373.

———. 1983. Geographic variation in *Chlorospingus ophthalmicus* in Colombia and Venezuela (Aves: Thraupidae). *Proc. Biol. Soc. Wash.* 96:103–109.

Olson, S. L., and J. P. Angle. 1977. Weights of some Puerto Rican birds. *Bull. Br. Ornithol. Club* 97:105–107.

O'Neill, J. P. 1966. Notes on the distribution of *Conothraupis speculigera* (Gould). *Condor* 68:598–600.

———. 1969. Distributional notes on the birds of Peru, including twelve species previously unreported from the Republic. *Occas. Pap. Mus. Zool. Louisiana State Univ.* 37:1–11.

———. 1974. *The birds of Balta, a Peruvian dry tropical forest locality, with an analysis of their origins and ecological relationships.* Unpublished Ph.D. dissertation, Baton Rouge, Louisiana State University.

O'Neill, J. P., and T. A. Parker III. 1981. New subspecies of *Pipreola riefferii* and *Chlorospingus ophthalmicus* from Peru. *Bull. Br. Ornithol. Club* 101:294–299.

O'Neill, J. P., and D. L. Pearson. 1974. Estudio preliminar de las aves de Yarinacocha, Departamento de Loreto, Peru. *Publ. Mus. Hist. Nat. 'Javier Prado' Ser. A Zool.* 25:1–13.

Oniki, Y. 1972. Some temperatures of Panamanian birds. *Condor* 74:209–215.

———. 1975. Temperatures of some Puerto Rican birds, with note of low temperatures in todies. *Condor* 77:344.

Oniki, Y., and E. O. Willis. 1972. Studies of ant-following birds north of the eastern Amazon. *Acta Amazonica* (Manaus) 2:127–151.

Orces, V. G. 1944. Notas sobre la distribución geográfica de algunas aves neotropicas. *Flora* 4:103–123.

Parker, T. A., III. 1976. An introduction to bird-finding in Peru: Part 2. The Carpish Pass Region of the Eastern Andes and Central Highway. *Birding* 8:205–216.

Parker, T. A., III., and J. P. O'Neill. 1980. Notes on little known birds of the upper Urubamba Valley, southern Peru. *Auk* 97:167–176.

Parker, T. A., III., and S. A. Parker. 1982. Behavioral and distributional notes on some unusual birds of a lower montane cloud forest in Peru. *Bull. Br. Ornithol. Club* 102:63–70.

Parker, T. A., III, S. A. Parker, and M. A. Plenge. 1982. *An annotated checklist of Peruvian birds.* Vermillion, South Dakota: Buteo Books.

Parker, T. A., III, J. V. Remsen, Jr., and J. A. Heindel. 1980. Seven bird species new to Bolivia. *Bull. Br. Ornithol. Club* 100:160–162.

Parker, T. A., III, T. S. Schulenberg, G. R. Graves, and M. J. Braun. 1985. The avifauna of the Huancabamba region, northern Peru. In Neotropical ornithology, eds. P. A. Buckley et al. *Am. Ornithol. Union Ornithol. Monogr.* 36:169–197.

Parkes, K. C. 1969a. The Blue-backed Tanager (*Cyanicterus cyanicterus*), a genus new to Venezuela, with notes on its plumages. *Auk* 86:568–569.

———. 1969b. Some undescribed subspecies of tanagers from South America. *Bull. Br. Ornithol. Club* 89:17–20.

———. 1977. An undescribed subspecies of the Red-legged Honeycreeper *Cyanerpes cyaneus*. *Bull. Br. Ornithol. Club* 97:65–68.

Parkes, K. C., and P. S. Humphrey. 1963. Geographic variations and plumage sequence of the tanager *Hemithraupis flavicollis* in the Guianas and adjacent Brazil. *Proc. Biol. Soc. Wash.* 76:81–84.

Patterson, B., and R. Allen. 1968. A Maine nest of the Scarlet Tanager. *Wilson Bull.* 80:495.

Paynter, R. A., Jr. 1955. The ornithogeography of the Yucatán Peninsula. *Bull. Peabody Mus. Nat. Hist. Yale Univ.* 9:1–347.
Paynter, R. A., Jr., and R. W. Storer. 1970. Introduction pp. v–x. In *Check-list of birds of the world*. Vol. *13*; ed. R. A. Paynter, Jr. Cambridge: Mus. Comp. Zool. Harv. Univ.
Pearson, D. L. 1969. Vertical stratification and biomass distribution of birds in a tropical dry forest. Unpublished M.S. thesis, Baton Rouge, Louisiana State University.
———. 1971. Vertical stratification of birds in a tropical dry forest. *Condor* 73:46–55.
———. 1972. Un estudio de las aves de Limoncocha, Provincia de Napo, Ecuador. *Bol. Inf. Cient. Nac.* (Quito) 13:1–14.
———. 1975a. The relation of foliage complexity to ecological diversity of three Amazonian bird communities. *Condor* 77:453–466.
———. 1975b. Range extensions and new records for bird species in Ecuador, Peru, and Bolivia. *Condor* 77:96–99.
———. 1975c. Un estudio de las aves de Tumi Chucua, Departmento de Beni, Bolivia. *Pumapunku* (La Paz) 8:50–56.
———. 1977. A pantropical comparison of bird community structure on six lowland forest sites. *Condor* 79:232–244.
Peck, M. E. 1910. The effect of natural enemies on the nesting habits of some British Honduras birds. *Condor* 12:53–60.
Peixoto Velho, P. P. 1932. Descripção de alguns ovos de aves do Brasil existentes nas collecções do museu. *Bol. Mus. Nac. Rio de J.* 8:49–60.
Pelzeln, A. von. 1869. *Zur Ornithologie Brasiliens*. Wien: A. Pichler's Witwe & Sohn.
Penard, F. P., and A. P. Penard. 1910. *De vögels van Guyana (Suriname, Cayenne en Demerara)*, Vol. 2. Paramaribo: Penard.
Pereyra, J. A. 1938. Aves de la zona ribereña nordeste de la Provincia de Buenos Aires. *Mem. Jard. Zool.* (La Plata) 9:1–304.
———. 1951. Avifauna Argentina. *Hornero* 9:291–347.
Peters, J. L. 1929. An ornithological survey in the Caribbean lowlands of Honduras. *Bull. Mus. Comp. Zool. Harv. Univ.* 69:397–478.
Peters, J. L., and J. A. Griswold, Jr. 1943. Birds of the Harvard Peruvian Expedition. *Bull. Mus. Comp. Zool. Harv. Univ.* 92:281–327.
Peterson, R. T. 1947. *A field guide to the birds*. Boston: Houghton Mifflin.
———. 1969. *A field guide to western birds*. Boston: Houghton Mifflin.
Peterson, R. T., and E. L. Chalif. 1973. *A field guide to Mexican birds*. Boston: Houghton Mifflin.
Phelps, K. D. 1954. *Cien de las más conocidas aves Venezolanas*. Caracas: Editorial Lectura.
Pinto, O. M. de O. 1932. Resultados ornithológicos de uma excursão pelo oeste de São Paulo e sul de Matto-Grosso. *Rev. Mus. Paulista* (São Paulo) 17:691–826.
———. 1944a. *Catálogo das aves do Brasil*, Vol. 2. São Paulo: Depto. Zool.
———. 1944b. Sôbre as aves do Distrito de Monte Alegre, Municipio de Ampara (São Paulo, Brasil). *Pap. Avulsos Zool.* (São Paulo) 4:117–150.
———. 1951. Aves do Itatiaia. *Pap. Avulsos Zool.* (São Paulo) 10:155–208.
———. 1953. Sôbre a coleção Carlos Estevao de peles, ninhos e ovos das aves de Belém (Pará). *Pap. Avulsos Zool.* (São Paulo) 11:111–222.
———. 1954. Resultados ornitológicos de duas viagens científicas ao Estado de Alagoas. *Pap. Avulsos Zool.* (São Paulo) 12:1–98.
———. 1966. Cadernos de Amazônia, 8, estudo critico e catalogo remissivo das aves de Território Federal de Roraima, Manaus. *Inst. Nac. de Pesquisas da Amazônia* 8:1–176.
Pinto, O., and E. Camargo. 1957. Sôbre uma coleção de aves da região de Cachimbo (Sul do Estado do Pará). *Pap. Avulsos Zool.* (São Paulo) 13:51–69.
———. 1961. Resutados ornitológicos de quatro recentes expedições do Departamento de Zoologia ao nordeste do Brasil, com a descrição de seis novas subespecies. *Arq. Zool.* (São Paulo) 11:193–284.
Plenge, M. A. 1974. Notes on some birds in west-central Peru. *Condor* 76:326–330.
Poole, E. L. 1938. Weights and wing areas in North American birds. *Auk* 55:511–517.
Pough, R. H. 1946. *Audubon bird guide*. New York: Doubleday.
Powell, G. V. N. 1979. Structure and dynamics of interspecific flocks in a neotropical mid-elevation forest. *Auk* 96:375–390.
———. 1985. Sociobiology and adaptive significance of interspecific foraging flocks in the Neotropics. In Neotropical ornithology, eds. P. A. Buckley et al. *Am. Ornithol. Union Ornithol. Monogr.* 36:713–732.
Pregill, G. K., and S. L. Olson. 1981. Zoogeography of West Indian vertebrates in relation to Pleistocene climatic cycles. *Ann. Rev. Ecol. Syst.* 12:75–98.
Prescott, K. W. 1964. Constancy of incubation for the Scarlet Tanager. *Wilson Bull.* 76:37–42.
———. 1965. *The Scarlet Tanager*. Investigations 2. Trenton: New Jersey State Museum.

———. 1974. Summer Tanager southern range extension in Chile. *Auk* 91:617–618.
Raffaele, H. A. 1983. *A guide to the birds of Puerto Rico and the Virgin Islands.* San Juan: Fondo Educativo Interamericano.
Raikow, R. W. 1978. Appendicular myology and relationships of the New World nine-primaried oscines (Aves: Passeriformes). *Bull. Carnegie Mus.* 7:1–43.
Ramo, C., and B. Busto. 1984. Nidificación de los passeriformes en los llanos de Apure (Venezuela). *Biotropica* 16:59–68.
Rand, A. L., and M. A. Traylor. 1954. *Manual de las aves de El Salvador.* San Salvador: Univ. El Salvador.
Reinhardt, J. 1870. Kundskab om Fuglefaunaen i Brasiliens Campos. *Vidensk. Medd. Naturhist. Foren. i Kjobenhavn.*
Remsen, J. V., Jr. 1976. Observations of vocal mimicry in the Thick-billed Euphonia. *Wilson Bull.* 88:487–488.
———. 1984. Natural history notes on some poorly known Bolivian birds. Part 2. *Gerfaut* 74:163–179.
———. 1985. Community organization and ecology of birds of high elevation humid forest of the Bolivian Andes. In Neotropical ornithology, eds. P. A. Buckley et al. *Am. Ornithol. Union Ornithol. Monogr.* 36:733–757.
———. Nuevos registros de aves para el Departmento Cochabamba. *Com. Mus. Nac. Hist. Nat.* (Bolivia), in press.
Remsen, J. V., Jr., and T. A. Parker III. 1983. Contribution of river-created habitats to bird species richness in Amazonia. *Biotropica* 15:223–231.
———. 1984. Arboreal dead-leaf searching birds of the Neotropics. *Condor* 86:36–41.
Remsen, J. V., Jr., and R. S. Ridgely. 1980. Additions to the avifauna of Bolivia. *Condor* 82:69–75.
Remsen, J. V., Jr., and M. A. Traylor, Jr. 1983. Additions to the avifauna of Bolivia, Part 2. *Condor* 85:95–98.
Remsen, J. V., Jr., M. A. Traylor, Jr., and K. C. Parkes. Range extensions for some Bolivian birds (Tyrannidae to Passeridae). *Bull. Br. Ornithol. Club,* in press.
Renssen, T. A. 1974. Twelve bird species new for Surinam. *Ardea* 62:118–122.
Reynard, G. B. 1981. *Bird songs in the Dominican Republic* (sound recording). Ithaca, N.Y.: Laboratory of Ornithology, Cornell Univ.
———. 1982. Whisper song of the Stripe-headed Tanager. *Broadsheet* 38. Jamaica, W.I.: Gosse Bird Club.
Richmond, C. W. 1893. Notes on a collection of birds from eastern Nicaragua and the Río Frío, Costa Rica, with a description of a supposed new trogon. *Proc. U.S. Nat. Mus.* 16:479–530.
Ricklefs, R. E. 1968. Patterns of growth in birds. *Ibis* 110:419–451.
———. 1976. Growth rates of birds in the humid New World tropics. *Ibis* 118:179–207.
———. 1977. Reactions of some Panamanian birds to human intrusion at the nest. *Condor* 79:376–379.
Ridgely, R. S. 1976. *A guide to the birds of Panama.* Princeton: Princeton University Press.
———. 1980. Notes on some rare or previously unrecorded birds in Ecuador. *Am. Birds* 34:242–248.
Ridgely, R. S., and S. J. C. Gaulin. 1980. The birds of Finca Merenberg, Huila Department, Colombia. *Condor* 82:379–391.
Ridgway, R. 1902. *The birds of North and Middle America*, Part 2. Washington, D.C.: Smithsonian Institution.
Robbins, M. B., T. A. Parker III, and S. E. Allen. 1985. The avifauna of Cerro Pirre, Darién, eastern Panama. In *Neotropical ornithology,* eds. P. A. Buckley et al. Am. Ornithol. Union Ornithol. Monogr. 36:198–231.
Robins, C. R., and W. B. Heed. 1951. Bird notes from La Joya de Salas, Tamaulipas. *Wilson Bull.* 63:263–270.
Rogers, D. T., Jr., and E. P. Odum. 1966. A study of autumnal postmigrant weights and vernal flattening of North American migrants in the tropics. *Wilson Bull.* 78:415–433.
Roles, D. G. 1971. Breeding the Thick-billed Euphonia at the Jersey Zoo Park (*Tanagra laniirostris*). *Avic. Mag.* 77:101–102.
Rosenberg, K. V., R. D. Ohmart, and B. K. Anderson. 1982. Community organization of riparian breeding birds: response to an annual resource peak. *Auk* 99:260–274.
Rowley, J. S. 1962. Nesting of the birds of Morelos, Mexico. *Condor* 64:253–272.
———. 1966. Breeding records of birds of the Sierra Madre del Sur, Oaxaca, Mexico. *Proc. West. Found. Vertebr. Zool.* 1:107–204.
———. 1984. Breeding records of land birds in Oaxaca, Mexico. *Proc. West. Found. Vertebr. Zool.* 2:76–221.
Ruschi. 1979. *Aves do Brasil.* São Paulo: Ed. Rios.
Russell, S. M. 1964. A distributional study of the birds of British Honduras. *Am. Ornithol. Union Ornithol. Monogr.* 1.
———. 1970. Avifauna in British Honduras. In *A symposium held at the Smithsonian Institution 13–15 April 1966*, eds. H. K. Buechner and J. H. Buechner. *Smithson. Contrib. Zool.* 26:45–49.
———. 1980. Distribution and abundance of North American migrants in lowlands of northern Colombia. In *Migrant birds in the*

Neotropics: ecology, behavior, distribution, and conservation, pp. 249–252, eds. A. Keast and E. S. Morton. Washington, D.C.: Smithsonian Institution Press.

Sabo, S. R., and R. T. Holmes. 1983. Foraging niches and the structure of forest bird communities in contrasting montane habitats. *Condor* 85:121–138.

Salt, G. W. 1957. An analysis of avifaunas in the Teton Mountains and Jackson Hole, Wyoming. *Condor* 59:373–393.

Salvin, O., and F. D. Godman. 1879–1904. *Biológia Centrali-Americana: Aves*, Vol. 1–3.

Santos, E. 1948. *Pássaros do Brasil*. Rio de Janeiro: F. Briguiet.

Scamell, K. M. 1970. Breeding the Lemon-rumped Tanager (*Ramphocelus icteronotus*). *Avic. Mag.* 76:216–219.

Schaefer, E. 1953. Contribution to the life history of the Swallow-Tanager. *Auk* 70:403–460.

Schäfer, E., and W. H. Phelps, Jr. 1954. Las aves del Parque Nacional 'Henri Pittier' (Rancho Grande) y sus funciones ecológicas. *Bol. Soc. Venez. Cienc. Nat.* 16:3–167.

Schaldach, W. J., Jr. 1963. The avifauna of Colima and adjacent Jalisco, Mexico. *Proc. West. Found. Vertebr. Zool.* 1:1–100.

———. 1969. Further notes on the avifauna of Colima and adjacent Jalisco, Mexico. *An. Inst. Biol. Univ. Nac. Auton. Mex. Ser. Zool.* 40:299–316.

Schmitt, C. G., D. C. Schmitt, J. V. Remsen, Jr., and B. D. Glick. New bird records for Departmento Santa Cruz, Bolivia. *Hornero*, in press.

Schubart, O., A. C. Aguirre, and H. Sick. 1965. Contribução para o conhecimento da alimentação das aves Brasileiras. *Arq. Zool.* (São Paulo) 12:95–249.

Schulenberg, T. S. 1985. An intergeneric hybrid conebill (*Conirostrum* x *Oreomanes*) from Peru. In *Neotropical ornithology*, eds. P. A. Buckley et al. Am. Ornithol. Union Ornithol. Monogr. 36.

Schulenberg, T. S., and L. C. Binford. 1985. A new species of tanager (Emberizidae, Thraupinae, *Tangara*) from southern Peru. *Wilson Bull.* 97:413–420.

Schulenberg, T. S., and M. A. Plenge. 1980. The type locality and taxonomy of *Anisognathus flavinucha somptuosus*. *Bull. Br. Ornithol. Club* 100:147–149.

Schulenberg, T. S., and J. V. Remsen, Jr. 1982. Eleven bird species new to Bolivia. *Bull. Br. Ornithol. Club* 102:52–57.

Schulenberg, T. S., and M. D. Williams. 1982. A new species of antpitta (*Grallaria*) from northern Peru. *Wilson Bull.* 94:105–113.

Sclater, P. L. 1875. Synopsis of the species of the subfamily Diglossinae. *Ibis* 3rd Ser. 5:204–221.

———. 1886. Catalogue of the birds in the British Museum, Vol 2. London: British Museum.

Sclater, P. L., and W. H. Hudson. 1888. *Argentine ornithology*, Vol 1. London: R. H. Porter.

Sclater, P. L., and O. Salvin. 1859. On the ornithology of Central America. *Ibis* 1st Ser. 1:1–22.

———. 1879. On the birds collected by the late Mr. T. K. Salmon in the State of Antioquia, United States of Colombia. *Proc. Zool. Soc. Lond.* 1879:486–550.

Short, L. L. 1971. Aves nuevas o poco comunes de corrientes, Republica Argentina. *Rev. Mus. Argent. Cienc. Nat. 'Bernardino Rivadavia'* 9:283–309.

———. 1972. Two avian species new to Paraguay. *Auk* 89:895.

———. 1975. A zoogeographic analysis of the South American chaco avifauna. *Bull. Am. Mus. Nat. Hist.* 154:163–352.

———. 1976. Notes on a collection of birds from the Paraguayan chaco. *Am. Mus. Novit.* 2597:1–16.

Short, L. L., and J. J. Morony, Jr. 1969. Notes on some birds of central Peru. *Bull. Br. Ornithol. Club* 89:112–115.

Shy, E. 1983. The relation of geographical variation in song to habitat characteristics and body size in North American tanagers (Thraupinae: *Piranga*). *Behav. Ecol. Sociobiol.* 12:71–76.

———. 1984a. The structure of song and its geographical variation in the Scarlet Tanager (*Piranga olivacea*). *Am. Midl. Nat.* 112:119–130.

———. 1984b. Sympatry and allopatry of song in North American tanagers. *Behav. Ecol. Sociobiol.* 15:189–195.

———. 1984c. Habitat shift and geographical variation in North American tanagers (Thraupinae: *Piranga*). *Oecologia* 63:281–285.

———. Songs of Summer Tanagers (*Piranga rubra*): structure and geographical variation. *Am. Midl. Nat.*, in press.

Sibley, C. G. 1955. Nesting of the Western Tanager in the Santa Cruz Mountains, California. *Condor* 57:307.

———. 1970. A comparative study of the egg-white protein of passerine birds. *Bull. Peabody Mus. Nat. Hist. Yale Univ.* 32:1–131.

———. 1973. The relationships of the Swallow-tanager *Tersina viridis*. *Bull. Br. Ornithol. Club* 93:75–78.

Sibley, C. G., and J. E. Ahlquist. The phylogeny and classification of the passerine birds, based on comparisons of the genetic material, DNA. In *Proc. 18th Int. Ornithol. Congr.*, ed. V. D. Ilyichev. Moscow: Nauka Publ., in press.

Sick, H. 1955. O aspecto fitofisionômico da paisagem do médio rio das Mortes, Mato Grosso e a avifauna região. *Arq. Mus. Nac. Rio de J.* 42:541–576.
———. 1957a. Anting by two tanagers in Brazil. *Wilson Bull.* 69:187–188.
———. 1957b. Robhaarpilze als Nestbaumaterial brasilianischer Vogel. *J. Ornithol.* 98:421–431.
———. 1958. Resultados de uma excursão ornitológica do Museu Nacional a Brasilia, novo Distrito Federal, Goiás, com a descrição de um novo representante de *Scytalopus* (Rhinocryptidae, aves) (1). *Bol. Mus. Nac. Rio de J. (Zool.)* 185:1–41.
———. 1960. The honeycreeper *Dacnis albiventris* in Brazil. *Condor* 62:66–67.
———. 1968. Vogelwanderungen im kontinentalen Sudamerika. *Vogelwarte* 24:217–243.
———. 1979. Notes on some Brazilian birds. *Bull. Br. Ornithol. Club* 99:115–120.
———. 1985. *Ornitologia Brasileira, uma introdução*. Brasília: Editora Univ. de Brasília.
Sick, H., and L. F. Pabst. 1968. As aves do Rio de Janeiro (Guanabara) (lista sistemática anotada). *Arq. Mus. Nac. Rio de J.* 53:99–160.
Silva, W. R. 1980. Notas sobre o comportamento alimentar de três espécies de traupídeos (Passeriformes: Thraupidae) em *Cecropia concolor* na região de Manaus. *Acta Amazonica* 10:427–429.
Simmons, K. E. L. 1957. The taxonomic significance of the head-scratching methods of birds. *Ibis* 99:178–181.
———. 1961. Problems of head-scratching in birds. *Ibis* 103a:37–49.
Skutch, A. F. 1953. How the male bird discovers the nestlings. *Ibis* 95:1–37, 505–542.
———. 1954. Life histories of Central American birds. *Pacific Coast Avif.* No. 31. Berkeley: Cooper Ornithol. Soc.
———. 1961. Helpers among birds. *Condor* 63:198–226.
———. 1962a. On the habits of the Queo, *Rhodinocichla rosea*. *Auk* 79:633–639.
———. 1962b. Life histories of honeycreepers. *Condor* 64:92–116.
———. 1967a. Life histories of Central American highland birds. *Publ. Nuttall Ornithol. Club.* No. 7.
———. 1967b. Cape May Warbler in Costa Rica. *Wilson Bull.* 79:118–119.
———. 1967c. Adaptive limitation of the reproductive rate of birds. *Ibis* 109:579–599.
———. 1968. The nesting of some Venezuelan birds. *Condor* 70:66–82.
———. 1969. A study of the Rufous-fronted Thornbird and associated birds. *Wilson Bull.* 81:123–139.
———. 1972. Studies of tropical American birds. *Publ. Nuttall Ornithol. Club.* No 10.
———. 1976. *Parent birds and their young*. Austin and London: University of Texas Press.
———. 1977. *A birdwatcher's adventures in tropical America*. Austin and London: University of Texas Press.
———. 1980. Arils as food of tropical American birds. *Condor* 82:31–42.
———. 1985. Clutch size, nesting success, and predation on nests of neotropical birds, reviewed. In Neotropical ornithology, eds. P. A. Buckley et al. *Am. Ornithol. Union Ornithol. Monogr.* 36:575–594.
Slud, P. 1960. The birds of finca 'La Selva,' Costa Rica: A tropical wet forest locality. *Bull. Am. Mus. Nat. Hist.* 121:49–148.
———. 1964. The birds of Costa Rica: Distribution and ecology. *Bull. Am. Mus. Nat. Hist.* 128:1–430.
———. 1980. The birds of Hacienda Palo Verde, Guanacaste, Costa Rica. *Smithson. Contrib. Zool.* 292:1–92.
Smithe, F. B. 1966. *The birds of Tikal*. Garden City, N.Y.: Natural History Press.
———. 1975 plus supplements. *Naturalist's color guide*. New York: Am. Mus. Nat. Hist.
Smyth, C. H. 1928. Descripción de una colección de huevos de aves argentinas. *Hornero* 4:1–16, 124–152.
Snethlage, E. 1907. Uber unteramazonische Vögel. *J. Ornithol.* 55:283–299.
———. 1913. Uber die Verbreitung der Vogelarten in Unteramazonien. *J. Ornithol.* 61:469–539.
———. 1935. Beiträge zur Brutbiologie brasilianische Vögel. *J. Ornithol.* 83:1–24, 532–562.
Snethlage, E., and K. Schreiner. 1929. Beiträge zur brasilianischen Oologie. *Verh. 6. Inter. Ornithol.-Kongr.* 1926:576–640.
Snethlage, H. 1927–1928. Meine Reise durch Nordostbrasilien. *J. Ornithol.* 75:453–484; 76:503–581, 668–738.
Snow, B. K. 1974. Vocal mimicry in the Violaceous Euphonia, *Euphonia violacea*. *Wilson Bull.* 86:179–180.
Snow, B. K., and D. W. Snow. 1971. The feeding ecology of tanagers and honeycreepers in Trinidad. *Auk* 88:291–322.
Snow, D. W., and C. T. Collins. 1962. Social breeding behavior of the Mexican Tanager. *Condor* 64:161.
Snow, D. W., and B. K. Snow. 1964. Breeding seasons and annual cycles of Trinidad land-birds. *Zoologica* (N.Y.) 49:1–39.
———. 1980. Relationships between hummingbirds and flowers in the Andes of Colombia. *Bull. Br. Mus. Nat. Hist.* (Zool.) 38:105–139.

Snyder, D. E. 1966. *The birds of Guyana*. Salem: Peabody Museum.

Steadman, D. W., S. L. Olson, J. C. Barber, C. A. Meister, and M. E. Melville. 1980. Weights of some West Indian birds. *Bull. Br. Ornithol. Club* 100:155–158.

Steinbacher, G. 1938. Zur brutbiologie der Orangebrusttangare (*Calospiza thoracica* Tem.) *Beitr. Fortpf. Biol. Vog.* 14:81–84.

Stewart, P. A., and R. W. Skinner. 1967. Weights of birds from Alabama and North Carolina. *Wilson Bull.* 79:37–42.

Stiles, F. G. 1980. Bird community structure in alder forests in Washington. *Condor* 82:20–30.

———. 1983. Birds, chap. 10. In *Costa Rican Natural History*, ed. D. H. Janzen. Chicago: University of Chicago Press.

Stiles, F. G., and H. A. Hespenheide. 1972. Observations of two rare Costa Rican finches. *Condor* 74:99–101.

Stone, W. 1918. Birds of the Panama Canal Zone, with special reference to a collection made by Mr. Lindsey L. Jewel. *Proc. Acad. Nat. Sci. Phila.* 70:239–280.

Storer, R. W. 1960. Notes on the systematics of the tanager genus *Conothraupis*. *Auk* 77:350–351.

———. 1969. What is a tanager? *Living Bird* 8:127–136.

———. 1970. Subfamily Thraupinae, pp 246–408. In *Check-list of birds of the world*, Vol. 13, ed. R. A. Paynter, Jr. Cambridge: Mus. Comp. Zool.

Strauch, J. G., Jr. 1977. Further bird weights from Panama. *Bull. Br. Ornithol. Club* 97:61–65.

Sutton, G. M. 1951a. *Mexican birds: First impressions*. Norman: University of Oklahoma Press.

———. 1951b. Dispersal of mistletoe by birds. *Wilson Bull.* 63:235–237.

Sutton, G. M., and T. D. Burleigh. 1940. Birds of Tamazunchale, San Luis Potosí. *Wilson Bull.* 52:221–233.

Sutton, G. M., and O. S. Pettingill, Jr. 1942. Birds of the Gomez Farias region, southwestern Tamaulipas. *Auk* 59:1–34.

Sutton, G. M., R. B. Lea, and E. P. Edwards. 1950. Notes on the ranges and breeding habits of certain Mexican birds. *Bird-Banding* 21:45–59.

Sworth, H. S. 1904. Birds of the Huachuca Mountains, Arizona. *Pacific Coast Avif.* No. 4. Berkeley: Cooper Ornithol. Soc.

Taczanowski, L. 1884a. *Ornithologie du Pérou*, Vol. 1. Berlin: Friedlander und Sohn.

———. 1884b. *Ornithologie du Pérou*, Vol. 2. Rennes: Oberthur.

Tallman, D. A. 1974. *Colonization of a semi-isolated temperate cloud forest: Preliminary interpretation of distributional patterns of birds in the Carpish region of the Department of Huánuco, Peru.* Unpublished M.S. thesis, Baton Rouge, Louisiana State University.

Tashian, R. E. 1952. Some birds from the Palenque region of northeastern Chiapas, Mexico. *Auk* 69:60–66.

———. 1953. The birds of southeastern Guatemala. *Condor* 55:198–210.

Tatschl, J. L. 1967. Breeding birds of the Sandia Mountains and their ecological distributions. *Condor* 69:479–490.

Taylor, R. G. L. 1955. *Introduction to the birds of Jamaica*. London: Macmillan.

Terborgh, J. W. 1971. Distribution on environmental gradients: theory and a preliminary interpretation of distributional patterns in the avifauna of the Cordillera Vilcabamba, Peru. *Ecology* 52:23–40.

Terborgh, J., and J. Faaborg. 1973. Turnover and ecological release in the avifauna of Mona Island, Puerto Rico. *Auk* 90:759–779.

Terborgh, J., and J. S. Weske. 1969. Colonization of secondary habitats by Peruvian birds. *Ecology* 50:765–782.

———. 1975. The role of competition in the distribution of Andean birds. *Ecology* 56:562–576.

Terres, J. K. 1980. *The Audubon Society encyclopedia of North American birds*. New York: Alfred A. Knopf.

Thomas, B. T. 1979. The birds of a ranch in the Venezuelan llanos. In *Vertebrate Ecology in the northern Neotropics*, ed. J. F. Eisenberg, pp. 213–232. Washington, D.C.: Smithsonian Institution Press.

———. 1982. Weights of some Venezuelan birds. *Bull. Br. Ornithol. Club.* 102:48–52.

Thomas, R. H. 1941. 'Anting' by Summer Tanager. *Auk* 58:102.

Todd, W. E. C., and M. A. Carriker, Jr. 1922. The birds of the Santa Marta region of Colombia: A study in altitudinal distribution. *Ann. Carnegie Mus.* 14:3–582.

Tostain, O. 1980. Contribution a l'ornithologie de la Guyane francaise. *Oiseau et Rev. Fr. Ornithol.* 50:47–62.

Traylor, M. A. 1941. Birds from the Yucatán Peninsula. *Field Mus. Nat. Hist. Publ. Zool. Ser.* 24:195–225.

van Rossem, A. J. 1945. A distributional survey of the birds of Sonora, Mexico. *Occas. Pap. Mus. Zool. Louisiana State Univ.* 21:1–379.

Verrill, A. E., and A. H. Verrill. 1909. Notes on the birds of San Domingo, with a list of the species, including a new hawk. *Proc. Acad. Nat. Sci. Phila.* 61:352–366.

Vigil, C. 1973. *Aves Argentinas y Sudamericanas*. Buenos Aires: Editorial Atlantida.

Voss, W. A. 1977a. Aves silvestres livres observadas no Parque Zoológica em Sapucaia do Sul, RS, Brasil. *Pesquisas Zool.* 30:1–29.

———. 1977b. Comunicação sobre a ocorrência do Sanhaçu-do-Coqueiro, *Thraupis palmarum* (Wied), na cidade de Porto Alegre-RS. *Pesquisas Zool.* 30:32.

Voss, W. A., and M. Sander. 1980. Frutos de arvores nativas na alimentação das aves. *Trigo e Soja* (Porto Alegre) 51:26-30.

———. 1981. Frutos e sementes vários na alimentação das aves livres. *Trigo e Soja* (Porto Alegre) 58:28–31.

Vuilleumier, F. 1969. Systematics and evolution in *Diglossa* (Aves, Coerebidal). *Am. Mus. Novit.* 2381:1–44.

———. 1970. L'organisation sociale des bandes vagabondes d'oiseaux dans les Andes du Pérou central. *Revue Suisse Zool.* 77:209–235.

———. 1984a. Zoogeography of Andean birds: two major barriers; and speciation and taxonomy of the *Diglossa carbonaria* superspecies. *Nat. Geog. Soc. Res. Rep.* 16:713–731.

———. 1984b. Patchy distribution and systematics of *Oreomanes fraseri* (Aves ?Coerebidae) of Andean *Polylepis* woodlands. *Am. Mus. Novit.* 2777:1–17.

Vuilleumier, F., and D. N. Ewert. 1978. The distribution of birds in Venezuelan Paramos. *Bull. Am. Mus. Nat. Hist.* 162:49–90.

Wells, J. G. 1886. A catalogue of the birds of Grenada, West Indies, with observations thereon. *Proc. U.S. Nat. Mus.* 9:609–633.

Weske, J. S. 1972. *The distribution of the avifauna in the Apurímac Valley of Peru with respect to environmental gradients, habitat, and related species.* Unpublished Ph.D. dissertation. Norman: University of Oklahoma.

Weske, J. S., and J. W. Terborgh. 1974. *Hemispingus parodii,* a new species of tanager from Peru. *Wilson Bull.* 86:97–103.

Wetmore, A. 1926. Observations on the birds of Argentina, Paraguay, Uruguay, and Chile. *Bull. U.S. Nat. Mus.* 133:1–448.

———. 1927. *The birds of Porto Rico and the Virgin Islands—Psittaciformes to Passeriformes. Scientific survey of Porto Rico and the Virgin Islands,* Vol. 9, Part 4. New York: New York Academy of Sciences.

———. 1939. Observations on the birds of northern Venezuela. *Proc. U.S. Nat. Mus.* 87:173–260.

———. 1941. Notes on birds of the Guatemalan highlands. *Proc. U.S. Nat. Mus.* 89:523–581.

———. 1943. The birds of southern Veracruz, Mexico. *Proc. U.S. Nat. Mus.* 93:215–340.

———. 1944. A collection of birds from northern Guanacaste, Costa Rica. *Proc. U.S. Nat. Mus.* 95:25–80.

Wetmore, A., and F. C. Lincoln. 1933. Additional notes on the birds of Haiti and the Dominican Republic. *Proc. U.S. Nat. Mus.* 82:1–68.

Wetmore, A., and B. H. Swales. 1931. The birds of Haiti and the Dominican Republic. *Bull. U.S. Nat. Mus.* 155:1–483.

Wetmore, A., R. F. Pasquier, and S. L. Olson. 1984. *The birds of the Republic of Panamá. Part 4. Passeriformes: Hirundinidae (Swallows) to Fringillidae (Finches).* Washington, D.C.: Smithsonian Institution Press.

Wheelwright, N. T., W. A. Haber, K. G. Murray, and C. Guindon. 1984. Tropical fruit-eating birds and their food plants: survey of a Costa Rica lower montane forest. *Biotropica* 16:173–192.

White, E. W., and P. L. Sclater. 1883. Supplementary notes on the birds of the Argentine Republic. *Proc. Zool. Soc. Lond.* 6:37–43.

Whitaker, L. M. 1957. A résumé of anting, with particular reference to a captive Orchard Oriole. *Wilson Bull.* 69:195–262.

Wied, M. von. 1830. *Bietr. Naturg. Bras.* 3 volumes.

Wiedenfeld, D. A., T. S. Schulenberg, and M. B. Robbins. 1985. Birds of a tropical deciduous forest in extreme northwestern Peru. In Neotropical ornithology, eds. P. A. Buckley et al. *Am. Ornithol. Union Ornithol. Monogr.* 16:305–316.

Wiggins, I. L., and B. L. Wiggins. 1939. An unusual nesting site of the Western Tanager. *Condor* 41:80–81.

Williams, C. B. 1922. Notes on the food and habits of some Trinidad birds. *Bull. Dept. Agric. Trinidad and Tobago* 20:123–185.

Willis, E. O. 1960a. A study of the foraging behavior of two species of ant-tanagers. *Auk* 77:150–170.

———. 1960b. Red-crowned Ant-Tanagers, Tawny-crowned Greenlets, and forest flocks. *Wilson Bull.* 72:105–106.

———. 1960c. Voice, courtship, and territorial behavior of ant-tanagers in British Honduras. *Condor* 62:73–87.

———. 1961. A study of nesting ant-tanagers in British Honduras. *Condor* 63:479–503.

———. 1966a. The role of migrant birds at swarms of army ants. *Living Bird* 5:187–231.

———. 1966b. Ecology and behavior of the Crested Ant-Tanager. *Condor* 68:56–71.

———. 1966c. Competitive exclusion and birds at fruiting trees in western Colombia. *Auk* 83:479–480.

———. 1972a. Taxonomy, ecology, and behavior of the Sooty Ant-Tanager (*Habia gutturalis*) and other ant-tanagers (aves). *Am. Mus. Novit.* 2480:1–38.

———. 1972b. The behavior of Spotted Antbirds. *Am. Ornithol. Union Ornithol. Monogr.* 10.
———. 1976a. Effects of a cold wave on an Amazonian avifauna in the upper Paraguay drainage, western Mato Grosso, and suggestions on Oscine-Suboscine relationships. *Acta Amazonica* 6:379–394.
———. 1976b. Similarity of a tanager (*Orchesticus abeillei*) and an ovenbird (*Philydor rufus*): a possible case of mimicry. *Ciencia e Cultura* 28:1492–1493.
———. 1977. Lista preliminar das aves da parte noroeste e áreas vizinhas da Reserva Ducke, Amazonas, Brasil. *Rev. Bras. Biol.* 37:585–601.
———. 1979. The composition of avian communities in remanescent woodlots in southern Brazil. *Pap. Avulsos Zool.* (São Paulo) 33:1–25.
———. 1980. Ecological roles of migratory and resident birds on Barro Colorado Island, Panama. In *Migrant birds in the Neotropics: ecology, behavior, distribution, and conservation*, eds. A. Keast and E. S. Morton. Washington, D.C.: Smithsonian Institution Press.
Willis, E. O., and E. Eisenmann. 1979. A revised list of birds of Barro Colorado Island, Panama. *Smithson. Contrib. Zool.* 291:1–31.
Witt, H. 1978. Banding Orangequits (*Euneornis campestris*)—more than just tagging. *Broadsheet* 31:6–8. Jamaica, W.I.: Gosse Bird Club.
Wolf, L. L. 1976. Avifauna of the Cerro de la Muerte region, Costa Rica. *Am. Mus. Novit.* 2060:1–37.
Worth, C. B. 1939. Nesting of some Panamanian birds. *Auk* 56:306–310.
Wyatt, C. W. 1871. Notes on some of the birds of the United States of Columbia. *Ibis* 1:319–335.
Young, C. G. 1929. A contribution to the ornithology of the coastland of British Guiana, Part 3. *Ibis* 12th Ser. 5:221–261.
Zimmer, J. T. 1929a. A study of the Toothbilled Red Tanager, *Piranga flava*. *Field Mus. Nat. Hist. Publ. Zool. Ser.* 17:169–219.
———. 1929b. Variation and distribution in two species of *Diglossa*. *Auk* 46:21–37.
———. 1930. Birds of the Marshall Field Peruvian Expedition 1922–1923. *Field Mus. Nat. Hist. Publ. Zool. Ser.* 17:223–480.
———. 1942a. Studies of Peruvian birds. No. 43. Notes on the genera *Dacnis*, *Xenodacnis*, *Coereba*, *Conirostrum*, and *Oreomanes*. *Am. Mus. Novit.* 1193:1–16.
———. 1942b. Studies of Peruvian birds. No. 44. Notes on the genera *Diglossa* and *Cyanerpes*, with addenda to *Ochthoeca*. *Am. Mus. Novit.* 1203:1–7.
———. 1943a. Studies of Peruvian birds. No. 45. The genera *Tersina*, *Chlorophonia*, *Tanagra*, *Tanagrella*, *Chlorochrysa*, and *Pipraeidea*. *Am. Mus. Novit.* 1225:1–24.
———. 1943b. Studies of Peruvian birds. No. 46. The genus *Tangara*. Part 1. *Am. Mus. Novit.* 1245:1–14.
———. 1943c. Studies of Peruvian birds. No. 47. The genus *Tangara*. Part 2. *Am. Mus. Novit.* 1246:1–14.
———. 1944. Studies of Peruvian birds. No. 48. The genera *Iridisornis*, *Delothraupis*, *Anisognathus*, *Buthraupis*, *Compsocoma*, *Dubusia*, and *Thraupis*. *Am. Mus. Novit.* 1262:1–21.
———. 1945. Studies of Peruvian birds. No. 50. The genera *Ramphocelus*, *Piranga*, *Habia*, *Lanio*, and *Tachyphonus*. *Am. Mus. Novit.* 1304:1–26.
———. 1947a. Studies of Peruvian birds. No. 51. The genera *Chlorothraupis*, *Creurgops*, *Eucometis*, *Trichothraupis*, *Nemosia*, *Hemithraupis*, and *Thlypopsis*, with additional notes on *Piranga*. *Am. Mus. Novit.* 1345:1–23.
———. 1947b. Studies of Peruvian birds. No. 52. The genera *Sericossypha*, *Chlorospingus*, *Cnemoscopus*, *Hemispingus*, *Conothraupis*, *Chlorornis*, *Lamprospiza*, *Cissopis*, and *Schistochlamys*. *Am. Mus. Novit.* 1367:1–26.
Zimmerman, D. A. 1977. A sight record of the Magpie Tanager in Surinam. *Am. Birds* 31:233.
Zimmerman, D. A., and G. B. Harry. 1951. Summer birds of Autlan, Jalisco. *Wilson Bull.* 63:302–314.
Zotta, A. 1940. Notas ornitológicas. *Hornero* 7:359–365.

Index

Page numbers are systematically merged so that all references to a given tanager are listed under both the English and the scientific name in this index. Page numbers set in roman type locate the genus and species accounts. Italicized page numbers locate other references. The cross-reference "see" indicates use of variant nomenclature.

abbas, Thraupis, 182, 183, 190–192, Pl.15
abeillei, Orchesticus, 42–43, Pl.1
affinis, Euphonia, 222, 223, 226–227, *239,* Pl.20
albilatera, Diglossa, 350, 351, 363–364, Pl.31
albiventris, Dacnis, 327, 327–328, Pl.29
albocristata, Sericossypha, 30, 33, 56, 56–58, Pl.2
analis, Iridosornis, 214, 215, Pl.19
Anisognathus, 207, 212
  flavinuchus, 207, 210–211, Pl.18
  igniventris, 207, 209–210, Pl.18
  lacrymosus, 195, 207, 207–209, Pl.18
  melanogenys, see *207, 208–209,* Pl.18
  notabilis, 207, 212, Pl.18
anneae, Euphonia, 223, 224, 252, Pl.22
Antillean Euphonia, see *223, 243–245,* Pl.21
Ant-Tanager
  Black-cheeked, *138,* 144–145, Pl.11
  Crested, *138, 139,* 146–147, Pl.11
  Red-crowned, *33, 36, 138, 139,* 139–142, Pl.11
  Red-throated, *138,* 142–144, Pl.11
  Sooty, *138,* 145–146, Pl.11
arcaei, Buthraupis, 199, 199–200, Pl.16
argyrofenges, Tangara, 268, 271, 272, 322–323, Pl.28
Arnault's Tanager, see *271*
arthus, Tangara, 268, 270, 289–290, Pl.25
Ash-throated Bush-Tanager, see *70*
Ashy-throated Bush-Tanager, *59,* 70–71, Pl.4
atrimaxillaris, Habia, 138, 144–145, Pl.11
atropileus, Hemispingus, 72, 73–75, 77, Pl.4
aurantius, Lanio, 114, 117–118, Pl.8
aureata, Euphonia, see *223, 242–243,* Pl.21
aureocincta, Buthraupis, 199, 202–203, Pl.16
aureodorsalis, Buthraupis, 18, 199, 205, Pl.17
Azure-rumped Tanager, *268, 269,* 273–274, Pl.24
Azure-shouldered Tanager, *182, 186,* 188–190, Pl.15

Bangsia, see *198*
baritula, Diglossa, 38, 350, 351, 351–355, Pl.30

Bay-headed Tanager, *267, 268, 270,* 301–303, *303,* Pl.26
berlepschi, Dacnis, 327, 337, Pl.29
Beryl-spangled Tanager, *268, 271,* 319, Pl.27
bidentata, Piranga, 147, 148–149, Pl.12
Black-and-gold Tanager, *199,* 200–201, Pl.16
Black-and-white Tanager, *31, 50,* 50–51, Pl.1
Black-and-yellow Tanager, *95,* 95–96, Pl.6
Black-backed Tanager, *268, 271,* 306–308, *308,* Pl.26
Black-banded Tanager, see *316*
Black-bellied Tanager, see *171*
Black-capped
  Hemispingus, *72, 73*–75, 77, Pl.4
  Tanager, *268, 271, 272,* 321, Pl.28
Black-cheeked
  Ant-Tanager, *138,* 144–145, Pl.11
  Mountain-Tanager, see *208*
Black-chested Mountain-Tanager, *199,* 204, Pl.17
Black-chinned Mountain-Tanager, *207,* 212, Pl.18
Black-crowned Palm-Tanager, *100,* 100–101, *101,* Pl.7
Black-eared Hemispingus, *72, 73,* 78–79, Pl.5
Black-faced
  Dacnis, *327,* 328–330, Pl.29
  Tanager, *31, 32, 43, 44,* 45–46, Pl.1
Black Flowerpiercer, see *350, 358, 359,* Pl.31
Black-goggled Tanager, *32, 37, 136,* 136–138, Pl.10
Black-headed
  Hemispingus, *36, 72, 73,* 80–81, Pl.5
  Tanager, *268, 272,* 323–324, Pl.28
Black-legged Dacnis, *327,* 332-333, Pl.29
Black-throated
  Flowerpiercer, see *350*
  Shrike-Tanager, *114,* 117–118, Pl.8
Blue-and-black Tanager, *268, 271,* 320, Pl.27
Blue-and-gold Tanager, *199,* 199–200, Pl.16
Blue-and-yellow Tanager, *32, 178, 182, 183,* 195–197, Pl.16

Blue-backed Tanager, 197–198, Pl.16
Blue-browed Tanager, 268, 271, 312–313, Pl.27
Blue-capped Tanager, 182, 194–195, 208, Pl.16
Blue-crowned Chlorophonia, 258, 262–264, Pl.23
Blue Dacnis, 37, 327, 334–336, 337, Pl.29
Blue-gray Tanager, 30, 32, 36, 38, 182, 183, 183–185, 186, 192, Pl.15
Blue-hooded Euphonia, 32, 223, 224, 241–245, Pl.21
Blue-naped Chlorophonia, 32, 258, 259–260, Pl.23
Blue-necked Tanager, 268, 271, 313–314, Pl.27
Blue-whiskered Tanager, 268, 270, 285–286, Pl.25
Blue-winged Mountain-Tanager, 207, 210–211, Pl.18
Bluish Flowerpiercer, 350, 366, 367, Pl.32
bonariensis, Thraupis, 32, 178, 182, 183, 195–197, Pl.16
Brassy-breasted Tanager, 268, 269, 282–283, Pl.24
Brazilian
  Silverbeak, see 173
  Tanager, 166, 167, 169, 173–175, Pl.14
bresilius, Ramphocelus, 166, 167, 169, 173–175, Pl.14
Bronze-green Euphonia, 223, 224, 249–250, Pl.22
Brown-flanked Tanager, 84, 86–87, Pl.5
Brown Tanager, 42–43, Pl.1
brunneiventris, Diglossa, see 350, 358, 359-360, 361, Pl.31
Buff-bellied Tanager, 84, 88–89, Pl.6
Buff-breasted Mountain-Tanager, 218, 218–219, Pl.19
Burnished-buff Tanager, 268, 271, 304–306, Pl.26
Bush-Tanager
  Ash-throated, see 70
  Ashy-throated, 59, 70–71, Pl.4
  Common, 33, 59, 60, 60–63, 64, 65, 317, Pl.3
  Dark-breasted, see 68
  Dotted, 59, 60, 64–65, Pl.3
  Dusky, 59, 65–66, Pl.3
  Dusky-bellied, see 65
  Gray-hooded, 36, 71–72, Pl.4
  Pirre, 59, 64, 318, Pl.3
  Sooty-capped, 59, 60, 66, 66–67, Pl.3
  Tacarcuna, 59, 63–64, Pl.3
  Yellow-green, 59, 69–70, Pl.4
  Yellow-throated, 59, 60, 68–69, Pl.3
  Yellow-whiskered, 59, 60, 67–68, 68, Pl.3
  Zeledon's, 59, 60, 66, Pl.3
Buthraupis, 37, 38, 55, 197, 198–199, 206
  arcaei, 199, 199–200, Pl.16
  aureocincta, 199, 202–203, Pl.16
  aureodorsalis, 18, 199, 205, Pl.17

edwardsi, 199, 201–202, Pl.16
eximia, 199, 204, Pl.17
melanochlamys, 199, 200–201, Pl.16
montana, 38, 199, 203–204, Pl.17
rothschildi, 199, 201, Pl.16
wetmorei, 199, 206, Pl.17

cabanisi, Tangara, 268, 269, 273–274, Pl.24
caerulescens, Diglossa, 350, 366, 367, Pl.32
caeruleus, Cyanerpes, 340, 343–344, Pl.30
calliparaea, Chlorochrysa, 264, 265–266, Pl.23
callophrys
  Chlorophonia, see 258, 263–264, Pl.23
  Tangara, 268, 272, 327, Pl.28
  Hemispingus, see 72, 73, 74–75, Pl.4
Calochaetes, 165
  coccineus, 165–166, Pl.13
Calyptophilus, 102
  frugivorus, 37, 102, 102–103, Pl.7
  tertius, see 102
campestris, Euneornis, 369–370, Pl.32
canigularis, Chlorospingus, 59, 70–71, Pl.4
carbo, Ramphocelus, 38, 166, 169, 171, 171–173, Pl.14
carbonaria, Diglossa, 33, 350, 351, 356, 358-362, Pl.31
Carbonated Flowerpiercer, 33, 350, 351, 356, 358-362, Pl.31
carmioli, Chlorothraupis, 107, 107–108, Pl.7
Carmiol's Tanager, see 107
cassinii, Mitrospingus, 33, 38, 105, 105–106, Pl.7
castaneoventris, Delothraupis, 218, 219–220, Pl.19
cayana
  Dacnis, 37, 327, 334–336, 337, Pl.29
  Tangara, 268, 271, 304–306, Pl.26
cayennensis, Euphonia, 223, 224, 256–257, Pl.22
chalybea, Euphonia, 223, 224, 239–241, Pl.21
Chat Tanager, 37, 102, 102–103, Pl.7
Cherry-throated Tanager, 97, 99, Pl.6
Chestnut-backed Tanager, 268, 271, 306, 307, 308–309, Pl.26
Chestnut-bellied
  Euphonia, 223, 224, 256–257, Pl.22
  Flowerpiercer, see 350, 355, 356, Pl.31
  Mountain-Tanager, 218, 219–220, Pl.19
Chestnut-breasted Chlorophonia, 258, 259, 261–262, Pl.23
Chestnut-headed Tanager, 83–84, Pl.5
chilensis, Tangara, 268, 269, 277–279, Pl.24
chloricterus, Orthogonys, 37, 110, 110–111, Pl.7
Chlorochrysa, 264
  calliparaea, 264, 265–266, Pl.23
  nitidissima, 264, 266–267, Pl.23
  phoenicotis, 264, 265, Pl.23
Chlorophanes, 34, 35, 337
  purpurascens, see 337
  spiza, 264, 337–340, Pl.30

Chlorophonia
  Blue-crowned, *258*, 262–264, Pl.23
  Blue-naped, *32*, *258*, 259–260, Pl.23
  Chestnut-breasted, *258*, *259*, 261–262, Pl.23
  Golden-browed, see *258, 263–264*, Pl.23
  Yellow-collared, *258*, *259*, 259, Pl.23
Chlorophonia, *35*, *39*, *222*, 258–259
  callophrys, see *258, 263–264*, Pl.23
  cyanea, *32*, *258*, 259–260, Pl.23
  flavirostris, *258*, *259*, 259, Pl.23
  occipitalis, *258*, 262–264, Pl.23
  pyrrhophrys, *258*, *259*, 261–262, Pl.23
Chlorornis, 54–55
  riefferii, *54*, 55, Pl.2
Chlorospingus, *33*, *37*, *39*, *58*, 58–60, *70*, *71*, *200*
  canigularis, *59*, 70–71, Pl.4
  flavigularis, *59*, *60*, 68–69, Pl.3
  flavovirens, *59*, 69–70, Pl.4
  inornatus, *59*, *64*, *318*, Pl.3
  ophthalmicus, *33*, *59*, *60*, 60–63, *64*, *65*, *317*, Pl.3
  parvirostris, *59*, *60*, 67-68, *68*, Pl.3
  pileatus, *59*, *60*, *66*, 66–67, Pl.3
  punctulatus, *59*, *60*, 64–65, Pl.3
  semifuscus, *59*, 65–66, Pl.3
  tacarcunae, *59*, 63–64, Pl.3
  zeledoni, *59*, *60*, 66, Pl.3
Chlorothraupis, *30*, *31*, *37*, *107*, *110*, *197*
  carmioli, *107*, 107–108, Pl.7
  olivacea, *107*, 109, Pl.7
  stolzmanni, *107*, 109–110, Pl.7
chlorotica, *Euphonia*, *222*, *223*, 229–230, Pl.20
chrysomelas, *Chrysothlypis*, *95*, 95–96, Pl.6
chrysopasta, *Euphonia*, *223*, *224*, 247–249, Pl.22
Chrysothlypis, *37*, 95
  chrysomelas, *95*, 95–96, Pl.6
  salmoni, *95*, 96–97, Pl.6
chrysotis, *Tangara*, *268*, *270*, 292–293, Pl.25
Cinnamon-bellied Flowerpiercer, see *350*, *352*, Pl.30
Cinnamon Tanager, 43–44, Pl.1
Cissopis, 51
  leveriana, *30*, 53–54, Pl.2
Cnemoscopus, 71
  rubrirostris, *36*, 71–72, Pl.4
coccineus, *Calochaetes*, 165–166, Pl.13
Common
  Bush-Tanager, *33*, *59*, *60*, 60–63, *64*, *65*, *317*, Pl.3
  Silverbeak, see *171*
Compsocoma, see *207*
Compsothraupis, 56
  loricata, *56*, 56, Pl.2
concinna, *Euphonia*, *223*, 232, Pl.20
Cone-billed Tanager, *50*, 51, Pl.1
Conebill, Giant, *348*, 348–350, Pl.30
Conothraupis, 50
  mesoleuca, *50*, 51, Pl.1

speculigera, *31*, *50*, 50–51, Pl.1
coronatus, *Tachyphonus*, *38*, *122*, *123*, 131–132, Pl.10
Crested Ant-Tanager, *138*, *139*, 146–147, Pl.11
Creurgops, *31*, *36*, *42*, 119
  dentata, *119*, 120, Pl.9
  verticalis, *119*, 119–120, Pl.9
Crimson-backed
  Silverbeak, see *168*
  Tanager, *166*, 168–170, Pl.14
Crimson-collared Tanager, *166*, 167, Pl.13
cristata, *Habia*, *138*, *139*, 146–147, Pl.11
cristatus, *Tachyphonus*, *122*, 123–125, Pl.9
cucullata, *Tangara*, *267*, *268*, 270, 306, Pl.26
cyanea
  Chlorophonia, *32*, *258*, 259–260, Pl.23
  Diglossa, *350*, *366*, *367*, 368–369, Pl.32
Cyanerpes, *31*, *35*, *36*, 340
  caeruleus, *340*, 343–344, Pl.30
  cyaneus, *337*, *340*, *342*, 344–347, Pl.30
  lucidus, *340*, 342–343, Pl.30
  nitidus, *30*, *340*, 340–341, Pl.30
cyaneus, *Cyanerpes*, *337*, *340*, *342*, 344–347, Pl.30
cyanicollis, *Tangara*, *268*, *271*, 313–314, Pl.27
Cyanicterus, 197
  cyanicterus, 197–198, Pl.16
cyanicterus, *Cyanicterus*, 197–198, Pl.16
cyanocephala
  Tangara, *268*, *269*, 282–283, Pl.24
  Thraupis, *182*, 194–195, *208*, Pl.16
cyanoptera
  Tangara, *268*, *272*, 323–324, Pl.28
  Thraupis, *182*, *186*, 188–190, Pl.15
cyanotis, *Tangara*, *268*, *271*, 312–313, Pl.27
cyanoventris, *Tangara*, *268*, *269*, 283–285, Pl.24
Cypsnagra, *37*, 46
  hirundinacea, *46*, 48–49, Pl.1

Dacnis
  Black-faced, *327*, 328–330, Pl.29
  Black-legged, *327*, 332–333, Pl.29
  Blue, *37*, *327*, 334–336, *337*, Pl.29
  Scarlet-breasted, *327*, *337*, Pl.29
  Scarlet-thighed, *327*, 332–334, Pl.29
  Tit-like, 347–348, Pl.30
  Turquoise, *327*, 331–332, Pl.29
  Viridian, *327*, 336–337, Pl.29
  White-bellied, *327*, 327–328, Pl.29
  Yellow-bellied, *327*, 330–331, Pl.29
Dacnis, *35*, 327
  albiventris, *327*, 327–328, Pl.29
  berlepschi, *327*, *337*, Pl.29
  cayana, *37*, *327*, 334–336, *337*, Pl.29
  flaviventer, *327*, 330–331, Pl.29
  hartlaubi, *327*, 331–332, Pl.29
  lineata, *327*, 328–330, Pl.29
  nigripes, *327*, 332–333, Pl.29
  venusta, *327*, 332–334, Pl.29
  viguieri, *327*, 336–337, Pl.29

Dacnis-Tanager, Turquoise, see *331*
Dark-breasted Bush-Tanager, see *68*
Deep-blue Flowerpiercer, *350, 365*, 366, Pl.32
delatrii, Tachyphonus, 107, 122, 123, 130–131, Pl.10
Delothraupis, 218
  castaneoventris, 218, 219–220, Pl.19
dentata, Creurgops, 119, 120, Pl.9
desmaresti, Tangara, 268, 269, 282–283, Pl.24
diadematus, Stephanophorus, 212–214, Pl.18
Diademed Tanager, 212–214, Pl.18
Diglossa, 19, 31, 34, 38, 86, 350–351, *355, 359, 360*
  albilatera, 350, 351, 363–364, Pl.31
  baritula, 38, 350, 351, 351–355, Pl.30
  brunneiventris, see *350, 358,* 359–360, *361,* Pl.31
  caerulescens, 350, 366, 367, Pl.32
  carbonaria, 33, 350, 351, 356, 358–362, Pl.31
  cyanea, 350, 366, 367, 368–369, Pl.32
  duidae, 350, 351, 364, Pl.31
  glauca, 350, 365, 366, Pl.32
  gloriosa, see *350, 358, 362,* Pl.31
  gloriosissima, see *350, 355, 356,* Pl.31
  humeralis, see *350, 358–359,* Pl.31
  indigotiça, 350, 365, Pl.32
  lafresnayii, 33, 350, 351, 354–358, Pl.31
  major, 350, 351, 364–365, Pl.31
  mystacalis, see *350, 355,* 357–358, Pl.31
  plumbea, see *350,* 353–354, Pl.30
  sittoides, see *350, 354,* Pl.30
  venezuelensis, 350, 351, 362–363, Pl.31
dimidiatus, Ramphocelus, 166, 168–170, Pl.14
dominicensis, Spindalis, see *179, 180,* Pl.15
Dotted
  Bush-Tanager, *59, 60,* 64–65, Pl.3
  Tanager, *268, 270,* 299–300, Pl.25
dowii, Tangara, 18, 268, 271, 316–319, Pl.27
Drab Hemispingus, *36, 72, 73, 76,* 81–82, Pl.5
Dubusia, 218, *220*
  taeniata, 218, 218–219, Pl.19
duidae, Diglossa, 350, 351, 364, Pl.31
Dusky-bellied Bush-Tanager, see *65*
Dusky Bush-Tanager, *59,* 65–66, Pl.3
Dusky-faced Tanager, *33, 38, 105,* 105–106, Pl.7

Eastern
  Chat Tanager, see *102*
  Stripe-headed Tanager, see *179, 180,* Pl.15
edwardsi, Buthraupis, 199, 201–202, Pl.16
elegantissima, Euphonia, see *223,* 241–242, Pl.21
Emerald Tanager, *268, 270,* 287–289, Pl.25
episcopus, Thraupis, 30, 32, 36, 38, 182, 183, 183–185, *186, 192,* Pl.15

erythrocephala, Piranga, 147, 164, Pl.13
Erythrothlypis, see *95*
Eucometis, 112, *136*
  penicillata, 37, 112–114, Pl.8
Euneornis, 369
  campestris, 369–370, Pl.32
Euphonia
  Antillean, see *223, 243–245,* Pl.21
  Blue-hooded, *32, 223, 224,* 241–245, Pl.21
  Bronze-green, *223, 224,* 249–250, Pl.22
  Chestnut-bellied, *223, 224,* 256–257, Pl.22
  Finsch's, *223,* 233, Pl.20
  Fulvous-vented, *222, 223, 224,* 245–246, Pl.21
  Golden-bellied, see *247*
  Golden-rumped, see *223, 242–243,* Pl.21
  Golden-sided, *223, 224,* 256–257, Pl.22
  Green-chinned, *223, 224,* 239–241, Pl.21
  Green-throated, see *239*
  Jamaican, *222, 223,* 224–225, Pl.20
  Olive-backed, *223, 224, 247, 249,* Pl.21
  Orange-bellied, *222, 223, 224,* 252–254, Pl.22
  Orange-crowned, *223,* 232–233, Pl.20
  Plumbeous, *30, 222, 223,* 225–226, Pl.20
  Purple-throated, *222, 223,* 229–230, Pl.20
  Rufous-bellied, *223, 224,* 254–256, Pl.22
  Scrub, *222, 223,* 226–227, *239,* Pl.20
  Spot-crowned, *223, 224,* 246, Pl.21
  Tawny-capped, *223, 224,* 252, Pl.22
  Thick-billed, *223, 233,* 236–238, *239,* Pl.21
  Trinidad, *222, 223, 225, 229,* 230–232, *233,* Pl.20
  Velvet-fronted, *223,* 232, Pl.20
  Violaceous, *222, 223, 224,* 233–236, *239,* Pl.21
  White-lored, *223, 224,* 247–249, Pl.22
  White-vented, *223, 224,* 250–252, Pl.22
  Yellow-crowned, *222, 223,* 228–229, Pl.20
  Yellow-throated, *223, 224, 227,* 238–239, Pl.21
Euphonia, 19, 30, 35, 36, 37, 39, 220, 222–224, 225, 229, 237, 250, 254, 258
  affinis, 223, 226–227, *239,* Pl.20
  anneae, 223, 224, 252, Pl.22
  aureata, see *223, 242–243,* Pl.21
  cayennensis, 223, 224, 256–257, Pl.22
  chalybea, 223, 224, 239–241, Pl.21
  chlorotica, 222, 223, 229–230, Pl.20
  chrysopasta, 223, 224, 247–249, Pl.22
  concinna, 223, 232, Pl.20
  elegantissima, see *223,* 241–242, Pl.21
  finschi, 223, 233, Pl.20
  fulvicrissa, 222, 223, 224, 245–246, Pl.21
  gouldi, 223, 224, 247, 249, Pl.21
  hirundinacea, 223, 224, 227, 238–239, Pl.21

imitans, *223, 224*, 246, Pl.21
jamaica, *222, 223*, 224–225, Pl.20
laniirostris, *223, 233*, 236–238, *239*, Pl.21
luteicapilla, *222, 223*, 228–229, Pl.20
mesochrysa, *223, 224*, 249–250, Pl.22
minuta, *223, 224*, 250–252, Pl.22
musica, *32, 223, 224*, 241–245, Pl.21
pectoralis, *223, 224*, 256–257, Pl.22
plumbea, *30, 222, 223*, 225–226, Pl.20
rufiventris, *223, 224*, 254–256, Pl.22
saturata, *223*, 232–233, Pl.20
trinitatis, *222, 223, 225, 229*, 230–232, *233*, Pl.20
violacea, *222, 223, 224*, 233–236, *239*, Pl.21
xanthogaster, *222, 223, 224*, 252–254, Pl.22
eximia, Buthraupis, *199*, 204, Pl.17

fasciata, Neothraupis, *46*, 46–48, Pl.1
fastuosa, Tangara, 268, 269, 279–280, Pl.24
Fawn-breasted Tanager, *32, 220*, 220–222, Pl.19
Finsch's Euphonia, *223*, 233, Pl.20
finschi, Euphonia, *223*, 233, Pl.20
Flame-colored Tanager, *147*, 148–149, Pl.12
Flame-crested Tanager, *122*, 123–125, Pl.9
Flame-faced Tanager, *165, 268, 270*, 293–294, Pl.25
Flame-rumped
 Silverbeak, see *178*
 Tanager, *166*, 176–178, Pl.14
flammigerus, Ramphocelus, *166*, 176–178, Pl.14
flava, Piranga, 147, 148, 149–154, Pl.12
flavicollis, Hemithraupis, *90*, 93–95, Pl.6
flavigularis, Chlorospingus, *59, 60*, 68–69, Pl.3
flavinuchus, Anisognathus, 207, 210–211, Pl.18
flavirostris, Chlorophonia, 258, 259, 259, Pl.23
flaviventer, Dacnis, 327, 330–331, Pl.29
flavovirens, Chlorospingus, 59, 69–70, Pl.4
florida, Tangara, 268, 270, 287–289, Pl.25
Flowerpiercer
 Black, see *350, 358–359*, Pl.31
 Black-throated, see *350, 358, 359–360, 361*, Pl.31
 Bluish, *350, 366*, 367, Pl.32
 Carbonated, *33, 350, 351, 356*, 358–362, Pl.31
 Cinnamon-bellied, see *350, 352*, Pl.30
 Chestnut-bellied, see *350, 355, 356*, Pl.31
 Deep-blue, *350, 365*, 366, Pl.32
 Glossy, *33, 350, 351*, 354–358, Pl.31
 Gray-bellied, see *350, 360*, Pl.31
 Greater, *350, 351*, 364–365, Pl.31
 Indigo, *350*, 365, Pl.32
 Masked, *350, 366, 367*, 368–369, Pl.32
 Merida, see *350, 358, 362*, Pl.31
 Moustached, see *350, 355, 357–358*, Pl.31
 Rusty, see *350, 354*, Pl.30
 Scaled, *350, 351*, 364, Pl.31
 Slaty, *38, 350, 351*, 351–355, Pl.30
 Venezuelan, *350, 351*, 362–363, Pl.31
 White-sided, *350, 351*, 363–364, Pl.31
fraseri, Oreomanes, 348, 348–350, Pl.30
frontalis, Hemispingus, 72, 73, 77–78, Pl.4
frugivorus, Calyptophilus, 37, 102, 102–103, Pl.7
fucosa, Tangara, see *18, 268, 318–319*, Pl.27
fulviceps, Thlypopsis, 84, 84–85, Pl.5
fulvicrissa, Euphonia, 222, 223, 224, 245–246, Pl.21
Fulvous-crested Tanager, *122, 123*, 126–128, Pl.9
Fulvous-headed Tanager, *84*, 84–85, Pl.5
Fulvous Shrike-Tanager, *114*, 115–116, Pl.8
Fulvous-vented Euphonia, *222, 223, 224*, 245–246, Pl.21
fulvus, Lanio, 114, 115–116, Pl.8
fuscicauda, Habia, 138, 142–144, Pl.11

Giant Conebill, *348*, 348–350, Pl.30
Gilt-edged Tanager, *268, 269*, 283–285, Pl.24
glauca, Diglossa, 350, 365, 366, Pl.32
glaucocolpa, Thraupis, see *182, 186, 188*, Pl.15
Glaucous Tanager, see *182, 186, 188*, Pl.15
Glistening-green Tanager, *264*, 265, Pl.23
gloriosa, Diglossa, see *350, 358, 362*, Pl.31
gloriosissima, Diglossa, see *350, 355, 356*, Pl.31
Glossy Flowerpiercer, *33, 350, 351*, 354–358, Pl.31
goeringi, Hemispingus, 72, 79, Pl.5
Golden-backed Mountain-Tanager, *18, 199*, 205, Pl.17
Golden-bellied Euphonia, see *247*
Golden-browed Chlorophonia, see *258, 263–264*, Pl.23
Golden-chested Tanager, *199*, 201, Pl.16
Golden-chevroned Tanager, *182, 189*, 190–191, Pl.15
Golden-collared
 Honeycreeper, *268, 272*, 324, Pl.28
 Tanager, *214*, 215–216, Pl.19
Golden-crowned Tanager, *214*, 216–218, Pl.19
Golden-eared Tanager, *268, 270*, 292–293, Pl.25
Golden-hooded Tanager, *268, 271*, 314–316, Pl.27
Golden-masked Tanager, see *314*
Golden-naped Tanager, *268, 271*, 310–311, Pl.27
Golden-rumped Euphonia, see *223, 242–243*, Pl.21
Golden-sided Euphonia, *223, 224*, 256–257, Pl.22
Golden Tanager, *268, 270*, 289–290, Pl.25
Gold-ringed Tanager, *199*, 202–203, Pl.16
gouldi, Euphonia, 223, 224, 247, 249, Pl.21

Grass-green Tanager, *54*, 55, Pl.2
Gray-and-gold Tanager, *268*, *269*, 274–275, Pl.24
Gray-bellied Flowerpiercer, see *350*, *360*, Pl.31
Gray-capped Hemispingus, *72*, 77, Pl.4
Gray-crowned Palm-Tanager, 101–102, Pl.7
Gray-headed Tanager, *37*, 112–114, Pl.8
Gray-hooded Bush-Tanager, *36*, 71–72, Pl.4
Greater Flowerpiercer, *350*, *351*, 364–365, Pl.31
Green-and-gold Tanager, *268*, *270*, 286–287, Pl.25
Green-capped Tanager, *18*, *268*, *271*, 373, Pl.32
Green-chinned Euphonia, *223*, *224*, 239–241, Pl.21
Green-headed Tanager, *268*, *269*, 280–281, Pl.24
Green Honeycreeper, *264*, 337–340, Pl.30
Green-naped Tanager, see *18*, *268*, *318–319*, Pl.27
Green-throated
  Euphonia, see *239*
  Tanager, see *322*
guira, *Hemithraupis*, *36*, *90*, 90–92, *92*, Pl.6
Guira Tanager, *36*, *90*, 90–92, *92*, Pl.6
guttata, *Tangara*, *267*, *268*, *270*, 297–299, Pl.25
gutturalis, *Habia*, *138*, 145–146, Pl.11
gyrola, *Tangara*, *267*, *268*, *270*, 301–303, *303*, Pl.26

Habia, *31*, *33*, *37*, *38*, *39*, *107*, *136*, 138–139
  atrimaxillaris, *138*, 144–145, Pl.11
  cristata, *138*, *139*, 146–147, Pl.11
  fuscicauda, *138*, 142–144, Pl.11
  gutturalis, *138*, 145–146, Pl.11
  rubica, *33*, *36*, *138*, *139*, 139–142, Pl.11
hartlaubi, *Dacnis*, *327*, 331–332, Pl.29
heinei, *Tangara*, *268*, *271*, *272*, 321, Pl.28
Hemispingus
  Black-capped, *72*, 73–75, 77, Pl.4
  Black-eared, *72*, *73*, 78–79, Pl.5
  Black-headed, *36*, *72*, *73*, 80–81, Pl.5
  Drab, *36*, *72*, *73*, *76*, 81–82, Pl.5
  Gray-capped, *72*, 77, Pl.4
  Oleaginous, *72*, *73*, 77–78, Pl.4
  Orange-browed, see *72*, *73*, *74–75*, Pl.4
  Parodi's, *18*, *72*, *73*, 75, Pl.4
  Rufous-browed, *18*, *72*, *73*, 79–80, Pl.5
  Slaty-backed, *72*, 79, Pl.5
  Superciliaried, *72*, 75–76, Pl.4
  Three-striped, *72*, 82–83, Pl.5
Hemispingus, *30*, *35*, *38*, *71*, 72–73, *80*
  atropileus, *72*, 73–75, 77, Pl.4
  calophrys, see *72*, *73*, *74–75*, Pl.4
  frontalis, *72*, *73*, 77–78, Pl.4
  goeringi, *72*, 79, Pl.5
  melanotis, *72*, *73*, 78–79, Pl.5
  parodii, *18*, *72*, *73*, 75, Pl.4

reyi, *72*, 77, Pl.4
rufosuperciliaris, *18*, *72*, *73*, 79–80, Pl.5
superciliaris, *72*, 75–76, Pl.4
trifasciatus, *72*, 82–83, Pl.5
verticalis, *36*, *72*, *73*, 80–81, Pl.5
xanthophthalmus, *36*, *72*, *73*, *76*, 81–82, Pl.5
Hemithraupis, *90*, *95*
  flavicollis, *90*, 93–95, Pl.6
  guira, *36*, *90*, 90–92, *92*, Pl.6
  ruficapilla, *90*, 92, Pl.6
hepatica, *Piranga*, see *147*, *149–150*, Pl.12
Hepatic Tanager, *147*, *148*, 149–154, Pl.12
Hepatic-Tanager
  Highland, see *147*, *149*, *150–152*, Pl.12
  Lowland, see *147*, *149*, *152–154*, Pl.12
  Northern, see *147*, *149*, *149–150*, Pl.12
Heterospingus, 120
  rubrifrons, see *120*, *121*, Pl.9
  xanthopygius, *120*, 121–122, Pl.9
Highland Hepatic-Tanager, see *147*, *149*, *150–152*, Pl.12
hirundinacea
  Cypsnagra, *46*, 48–49, Pl.1
  Euphonia, *223*, *224*, *227*, 238–239, Pl.21
Honeycreeper
  Golden-collared, *268*, *272*, 324, Pl.28
  Green, *264*, 337–340, Pl.30
  Purple, *340*, 343–344, Pl.30
  Red-legged, *337*, *340*, *342*, 344–347, Pl.30
  Shining, *340*, 342–343, Pl.30
  Short-billed, *30*, *340*, 340–341, Pl.30
Hooded
  Mountain-Tanager, *38*, *199*, 203–204, Pl.17
  Tanager (*Nemosia pileata*), *97*, 97–98, Pl.6
  Tanager (*Tangara cucullata*), see *306*
Huallaga
  Silverbeak, see *171*
  Tanager, *166*, 171, Pl.14
humeralis, *Diglossa*, see *350*, *358*, *359*, Pl.31

icterocephala, *Tangara*, *268*, *269*, *270*, *288*, 290–291, Pl.25
icteronotus, *Ramphocelus*, see *166*, *176–178*, Pl.14
igniventris, *Anisognathus*, *207*, 209–210, Pl.18
imitans, *Euphonia*, *223*, *224*, 246, Pl.21
Indigo Flowerpiercer, *350*, 365, Pl.32
indigotica, *Diglossa*, *350*, 365, Pl.32
inornata
  Tangara, *268*, *269*, *272–273*, Pl.24
  Thlypopsis, *84*, 88–89, Pl.6
inornatus, *Chlorospingus*, *59*, 64, *318*, Pl.3
Iridophanes, see *272*, *324*
Iridosornis, *37*, 214
  analis, *214*, 215, Pl.19
  jelskii, *214*, 215–216, Pl.19
  porphyrocephala, *214*, 214–215, Pl.19

reinhardti, see *214, 216, 217–218*, Pl.19
rufivertex, *214*, 216–218, Pl.19

jamaica, *Euphonia*, *222, 223*, 224–225, Pl.20
Jamaican
  Euphonia, *222, 223*, 224–225, Pl.20
  Stripe-headed Tanager, see *179, 181, 182*, Pl.15
jelskii, *Iridosornis*, *214*, 215–216, Pl.19
johannae, *Tangara*, *268, 270*, 285–286, Pl.25

labradorides, *Tangara*, *268, 271*, 311–312, Pl.27
Lacrimose Mountain-Tanager, *195, 207*, 207–209, Pl.18
lacrymosus, *Anisognathus*, *195, 207*, 207–209, Pl.18
lafresnayii, *Diglossa*, *33, 350, 351*, 354–358, Pl.31
Lamprospiza, 51
  melanoleuca, 51–53, Pl.2
laniirostris, *Euphonia*, *223, 233*, 236–238, *239*, Pl.21
Lanio, *31, 37*, 114, *117*
  aurantius, *114*, 117–118, Pl.8
  fulvus, *114*, 115–116, Pl.8
  leucothorax, *114*, 118–119, Pl.8
  versicolor, *114*, 116–117, Pl.8
larvata, *Tangara*, *268, 271*, 314–316, Pl.27
lavinia, *Tangara*, *268, 270*, 303–304, Pl.26
Lemon-browed Tanager, see *109*
Lemon-rumped
  Silverbeak, see *176*
  Tanager, *166*, 176–178, Pl.14
Lemon-spectacled Tanager, *107*, 109, Pl.7
Lesser Antillean Tanager, *267, 268, 270*, 306, Pl.26
leucoptera, *Piranga*, *36, 147*, 162–164, *198*, Pl.13
leucothorax, *Lanio*, *114*, 118–119, Pl.8
leveriana, *Cissopis*, *30*, 53–54, Pl.2
lineata, *Dacnis*, *327*, 328–330, Pl.29
loricata
  Compsothraupis, *56*, 56, Pl.2
  Sericossypha, see *56*
Lowland Hepatic-Tanager, see *147, 149, 152–154*, Pl.12
lucidus, *Cyanerpes*, *340*, 342–343, Pl.30
luctuosus, *Tachyphonus*, *36, 122*, 128–130, Pl.10
ludoviciana, *Piranga*, *147, 148*, 159–162, Pl.13
lutea, *Piranga*, see *147, 149, 150–152*, Pl.12
luteicapilla, *Euphonia*, *222, 223*, 228–229, Pl.20

Magpie Tanager, *30*, 53–54, Pl.2
major, *Diglossa*, *350, 351*, 364–365, Pl.31

Masked
  Flowerpiercer, *350, 366, 367*, 368–369, Pl.32
  Mountain-Tanager, *199*, 206, Pl.17
  Tanager, *268, 271*, 316, Pl.27
Masked Crimson
  Silverbeak, see *168*
  Tanager, *36, 166, 167*, 168–169, Pl.13
melanochlamys, *Buthraupis*, *199*, 200–201, Pl.16
melanogaster, *Ramphocelus*, *166*, 171, Pl.14
melanogenys, *Anisognathus*, see *207, 208–209*, Pl.18
melanoleuca, *Lamprospiza*, 51–53, Pl.2
melanonota, *Pipraeidea*, *32, 220*, 220–222, Pl.19
melanopis, *Schistochlamys*, *31, 32, 43, 44*, 45–46, Pl.1
melanops, *Trichothraupis*, *32, 37, 136*, 136–138, Pl.10
melanotis, *Hemispingus*, *72, 73*, 78–79, Pl.5
Merida Flowerpiercer, see *350, 358, 362*, Pl.31
mesochrysa, *Euphonia*, *223, 224*, 249–250, Pl.22
mesoleuca, *Conothraupis*, *50*, 51, Pl.1
Metallic-green Tanager, *268, 271*, 311–312, Pl.27
mexicana, *Tangara*, *33, 268, 269*, 275–277, *327*, Pl.24
meyerdeschauenseei, *Tangara*, *18, 268, 271*, 373, Pl.32
minuta, *Euphonia*, *223, 224*, 250–252, Pl.22
Mitrospingus, 105
  cassinii, *33, 38, 105*, 105–106, Pl.7
  oleagineus, *105*, 106–107, Pl.7
montana, *Buthraupis*, *38, 199*, 203–204, Pl.17
Moss-backed Tanager, *199*, 201–202, Pl.16
Mountain-Tanager
  Black-cheeked, see *208*
  Black-chested, *199*, 204, Pl.17
  Black-chinned, *207*, 212, Pl.18
  Blue-winged, *207*, 210–211, Pl.18
  Buff-breasted, *218*, 218–219, Pl.19
  Chestnut-bellied, *218*, 219–220, Pl.19
  Golden-backed, *18, 199*, 205, Pl.17
  Hooded, *38, 199*, 203–204, Pl.17
  Lacrimose, *195, 207*, 207–209, Pl.18
  Masked, *199*, 206, Pl.17
  Santa Marta, see *207, 208–209*, Pl.18
  Scarlet-bellied, *207*, 209–210, Pl.18
Moustached Flowerpiercer, see *350, 355, 357–358*, Pl.31
Multicolored Tanager, *264*, 266–267, Pl.23
musica, *Euphonia*, *32, 223, 224*, 241–245, Pl.21
mystacalis, *Diglossa*, see *350, 355, 357–358*, Pl.31

nattereri, *Tachyphonus*, see *122, 123, 125*, Pl.9
Natterer's Tanager, see *122, 123, 125*, Pl.9

Nemosia, 97
  pileata, *97*, 97–98, Pl.6
  rourei, *97*, 99, Pl.6
Neothraupis, 46
  fasciata, *46*, 46–48, Pl.1
Nephelornis, 372
  oneilli, *18*, 372–373, Pl.32
Nesospingus, 58
  speculiferus, 58–59, Pl.3
nigricephala, *Spindalis*, see *179, 181, 182*, Pl.15
nigripes, *Dacnis*, *327*, 332–333, Pl.29
nigrocincta, *Tangara*, *268, 271*, 316, Pl.27
nigrogularis, *Ramphocelus*, *36, 166, 167*, 168–169, Pl.13
nigroviridis, *Tangara*, *268, 271*, 319, Pl.27
nitidissima, *Chlorochrysa*, *264*, 266–267, Pl.23
nitidus, *Cyanerpes*, *30, 340*, 340–341, Pl.30
Northern Hepatic-Tanager, see *147, 149–150*, Pl.12
notabilis, *Anisognathus*, *207*, 212, Pl.18

occipitalis, *Chlorophonia*, *258*, 262–264, Pl.23
Ochre-breasted Tanager, *107*, 109–110, Pl.7
oleagineus, *Mitrospingus*, *105*, 106–107, Pl.7
Oleaginous Hemispingus, *72, 73*, 77–78, Pl.4
olivacea
  Chlorothraupis, *107*, 109, Pl.7
  Piranga, *38, 147, 148, 154*, 157–159, *161*, Pl.12
Olive-backed
  Euphonia, *223, 224, 247, 249*, Pl.21
  Tanager, *105*, 106–107, Pl.7
Olive-green Tanager, *37, 110*, 110–111, Pl.7
Olive Tanager, *107*, 107–108, Pl.7
oneilli, *Nephelornis*, *18*, 372–373, Pl.32
Opal-crowned Tanager, *268, 272, 327*, Pl.28
Opal-rumped Tanager, *268, 272*, 325–327, Pl.28
ophthalmicus, *Chlorospingus*, *33, 59, 60*, 60–63, *64, 65, 317*, Pl.3
Orange-bellied Euphonia, *222, 223, 224*, 252–254, Pl.22
Orange-browed Hemispingus, see *72, 73*, 74–75, Pl.4
Orange-crowned Euphonia, *223*, 232–233, Pl.20
Orange-eared Tanager, *264*, 265–266, Pl.23
Orange-headed Tanager, *84*, 87–88, *90*, Pl.5
Orangequit, 369–370, Pl.32
Orange-throated Tanager, 206–207, Pl.17
Orchesticus, 42
  abeillei, 42–43, Pl.1
Oreomanes, 348
  fraseri, *348*, 348–350, Pl.30
ornata
  Thlypopsis, *84*, 85–86, *86*, Pl.5
  Thraupis, *182, 189*, 190–191, Pl.15

Orthogonys, 110
  chloricterus, *37, 110*, 110–111, Pl.7

palmarum
  Phaenicophilus, *100*, 100–101, *101*, Pl.7
  Thraupis, *32, 36, 38, 39, 182, 183*, 192–194, *306*, Pl.15
palmeri, *Tangara*, *268, 269*, 274–275, Pl.24
Palm Tanager, *32, 36, 38, 39, 182, 183*, 192–194, *306*, Pl.15
Palm-Tanager
  Black-crowned, *100*, 100-101, *101*, Pl.7
  Gray-crowned, 101–102, Pl.7
Paradise Tanager, *268, 269*, 277–279, Pl.24
Pardusco, *18*, 372–373, Pl.32
parina, *Xenodacnis*, 347–348, Pl.30
parodii, *Hemispingus*, *18, 72, 73*, 75, Pl.4
Parodi's Hemispingus, *18, 72, 73*, 75, Pl.4
parvirostris, *Chlorospingus*, *59, 60*, 67–68, *68*, Pl.3
parzudakii, *Tangara*, *165, 268, 270*, 293–294, Pl.25
passerinii, *Ramphocelus*, *166, 167*, 175–176, Pl.14
pectoralis
  Euphonia, *223, 224*, 256–257, Pl.22
  Thlypopsis, *84*, 86–87, Pl.5
penicillata, *Eucometis*, *37*, 112–114, Pl.8
peruviana, *Tangara*, *268, 271*, 306–308, *308*, Pl.26
Phaenicophilus, 100
  palmarum, *100*, 100–101, *101*, Pl.7
  poliocephalus, 101–102, Pl.7
Phlogothraupis, see *167*
phoenicius, *Tachyphonus*, *122, 123*, 135, Pl.10
phoenicotis, *Chlorochrysa*, *264*, 265, Pl.23
pileata, *Nemosia*, *97*, 97–98, Pl.6
pileatus, *Chlorospingus*, *59, 60, 66*, 66–67, Pl.3
Pipraeidea, 220
  melanonota, *32, 220*, 220–222, Pl.19
Piranga, *20, 31, 33, 36, 37*, 147–148, *165, 185, 213*
  bidentata, *147*, 148–149, Pl.12
  erythrocephala, *147*, 164, Pl.13
  flava, *147, 148*, 149–154, Pl.12
  hepatica, *147*, 149–150, Pl.12
  leucoptera, *36, 147*, 162–164, *198*, Pl.13
  ludoviciana, *147, 148*, 159–162, Pl.13
  lutea, see *147, 149, 150–152*, Pl.12
  olivacea, *38, 147, 148, 154*, 157–159, *161*, Pl.12
  roseogularis, *147*, 157, Pl.12
  rubra, *38, 147, 148, 150*, 154–157, Pl.12
  rubriceps, *147*, 164–165, Pl.13
Pirre Bush-Tanager, *59, 64, 318*, Pl.3
Plain-colored Tanager, *268, 269*, 272–273, Pl.24
plumbea
  Diglossa, see *350, 353–354*, Pl.30

Euphonia, 30, 222, 223, 225–226, Pl.20
Plumbeous Euphonia, *30, 222, 223,* 225–226, Pl.20
poliocephalus, Phaenicophilus, 101–102, Pl.7
porphyrocephala, Iridosornis, 214, 214–215, Pl.19
preciosa, Tangara, 268, 271, 306, 307, 308–309, Pl.26
Pseudodacnis, see *331*
Puerto Rican Tanager, 58–59, Pl.3
pulcherrima, Tangara, 268, 272, 324, Pl.28
punctata, Tangara, 268, 270, 295–297, Pl.25
punctulatus, Chlorospingus, 59, 60, 64–65, Pl.3
Purple Honeycreeper, *340,* 343–344, Pl.30
Purple-throated Euphonia, *222, 223,* 229–230, Pl.20
Purplish-mantled Tanager, *214,* 214–215, Pl.19
Pyrrhocoma, 83
 ruficeps, 83–84, Pl.5
pyrrhophrys, Chlorophonia, 258, 259, 261–262, Pl.23
Pyrrhuphonia, see *222*

Ramphocelus, 38, 165, 166–167, *177*
 bresilius, 166, 167, 169, 173–175, Pl.14
 carbo, 38, 166, 169, 171, 171–173, Pl.14
 dimidiatus, 166, 168–170, Pl.14
 flammigerus, 166, 176–178, Pl.14
 icteronotus, see *166, 176–178,* Pl.14
 melanogaster, 166, 171, Pl.14
 nigrogularis, 36, 166, 167, 168–169, Pl.13
 passerinii, 166, 167, 175–176, Pl.14
 sanguinolentus, 166, 167, 167, Pl.13
Red-billed Pied Tanager, 51–53, Pl.2
Red-crowned Ant-Tanager, *33, 36, 138, 139,* 139–142, Pl.11
Red-headed Tanager, *147,* 164, Pl.13
Red-hooded Tanager, *147,* 164–165, Pl.13
Red-legged Honeycreeper, *337, 340, 342,* 344–347, Pl.30
Red-necked Tanager, *268, 269,* 282–283, Pl.24
Red-shouldered Tanager, *122, 123,* 135, Pl.10
Red-throated Ant-Tanager, *138,* 142–144, Pl.11
reinhardti, Iridosornis, see *214, 216,* 217–218, Pl.19
reyi, Hemispingus, 72, 77, Pl.4
Rhodinocichla, 37, 103
 rosea, 37, 39, 102, 103–105, Pl.7
riefferii, Chlorornis, 54, 55, Pl.2
rosea, Rhodinocichla, 37, 39, 102, 103–105, Pl.7
Rose-breasted Thrush-Tanager, see *103*
roseogularis, Piranga, 147, 157, Pl.12
Rose-throated Tanager, *147,* 157, Pl.12
Rosy Thrush-Tanager, *37, 39, 102,* 103–105, Pl.7

rothschildi, Buthraupis, 199, 201, Pl.16
rourei, Nemosia, 97, 99, Pl.6
rubica, Habia, 33, 36, 138, 139, 139–142, Pl.11
rubra, Piranga, 38, 147, 148, 150, 154–157, Pl.12
rubriceps, Piranga, 147, 164–165, Pl.13
rubrifrons, Heterospingus, see *120, 121,* Pl.9
rubrirostris, Cnemoscopus, 36, 71–72, Pl.4
Ruby-crowned Tanager, *38, 122, 123,* 131–132, Pl.10
ruficapilla, Hemithraupis, 90, 92–93, Pl.6
ruficapillus, Schistochlamys, 43–44, Pl.1
ruficeps
 Pyrrhocoma, 83–84, Pl.5
 Thlypopsis, 84, 89–90, Pl.6
ruficervix, Tangara, 268, 271, 310–311, Pl.27
rufigenis, Tangara, 268, 270, 310, Pl.26
rufigula, Tangara, 268, 270, 300–301, Pl.25
rufiventer, Tachyphonus, 122, 125–126, Pl.9
rufiventris, Euphonia, 223, 224, 254–256, Pl.22
rufivertex, Iridosornis, 214, 216–218, Pl.19
rufosuperciliaris, Hemispingus, 18, 72, 73, 79–80, Pl.5
Rufous-bellied Euphonia, *223, 224,* 254–256, Pl.22
Rufous-browed Hemispingus, *18, 72, 73,* 79–80, Pl.5
Rufous-cheeked Tanager, *268, 270,* 310, Pl.26
Rufous-chested Tanager, *84,* 85–86, *86,* Pl.5
Rufous-crested Tanager, *119,* 119–120, Pl.9
Rufous-headed Tanager, *90,* 92–93, Pl.6
Rufous-throated Tanager, *268, 270,* 300–301, Pl.25
Rufous-winged Tanager, *268, 270,* 303–304, Pl.26
rufus, Tachyphonus, 32, 37, 122, 123, 133–135, Pl.10
Rust-and-yellow Tanager, *84,* 89–90, Pl.6
Rusty Flowerpiercer, see *350, 354,* Pl.30

Saffron-crowned Tanager, *268, 270,* 291–292, Pl.25
salmoni, Chrysothlypis, 95, 96–97, Pl.6
sanguinolentus, Ramphocelus, 166, 167, *167,* Pl.13
Santa Marta Mountain-Tanager, see *207, 208–209,* Pl.18
saturata, Euphonia, 223, 232–233, Pl.20
Sayaca Tanager, *182, 183,* 186–188, *188, 189, 190, 307,* Pl.15
sayaca, Thraupis, 182, 183, 186–188, *188, 189, 190, 307,* Pl.15
Scaled Flowerpiercer, *350, 351,* 364, Pl.31
Scarlet-and-white Tanager, *95,* 96–97, Pl.6
Scarlet-bellied Mountain-Tanager, *207,* 209–210, Pl.18
Scarlet-breasted Dacnis, *327,* 337, Pl.29

Scarlet-browed Tanager, see *120, 121–122*, Pl.9
Scarlet-rumped Tanager, *166, 167*, 175–176, Pl.14
Scarlet Tanager, *38, 147, 148, 154*, 157–159, *161*, Pl.12
Scarlet-thighed Dacnis, *327*, 332–334, Pl.29
Scarlet-throated Tanager, *56*, 56, Pl.2
Schistochlamys, 37, 43
  melanopis, *31, 32, 43, 44*, 45–46, Pl.1
  ruficapillus, *43*, 43–44, Pl.1
schrankii, *Tangara*, *268, 270*, 286–287, Pl.25
Scrub
  Euphonia, *222, 223*, 226–227, *239*, Pl.20
  Tanager, *268, 271*, 309–310, Pl.26
seledon, *Tangara*, *268, 269*, 280–281, Pl.24
semifuscus, *Chlorospingus*, *59*, 65–66, Pl.3
Sericossypha, 56
  albocristata, *30, 33, 56*, 56–58, Pl.2
  loricata, see *56*
Seven-colored Tanager, *268, 269*, 279–280, Pl.24
Shining Honeycreeper, *340*, 342–343, Pl.30
Short-billed
  Bush-Tanager, see *67*
  Honeycreeper, *30, 340*, 340–341, Pl.30
Shrike-Tanager
  Black-throated, *114*, 117–118, Pl.8
  Fulvous, *114*, 115–116, Pl.8
  White-throated, *114*, 118–119, Pl.8
  White-winged, *114*, 116–117, Pl.8
Silverbeak
  Brazilian, see *173*
  Common, see *171*
  Crimson-backed, see *169*
  Flame-rumped, see *178*
  Huallaga, see *171*
  Lemon-rumped, see *176*
  Masked Crimson, see *168*
Silver-beaked Tanager, *38, 166, 169, 171*, 171–173, Pl.14
Silver-throated Tanager, *268, 269, 270, 288*, 290–291, Pl.25
Silvery-backed Tanager, *268, 271, 272*, 322, Pl.28
Silvery Tanager, see *322*
sittoides, *Diglossa*, see *350*, 354–355, Pl.30
Slaty
  Flowerpiercer, *38, 350, 351*, 351–355, Pl.30
  Tanager, *119*, 120, Pl.9
Slaty-backed Hemispingus, *72*, 79, Pl.5
Sooty Ant-Tanager, *138*, 145–146, Pl.11
Sooty-capped Bush-Tanager, *59, 60, 66*, 66–67, Pl.3
sordida, *Thlypopsis*, *84*, 87–88, *90*, Pl.5
Spangle-cheeked Tanager, *18, 268, 271*, 316–319, Pl.27
Speckled Tanager, *267, 268, 270*, 297–299, Pl.25
speculiferus, *Nesospingus*, 58–59, Pl.3

speculigera, *Conothraupis*, *31, 50*, 50–51, Pl.1
Spindalis, 178
  dominicensis, see *179, 180*, Pl.15
  nigricephala, see *179, 181, 182*, Pl.15
  zena, 178–182, Pl.15
spiza, *Chlorophanes*, *264*, 337–340, Pl.30
Spot-crowned Euphonia, *223, 224*, 246, Pl.21
Spotted Tanager, *268, 270*, 295–297, Pl.25
Stephanophorus, 212
  diadematus, 212–214, Pl.18
sterrhopteron, *Wetmorethraupis*, 206–207, Pl.17
stolzmanni, *Chlorothraupis*, *107*, 109–110, Pl.7
Straw-backed Tanager, *268, 271, 272*, 322–323, Pl.28
Stripe-backed Tanager, see *148*
Stripe-headed Tanager, 178–182, Pl.15
  Eastern, see *179, 180*, Pl.15
  Jamaican, see *179, 181, 182*, Pl.15
  Western, see *179–180*, Pl.15
Sulphur-rumped Tanager, *120*, 121–122, Pl.9
Summer Tanager, *38, 147, 148, 150*, 154–157, Pl.12
Superciliaried Hemispingus, *72*, 75–76, Pl.4
superciliaris, *Hemispingus*, *72*, 75–76, Pl.4
surinamus, *Tachyphonus*, *122, 123*, 126–128, Pl.9
Swallow-Tanager, *31, 33, 37, 38, 39*, 370–372, Pl.32

Tacarcuna Bush-Tanager, *59*, 63–64, Pl.3
tacarcunae, *Chlorospingus*, *59*, 63–64, Pl.3
Tachyphonus, *31, 36, 37, 42, 46, 47, 48, 120*, 122–123, *136, 197*
  coronatus, *38, 122, 123*, 131–132, Pl.10
  cristatus, *122*, 123–125, Pl.9
  delatrii, *107, 122, 123*, 130–131, Pl.10
  luctuosus, *36, 122*, 128–130, Pl.10
  nattereri, see *122, 123, 125*, Pl.9
  phoenicius, *122, 123*, 135, Pl.10
  rufiventer, *122*, 125–126, Pl.9
  rufus, *32, 37, 122, 123*, 133–135, Pl.10
  surinamus, *122, 123*, 126–128, Pl.9
taeniata, *Dubusia*, *218*, 218–219, Pl.19
Tanagrella, see *272*
Tangara, *19, 30, 35, 36, 37, 39, 120, 200, 220, 249, 252, 254, 264, 267–272, 292, 294, 297, 310, 311, 322, 327, 332, 337, 340*
  argyrofenges, *268, 271, 272*, 322–323, Pl.28
  arthus, *268, 270*, 289–290, Pl.25
  cabanisi, *268, 269*, 273–274, Pl.24
  callophrys, *268, 272*, 327, Pl.28
  cayana, *268, 271*, 304–306, Pl.26
  chilensis, *268, 269*, 277–279, Pl.24
  chrysotis, *268, 270*, 292–293, Pl.25
  cucullata, *267, 268, 270*, 306, Pl.26

cyanicollis, *268*, *271*, 313–314, Pl.27
cyanocephala, *268*, *269*, 282–283, Pl.24
cyanoptera, *268*, *272*, 323–324, Pl.28
cyanotis, *268*, *271*, 312–313, Pl.27
cyanoventris, *268*, *269*, 283–285, Pl.24
desmaresti, *268*, *269*, 282–283, Pl.24
dowii, *18*, *268*, *271*, 316–319, Pl.27
fastuosa, *268*, *269*, 279–280, Pl.24
florida, *268*, *270*, 287–289, Pl.25
fucosa, see *18*, *268*, *318–319*, Pl.27
guttata, *267*, *268*, *270*, 297–299, Pl.25
gyrola, *267*, *268*, *270*, 301–303, *303*, Pl.26
heinei, *268*, *271*, *272*, 321, Pl.28
icterocephala, *268*, *269*, *270*, *288*, 290–291, Pl.25
inornata, *268*, *269*, 272–273, Pl.24
johannae, *268*, *270*, 285–286, Pl.25
labradorides, *268*, *271*, 311–312, Pl.27
larvata, *268*, *271*, 314–316, Pl.27
lavinia, *268*, *270*, 303–304, Pl.26
mexicana, *33*, *268*, *269*, 275–277, *327*, Pl.24
meyerdeschauenseei, *18*, *268*, *271*, 373, Pl.32
nigrocincta, *268*, *271*, 316, Pl.27
nigroviridis, *268*, *271*, 319, Pl.27
palmeri, *268*, *269*, 274–275, Pl.24
parzudakii, *165*, *268*, *270*, 293–294, Pl.25
peruviana, *268*, *271*, 306–308, *308*, Pl.26
preciosa, *268*, *271*, *306*, *307*, 308–309, Pl.26
pulcherrima, *268*, *272*, 324, Pl.28
punctata, *268*, *270*, 295–297, Pl.25
ruficervix, *268*, *271*, 310–311, Pl.27
rufigenis, *268*, *270*, 310, Pl.26
rufigula, *268*, *270*, 300–301, Pl.25
schrankii, *268*, *270*, 286–287, Pl.25
seledon, *268*, *269*, 280–281, Pl.24
varia, *268*, *270*, 299–300, Pl.25
vassorii, *268*, *271*, 320, Pl.27
velia, *268*, *272*, 325–327, Pl.28
viridicollis, *268*, *271*, *272*, 322, Pl.28
vitriolina, *268*, *271*, 309–310, Pl.26
xanthocephala, *268*, *270*, 291–292, Pl.25
xanthogastra, *268*, *270*, 294–295, Pl.25
Tawny-capped Euphonia, *223*, *224*, 252, Pl.22
Tawny-crested Tanager, *107*, *122*, *123*, 130–131, Pl.10
Tersina, *18*, 370
   viridis, *31*, *33*, *37*, *38*, *39*, 370–372, Pl.32
tertius, *Calyptophilus*, see *102*
Thick-billed Euphonia, *223*, *233*, 236–238, *239*, Pl.21
Thlypopsis, *37*, *83*, 84
   fulviceps, *84*, 84–85, Pl.5
   inornata, *84*, 88–89, Pl.6
   ornata, *84*, 85–86, *86*, Pl.5
   pectoralis, *84*, 86–87, Pl.5
   ruficeps, *84*, 89–90, Pl.6
   sordida, *84*, 87–88, *90*, Pl.5

Thraupis, *31*, *34*, *35*, *37*, *56*, *178*, 182–183, *189*
   abbas, *182*, *183*, 190–192, Pl.15
   bonariensis, *32*, *178*, *182*, *183*, 195–197, Pl.16
   cyanocephala, *182*, 194–195, *208*, Pl.16
   cyanoptera, *182*, *186*, 188–190, Pl.15
   episcopus, *30*, *32*, *36*, *38*, *182*, *183*, 183–185, *186*, *192*, Pl.15
   glaucocolpa, see *182*, *186*, *188*, Pl.15
   ornata, *182*, *189*, 190–191, Pl.15
   palmarum, *32*, *36*, *38*, *39*, *182*, *183*, 192–194, *306*, Pl.15
   sayaca, *182*, *183*, 186–188, *188*, *189*, *190*, *307*, Pl.15
Three-striped Hemispingus, 72, 82–83, Pl.5
Thrush-Tanager
   Rose-breasted, see *103*
   Rosy, *37*, *39*, *102*, 103–105, Pl.7
Tit-like Dacnis, 347–348, Pl.30
Trichothraupis, *31*, 136, *212*
   melanops, *32*, *37*, *136*, 136–138, Pl.10
trifasciatus, *Hemispingus*, 72, 82–83, Pl.5
Trinidad Euphonia, *222*, *223*, *225*, *229*, 230–232, *233*, Pl.20
trinitatus, Euphonia, *222*, *223*, *225*, *229*, 230–232, *233*, Pl.20
Turquoise
   Dacnis, *327*, 331–332, Pl.29
   Dacnis-Tanager, see *331*
   Tanager, *33*, *268*, *269*, 275–277, *327*, Pl.24

varia, Tangara, *268*, *270*, 299–300, Pl.25
vassorii, Tangara, *268*, *271*, 320, Pl.27
velia, Tangara, *268*, *272*, 325–327, Pl.28
Velvet-fronted Euphonia, *223*, 232, Pl.20
Venezuelan Flowerpiercer, *350*, *351*, 362–363, Pl.31
venezuelensis, Diglossa, *350*, *351*, 362–363, Pl.31
venusta, Dacnis, *327*, 332–334, Pl.29
Vermilion Tanager, 165–166, Pl.13
versicolor, Lanio, *114*, 116–117, Pl.8
verticalis
   Creurgops, *119*, 119–120, Pl.9
   Hemispingus, *36*, *72*, *73*, 80–81, Pl.5
viguieri, Dacnis, *327*, 336–337, Pl.29
violacea, Euphonia, *222*, *223*, *224*, 233–236, *239*, Pl.21
Violaceous Euphonia, *222*, *223*, *224*, 233–236, *239*, Pl.21
Viridian Dacnis, *327*, 336–337, Pl.29
viridicollis, Tangara, *268*, *271*, *272*, 322, Pl.28
viridis, Tersina, *31*, *33*, *37*, *38*, *39*, 370–372, Pl.32
vitriolina, Tangara, *268*, *271*, 309–310, Pl.26

Western
   Chat Tanager, see *102*

Western (continued)
  Stripe-headed Tanager, see *179–180*, Pl.15
  Tanager, *147, 148*, 159–162, Pl.13
wetmorei, Buthraupis, 199, 206, Pl.17
Wetmorethraupis, 206
  sterrhopteron, 206–207, Pl.17
White-banded Tanager, *46*, 46–48, Pl.1
White-bellied Dacnis, *327*, 327–328, Pl.29
White-capped Tanager, *30, 33, 56*, 56–57, Pl.2
White-lined Tanager, *32, 37, 122, 123*, 133–135, Pl.10
White-lored Euphonia, *223, 224*, 247–249, Pl.22
White-rumped Tanager, *46*, 48–49, Pl.1
White-shouldered Tanager, *36, 122*, 128–130, Pl.10
White-sided Flowerpiercer, *350, 351*, 363–364, Pl.31
White-throated Shrike-Tanager, *114*, 118–119, Pl.8
White-vented Euphonia, *223, 224*, 250–252, Pl.22
White-winged
  Shrike-Tanager, *114*, 116–117, Pl.8
  Tanager, *36, 147*, 162–164, *198*, Pl.13

xanthocephala, Tangara, 268, 270, 291–292, Pl.25
xanthogaster, Euphonia, 222, 223, 224, 252–254, Pl.22
xanthogastra, Tangara, 268, 270, 294–295, Pl.25
xanthophthalmus, Hemispingus, 36, 72, 73, 76, 81–82, Pl.5
xanthopygius, Heterospingus, 120, 121–122, Pl.9
Xenodacnis, 38, 347
  parina, 347–348, Pl.30

Yellow-backed Tanager, *90*, 93–95, Pl.6
Yellow-bellied
  Dacnis, *327*, 330–331, Pl.29
  Tanager, *268, 270*, 294–295, Pl.25
Yellow-browed Tanager, see *109*
Yellow-collared Chlorophonia, *258, 259*, 259, Pl.23
Yellow-crested Tanager, *122*, 125–126, Pl.9
Yellow-crowned Euphonia, *222, 223*, 228–229, Pl.20
Yellow-green Bush-Tanager, *59*, 69–70, Pl.4
Yellow-scarfed Tanager, see *214, 216, 217–218*, Pl.19
Yellow-throated
  Bush-Tanager, *59, 60*, 68–69, Pl.3
  Euphonia, *223, 224, 227*, 238–239, Pl.21
  Tanager, *214*, 215, Pl.19
Yellow-whiskered Bush-Tanager, *59, 60*, 67–68, *68*, Pl.3
Yellow-winged Tanager, *182, 183*, 190–192, Pl.15

zeledoni, Chlorospingus, 59, 60, 66, Pl.3
Zeledon's Bush-Tanager, *59, 60*, 66, Pl.3
zena, Spindalis, 178–182, Pl.15